W9-AHO-297

A Library of Film Criticism

Frederick Ungar Publishing Co.
New York

A Library of Film Criticism

AMERICAN FILM DIRECTORS

Compiled and edited by

Stanley Hochman

With Filmographies and
Index of Critics and Films

To David

Printed in the United States of America
Library of Congress Catalog Card No. 73–92923
ISBN 0-8044-3120-5

Copyright Acknowledgments

Selections in this volume are quoted with the approval of the copyright owners as listed below and may not be reprinted elsewhere without their consent. The exact source is given at the end of each selection. Every effort has been made to trace and acknowledge copyright owners. If any acknowledgment has been inadvertently omitted, the necessary correction will be made in the next printing.

ACROPOLIS BOOKS LTD. For selections excerpted with permission from *The American Film Heritage* copyright © 1972 by the American Film Institute, published by Acropolis Books Ltd.

AMERICA. For excerpts from articles by Moira Walsh. Copyright © 1956, 1965 by America Press, Inc. All rights reserved. Reprinted by permission.

AMERICAN DIALOG. For its generous permission to reprint excerpts from numerous articles first published in *New Masses*.

ATHENEUM PUBLISHERS, INC. For excerpt from *Tynan Right & Left* by Kenneth Tynan. Copyright © 1964 by Kenneth Tynan. Reprinted by permission of Atheneum Publishers, New York.

THE ATLANTIC MONTHLY. For excerpts from articles by David Denby and by Dan Wakefield.

AVON BOOKS. For excerpt from *The Cinema of Alfred Hitchcock* by Peter Bogdanovich, by arrangement with Avon Books. Copyright © 1974 by Peter Bogdanovich.

A. S. BARNES & COMPANY, INC. For excerpts from *Cinema of Joseph von Sternberg* by John Baxter; from *Horror in the Cinema* by Ivan Butler; from *Seventy Years of Cinema* by Peter Cowie; from *Cinema of Fritz Lang* by Paul M. Jensen; from *Mack Sennett's Keystone* by Kalton C. Lahue; from *Cinema of John Frankenheimer* by Gerald Pratley; from *Hitchcock's Films* by Robin Wood.

continued on page 565

Contents

FOREWORD

The increasing emphasis on the movies as a significant, modern art form has created a growing demand for ready access to information that places contemporary trends and developments in the proper perspective. *American Film Directors*, the first volume in a projected series entitled A LIBRARY OF FILM CRITICISM, is a response to the needs of the growing number of sophisticated film buffs and of students enrolled in the cinema history and technique courses in hundreds of American colleges and universities. Future volumes will focus on the achievements of leading directors of Europe and the Orient.

Like the art on which it focuses, movie criticism is a discipline still in its relative infancy. At the turn of the century, few could have speculated that Edison's little toy would give birth to an art that would challenge our literary and dramatic traditions and that could be seriously discussed in polite society. Keeping just proportion in mind, the early Kinetoscope Parlors, in which for a penny you could watch the gyrations of Fatima, had somewhat the unsavory reputation of the peepshows that today line our downtown areas. And when movies were first released from the little box and projected onto a screen, they were still considered merely a technical marvel—at best a harmless entertainment for the uneducated masses that were swarming to our shores, at worst a moral threat.

"There are better ways of stocking the mind than by flashing before the eye a kaleidoscopic jumble of unrelated information. There is danger in any form of amusement or instruction which merely gluts the mind," complained educator Alfred M. Hitchcock in 1915. True, the movies had learned to tell a story with Edwin S. Porter's *The Life of an American Fireman* (1902), but for a long time they contented themselves with filming star vaudeville turns and just about anything that moved. (In our own day Andy Warhol seems to have reversed the process by filming things that—hopefully—never move: *Empire* (1964) gave us several hours of the Empire State Building.)

But men of genius soon began to see that in the correct hands what Leo Tolstoy called "this little clicking contraption with the revolving handle" could bring about a revolution in the lives of narrative artists. For his own part, the Russian master welcomed it. "The swift change of scene, this blending of emotion and experience—it is much better than the heavy, long-drawn-out kind of writing to which we are accustomed. It is closer to life."

The turning point for many was D.W. Griffith's *The Birth of a Nation* (1915). "I am sure that I shall speak of an experience that came to a large number of Americans, who had given up the movies as hopeless, when I say that *The Birth of a Nation* revived in me the conviction that the screen has before it a great future, a splendid mission, a message to deliver to humanity that may atone eventually for its juvenile sins of omission and commission," wrote Edward S. Van Zile in *That Marvel—The Movie* (1923). In this country at least, Griffith's epic launched both the art of the film and the art of film criticism. It opened the eyes of intellectuals to the possibilities inherent in a discipline that could instruct, entertain, and elevate by means of images alone. The poet Vachel Lindsay rallied to the cause with *The Art of the Moving Picture* in 1915. Griffith's *Intolerance* mere sensationalism? Why, it was the very essence of cinema art, he argued in the book's 1922 revision. "This photoplay is given power not by straining for the depth of passion, but depth of what might be called tableau-emotion, a much more elusive thing."

Of course, not all those who wrote about the movies were—or are—intellectuals. From their inception the movies have been a popular art in both senses of the word. Too much of what passes for criticism is mere reviewing in which the writer reveals that he has no conception of film as an art and a means of social commentary. He or she is often content merely to keep the reader informed of what is playing at the local Bijou.

Nevertheless, from the very beginning the movies have had perceptive critics, much of whose work appeared anonymously. It was not until almost 1925 that the signed reviews of Mordaunt Hall began to appear in *The New York Times*. Much of the film criticism in *Photoplay* was unsigned, but the reader of this book will find some admirably perspicacious articles from that pioneer venture written by Burns Mantle and even Theodore Dreiser. A particularly valuable source for early film commentary has been the *National Board of Review*, which featured the work of early critics such as James Shelley Hamilton.

Examples of "popular" criticism have been included in the present volume in order to convey the flavor of a period—and sometimes to show what an intelligent director was up against. However, the concentration has been on those writers on film whose approach shows a valid conception—whether or not one agrees with it—of film as a separate artistic discipline that obeys the demands of an art which is primarily visual. The chronological arrangement of these excerpts shows the response of both directors and their critics to the eruption and taming of sound and color (which once more threatened to turn the movies into little more than a technical marvel). The material is presented "as is"; though obvious typos have been corrected, no attempt has been made to impose stylistic conformity on spelling variations or exotic punctuation and syntax.

It is less easy to assign the final responsibility for a film than for a novel or even a play. Nevertheless, critics agree that most major films show the impress of the personality of a given director—that a John Ford film is as identifiable as a William Faulkner novel. One realizes, of course, that to some extent directors are at the mercy of their actors, writers, studios, etc., but to a remarkable degree remarkable men have achieved remarkable work within these limitations—though sometimes only for a short period. Even the most obvious potboiler forced on a director can convey a strong cinematographic sensibility, as Ado Kyrou points out in his discussion of Frank Borzage. Therefore, while the emphasis of the excerpts gathered here is on a director's major films, we have not hesitated to focus on "disasters" which a director has been willing to accept for extra-artistic reasons or which document his artistic decline.

In the present volume, attention has been concentrated on 65 American directors whose reputations had been established by the mid-1960s. Needless to say not everyone will agree with the selection made. To some degree it reflects personal preference, but to a larger extent it reflects the consensus of the many critical works consulted. Men such as Maurice Tourneur, Victor Seastrom, and F. W. Murnau cannot, of course, be considered American directors, but the films they made in this country were so influential that their elimination would distort the overall picture.

In the following pages, the chronologically arranged excerpts under each director's name are drawn from specialized periodicals, general publications, collections of film criticism, private clipping files—which explains the occasional absence of page numbers—and books on individual directors. Our purpose has been to convey an overall picture of the critical ups and downs of these film-makers over the years—sometimes more than half a century—and to indicate sources of further study to students and scholars. Sometimes selections were chosen because they comment on one another as well as on the film. Sometimes a film was concentrated on because it provided an opportunity to show how several major critics responded to a single work, i.e., Philip T. Hartung, John Simon, and Stanley Kauffmanm on George Stevens's *The Greatest Story Ever Told*.

This book would not have been possible without the kind help of the expert staffs at the New York Public Library and the Film Study Center of the Museum of Modern Art. Someday, perhaps, their budgets will be as limitless as their patience.

STANLEY HOCHMAN

DIRECTORS INCLUDED

Frank Borzage
Richard Brooks
Clarence Brown
Tod Browning
Frank Capra
John Cassavetes
Charles Chaplin
James Cruze
George Cukor
Michael Curtiz
Cecil B. De Mille
William Dieterle
Allan Dwan
Robert J. Flaherty
Victor Fleming
John Ford
John Frankenheimer
D.W. Griffith
Henry Hathaway
Howard Hawks
Alfred Hitchcock
John Huston
Thomas H. Ince
Rex Ingram
Elia Kazan
Buster Keaton
Henry King
Stanley Kramer
Stanley Kubrick
Gregory La Cava
Fritz Lang
Mervyn Le Roy
Anatole Litvak
Frank Lloyd
Pare Lorentz
Ernst Lubitsch
Sidney Lumet
Leo McCarey
Rouben Mamoulian
Joseph L. Mankiewicz
Lewis Milestone
Vincente Minnelli
F.W. Murnau
Mike Nichols
Arthur Penn
Edwin S. Porter
Otto Preminger
Robert Rossen
Victor Seastrom
Mack Sennett
Josef von Sternberg
George Stevens
Erich von Stroheim
John Sturges
Preston Sturges
Maurice Tourneur
W.S. Van Dyke
King Vidor
Raoul Walsh
Andy Warhol
Orson Welles
William Wellman
Billy Wilder
William Wyler
Fred Zinnemann

PERIODICALS CONSULTED

America
The Arts
The Atlantic Monthly
British Film Institute Monthly Bulletin
Cahiers du Cinéma
Cahiers du Cinéma in English
Cahiers du Sud
Cinema Arts
Cinema Magazine
Close Up
Commentary
Commonweal
Le Crapouillot
Cue
Daily Worker
Encounter
Film (England)
Film Comment
Film Culture
Film Daily
Film Heritage
Film Journal (Australia)
Film Society Review
Film Spectator
Film Quarterly
Films
Films and Filming
Films in Review (NBR)
Hollywood Spectator
Judge
Life
Literary Digest
London Times
Los Angeles Times
McCall's
Motion Picture Herald
Motion Picture Magazine
Motion Picture News
Moving Picture World
The Nation
National Board of Review
New Masses
The New Republic
Newsweek
New Theatre
New York Dramatic Mirror
New York Herald Tribune
New York Journal American
New York Sun
New York Times
New York Times Magazine
New York World Telegram
New York World Telegram and Sun
Pacific Coast Musician
Photoplay
Picture Play
PM
The Reporter
Revue du Cinéma
The Screen Writer
Scribner's
Show
Sight & Sound
The Spectator (London)

Stage
Sunday Times (London)
TAC
Theatre Arts
Theatre Magazine
Vanity Fair
Variety
Village Voice
Vogue
World Film News

Some of the above titles are abbreviated as follows:

BFI Bulletin	British Film Institute Monthly Film Bulletin
HS	Hollywood Spectator
LT	London Times
LAT	Los Angeles Times
NBR	National Board of Review
NYDM	New York Dramatic Mirror
NYHT	New York Herald Tribune
NYJA	New York Journal American
NYS	New York Sun
NYT	New York Times
NYT mag	New York Times Magazine
NYWT	New York World Telegram
NYWTS	New York World Telegram & Sun
VV	Village Voice

BORZAGE, FRANK (1893–1961)

The primary stages of the film version of Zoé Atkins's play *Daddy's Gone a-Hunting* are thoughtfully directed, with the action pictured from interesting angles. Unfortunately, this good work does not atone for the weakness of the story as it appears on the screen. The activities of the principal main character, Julian, cause one to think of him as a masculine Sandra. He is a weak, thoughtless individual, who is only brought to his senses by the death of his little girl. . . . Occasionally Frank Borzage, the director, slides over years with a facility that is astonishing. In one sequence one knows that Julian is embracing the girl with whom he is in love, and the next instant he is lifting up his little daughter, who must be 6 years old. He lays down his brush and pen and decides that he must study art in Paris, and in less time than it takes to tell he is on his way to the French capital. He is tired of doing commercial work.

Mordaunt Hall. *NYT*. Feb. 24, 1925, p. 17

[In *Seventh Heaven*] Janet Gaynor as Diane and Charles Farrell as Chico played directly in terms of the screen. They made the shameless, frank appeal of youth and beauty which dissolves the strictures of the old in warm memories and evokes the helpless rapture of the young. They were graceful with the grace of beautiful animals. This Chico was shy as a young man might be shy and Diane's shyness was a trembling sweet thing to see. Neither of them acted shyness. They reached for each other hesitatingly and Diane's lips lifted upwards for Chico's neck. Not since Lois Moran kissed her lover on the cheek in the tree shaded canoe in *Stella Dallas* has young love been so delicately portrayed on the screen.

Thank Heavens they were not hampered by any tired, jaded words. They expressed themselves entirely in terms of motion. Thus their method was one of simplification and by that simplification they liberated the imagination of the spectator so that he could take active part in the scene. Having nothing to observe but their bodily grace he was able to watch an exquisite pantomiming of an instinctive attraction which was completely self-expressive without any further aid. Words would have been as much out of place as song in the performance of a ballet dancer. . . .

These love scenes between Chico and Diane are the whole picture. This for the reason that they are the most perfectly realized in terms of their own medium. The rest of the picture is picturesque setting with the novelty of having a Parisian sewer worker fall in love with a street waif who is melodramatically abused by a thieving sister who drinks absinthe just as if there were prohibition in France as well as in America. The celestial symbolism is no whit better in the picture than it was in the play, a matter for Charles Rann Kennedy to wax enthusiastic about. Yet it furnishes the opportunity for a rather fine stair sequence where you get a sense of continual movement by having the camera apparently rise with the ascending couple right through the solid floors. What a way that would have been of making the famous stairway scene from "Sappho" immortal on the screen!

The external movement of the story, always the least significant movement in a cinegraphic composition, is supplied by the declaration of war and the celebrated advance of the taxi-cab army to stem the Germans at the Marne. Here we become much and amusingly concerned with the fate of "Eloise", the decrepit old taxi which was just about due to be pensioned for life in a quiet storage garage. This is good humor and, in the final collapse of the old war chariot, an interesting illustration of how the slapstick method can be used to evoke pathos.

NBR. June 1927, p. 12

Continuing the adventures of those Babes in the Wood—Janet Gaynor and Charles Farrell. Thanks again to the sympathetic direction of Frank Borzage, here is a picture [*Street Angel*] that is as human and as appealing as *Seventh Heaven*. Miss Gaynor plays a little Italian circus performer, whose innocence and poverty force her to attempt the last resources of desperate girls. How a tramp artist, played by Farrell, rescues her; how they are separated and reunited, forms the basis of a tear-wringing romance.

You'll like the simple, sincere playing of these two youngsters, the picturesque backgrounds and the fantasy-like treatment of the story. These two kids strike a fresh, new note on the screen. Natalie Kingston and Henry Armetta give good performances. Don't miss this one.

Photoplay. April 1928, p. 52

It's a pleasantry in the best possible taste to put a symbol into a work of art. It becomes an admirable pleasantry and one worthy of Joyeux-Drille when the symbolic part of the work passes almost unnoticed, or is nonexistent, and when intelligent people race after the ghost of a symbol. Such is the case with *The River*: for many people, with whom I do not agree, no doubt because of the title (*La Femme au Corbeau*), as well as their mental laziness, the raven (*corbeau*) is a symbol (Good God, of what!). They just haven't understood a thing. But that's not all;

a gentleman—natural reserve forbids me to give his name and titles to respect—doesn't trouble himself with symbols but inflicts the following upon us: "In this Frank Borzage film there are a color and an atmosphere of the solitudes of the North that are of the first order. One is reminded of Jack London, sometimes of Louis Hémon" (with all due respect?).

Not one pen pusher has noticed the presence of the river. If you want a symbol, there's one for you. Moral: the importance of a title. . . .

This film was forbidden in a goodly number of American states. To my knowledge it is the first film that tackles a subject as delicate as female frigidity. In it Mary Duncan is a splendidly American gold-digger and flirt until the day that her body finds the body of a young man that she is to love. It's the somewhat special type of woman who doesn't grow in our debauched countries, but I find that everything becomes luminous from the moment in which Mary Duncan replies no to Charles Farrell, who asks her if she is the wife or the mistress of Marsdon. Once more she is, physically, a frightened virgin before a male who has the advantage of her.

This very beautiful film fully satisfied me. Note should be taken of the breasts of Mary Duncan in her spring dress, of Charles Farrell's dip, of the wait for Farrell's return, of the declaration, of the cutting of the trees, of Mary Duncan warming Farrell with her body, of Mary Duncan's dive. Mary Duncan as a whole and in detail. This film by Frank Borzage is of a sustained beauty and—at least in the French version—does not show the disagreeable artistic side of his other films.

Michel J. Arnaud. *Revue du Cinéma.*
May 1929, unpaged

Bravely as it is produced for the most part, there is too much sentiment and not enough strength in the pictorial conception of Ernest Hemingway's novel, *A Farewell to Arms*. . . . Notwithstanding the undeniable artistry of the photography, the fine recording of voices and Frank Borzage's occasional excellent directorial ideas, one misses the author's vivid descriptions and the telling dialogue between Lieutenant Frederic Henry and the Italian officers. It is Mr. Borzage rather than Mr. Hemingway who prevails in this film and the incidents frequently are unfurled in a jerky fashion. . . .

The film account skips too quickly from one episode to another and the hardships and other experiences of Lieutenant Henry are passed over too abruptly, being suggested rather than told. Here and there Mr. Borzage has some sterling sequences, such as after Lieutenant Henry is wounded and is being carried on a stretcher to the ambulance and from the ambulance to the hospital. In some scenes he does not show the wounded man, but contents himself by depicting what the wounded man sees—the faces from above him, the temporary hospital ceiling and so forth. . . .

Often one is confused as to where the players are, and when Henry decides to escape from Italy to Switzerland the glimpse of his getting into a boat is much too like many another Hollywood scene. Then, too, Mr. Borzage is too partial to a deluge of rain instead of a drizzle.

The first meeting of Catherine and Henry is set forth satisfactorily, but subsequently the picture appears to gather speed, as though the director feared he could not get in all the details he wished. . . .

Several of the strong dramatic incidents of the novel are not included in the film, obviously because the producers did not wish to offend Italians. Here there is a note of victory coupled with the presumed death of Catherine, for Henry carries Catherine's inert form from her cot to a window as the throngs outside are celebrating the armistice.

Mordaunt Hall. *NYT*. Dec. 9, 1932, p. 26

Asked to write his own criticism of the movie adaptation of his *A Farewell to Arms*, Mr. Hemingway probably would give it no more credit than one could find in a few four-letter Anglo-Saxon words; yet, compared with other adaptations and other movies of the year, Mr. Hemingway might as easily discover that he has been done very well by indeed. . . .

As seems inevitable with adaptors, the authors of the movie allowed their respect for Hemingway to carry them astray. Any license is permissible in adaptation as long as it does not destroy the focus of the story. I think they were wise in leaving out most of the war and making the simple love story of the tale the main body of the movie; it wasn't necessary to "follow the book", as long as they developed their story logically. But, for adaptors, they did as well as they probably could. . . . In the first good scene, and one which is as genuinely moving as any you will ever see in a movie, the director wisely takes the emphasis of the story away from the hero and gives it to the heroine. I say wisely, simply because there are so few leading men in movies or theatre with enough maturity and talent to be convincing, and while this emphasis does emasculate the virility of the tale, it would have been too much to have expected Gary Cooper to have carried the burden of the drama.

This first good scene, incidentally, is as tender and beautifully done as any author could ask. It is a brief episode. The young officer seduces his casual acquaintance in a cemetery; in the lucid prose of the author, she asks him his name; she sadly quotes: "and the young lady sat in the park warming her lost innocence"; she asks him to be good to her. Director Borzage surrounds his couple with a soft grey photographic frame and stringed music, and Helen Hayes takes the movie, wraps it up, and carries it home with her. After this scene, a director would have been criminally insane to have bothered with his leading man. And from this point on, had the authors let the war dialogue go and watched only their lovers, they would have had a simpler but truer show.

Pare Lorentz. *Vanity Fair.* Jan. 1933, p. 62

No Greater Glory has attempted to tell in celluloid what the death-dealing academicians have propagated through the centuries in books, essays and sermons—the theory that there resides *innately in human beings the instinct to wage war*, and that there is no greater glory than to die for one's country. To graphically prove this main thesis Columbia Pictures have telescoped down the wars of all time to a close-up of the origin and development of a gang fight between two "big injun" groups. . . .

As a piece of filmmaking, *No Greater Glory* is no contribution. The kids play well—as well as 12-year-olds can possibly play with dialogue rarely uttered even from the lips of 30-year-olds. The photography is better than most. But the film as a whole suffers from what all Hollywood "problem" (topical, realistic) films are destined to suffer from: the insurmountable difficulty of bridging the contradiction between the nature of the movie as an art form and its content. For, all of Hollywood to the contrary, cinematography is an art of "seeing," an art impossible in a system of society dependent on "blinders."

Tom Brandon. *New Masses.* May 29, 1934, pp. 29, 30

There is no end to a quarter other than the films you've seen. But in the dying moments of this critic's quarter came *Desire*, in which Frank Borzage's direction has been trimmed and polished by a Lubitsch in his best form since *Trouble in Paradise*. That is a strong sentence, and it was meant to be. After the tribe of knockabouts, gagmen, wisecrackers, the purveyors of "smart" comedy, Mr. Lubitsch's picture is like—I almost said—a breath of spring. It's not that, but it makes this indoor confinement less painful. For to the strong light, the trees and the mountains of southern California (here called Spain, so that the audience may admire aloud with fewer misgivings) is added a sure, beautifully written piece about the usual Lubitsch trifles, about crooks and fake countesses breathless before the dawn of romance. Somehow Mr. Lubitsch's style has regained enough strength to make this stuff take on a vintage body long after the captains of industry and the kings of jazz depart.

Alistair Cooke. *Sight & Sound.* Spring 1936, p. 25

[*The Green Light*]. A somber and sincere study of the spiritual life of a surgeon, made particularly impressive by excellent performances by Cedric Hardwicke, and Errol Flynn. Director Frank Borzage uses taste and judgment in keeping the dialogue subordinated to the action, and the philosophical overtone intact. *A mature and thoughtful translation of a best-seller.*

Stage. Feb. 1937, p. 16

Love stories—though not so much now as they used to be—are generally considered the properest kind of stuff for the movies: popular appeal and all that. Yet how many pictures are remembered because they were love stories—anything more than the boy-and-girl pattern that is so taken for granted that it has to be decked out with other elements to be even entertaining? Very few, and *Three Comrades* is likely to be one of them. . . .

A remarkably high combination of talents has made it all very impressive and moving—good writing, a good man at the camera, good actors, and presiding over them a good director. Sometimes there seems to be a bit too much talk, but there are some things that can only be said in words and Scott Fitzgerald (it must be he) has a gift for words well above the average of movie dialogue. When there is only something to watch, without the need of words, the director and camera man have their own kind of eloquence—such unforgetable bits as the pursuit of the boy who shot Gottfried, the glimpse from under the muffling blanket of the girl's stricken face, the startling downswoop of the camera's eye upon the girl getting up from bed and across the room to remove the burden of her illness from those who love her. Those are high moments in a film that is full of beauty.

It is hard to say where Frank Borzage directing and Joseph Ruttenberg at the camera and the fine cast of actors supplement one another, so perfectly the work of them all merges together.

NBR. June 1938, pp. 10–11

Suffocating to meet nose to nose (it is over two hours of Virginia Dare wine, women, and song), *Stage Door Canteen* is beautiful as a preview of a period piece. Any film is, but this one carries a saturation of mannerisms of fourth-decade entertainment, patriotism, and sub-idealized lovemaking which could supply almost twenty others. The best of the patriotism is implicit rather than overt. The lovemaking is strictly church-supper. The entertainment is best. Lack of space, libel laws, and a fondness for entertainers, all prevent any detail on the subject; but we can safely remember that every piece of entertainment, like every political speech or swatch of advertising copy, has nightmarish accuracy as a triple-distilled image of a collective dream, habit, or desire. . . . *Stage Door Canteen* is achingly long; a lot of dialogue is dragged in by heels who should never have been hired even to drag it out; and Frank Borzage should have used a spare cameraman with first-rate eyes to work the Canteen floor for its wonderful possibilities. Yet this is a nice harmless picture for the whole family; and it is a gold mine for those who are willing to go to it in the wrong spirit. [1943]

James Agee. *Agee on Film* (Beacon, 1964), pp. 41–42

The *Moonrise* (meaningless title) is the latest film of Frank Borzage, who did well in the 'thirties with such films as *A Farewell to Arms* and *Man's Castle*, but then turned his hand to so many potboilers that one had almost forgotten his existence. Now his new film, *Moonrise*, made independently with very limited resources at a small Hollywood studio, shows that Borzage as a creative personality is still very much alive. The story is told with a unity of mood, sombre and poignant, set by some impressionistic opening passages and sustained by the slow yet firmly compressed style and the strong, low-toned images. Borzage is a romanticist, but he does not over-simplify; the scene where the lovers visit a fairground and circumstances cause the nervous, inarticulate young man to undergo a whole series of conflicting tensions is done with remarkable skill. He brings a sardonic humour to the portrait of a little town, lethargic and turned in on itself, and finds a poetic contrast in the derelict mansion on the edge of the swamp where Danny meets his girl at night and dances with her. There is a touching sadness also in the strange deaf-mute to whom Danny is attracted because he too is an outcast. One regrets only a brief emotional flaw caused by Ethel Barrymore, who plays Danny's grandmother with a portentous theatricality and the intonation of a female King Lear. [1949]

Gavin Lambert in *Shots in the Dark*, edited by E. C. Ansley and others (Allan Wingate, 1951), p. 89

This former cowboy of Ince's films, who learned his craft as a director as an assistant to Griffith, is undeniably the cinema's greatest poet of the couple. The majority of his films are exciting, some are masterpieces. Even after he understood that it was impossible to work "honestly" in a craft where everything is decided in advance, in which the director no longer has the latitude to express himself freely, he made some potboilers (he used to say that most directors took themselves too seriously) in which in spite of all we find timid notations that carry the mark of a strong cinematographic sensibility.

It's hard to make those who haven't seen his films understand their irresistible charm. Borzage believes in mad love, he has confidence in lovers. Love isn't a simple amusement, it surpasses in force all our senses, it is luminous and it transfigures those who suffer in this unworthy world. Unlike Vidor, Borzage does not see love in bloody colors. This is no doubt because his admirable lovers look to the future with hope: they fight against the conditions of their lives, suffer as we all do, but they are strong, inflexible, they are happy.

A single image from *A Man's Castle* suffices to give us an idea of Borzage's very personal tone: a young woman has just been married and she wears a beautiful white robe garnished with little flounces; she is proud of it and would like everybody to know that she is happy; she therefore sets out down the road early in the morning without changing her dress. Only Vigo or Chaplin would have been able to conceive of such potential poetry.

It may be that my description of Borzage's work is incomplete, since I have not seen some of his films. Where this very skillful director is concerned, I place less confidence than usual in criticism that I have read or overheard. *Seventh Heaven* and *The River* should of themselves suffice to place Borzage in the front rank of the true poets of love.

Humoresque (1920), *Song of Love* (1923–24), and *Lady* (1925) brought a new "climate" to the cinema. At a time when Stroheim caused talk about himself by means of rolling drums and eyes, Borzage, without noise, took a counter-approach, describing luminously beautiful couples at war with an ugly world. We had to wait for *Seventh Heaven* (1927) to clearly understand Borzage's importance. The film was badly received in France because it was situated in a fanciful Paris, like that of *Monsieur Verdoux*. Touchy and carping, the French have the bad habit of looking for documentary truth; if they don't find it they totally reject a masterpiece, being incapable of understanding that "Paris" only stands for a "big city." The scenario was by Benjamin Glazer, but we know that Borzage always collaborated on the scenarios of films close to his heart.

Ado Kyrou. *Amour, Erotisme et Cinéma*
(Le Terrain Vague, 1957), pp. 361–62

Borzage the director was an excellent coordinator. In addition to his careful visual style, he was able to give added depth and understanding to his performers because of his own acting background. (Charles Farrell and Janet Gaynor were never again as good as they were in *Seventh Heaven* and *Street Angel*, and Margaret Sullavan received much of her acclaim from her Borzage films.)

But Borzage was also a skillful story teller; more so, perhaps, because he was able to do so much with his one basic plot. This typical

Borzage plot concerns two lovers who meet under mutual hardship or under what is to become hardship. Facing adversity together, they are often separated by outside forces until their lives are resolved when they overcome the flaws of the larger universe. This is the plot of *Seventh Heaven*, a sentimental film, and the forerunner of what seem to be numerous imitations by other directors. Borzage himself directed two remakes of this film for Fox: *Street Angel* (1928) which suffers from an almost unbearable Germanic heaviness; and *The River* (1929), which was photographically more stunning than *Seventh Heaven*, though never able to achieve the audacious heights of the original. . . .

Burton J. Shapiro in *The American Film Heritage*, edited by the American Film Institute (Acropolis, 1972), pp. 172–73

BROOKS, RICHARD (1912–)

Not the least remarkable aspect of *Crisis*, the first film directed by Richard Brooks—a former radio writer, the author of the novel *The Brick Foxhole*, from which *Crossfire* was taken, and a collaborator on the scripts of *Brute Force, Mystery Street* and *Key Largo*—is the evidence it gives of a writer being allowed freedom in the cinema. Brooks wrote the screenplay from a story by George Tabori and *Crisis* is predominantly a writer's film: its principal strength resides in the dialogue, and as a piece of filmmaking it is a little lacking in the refinements of authority. The drama of *Crisis* is the confrontation of a fanatic, cunning, Latin American dictator, threatened with death from a brain tumour, and the American surgeon kidnapped and obliged to operate on him. Round this situation, Brooks has composed a shrewd and persuasive picture of a minor fascist state on the brink of civil war. . . . The main emphasis, however, is kept on the prolonged duel—at one point crystallised in a gripping, horrific sequence of an operation rehearsal—between the surgeon and the dictator: between the humane, civilized liberal and the savage authoritarian. These are portraits of an incisiveness and density rare in the cinema, and the actors, Cary Grant and Jose Ferrer, realise them perfectly. The ingenious ending, which seems at first a cynical epilogue to the dictator's death, serves to throw the whole conflict into sharp relief, and to illuminate the predicament of a sentient individual pressed by the forces of political violence.

Apart from some lack of flow in the handling, *Crisis* is slightly flawed by the weaker characterisations of the surgeon's and the dictator's wives, two figures who are often on the screen, but not very well played and less firmly written than the other parts. But the film as a whole is original, arresting and considered—and so far probably the most striking example of Dore Schary's policy at MGM of encouraging the development of new talents.

Gavin Lambert. *Sight & Sound.* Dec. 1950, p. 334

This unconvincing mixture [*Battle Circus*] of love, war and studio heroics introduces itself, most inappositely, as "a story of the indomitable human spirit." Nurse McCara's pursuit of the Major might perhaps be called indomitable—"these refugees are becoming quite a problem," she complains at one point, when her duties temporarily keep her from him—but that presumably was not the intention. Scenes of the helicopter rescues and of the taking down and putting up of the unit's tents have a slight documentary interest, but the general tone of the picture is neither realistic nor dramatic; the dialogue adopts a synthetic tough-smart manner, the characters are one-dimensional (both Humphrey Bogart and June Allyson seem ill at ease in their parts), and the film builds laboriously up to an ending which takes the form of a disconcerting anti-climax. It is disappointing that Richard Brooks, whose early work as a scriptwriter and, with his first film, *Crisis*, as a director, suggested considerable promise, should have descended to such a glib, uninteresting piece of film-making.

BFI Bulletin. May 1953, p. 64

Now, utilizing the shocking disclosures made by Evan Hunter in his novel, M.G.M. has launched *The Blackboard Jungle*, directed by Richard Brooks, in order to capitalize on one of the most serious social problems in the United States. Juvenile delinquency is on a steady increase in the great centers, and the polemics between the supporters of the old and of the progressive schools are reaching new heights. This film is therefore a very timely one. With the background of a typical American city, the repelling conditions of some schools are frankly exposed with a "shock treatment" system which is unfortunately too superficial to convey to its audiences the real causes of this appalling situation. We see rapes, muggings, poison-pen letters, knife-stabbings, petty robberies, but we are not made aware, at least in this film, as to the main causes of these evils. The fact that Mr. Brooks, for example, has tolerated the histrionics of a young actor (Vic Morrow) based on an unconvincing imitation of Marlon Brando's style, proves that this film has been made more with an idea to exploit a new item than to deal seriously with a phenomenon which the camera could have expressed and fixed, with realistic ferocity, so that a substantial contribution to the accurate knowledge of a social aspect of great importance be made.

This is all the more unfortunate in as much as we think that scholastic education and juvenile delinquency should be dealt with in motion pictures. *The Blackboard Jungle* could just as well have been the first good film of this kind. Actually, it will be remembered chiefly for its timely production and release.

G. N. Fenin. *Film Culture.* May-June 1955, p. 26

Nobody is satisfied with Hollywood's approach to delinquency, but who has a better one? The psychiatrically-oriented social workers and teachers are advised that they will be included in the delinquent's hostility to authority and that they must get through to the boy. But is the boy mistaken in feeling that they are trying to give him a snow job and that they are part of the apparatus of deadly adjustment to what he is reacting against? *Blackboard Jungle* says the boy *is* mistaken, and though in many ways a good film, like *The Wild One* it's a snow job. . . . *Blackboard Jungle* lifts a group of mixed-up kids from the headlines and tries to devise a dramatic structure for them out of the social problem drama. Delinquency is treated as a problem with a definite solution: the separation of the salvageable from the hopeless, and the drama is the teacher's effort to reach the salvageable. (Like the newspaper, both films avoid discussion of why the boys form their own organizations, with rigid authority, strict codes, and leaders.) Although the script of *Blackboard Jungle* is sane and intelligible, the thematic resolution (like the end of *The Wild One*) is an uneasy dodge—not because it isn't well worked out, but because the film draws its impact from a situation that can't be so easily worked out. . . . Somehow it's no surprise when we excavate the short story on which the rather shoddy novel was based to find that in the original version, "To Break the Wall," the teacher did *not* break through. . . . [1955]

Pauline Kael. *I Lost It at the Movies* (Little, Brown, 1965), pp. 58–59

After Richard Brooks' direction and adaptation of *The Brothers Karamazov*, one was just a bit more apprehensive than usual when it was first announced that he was to perform the same tasks for Tennessee Williams' *Cat on a Hot Tin Roof*.

However, this film is quite distinguished in a surprising way, because it manages to be adult in theme, entertaining in presentation, and to an extent, faithful to the original work. The film exists on its own four feet, so to speak, without the censorial agony of trying to bring the hot tin roof of homosexual implications upon the screen. *Cat on a Hot Tin Roof* is one of the best presentations of neurotic family life in the Deep South—a genre seemingly at its height this year with *God's Little Acre* and *Hot Spell* very recently in our memories.

. . . Here, it is Brick's confusion about the relationship of his wife and his best friend, Skipper, that drives him to drink and self-enforced celibacy. The fact that Skipper is dead only intensifies this guilty confusion, but all verbal intimation of latent sexual aberration is absent. Since this was the chief matter of Brick's violent arguments with his father, the terrifyingly self-confident landowner, "Big Daddy" Pollitt, director Brooks has resorted to the use of the camera to add impact to arguments which lack the shock value of hidden scandal. The thing that matters most in the film is not whether "Big Daddy" will live or die, but whether Maggie and Brick will be reconciled and become heirs to his wealth.

It also matters that we, as spectators, should be kept interested in these events and incredible people, and what results is cinematic style at its slickest. One gets a picture of the contemporary South that does not exist, really, but its images hold us constantly. . . .

Albert Johnson. *Film Quarterly*. Winter 1958, pp. 54–55

Money is the root of virtually all evil. That appears the dominating theme of the movie version of *The Brothers Karamazov* which came to the Music Hall yesterday.

For, out of the fast and tangled stretches of Fyodor Dostoevski's classic tale of greed and hatred and vengeance among a nineteenth-century Russian father and his three legitimate and one illegitimate son, that is the most conspicuous cause for the violent passions that director-writer Richard Brooks has found. Money, in this particular picture, seems to outrank lust—or love.

To be sure, lust and love figure strongly in the barbaric doings that go on in this king-sized and handsome color picture produced by Pando S. Berman for Metro-Goldwyn-Mayer. . . . But it is mostly the matter of money—who owes what to whom and how is a fellow going to pay debts when he has run out of sources of funds—that keeps popping up throughout the drama and making folks mad and miserable. It is really the crux of the conflict between the father and the eldest son.

In the Dostoevski novel there are many other factors that combine to move and account for the reactions of the complex characters. But since Mr. Brooks had but two hours—two hours and twenty-six minutes to be precise—in which to digest the principal movements of the several hundred pages of the book, he did well to emphasize money as the cold, materialistic device of a crude and degenerate society that does most to warp and corrupt men.

Except for a halfway happy ending that blunts the drama's irony, he has done a good job of compressing the substance of the book. The greed and lust and love are in it, and also a little sense of spiritual compassion and intellectual sterility.

Bosley Crowther. *NYT*. Feb. 21, 1958, p. 18

The film [*Cat on a Hot Tin Roof*] will undoubtedly be popular because of a sexual frankness remarkable in American movies—for example, Big Mama pounds the bed to indicate to her daughter-in-law the place where marriages fail; but artistically it arrives at even less point than the play, the change in Brick toward Maggie is even less convincing, and the sweet adjustment of Big Daddy to his sentence is spurious.

Brooks, who also directed, has shoved the action around the big house in an obvious manner, presumably to demonstrate the advantages of films over the restrictions of one stage set. He has allowed the Gooper brood to caricature their adulation of Big Daddy so wildly that, against his attempt to create hard reality in other scenes, it is as if cartoon sequences had been woven into the film. His one accomplishment is with Elizabeth Taylor as Maggie. The lovely Miss Taylor lacks the inner fire from which all else grows and without which nothing can really live; but she is a diligent pupil and, with Brooks' help, has worked so hard that she gives a certain surface to her performance. [1958]

Stanley Kauffmann. *A World on Film*
(Harper, 1966), p. 80

Richard Brooks, who adapted the novel, and directed this film, says Lewis told him long ago that he would do well, in making a movie of *Elmer Gantry*, "to avoid my mistakes—benefit from hindsight." Lewis was probably referring to the anti-religious diatribes that disfigured the novel. Brooks *has* eschewed these. He has also discarded about half the novel, and changed many of the characters.

The result is a so-so vehicle for Burt Lancaster, who plays the title role. Lancaster gives an even more flamboyant performance than usual, and his Gantry is an even greater psychological confusion than Lewis' was. Brooks makes him latch on to Sister Sharon Falconer's evangelistic troupe because he falls in love with her. Brooks also makes Sharon be a *sincere* evangelist, which, in the novel, she was anything but.

One wonders why Brooks, and Producer Bernard Smith, went to so much trouble over such superficially handled material. After all, the *real* drama about a corrupt revivalist is more in the lives he affects than in the greeds and delusions of the man himself. Sinclair Lewis evaded these real issues and was content merely to expose a crude and obvious fraud. Brooks repeats this mistake.

Colton Washburn. *Films in Review*.
Aug.-Sept. 1960, pp. 431–32

[*Sweet Bird of Youth.*] In cold print, the effect of this dramatic deluge was overwhelming; and if one wasn't taken totally in, one was certainly carried unprotestingly along. On film, in Richard Brooks' adaptation, its effect is perhaps more immediately satisfying and less wholly so. For in scaling down the highly-charged tone of Williams' writing, from *fortissimo* to *vibrato* if you like, in curbing its more melodramatic moments and generally pruning and re-shaping it, the director has gained one thing at the cost of another. Isolated scenes are better, so is some of the characterisation, but motivation suffers, as does the stark overall mood of the piece. . . . But by substituting a mere beating for the total horror of castration, the point of Williams' motivation has been cruelly blunted (the boy, after all, was a stud bull, a regular sexual acrobat), the gathering momentum is dissipated, and one goes away from what is a generally gripping entertainment muttering "phoney, phoney, compromise, compromise."

A pity. A real pity. For up to about five minutes before this idiotic event, *Sweet Bird* is full of power, jagged humour and not a little compassion. But banal ending apart, seven-eighths of it is still well worth the watching.

John Cutts. *Films and Filming*. June 1962, p. 35

Conrad wrote: "I stood by with my hand on the davit. I was very quiet. . . . I heard the boat alongside go bump, bump, and not another sound down in there for a while, but the ship under me was full of talking noises."

When Richard Brooks reaches that moment in his film version of *Lord Jim* he has the *Patna* tossing desperately in an Indian Ocean squall and Jim fighting against walls of water that come seething over the bridge to beat the breath from his body and the wits from his head.

Why? The storm does not make the scene more dramatic; it makes it less dramatic. It does not make Jim's leap to safety more infamous, but less so. I can suppose only that Mr. Brooks was abiding by some tenet of screen melodrama that a scene of crisis on the high seas must be accompanied by gale-force winds. In this case, however, it has the additional usefulness of signaling that the movie will show no glimmer of understanding of what Conrad was writing about.

Brooks has caught on to the notion that Jim is in flight from a reputation for cowardice and that his subsequent career is an attempt to live down that shameful leap from the *Patna*. Indeed, he can produce Jim's very words to show that this was so, for Conrad was ever cunning at keeping the ace of his stories up his sleeve. You will not find in the picture—as you will not find it set down in the book—that Jim never really cared a tinker's curse about the world's opinion. He had let *himself* down; he knew himself to be that one man in ten thousand, a perfect hero, and yet there was that wretched little incident caught like a flaw deep in the jewel. The secret sharer, that other who occupies the deepest sanctuaries of a man's soul—he was the enemy; not the ragtag and bobtail of the Eastern ports. . . .

Brooks's offense is that he does not cope with the theme of the great work whose name he has appropriated, but that is really his only offense. Otherwise he has made a rousing tropical adventure tale, about at the level of *Treasure Island*, and centered upon the resourceful figure of a slightly world-soiled Jack Hawkins. . . .

Robert Hatch. *Nation*. March 22, 1965, p. 315

The Professionals referred to in the film of the same name are four tough, hardened-by-experience men who are hired by a wealthy southwestern rancher to bring back his wife being held for ransom by the "bloodiest cutthroat in Mexico." . . .

The adventures of these four men, their encounters with roving bandits, their hunt for Palance and his gang in the Mexican mountains, their stealing into the hacienda hideaway to free Bellamy's wife, Maria, and the trip back with Palance and gang in hot pursuit are full of excitement and suspense. Richard Brooks' direction is fine. He has made not only a lively action film that uses the rugged scenery well in Technicolor, but has also come through with a strong movie of vivid characterization. The four men are more than toughs; they are individuals, with Strode and Ryan displaying some gentleness, beneath their hardness, and Lancaster and Marvin showing a touch of sentiment underneath their pugnacity and cynicism.

The script, however, which Brooks wrote from Frank O'Rourke's *A Mule for the Marquesa*, blows both hot and cold; and while it often makes good sense, particularly the discussions about revolution, . . . the talk gets rather pretentious at times and even down-right silly with a lot of sentimental guff during the shoot-it-out scene between Palance and Lancaster. . . . Claudia Cardinale . . . is no Helen of Troy, but neither is she a baby-faced western heroine. Neither is *The Professionals*, with its good cast and fancy dialogue, any run-of-the-mill western.

Philip T. Hartung. *Commonweal*.
Nov. 18, 1966, p. 201

Richard Brooks has transformed Capote's journalistic caper [*In Cold Blood*] into a tract against capital punishment. A journalist . . . is superimposed on the film as the writer-director's liberal humane mouthpiece. Capote himself seemed singularly uncommitted on the issue. However, Brooks seems to have sacrificed too much of the book in order to make the murderers more sympathetic.

It is not a question of dropping some of Capote's details; Brooks has dropped entire dimensions of the book. The Clutters, for example, take up much of Capote's book, as do the neighbors around them. Nancy Clutter goes steady with a boy of whom her father disapproves because of the boy's Catholicism. The boy is treated as a suspect after the murder. Nancy's mother has been sick for years, and one day she bursts into tears in a neighbor's arms because she feels that in these years when the children are growing up she is so ill that the children will remember her in years after only as a ghost in the house. . . .

None of these "details" turn up in the movie. The first half of the film looks promising; the second half becomes boring. The trouble is that Brooks has focused almost entirely on the killers and their sick minds and childhood dreams. Consequently the movie is motivated by the kind of facile Freudianism that is supposed to have gone out in the forties. . . . The whiplash documentary style of much of the photography clashes with the tired German expressionism of dreams and hallucinations, and the mixture is a bit dishonest besides, in that it places an aura of subjectivity around the killers and around no one else. In the book the dead and even the detectives were allowed the dignity of their own dreams and reveries. [1967]

Andrew Sarris. *Confessions of a Cultist* (S&S, 1970), pp. 328–29

I have not read the book *In Cold Blood*, but, I'm afraid, I have seen the movie. Not that it is so bad as Hollywood products go; in fact, it marks a slight step up for its director, Richard Brooks, best remembered for reducing *Lord Jim* to pablum and *The Brothers Karamazov* to pulp. He has served as his own screenwriter, and from even a cursory scanning of the book I can tell he meant to be faithful to it but was defeated by three problems: the book's superabundance of detail, much of it barely relevant but arguably more interesting than the more pertinent stuff; the shifting, inchoate, self-contradictory sympathies and antipathies lurking under Capote's mask of impassivity; and the need to make it all "filmic," as that term is conventionally understood—having the proper suspense, climaxes, visual effects, and so on.

To handle the detail correctly, Brooks went to the exact locations—only to prove, once again, that the camera photographs the photographer. Yes, this is the Clutter home; yes, that was shot in the actual courtroom; but Brooks does not capture the *genius loci*. He can show you what a place looks like, not how it feels to be or live in it. The significant detail is missing—whether it is something about the upholstery of a chair or the precise proportions of a room. Few of the places he shows us seem used: the people and their ambience assume no other relationship except the flimsy one of contiguity. [1968]

John Simon. *Movies into Film* (Dial, 1971), p. 171

BROWN, CLARENCE (1890–)

This tale [*The Signal Tower*] by Wadsworth Camp, of an isolated signal tower in a desolate section of a mountain railroad, might easily be trite melodrama. In the hands of Director Clarence Brown it becomes a compelling story. Brown has given vitality to his characters through carefully built incident. They live and consequently their movements become real and holding. The director has touched upon the home life of a young towerman and his wife with keen insight. Then there is a derelict telegrapher, who comes to board with them. This man is no out and out scoundrel. He is just a happy-go-lucky oaf. Wallace Beery gives a striking characterization of this hulking wanderer, Rockcliffe Fellowes is excellent as the towerman-husband and Virginia Valli gives a compelling performance of his young wife.

Photoplay. Aug. 1924, p. 48

The Goose Woman is a story of a woman's change of heart. This theme, it is obvious, is not a new one in motion pictures but it *is* unusual to see the influences that change character and cause action, so clearly and interestingly disclosed. Seldom has the deeper significance of a situation been brought out so completely as in this story of the workings of Marie de Nardi's mind and heart. One must qualify this statement, however, by noting that the actual change of heart, when the mother changes from hatred to love of her son, is the weakest part of the photoplay.

Both the acting of Louise Dresser, who took the part of Marie de Nardi, and the work of the director, Clarence Brown, contribute to the success of the film. Miss Dresser has that presence and dignity which is a hall mark of good acting on either the screen or the stage. Through a long sequence of scenes in which she is constantly to the fore her command of the situation never slackens. Her knowledge of the technique of motion picture art gives an artistic maturity to the photoplay and one feels that both Miss Dresser and the director have happily well over-shot the mark of the twelve year old intellect. . . .

Some of the praise for these effects and artistry must be shared with the director. One can, by looking closely, see his hand in the touches that built up the effect of squalor and ugliness of the home of Marie de Nardi. Or, when the District Attorney, in order to impress the court, has the dirty Goose Woman groomed into the charming person she once was, the details of dirty nails being cleaned, for example, are both humorous and realistic.

NBR. Nov.-Dec. 1925, p. 3

Produced with admirable artistry, both in the unfurling of the chronicle and in the character delineation, *Flesh and the Devil*, a picture based on Hermann Sudermann's novel *The Undying Past*, is a compelling piece of work in which there are but few conventional movie notes. There is, it is true, a flood of sunshine and a wealth of flowers for the final sequence, but in the previous chapter tragedy had stalked into the picture.

In this photoplay Clarence Brown has mingled adroitly hard and fast realism with soft and poetic glimpses. Sometimes he appears to have given just a little too much consideration to doing something different, but his ideas are eminently successful most of the time. . . .

Mr. Brown gives a most impressive idea of the duel, moving his camera back so that the two figures are silhouetted against the sky-line. There are a couple of puffs of smoke, and all that denotes the result of the pistol shots is the next scene, wherein Felicitas is looking at herself in a mirror as she tries on a mourning veil. . . .

Mordaunt Hall. *NYT*. Jan. 10, 1927, p. 20

In a way, *The Trail of '98* has the sweep of *The Covered Wagon*. You follow Brown's fortune seekers with breathless interest from the moment their steamboat puffs its way out of the Golden Gate, laden with gold maddened humans from every corner of the globe, until the last fadeout after the burning of Dawson City.

The whole gold rush trail is here—over the snowy perils of Chilkoot Pass and through the river rapids. The menace is always Old Man Mercury, hovering at forty or below zero.

The Trail of '98 is that dream of all megaphone wielders: a purely director's picture. Still, the story of the six principal protagonists—played by Dolores Del Rio, Ralph Forbes, Karl Dane, Harry Carey, Tully Marshall, and George Cooper—is never lost. Basically, it is the romance of two adventurers in the Yukon, one a young Scotchman, the other the granddaughter of an old Jew making a quest for fortune.

It has tremendous interest as Brown pictures it—the last stand of roistering, hard-fisted pioneer America.

Photoplay. April 1928, p. 52

Clarence Brown is another American director who has shown short flashes of cinema in between long stretches of picture-sense. Some time ago, in 1925, his clever handling of *The Goose Woman* and of Louise Dresser aroused some interest. During the first portion of this film, while Miss Dresser played the drink-sodden prima donna who had fallen beside the way, Clarence Brown's direction was remarkable. He made her live in the filthiest squalidity with gin bottles and geese, and at night she would hunch up her back over her precious book of press-cuttings, to read over the reports of her glorious days. So far the film was excellent, handled with sympathy, but the latter half was quite ridiculous, Miss Dresser, the direction, and the film going to pieces. Among the many films credited to Clarence Brown were *The Light in the Dark* (1922); *The Eagle*, with Valentino at his best; *Smouldering Fires*, with Pauline Frederick, in 1925; and *The Trail of '98*, a film that was meant to be an epic, but succeeded in being a first-class super film, without interest to the intelligent-minded. *Flesh and the Devil*, however, made in 1926, was a film of more than passing cleverness. It was, it is true, another example of the committee-produced picture, with John Gilbert, Lars Hanson and Greta Garbo as the star appeal, but it contained short sequences that strengthened Clarence Brown's claim as a director. The copy shown in this country was maltreated, either by the censor or by special English editing, but it sufficed to show that in its original version *Flesh and the Devil* had some pretensions to be called a good film. The theme was sheer, undiluted sex, and Brown used a series of close ups to get this across with considerable effect. Notable also was his use of angles, different indeed from either the customary German or American method, and the happiness with which he settled the characters in their environment.

Paul Rotha. *The Film Till Now* (Jonathan Cape, 1930), pp. 129–30

Frances Marion, who has been entrusted with making more important scenarios than probably any other writer for the screen, faithfully followed the text of the play [*Anna Christie*], adding a few connecting scenes that are quite in key with what O'Neill wrote. The result is a very talkie, uncinematic affair, more old-fashioned than the silent movies. If it were not so well acted it would be pretty tiresome. The action goes forward by jerks, one scene of talk talk talk, followed by a fadeout and a time-elapse title, in effect just like the falling of a curtain, then more talk. That a great deal of it is good talk does not liven it up very much, nor does the obviously studio-constructed sky-line help to remove the feeling of watching something on a stage. "Dat ole davil sea," is present only in the conversation of old Chris.

NBR. Feb. 1930, p. 12

To appreciate Milestone's achievement in this environment, one may refer to W. S. Van Dyke and *White Shadows*. Here is a minimum achievement with potential material. Or, we may refer to Clarence Brown. He has shown himself an apt chameleon. There are three kinds of this creature: the passive, like Herbert Brenon; the apt, like Brown;

and the selective, like Jacques Feyder, a foreign importation whom Hollywood has never learned to use despite his responsiveness. Brown in *Flesh and the Devil* showed an aptitude for a maturer idiom, which controlled him rather than submitted to him. In *Emma*, Brown has illustrated that directorial integrity may keep a sentimental idea chaste, when a chaste personality like Marie Dressler is the pivot. In *A Free Soul* he assembled his film as Frankenstein assembled his monster, though for the Academy of Motion Picture Arts and Sciences, to more self-satisfying consequences.

Harry Alan Potamkin. *Vanity Fair*. March 1932, p. 52

It is in the sense this film conveys of human beings caught in the swift machinery of modern living that *Night Flight* soars above other pictures of its kind. The production is of course beautifully adequate in its photography and settings and especially in the workman-like effectiveness of its scenario. The cast, with all its resplendent names, might have been more of a hindrance than a help—high-calibered stars have a way of knocking the values of a story out of gear with their over-accented personalities; but Clarence Brown has achieved something like a miracle of fusion in keeping his cast subordinate to his story without sacrificing any of their excellence as actors. Even so, it is sometimes hard not to be conscious of the ghosts of other pictures hovering too near—one has seen the Barrymores so many, many times, for instance, that every new film they appear in is haunted with echoes of other films.

James Shelley Hamilton. *NBR*. Nov. 1933, p. 12

Miss Garbo, the first lady of the screen, sins, suffers and perishes illustriously in the new, ably produced and comparatively mature version of the Tolstoy classic. . . . Having put on a couple of mental years since the 1927 version of *Anna Karenina*, which called itself *Love* and meant it, the cinema now is able to stab tentatively below the surface of Tolstoy's passion tales and hint at the social criticism which is implicit in them. Samuel Goldwyn's screen edition of *Resurrection* last year discussed Tolstoy's theories of social reform, and now *Anna Karenina* widens the iris of the camera so as to link the plight of the lovers to the decadent and hypocritical society which doomed them. The photoplay is a dignified and effective drama which becomes significant because of that tragic, lonely and glamourous blend which is the Garbo personality.

André Sennwald. *NYT*. Aug. 31, 1935, p. 16

What the screen really makes out of *Ah, Wilderness* is a first-class atmosphere piece. It calls up more matters than it knows of by its sure reconstruction of the day-to-day life of the New England country in a time (1906) that is as dead but as vivid in the general memory as the smell of leaves burning in piles along the gravel walks, this fall or when you were a kid. Practically all of it that is good is background, in the way of local color. Not only the sets of stiff cluttered rooms, lawns, gas buggies, picnics, but the incidental life of the place. Take the high-school graduation, shifting rapidly from the audience of proud parents to the speakers, quartets ("Asleep in the Deep"), the valedictorian, and the serious young chit in pigtails, fighting a very sick clarinet with a wild roving eye of reproach for her accompanist. Or the barroom scene (the fast baby here was perfectly fine); or the scenes at table, or on the morning of the Fourth (a little overdone), or at the school sociable. And at times, what with the genius that often goes into Metro production—cameras, set crews, and particularly the musical arranging of Herbert Stothart, always appropriate and frequently an inspired counterpoint to the action—at times the picture is beautiful, as in the spooning at night on the Common, with the trees quiet and dark over the grass, framing a white Georgian church as sweet as music. Much of the film is silly, but *Ah, Wilderness* remains a job of picture making, in craftsmanship and feeling, that is wonderful to see. [1935]

Otis Ferguson. *The Film Criticism of O.F.*
(Temple, 1971), pp. 108–09

Clarence Brown, who is in the myth business himself (remember the Russia of *Anna Karenina*), has taken his spring vacation with Eugene O'Neill and in *Ah, Wilderness* they wander back with never a false step into a Connecticut of thirty years ago. It must be O'Neill's script and the tender authenticity of his dialogue that give it undeniable distinction. Yet in retrospect Brown is never mawkish, is more than ingenious in the graduation scene, is neat and economical with the big scene of the play, a dinner table conversation that might have grown wooly in the screen version. And the acting of, especially, Eric Linden and Lionel Barrymore save Wallace Beery from the woeful emphasis he receives from being in the film at all, or even from the shock *we* receive at finding him within bellowing distance of Connecticut.

Alistair Cooke, *Sight & Sound.*
Spring 1936, p. 23

Possessed. This is another of the familiar formulae in which the small town girl, a factory worker, yearns for the attractions of a life of ease and luxury. She is determined to get what she wants. She finds her way to New York and there meets a rich and socially prominent bachelor who, however, is averse to matrimony. The girl gets what she wants and after a considerable period without benefit of clergy they are married and, presumably, live happily ever after. The story is destructive to character and conduct because it accepts and condones the girl's conduct and shows that it apparently led to a successful accomplishment of her wishes. It tends to glorify vice and to make virtue appear stupid.

Martin Quigley. *Decency in Motion Pictures* (Macmillan, 1937), pp. 36–37

Idiot's Delight assumed the task of discoursing on the subject that affects us most vitally today—fascist war. As such it must be judged more exactingly than the usual "subjectless" program filler. If it had succeeded its credit would have been highest. As a deliberate and inarguable failure it can arouse only a deep sense of pity for a lost opportunity and scorn for its cowardice. Surely the path this film walked, methodically shedding whatever barbs the original stage play possessed, is one of the most ignominious and humiliating ever laid out by an American film company. How neatly and deftly are Germany and Italy absolved of present war responsibility, in terms of the film! This ingenuity would be something to marvel at if it didn't take us closer to the grave! For one brief, humbling moment Germany is hastily indicted for subscribing to philosophies of hatred and destruction, but never as far as relates to the immediate war situation that is the subject of the film.

Robert Stebbins. *TAC*. March 1939, p. 23

The Human Comedy is an effort to create, through a series of lyrically casual, almost plotless scenes, the image of a good family in a good town in wartime. Most of my friends detest it. A good many millions of other people, I suspect, will like it, as they like the Andy Hardy films and Rupert Hughes's *The Old Nest*, whose traditions it returns to rather more than improves on. I do not agree with either side. I think my friends are too frightened of tearjerkers to grant that they can be not only valid but great, and that the audience at large is too friendly, too gullible, too eager to be seduced. The picture is mainly a mess, but as a mixture of typical with atypical failure, and in its rare successes, it interests me more than any other film I have seen for a good while.

Many of its faults, and most of its virtues, are those of its author. What angers me is that Saroyan's original story, cut perhaps twenty per cent and sternly dry-cleaned, might have been the basis for a film which, though I might not wholly have liked or agreed with it, would have had a great deal of beauty and importance. That, of course, would have had to depend on every detail of its screen treatment; and in nearly every respect the treatment it gets wobbles between that stultifying kind of slick-paper competence which is worse than no competence at all and unforgivable errors of taste and judgment. The best one can say of it, with few exceptions, is that it tries on the whole to be "faithful" to Saroyan; not invariably a good idea. The worst, in my opinion, lies less in its active failures of taste or of plain sense than in its easygoing, self-pleased, Mortimer Snerdish neglect of some magnificent opportunities. [1943]

James Agee. *Agee on Film* (Beacon, 1964), p. 30

Intruder in the Dust bears little resemblance in directorial style to the bulk of Brown's glamorous, star-ridden productions. But surely it is the years of range and experience which have given him a control of the medium so calm, sure, and—apparently—easy that he can make a complex story seem simple and straightforward, without any of that straining for effect or vulgar overemphasis which is Hollywood's usual approach to a "classic" (for example, the way Richard Brooks overloaded *Elmer Gantry* with gigantic sets, enormous crowds, fires, riots, and human stampedes). As Karel Reisz pointed out in his analysis of *Intruder in the Dust*, Brown's "deliberate, unspectacular direction" often extends and sharpens the impact of the novel by capturing in a single image the effects that Faulkner had to catalogue one by one; but, of course, the movie simplifies the internal conflicts, the long passages of minute analysis of motives and reactions. As Reisz says, "This, perhaps, is inevitable. But it means that the novelist's most sensitive instrument of perception has been lost." It is evidence of Brown's craftsmanship that he achieved in a single take the sequence which most impressed European critics: the gathering of the crowd in the town square—expectant, waiting for the lynching.

Pauline Kael. *Kiss Kiss Bang Bang* (Little, Brown, 1968), p. 285

BROWNING, TOD (1882–1962)

Not often does one see so powerful a photodrama as *The Unholy Three*. . . . It is a stirring story stocked with original twists and situations, a picture that teems with surprises and one in which the suspense is kept as taut as the string of a bow. After viewing this production the figures that have passed upon the screen still cling to one's mind, and one feels like talking about the strange and unusual tale.

The Unholy Three is at first concerned with the sideshow of a circus, but the whole plot is quite different from any other narrative with such a background. The atmosphere, inside and outside the freak's tent, is wonderfully impressive, and the characters and their actions are so realistic. Tod Browning, the director of this film, and the scenarist have cooperated magnificently on this effort, which was adapted from a story by C. A. Robbins. Added to this, the cast is one in which the players are thoroughly suited to their respective roles. The principals are Lon Chaney, Mae Busch, Matt Moore, Victor McLaglen and a midget, Harry Earles. . . .

There is nothing ludicrous or slapstick about a single scene. It all seems plausible, and the way in which the story is worked out, with the possible exception of the introducing of a giant gorilla, is a credit to the director. Even this particular stretch is quite effective. . . .

This pictorial effort is a startling original achievement which takes its place with the very best productions that have been made. It is encouraging to witness something so different from the usual run of films.

NYT. Aug. 4, 1925, p. 14

Then there is Tod Browning who made *The Unholy Three* and *The Blackbird*, although the latter was only in essence a repetition of the first. Browning has a peculiar gift for managing dramatic suspense, only rivalled by some of the Germans, though achieved by methods less obvious than theirs. He has whatever it was that made Stevenson a notable writer in spite of his being a second-rate mind.

Iris Barry. *Let's Go to the Movies*
(Payson & Clarke, 1926), p. 227

Mr. Browning has provided [in *The Unknown*] a skillful vehicle for the display of Lon Chaney's peculiar talents. An armless wonder whose arms are really only well concealed for use in secret, criminal violence, is in love with the beautiful girl at whom he hurls dangerous knives with his prehensible toes. She likes him just because he is armless unlike the other men of the circus whose arms and hands constantly threaten her with unwelcome attentions. When she sees his hand, which has a double thumb, strangling her father, he has his arms amputated in order to be truly perfect in her eyes, as well as to be rid of the tell-tale double thumb. But now her avowed love for the circus strong man blights his hopes and makes him seek revenge. He plots to have the horses in the strong man's big act tear his arms out of their sockets but he is killed in the attempt. It is a grewsome, inhuman tale rather artificially built up but likely to please those who want to see Lon Chaney do his stuff.

NBR. July 1927, p. 11

What immediately astonishes us [in *The Big City*], what puts us squarely onto a terrain different from what we are accustomed to, is this inconceivable mixture of rival bands and the police in constant encounter. Everybody smiles, everybody suspects everybody else, shakes hands and waits for an opportune moment that will justify a brutal and rapid action. Until then these men show enormous tranquility and are constantly sure of having taken in the other guy.

In these films of mathematical construction, we have to watch all corners of the screen because something is going on there. Though the principal actions are centered on, don't forget to attach great importance to that back of the hand that settles a derby or that finger that distractedly lifts a key from the lock. No close-ups are used to underline these basic acts because they would be too easily perceptible and we would have no occasion to congratulate ourselves on our perspicacity. The gesture, the conduct of each man, the tactic of the bands, everything is extraordinarily combined. There is a dazzling logic in it all. Yes, it's the logic that strikes me as admirable; just as in dreams or in madness it is the *excess* of logic in a world unrelated with ours that leaves us completely confounded. . . .

These general remarks can also apply to *Underworld*. But whereas in that film the protagonists or their characters leave their mark on the action, here it is the value of the combinations that is interesting. We watch a magnificent game of checkers in which the pieces [*dames*] are not restricted by the board in their attack. It should be added that the *dames* have too much importance in this gangster film since Betty Compson and Marceline Day manage to convert Lon Chaney and James Murray, and this is really too much.

Such as it is, this film is remarkable, but is no doubt considerably inferior to the too little appreciated recent works of Tod Browning—*The Road to Mandalay, The Black Bird,* and *The Show*.

Louis Chavance. *Revue du Cinéma.*
Feb. 1929, unpaged

Not since *The Lost World, King Kong*, and *The Invisible Man* have the camera wizards enjoyed such a field day. By use of the split screen, glass shots, oversize sets and other trick devices cherished of their kind, they have pieced together a photoplay [*The Devil Doll*] which is grotesque, slightly horrible and consistently interesting. A freak film, of course, and one which may overburden Junior's imagination, but an entertaining exhibition of photographic hocus-pocus for all that. . . .

Mr. Barrymore's appearance in a wig, skirt and tremulous lower lip has its novelty value, and there are a few scenes, played by Rafaela Ottiana and other unprocessed grown-ups, which have melodramatic virtues. But the picture relies mainly, and with understandable assurance, upon such ingenious bits as Miss Ford's demonstration of Alpine skill in climbing (via a slipper, footstool, bench and drawer handles) to the top of a dressing table; or Mr. Hohl's ludicrous impersonation of a Christmas tree ornament; or the Apache dance with a table-top serving as a ball room. Tod Browning, who may be remembered for *The Unholy Three, Dracula* and similar pleasantries, has invested these essentially ridiculous episodes with a menacing, chilling quality which makes it impossible for you to consider them too lightly. That, naturally, is as it should be in a horror film.

Frank S. Nugent. *NYT*. Aug. 8, 1936, p. 5

This picture [*Freaks*] is selected for mention not because it may be said definitely to be in violation of one or more principles of morality but rather because it represents a type that provokes apprehension. It is a story concerned with the life and loves of circus freaks and because of the human abnormalities involved its unwholesome shockery creates morbid audience reactions. It is a skillfully presented production but of a character which in consideration of the susceptibilities of mass audiences should be avoided. Represented in this picture and appearing in some degree in many others is the horror element—this growing out of the procedure of the melodramatic mystery play. This element may not be considered as unreservedly objectionable but its use must be governed by reasonable judgment as to the character of the material, the degree of detail and emphasis given to it and a commonsense understanding of mass audience psychology.

Martin Quigley. *Decency in Motion Pictures* (Macmillan, 1937), pp. 34–35

Tod Browning's *Dracula* is the obvious leader of the American vampire product, though it was far from the classic of terror it might have been. A too literal adaptation of the play (*not* the book) resulted in a plodding, talkative development, with much of the vital action taking place off-screen.

However, it did have some superb moments—and the opening two reels contain some of the best horror of the American cinema. Perhaps the credit for this should go to the cameraman (Freund) rather than to Browning, for the atmosphere of obscure, mystic terror of these scenes is reminiscent of the earlier German fantasies. Particularly memorable are the first scenes in the crypt of Dracula's castle. The camera seems to float around the misty walls, almost like a phantom, and Dracula's emergence from his coffin is recorded casually, without any attempt to shock. The gliding movements of Dracula's three wraith-like sisters as they pass among the last rays of light of the dying day, and the bloated rats scampering in and out of the coffins, are also devoid of sensationalism.

William K Everson. *Films in Review.*
Jan. 1954, p. 15

There is little to be said about *Freaks* (1932), Tod Browning's celebrated film, except that it does not merit that reputation for cruelty accorded it by the litany of belated surrealists. On the contrary, what I found touching was the human being's prodigious capacity for adaptation. Seeing the armless man light a cigarette by using only his mouth leaves us breathless with admiration. This story shows the infinite ingenuity and the greatness of man. But enough moralizing. *Freaks* is a very honest film that can be seen with more pleasure than horror.

Jean Douchet. *Cahiers du Cinéma.*
Nov. 1962, p. 32

Dracula, although masterfully directed by Tod Browning and boasting the brilliant camera work of the German Karl Freund, seems somewhat dated today and does not stand up as well as does *Frankenstein*, but it is still an effective work. Stoker's original tale is too all-encompassing for a literal translation to the screen, but his basic theme was closely followed. As in the book itself, the opening portions of the film were considerably superior to the closing ones. Castle Dracula was a massive, ancient ruin filled with cobwebs and mystery, sweeping stone staircases and enormous cold fireplaces, a perfect setting for the unnamable horror it concealed. The countryside was blasted and arid, the villagers terrified of the monstrosities dwelling in the fortress on the mountaintop. From the opening scene with Renfield and a terrified coach driver riding through the barren countryside, a sense of horror settles upon the screen. . . .

There are various reasons why the film has lost some of its effectiveness today. Styles in acting and direction have undergone considerable alteration in the past thirty years and more. Much of the performance in *Dracula* today seems considerably overdone, a result, too, of too literal transference from the stage, where broadness of performance is a necessity. The action seems somewhat static, more in keeping with stage production rather than the greater freedom of the film. In many portions the sound was faulty and the photography indistinct. An air of constant silence hovers over the film, for this was before the days of the crashing musical score which is now an integral part of every film. In some scenes—particularly those in which Lugosi, eyes glowing and fangs gleaming, approaches his victim—the complete silence enhanced the air of horror, but today the total lack of musical scoring creates an air of monotony, particularly in the opening scenes at Castle Dracula. The black and white photography, on the other hand, is a decided asset to the film, creating a nightmarish world of black, white, and gray shadows.

Drake Douglas. *Horror* (Macmillan, 1966), pp. 47–48

It is difficult, on re-viewing the film [*Dracula*] nowadays, to see it through the eyes of the early thirties. The dialogue, even by former standards, is deadeningly slow, and long stretches never break away from the confines of the stage. Much of the camerawork is uninspired and static, though there is one travelling shot, through the Doctor's sanatorium grounds, which is remarkable for those days of enclosed booths. The sea journey to Whitby promises much, but then cuts straight to the finding of the dead crew. Almost every climax, in fact, is cut before it reaches its peak. Even leaving things to the imagination can be overdone. The final destruction of Dracula is handled with such reticence that one is unsure of what is happening at all. The epilogue, showing the actor who played the professor (Edward van Sloan) as himself standing in front of a portion of blank screen and warning the audience that there are such things as vampires, does not come off because the audience does not realise that they are supposed to be looking at someone in a cinema talking directly to them. It worked in the theatre because the curtain had fallen and risen again to show the cast in the familiar line-up.

Nevertheless, even when much of the film is written off, enough remains of a kind of macabre poetry to leave a stronger impression in the memory than many slicker examples since. The opening sequence is splendid. The young agent arriving in the little mid-European village as the sun sets, the frightened inhabitants shutting themselves up as the light thickens, the clattering old cab, the first sight of the gaunt coachman who takes over for the final part of the journey, the misty ruined castle, the rats and dust, the Count and his three wraith-like concubines grouped on the wide stairs, all this is highly atmospheric, and magnificently photographed by Karl Freund. It is with the start of the Count's dialogue that the magic falls. Even in the rest of the film there are effective moments—the Count's "invisibility" in a silver box, the un-dead Lucy wandering spectre-like in the shadows, the dark arches of Dracula's Hampstead cellar, even the very unlikely London of swirling fogs. The mistiest parts are, in fact, the best; when the lights go up the interest goes down. . . .

Ivan Butler. *Horror in the Cinema* (Barnes, 1967–70), pp. 40–42

CAPRA, FRANK (1897–   )

A Lady For a Day is a well-produced bit of O. Henry hokum that gains rather than suffers from a troupe of second-rate actors. Originally a short story by Damon Runyon, the Cinderella theme is dressed up in sentimental, holiday clothes by Frank Capra. The mythical golden-hearted Broadway in the story is a realistic fairyland because Capra has learned from the Russians (and improved, because he has been steadily directing pictures instead of conferring importantly ten months a year and working two).

May Robson uses the cheapest tricks in the actor's bag. . . . Warren William is a lightweight with little charm, and Ned Sparks is an old-time comedian who can't deliver a line without winking broadly at the audiences and falling down a flight of stairs. Fortunately, these people fit into Capra's design for *A Lady For a Day*, because he needs only bit players to fill in his fine photography, his genuine atmospheric feeling of a Broadway teeming with philanthropic killers and soft-hearted hoofers. . . .

Frank Capra has worked in a good movie school. He has made dozens of unpretenious and inexpensive "action" pictures. *A Lady For a Day* shows the ease he has gained by having to work fast, cheaply, and with minor players. Admitting a good manuscript, nevertheless, under poor direction, it could have been turned into an exaggerated, blundering maudlin, Broadway sob story. He made it an amusing, sentimental tale.

Pare Lorentz. *Vanity Fair*. Oct. 1933, p. 40

It seems to me that the best of recent pictures was *It Happened One Night*. It was far superior to such great opuses as *Viva Villa*! and *The House of Rothschild*. It was directed by Frank Capra and they tell me Frank Capra has never had a failure. This may be attributed to the fact that he is in control of his productions from the first detail to the last fadeout. He picks his story, takes his time and invariably turns out something that can be sat through with pleasure. I don't vouch for his entire output but I know that *It Happened One Night* was something to revive your faith in a medium which could belong among the great arts. . . . For freshness of treatment and humor of presentation, we have had nothing to equal it in a long time.

Robert Forsythe. *New Masses*. July 3, 1934, p. 44

Frank Capra is not the genius of the age, but he is a careful, talented director who has made a Hollywood success and earned an office of his own, and still not been taken in by blobs of gilt. Thus far he has used his prerogatives as a sure-fire moneymaker to hold out on one important thing: it will either be good comedy before he is through with it, or he won't be through with it. . . .

And where Mr. Capra himself stands out, after you have granted him intelligence, technical skill, a sense of character, is for his mastery of two of the most vital factors in comedy: timing and accent. There is no need to be too intellectual on this: it is merely the old difference between the man who can, and the man who can't, tell a joke—extended from the point in a two-line gag to the interwoven points of a sequence, and from the innumerable separate parts of a picture to their relative duration, the way they run into one another and carry along the mood without spilling a drop. And it is largely this precision and instinct for where the swing of the words or of the body should be, that makes everything so natural and irresistible here. (The René Clair pictures show the same thing, more complex, more highly developed.) *Broadway Bill* has faults, there's no denying that—an almost unbelievably false uplift in the end, a song about the split-pea soup and the succotash that is given too much extension, and Mr. Capra tends to repeat things out of his old pictures. In substance it is a little thing. But we can finish with it quickly and definitely by saying that it will be a long day before we see so little made into so much: it is gay and charming and will make you happy, and I am sorry to say I do not know recommendations much higher. [1934]

Otis Ferguson. *The Film Criticism of O.F.* (Temple, 1971), pp. 58–59

Among the more gratifying phenomena of the current season has been the growing recognition of *It Happened One Night*, the Frank Capra production of last year, as one of the few potential classics of the recent cinema. . . . There had been a whole succession of pictures based on the picaresque aspects of the cross-country bus; neither Claudette Colbert nor Clark Gable was a reigning favorite with the great popular public; and Frank Capra was merely one of several better than average Hollywood directors. In brief, the wholly spontaneous response with which the picture was received could be traced to no novelty or originality in its component elements. A second viewing of it confirms this truth at the same time that it enforces the realization of how difficult it is, at the present stage of motion picture production and appreciation, to determine what it is precisely which makes a good photoplay. It is true that the story, which is a mixture of both farcical and realistic situations, is exceptionally well put together from almost every point of view. It is developed with the galloping pace that good farce requires, and the timing of individual scenes is invariably well managed. But it is hard to distinguish between the work of the scriptwriters and the work of the director, who is perhaps even more responsible for maintaining an unerring accuracy of tempo throughout. . . . As for the content of the film, which may possibly be distinguished from the treatment, one can remark only that is is authentically indigenous without being in any way novel or striking. An honest documentation of familiar American actualities becomes, in a Hollywood film, more absorbing than intrigue in Monte Carlo or pig-sticking in Bengal. Also one might point out that the manner in which this material is utilized for comic purposes strikes a nice balance between pure farce and serious social satire. The result of the balance is something less tiresome than the first, and less precarious to the comic intention than the second. But the effort to fix and label the particular quality which separates this film from the dozen or more substantially like it in recent years is bound to end only in an admission of critical humiliation. A good photoplay, like a good book or a good piece of music, remains always something of a miracle—in the least sentimental sense of that word. Beyond a certain point the mind is forced to bow down before its own inability to unravel and put together again all the parts of the shining and imponderable whole with which it is dealing.

William Troy. *Nation*. April 10, 1935, p. 426

Frank Capra, from all evidence we have been able to gather, is solely responsible for *Lost Horizon*, having supervised every stage of its vast production. And great must the blame be. After *Mr. Deeds Goes to Town*, the all-pervasive triteness of *Lost Horizon* is a disagreeable shock. From the novel by James Hilton we had learned what to expect. Capra's enthusiasm for the novel and his selection of it for filmization was entirely in keeping with his psychological development. From *Broadway Bill* thrugh *Mr. Deeds*, Capra plainly showed his distress that the world was out of joint, that mass misery is the foundation of the fortunes of the few. His distress was manifestly sincere, his concern genuine, and remains so even on the basis of *Lost Horizon*. He obviously wished he could do something about it. In *Broadway Bill*, Walter Connelly sells his huge interests, gives up money grubbing and goes off with his favorite son-in-law to follow the ponies. Mr. Deeds gives most of his millions to several thousand dispossessed farmers, and retires to "Mandrake Falls, where the scenery enthralls, where no hardship e'er befalls, welcome to Mandrake Falls."

Shangri-La is Mandrake Falls without the United Cigar Store. It has more books than the Congressional Library and a shady approximation of a Tibetan horn that hardly compensates for Mr. Deeds' tuba. As for authentic feeling for the Tibetan scene one is reminded of a British critic's comment on *Mary of Scotland*, "the inaccuracies must have involved tremendous research." One would require but a single sequence, almost a single frame, from *Storm Over Asia* or *Son of Mongolia* to shame the highly publicized "fidelities" of *Lost Horizon*.

Some time last year we concluded our review of *Mr. Deeds* with a fervent wish that in his next picture, *Lost Horizon*, Capra would "in some unaccountable way avoid the chauvinist, jingo pitfalls" that would face him. It is among the more regrettable features of *Lost Horizon* that he fails completely. As evidence we can point to the Chinaman who leers lasciviously at the film's shady lady, Isabel Jewell during the refueling scene. . . . At this date, it is perhaps unnecessary to discuss so completely an escapist philosophy as that summed up in Shangri-La (a refuge for all the delicate perishable beauties of the world to which men will turn after their civilization is destroyed). It is perhaps supererogatory to point out that today the preservation of culture is a process of complete participation in the struggles of the world. The Spanish workers who at this moment are defending with their lives their great artistic heritage understand this.

Robert Stebbins. *New Theatre*. April 1937, pp. 27–28

Just now Mr. Capra is the most sensitive of all men riding herd over Hollywood cameras; and the scenarist who works with him, Robert Riskin, has earned enough laurels in celluloid to give him first call. Yet the two of them cannot move [*Lost Horizon*] past the first three reels without recourse to fresh invention, and only by shooting a remarkable escape sequence—all marvelously contrived among Tibetan glaciers—can they climax their story. The result is a conglomeration of the Capra-Riskin magic, all mixed with Mr. Hilton's insecure metaphysics—a sandwich of strong bread provided by the director and the writer to enfold the thin slice of Hiltonian aesthetics. . . . The basis of Mr. Hilton's escapist dreams was not unrelated to that of Senator Carter Glass—be it enacted: for man to be happy, there must be plenty of gold lying around loose. I submit, however enchanting such an idea grows in print, it can hardly lend itself to the epic mood of film. . . .

Contrast the work of *Lost Horizon* and its superlative three reels of an aeroplane flight over the Himalayan ranges (the finest background projection and cutting effects ever achieved in an air sequence) with the true Capra vein of *Mr. Deeds Goes to Town*. In that graceful picture, the High Lama of a Down East village—he happens to be a tuba-player—received a bequest of many millions of dollars, which he promptly proceeded to give away in New York City. There was more genuine fantasy in that film than ever was found in Mr. Hilton's book.

Lawrence Stallings. *Stage*. April 1937, pp. 53–54

Frank Capra, though sensitive and civilized, still remains the O. Henry of the films. If he could only forget his early Sennett training and dip a large ladle in the bowl of life, he might still climb the mountain of great art.

Jim Tully. *Cinema Arts*. June 1937, p. 42

Capra's best pictures are marked by a sense of humor, an awareness of American life, and a shrewd use of topical events, all these being traits developed from his early association with screen-comedy specialists. *Lady for a Day* depicted in a light vein a 1933 phenomenon of the depression: Apple Annie. *It Happened One Night* exploited the latest American innovation in living—bus travel and tourist camps—for a romantic tale. The witty *Mr. Deeds Goes to Town* pitted happiness against money before a semipolitical American background. In all of these pictures Capra has shown himself to be a professional craftsman more interested in what he has to say than in the way it is said. Cutting, composition, and rhythm in the more profound sense are rarely seen in his work. His forte is humorous characterization, the light incident, local color, and sentiment. When he has a more serious story that demands strong imaginative treatment, such as *Lost Horizon*, he is out of his realm. Gags, ingenious pieces of business, novel story twists—these are his main tools in trade. Perhaps more than any other director he could be called the O. Henry of the screen. . . .

Frank Capra is a fully experienced and mature director: his technique is formulated, his purpose is clear. He knows what he wants to do and what he is after. Intergrity in the selection of his material, seriousness of approach, simple and unpretentious rendition, and emphasis on fresh incident, characterizations, and clever twists—these make his efforts easily appreciated, readily understood, widely enjoyed. His aims and interests fortunately coincide with commercial standards; so well, indeed, that his success has obscured his weaknesses and made a virtue of superficiality. His films, like O. Henry's stories, will be enjoyed as pastimes by millions, and as such are undeniably important. [1939]

Lewis Jacobs. *The Rise of the American Film* (Teachers College, 1968), pp. 475–76, 478–79

Frank Capra's *Mr. Smith Goes to Washington* is going to be the big movie explosion of the year, and reviewers are going to think twice and think sourly before they'll want to put it down for the clumsy and irritating thing it is. It is a mixture of tough, factual patter about Congressional cloakrooms and pressure groups, and a naïve but shameless hooraw for the American relic—Parson Weems at a flag-raising. It seems just the time for it, just the time of excitement when a barker in good voice could mount the tub, point toward the flag, say ubbuh-ubbah-ubbah and a pluribus union? and the windows would shake. But where all this time is Director Capra?

I'm afraid Mr. Capra began to leave this world at some point during the production of *Mr. Deeds Goes to Town*, his best picture. Among those who admired him from the start I know only Alistair Cooke who called the turn when *Deeds* came out. Writing in England, Cooke confessed to "an uneasy feeling he's on his way out. He's started to make movies about themes instead of people." When *Lost Horizon* appeared, I thought our Mr. Capra was only out to lunch, but Cooke had it. *You Can't Take It with You* in the following year (1938) made it pretty evident that Capra had forgotten about people for good. He had found out about thought and was going up into the clouds to think some. From now on, his continued box-office triumph and the air up there being what they are, he is a sure thing to stay, banking checks, reading *Variety*, and occasionally getting overcast and raining on us. Well, he was a great guy. [1939]

Otis Ferguson. *The Film Criticism of O.F.*
(Temple, 1971), p. 273

Since Mr. Capra has got people into the habit of seeing meanings and lessons in his pictures they are sometimes apt to examine what he does with more probing an eye than may be called for. *Meet John Doe* can easily be taken for just a dramatic story, with a powerful and unscrupulous man plotting to use the sentimentality and gullibility of ordinary people for his own ends. Is it necessary to take this as Mr. Capra's solemn conviction that sentimentality and gullibility are the chief American characteristics, and that if they are used in the right way all will be well with us and with the world?

Anyway, Capra is as skilled as ever in keeping things moving along briskly and dramatically—though here and there are some pretty long speeches which for all his artful manipulation have something of the effect of a set aria in an opera. He is still gifted in making characters, particularly background characters, vivid and alive—though there is a reporter in this picture who appears to perform on the principle that tripping over a spitoon is always funny. Sentimentalities are neatly balanced with sharp commentaries on sentimentality. Folkways are brilliantly pictured again and again, particularly in the small-town mayor's befuddled antics, and in the broadcast of the John Doe convention. Such a characterization as James Gleason's is deep and revealing.

But it's a pity Mr. Capra, with so much good stuff to work with, had to fumble the point of it.

James Shelley Hamilton. *NBR*. April 1941, p. 15

You Can't Take It with You created a sensation in Hollywood, influencing other directors to a surprising degree. There was no "production value," meaning glamour and lavish décor and elegant dresses, in this study of a lower-middle-class family, each of whose members was characterized by fads and hobbies that made them twice as natural as most screen people. The informality of Capra's approach, the serene curiosity with which he looked at his countrymen, the simplicity of sentiment, were something new and refreshing. In countless films since then, scores of directors have tried, with more or less success, to apply that "Capra touch" to their pictures.

Egon Larsen. *Spotlight on Films* (Max Parrish, 1950), pp. 106–07

We respond finally to the classic Capra hero, whether Mr. Smith or John Doe, the uniquely American Everyman, with a kind of reluctant longing. He is our conscience *manqué*, the image of our childhood selves, reminding us, as we do not wish to be reminded, of the ways and degrees to which we have failed this image; all reaching some comic apotheosis in the figure of Jimmy Stewart, as Mr. Smith, in Washington, quite literally, a big Boy Scout.

What moderates the merely Sunday school piety of the Capra hero, what keeps his meaning just short of the moralizing "essay" on the page before the murder case in our Sunday supplements, is always some specifically foolish, specifically human trait which becomes the comic correlative of virtue: Mr. Deeds plays his tuba, John Doe plays his baseball, and Mr. Smith is not simply a patriot, but an absurdly fanatical one, who cannot pass the Washington Monument, however casually, without adopting some posture of ridiculously extravagant reverence. The virtue of the characters seems inseparable from their absurdity, and, bound up as it is with this absurdity, passes from the ideality of the Sunday moral to the reality of a concrete human embodiment. It becomes a human possibility: that is to say, the peculiar impact of the Capra hero is as an assertion that it is possible to be that good . . . and human, too.

It is the formularized happy ending which has always seemed the fatal weakness of Capra's films; the apparent belief that everything will turn out all right in the end serves, finally, only to nullify any serious moral concern. Yet this convention of the happy ending seems, on closer look, to be curiously quarantined in Capra's films, and the observance of it has often been strangely perfunctory. Only *Mr. Deeds Goes to Town* appears comfortably to adopt a happy ending, and, while this film remains the prototype of the others, much of their interest derives from the variations they work on the original pattern. In *Mr. Smith Goes to Washington*, the dramatic climax is brought off with such astonishing abruptness as to be over before we can consciously comprehend it. [1962]

William S. Pechter. *Twenty-four Times a Second* (Harper, 1971), pp. 126–27

Before creating the screwball comedy, Capra seemed comfortable with the shyster mania that prevailed between 1931 and 1933. *Platinum Blonde* (Columbia, 1931) showed his initial sympathy with, and attraction to, newspapermen and their racy urban milieu. His hero was an urban Mr. Deeds, an individualist ace reporter with disdain for a world of "phonies." By 1936, the "phonies" would include those very newspapermen. In 1932, Capra directed a movie about bank failures entitled *American Madness*, with Walter Huston the beleaguered and incorruptible banker, kept afloat during the panic by the faith of his depositors. That kind of faith was typical of Capra.

His next vehicle, *Lady for a Day*, was taken from a Damon Runyon story ("Madam La Guimp"), and the choice of material indicated Capra's continued affection for the shyster city. Runyon's world was peopled by the breezy and sleazy of a Broadway long since gone. Capra revelled in the efforts of various blondes, race touts, and gamblers to pass off "Apple Annie" as a lady of wealth to secure her daughter's marriage to royalty. Eventually, the police and Mayor and Governor of New York pitch in to bring off the deception. It was all urban, this unity—a cheerful combine of all the types Capra would turn against in *Deeds*. A different city—cynical and destructive—appeared in his work from 1934 on.

In the late thirties, Capra evolved the shyster into a vaguely fascistic threat. The urban sharper become the Wall Street giant, communications mogul, munitions kingpin, and reactionary political force embodied in the corpulent and bespectacled figure of Edward Arnold. Capra's emphasis upon the melting of class tensions changed as the decade ended. Class amiability, the end of *It Happened One Night* and *You Can't Take It With You* (and non-Capra works like *My Man Godfrey* and *Easy Living*), became a means. If the mid-thirties witnessed a stress on the resolution of social tensions, Capra, by 1939, fancied that resolution to be an accomplished fact. And so the common decency of all Americans, rich and poor, got turned, in *Mr. Smith* and *Meet John Doe*, against threats to our most sacred national institutions. Capra was exchanging the symbols and dynamics of the thirties for those of the forties.

Andrew Bergman. *We're in the Money*
(NYU, 1971), pp. 135–36

Capra's talkie comedy *Platinum Blonde* (1931) continued the message that money corrupts but said it much more snappily. Capra says the story was "stolen" from *The Front Page* (1931), though there aren't really many similarities. . . .

Platinum Blonde doesn't work as well as the later Capra films. After long prefatory scenes, the premise is set up, a bit late, in a short expository dialogue between Harlow and another character. It's too abrupt and perfunctory. And the reporter's slugging instinct becomes tiresome. It gets ludicrous when he even threatens his foolishly loyal girl-back-home: "I should sock you right in that funny little nose." The moral of the film is obvious, but the reporter announces it anyway when he leaves Harlow on his way back to the simple life. "I know I'm out of my crowd," he says. "I'll stay in my own back yard from now on." (It was a common theme in the thirties—culminating, perhaps, in Dorothy's promise to Aunt Em never to run away again in *The Wizard of Oz*. Know your place, and stay there.)

It would not be fair to say that the rich were universally villainous in the Capra films. If they could behave like regular people, they got approval. In his film *American Madness* (1932), Capra celebrates a bank president who hasn't forgotten the little folk who put him in authority. Likewise, they do not forget him. They come marching to his rescue when the bank is failing and the sneaky board of directors is clamoring for the president's resignation. In his autobiography, Capra calls this his first realistic, nonescapist film. It dealt with the realities of Depression America. Of course, it did not deal with them in the most harshly realistic of terms. It saw a light at the end of the tunnel; it saw hope so long as people kept their heads and didn't panic.

Tom Shales in *The American Film Heritage*,
edited by the American Film Institute
(Acropolis, 1972), p. 120

CASSAVETES, JOHN (1929–)

In *Shadows*, things just happen; the film makes no attempt to discriminate or differentiate between the several qualities of experience it describes. This isn't to say that the film fails to interpret this experience, only that nowhere in *Shadows* does one see any evidence of the recognition that, perhaps, at some level, experience may be susceptible to some understanding, to some mental apprehension.

Yet I don't so much object to *Shadows'* mindlessness as to its formlessness, regardless of the practical excuses that may be advanced for the film's rambling incoherence. . . . It's not the lack of conventional shaping in *Shadows* that I object to; after all, since the film is intended as an assault on certain artistic conventions, why not an assault on conventional notions of form as well? Some of Lionel Abel's remarks on *The Connection* seem to apply to *Shadows* with equal justice. Much of the film is cruelly, almost unendurably boring, and its implied challenge seems to be that since it is purporting to depict life itself, unfettered by the intrusion of art, you, the audience, are free to leave any time you become convinced that your own life is this interesting and this sensitively observed. I was on the verge of leaving countless times, but what, I believe, finally held me to the end was so conventional an element as suspense: how will it all turn out? As the film meanders to a close, one may, in fact, observe a few other conventionalities as well: a dreadfully Victorian scene of postseduction *tristesse* ("I never knew it could be so awful") and a heavily moralizing example of a Negro-hater getting his just deserts, among them. The great mistake of *Shadows* is, it seems to me, to fail to realize that fresh ways of seeing are useless, or, at best, merely diverting, unless they are allied with fresh modes of perception. [1960]

William S. Pechter. *Twenty-four Times a Second* (Harper, 1971), pp. 9–10

It is said that *Shadows* is a completely improvised film: that no script was prepared and that John Cassavetes, himself an actor turned director, did no more than help the players to work out what they wanted to do. I don't quite believe in miracles. It is obvious that the company worked from a well-understood story line and equally obvious that each actor knew in advance what sort of character he was impersonating. But the details of action, the dialogue, the camera work are undoubtedly spontaneous, and the result is a picture of startling immediacy and shocking power.

Most important, it is a *movie*, a story told in film that could not have been told in any other way. The photography is rough by studio standards—there are moments when the camera seems even to have lost the action and to be scurrying around after the performers—but the gain in authenticity and in the sense of an urgent, inevitable flow of events, far outweighs the occasional cramped composition, awkward transition, or flaring light. You feel that you are present—an original excitement of the movies that has now almost been abandoned for calculated effects.

Robert Hatch. *Nation*. April 15, 1961, p. 330

In *Too Late Blues*, Cassavetes worked with a specific shooting script, but he still managed to endow his film with an unobtrusive air of improvisation, especially in two sequences. First, a baseball game is played with some youngsters in the park, a daytime exploit in which the musicians, all agrumble and anti-Nature, suddenly find themselves. Cassavetes turns this sunny episode into a light-hearted, unsquare fantasy, exemplifying more than anything else, the incongruous impulses of Ghost and the childlike loyalty of Jess and the rest of the group toward his desires. Secondly, there is the long, brilliant sequence in the poolroom, when Sheehan is goaded toward provoking a fight with the musicians. The interaction of performers, fluidly moving, subtle camerawork (by Lionel Lindon) and interweaving sound of cue balls, clinking glasses, and conversation, the sudden whisperings and close-ups of Sheehan and his provocant, Benny (Everett Chambers)—these create a stunning visual progress from euphoria to gloom. It is the single sequence in *Too Late Blues* that most exhibits Cassavetes' flashbulb imagination and feeling for cinematic drama, and from this moment on the film's tone shifts toward tragedy. The image of Ghost completely yielding to Sheehan's hammerlock hold is a painful shock to the characters in the film as well as to the spectator; the tradition of the screen hero-as-coward has heretofore been much too Conradian for Hollywood producers, making his appearance in this film totally unexpected.

Albert Johnson. *Film Quarterly*. Winter 1961–62, p. 50

Ultimately, however, *Faces* emerges for me as the revelation of 1968, not the best movie to be sure, but certainly the most surprising. . . . After its somewhat strained beginning, *Faces* not only works, it soars. The turning point is the first desperately domestic conversation between John Marley and Lynn Carlin, a conversation swept along on its banal course by gales of nervous laughter, a conversation accompanied by physical withdrawal behind the luxurious barriers of space, walls, doors, and furniture, a conversation that in its lack of topical details and symbolic overtones is perhaps closer to aimless soap opera than to deliberate drama. But it works in ways that are mysterious to behold, as if for once a soap opera was allowed to unfold out of its own limited logic for two hours without interruption for commercials or station identification. What we have in *Faces*, therefore, is not only a failure to communicate but a reluctance to terminate, and this reluctance is one of the reasons *Faces* achieves an otherwise inexplicable intensity of feeling that transcends the too easily satirized milieu of affluently superficial Southern California. Although it is concerned almost exclusively with the lecherous delusions of pick-ups and pick-me-ups, *Faces* is never sordid or squalid. Cassavetes stays with his tormented, alienated characters until they break through the other side of slice-of-life naturalism into emotional and artistic truth. [1968]

Andrew Sarris. *Confessions of a Cultist* (S&S, 1970), p. 407

Like *The Graduate*, *Faces* detests middle age and will doubtless win a grateful audience among the young. The only likeable character is a benign hippie who serves as the mouthpiece for the deep thoughts of John Cassavetes, its writer and director. Italian and Czech films invest the old at least with pathos; the American film these days takes a savage delight in stripping the old of all trace of dignity.

Faces catches a marriage in a state of decay. The husband leaves his wife and visits a call girl; the wife goes to a discothèque with other wives, returns with the hippie, sleeps with him, and attempts suicide. The hippie saves her life. The husband comes back in the morning and surprises the hippie. Husband and wife end locked in reciprocal sterility.

"The mass of men," wrote Thoreau, "lead lives of quiet desperation." In California they lead lives of noisy desperation. Cassavetes's camera, fluid and inquisitive, records this desperation in harsh close-ups given a specious authenticity by the anonymous excellence of the cast and by the grainy quality of the film. His dialogue exploits the sounds of despair underneath banality; his pace is hectic and pitiless.

Arthur Schlesinger, Jr. *Vogue*. Jan. 1969, p. 66

Cassavetes' approach to making a film is not unlike Andy Warhol's in *The Chelsea Girls* and Norman Mailer's in *Wild 90* and *Beyond the Law*; by depending on the inspiration of the amateurs and professionals in their casts, they attempt to get at something more truthful than ordinary movies do. And the actors act away. The movie equivalent of primitive painters may be movie-makers like these, who expect the movie to happen when the camera is on. Their movies become the games actors play (and this can be true even when there is a conventional script, as in *Rachel, Rachel*). They are likely to go for material that they feel is being left out of commercial films, but they make their movies in terms of what impressed them in their childhood—the stars—and ignore the other elements of movies. In Warhol and in Mailer, the best moments may be when the actors have a good time performing for the camera. Cassavetes has a good, clear sense of structure; he uses a script and allows improvisation only within strict limits, and as a result, *Faces*—which is like an upper-middle-class, straight version of *The Chelsea Girls*—has the unified style of an agonizing honesty. Many professional and non-professional actors have something they're particularly good at, and in this kind of movie they may get a chance to show it. . . . But these actors may be inadequate or awful in the rest of the film, because, working out of themselves this way, they can't create a character. Their performances don't have enough range, so one tends to tire of them before the movie is finished. . . .

Pauline Kael. *Going Steady* (Little, Brown, 1970), pp. 196–97

Although *Husbands* is better than Cassavetes' 1968 film, *Faces*, it is an artistic feat of the same kind. He has again done extraordinary things with the most ordinary characters and actors imaginable. Archie, Harry and Gus don't have the wherewithal to understand why they've done what they have. They're uncomplicated men who've lived unexamined lives. Their actions are truly a phylogenic reflex. But while Cassavetes hasn't inflated their sensibilities, he hasn't made fools out of them either. The comedy of his film is warm-blooded. His camera has fondled his middle-class characters with tight close-ups, as it did in *Faces*.

This kindheartedness is a bit hard to figure, for when he's away from his camera Cassavetes does his best to convince us he's a nasty man. The people he makes films about are the same people who go to see his films. Yet in his interviews he makes it clear he only has contempt for them as an audience. Perhaps he assumes this attitude to conceal his rather old-fashioned aesthetic principles. He seems to be the kind of artist who believes you can't satirize people you don't really love. On the other hand, though, his surliness may be just the self-defensive reaction of a genuine eccentric. I can't think of any emotion more eccentric and vulnerable these days than compassion for the middle classes.

Colin L. Westerbeck, Jr. *Commonweal.* Feb. 12, 1971, p. 469

In *Husbands* we have a decided pro-male emotional commitment, whatever its terms. To me, the doggedness of Cassavetes and his colleagues in this regard verges on the morbidly sentimental. Perhaps, despite all the genuine warmheartedness, the genuine enough good-guyness, *Husbands* proves for Gazzara, Falk, and Cassavetes too much an occasion of condescension. Morbid sentimentality is one symptomatic superstructure of the restless unconscious, of deliberately suppressed impulses. I wouldn't say that Gus, Harry, and Archie, as conceived, are necessarily suppressing homosexual yearnings; no, but I would say that they are suppressing *something.* Could it be just plain, old, undenominated "sexuality"?—what Freud calls the polymorphous perverse as characteristic of the earliest stages of growth? The trio's behavior in London, where they climax their binge by bedding pickups from the gambling casino, displays not only symptoms of naïve American-guy boorishness but also clear-cut puritan inhibitions and a kind of ingrained infantilism. Archie, as was noted, is elected to illustrate the latter: he shrinks from tongue-kissing as if it meant sexual dishonor. Is all this an account of *male* sexual maladroitness? Scene by scene, action by action, a prevalent atmosphere of built-in frustration is created as evidence against the sexual normalcy, adequacy, and adulthood of these three husbands. Their very squareness becomes, as identifiable sexual mores, the sign and proof of their own lack of erotic style—alas! their poor-dope ineligibility. Cassavetes' earnest emotion has ultrasentimentalized itself. Neither the framework of life nor the film's inner statistics give support, shape, and conviction to the moral empathy so obviously required of the spectator.

Parker Tyler. *Screening the Sexes* (Holt, 1972), pp. 113–14

John Cassavetes, actor and director, who is justly considered as one of the fathers of American *cinéma-vérité* because of his first film, *Shadows*, has to his credit two other exceptional films, *Faces* (1968) and *Husbands* (1970). He has now directed *Minnie and Moskowitz* in the same style.

Once more the spectator has the impression of a hidden camera that has seized a slice of life that is both banal and painful. It is the absolute contrary of traditional Hollywood cinema, which is now moribund. Actually, everything is very planned, and this aesthetic of authenticity demands a subtle elaboration.

On the level of style, the success is very great, but on the level of story there is something wrong, something that doesn't work and that worked so well in *Faces* and *Husbands*. In truth, the opposition between Seymour and Minnie is such that we are not convinced that they can come to some agreement.

We believe in their meeting, in Seymour's mad love for Minnie, in Minnie's softening toward Seymour, in a brief affair—but not in the "happy end," which is literal. I mean by that that we see the image "they married and had many children."

This is a shame because the film abounds in dazzling bits and the actors are remarkable, especially Gena Rowland, who is Mrs. Cassavetes in real life. Its too bad that the fatality of the tale seems artificial because the two portraits are profoundly true. But if only for the wonderful meeting between the two future mothers-in-law much can be pardoned Cassavetes, who was temporarily led astray by too much talent and facility.

Jacques Doniol-Valcroze. *L'Express.*
Dec. 25, 1972, p. 45

CHAPLIN, CHARLES (1889–)

The Tramp (Essanay, April 12).—You would really be surprised to see how much fun Charles Chaplin gets out of a brick, or a pitchfork, or whatever he takes up. And later, when he is sent out to milk the cow and, by mistake, meets the bull, as in the old yarn, the house rocks with laughter. Certainly the work of Charles Chaplin has never been any funnier than here, and that is saying as much as is, within the circumstances, possible. Pity that he must carry the whole film himself. One laughs at the other characters, but only when they are being knocked down, or when he plays some trick on them. . . . The very end is rather dramatic . . . and falls flat by reason of its contrast, with the tempo of what had preceded. Also the photography at times might have been clearer, and there were instances when working a little closer to the camera would have brought the comedy of his expressions out better.

NYDM. April 28, 1915, p. 39

Did you see *The Immigrant*? I not only saw *The Immigrant*, but I saw some light, disparaging reviews of it—one or two by metropolitan critics. Henceforth, these persons can never make me believe anything they write, for the subject of their malministrations is a transparent intermezzo well repaying their closest analysis. In its roughness and apparent simplicity it is as much a jewel as a story by O. Henry, and no full-time farce seen on our stage in years has been more adroitly, more perfectly worked out.

It has, to an extraordinary degree, those elements of surprise which are necessary in every play and which put the capstone of humor on comedy, because they add to the ludicrous the deliciousness of the unexpected . . . There is one flash of Chaplin's inimitable pathos in this picture: that rollicking moment in which, lifting the petite hand of la Purviance, he discovers clutched within it the black-bordered handerchief which tells the story of her mother's death. Simply, sincerely, and with a look of infinite pity he lowers her hand. The moment, genuinely affecting though sandwiched in boisterousness, is a little flash of genius.

Julian Johnson. *Photoplay*. Sept. 1917, pp. 99–100

A couple of years ago it would have been deemed treasonable to cast the smallest of critical stones at Chaplin. He was the biggest thing in laughs in the whole of America. . . .

But today is not a couple of years ago—and a review of Chaplin's last release, *Sunnyside*, fills the analytical mind with grim foreboding. It wasn't a success, to put it bluntly. And, honestly, when you consider all the Chaplin films in the order of their manufacture, can you truthfully call them great art? Even if you allow that *A Dog's Life* was funny —which many people deny—and even if you affirm that *Shoulder Arms* was not an uncouth reflection on army life but a clever satire, you must admit that these two films were, in essence, but a rehash of the earlier *Carmen*, just as *Carmen* was a recooking of *Behind the Screen*, and so on and so on.

In other words, I contend that the extraordinary Chaplin vogue is based upon the simple law of repetition—that each film contains precisely the same elements—that the appeal of every Chaplin picture is to the lowest human instincts—and that, in the natural course of events, the Chaplin vogue in five years will be a thing of remote antiquity.

Harcourt Farmer. *Theatre Magazine*. Oct. 1919, p. 249

The blemish on *The Kid* is the same that has marred many of Chaplin's other pictures—vulgarity, or coarseness. There is only a little of it in the present work, just two scenes that will be found particularly offensive by some. They are funny. That cannot be denied. One laughs at them, but many try not to, and are provoked with themselves and Chaplin for their laughing. This is not good. The laugh that offends good taste doesn't win. And these scenes would never be missed from *The Kid*. It has plenty of unadulterated fun to go far and long without them. Why can't Chaplin leave out such stuff? Why don't the exhibitors delete it?

There is less pure horseplay in *The Kid* than in the other Chaplins. The comedian depends chiefly upon his inimitable pantomime, and it scores every time. He also gets many laughs from the ludicrous situations which he concocts. There's nothing clumsy about the picture's continuity. Its "comedy relief" actually comes as a well-timed relief.

NYT. Jan. 22, 1921, p. 9

In spite of all the people who take literature seriously (and even take only that seriously), I prefer Chaplin's *Shoulder Arms* to Barbusse's *Under Fire*, and to his imitators, and to the *J'Accuse* film. *Shoulder Arms* doesn't bombard anything and doesn't accuse anybody, but it is much more relentless.

The sufferings of the American Sammy doing his training and dreaming of the glorious trenches are explored without any romantic feeling or any preaching. Irony is far stronger than sermonizing. And humor is a wonderful thing: it has irony in it, and many other ingredients too. This little cinematographic picture is one of the most truthful that the War inspired in any peace-loving man. The farcial atmosphere of the film, its amusing details and jokes, its scenario on the lines of a sketch, only accentuate the cruel satire of the fantasy. It never declaims, not even against declaiming. . . .

This film justifies all that one can expect from the cinema.

There we are really in a country which is splendidly illimitable. And moreover we have Chaplin, who by force of his personal genius, is something above the art of the cinema. We should never have dared to hope so much from it.

And shall I astonish Forbes Robertson much by telling him that Charlie Chaplin is a Shakespearean actor?

Louis Delluc. *Charlie Chaplin* (Bodley Head, 1922), pp. 93–95

Dear Mr. Chaplin: You get hundreds of letters every week no doubt, but I have seen your last picture [*Pay Day*]—which they say completes your contracts and leaves you free to do what you like—and I must write to say that I hope this will indeed be the last of its kind and that now you will go on to a larger field. How many people have said this to you I have no way of knowing. But your friends, I am sure, in so far as they are able to see, must have said it often.

This is how it stands. You have created one of the great clowns of all time. This Charlie of yours needs no portrait anywhere: he *is* foolish, pathetic, irrepressible, flickering, comical, lovable beyond all words; he is light as air; he is a blunderer with a heart not solid but worn like a flower on a child's sleeve; a sexless gallantry; he is a tireless curiosity drawn to things as a monkey to a peephole or a moth to a flame; a gentle blithe dreamer and acrobat; a mask; he is a little, grotesque music; a dear laughter carried lightly in everybody's breast; a gay, shy classic; a world figment.

But you have finished your creation. It was perfect long ago. Already it begins to slow down. It shows a falling off in invention and zest; it shows a kind of boredom in you despite the great art with which you sustain the flow of it, the lightness, the airy intensity. Better still it is than all the clowns in the world put together could do, or comic artists anywhere; but it is yet not quite its own best; it is a little weak judged by itself. You have the achievement of it, however, to rest on, whatever happens, whatever you turn to. And you have your own genius and accomplishments to go forward on. . . .

But with all this you have done only one thing. Why not go on? There are so many things that you could do. There is *Liliom* for example. What could you not do with that part where Mr. Schildkraut made it a role that was expert only, always crowded in motif and business and nearly always touched with vulgarity and insistence? You could do *He Who Gets Slapped.* Or with study you could do *Peer Gynt*, and many other parts. But better than all of these, you could do new things written by you or for you, things in which you would use your full endowment, comic and otherwise. And finally you might do the one most important of all things so far as moving pictures go, and that is to develop things calculated strictly for it and for no other art, made up out of its essential quality, which is visual motion and not mere stage drama photographed. In sum, you might really create in terms of moving pictures as you have already created in terms of character.

Stark Young. *The New Republic.*
Aug. 23, 1922, p. 358

Charlie Chaplin is the first man to create a drama that is purely cineplastic, in which the action does not illustrate a sentimental fiction or a moralistic intention but creates a monumental whole; projecting from the inner consciousness a personal vision of the object in a form that is actually visible, in a setting that is actually material and perceptible. There, as it seems to me, we have something very great, an achievement comparable with Titian's concentration of all the sound-elements in time, thus creating from them their very soul and sculpturing it before us. Apparently most people do not perceive this because Chaplin is a clown, and because a poet is, by definition, a solemn person who brings us to knowledge through the door of boredom. Yet to me Chaplin is a poet, even a great poet, a creator of myths, symbols, and ideas, the discoverer of a new and unknown world. I could not even begin to say how much Chaplin has taught me—and always without boring me. Indeed I do not know, for it is too essential to be defined. Every time I see him I have a sense of equilibrium and of certitude which liberates my judgment and sets my ideas swarming. Chaplin reveals to me what is in me, what is truest in me, what is most human. That a man should thus be able to speak to another—is that not strange and unusual?

Elie Faure. *The Art of Cineplastics*
(Four Seas, 1923), pp. 48–49

In *A Woman of Paris,* Mr. Chaplin as the writer and director has not done anything radical or anything esoteric; he has merely used his intelligence to the highest degree, an act which has ceased to be expected of motion picture people for many years. He has written and directed a story in which all the characters act upon motives which the spectator immediately recognizes as natural and sincere, and therefore *A Woman of Paris* breathes an atmosphere of reality, and thereby holds the attention of any perceptive audience in thrall.

As a director Mr. Chaplin has attained to a great achievement, because he has succeeded in contributing his own fascinating personality and subtle intelligence to his actors in their given situation. . . .

A Woman of Paris has the one quality which almost every other motion picture that has been made to date lacks—restraint. The acting is moving without being fierce; the story is simple and realistic without ever being inane; the settings are pleasing and adequate without ever being colossally stupid. The result is a picture of dignity and intelligence, and the effect is startling because it is so unusual.

The achievement of Mr. Chaplin indicates what should be obvious, that 10,000 in the cast do not necessarily make a moving drama, and directors of pictures made on that principle would do well to see this picture often and take it to heart if it is the artistic motion picture that they are striving for. The action is very simple and to tell the story would be unprofitable, because the story is not at all unusual, which is the very thing that makes it humanely interesting. But to attain the simplicity and even flow which his picture has must have cost Mr. Chaplin much effort. He, as the director, undoubtedly deserves much of the credit for the natural relations of his characters to each other as brought out by Edna Purviance, Adolph Menjou and Carl Miller. It is easy to see that these actors are doing exactly what they are told, and doing it as they would in their homes, if they happened to live in such homes as Mr. Chaplin, the writer, has devised for them.

Incidentally, *A Woman of Paris* has some bits of comedy that are typical of what has made Charlie Chaplin justly famous, but the comedy is never forced in for relief but takes place as the natural thing in the situation. There is also an underlying vein of satire which is a healthy sign in any study of the interrelations of human beings in modern life.

NBR. Oct.-Nov. 1923, p. 5

In this early day Charlie had already mastered his principles. He knew that the broad lines are funny and that the fragments—which are delicious—must "point" the main line of laughter. I recall, for example, an exquisite moment at the end of [*His Night Out*]. Turpin is staggering down the street, dragging Charlie by the collar. Essentially the funny thing is that one drunkard should so gravely, so soberly, so obstinately take care of another and should convert himself into a policeman to do it; it is funny that they should be going nowhere, and go so doggedly. The lurching-forward body of Turpin, the singular angle formed with it by Charlie's body almost flat on the ground, added to the spectacle. And once as they went along Charlie's right hand fell to one side, and as idly as a girl plucks a water-lily from over the side of a canoe he plucked a daisy from the grass border of the path, and smelled it. The function of that gesture was to make everything that went before, and everything that came after, seem funnier; and it succeeded by creating another, incongruous image out of the picture before our eyes. The entire world, a moment earlier, had been aslant and distorted and wholly male; it righted itself suddenly and created a soft idyll of tenderness. Nearly everything of Charlie is in that moment, and I know no better way to express its elusive quality than to say that as I sat watching the film a second time, about two hours later, the repetition of the gesture came with all the effect of surprise, although I had been wondering whether he could do it so perfectly again.

This was the Charlie whom little children came to know before any other and whose name they added to their prayers. He was then popular with the people; he was soon to become universally known and admired—the Charlie of *The Bank* and of *Shoulder Arms*; and finally he became "the great artist" in *The Kid*. The second period is pure development; the third is change; and the adherents of each join with the earlier enthusiasts to instruct and alarm their idol. No doubt the middle phase is the one which is richest in memory. It includes the masterpieces *A Dog's Life*, *The Pawnshop*, *The Vagabond*, *Easy Street*, as well as the two I have just mentioned, and, if I am not mistaken, the *genre* pictures like *The Floorwalker*, *The Fireman*, *The Immigrant*, and the fantastic *Cure*. [1924]

Gilbert Seldes. *The Seven Lively Arts*
(Sagamore, 1957, rev.), pp. 38–39

And it is well to bear in mind that Chaplin's enormous success is due entirely to his personality and the sheer force of his acting ability. To the technique of the motion picture, its development as an art in terms of pure cinema, Chaplin has contributed little except here and there in *The Woman of Paris*. As a matter of fact his technique is old-fashioned, photographic rather than cinematic. Compare, for instance, the scene [in *The Circus*] of Chaplin on the tightrope with similar scenes from *Variety*. We simply see Chaplin on a tight-rope, we do not feel him there. There is none of the dizziness, the suspense which we sense when boss Heller is debating whether he should dash his rival to death or not. We are entirely absorbed in the ludicrous aspect of the situation, the monkey business, literally speaking, never for a moment in the kinetics except through subsequent suggestion. In one respect the old-fashioned technique celebrates a triumph. We refer to the final scene where Chaplin, having married off the bareback rider whom he loves to his rival, sits in the desolate circle of his despair and chews the cud of fate. That is indeed a marvellous scene which should never have been spoiled by the subsequent close-up. Shot in the middle distance, with the hazy outline of a town behind it, this scene has a symbolic and (we might as well admit it) a philosophic significance scarcely equalled in the annals of the screen.

NBR. Feb. 1928, p. 7

This remarkable picture [*A Woman of Paris*], which has very striking merits, is quite incorrectly judged by us as regards the nature of its significance. According to my point of view, its significance is in no sense practical, but of a purely stimulative character. The *Woman of Paris* is for us significant in a purely abstract sense, as a stage of accomplishment possible of attainment in any domain whatsoever. In this respect its significance for the cinema is of exactly the same order as the Doric temple, a well-executed somersault or the Brooklyn bridge.

In our country it was received as a phenomenon of practical advantage to us; in fact, as an object for imitation and even plagiarism. Examples of such an attitude are among the sad pages of our cinema history: elements of reaction and retrogression along the line of the general development of the ideology of the forms of the Soviet cinema.

Sergei Eisenstein. *Close Up*. May 1929, p. 11

Modern Times has several new angles, principally those of the factory and the occasional offstage reports of strikes and misery (the girl's father was shot in a demonstration). But they are incidental. Even in taking René Clair's conveyor-belt idea, for example, you can almost hear Chaplin, where Clair directed a complex hubbub, saying to one of his old trusties: You drop the wrench, I kick you in the pants, you take it big, and we cut to chase, got it? It has the thread of a story: Chaplin's meeting up with the orphan girl, very wild and sweet, and their career together. For the rest it is disconnected comedy stuff: the embarrassing situation, the embroilment and chase, and the specialty number, *e.g.*, the roller skates, the completely wonderful song-and-dance bit, the Chaplin idyll of a cottage and an automatic cow, beautiful with humor and sentiment. These things and the minor business all along the way—in jails, cafeterias, with oil cans, trays, swinging doors, refractory machinery—are duplicates, they take you back.

But such matters would not call for discussion if all together they did not set up a definite mood, a disturbing sense of the quaint. Chaplin himself is not dated, never will be; he is a reservoir of humor, master of an infinite array of dodges, agile in both mind and body; he is not only a character but a complex character, with the perfect ability to make evident all the shades of his odd and charming feelings; not only a touching character, but a first-class buffoon and I guess the master of our time in dumb show. But this does not make him a first-class picture maker. He may personally surmount his period, but as director-producer he can't carry his whole show with him, and I'll take bets that if he keeps on refusing to learn any more than he learned when the movies themselves were just learning, each successive picture he makes will seem, on release, to fall short of what went before. The general reaction to this one anyway is the wonder that these primitive formulas can be so genuinely comic and endearing. [1936]

Otis Ferguson. *The Film Criticism of O.F.* (Temple, 1971), p. 118

The Woman is a rather disturbing piece of broad comedy in which Charlie disguises himself as a woman and cuts off his mustache, in order to circumvent the opposition of his sweetheart's uncle. Of course the uncle at once begins to flirt with the supposed girl; and there is something about Chaplin's face when one sees it clean-shaven which is unexpected and utterly unfamiliar. One catches a glimpse of one aspect of the man about which volumes could be written, an almost equivocal and feminine quality born of humiliation, which can be detected in later films. That is why *The Woman* is so important, as a sort of curiosity. Otherwise, it is still a prentice piece with few first-rate inventions in it, but exhibiting a curious sureness of touch at least as impressive as the slightly dubious quality of some of the humor and some of the incidents.

Maurice Bardèche and Robert Brasillach. *The History of Motion Pictures* (Norton and MOMA, 1938), p. 119

The Great Dictator is its own kind of film, a completely Chaplin kind, and no other kind in the world. It is not only the climax of Chaplin, so far, but a resumé of Chaplin's whole growth, in his picture-making and in the evolution of his social conscience—a statement that is practically a quotation from Terry Ramsaye, who so far as I know is the only commentator who has noted this fact, as well as the fact that you must go back to Griffith's *Intolerance* for another motion picture that is so completely one man's personal expression of his attitude on something about which he feels deeply and passionately.

There is practically no plot: a Jewish barber looks so much like

Hynkel (Hitler) that eventually he is mistaken for the dictator and finds himself in the dictator's shoes about to broadcast to the nation. The rest of the picture is a rambling, episodic sort of thing that a Chaplin picture has always been. . . . From the prologue in the Old War (it might have been something out of *Shoulder Arms*), through the barbershop days when Hynkel forgot the Jews for a bit, till his escape from the prison camp in the uniform that made him mistaken for the Phooey, the picture might have been made before talk came to the films—it is, in truth, a lot like an early talkie.

But without talk Chaplin couldn't have been Hynkel. The gods in their wisdom made Chaplin hit upon a make-up from his earliest days that destined him to be the inevitable parody of Hitler in appearance, but something even higher in the right ordering of things bestowed on him the gift to conceive and utter the astonishing, devastating speech that spurts from his lips when he is Hitler vocal. . . . [T]he bitterest venom of his characterization comes out in the indescribable jargon, utterly untranslatable yet completely understandable, which is the utterance of Hynkel in his greatest furies, and which is certainly one of the most remarkable things that the talkies—or anything else—has ever presented in the form of speech. . . .

It is easy to find technical shortcomings in *The Great Dictator*, ways in which it doesn't line up with the stream-lined slickness of continuity, photography, sets, lesser characters, that have become a commonplace in our studios. As a job of picture-making Chaplin has been content to do things just about as he has always done them. He has been himself, but with a further reach. And his grasp has equalled his reach. What other man in motion pictures has put so much time, so much money, so many gifts, into the sincerest expression he could achieve of what he feels about the most important thing in the world today? That will be remembered long after all the other pictures of this year have been forgotten.

James Shelley Hamilton. *NBR*. Nov. 1940, pp. 10–12

I find it difficult to understand how after five years of Hilter terror (and in the year XV of Mussolini's regime) the sensitive creator of *The Gold Rush* and *Modern Times* could still have considered Fascists and Fascism as something just funny. At any rate the fact remains that in the last phase of his production [*The Great Dictator*] Chaplin failed to translate Nazi violence and persecution into satire. Perhaps he felt himself too immediately touched by the events; it may be that he found himself unable to keep up the stylized manner against the ever-increasing naturalism of the materials with which he was working. Look at his

Herring and Garbitch. In them is nothing of the mythological sublimity of those swarthy, eye-rolling monsters that Charlie used to fight and defeat in his earlier films. Rather there is a painful resemblance between this Garbitch and the Goebbels of *Confessions of a Nazi Spy*. Nothing of "Wotan's Mickey Mouse," as the people call Goebbels after a very Chaplinesque forumula, nothing of the wretched little intellectual in the uniform of the smart warrior, the poor herald of a strong blond race, the actress-hunter. The real Goering's imposing facade becomes irresistibly comic only when he poses, as he does in reality, as the steel-hard air hero. Remember him breeding prehistoric auroches on his estate near Berlin and hunting them with ancient spears; remember this official patrol of the arts and his pornographic fresco gallery as described by Nevile Henderson and realize what chances for satire the film has missed.

Rudolf Arnheim. *Films*. Winter 1940, pp. 32–33

Chaplin's genius affects our innermost feelings because he draws his strength from the power of the idea developed in an environment which he re-creates for us through his own interpretation. A courageous observer of people and events, Chaplin has every right to be harsh and biting with the people at whom he directs his shafts, because he does it with wit and integrity. But his genius almost always takes the form of that smiling kindness, that sensibility without sentimentality which has marked all his work from *A Dog's Life* and *Charlie the Soldier* up to the great cry of outraged conscience expressed in *The Dictator*. In this last film, Chaplin uses the sharp edge of satire to triumph through ridicule. In *Modern Times*, he uses his own methods to fight against the exploitation of the individual by those who control for their own profit the machines which are really a part of the natural evolution of progress for the betterment of man's condition.

The diversity of Charlie Chaplin's work finds unity in the fact that it is the product of a talent which has been put to work serving the cause of ideas made up of human kindness and drawn from observations close to life in an attempt to make the latter better and finer. Under these conditions, the social aim of the dramatic film is superbly achieved. Charlie Chaplin's work, like that of Molière, to which it is akin, will never die because his genius enabled him to draw universal conclusions from his observations of the human environment.

Jean Benoît-Levy. *The Art of the Motion Picture* (Coward-McCann, 1946), pp. 146–47

Not even the cinematic genius of Griffith's early films was so absolute and invulnerable as Chaplin's first screen comedies. It was not merely that Charlie had created an authentic clown of world stature—a clown whose genius was recognizable even in flat silhouette—but that he immediately created in film a pattern perfectly adapted to it as a technical medium. As an actor, Chaplin used an art equivalent to dance-pantomime and as such, in his first series of short comedies prior to his "feature films" (which grew longer and longer), his art was actually a precursor to the mathematical precision and breathtaking pace of the animated cartoon in Walt Disney's heyday. We should not hesitate to place Mickey Mouse and Donald Duck beside their legitimate predecessor; indeed, the miracle was that Chaplin's style was as "correct" in the animal and mathematical senses as that of Mickey, Donald, Bugs Bunny, et al. Time and its inevitable concomitant of human experience, however, have witnessed a recession of musical completeness and brilliance in Chaplin's art. What at first seemed mere slapstick action was eventually recognized as the exact correlation of tempo, emphasis, and climax. Recession took place not because of any deterioration in the integral mechanism of the artist himself, but because of what film terms "the scenario"—that is, plot and theme. Chaplin's art, as expression of the entire work, has gradually lost *animal* integrity as it has striven to gain *intellectual* integrity; it has lost human integrity in one field, the *aesthetic*, as it has striven to gain it in another, *the moral.* [1947]

Parker Tyler. *Sex Psyche Etcetera in the Film*
(Horizon, 1969), pp. 161–62

The sign of great works is that they surpass the designs of their authors. There is no doubt that we find in *Hamlet* much more than Shakespeare clearly intended, and the same can be said for Molière's *Dom Juan*.

This is also true of *Monsieur Verdoux*, the most recent film of Charlie Chaplin. I don't think that it is going too far to associate it with famous examples. It is worthy of it, if only by its nature and by the nature of its intentions. If ever the word genius could be pronounced where movies are concerned, Chaplin is an example, and perhaps the only one. The genesis of this film is attributed to an "idea" by Orson Welles. . . . And the public knows that Welles in turn took the idea from the Landru case. Perhaps. But it was neither Landru nor his "case" that had genius. The genius is Chaplin's. And though Welles may abound in "ideas of genius," it is Chaplin who is the genius. . . . With Chaplin the cinema achieves its true nature, because Chaplin *creates* his material. He is even the sole author of his film, including the words and the music. This strikes me as the ideal (the *terminus ad quem*) toward which moviemakers are tending. In addition, Chaplin is the film's actor, just as Shakespeare and Molière were, and though this may not be a necessity, it is not a negligible point. . . .

Chaplin creates a film, and not a novel or a play. His work is not reducible to a book or to theater. He has created cinema. One may easily conceive of a *Monsieur Verdoux* in a circus arena or on the stage. But it so happens that Chaplin has made him speak the language of the cinema and no other, just as Molière in *Dom Juan* used the language of the theater, and no other, and Mozart used the language of opera for his work. This is so true that *Verdoux*, even silent (I hope the experiment of running it without sound will be tried) would be by and large easily understood in the four corners of the world and thus retain the fundamental universal character that is the sign of cinema. . . .

[For example] M. Verdoux enters the bedroom of one of his wives in the evening and leaves it in the morning. Nothing has been said of what he has done in the interval, but we see him prepare the table for breakfast, first setting two plates and then taking one away. In a close shot we see first two plates and then one. It becomes evident that Verdoux has killed the woman. We can shut our ears, but not our eyes. That's cinema: an action experienced in images.

Gabriel Audisio. *Cahiers du Sud*. No. 288, 1948, pp. 332–34

What sets *Limelight* completely apart from the Chaplin tradition, and what damages it most seriously, is not its pretentious flirtation with weight, but its hopeless capitulation to words. The man who originally fought the coming of sound, who dared to produce at least two silent films long after sound had triumphed, and who, even when be began to speak, still struggled to keep the mobile image dominant over the sound track, has changed his mind. He has not only gone over to what he once considered the enemy; he has gone over with love.

From the first reel of *Limelight* it is perfectly clear that Chaplin now wants to talk, that he *loves* to talk, that in this film he intends to do little *but* talk. Where a development in the story line might easily be conveyed by a small visual effect, he prefers to make a speech about it. Where the 1917 music-hall background obviously opens the door to extensive onstage pantomime, he prefers to stand still and sing a song. This is not a compromise between the old and the new, an adjustment to inevitable and necessary change; it is a disturbing rejection of the nature of the medium itself.

Walter Kerr. *Theatre Arts*. Nov. 1952, p. 73

It is not good for a man to become a myth in his lifetime; particularly it is not good for an entertainer. He loses touch with his audience; he forgets, because many have called him great, that no one has called him infallible; no voice can reach him but the voice of the cult. He sees that people still attend him and does not know that they are listening for old echoes. No comedian should become so eminent as to feel that humor no longer becomes him.

Do not assume from this that you would walk out on *Limelight*. No one walks out on Chaplin. He is still the most commanding personality the screen has ever known, and his body is still an instrument of uncanny eloquence. But the power to communicate is not necessarily the power to say something. By what misfortune does it happen that the world's greatest showman now detains us against our will?

Robert Hatch. *Reporter*. Nov. 25, 1952, p. 37

Much of the unofficial publicity connected with *A King in New York* has emphasized its criticisms of the United States: the fingerprinting of aliens, the rock-'n'-roll craze, television commercials, the treatment of suspected subversives. But most of these evils have been much more blatantly condemned in American films: a small-town librarian's suspected subversion in *Storm Center*, TV commercials in *Will Success Spoil Rock Hunter?*, and rock 'n' roll in a dance sequence in the film version of *Silk Stockings*. I did not find *A King in New York* a satirical movie; it was, rather, a sad movie with moments, as one would expect in a Chaplin film, of wonderful humor. . . .

Still, there are some hilarious moments. The funniest sequence takes place at the movies, when "flash" previews break upon the rock-'n'-roll audience to proclaim the imminent maturity of the American film. Chaplin's miming is still capable of giving great joy: His attempt to order caviar in a noisy restaurant, his keyhole peeping, and his excruciatingly funny efforts to extricate his finger from the nozzle of a fire hose are touches of the old genius.

But the film contains major disappointments. First of all, the dialogue is frequently absurd ("To part is to die a little," murmurs the cliché-ridden king, and one wonders why he persists in reciting Hamlet's "To be or not to be" soliloquy, especially to misquote it). Second, there are technical flaws: the obvious London settings ("stalls" signs in the movie house, the "lift"), and the unattractive hotel suite where too many phone calls and too many knocks on the door remind one of a series of vaudeville routines. . . .

There are flashes of the old Charlie Chaplin, of course. But at the center is Mr. Chaplin—writer, actor, director, producer, composer. (One must add that the music is superb.) Unhappily he is a sadder and an older man; the real punch is gone. His dethroned king is an ironically apt image.

Marvin Felheim. *Reporter*. Oct. 17, 1957, p. 43

A qualitative judgment of *A King in New York* is impossible, since this film, like all of Chaplin's, depends for its final effect on the responses of the individual observer. The rewards correspond in direct ratio to the amount of intellectual effort which the spectator is willing to expend. Such early works as *The Gold Rush* and *City Lights* were more immediately gratifying: to the casual observer, unwilling to search for deeper meanings, the hilarious comedy of these films made them satisfactory on the most elementary level. *Monsieur Verdoux* and *Limelight* were another matter; these films were serious even on the surface and most displeasing to observers disinclined to think about their content. On a superficial level, without considering its intellectual meanings, *A King in New York* is much more amusing. Its proportions are approximately three parts farce to one part drama. Most of the comedy is successful (although never as hilarious as, for example, *Modern Times*); at least half of the dramatic scenes obtain the proper emotional effect. The remaining scenes—constituting about a fourth of the film—aim at comic or emotional effects which they fail, for various reasons, to achieve. These are not bad proportions for a comedy, particularly since the film is logically constructed and skillfully edited, although the weak moments and the serious ending are qualifications which must inevitably limit its popular appeal. If the subject were non-political and the creator someone other than a world celebrity, the film could be critically evaluated as a clever comedy with a number of defects, and consequently, a moderate success.

Eugene Archer. *Film Culture*. Jan. 1958, p. 4

Even today *Monsieur Verdoux* will seem a failure to anyone who has taken half a dozen lessons in film technique. Things were much worse, however, back in 1947 when Chaplin was squeezed between the patrons of Hollywood illusionism on the one hand and the partisans of Italian neorealism on the other. *Verdoux* is neither slick enough for the dream merchants nor sincere enough for the humanists, and this is not necessarily all to the good, as Agee seemed to suggest. There are distinct pleasures in both stylistic elaboration of a dream apparatus and the God-given ambiguity and accident of raw realism.

These pleasures are not to be found in *Verdoux* or in the rest of Chaplin. What we get instead is the genius of economy and essentiality, and it follows that the most drab moments in *Verdoux* are also the most functional. Indeed, the opening exposition involving the family of a Verdoux victim is about as bad as anything I have ever seen in the professional cinema. Yet after repeated reviewings, the badness seems not only integral to Chaplin's conception but decidedly Brechtian in the bargain. Chaplin has stacked the deck shamelessly and crudely, but as soon as he makes his first entrance in his rose garden with his meticulous hands and pliers ravishing sweet nature, all is forgiven, particularly the smoking remains of his wife in the incinerator. [1964]

Andrew Sarris. *Confessions of a Cultist* (S&S, 1970), pp. 145–46

I wish I could say some nice things about the new Chaplin movie, mainly because I think he is one of the greatest movie makers of all times. But *A Countess from Hong Kong* is so old-fashioned and dull that one can hardly believe it was made now. Sophia Loren is quite attractive at times as the dance hall girl who hides in Marlon Brando's suite on a luxury liner to escape from Hong Kong, and Brando is lethargic as the not-yet-divorced diplomat who doesn't want to get involved; so the two of them spend most of their time running coyly from parlor to bedroom to bath. The running, the dialogue, and even the score Chaplin wrote are incredible. Most times the cast, including Sydney Chaplin and Tippi Hedren just look pained as if they were asked to perform in one of those outmoded and superficial plays of the twenties like *Getting Gertie's Garter* or *Parlor, Bedroom and Bath.* No wonder dead-panned Brando says at one point, "I didn't smile; that was a gas pain." It probably really was.

Philip T. Hartung. *Commonweal.* April 14, 1967, p. 128

CRUZE, JAMES (1884–1942)

[*The Roaring Road*] is supposed to star Wallace Reid, but according to the number of close-ups of Theodore Roberts smoking a cigar, I should say it was starring a new brand of tobacco. Although I quarrel with the infrequency with which the handsome Wally is allowed to come within camera range, I cannot but admit that the production as a whole is a mighty interesting piece of work. The story also was recounted in last month's *Magazine*, so you know it concerns a peppery young auto salesman, his red-peppery employer, his daughter and an auto race. The race between the machine and a train has been well handled by Director Cruze. Every ounce of suspense, interest and thrill is maintained until the very end, while all the comedy possible is extracted from the conflict of the two men's hot tempers. Some of the photography is unnecessarily harsh on Ann Little and Wally Reid is conspicuous because of the distance they keep him from the camera, otherwise *The Roaring Road* is satisfactory. . . .

Hazel Simpson Naylor. *Motion Picture Magazine*, July 1919, p. 62

James Cruze treated *Hollywood* as a fantasy rather than as a grimly realistic drama. Together with Tom Geraghty, he kidded his subject from start to finish, introducing elements of the wildest absurdity. In this way he avoided the semblance of propaganda; he never attempted to defend Hollywood, or the art of the motion picture; he never preached or moralized or drew conclusions.

In one episode he visualized a dream in which the Centerville pants presser imagined himself a knight errant who had journeyed to the Twentieth Century Babylon to rescue his girl from the clutches of that dread dragon, the Cinema. It was utter insanity. The various stars, garbed as sheiks, licentious club-men, aristocratic roués, bathing girls, apaches, and the like, moved about in weird confusion through a distorted nightmare. There was slow motion photography, reverse action and double exposure; no sense was made at any given point.

In another scene, Angela was shown making a futile application for work at the Christie Comedies studio. When she joined the line before the casting director's window, a corpulent gentleman stepped aside and politely gave her his place. When she had been firmly refused, the fat man walked up to make his plea but the window was slammed in his face and the word "CLOSED" displayed before his eyes. The camera was moved into a close-up, and Fatty Arbuckle was shown gazing at that one final word.

Robert E. Sherwood. *The Best Moving Pictures of 1922–23* (Small, Maynard, 1923), p. 83

While *The Covered Wagon* was not strictly first-rate photodrama, James Cruze in his handling of the story showed more than the average amount of directorial intelligence. Cruze's best photoplay was *One Glorious Day*, a film which, by the way, ranks as one of the very finest celluloid gems which has yet found its way upon the screen. Given the proper material, Cruze could no doubt do better things but instead we find him dabbling with such conglomerations as *The Old Homestead*.

Tamar Lane. *What's Wrong with the Movies* (Waverly, 1923), p. 69

A hundred or more prairie-schooners, several hundred yokes of oxen and teams of horses, a small itinerant city of people, a plot built on an historical event which most people have heard about and will be keen to see presented on the screen in which is incorporated a prairie fire, a big Indian attack and a big buffalo hunt—well, you have there the paraphernalia and the dramatic material for a spectacular motion picture *par excellence*. And this is what was gathered together, all under one tent, for the making of *The Covered Wagon*.

The result is that this much heralded picture is successful in holding the interest over a distance of ten thousand feet of film. It could have been shortened without hurting the picture, indeed probably to its benefit, but as it stands it is one of the best motion pictures of its kind so far produced.

James Cruze, the director, has stuck to his last and done a business-like job. Emerson Hough's story of the trek of the settlers who in the late forties adventured across the continent to develop virgin lands in Oregon, leaving some of their numbers to push on into California to take part in the gold rush, called for the broadest treatment for panoramic effects, and for terse and vivid narration. All of these Mr. Cruze has given *The Covered Wagon*. . . .

Outstanding in the picture are the scenes portraying the episode of the covered wagons being floated across the river Platte, with their yokes and teams swimming on ahead, and the free live stock being herded into the water behind. This is a vivid bit of what the pioneers were up against and what their resourcefulness was. The Indian attack is not so successful; better Indian attacks have been done in pictures. Possibly Mr. Cruze realized that it was old stuff and decided not to take much trouble with it, but such things as a burning wagon, obviously empty of the stores and household belongings that would surely have been in it, being pulled from the wagon ring of barricade, are inexcusable. For the skimping of a few dollars for an old bed or chest the authenticity of a scene costing many thousands of dollars was lost. And the buffalo hunt is hardly convincing, since with all the guns that the hunters fire point-blank at the numerous herd, it seems hardly possible that only one buffalo would have been killed—by a knife which an old plainsman stabs it with as he throws himself from his horse. These things may be minor, but they do tend to destroy the necessary illusion at the points where they occur. The incident where the old plainsman meets Kit Carson and on behalf of old friendship and old dangers faced together, proceeds with Carson to imbibe too freely, is one of the fine human touches in the picture.

NBR. March 1923, p. 2

Seeing yourself as others see you is said to be good medicine. Showing yourself as others might see you if they had a six-cylinder sense of humor certainly is good fun. James Cruze has tried the latter experiment in *Hollywood*, made from a story by Frank Condon originally published in *Photoplay*, and the result is one of the most successful of Paramount pictures. Angela Whitaker felt the urge to twinkle in Hollywood. So she took her ill and aged grandfather, and made the trip. Angela didn't get a job. Grandpa did. Angela's beau and her family felt something must be wrong, so they followed after, and got jobs, too.

All the motion picture people you ever heard of are in this picture. By laughing at himself and his crowd Mr. Cruze has turned out a rattling good film.

Photoplay. Oct. 1923, p. 72

Unfortunately, it is only too rare that one sees a celluloid gem as well-nigh perfect as [*Merton of the Movies*], for in it the acting is performed by all the players with an obvious comprehension of the characters and of the narrative as a whole. Nothing is exaggerated, and there is all the humor and pathos it is possible to extract from the story, the various nuances being perfectly balanced. The assembling of the scenes is accomplished effectively, and the dissolves, fade-outs and flashbacks come as pleasant surprises.

In every adaptation of a play there are spots where the picture can atone for what it lacks in color and sound, and in *Merton of the Movies* Mr. Cruze has not lost an opportunity. The introductory sequence shows a scene of the "great open spaces where men are men," and one sees Merton as a cowboy, high on a cliff, espying a bewigged beauty about to become the victim of bandits. Heroically he descends by a rope, faces the brigands, rolling a cigarette with one hand. One of the villains prods him with a pistol. Merton smiles, and with a William S. Hart movement he suddenly snatches the weapon from the startled blackguard.

This scene dissolves into reality, showing Merton in a rear room of the town grocery shop with his arm around the neck of a store dummy. "You cur," he hisses at a male effigy. His various dreams of success as an actor are cleverly illustrated. Then there is the Sunday morning when he has his picture taken in cowboy's rig, and the old gray mare finally running away with him, throwing him off her back just as the congregation is leaving the church.

NYT. Sept. 8, 1924, p. 15

Harry Leon Wilson's superb satire of movieland [*Merton of the Movies*] has reached the screen minus a considerable measure of its tang. James Cruze's version avoids the biting satire and centers upon the pathos of the dreaming small-town boy who wanted to do better and bigger things on the screen. The adaptation follows Merton Gill from Illinois to Hollywood, traces his tragic collision with the world of celluloid make-believe, and reveals his ultimate success—as a burlesque comic foil for a cross-eyed comedian. In this the screen *Merton of the Movies* is pretty satisfying. But you will miss the pointed satire of filmdom. You will resent too, the making of Flips Montague into a soubrette, although Violo Dane has a good moment or two. We would rather have had Charlie Ray as Merton than Glenn Hunter.

Photoplay. Oct. 1924, p. 52

On the other hand, though James Cruze has not, as far as I know, been hailed by the more intelligent critics as a great director, any picture which he makes is generally worth seeing. Good as he is at outdoor stuff, he is best at American domestic comedy, such, for instance, as *The Goose Hangs High* and *To the Ladies*. Cruze practically cannot make a bad picture.

Iris Barry. *Let's Go to the Movies* (Payson & Clarke, 1926), pp. 226–27

So much happened last night at the Rivoli Theatre, the scene of the launching of James Cruze's great picture, *Old Ironsides*, that it seemed like a very full evening. . . . [A]s an additional feature of the entertainment, the scene that ended the first half of the picture was a startling surprise for the standard screen disappeared and the whole stage, from the proscenium arch to the boards, was filled with a moving picture of a replica of Old Ironsides. This brought every man and woman in the audience to their feet and Dr. Hugo Riesenfeld's orchestra and a chorus of voices further stirred the spectators with "Ship of State."

Some conception of the magnificent effect of this enlarged screen can be gained from its dimensions, which are 30 by 40 feet, whereas the usual screen in the Rivoli is about 12 by 18. Following the intermission most of the scenes of *Old Ironsides* were depicted by this apparatus, a device discovered by Glen Allvine of the Famous Players-Lasky Corporation. Mr. Allvine said that he called the idea or invention a magnascope. It is a magnifying lens attached to the ordinary projection machine.

This wide angle screen was tremendously effective in the scenes of fighting aboard the old frigate off the coast of Tripoli, and also in those pictures of the imposing productions of the forts, with old-fashioned guns booming and the missiles splashing in the sea.

In this picture Mr. Cruze, for the first time, gives a true conception of a frigate at sea. It was no millpond when these "shots" were photographed, the ocean being covered with white caps.

The story has its full share of hokum, but it is the sort of stuff that one enjoys. . . .

Mr. Cruze exhibits his skill by "shots" from all angles, and some of the most striking ones are those pictured from the masts of the Constitution. He has also introduced some sterling miniature photographs, which, in this case, fit in nicely with the other scenes.

Mordaunt Hall. *NYT*. Dec. 7, 1926, p. 20

Among the fifteen or twenty million who now daily rest on the plush seats of our country's motion picture theatres there must be many whose ancestors trod salt-stained decks on the deep sea and sucked in, instead of pollyanna, wind and foam and adventure of a stirring reality. Whether there are enough of these folks to provide an overflowing box-office for *Old Ironsides* remains, of course, to be seen, but we have much thanks to return to Messrs. Stallings, Cruze, Zukor and Lasky for giving us the ships of the film *Old Ironsides* and for giving them in correct nautical detail, with a fine feeling for their personalities, in a medium so singularly equipped as the motion picture is to render them with vividness, as they were and as they must have appeared. This is the first time it has been carefully done in an American film. . . .

Also the sea beneath and around the ship has never been shot with a motion picture camera for the purposes of a dramatic picture in a way to equal the cinematics of *Old Ironsides*; nor has the motion of the hull under sail—the ship in her living power and action, cutting her way through the waters—been at any previous time put upon the screen in a comparable way. Through special camera device, it would appear, the horizon stands steady, while the ship rises and plunges and the wave from her cutwater rolls out to leeward from her side, or the horizon itself, seen through an interstice of the sails, soars and falls away, giving us in both instances the almost perfect sensation of one who actually stands upon a heaving deck. . . .

Director Cruze's big test as an admiral comes when "Constitution" and her consorts sail into Tripoli harbor to avenge the loss of "Philadelphia," captured by the Moors and retaken and burned by Decatur. In her victorious engagement with the Tripolitan frigate sent out to meet her, he handles his ships and camera in a seamanlike manner, and for many moments together we forget that it is a movie, simply because the movie stuff is shut under hatches. The shots of "Constitution's" top-hanger coming down under the fire of the forts, of "Old Ironsides," her royal and top-masts hanging, enveloped in smoke through which jet out the flashes from her gunports (and it doesn't appear to be mere fire-works' powder either), of her decks in action with the long line of heavy broadside ordinance being worked, of the boarding actions, of her slowly crumbling Tripolitan adversary drifting away and burning—particularly a great shot of her spars and sails coming down on her deck and her crew struggling out from beneath the smothering fall of heavy canvas and gear—are all very fine, being full of the sense of reality. Here again is the best the screen has given us of an old-fashioned naval engagement.

NBR. Jan. 1927, pp. 6–8

The American cinema came of age when it produced *The Covered Wagon*, a film not in itself a major bit of work, not imaginative, not fully considered, but of immense historical interest as the first commercial picture to play straight for the ideals and loyalties of the public and build them into the structure on the screen. There was romance in Cruze's film, and comedy and sobstuff, and old-fashioned drama, but these things did not matter; what mattered was the idea behind the story, the courage of that trek westwards to open out new country for a young race. The hero and heroine were figureheads of a generation; the audience looked past them and saw youth fighting for a new home and fresh beginnings. The best in mass emotions rose to back them; enthusiasms which the cinema had never touched till then came into play.

The Covered Wagon was, aptly enough, a pioneer among films, blazing the trail for adventure. There had been earlier films with an impersonal theme—Flaherty's *Nanook* the greatest of them all, with a sheer statement of drama that has never been equalled to this day. But *Nanook* did not impinge closely enough on emotion to win the suffrage of the public; its theme was too pure, too remote from audience psychology. It had successors; it was not sterile. Flaherty's own *Moana* sprang from it, and *Tabu*, which Flaherty made with Murnau just before Murnau's death; Schoedsack's and Cooper's *Grass* and *Chang,* and Schoedsack's individual *Rango*; and some of the best non-fictional work of our British directors—peculiarly Grierson's *Drifters*—suggests a direct stimulation from this early source. But it was *The Covered Wagon* that made *Chang* and *Moana* and *Stark Love* possible, by breaking down old inhibitions and insisting that there are other things exciting in the world besides the graft and jealousies and flirtations of men.

C. A. Lejeune. *Cinema* (Alexander Maclehose, 1931), pp. 179–80

James Cruze, who had become a film actor in 1908, starring in the Thanhouser serials in 1910, directed his first picture in 1918: *Too Many Millions.* Since then he has directed about one hundred fifteen feature-length pictures. It is as the director of the renowned *The Covered Wagon*, a historical spectacle of the pioneers' westward trek, that he is popularly remembered today, but it is Cruze's flair for satire and domestic comedies that has made him a notable director. At his best he had a style that was direct, light, bantering, and breezy, and he turned out picture after picture with facility and ease. Cruze never reached real importance because the early promise he showed as a screen satirist faded as he became merely another maker of pot-boilers. He himself declared that his main fault was an overanxiety to please, and that he had "no guts." In his heyday, however, he did evidence a talent that was original and might have continued to produce significant films if he had been less compromising. Cruze's films of the post-war period, like DeMille's and Chaplin's, are said to have been the models that Lubitsch studied when he came to America. [1939]

Lewis Jacobs. *The Rise of the American Film*
(Teachers College, 1968), p. 374

Today, the more than a hundred films directed by James Cruze have vanished from memory, except for *The Covered Wagon*. Cruze had been an actor in the cinema since 1908, and his first assignment as director was *Too Many Millions* in 1918. Although its plot line appears rather ponderous now, *The Covered Wagon* was surely the most accurate of the early Westerns. Cruze's thirst for realism prompted him to commission some fifty experts to research into the story and to establish the costumes and locations. Eventually the exteriors were shot in Snake Valley, Nevada, more than eighty miles from the nearest railroad station. The great trek westward by the pioneers is the theme of *The Covered Wagon*. Some aim for Oregon, some for California. The journey quickly thins out the wagon train. Hardship, homesickness, clashes with the Indians, and snow all take their toll.

One of the most famous scenes is the fording of the river. "It's most important of all to get the babies across," says an old timer, "They'll be the real pioneers." This unselfish attitude colored much of the film, and the undertow of patriotism was probably as much responsible as the spectacular elements for the huge commercial success of *The Covered Wagon*.

Peter Cowie. *Seventy Years of Cinema*
(Barnes, 1969), p. 62

CUKOR, GEORGE (1899–)

[In *Dinner at Eight*] Mr. Cukor, and his supervisor, Mr. Selznick, had an expensive and successful play on their hands. The forms of the play presented a difficult problem of direction. Like *Grand Hotel*, the novelty and pace of *Dinner at Eight* accounted for part of its success. Both really are more movies than plays. Using a revolving stage, Mr. Kaufman, with his usual precise, machine-like direction, presented an amazing number of scenes, in which the customers saw thumb-nail dramas in the lives of six couples, at a smooth, swift pace; so effortless and swiftly that the characters seemed almost like people in a newsreel.

Now this kaleidoscopic, cross-section method of story-telling is novel on the stage. It is the very basic principle, however, of movie-making.

The camera can go anywhere. What is a tough assignment for a crew of stage hands is child's play in the hands of a third assistant camera man.

What Mr. Cukor had was an old-fashioned movie scenario on his hands. Yet he chose, wisely, considering his unexciting record, to take no chances with directorial experimentation. He set up his camera on a stage, and photographed *Dinner at Eight* just exactly as it appeared in the Music Box Theatre last year. You will get no atmospheric camera studies, no photomontage, no music, no outdoor scenes in this picture.

Of course, you cannot focus a camera on a stage from what would be thirteenth row center and register as much as your eyes naturally encompass. It was necessary, then, to freeze the movie characters in their important scenes and show close-up shots of them delivering their lines. This, unfortunately, slows down the pace of the picture, and you'll find the paradox in *Dinner at Eight*—one based on sheer mechanics—of a picture, which can be put together in a laboratory, moving slower on the screen that it did on the stage.

Pare Lorentz. *Vanity Fair*. Oct. 1933, p. 39

If to put a book on the screen with all the effectiveness that sympathy and good taste and careful artifice can devise is to make a fine motion picture, then *Little Women* is a fine picture. Only faintly does the Hollywood temptation to gild the lily obtrude: something of the homely shabbiness of the March home is missing—the attic to which Jo fled with her griefs irresistibly suggests a carefully stocked antique shop—Concord has rather more of opulent handsomeness that one expects of the home of Emerson and Thoreau and Bronson Alcott during the Civil War. But restraining this tendency toward richness is a sincere feeling for the life of that far-off time, and that feeling triumphs eloquently.

The story doesn't need retelling here. It is the simple tale, warm and human and innocent, of how four sisters grew up, with their good times and sad times. Inevitably, with the condensation needed for the screen, the sad times seem to predominate. Beth's illness and death, for instance, without the leisurely pace of the book to separate them, seems unduly drawn out and tearful. So much of Miss Alcott's cheerful robustness of humor has had to be left out that the picture has a "soft" quality absent from the book. But here again the director's restraint saves the day: with all the tears there is no mawkishness—it is all sincere and genuine. . . .

The picture should go into the archives of Americana because it preserves something precious in our tradition that can never come back again. Without being intended as an historical film it does really record, with surprising faithfulness, a period in America that many people think was most characteristically and ideally American. Here the simple sturdy virtues live as we like to think they lived in earlier times. Fortunately, for such as dislike "lessons," they are not underlined and labeled, but are intrinsic in a film that on the surface is above everything else entertaining, and appealing.

James Shelley Hamilton. *NBR*. Dec. 1933, pp. 9–10

"I have in my heart of hearts," said Dickens, "a favorite child and his name is David Copperfield." The classic story of David's triumphs and sorrows, and of the amazing people who were his friends and enemies, has been made into a gorgeous photoplay which encompasses the rich and kindly humanity of the original so brilliantly that it becomes a screen masterpiece in its own right. The immortal people of *David Copperfield*, of whom G. K. Chesterton has said that they are more actual than the man who made them, troop across the Capitol's screen like animated duplicates of the famous Phiz drawings, an irresistible and heartwarming procession. It is my belief that this cinema edition of *David Copperfield* is the most profoundly satisfying screen manipulation of a great novel that the camera has ever given us. . . .

Although it is a film of enormous length, according to screen standards two hours and ten minutes—Hugh Walpole's screen play has been arranged with such uncanny correctness, and each of the myriad episodes which go into the making of the varied canvas has been performed so perfectly, that the photoplay slips by in an unwearying cavalcade. It is astonishing to discover how much of the novel has found its way to the screen. Some of it has been telescoped for brevity, some of it has been omitted out of sheer painful necessity, but the total impression is one of amazing completeness and accuracy. Pausing only once or twice for the briefest of subtitles, the work flows on its invincibly entertaining way from beginning to end.

Like Dickens himself, it is able to invest each character in this complex story with such a completeness of personality that none is too minor to take his place in the unforgettable gallery. Certainly it is in the great narrative tradition of the cinema. A new year which has already been enriched by several distinguished photoplays now adds a genuine masterpiece to its record with *David Copperfield*.

André Sennwald. *NYT*. Jan. 19, 1935, p. 8

Now and then a film comes along which nearly all the critics acclaim, nearly all the intelligentsia admire, practically all the multitudes of the film audience line up in long queues waiting their turn to see, and so everyone is made happy and the causes of art and mammon are celebrated with one trumpet blast of victory. Such a picture, contrary to the dissenting voice of a few very pernickety ones, may be art. This production of *Camille* is, and not altogether because of the sumptuously human, moving performance of Miss Greta Garbo, a performance hardly equaled, never exceeded in the history of the screen. . . .

. . . *Camille* has the charm of giving out something that is documentary, which greatly enhances the atmosphere of reality. Through all its long, splendid scenes with their variety and feeling of what must have been the Paris of the times—the springtide streets, the gilded glittering rooms, the spacious opera, the ornateness, extravagance and overcrowded luxury of the places and haunts of the life of joy, it steadily builds up the impression of being a spectacle of manners and fashions, and so a socially true background for its characters to move against. It makes one think of Anna Sten and *Nana*, and how that film, with material so much richer, so much more dramatic as sociology, similar too in the world with which it dealt and with a leading character whose counterparts Zola had studied down to their polished fingernails, so utterly failed in giving one the feeling either of reality or importance. But *Camille*, the thing of sometimes tinselly fiction and romantic effulgence, becomes in this production, so far superior to the sappy, plushy *Camilles* that clutter here and there the path of the screen, attains the moving dignity of the authentic.

Of *Camille* we come to know, old-fashioned though it may be, if it is, that it has the vitality of a love story powerful enough to give us an increased understanding of the human heart, directed somehow to a new understanding of ourselves as not such hard-boiled creatures, after all, of a new steel-clad, rational day. Indeed we may see in this old baggage of tragic romance something of the glamorous, the tawdry and the sad in the perspective of what we are pleased to call life.

NBR. Feb. 1937, pp. 13–14

The present movie season is not only good but in unexpected ways. As to *Camille*, the surprise is to find a story that should by rights be old hat coming to such insistent life on the day's screen. On the screen, of course, there is no such easy thing as material's just "coming" to life: the life has to be put there, and lived in make-believe, all of which takes understanding, faith, and craftsmanship. The story of a farm girl whose loveliness and adaptable wisdom had promoted her into a nineteenth-century Paris figure, exquisite, obtainable, and expensive as to surface, but inwardly consumed with a certain sickness and spiritual uncertainty; her surrender to and partly wasted sacrifice for simple love—this could have been made into many things: the perfunctory observance of a theater classic, a costume piece, a vehicle for some heedless star. But although George Cukor's direction has seemed to be on the consciously classic side previously, his work here with the cast, material (treatment credited to Zoë Akins, Frances Marion, James Hilton), and technical staff (the top MGM crew: Herbert Stothart, William Daniels and Karl Freund, Cedric Gibbons, etc.) is a firm and straight-out piece of film work.

The life of the times grows up unobtrusively around the people as they take their dramatic position in the story, so that the complexities of an unfamiliar code of living and way of life become the simple background. This has flaws (some of the outdoors is needlessly artificial), but the point is that it serves functionally rather than as a separate effect in itself. In the same way the people become part of the life there. [1937]

Otis Ferguson. *The Film Criticism of O.F.* (Temple, 1971), p. 170

This clinical study [*The Women*] of the domestic problems of the idle rich, which was hilarious on stage, hasn't transferred very well to the screen—in large measure because of the heavy direction of George Cukor, who doesn't seem to know a laugh-line from the kitchen sink, and the "acting" of Norma Shearer, who plays the leading, or sweet wife, role, and is so lovely and so tragic that you expect the tumbrils to roll any moment over the cobblestones for her or Romeo to come traipsing down to her tomb with a drawn sword. Neither of these things happens, however. Our Norma bitches up the other woman (Joan Crawford, and never prettier) with the help of Rosalind Russell . . . Miss Goddard, by the way, is *The Women*'s only convincing woman. The others look and sound as if they came fresh from a night-club press agent's dream.

Gordon Sager, *TAC*. Oct. 1939, p. 31

Consider in passing what happened to *Romeo and Juliet*. It is impossible to realize how bad this film was unless you reflect upon how good it might have been. The music—Tschaikovsky's—fitted the production perfectly—that is to say, it was music of the indoors, heavy with scent, unventilated, introverted, consorting well with the glorified seraglio that was the set-designer's picture of ancient Verona. Tschaikovsky's main musical theme has since come out in its true colors as a crooner's nostalgic drag called "Our Love." This is the musical accompaniment, if you please, of a play by Shakespeare which presents one of the purest love-stories of all time—full of stark, sharp terrifying beauty. One can't represent such a love with Tschaikovsky's music. One might as well try to etch with a paintbrush. I would not have had any other music in that particular production, all the same. For that, it was perfect. But in another production, I should certainly like to entrust the music to a good modern composer. Shakespeare's strangely universal genius needs to be interpreted anew in every age—by the most modern means. The recent film *Romeo and Juliet* was thirty years out of date all the way through.

Alberto Cavalcanti. *Films*. Nov. 1939, p. 35

A *raffiné*, George Cukor is often too much so. A great artistic finesse, a very subtle taste.

Cukor came from the theater and waited for sound movies to make his cinema debut. His theatrical background is incontestable: Cukor is static, he leans on dialogue and acting. But the admirable continuity of his films, their smoothness, makes for excellent cinema. His films are carefully done, consciously artistic, literary, poetic to the point of being effeminate. Cukor likes to work (generally at MGM) with women actors and writers. Didn't he make a film called *The Women*? He is intent on penetrating female psychology, and he directs Hollywood's greatest stars, especially Hepburn.

Henri Colpi. *Le cinéma et ses hommes* (Causse, Graille & Castelnau, 1947), p. 152

The faults and virtues of *Adam's Rib* are implied in its punning title—funny, but not quite funny enough and more than a little self-conscious. . . . Cukor has directed with a deliberate, polished theatricality which emphasizes the artificiality of the piece. The camera often remains anchored for quite an appreciable time so that the screen becomes simply a frame for the two stars, and theatricality is heightened by the device of a stage curtain, with the title "that evening," used to separate court and home scenes. Hepburn and Tracy are masters of the artificial comedy, but once or twice they seem to strain a little too hard after the light touch. The script, which contains several promising situations, but fails on the whole to exploit them by good lines, can be blamed for trading on the personality of the stars to carry off some domestic scenes which in other hands might have proved unbearably whimsical. This is synthetic rather than artificial, and for once it is a relief to turn from the stars to the secondary couple, the dumb husband-shooter and her morose near-victim. Tom Ewell has some laconic moments in the court room, but the real discovery of the film is Judy Holliday. The part could have been quite ordinary, but she makes it both touching and comic: a remarkable performance.

BFI Bulletin. Feb.-March 1950, p. 22

Even allowing for the assumed prejudices of self-styled intellectuals against expensive enterprises of any kind, *My Fair Lady* must be described in all candor as an evening of disenchantment. As a longtime admirer of George Cukor's directorial style, I had expected something more in the way of creative adaptation. Unfortunately, *My Fair Lady* is to Cukor's career what *Porgy and Bess* is to Preminger's, a producer's package overstuffed with all the snob stage values so dear to the garment center-garden club tastes of the Warners and the Goldwyns. With justice less poetic than prosaic, Cukor, long slandered as a "woman's director," will probably receive an overdue fistful of awards for one of his weakest jobs of direction. With so much capital invested, *My Fair Lady* has been approached so reverently that transference has degenerated into transcription. This property has not been so much adapted as elegantly embalmed, and yet, with few exceptions, the film fails dismally to repeat the click effects of the stage show. [1964]

Andrew Sarris. *Confessions of a Cultist* (S&S, 1970), p. 176

Since Cukor did not have any say over the screenplay or the casting of the film, and since these two elements so often give Cukor films their character, *Justine* can be considered a film of marginal importance to his career. . . .

Perhaps no one could turn Durrell's books into a workable screenplay of average length, but certainly [Lawrence] Marcus hasn't. The script is utter confusion even to someone who has read all the books. With the exceptions of Anouk Aimée, Anna Karina, and Dirk Bogarde, the film is entirely miscast. Against these odds Cukor fails to re-create the author's world of fetid sensuality, political intrigue, and moral fatigue. Nor does he capture the sense of magic inherent in the constantly shifting identities and relationships of the characters. Durrell's sensibility goes against the grain of Cukor's. The writer is flamboyant, purple-prosed, in love with the sound of words, and to bring his world to life on film one needs a director with a true sensual response to the plasticity of the medium. It needs a bit of the kind of showing off that Cukor's approach prevents.

Garey Carey. *Cukor & Co.* (MOMA, 1971), pp. 152–53

There are, in our film legacy, too many instances of moral frivolity about homosexuality, too many cases where it is literally used as a Halloween masquerade to play slyly on the subject of the homosexual as if he were not real but a sort of charade person. Thus, the sophisticated Hollywood director George Cukor, who had discovered Katharine Hepburn and developed her into a star, used her for the kind of thing that Mart Crowley terms, where a certain sort of director is involved, "getting his jollies." For such directors, homosexuality becomes a professional in-joke that will entertain the public while leaving it in its natural, semiblind state of prejudice about the facts of homosexuality. True enough, that day is about over. Now it is "in" to exploit the homosexual's non-Halloween personality. According to Cukor's own statement (made at the Museum of Modern Art on the occasion of introducing a retrospective of his films) he regretted the movie *Sylvia Scarlett*, in which Hepburn masquerades as a boy. The reason was undisclosed, but Cukor indicated that all concerned thought the movie a loss, a sort of tactical misstep.

Parker Tyler. *Screening the Sexes* (Holt, 1972), pp. 212–13

CURTIZ, MICHAEL (1888–1962)

The price of Red Sea crossings is coming down. When one of them is thrown in as a mere incident in a romantic love affair between a Jewish slave maiden and a son of a Pharaoh, the mind harks back almost incredulously to the prodigious publicity noises which emanated from the double exposure and miniature departments of the DeMille studios while the *Ten Commandments* was in process. . . .

Nor is the crossing of the Red Sea the only thing that makes the *Moon of Israel* memorable. Imaginative direction and the fine handling of crowds mark all the spectacle scenes and leave a vivid impression of the splendor and magnificence of Egyptian civilization under the rule of the Pharaohs. It is in this combination of noteworthy mass effects and an intriguing love story that the strength of the picture lies.

NBR. July 1927, p. 8

Two falsehoods are presented [in *The Cabin in the Cotton*] to strengthen the drama of conciliation: the tenants steal the planters' cotton and seek to set up their own broker in Memphis (how long could a tenant conceal the bales before he were apprehended?), the collaborator of the hyphenate in making the peace is the district attorney—an agent of the planters who is presented as a friend of the tenants! There are other details equally suspect. Yet, it would be sectarian and dishonest not to say that this film, in its argument and mood, balances the sympathy to the credit of the tenants. That is assuredly a victory! a concession to a rising temper. The tenants are facially well-chosen, not non-professional players but professionals chosen and controlled upon the documentary principle—director Curtiz has evidently learned something from the Russians. For the first time, in my immediate recollection, the movie has dared to approach lynching as a contemporary American custom. Here the victim is a white peasant who has been sorely driven to the murder of a planter. More should have been made of the scene since it submits the climax to the hyphenate's evolving attitude. We must recognize also that this is not a typical instance. The typical instance is lynching not on a "real" but a framed charge; the most frequent instances are the organized mob-murders of Negroes, but that is an indisputable fact to which our conscience is too sensitive —we can argue the lynching in *The Cabin in the Cotton* as rare and therefore chance. Still, the incomplete presentation of the pursuit and lynching of a white man by wealthy men of his own race is an incipient suggestion of the fact that lynchings are economic. Therefore, for all its distortion of the social theme it particularizes, *The Cabin in the Cotton* is an advance in the movie's content. A more truthful production would have sought its material in works like *Georgia Nigger*, *To Make My Bread*, *Call Home the Heart*, *Strike*! or *Gathering Storm*.

H. A. Potamkin. *Close Up*. March 1933, pp. 34–36

This last Warner picture, *Black Fury*, has not got the subject of strikes reduced to final terms (in fact its strike is a phony, its villains are not the actual owners at all), but still it is the most powerful strike picture that has yet been made—so far as I am aware, and I am aware of the better known Soviet jobs in the field. Pudovkin has produced the most massive and beautiful works of this kind; but even his best film, *Mother*, was lacking in the suppleness of personal development, the direct and hard-hitting action where action is needed, that are required to give a picture its air of easy, continuous motion and real life, and to sway its audiences.

Black Fury has this motion and this air of life, whatever we may think of its social content (and from the row being kicked up on several sides, we may think some very thoughtful things indeed). . . .

It may not be taken as the study of a typical strike: it does not show why strikes are generally made, or even how. It is a story of the suffering in the life of a single man—his betrayals, the battering of his poor muddy wits, the unquenchability of his vigor and loyalties. To this story certain conditions of life in a striking town are essential: it derives its force and persuasion from the fine tangible way in which these conditions are built up around plot situations and brought to bear on the central figure. And because this central figure is made dominant and real, laying a strong hand on his audience, including it in his humiliations and rough-and-tumble victories, all these incidents will be seen through his eyes and taken at his valuation. [1935]

Otis Ferguson. *The Film Criticism of O.F.* (Temple, 1971), p. 73

The Frères Warner, bless 'em, may not give a hang for history, but they do know how to turn out a smashing and spectacular adventure film. *The Charge of the Light Brigade*, which has taken what will unquestionably prove to be a long-term lease of the Strand, is the 1936 model of *Lives of a Bengal Lancer*. Like its magnificently melodramatic predecessor, it is a virile and picturesque saga of blood and empire in India, with the usual treacherous Amir lurking in one corner, the immaculately heroic Lancers in another and the middle ground a vivid splash of leopard hunts, native uprisings and outpost massacres. . . . And a picture, which already might have been accounted a larruping action tale, crashes into its spectacular climax when the gallant 600, spread across a flat valley rimmed with enemy batteries, charged with sabers forward and lances leveled through a deadly thunder of cannon and rifle fire. Tennyson described the charge and the Warner cameras have photographed it just that way. It's a sight to see.

Frank S. Nugent. *NYT*. Nov. 2, 1936, p. 24

Mostly the picture [*The Adventures of Robin Hood*] is full of movement, some of it dashing in the fine romantic costume style, some of it just sprightly. The excitement comes from fast action—galloping steeds, men swinging Tarzan-like down from trees, hurling tables and chairs, rapid running sword-play, the sudden whiz of Robin's arrows coming from no-where to startle his enemies—more than from any fear that Robin might be worsted. Robin is more than equal to any danger, incredibly strong and swift and sure, politely arrogant, always flashing a smile. Somehow the whole thing has an air of being a costume party, a jolly and rather athletic one, with a lot of well-bred Englishmen playing at being in the greenwood. Their bright, fresh clothes, their house-party kind of conversation, the clean castles and neat forests, might all have been something an affluent host arranged for the entertainment of summer guests. Only Alan Hale looks and acts as if he could be at home in the woods.

There is some charming color in the film, and quite a lot of brilliant dazzle. Some of the actors, like Montagu Love and Claude Rains, might have stepped out of a history book. The others live up to the picture-book quality of the film, which has the supreme virtue of a movie—except for some tedious and modernish love-making it keeps moving.

James Shelley Hamilton. *NBR*. June 1938, pp. 14–15

. . . *Casablanca*, a ginspiked tale of refugees, agents and counter-agents, who pivot around the *Cafe Americain* in a North African port waiting for their precious visas to Lisbon and New York. This one is an excellent example of the kind of film Hollywood, and Warner Brothers in particular, does extremely well. All the characters, as well as the situations in it, are stock, and you know how it's all going to turn out, but, despite the papier-mâché Casablanca (who, in Hollywood, has ever put the sultriness and heat of North Africa on the screen like von Sternberg did in *Morocco*?) and the clichés of casting, which give each character's destiny away, it manages, by virtue of some of its dialogue to be occasionally believable. Its humour is what really saves it, being a mixture of Central European irony of attack and racy Broadway-Hollywood Boulevard cynicism. It is also the first outspokenly anti-Vichy film, and it's about time.

Herman G. Weinberg. *Sight & Sound*.
Spring 1943, pp. 95–96

If the history of France were written according to the American films devoted to it, our country would be described as peopled by imbeciles and Vichyites convinced of German victory. The French could become patriots but only out of love for a secret agent; in that case they were dragged into incredible adventures in which there were stupid Germans or romantic Italians. This curious historical conception inspired *Five Graves to Cairo* by the Austrian Billy Wilder and Michael Curtiz' *Casablanca*, which in 1942 won seven or eight Oscars. Such were the films that were set in Occupied France, and their ridiculousness prevented them from being shown here.

Georges Sadoul. *Histoire d'un art: le cinéma*
(Flammarion, 1949), p. 330

Warners, who hold the screen rights of Ernest Hemingway's *To Have and Have Not*, have certainly got value for their money. The book was first filmed, in 1944, with a script credit to William Faulkner; the title was retained, but the story was transmuted into a wartime crisis of awakening patriotism. In *Key Largo*, a denouement borrowed from the novel was attached rather arbitrarily to Maxwell Anderson's play. Now *The Breaking Point*, scripted by Ranald MacDougall, makes a determined effort to come within striking distance of Hemingway's original theme. . . .

The script, after outlining a situation whose main spring is a moral crisis, abandons its exploration, and the story is played out on a level of melodramatic excitement. Weakness in the writing is particularly apparent in Morgan's last scene with his wife, when the dialogue sounds almost like a parody of some of Hemingway's less happy mannerisms. With material so overworked, Michael Curtiz' slick, rather mechanical, style is inadequate. He achieves one or two effective moments of tension, but yields too often to his taste for a formalized arty shot. A case in point is the last shot of the film: a Negro, Morgan's friend and only crew member, has been killed by the gang; at the end, his small son stands alone, in the dark, on the solitary dock. This could have been a moving conclusion, but it is so manoeuvred into position, has so little connection with what has gone before, that it becomes merely a director's flourish. This clever artifice without emotional justification is typical of the level at which the director has approached his subject; only Garfield's playing consistently suggests greater depths and resources.

Penelope Houston. *Sight & Sound.*
Feb. 1951, p. 413

Mika Waltari's novel, on which this film-spectacle [*The Egyptian*] is based, supplied the reader with enough occurrences and customs of Akhnaton's time—the most fascinating period in Egyptian history—to hide some of the more obvious contrivances of the story. The film does not do this.

There are other imperfections. Michael Curtiz, who directed, neither restrained the mugging of such extroverted players as Victor Mature and Peter Ustinov, nor elicited life from such introverted ones as Edmund Purdom, Jean Simmons, Gene Tierney, Michael Wilding and Bella Darvi (even though the last named was rigged out like a latter day Theda Bara).

Carolyn Harrow. *Films in Review.*
Oct. 1954, p. 433

But although Curtiz may mangle the English language, his movies are usually nicely articulated on the screen. He is a camera expert who can make a move take form and rhythm through moving camera shots, movement before the camera and ingenious camera angles. Some of Curtiz's kinetic camera effects can be seen in the atmospheric *Casablanca*; *Black Fury* with its raw bohunk realism; the swashbuckling *The Sea Hawk* and *The Adventures of Robin Hood*; the punchy fight film *Kid Galahad*; and the bouncy musical *Yankee Doodle Dandy*.

One of Curtiz's movies, *The Charge of the Light Brigade*, which he directed for Warners in 1936 and which has been seen extensively on television in recent years, is in my opinion one of the most dynamic Hollywood films ever made. It is a straightforward and strikingly carried-off exercise in motion, culminating in the final, head-on charge, and, as such, for camerawork, cutting and over-all pace, ranks with some of the best things done in this field. The entire picture is essentially one elongated spiral of slowly but surely intensifying momentum, building up to the electrifying charge at the end. *The Charge of the Light Brigade* does not pretend to be anything but an action adventure story. It is not a great human document—and how many American movies are?—but for downright technical virtuosity it would be hard to find anything to remotely equal it in the work of a Wyler, Wilder, Stevens or Huston. Curtiz was assisted in this production by action expert B. Reeves Eason and cutter George Amy . . . and they managed, between them, to achieve, fortuitously perhaps, a high mark in the American Action movie.

Ezra Goodman. *The Fifty-Year Decline and Fall of Hollywood* (S&S, 1961), p. 211

Perhaps more than any other director, Curtiz reflected the strengths and weaknesses of the studio system in Hollywood. This most amiable of Warners' technicians faithfully served the studio's contract players from Dolores Costello to Doris Day. When one speaks of a typical Warners' film in the thirties and forties, one is generally speaking of a typical Curtiz film of those periods. . . . After *Force of Arms*, his career went to the dogs. If many of the early Curtiz films are hardly worth remembering, none of the later ones are even worth seeing. What the collapse of studio discipline meant to Curtiz and to Hollywood was the bottom dropping out of routine film-making. The director's one enduring masterpiece is, of course, *Casablanca*, the happiest of happy accidents, and the most decisive exception to the auteur theory.

Andrew Sarris. *The American Cinema* (Dutton, 1968), pp. 175–76

No, *Casablanca* was in its time (1942), and looks now just like, a routine, surefire piece of commercial film-making. No pretensions to art, and precious few to originality. Warner Brothers going happily, uncomplicatedly through the motions, with all the usual people, Don Siegel in the montage department, and all right with the world. So why, then, does the film have an almost legendary stature? Why does it still live up to its fame and, above all, why does it still, almost infallibly, work? If it sums up ideally the feeling of "they don't make pictures like that any more," why does it, and why don't they?

Complicated, but not unanswerable. In fact there are so many answers one hardly knows where to start. The film's secret can be seen, most immediately, in its combination of extreme sophistication, of a sort, and extreme innocence, of a sort. The sophistication lies mainly in what it takes for granted at a purely technical, organisational level. It is the sophistication of complete confidence, in which no one has to prove anything, defend anything: there is simply an unquestioned way of doing things, and that's it. There is a whole hyper-efficient studio machine behind the film, a palpable presence in every frame. Clearly just about everybody (apart from Ingrid Bergman) is on the company payroll: they are all there, waiting to be used. The actors particularly, but also the technicians, from director down, are not called upon to justify themselves specifically in this one instance. They are cast to do what they have always done, and what everyone knows perfectly well they can do. . . .

Then there is the directorial side. Studio style, of course; nothing personal. But it was a studio style which served its required end very well. Brisk, to the point, confident enough to do everything as simply and cheaply as it well could be done. "Local colour" is provided by a couple of little scenes apparently shot in a left-over or made-over Casbah set, plus some summary interludes with maps, stock-shots and the montage artistry of Mr. Siegel. Otherwise the film takes place almost entirely in interiors, or at night, against backgrounds so simple and shadowy that they could be anywhere, any time. No director now would dare to do it that way. If you were making a film called *Casablanca* you would have to go to Casablanca, or somewhere that would pass for it, and then provide tangible evidence that you had been in the shape of picturesque detail, quite irrelevant to the story but obedient to the theory that part of the something-for-everybody ethos is vicarious travel for those who don't like the stars and find the story too difficult, or too dull, to follow.

Arkadin. *Sight & Sound*. Autumn 1968, p. 211

Black Fury was one of the real frauds of the thirties, a fact recognized by many contemporaries. Not that it did not get some auspicious notices: New York's Democratic Senator Robert F. Wagner thought it a "vivid portrayal of a coal mine strike" and John L. Lewis, "a great contribution to the comprehension of the deep-seated problem involved in industrial relationships." *The New Republic* hailed it as "the most powerful strike picture that has yet been made," while New York's censor board threatened to cut its "inflammatory scenes."

The object of this adulation and fear was a film about a good-natured Polish miner who is manipulated by a shyster detective agency into leading a Pennsylvania wildcat strike. *Black Fury* had all the trappings of a proletarian drama: the realistic coal town setting, the working class camaraderie, the brutality of industrial police. Yet it was simply a fairy tale, weighed down by shyster motifs and sure of the intrinsic solidarity between benevolent capitalism and conservative unionism. In its basic assumptions of social unity, *Black Fury* had more ties to "screwball" comedy . . . than to earlier topical films. . . .

In setting up its labor confrontation, *Black Fury* raises some real problems and then proceeds to pretend that they are hallucinatory. Dissident miners complain that their leadership is stodgy and stale, collecting big salaries, and selling out their interests by promising the mine-owners no labor difficulties. The film embraced the premises of the shyster films by ascribing this discontent entirely to manipulation by the crooked strikebreaking agency, which needs conflict to remain in business. If assaults upon established trade union leadership had to be engineered entirely by shysters, then the fabric of industrial relationships must be sound, so long as corruption could be combatted. Small wonder that John L. Lewis found *Black Fury* so compelling a document.

Once the premises have been so thoroughly falsified, the film's "realism" seems an irrelevancy. . . .

Andrew Bergman. *We're in the Money*
(NYU, 1971), pp. 105–06

Ironically, [*The Mystery of the*] *Wax Museum* is less familiar to today's audience than is the generally inferior remake, *House of Wax*, directed by Andre de Toth and released by Warners in 1953. (Roger Corman also used the basic story for one of his own variations, *A Bucket of Blood*, in 1959.) In one dramatic respect, *House of Wax* has an advantage: the 3-D process, refined for the film's 1971 reissue. It also benefits from the score by David Buttolph. Though his music is not exceptional, at least it's there. *Wax Museum* has only three bursts of music: the opening credits, the fade-out, and a scene in which an on-screen radio is chirping out "A Shanty in Old Shanty Town." Then, too, the 1933 script was littered with loose ends of plot and needless people, all streamlined out of the fifties' slicker rewrite.

But what it may lack in these miscellaneous sophistications, *Wax Museum* makes up for in lurid details and characterization, the latter best represented by Atwill's demented artist (a character not dissimilar to the scarred composer of *The Phantom of the Opera*), leering at his wax creatures and acclaiming "the texture of that flesh" in gruesome tones, and by Glenda Farrell, as the hot-shottiest of tough girl reporters. . . .

Wax Museum's most telling details, though, are its horrific ones—the fire at the beginning, with the lifelike figures melting into grisly oozes; nighttime in the city morgue, with a dead body suddenly popping up as a side effect of embalming fluid; one of Atwill's workers lovingly sliding a dagger into the body of Marat as the New York wax museum readies for its opening; chases through shadows as the ghoulish sculptor collects bodies for his exhibit; and, of course, the shock when Atwill's homemade wax face crumbles to the floor and exposes the hidden demon.

Part of the film's suspense, too, derives from the wax figures themselves. We can't be blamed for wondering which are really fakes and which are actually live actors holding their breaths. If you watch closely, however, during a scene in which Atwill conducts a tour of his museum, you may be able to see Queen Victoria blink.

Tom Shales in *The American Film Heritage*, edited by the American Film Institute (Acropolis, 1972), pp. 29, 31

Four bullets shatter a full-length mirror. A man, doubled over as if kicked in the groin, staggers toward the camera and falls before a flickering fireplace. Like Charles Foster Kane, he mutters one cryptic word before dying: "Mildred." Abruptly changing locale, the camera cranes down past flickering neon signs as a woman in a broadshouldered fur coat walks listlessly across the rain-soaked boards of the Santa Monica pier. Smeared mascara belies her impassive expression as she stares down at the swirling, inviting water. Mildred Pierce is about to commit suicide.

From these first shots it is immediately obvious that *Mildred Pierce* (1945) is to be different—blacker, more pessimistic—than the average representative of the war years' most popular genre: the woman's picture. Designed as morale builders for the lonely females left working on the home front, this group of films invariably featured noble heroines enduring great hardship and strife to eventually win security and happiness (i.e., Love). While in some ways following the pattern (certainly Mildred is inflicted with sufficient suffering), *Mildred Pierce* perverts the comforting fantasy by exposing Work, Success, Marriage and even Mother Love as false, unrewarding ideals.

Such overt criticism of traditional American values was not missed by contemporary critics. John McManus, movie reviewer for *PM*, felt that the film should be withdrawn from foreign distribution because of its unfavorable image of domestic life. *Newsweek* called it, "A bitter commentary on suburbia . . ." and criticized the lack of moral distinction between the characters. Manny Farber, in *The New Republic*, echoed this criticism and noted with displeasure that the film's director and writer seemed primarily concerned with showing how "lascivious, zealous to make money, untrustworthy, loveless, and discontented Americans are." Among the major critics, only James Agee and Parker Tyler stood against the general condemnation, unreservedly praising what they viewed as its honesty and closeness to "life as it is lived." [1972]

John Davis. *The Velvet Light Trap*. No. 6, p. 27

DE MILLE, CECIL B. (1881–1959)

Without risking dangerous comparisons, it is only fair to place *The Squaw Man* among the few really satisfactory film adaptations of plays. In point of sustained interest it gives place to none; the acting offers no cause for criticism, the settings are notably appropriate, and best of all, there is a real story told in photographed action, not in lengthy subtitles, illustrated by fragmentary scenes.

NYDM. February 25, 1914

Though it is not faultless, *Joan the Woman* is the best sun-spectacle since *The Birth of a Nation*, and in the opinion of the writer only that sweeping review of arms and hearts has excelled it. *The Birth of a Nation* trumps all the picture spectacles yet made for its insistent humanity; its irresistible combination of power and simplicity, tempest and tenderness. Mechanically as well as photographically *Joan* equals but does not surpass *Civilization*, that photographic and mechanic milestone of flivver story; in legend and development of dramatic interest it would be absurd to mention *Civilization* in this connection. Mr. Griffith's radiant crazy-quilt, *Intolerance*, is also put by. . . .

The material side of the picture is splendidly taken care of. The reduction of a feudal fortress, the sweep of a great field of knights to the charge are big incidents. The flash to mouth of a hundred brass trumpets, the glitter of five times as many pennanted lances, the arching of what seemed a thousand great swords demonstrate overwhelmingly the drama of arms in the mailed centuries. . . .

Mr. DeMille has not Mr. Griffith's almost demoniac faculty of making even an extra do in a picture just what he would do in life. *Joan the Woman* could stand a bit more humanity here and there. Nevertheless, it is a big and splendid thing. . . .

Julian Johnson. *Photoplay*. March 1917, pp. 113–16

Paris has greeted *The Cheat* with violent admiration. This has somewhat surprised Americans. They were right to be surprised since *The Cheat* is an event of the tenth order in the ranks of their artistic production. But Paris was not wrong to admire it since for the first time it was seeing a film that merited the name of film. If the French are little by little beginning to understand a few bits of cinema, the thanks is due to *The Cheat*.

Nevertheless, let's see the matter clearly. Not to please the Americans but to please truth—and there is not much of a difference—let's admit that *The Cheat* is especially noteworthy because it is complete.

Works of genius are not often complete. Here, there is no genius. The very judiciously chosen and united elements have been balanced with infinite skill which gets from each only what it can—and not, of course, all that it can.

No musician would call Puccini's *Tosca* a work of genius. However, all recognize that is a complete whole organized with skill and admirable mastery. The synthesis of a well composed scenario and music without useless discretion but characterized without insolence and written so that a singer of second order is enough and a really sublime singer will shine strangely—without however wasting the secret treasures of his genius—has contributed to the end result.

The Cheat is the *Tosca* of films.

Louis Delluc. *Cinéma & Cie* (Grasset, 1919), pp. 16–17

Just now Director DeMille is at the extra-seasoning stage. Having achieved a reputation as the great modern concocter of the sex stew by adding a piquant dash here and there to *Don't Change Your Husband*, and a little something more to *Male and Female*, he spills the spice box into *Why Change Your Wife?* and the result is a rare concoction—the most gorgeously sensual film of the month; in decoration the most costly; in physical allure the most fascinating; in effect the most immoral.

Some day, so sure as we both shall live, and sooner than we now surmise, I'm thinking, we shall see a reaction against the society sex film. Largely because the more highly seasoned it becomes the more untrue it is and the more insidiously dangerous to a public that has a quietly effective way of protecting itself. . . .

Just as a picture, however, this screened yarn of a rich young husband, who, objecting to his wife's plainness and her thrift, thought to buy a few thin, lacy things for her to wear, and then fell in love with the model who showed them to him, is effectively told and pictured. It has the fault of all artificial stories, but its characters are interesting. Divorcing the wife and marrying the lingerie model, young husband discovers his mistake about the same time his first wife decides to do a little wild dressing on her own account. . . .

The settings and the costumes of the actors are, as previously noted, gorgeous . . . Gloria Swanson and Bebe Daniels, besides being histrionically competent, were glorious camera subjects, wrapped and unwrapped in a million dollars' worth of lace and lingerie. The Sennetts and the Sunshine boys may outdo Mr. DeMille as masters of the lower limb displays, but he completely distances them in the technique of the torso. William DeMille furnished the text for *Why Change Your Wife?*

Burns Mantle. *Photoplay*. May 1920, pp. 64–65

It is easy to imagine that Mr. DeMille had a great deal of fun making [*Fool's Paradise*]. It contains practically everything he has given evidence of loving to put on the screen—expensive and spectacular scenes, theatrical sentimentality, melodrama in exotic settings, and various other elaborations and embellishments of an unresisting plot. . . .

Now in all this there are many striking photographic effects, some expressive bits of cinematography, not a little childish symbolism, as, for example, when a broken heart is represented by a broken heart-shaped object, and a few scenes that approach verisimilitude through the accurate pantomime of Theodore Kosloff, Dorothy Dalton and Conrad Nagel, especially and most often through the pantomime of Mr. Kosloff. But, of course, the impression of the whole picture is one of artificiality, the spectator feeling somewhat as he does when sitting before one of the gorgeous revues that come to the New York stage every Summer, admiring but always conscious that the entertainment before him is a spectacle.

And no matter how much you may enjoy a spectacle, *Fool's Paradise* many make you wish that the studio workmanship of Mr. DeMille could be combined with the dramatic imagination and sincerity of, say, Ernst Lubitsch. What a picture would result!

NYT. Dec. 10, 1921, p. 11

Looking aside for the moment from the spectacular side of this newest DeMille achievement [*Manslaughter*]—its reproduction of decadent Rome under the Caesars, its lavishness displayed in the cabaret sets, and the opulence suggestive of the manner in which the idle rich live—looking aside from all these typically DeMille effects, we must give him credit for building the most direct action which has graced the screen in many a day. It is direct story-telling, think what you may about the theatrical character of the plot. It moves and by moving holds your attention through a chain of events dramatic, perhaps impossible, but which points a moral notwithstanding.

Laurence Reid. *The Motion Picture News*. Sept. 30, 1922

Cecil B. De Mille, whose pictures are second only to Griffith's as box-office attractions, makes little or no attempt at all to produce first-rate shadow plays. While *Joan the Woman* and *Don't Change Your Wife* [*sic*] prove beyond a doubt that he has within him the abilities to make commendable screen drama, he is content to play down to the shopgirl and yokel intellect. De Mille is long on talking about the wonders of the new art but short in making any effort to put them into practice. He believes in making every production a circus, a sight for the gullible multitude. The man in the street has come to look upon a De Mille opus in the same manner he regards the Winter Garden or the Follies—he knows he is going to see a good leg show. The feminine portion of the country, especially in Kalamazoo and Keokuk, looks forward to a C. B. extravaganza as the fashion parade of Fifth Avenue and the Rue de la Paix brought to their very door. De Mille is the best showman-director in the business. He knows full well all the weakness of his gallery and he plays to them for all he is worth. Much of his success has been gained through giving the plebeian multitudes a close-up of what they believe to be elite society. To anyone who knows the slightest thing about the real habits of the aristocracy his films and their high-falutin characters are an immense joke. Nobody is more aware of this than De Mille, himself. He realizes that society presented true to life on the screen would not only be a disappointment to the average John and Mary but it would be extremely uninteresting. So he gives them society not as it actually is but as they believe and hope it to be. De Mille is the hokum merchant par excellence of the studio world and usually gives one, if nothing else, a very enjoyable evening's entertainment, but there is seldom much savoring of first-rate drama in his films and they certainly will not bear anything resembling criticism of a higher form. His stories are far-fetched, the situations forced and full of glaring inconsistencies, his characters unlifelike and mere puppets on a string manipulated rather adroitly. What he could do with a first-rate play minus the usual hokum and frillery is a matter of conjecture. . . .

Tamar Lane. *What's Wrong with the Movies*
(Waverly, 1923), pp. 64–66

I am not an admirer of Mr. Cecil B. de Mille, though I will admit that he has a perfect genius for vulgarity in every sense of the word. I do not mean that his pictures are always unpleasant—far from it! Many of them are so moral that they might make even a Presbyterian minister feel like abandoning the paths of righteousness. Mr. de Mille obviously likes toying with the Infinite. *The Ten Commandments* is his wash-pot, and over Reincarnation he has cast out his shoe. I shall never feel the same either about the decalogue or about reincarnation now that I have seen what Mr. de Mille has done with them. There are those, I know, who contend that because Mr. de Mille, however bad they may be, shows his pictures so smartly, keeps them moving so brightly, that people cannot leave the cinema while they are being shown, however angry they make them, he is therefore a good director. But frankly I do not believe it. I think his is the kind of picture which grips the eye at the moment, but which on reflection (and I believe that nearly everyone does reflect a little after seeing a picture) one is bound to shrug off as silly because his psychological values, even in their own convention, are false, and there is so little real reason why any of his characters should do anything that they do. So afterwards one feels that one has been sold. This, I contend, brings the whole cinema into contempt.

Iris Barry. *Let's Go to the Movies* (Payson & Clarke, 1926), pp. 231–32

The Supreme theme has been used. Jesus has come to the screen and DeMille has given us a picture which will tend to standardize the world's conception of the New Testament. It was a great thing that Cecil DeMille conceived and executed—something that will live for a long, long time and which will gross more money than any other picture ever made. DeMille has one of the best business minds in pictures and making *King of Kings* was the most brilliant stroke of his successful business career.

Welford Beaton. *Film Spectator*. June 11, 1927

The public wanted to see how the rich lived and whether the furnishings they read about were actually real, and DeMille showed them objects of their dreams in actual use. With his acutely developed sense of showmanship, he knew to a hair the value of over-emphasis and over-elaboration, and where to draw the line; his interiors, exaggerated as they often were, were nevertheless convincing; anyone of them might have been in the home of a multi-millionaire, and many of them undoubtedly were after DeMille pointed the way.

If the DeMille era materially influenced the design of American homes, his services in this field aroused less attention than his contribution to the art of dress. . . . From time to time, a few movie producers had made tentative attempts to invade [the fashion] field. . . . These attempts were . . . interesting but inadequate, until DeMille assembled his forces to level the walls of Fashion.

He accomplished his victory by a combination of simplicity and strategy. He transferred the fashion show to his photoplays, and lured from the sacred temples the most celebrated priests and priestesses of the Sacred Art of Dress, and thereafter the actresses in his plays were outfitted literally from head to foot by artists. . . .

DeMille had discovered no new principle of screen dramaturgy. He found only a new formula, but so efficiently did it work that his pictures thronged the box offices. His fame soon equalled and presently surpassed that of Griffith. . . .

Benjamin B. Hampton. *A History of the Movies* (Covici, Friede, 1931), pp. 222–24

Adapted from the old play by Wilson Barrett, *The Sign of the Cross* is once more raised by the movies. Nothing could be more logical than that is should be raised at the Rialto by Cecil B. DeMille, who has already offered us such spectacles as *The Ten Commandments* and *The King of Kings*.

Mr. DeMille paints a quite effective, expansive, glittering pageant of Rome under Nero. He likewise offers a pageant of the sufferings of the Christian martyrs. And through it runs the love story of a lovely Christian girl and a Roman Prefect who chooses to die with her in the arena rather than go on living.

It is needless to say, big, beautiful and rather cruel. Call it a gaudy, phony Roman holiday as celebrated by the movies if you wish. Say that Mr. DeMille's perverse imagination is almost funny in spots, it still remains a good show. . . .

I note that Mr. DeMille makes this tribute to the early Christian martyrs after a trip through Communist Russia, where religion, as we know it, is distinguished by the fact that it is being rapidly extinguished. At least, I gather that he means *The Sign of the Cross* as a tribute to Christianity and the beauty, kindness and courage that it represents. One never knows these days what is really meant.

John S. Cohen, Jr. *NYS*. Dec. 1, 1932

In the fairly early days of the silent pictures Cecil B. De Mille made a photoplay based upon Sir James M. Barrie's *The Admirable Crichton* and called it, much to the amusement of those who looked down upon the cinema, *Male and Female*. As it emerged under the celebrated director's lavish touch, the film, along with a spectacular shipwreck, narrated the Barrie story of the English menial who became a master of men when cast away on a primitive island. Now in his lastest picture, Mr. De Mille returns to something of the same theme in a cumbersome sort of melodrama called *Four Frightened People*. Altho the work, despite some mildly entertaining jungle scenes, is a pretty routine one, it is obvious that it contains some potentially effective dramatic ideas.

"Argus." *Literary Digest*. Feb. 10, 1934, p. 27

It is remarkable how Cecil B. deMille can photograph so much on such a vast scale and still say nothing. *Cleopatra* is, of course, not history; it is so badly done and is so noisy that it can't be classed as "entertainment"; and it reeks of so much pseudo-artistry, vulgarity, philistinism, sadism, that it can only be compared with the lowest form of contemporary culture: Hitlerism. This is the type of "culture" that will be fed to the audience of Fascist America.

Irving Lerner. *New Masses*. Aug. 28, 1934, p. 30

The Sign of the Cross. A conspicuous incident is a dance scene of a suggestive, erotic character. It is played principally by two persons, a lewd pagan dancer and an innocent Christian girl. The apparent dramatic intention is to contrast the evil character of the dancer and the innocence of the girl. The scene is objectionable because it transgresses the limits of legitimate dramatic requirements and becomes an incident liable to an evil audience effect.

Martin Quigley. *Decency in Motion Pictures* (Macmillan, 1937), p. 39

It is easy to turn to Mr. De Mille. In his film of *The Plainsman* he has made Gary Cooper into Wild Bill Hickok with Miss Jean Arthur as Calamity Jane. A monstrous peep-show, peopled with horses and Indians, it is priceless fare for the cameras. Since Griffith's day, effects have been achieved so that no longer does one need to cut from a close-up of a Cheyenne riflemen to a long shot of the Seventh Cavalry's leading guidon; and Mr. De Mille has provided a treat for all those who remember the halcyon days. By skill and process trickery, one can now see—in one embracing two-inch shot—both the Injun and the flag. Booms and cranes, too, have considerably intensified the suspense of that rocky hillock where troopers shoot down Indian horsemen who career through the muddy waters of the Kaw. The material, however, remains the same, timeless and exciting.

Lawrence Stallings. *Stage.* April 1937, pp. 56–57

When, after the war, the movie makers had become self-assured and were using the medium to create "sensations," Cecil B. DeMille, mentor of erotica and display, became the leader.

From 1919 to 1924 DeMille exerted enormous influence. He was copied and envied by all, although a far greater figure—a man head and shoulders above him in talent—Erich von Stroheim, was then making extraordinary films. . . .

Cecil B. DeMille was a showman, and he flourished at a time when showmanship was the nation's way of life. To neglect or minimize his importance in an evaluation of the film directors of the post-war years, on the grounds that his works were superficial and added nothing to film art, would be to ignore the standards of a public who looked upon him as the model. . . .

DeMille introduced "style" into films, but so far as direction was concerned his style was largely theatrical. His respect for stagecraft blinded him to the possibilities of camera use and cutting except as means for trick effects. In his films the camera simply photographed the actor and the setting; it was a wholly reproductive instrument. Unable to think in terms of images, DeMille depended upon artists to illustrate the scenario in sketches as literally as possible; he conceived of a film not as a moving and changing medium but as a series of separate pictures. All his films therefore lacked a cinematic continuity—a failing only partly compensated for by sensuous diversions. [1939]

Lewis Jacobs. *The Rise of the American Film* (Teachers College, 1968), pp. 336–40

For more than twenty-five years the work of Cecil B. De Mille has been violently attacked by the critics. "Empty," "pretentious," "puerile," "gaudy," "tasteless," "hypocritical," "theatrical," "ignorant of film technique," and "negligible as contributions to the development of the medium"—these are but a few of the epithets that have denigrated De Mille and his pictures. Indeed, with the exception of D. W. Griffith and Eric von Stroheim, no other director has been exposed to such vicious abuse and character assassination. The "hate De Mille" cult has swelled to such proportions that he is regarded today by many critics as the worst director in Hollywood, and his very name has been anathemized in "advanced film circles."

As a result, De Mille's standing as a creative artist has been almost completely obscured. Students of the medium refuse to take his work seriously. In twenty-five years no periodical devoted to furthering appreciation of the cinema has featured an article analyzing his style, his form, his structure, his technique, or his influence upon other directors. People without a tenth of De Mille's filmic knowledge and less than a twentieth of his experience as a film maker, regard the man whose combined output grossed more millions of dollars than that of any other director except D. W. Griffith, as a tyro.

It has become accepted critical practice to condemn his works without examination, which is the very essence of prejudice.

Nothing else, at any rate, can explain the inability of critics to recognize what motion picture audiences have long known—namely that Cecil B. De Mille is one of the greatest masters of the screen. The public, we believe, is right in its judgment, the critics wrong.

Joseph and Harry Feldman. *Films in Review*. Dec. 1950, pp. 1–2

Cecil B. DeMille, who might lay claim to having falsified history as much as any man alive, is now at work on *The Ten Commandments* (in Vista Vision). He states: "It's amazing how much our story parallels the world situation today"—the parallel may be a bit elusive, but no doubt DeMille will make his point. Other film makers, suddenly confronted with Cinema-Scope, have been raiding his domain; they appear to be so dazzled by the width of the screen they feel it can only be filled by God. [1954]

Pauline Kael. *I Lost It at the Movies* (Little, Brown, 1965), p. 329

De Mille had something with which to replace the plus that a star name gave to a film. He had and has a form of extrasensory perception that makes him aware of an approaching tidal wave of public taste long before anyone else, least of all the public itself, has detected the faintest ripple—or perhaps he just knows how to take a ripple and magnify it into a tidal wave. In the prewar screen world, people were heroes, heroines, villains, and vamps, and anyone who was not in one of these categories need not apply. But in a picture De Mille had made in 1916, *The Cheat*, a "good" woman was forced by the exigencies of the plot to behave for part of the time like a vamp. The favorable response to this brew convinced him that a new public was coming to the movies: one which preferred such qualities as courage and weakness, evil and good, which had hitherto been offered neat, all mixed up together in a potent cocktail of human fallibility. . . .

What action took place against the background of the elegant De Mille world? Boy meets girl, of course, but they were considerably older boys and girls than the adolescent screen was used to. In fact, they were married couples tempted to stray from their connubial vows. Of all the innovations De Mille introduced to the screen of the postwar era, this was the most revolutionary. Before Cecil, "love" was the exclusive prerogative of the young and unmated; such married couples as were to be seen were drab, gray figures in the background . . . De Mille suddenly presented the movie audience with husbands and wives who were human, all too human, and he began his picture where his predecessors left off, with the honeymoon over and the man and woman sitting down to dinner together night after night, pondering their bargain.

Richard Griffith and Arthur Mayer. *The Movies* (S&S, 1957), pp. 123, 132–33

Probably no man did more to set the commercial tone of Hollywood in the early twenties than Cecil B. DeMille. . . . He was among the first to capitalize on Amerca's growing concern with the war in Europe, and he made a series of highly successful military adventures. The minute the war ended, he tested the shifting winds of popular interest and found its new direction before anyone else. It was, not surprisingly, sex again—but of a special sort. He made a glittery series of films in which he examined the new, ambiguous morality of the younger generation. Comic or melodramatic, the pictures revolved mainly around the question of marital fidelity. The endings were conventionally moral, but getting to them was half the fun, maybe more. Never had sexual license seemed more glamorous, more exciting than in such DeMille works as *Male and Female, For Better for Worse, Don't Change Your Husband, Why Change Your Wife?* and *Adam's Rib*. The films made a star out of Gloria Swanson and a place of glamour out of the American bathroom.

Richard Schickel. *Movies* (Basic, 1964), pp. 93–94

It is inevitable that the mere mention of Cecil B. de Mille will evoke complacent laughter in some quarters, and bristling patriotic speeches in others. If De Mille had the right enemies, he also had the wrong friends. De Mille was neither a primitive like Fuller nor a populist like Capra. Although he appealed to audiences, he never manipulated them. He remained faithful to the literary tradition of Cooper's *Leatherstocking Tales* and to the dramatic conventions of David Belasco. Griffith, Chaplin, Lubitsch, Murnau, Eisenstein, Ford, Hawks, Capra, Welles, Renoir, Ophuls, and all the others came and went without influencing his style in the slightest. Ironically, his films look much better today than their reputations would indicate. . . . He may have been the last American director who enjoyed telling a story for its own sake.

Andrew Sarris. *The American Cinema* (Dutton, 1968), p. 91

DIETERLE, WILLIAM (1893–1973)

I get heartily tired of referring to Hollywood as if it were something which automatically needed to be sneered at, as indeed it does. It is when you see *Fog Over Frisco* (which is no great shakes as a film and I don't want you to rush off to the nearest theater with that in mind) that you realize what can be done by the excellent people of Beverly Hills and Santa Monica when they let themselves go. It is a mystery melodrama and nobody will ever list it among the triumphs of the screen, but it reveals those qualities of pace and velocity and sharpness which make the Hollywood product acceptable even when the shallow content of ideas prompts you to scream. Since it makes no pretense of being a Super-Super-Magnificent, it was a treat to my sore eyes and tortured ears. The direction is firm, the photography is superb and the dialogue is right. The script calls for none of the fake sentiment and none of the county court house elaborateness which passes in the film colony as "class," and the result is something honest and exciting.

Robert Forsythe. *New Masses.* July 3, 1934, p. 44

The Story of Louis Pasteur is a picture which holds one—with the insistence of its theme, with the dignity and competence of the title role (Paul Muni) and of many small parts and situations—but which continually disappoints with a wasting of its substance, with a transmission of the feeling that whatever has been gained, too much has been lost, that what should be vital and arresting has been made hollow and dull, that we hereby are tendered something that is bright and stagey for something out of life.

The first criticism is that the story is undramatic, that Pasteur's conflict is either against intangible, nonscreenable forces, or against the solemn beards of the academy, who are too overdrawn, dull, and fatuous for a good fight. And the second criticism is one of overdrawing in general: Pasteur is too good and meek, his wife is too patient and sugary; Donald Woods as the assistant is Donald Woods, which is to say, damn; and the decent sentiment of the family scenes is so invariable as to be tiresome.

Most of the fault, that is, seems to lie in the story and dialogue, plus the way story and dialogue were in several instances invested in weak screen characters, plus the way William Dieterle as director did little to repair this. Dieterle's genius shows in the nimble (slightly formalized) arrangement of the introductory scenes and the details of his scenic construction, which is sometimes sweeping and lovely. Where he seems to be at a loss is in the handling of people, of tempering even a bad line with some special flair for pace and modulation—so that riding in a carriage and opening the front door, announcing a miracle or saying "I am at your service, sir," all come through stiffly, with all the best intentions in the world but just that lack of illusion which makes the difference between good and moving theater (*cf.* the movie *Arrowsmith*) and your daily paper. Coming from the same company that made *Ceiling Zero* and the newer *Petrified Forest* . . . the Pasteur film is an apt reminder that if the movies are good, this is enough, and it doesn't matter much where they got it. [1936]

Otis Ferguson. *The Film Criticism of O.F.* (Temple, 1971), pp. 116–17

During the so-called "dog days" of the American motion picture there were a few really great films produced. Important both as examples of cinema art and as social documents, they never grow out of date. That masterpiece of terrifying realism, *Greed*, obviously comes to mind. But even more extraordinary is Thomas Ince's *The Italian*, produced in 1914, which must be recorded as one of the finest social films ever made. These films were usually made by individual artists who turned to the cinema as a means of expression. When finance capital converted the movies into a motion picture industry, the largest and most efficient in the world, it became increasingly difficult for progressive artists to express themselves. . . .

With *The Life of Emile Zola* the Warner Brothers inaugurate a new era in the film industry. For the first time a commercial producer has given us a film with a broad political idea. It is a dignified and stirring motion picture. . . .

One could easily find fault with the film, with its presentation of the details of Zola's career. But then the film makes no pretensions to historical accuracy. And then, if in America there was a tradition of such films, such criticism at this time would be legitimate and desirable. But this is the first of its kind and, in a way, precious. . . .

Director William Dieterle gives the film several superb directorial touches. The sequence of the Dreyfus frame-up is magnificent. As the General Staff look down their list of officers for a goat, they come to the name of Alfred Dreyfus. A close-up of the ledger with the description "Jew" after the name. A finger comes into the frame and, the commander says: "I wonder how he ever became a member of the General Staff." And another voice says, "That's our man. Sandherr, take action at once." The parallel with Hitler Germany is obvious.

Peter Ellis. *New Masses*. Aug. 17, 1937, p. 29

Zola, now at the Carlton, will amost certainly turn out to be one of the great films of the year. Other films like *Lost Horizon* have been as big in scale; but none has been more weighty in theme and sincere at heart. Like most people who work at cinema, I see too many films: respecting most of them for the labour and the ingenuity I know they contain and, in one way or another, learning from all; but it is seldom enough that a film bowls you over. *Zola* is one of the fine ones which begin as a film and end as an experience: like *Potemkin, Earth, Deserter, Aran, Pasteur* and, with all its faults, *The Good Earth*.

On the sweeping canvas of late nineteenth century France, Hollywood has staged in this life of *Zola* as dramatic a battle for truth as ever the cinema managed in fact or fiction. Most people will wonder how they came to be interested, but, considered as a form of expiation, there is good reason for its fire. No one would be more likely to appreciate the disintegration that goes on in the successful artist and the pains of the artist in the face of vested interests than the writers and directors of Hollywood.

The quality of the film derives from this feeling of secret autobiography and, of course, from Muni. As a piece of acting his account of the character of Zola is enormously skilled: jumping from age to age of the man; changing his gait, his speech, his idiosyncrasies, his mind: developing his literary character with such an uncanny sense of detail that, before we know it, we are facing a picture that so pleasantly reminds one of H. G. Wells that it cannot be far from the great Zola himself.

John Grierson. *World Film News*. Nov. 1937, p. 18

[*Blockade*.] Although it is always possible that the right company could make a good fiction-picture out of current affairs in Spain, the odds against it are too infinite to monkey with. The dramatic arts have a special access to people's imaginations and nerve centers. And of all the arts, the movies play on the feelings of the most millions. Anything in films touching on things remote in space and time is fairly safe: anything that deals with matters of present hard feeling is just so much broken glass in any angry wound. If you made a true and good picture about Spain, the busy Catholics would be at their screaming and hopping around again; and if it were possible to dramatize the frank Catholic view, the easygoing millions of our democracy would rise out of its engrossing petty worries to give a great and awful yell. The movies aren't going to stir up any such trouble. And if they make a film on anything like Spain, they have to make it mostly hokum or just in fun. . . .

The story is the familiar one of the beautiful female spy (against her will, of course) and the young man of burning faith from the other (or right) side, who falls in love with her and indeed vice versa. . . . The enemy (designation carefully unknown) has got Miss Carroll and her weak father in their power: the Right (likewise undesignated) is rising up to fight for its homes and sheep and vineyards. Good stuff here: the mere quiet statement is enough. Then we get into the besieged town with Miss Carroll operating to destroy rescuing food-ships, and hating it. Then plot and counterplot from down under to high up, the ship comes in on a ruse, all are saved, and Mr. Fonda speaks some ringing deep lines for the rights of man, the right to work in and breathe freely the air of his own land, worth fighting for.

These last lines and the intent hunger-worn faces of the people as they watch for the ship (unusually fine types, though passed too mechanically through the cutting machine) are what the whole thing should have been, and wasn't. It could have been carried on some such sort of story perhaps; but in the case of Walter Wanger's production of William Dieterle's direction of John Howard Lawson's script, there is achieved a deadly numb level of shameless hokum out of which anything true or decent rises for a second only to confound itself. When it comes to what *Blockade* has to say for Spain to the common bewildered man, identification has been so smoothly rubbed out that to protest its content, as some of our hair-trigger Catholic friends are already naïvely doing, is to give away the fact of a deep and abounding ignorance, or of a stinking guilty conscience, and very probably of both. [1938]

Otis Ferguson. *The Film Criticism of O.F.* (Temple, 1971), pp. 222–23

Walter Wanger is to be congratulated for allowing John Howard Lawson, scenarist, and William Dieterle, director, to bring forth a modern miracle: *Blockade*. Variety calls it "a film with a purpose." It is much more than that.

Against a conventional spy melodrama-plot Lawson and Dieterle have given us a profound indictment of totalitarian war. It condemns the Fascist slaughter of innocent civilians, of women and children. "The world can stop it," says Henry Fonda. It cries out against the inhumanity of our so-called democratic nations which stand by and allow Italian and Nazi pirates to torpedo relief and food ships. "Where is the conscience of the world?" is the final accusation of the film.

Although *Blockade* does not take sides openly, Lawson and Dieterle make their sympathies for the Spanish people, the Loyalists, very clear. The united forces of reaction, therefore, are determined to sabotage the film. We, as members of the audience, must indicate our support of *Blockade*. *Blockade* must be seen, not only because it is a pro-Loyalist film, or because it establishes a precedent for future work along the same lines, but because Hollywood has given us a film which will be seen by millions of people and which, in effect, shouts, LIFT THE EMBARGO!

Peter Ellis. *TAC*. July 1938, p. 8

In many respects *Juarez* is similar to an equally distinguished work of the theatre, Robert Sherwood's *Abe Lincoln In Illinois*. The virtues and shortcomings of the Lincoln play find almost exact counterpart in the movie. The greatest merit of both is the remarkable human significance of content: Lincoln's profound words, gleaned from his writings and public addresses, and the noble utterance of Benito Juarez. Both are primarily rhetorical, both demand more of our hearing than of our sight.

Visually, the film is most expressive in the passage that depicts General Bazaine's last attempt to crush the Mexican peons, and in the incidents attending Maximilian's entrance into Vera Cruz. But in the main, the visual material is completely subsidiary, completely the handmaiden of the spoken and written word. To a certain type of film thinker, this is damnable practice and intolerable. We are of the opinion that the film, like the play, or the novel, is no one thing, that it is of age and that it may assume as many forms as its older companions in the arts. The film-goer should realize this in advance and be prepared to make the adjustment. The rewards will be great.

Juarez is an extraordinarily political film. There is very little in it that does not pertain to the immediate problems and plight of today's world. In this regard, in its intense politicalization, it bears great resemblance to another important film, *Alexander Nevsky*. There are moments in *Juarez*: for instance the speech of the English Ambassador to Mexico—"neutrality, and non-intervention"—when the crackle of today's newspapers fills your ears equally as much as the sounds coming from the screen.

But unlike most films of the Russian historical school, and even *Nevsky* is somewhat off the path in this respect, in *Juarez* you don't feel strongly enough the presence of the people. They are there, but vaguely. The film lives too much among the great ones. And political though it is, *Juarez* does not make clear that the way of democracy is the way of *all* peoples, not only of invaded Spain and Czechoslovakia, but of England and France, despite the governments that betray them. This is the one political weakness of the film.

Otherwise one can have nothing but praise for *Juarez*. May we extend our gratitude.

Robert Stebbins. *TAC*. May 1939, p. 12

Dieterle's *Hunchback of Notre Dame* is the most flagrant example of irrelevant waste, with Charles Laughton a gutta percha gargoyle, and the whole proceedings weakly devised, and without tension. *The Hunchback* obviously cost more than either *The Private Lives of Elizabeth and Essex* or *The Tower of London*, but they are of an equal tepid pretense. Max Beerbohm once had a friend who wanted to write a tragedy on the subject of Sardanapalus, but the Encyclopedia Britannica (his only source) opened to "Savonarola" instead. The ensuing masterpiece was larded with such stage directions as *Enter Guelphs and Ghibellines, fighting* and *Pippa passes*. It could serve as the next vehicle for Boris Karloff's benevolent mania without change.

Lincoln Kirstein. *Films*. Spring 1940

The devil, as you may not know, is an ornery fellow. It's not the task of a man with lead in his fingers to catch him, impale him on film, keep him fluttering so you can study him, recognize him when he taxis across *your* path.

But William Dieterle, who directed, fought and bled for *All That Money Can Buy*, the movie that came at last to the Music Hall yesterday and tips you off to the devil so you can spot him just before he nails *you*, hasn't got lead in his fingers, that is, anymore. He has now cast off the weighty meanings. No long pauses, no pregnant angles, no grave responsibilities to history now shackle him. He has a rollicking yarn to tell and he tells it, fantasy laid lightly upon reality, a wondrous fable against a background of it-does-so-happen-here.

All That Money Can Buy is an unorthodox movie. It deals with what the devil can do to a chap, and what a man can do to the devil. It created a pre-release furor. Some of those in the movie industry who saw it restively called it a dog; but some of them cried it was another catapult hurling the cinema up to its glorious destiny. Well, it's interesting and charming and beguiling. It has integrity and only honest intentions, even in the moments when it fails.

Cecelia Ager. *PM*. Oct. 17, 1941

The Man on America's Conscience, directed for M.-G.-M. by William Dieterle in 1944, was an example of a modern film which, while quite good of its kind, yet trod the same prejudiced rut. When it was first made in Hollywood it was called *Tennessee Johnson*, under which name it was released in America. The title referred to Johnson, one-time president of the U.S.A. (Apparently the U.S.A. thought that European filmgoers would find the title obscure and forthwith gave it a new one which was more obscure than ever). The film deals with the exciting period of the Reconstruction after the Civil War, and shows Andrew Johnson (excellently played by Van Heflin) as Abraham Lincoln's vice-president, and a man who faithfully follows in Lincoln's footsteps. . . .

Dieterle's film shows Johnson as the staunch upholder of the Southern bourgeoisie against the North, and the main part of the action is concerned with his clash with Thaddeus Stevens (played by Lionel Barrymore), a Northern politician who believes in giving the ex-slaves equal rights with the white Southerners. The sympathy of the entire film is, however, with Johnson, who stubbornly affirms that although the Civil War is over and although the slaves are admittedly now free, the South should be allowed to continue in the same tradition as before. The political implications of the whole film are obscure (especially to European filmgoers), but it is obvious that Stevens who stands up for Negroes is the villain of the piece, while Johnson who maintains that the coloured man should be kept in his proper place in American life is, in fact,the hero. . . .

The film may therefore be bracketed with *The Birth Of A Nation*; both deal with the same period and contain the same villain (Stevens in Dieterle's film and Stoneman in Griffith's). Griffith depicts him as an insincere careerist while Dieterle shows him as a scheming egotist. . . . [1948]

Peter Noble. *The Negro in Films* (Kennikat, 1969), pp. 208–209

In 1940 Robert Nathan wrote a novel under this title [*Portrait of Jennie*]. And often in the delicately spun narrative the author stopped to consider the imponderables of life and love. As an example, he asks: "Is there perhaps one soul among all others . . . who must love us or die? and whom we must love in turn until the end?"

To translate this ephemeral study into pictures was quite an undertaking for Director William Dieterle. For the little girl whom Joseph Cotten, the narrator, meets in Central Park one wintry twilight—here played by Jennifer Jones—exists only in the imagination. . . . There'll be some who will be confused by time's shuttling back and forth between the worlds of reality and infinity. But the film will have a message of consolation for many.

Frankie McKee Robins. *McCall's*. April 1949, p. 7

The film [*The Last Flight*] begins with furious air battle footage borrowed from *The Dawn Patrol* (1930). The frenzy of it is in sharp contrast to the rest of the film, although director William Dieterle never lets things get lazy. The characters may be lost, but the director isn't. The absence of traditional narrative structure doesn't really become apparent until, perhaps, the middle of the film. It leaves the audience stranded in much the same way as the pilots are. One of Dieterle's neatest touches is a slow dissolve after the battle footage, from a propeller gradually winding down to a meandering clock. Visually, it's effective, and it symbolizes the basic dilemma of the pilots. . . .

The director so cleverly avoids the static and theatrical that an overwritten script fails to slow the movie or turn it detrimentally languid. It moves. In the first half, there are several scenes of the five revellers at a table. Dieterle shows imagination and initiative at photographing these sessions. He keeps the camera active—not hyperactive, but active—moving in on individuals and moving out again, not to give dramatic emphasis to what they say, but on a sort of arbitrary basis, wisely in keeping with the screenplay and its avoidance of emotional climax in the severely structured scene. It is, we might say, an amoral way of shooting a picture. Here, it works. There can be no emotionalism beyond the devil-may-care attitude of the characters, and there isn't. Even Frank's comic-opera seduction of Nikki (which fails, of course) and Lockwood's sock to the Frank jaw are dealt with dispassionately, at least as compared to the other films of the period.

Tom Shales in *The American Film Heritage*,
edited by the American Film Institute
(Acropolis, 1972), pp. 176, 178

DWAN, ALLAN (1885–)

But what is . . . atmosphere alone? True, it is nothing unless it is spent on stories by a method that makes of them something filled with the completeness of life as our minds roam over it. And that the American movie has learned to do. It is our contribution. We have gone by experiment, by trial and error, by instinct, straight to the intricate, submental nature of the photoplay which [Hugo] Munsterberg recognized in his valuable analytical volume. We throw on the screen in half a minute a dozen aspects, great and small, immediate and remote, obvious and inferential, actual and reminiscent of the thing that is to be told.

It is a quality which resides first in the scenario and which the director must realize as he works. Alan Dwan, who makes his own scenarios, uses this thoroughgoing, Griffithian technique with sure effect in *Panthea*. He gathers that music room into our vision with undeniable sureness. He gives us Russia through a dozen small touches, crisp "flash-backs," intimate and pungent "close-ups." When he gets to the swiftest part of his story, he drives us through it unerringly by following physical actions to the minutest details. When, for instance, the police raid a dwelling, he shows not only the approach, the groups on both sides of the door, the violence of the entry and the scattering of the dwellers, but as the police charge upstairs after the hero, he smashes it home to us with a sudden flash of feet pounding the steps. Again he uses that same "close-up" expedient—and with an even greater, because characterizing, effect—when, after the officer has shot the hero, he kicks him over with his spurred boot to make sure he is harmless. Dwan catches in his "close-up" of the kicking boot itself and in the direction of the blow which is amazingly characteristic of the hard, perky, Prussian-like little officer. Such a detail serves no purpose in the tale. Eliminate it and every necessary step of the action would be there. But, when not dwelt on at such lengths as to seem to have a plot importance which it lacks, such a means builds up conviction and atmosphere to an astounding degree. It is things of this sort—intuitions of writer and director—which will give photoplays some of the quality of observation and character that make literature.

Kenneth MacGowan. *The New Republic*. Sept. 15, 1917

Fitzmaurice, Dwan, Holubar and Borzage are so busily engaged in ascertaining which one can spend the most money upon a production and get away with it that they have no time to be concerned about the welfare and amelioration of the silent drama. Any meritorious work these directors may have done in their various careers is now being swamped under by a series of piffle and balderbash.

Tamar Lane. *What's Wrong with the Movies* (Waverly, 1923), pp. 68–69

A story-book picture is *Robin Hood*, as gorgeous and glamorous a thing in innumerable scenes as the screen has yet shown. It is a splendid example of the one type of serious photoplay that has any future in a land where the fear of the censor works more efficiently than the fear of God, and it is hard to see how in many respects the future can improve on this particular example. It is romance—the romance of chivalry—in all the lovely trappings the heart can desire, and thrilling entertainment for the whole family group, from the oldest to youngest.

Naturally no one wants realism in a tale of the merry men of Sherwood Forest—and no one gets it in this picture. The realest looking things in it are the stones of the magnificent castles and the noble trees. The knights and fair ladies are what we would like our ideal knights and ladies to have been, moving beautifully through a story in which we know the wicked prince will be fittingly punished after the last exciting fight. The manners of the twelfth century are merely hinted at in the king's method of tackling his food, which has more the effect of proving Richard a jovial monarch than of being a bit of historical accuracy. Even the Crusade looks like a jolly pleasure jaunt. . . .

It is hard to tell to what extent the director, Allan Dwan, was responsible for the merit of a production into the making of which the talents and technical knowledge of many people have patiently gone. Whatever his share of the work was, he is entitled to due credit for having transferred an elaborate scenario from paper to the scenic background provided for its unfoldment on the screen.

To Arthur Edison must go a large share of the praise. It would appear that without the brand of photography he supplied much of the scenic grandeur and the tonal effects of the picture would never have been achieved.

NBR. Jan. 1923, p. 1

The pictorial translation of Felix Riesenberg's book, *East Side, West Side*, now on exhibition at the Roxy Theatre, is indubitably the best picture Allan Dwan has fashioned since he produced *Big Brother*. He has gone to great pains to set forth many of the incidents from the original story and quite a number of them are filmed with considerable skill. The only pity is that Mr. Dwan frequently permits his penchant for extravagancies to spoil otherwise effective episodes. He has, however, succeeded in eliciting really fine performances from both George O'Brien and Virginia Valli.

Two of the outstanding sequences in this picture are the sinking of a transatlantic steamship, which is inspired by the Titanic disaster, and a cave-in in a subway in course of construction. In the first of these chapters Mr. Dwan has adroitly coupled up miniature scenes of a vessel at sea with scenes aboard the liner before and after she crashes into the iceberg. This director has even filmed the slanting deck as the vessel is about to sink, and he shows the confusion of the passengers in trying to get into the lifeboats. One man is seen leaning over the rail of the sinking vessel while a coward hides under a seat in a lifeboat.

There is in this production a tendency to cater to the movie mind by arraying the feminine characters in flashy costumes and in having John Breen go to a none too impressive saloon in evening clothes with white gloves and a flower in the lapel of his coat. It is true that John is an ex-pugilist, but nevertheless, despite the fact that he is supposed to be disappointed in love, one would imagine that he would not make a shining mark of himself when going through a squalid section of the city. This is rather reminiscent of the old-time blood-and-thunder serials, wherein the hero and sometimes the villain usually wore immaculate black and white on their dangerous peregrinations.

Mr. Dwan also overdoes his comedy and he is occasionally guilty of permitting hysteria to conquer scenes. Tragic incidents appear to be forgotten very quickly by some sympathetic persons, and when Becka, the heroine, goes about her night club duties she sways rapidly from indifference to unusual solicitude for the patrons.

NYT. Oct. 18, 1927, p. 33

In a genre differing from that of Hawks' *A Girl in Every Port*, *East Side, West Side*, is also a great poetic success. The magnificent and terrible metaphysic of a big city serves as the background for the action. A formidable movement fills the images. The spectator is introduced into the heart of a frantic nest of men and Fords, and of intellectual adventures that make up today's America. Action, action, and still more action.

Revue du Cinéma. Dec. 1928, unpaged

A veteran of the American cinema, Allan Dwan is known as the director of numerous Douglas Fairbanks films, notably *Robin Hood* and *The Iron Mask*. In sound films for Fox, Dwan directed Shirley Temple and the Ritz Brothers. His films are of no interest, but exception can be made for *Heidi* and *Suez*.

Henri Colpi. *Le cinéma et ses hommes* (Causse, Graille & Castelnau, 1947), p. 156

The battle sequences in this film [*Sands of Iwo Jima*] are terrifyingly real but the personal dramatics make up a virtual compendium of war-picture cliches. Everything has been poured into this production from the toothy Jap shriveling up under a flamethrower spray to the U.S. marine mawkishly showing a picture of his kid back home. And there is, too, the tough-hided, soft-hearted top sergeant, the unmartial son of a fighting colonel, the company comic, some battling Irishmen and a sprinkling of Italians, Greeks and Jews. All these characters are readily recognizable, if not as real-life characters, then as standard cinema types. . . .

Best portions of this pic are the straight battle sequences, many of which were made up of footage taken at the actual fighting at Tarawa and Iwo Jima. With the latter celluloid neatly integrated into the studio and location lensing, the film is given an impact of authenticity when it shows the marines pulling towards shore on landing craft and establishing the beachheads under a rain of enemy fire. The authenticity is marred, however, when a Hollywood marine is sent out to find a bazooka and comes back maneuvering a tank.

Variety. Dec. 14, 1949

He is the last representative of the cinema of our ancestors. He has an inbred youthfulness and a sense of cinema that one could wish for in Martin Ritt or Sidney Lumet. He has for once and all been classified as a first-rate workman, the providence of producers who have gone broke. He has also been called the conscience of Hollywood.

He is all that and also much more and much better than that. His production is so large that it is hard to evaluate it properly, but he was able to retain the Triangle spirit and adapt it to the evolution of movies: sound, color, cinemascope. Our Dwan is still fit. But how, in only a few lines, can we talk of a director who has made innumerable films (among the silents, we French know only what the Cinémathèque has shown—in other words, only *Robin Hood*)? Let's look at his recent films, in which this veteran found in John Alton the cameraman of his dreams. In *Slightly Scarlet* each shot was a pictorial innovation. . . . The western especially gave Allan Dwan a chance to show his talent and we will not soon forget . . . *Silver Lode*, a violently anti-McCarthy political western with fine dialogue by Karen de Wolfe. This film made many "wise guys" snicker; they thought it too naïve and failed to understand that they had here one of the few films to treat lynching physically rather than intellectually. *Silver Lode* carried the theme to its conclusion: a false accusation aroused an entire town against John Payne. A false telegram made the whole town declare him . . . innocent. . . .

It is possible to prefer Allan Dwan to Raoul Walsh—that's a simple question of taste. But one must consider the old Allan as one of the great American directors—that's a question of discernment.

Jean Coursodon. *20 Ans de cinéma américain: 1940:60* (Editions C.I.B., 1961), pp. 70–71

A. Some of the French critics treat Dwan as Griffith's ghost.

B. But in a very marginal conception of his career. The French always seem to be most fascinated by those directors engulfed in the damnation of necessity. If Dwan is Griffith's ghost, and Ulmer is Murnau's ghost, what to do with the total Dwan-Ulmer output, which is more often ghastly than ghostly by any conventional standards? It is on this level that the *auteur* theory is most vulnerable to the charge of idiocy. The critic is placed in a delicate position. If he recommends *Woman They Almost Lynched* to the lay audience, he creates a false expectation of eyepopping art. To fully appreciate Dwan here, one must be able to perceive what a hundred other directors on Poverty Row would have done with this silly material, and this is difficult for the average moviegoer, who tries to see only the most essential films. Thus there is little point in arguing Dwan's case too strenuously, but somewhere, sometime, a reader may stumble on a minor Dwan film and remember vaguely that Dwan was worthy of a little attention despite his low estate, and the film might then burst into the pleasurable spectrum of tarnished creation. I have "pulled" Dwan on unsuspecting friends with gratifying results. [1962]

Andrew Sarris. *Confessions of a Cultist* (S&S, 1970), p. 45

Robin Hood greatly impressed audiences of its day with its Maxfield Parrish-style romantic atmosphere, its enormous sets, and its horde of costumed extras. Few seemed to notice that Fairbanks was a little subdued by it all, or at least forgot his subdued demeanor when, in the last part of the picture, he returned to his old dashing self, and the excitement he generated carried the film through to its smashing climax. Today, *Robin Hood* appears less entertaining and less well constructed than its masterful predecessor, *The Three Musketeers*. . . .

. . . The first half of the film moves much more slowly than we expect of a Fairbanks film; though it is enlivened with occasional touches of humor . . . the film shows little of Fairbanks' athletic grace, and the amount of intrigue as well as décor seem to have a strangling effect on him. Once Robin Hood is established in Sherwood Forest, the swashbuckling Fairbanks emerges, and the picture begins to move. If it was not clear from earlier films that Fairbanks was himself responsible for the creative use of the medium, it is surely evident here, where Allan Dwan's direction is on the whole pedestrian.

Eileen Bowser in *Film Notes*, edited by
Eileen Bowser (MOMA, 1969), p. 47

There will never again be a movie career like Allan Dwan's. Over fifty years, he directed at least 400 pictures, and produced, wrote or supervised as many more. Film history being the mess it is, his exact total is not likely to be known, but certainly two-thirds of that opus—almost the whole silent period—is virtually lost forever. The few examples that remain from those more carefree times make it clear that the years before 1929—when he had the most independence—were his most creative, valuable and successful.

This is not necessarily to diminish his talkies, but after the coming of sound the assignments were so often unworthy of him and the restrictions such that it is amazing he was able to produce as many good films as he did. Through it all, his professionalism, humour and enjoyment in the actual job of picture-making never lessened. The movies have been his vocation, and he has been true to that calling. . . . If there is no unifying theme nor imposing visual style to Dwan's work, it is certainly not devoid of personality and character. His approach to material has always been pragmatic, and his camerawork expressive but unadorned, in the most classical American tradition. The mischievous, occasionally even wicked, humour that runs through many of his films is that of a man amused by the pomposity and pretentions of the world, though he is equally tolerant of our most frivolous behaviour; never one to judge his characters, he still cannot resist deflating them. Yet, throughout his career, the lives of simple people have most often inspired his finest movies, from the open enthusiasm of Doug Fairbanks to the uncomplicated cowboys of his last films.

Only a man of inherent modesty—he claims that "a team" makes a movie, not one person—could have survived with such good spirit and without cynicism his years of inferior projects and crippling limitations. It has been his curse, as well as his peculiar glory, that he would prefer to shoot almost any old thing that came up rather than wait for just the right project; it was more fun that way, and since he has never had any pretensions, he would rather exercise his craft than not be out there at all.

Peter Bogdanovich. *Allan Dwan: The Last*
Pioneer (Praeger, 1971), pp. 6, 13

FLAHERTY, ROBERT J. (1884–1951)

Beside [*Nanook of the North*] the usual photoplay, the so-called "dramatic" work of the screen, becomes as thin and blank as the celluloid on which it is printed. And the photoplay cannot avoid the comparison that exposes its lack of substance. It is just as literal as the "travel" picture. Its settings, whether the background of nature or the constructions of a studio, merely duplicate the settings of ordinary human experience—or try to. And its people try to persuade spectators that they are just ordinary people, ordinary, that is, for the environment in which they happen to be placed. So the whole purpose of the photoplay, as a rule, is to reproduce life literally. And this is the purpose of the travel film. But the average photoplay does not reproduce life. Through the obvious artificialities of its treatment, through the unconcealed mechanics of its operation, through its reflection of a distorted or incomplete conception of life, rather than of life itself, it usually fails to be true to any aspect of human existence. It is not realistic in any sense. It remains fiction, something fabricated. It never achieves the illusion of reality. . . . No matter how intelligent a spectator may be, no matter how stubbornly he may refuse to make concessions to the screen because its pictures are "only the movies," he can enjoy *Nanook of the North.*

And this is because of the intelligence and skill and patience with which Mr. Flaherty has made his motion picture. It took more than just a man with a camera to make *Nanook of the North.* Mr. Flaherty had to wait for his light, he had to select his shots, he had to compose his scenes, he had to direct his people in order that Nanook's story might develop its full force of realism and drama on the screen. So it is due to Mr. Flaherty that Nanook, who lives his life by Hudson Bay, also lives at the Capitol.

NYT. June 12, 1922, p. 10

Technically, *Moana* indicates perhaps the most perfect way that the motion picture can go about doing this sort of thing. Photographically, the practice is one of compelling camera hues—lights, shades, composition—to give the same effect that the painter's brush can give. The sky has the appearance of being blue, the leaves of the trees green; the skin of the people seems brown and of a texture exquisitely molded, their garments strike one as patterns of rich color—the audience can feel and smell and see these things. Cinegraphically, the method is one of rhythm, like the prose that, using bright and exotic words, weaves them slowly and chimingly into a picture that charms and moves the reader. To perform all this with the camera, Mr. Flaherty has used no color photography nor any tricks. To construct it dramatically, he has chosen those activities and interests of his characters' lives that pictorially represent them, linking these pictures together in their natural sequence and inevitable dramatic implication. The idea has been to re-create the beings of the primitive Polynesians by letting us see them simply as they were, by cinegraphic means the least artificial, the most sumptuous, and suggestively the most indicative.

Thus, this picture shows thorough feeling for that rarely understood but vitally important essential in the use of photoplay medium, the need for constant pictorial interest. Mr. Flaherty's camera-eye roves over the tropical verdure and the daily comings and goings of these primitive folk and with inquisitiveness but always with good taste discloses them at their work and play, feasts and festivals, sometimes following them into their homes and often into the water where they are as much at ease as on land. And yet behind all this apparently casual and natural work of the camera is an alert and discriminating selection.

NBR. Nov.-Dec. 1925, p. 1

Among documentary films *Nanook of the North* is one of those that have held the screen for the longest time. Parisians especially have felt a fervent sympathy for this character whose mores were shown to be so far from their own. Love of contrast? Perhaps after having shivered at the sight of the hard living conditions in these almost polar regions the spectators re-entered their comfortable homes with more pleasure. There was not only curiosity in this élan of so many people; there was also a need to know and a surge of generosity. Everybody felt that they attenuated the cruelty of this hard life, that they sympathetically shared it. The success of *Nanook* is one that we must be pleased with. It shows in the present generations a feeling of humanity of which the cinema is the provoking agent. The success of *Nanook* stems from a healthy outlook; it does not exploit perverse sensibility.

Some have claimed that the film was "rigged." Obviously the very authentic hero of the film cooperated. But why deduct from this that when he constructs a house of ice before the camera he does it differently than he would do when alone in the veritable ice desert? . . . Rigged? But only wild animals who have been surprised by the camera do not rig their reactions. And even if the life of Nanook was reconstituted in a latitude somewhat more clement than that to which he was accustomed, would that diminish the interest or merit of the film?

André Delpeuch. *Le Cinéma* (Librairie Octave Doin, 1927), pp. 282–83

White Shadows in the South Seas comes close to greatness and misses. It exposes the predatory role of our aggressive, profit-seeking civilization. In an Eden of the South Seas the white man comes with booze, printed calico, disease and exploitation. But the picture goes only part of the way and has its goodly share of hokum. No danger that Hollywood has gone Bolshevik. Some unusually fine photography in this picture.

New Masses. Jan. 1929, p. 15

Robert Flaherty's new film, *Man of Aran*, has evoked the unanimous adulation of the bourgeois critics in Europe. Few films have been so praised. To a Marxist the reasons are quite clear. Here is a film to which the cultured bourgeoisie, ashamed of the productions of Hollywood, can give the cachet of a "work of art," yet a film patently in accord with the prevailing ideology of the capitalist class, and, unlike the indubitable screen masterpieces of the Soviet Union, not in the least dangerous socially. . . .

There is a deal of powerful photography. Unquestionably Flaherty is a superb cameraman. . . . But Flaherty's technical dexterity only underlines the basic falsity of the film.

In what does this falsity consist? In this: in Flaherty's deliberate portrayal of the islanders as primitives, twentieth century Neanderthals, cut off from all social relations, aloof from the social forces of modern capitalist society, and, with Nature as their only enemy. In actuality, the Aran people are as closely bound to capitalism and its problems as the Dublin or Belfast proletarians.

Brian O'Neill. *New Masses*. Oct. 30, 1934, p. 29

But *Man of Aran*, however real, would have made better truth if it had been handled with more of the art of fiction. In the first place, I do not think that for all the roughness of their clothes, their labor, and good stout speech, Mr. Flaherty's people have one-quarter as much of what it is really like as Synge's in *Riders to the Sea*. Here the material is so concentrated on the more vivid episodes of island life that the result is more idyllic than actual: there is no full conception of the long round of bitter days making up the less picturesque side. How you could remedy this and still make it dramatic is hard to know: there is small precedent in the movies. But certainly the film could with advantage be more varied than it is. There are only four or five phases of life touched on, if you exclude such incidents as the patching of the boat, and in working these out (especially the seaweed carrying, the putting of those at sea in relief against those on shore) repetition is too much favored over selection. [11-7-34]

Otis Ferguson. *The Film Criticism of O.F.* (Temple, 1971), pp. 54–55

It seems that in seeking things at the ends of the earth, Flaherty avoids the life around him when he gets there. Thus, what should be a documentary film (the creative treatment of the actual, honest reality) is transformed into a "poem" of pseudosymphonic structure. Even the thrilling sequence in *Man of Aran* of the sea breaking against the rocky shore resolves itself into glib "abstract cinema," visual excitement for its own sake.

Robert Flaherty has now reached a crucial period in his creative life. "What supreme pictures of the working class this man Flaherty is equipped to make!" says Mike Gold. And what an appreciative audience that same working class would be!

Or else—he can continue to thrill the boiled shirts of London and New York with another abstract film of man against the elements. Such films will continue to serve the imperialists faithfully; Mussolini will continue to award them silver cups; and Hitler will continue to distribute *Man of Aran* because it "illustrates the principles of simple living and strenuous endeavor which Hitler wishes the German people to adopt."

Peter Ellis. *New Theatre*. Dec. 1934, pp. 9, 29

Flaherty's *Elephant Boy* was something to weep over. Not because it was particularly sentimental, but because there must be so much footage blushing unseen on the cutting-room floor. This is a picture that should have been made entirely in India or else not at all. Time and again there are lovely shots full of sunlight and shadow and poetry. Then back we come to the studio set. Flaherty's Toomai of the Elephants might not have been good Kipling, but it would certainly have been good Flaherty. He found a perfect Indian boy for his Toomai, but then somebody taught him to speak English and his elephant to understand it and the result was so capitvating that the temptation to make the boy into a sort of Freddie Bartholomew of the jungle could not be resisted. Korda must be congratulated on commissioning Flaherty to go to India and make this picture. He should have had the courage to let him finish it. As it is, children will love it and adults will be disappointed and indulgent.

Alan Page. *Sight & Sound*. Spring 1937, p. 23

It will seem a pity to some that Flaherty, in dropping his old form and adopting the new, should have to begin on material which previous films have made familiar. Lorentz's pioneering *Plow That Broke The Plains*, and his masterpiece, *The River*, have told us before what wind and rain and wasteful greed have done to the soil of our country. *The Grapes of Wrath* has dramatized with heartbreaking power the tragic fate of the thousands of farmers dispossessed by erosion and forced into the serfdom of day labor on the great fruit and vegetable farms of California. A hundred films (it seems) have shown man sacrificed to the juggernaut of the machine. So the movies have made works like erosion, sharecropping, and technological unemployment come to life for us before. Now Flaherty [in *The Land*] does the same job over again, and he has to treat all three subjects at once, so that the film falls abruptly into three parts, with a brief, unemphatic coda which tries, not very successfully, to show what the government is doing to check erosion, stabilize farm prices, and put the farmer himself back on the land he owns.

In short, the picture lacks that wholeness and gradual building toward a climax which have hitherto contributed to the pleasure of seeing a Flaherty film. This is a fractured film, its skeleton is awry, the bones stick out through the skin. But I think Flaherty meant it that way. Edith Sitwell in her poems, Stravinsky in his music, deliberately adopted a jagged, staccato form to express the confusion and distress of their vision of the modern world. And Flaherty, travelling through his own country for the first time in many years, forsakes the graceful smoothness of his "primitive" films for a form which suggests the horror of his broken journey. "Here we saw this," he says, and passes on, but not indifferently. If ever there was a personal film, this is it. . . .

Richard Griffith. *NBR*. Dec. 1941, p. 12

With Flaherty it became an absolute principle that the story must be taken from the location, and that it should be (what he considers) the essential story of the location. His drama, therefore, is a drama of days and nights, of the round of the year's seasons, of the fundamental fights which give his people sustenance, or make their community life possible, or build up the dignity of the tribe.

Such an interpretation of subject-matter reflects, of course, Flaherty's particular philosophy of things. A succeding documentary exponent is in no way obliged to chase off to the ends of the earth in search of old-time simplicity, and the ancient dignities of man against the sky. Indeed, if I may for the moment represent the opposition, I hope the Neo-Rousseauism implicit in Flaherty's work dies with his own exceptional self. Theory of naturals apart, it represents an escapism, a wan and distant eye, which tends in lesser hands to sentimentalism. . . . For it is not only the fool that has his eyes on the ends of the earth. It is sometimes the poet. . . . Loving every Time but his own, and every Life but his own, he avoids coming to grips with the creative job in so far as it concerns society. In the business of ordering most present chaos, he does not use his powers. [1947]

John Grierson. *Grierson on Documentary* (California, 1966), pp. 147–48

The most notable event of the Autumn film season is the new Flaherty film, *Louisiana Story*, in which that poet, that Melville of the camera, returns to the lyricism of *Nanook* and *Moana* in a film of perfectly ineffable beauty, the like of which we have not seen since *Man of Aran*, and that was a long time ago. It is interesting to note that Flaherty's perennial theme, man vs. nature, is even maintained here, in a story that ostensibly tells of the effects on the lives of a primitive Accadian family in the swamps of the Louisiana bayous of the discovery of oil on their land. At first glance this would seem to be a *deux à deux* between man and technological progress but the latter is, in the geysers of oil spouting from the bowels of the earth, a force of nature still. Thus does Flaherty answer those of his critics (not the least of which is his idolator, Grierson) who have held that the theme of man vs. nature was almost an anachronism in the modern world of technological progress. . . .

Herman G. Weinberg. *Sight & Sound*. Autumn 1948, p. 119

Thus far we have put forward the view that expressionism of montage and image constitute the essence of cinema. And it is precisely on this generally accepted notion that directors from silent days, such as Erich von Stroheim, F. W. Murnau, and Robert Flaherty, have by implication cast a doubt. In their films, montage plays no part, unless it be the negative one of inevitable elimination where reality superabounds. The camera cannot see everything at once but it makes sure not to lose any part of what it chooses to see. What matters to Flaherty, confronted with Nanook hunting the seal, is the relation between Nanook and the animals; the actual length of the waiting period. Montage could suggest the time involved. Flaherty, however, confines himself to showing the actual waiting period: the length of the hunt is the very substance of the image, its true object. Thus in the film this episode requires one set-up. Will anyone deny that it is thereby much more moving than a montage by attraction? [1958–1965]

André Bazin. *What Is Cinema?* (California, 1967), pp. 26–27

But though one thinks of the places in which he filmed, Hudson Bay, Samoa, the Aran Islands, India, the United States, the Flaherty Country is of the mind, as characteristic in its climate as the Kafka Continent, Graham Greeneland or Dostoevskigrad. The Flaherty Country is one where all conflict is externalized. Nature is so savage in its elemental force that men must work together if they are to survive; hunger, a blizzard, a break in the ice or shipwreck may any moment bring death, so we must live purely under the shadow of eternity.

The Flaherty world was distasteful to many people, because its symbols belonged not to the proud world of modern science in which Nature, licked, was on the run and Everyman was master of his fate and captain of his soul, with the assistance of a good psycho-analyst or a plentiful supply of tranquillisers. Flaherty showed an unfashionable sanity in a world nursing its neuroses and gastric ulcers as signs of sensitivity. He had the childish tactlessness of the little boy in Hans Andersen who pointed out that the King was wearing no clothes.

It is interesting that though documentary film technicians pay a direct tribute to what Flaherty taught them about how to look through a camera, the feature-film men think of him as a writer. Orson Welles said Flaherty reminded him of Nathaniel Hawthorne or Thoreau; a strange selection, when Herman Melville lay so much closer at hand. Like Melville, Flaherty had always the sense of the individual embodying some universal principle.

Arthur Calder-Marshall. *The Innocent Eye*
(Harcourt, 1963), p. 249

In *Tabu*, the elements that are good are really good, and those that are bad are deplorable. If you take the defects into account and then completely disregard them, you'll be impressed, perhaps even moved as much as I was by the film. First of all, the musical score is almost distracting enough in itself to drive you out of the auditorium! There is no dialogue, so the music is supposed to enhance the general moods conveyed by facial expressions and actions. However, it is so exaggerated that it almost causes laughter when there should be tears. Also, the Tahitians are hopelessly type-cast and uniform. They look just like natives are supposed to look. Beautiful people are invariably good and the ugly ones are evil.

But if these things can be overlooked, the art of *Tabu* can be enjoyed to the fullest. Of course the film was originally conceived by Robert Flaherty whose objective was to present a documentary of how South Sea island culture is corrupted by civilization. He accomplished this goal marvelously because of his obvious admiration for, and deep understanding of, the natives. Their rituals, which might seem mere superstition in our culture, were included with all the seriousness which a native himself would give them.

Linda Lucas. *Film Society Review*. Sept. 1967, p. 15

FLEMING, VICTOR (1883–1949)

Lord Jim is an interesting example of what a fine story by a great writer can do for the screen when that story has been translated with a fair amount of accuracy and understanding into the language of motion pictures. In this picture, dealing with the character of a sensitive and romantic white man, under a cloud with his own people and practically condemned to live his life among an alien East Indian tribe, it is the master plot that stands out—a plot developing out of human character and circumstance, and moving along to that strange end of Fate, or Chance, the shadow of which forever hangs over the stories of Joseph Conrad.

To the extent that the photoplay gives the feel of this with considerable power, it is Conradian, and in so far as it is successful in that respect it has a quality that lifts it above the average run of pictures.

NBR. Nov.-Dec. 1925, p. 4

The western was perhaps America's nearest approach to real cinema. It was perfectly natural. It was, practically speaking, the Americans being themselves. Distinct from the sexual interplay of the drawing-room movie, the western had its birth in the early days of the one and two reelers, and rose to its zenith towards the end of the post-war period about 1922 or 1923. Since then, it has degenerated into a more sophisticated form, as with *The Winning of Barbara Worth* and *In Old Arizona*. It has almost been displaced by the steel-girder and the office eye-shade, the dance frock and the dumb-bell, together with the products of America's dancing youth. There is, it is true, some indication of the revival of the western in the dialogue cinema. Its natural scope for the use of synchronised sound, of horses' hoof-beats and of gun-shots, was the basis of Paramount's *The Virginian*, directed by Victor Fleming. The use of American natural landscape and types in this picture was highly creditable, and, despite the limitations imposed by dialogue, I have no hesitation in saying that it was amongst the best (if not the best) pictures to come from Hollywood since the opening of the dialogue period. *The Virginian*, because of its wonderful open-air atmosphere, lifted Victor Fleming in my estimation out of the rut of second-rate directors, although credit must also be given to J. Roy Hunt for his superb exterior photography.

Paul Rotha. *The Film Till Now* (Jonathan Cape, 1930), p. 132

Many a bottle of whisky is imbibed or smashed during the screening of the pictorial version of Upton Sinclair's novel, *The Wet Parade*, which came to the Rialto yesterday. This story of the ravages of John Barleycorn goes from the wet age to this year of grace—leaving the old devil Drink where he is now.

In the opening interlude there is the suicide of a Southern aristocrat, whose body is found in a pig-sty. After prohibition comes, a drunkard kills his wife, a young man is blinded by poisoned alcohol and a prohibition agent, impersonated by Jimmy Durante, is killed by a gangster's bullet.

Its bickerings and scenes in barrooms of men with unquenchable thirsts are bound to recall the old classic, "Ten Nights in a Barroom." After listening to the melodramatic incidents it is quite a relief to hear Mr. Durante's characteristic brand of humor. This picture, however, is endowed with several excellent performances, notably those given by Lewis Stone and Walter Huston. Both impersonate drunkards.

The Wet Parade runs for something like two hours, and while many of its scenes are undoubtedly interesting, it seems much too long. It attempts to tell of virtually everything in wet times and the present-day speakeasy, including references to capitalists who are willing to risk money in backing bootleggers. Some of it rings true, but it seems as if the inebriates were hand-picked cases. . . .

Mordaunt Hall. *NYT*. April 22, 1932, p. 23

As far West of Budapest as Hoboken is a good old-fashioned strip act titled *Red Dust*. Without explanations, which might lead to libel suits and other irritations, I confess to having enjoyed for a long time the simple, forthright acting of Miss Jean Harlow; and as the wrestling partner of Clark Gable in this picture she has a great deal of simple country fun.

Here again we have an old Hollywood formula but, where *Trouble in Paradise* suffers from pernicious anemia, *Red Dust* is lusty and fresh simply because, instead of one trader and one woman and one softy in the tropics, all suffering from damp rot and sex starvation, we have thrown in for good measure two ladies and three gentlemen, troubled with the same movie diseases. The good woman loses her honor to Mr. Gable and then her health. Her husband then takes her away from it all after she has taken a shot at Mr. Gable and as Miss Harlow's gentleman friend drinks himself to death the simple healthy couple remain on their rubber planatation to enjoy the climate and the advantages.

Pare Lorentz. *Vanity Fair*. Dec. 1932, p. 64

A story that offered no subtleties and all sorts of high adventure was realized in *Treasure Island*, which makes a picture so good in some ways that any but the most determined can see what fresh possibilities in the way of beauty and free movement lie in this new art of the screen. The frank swagger of the story was caught from the first, and somewhere near the first there was a fine sequence of the ship getting under weigh, one of the most lovely I have seen. Until this picture, everyone will perhaps have forgotten how shrewdly Stevenson worked in all the rich incidents of a time when, instead of organizing a strike—which is not fine and dashing, but the work of vicious malcontents—people took their damn ship away and struck for booty. The story and the good work of most of those in it were sadly enough spoiled at the end by the extended sentimentality that was allowed to spring up between Wallace Beery and Jackie Cooper; but the first three-quarters of it was still so lively and well established in its mood as to make the whole quite worth going to. [1934]

Otis Ferguson. *The Film Criticism of O.F.* (Temple, 1971), p. 47

Captains Courageous, Metro-Goldwyn-Mayer's superb translation of Kipling's novel, joins the year's gallery of distinguished films because Victor Fleming, its director, has never for a moment permitted his action to lag. And he has had the advantage, always, of a colorful and active background—the sea and the Gloucester fishermen whose schooners spank over it. Possibly I am in danger of being corrupted by subversive New Deal propaganda, but I share President Roosevelt's hankering for marine photography, and I have seen none more beautiful than that realized by the wizardry of Hal Rosson's camera. Trim Gloucester schooners, bowling along under a full head of sail, their decks awash and scuppers running—cameras achieve poetry too, sometimes.

But *Captains Courageous* is more than seascape and fascinating exposition of the fishing methods of the Gloucestermen. It has a soundly dramatic narrative as well, and one that has been brilliantly performed by young Freddie Bartholomew (not until now officially recognized by this reviewer), by Spencer Tracy, Lionel Barrymore, Melvyn Douglas and others. . . .

It's really a great motion picture, an odds-on favorite for near top-ranking in the year's ten best.

Frank S. Nugent. *Cinema Arts*. July 1937, p. 32

The Wizard of Oz was intended to hit the same audience as *Snow White*, and won't fail for lack of trying. It has dwarfs, music, Technicolor, freak characters, and Judy Garland. It can't be expected to have a sense of humor as well—and as for the light touch of fantasy, it weighs like a pound of fruitcake soaking wet. Children will not object to it, especially as it is a thing of many interesting gadgets; but it will be delightful for children mostly to their mothers, and any kid tall enough to reach up to a ticket window will be found at the Tarzan film down the street. The story of course has some lovely and wild ideas—men of straw and tin, a cowardly lion, a wizard who isn't a very good wizard—but the picture doesn't know what to do with them, except to be painfully literal and elaborate about everything—Cecil B. DeMille and the Seven Thousand Dwarfs by Actual Count. [1937]

Otis Ferguson. *The Film Criticism of O.F.* (Temple, 1971), p. 270

For *Test Pilot* is more than anything else a drama of love and friendship, often probing with extraordinary keenness into the nervous and psychological anatomy of those emotions, sometimes shying into a wordy bathos of cheap-fiction flapdoodle. There is some pseudo-poetic talk about a girl in blue in the sky—the Lorelei of the clouds with such a fatal allure for fliers—and again about the three roads to doom which lie ahead of anyone who loves a flier, which is pretty painfully fancy: even the authors must have realized there was something phoney about such talk, for they make the Spencer Tracy character kid it, casually but cuttingly.

But as a basis for these explorations into the workings of love, so daring and uncharted for the movies that no deviations from strict honesty would have been a miracle, are three very solid and real characters, essentially American and 1938, behaving for the most part not in the usual superficial boy-meets-girl fashion, but as such people, with their natures and backgrounds, would naturally behave in their surroundings of desperate speed and tension. . . .

Perhaps the most important thing about *Test Pilot* is that it is one of the examples of how the people of Hollywood, so berated for pretentious and expensive triviality, often, within the necessarily imposed framework of pleasing the millions, manage to work in strains of truth that might be expected to please only the few. The picture is so noisy with sure-fire elements—box-office cast, violent excitement, glycerine tears and such—that it may be hard to keep the ear attuned to the quieter, authentically human, things in it. But they are there, giving the picture an appeal on quite a different level from that of mere melodramatic thrill.

James Shelley Hamilton. *NBR*. May 1938, p. 11

As you may have heard, *Gone with the Wind*, the $3,900,000 super-picture in technicolor—playing time: three hours and thirty-seven minutes—has arrived. During years of preparation and twelve months of actual shooting, hundreds of people under David O. Selznick's supervision were at work to produce the epoch-making picture of our time. The result is a film which is a major event in the history of the industry but only a minor achievement in motion picture art. There are moments when the two categories meet on good terms, but the long stretches between are filled with mere spectacular efficiency. One admires an excellent cast and a hundred technical details, but one's heart seldom beats faster. While one waits to be carried away, critical thoughts have time to develop. The feeling grows that one is sitting in a Hollywood Duesenberg with nowhere to go. . . .

Of course one can easily conceive of a less polished and more exciting production of *Gone with the Wind*—for example, as an independent Erich von Stroheim would have done it. On the other hand, the fact that the hero and heroine of a super-picture are no longer merely noble and glamorous indicates a development which deserves high praise.

Franz Hoellering. *Nation*. December 30, 1939, p. 740

Victor Fleming, in his direction [of *Gone With the Wind*] has been content to tell his story as clearly as possible, with no fancy work or lingering on "touches." When the story calls for something impressive he does it, as in the scene in the railroad yard when Scarlett picking her way among scores of wounded soldiers lying on the ground, who look like thousands, suggests as much of the devastation of war as a terrific battle scene would have done. Or when Scarlett shoots the marauding Yankee, or when Mammy (so magnificently played by Hattie McDaniel) leads Melanie up the stairs to the room where Rhett is brooding over his dead child, and in a single scene sums up all the woe and despair that has filled the house for days. It is an achievement to have kept so long a narrative from never flagging, or getting wearisome. . . .

Faults could be found if one were looking at this film merely as a motion picture of Georgia in the war and reconstruction days; that it leaves too many important things untouched, that it has no historical perspective, that it provides no ethical or social comment on its characters or events, finally that it is still a novel more than it is a motion picture. But none of those things were intended, or really to be expected. It is enough that Margaret Mitchell's novel should have been put on the screen so satisfyingly for its millions of readers.

James Shelley Hamilton. *NBR*. Jan. 1940, pp. 19–20

Anyone reading the news reports of the Atlanta opening of *Gone With the Wind* will not deny the historical significance of this film. History itself, though, the history of the Civil War period, serves no more than a decorative purpose, a background painted with a distorted set of values and an even falser Technicolor. But history has rarely been told with even an approximation of truth in Hollywood, because the few men in control there have no interest in the real forces behind historical movements and the new forces that every new epoch sets into motion. *Gone With the Wind* deserves our attention because it is an overinflated example of the usual, the false move approach to history. Selznick's four-hour feature represents all Hollywood might do, and, unfortunately, most of what it usually does. In every foot of it is inscribed the tragic gap between possibility and achievement.

Lincoln Kirstein. *Films*. Spring 1940

. . . Like Griffith's historic film, [*Gone With the Wind*] dealt with the South, the Civil War and the efforts of the Negro to free himself from slavery. . . . Both were extraordinary from an artistic and technical point of view, both were heralded with almost fantastic publicity, both were remarkably long (*Gone With the Wind* lasted nearly four hours) and both were huge financial successes. Nevertheless it could be seen that the American film itself and film audiences generally had grown up considerably. No longer was it possible, as Griffith had done, to lay stress upon inflammatory appeal. Director Victor Fleming concentrated instead on the characters of Scarlett O'Hara and Rhett Butler, the "romantic leads," and his attitude to the black characters in the film was notable for its subtlety. Whether this was the subtlety of unconscious discrimination or that of a fully conscious desire to follow, a little more carefully, in the footsteps of Griffith, one cannot say. At any rate many critics felt that where Griffith's film ended Fleming's film began.

. . . The film succeeded admirably in continuing the popular Southern myth that the South had in fact won an ideological war, that, indeed, although the Negroes had been set free they still remained inescapably fettered as historic inferiors to the white race, socially, politically and economically. *Gone With The Wind* marked a high point in the Hollywood move to show that so far as the Negro was concerned United States opinion had reverted to the "Southern Mammy and Uncle Tom tradition." [1948]

Peter Noble. *The Negro in Films* (Kennikat, 1969), p. 75

A function of criticism is to find that which is good in a bad work and to find that which is bad in a good work, like what one's judgment of people should be. This is constructive criticism. *Joan of Arc* with Ingrid Bergman, by our own premise, is a bad film with one or two good things. Jose Ferrer as the Dauphin provides the film's only moments of strength. For the rest it is childishly oversimplified, its battles *papier-mâché*, its heroine far too worldly, its spiritual content that of a chromo art calendar. Maxwell Anderson's play, *Joan of Lorraine*, which discussed the ethical, moral and spiritual values to be learned from the Maid's life, was thrown out altogether, for the melodramatic "high-spots" of Joan's way to the stake, a pastiche in which Anderson collaborated for the screenplay. Such is expediency. I'm told that Wanger studied Dreyer's *Passion of Joan of Arc* for many weeks before shooting his film (he even lifted several of Dreyer's touches, the dropped chain at the stake; the opening moments of the trial; the sympathetic priest who brings her the cross at the stake, etc.), but it just goes to show you how little influence great films *really* have. . . . In the last analysis, whatever goes into the Hollywood grist mill, comes out the same way. It is a meat-grinder that will take beef and suet, pheasant and turnips, attar of roses and limburger, and turn it all into the same kind of hash that has served so many so well, for so long.

Herman G. Weinberg. *Sight & Sound*. Spring 1949, p. 18

Joan of Arc would be hardly more than *Robin Hood* without frequent and revolting appeals to the mawkishness of the spectator. For example, during the assault on the Tourelles fortress, the film shows us Jeanne at the head of her men, inciting them to combat. The battle is raging. Fleming was evidently aware of the necessity of a counterpart to the atrocities of combat—shown with a lip-smacking amount of detail; he had to show that Jeanne like the spectator is conscious of the atrocities and that sensible to them she regrets them (a sad paradox for the Christian conscience of a holy warrior!). Fleming therefore shows us a mortally wounded soldier who collapses at Jeanne's feet. Close-up of Jeanne's face: full of horror and pity, her eyes rest for a moment on the soldier. She quickly recovers from this moment of weakness; her eyes are raised to heaven and her voice again exhorts those still living to continue the fight. . . . This short scene—there are many others—is odious, almost obscene because of the crude means used. . . .

A Versailles ciné-club recently ran several passages from the Fleming film before *La Passion de Jeanne d'Arc*. The comparison in favor of the silent film was crushing. Carl Dreyer's masterpiece, though its language is dated, is still as valid as ever from the point of view of style. Everything in the Fleming film shows its total aesthetic lack and impersonality. *Joan of Arc* gives us only a superficial knowledge of Jeanne and avoids an attempt at interpreting a quasi-mythological personality. An excessive striving for effect, the abuse of both "dramatization" and the picturesque, the mediocrity of the *mise en scène* are the principle causes of its failure. Just as in Joan the Conqueror replaces the Saint, in the film the sublime is replaced by the picturesque. Exterior heroism covers spiritual ascesis.

Vincent Pinel in *Jeanne d'Arc au Cinéma*
(Michel Estève, 1968), pp. 62, 63

FORD, JOHN (1895–1973)

If the business of the screen as a dramatic art is to give us the essence of people as they are, the excitement and thrill of situation as it may really occur, and to use the imagination and the instrument through which it works in doing this so as to raise up before us the thing we call reality, then *Men Without Women* is a top grade film, one of the very best that the audible screen so far has given us.

For this swift, unornamented and visually compressed motion picture of what happened to the crew of a submarine sent to the bottom in a collision, seeks to handle only the material of probability, to use human nature so as to illuminate its meaning in a moment of stark disaster, and to select the stuff it would use so as to give us the complete scene as far as we need to have it to gain a vivid, veritable impression. . . .

The scenes that follow at this point are greatly enhanced by the care which has been taken to give the details of a submarine visual accurateness—to make one see how the air is supplied, what happens when it is cut off, how it may be cut off; to see how the mechanism is a steel web the keeping intact of which is of paramount necessity to the life of the men in it; to understand the cool, swift and expert judgment demanded of those who have to know and work this mechanism as a means of saving their lives. Valves, wheels, dials, pipes and the complicated breeches of the torpedo tubes are given a dramatic meaning because pains have been taken to make us understand their operation and uses.

NBR. March 1930, p. 8

A little rough, sir; but we overlook that, you understand? When a man can't walk up the gangway, after shore leave, we know he's all right. As fine a pack of fighting men as you will ever meet, sir.

We deplore.

John Ford's film, *Men Without Women*, tells of a crew imprisoned in a floundered submarine. One man, the youngest of the lot, makes a little ship, from a block of wood, and sails it in the rising water.

The model shots are well done; the sound is well done; some of the acting is overdone. The men talking of the girls whom they have left behind; the he-men getting tearful and shaking hands. Yet, many times more exciting than the about-to-snow *Atlantic* (you don't understand, sir, she is going to have a child).

John Ford has managed not to go down with the ship.

And no officers wasting time in pulling harsh faces.

Oswell Blakeston. *Close Up*. April 1930, p. 333

The Iron Horse was a good film in its time because it did, in spite of the extraneous love-story and the commonplace photography, keep the idea of the railway uppermost throughout the production, bringing out with all the power at its command the drama of these two tracks, the Central Pacific and the Union Pacific, fighting nearer to one another day by day across a continent. Lincoln comes, does his work for the railway, passes. He is assassinated, but the rails go on. The Indians come, wreck the railway, are shot down. The work begins again, and the rails go on. Men are ambushed and killed. Others take their places, soldiers of North and South, Irishmen, Chinese, Italians, digging and shovelling and laying track, and the rails go on.

The Iron Horse has a prodigious energy; a force deriving from its theme and unchecked by its statement.

C. A. Lejeune. *Cinema* (Alexander Maclehose, 1931), pp. 183–84

[*Arrowsmith*] will greatly disappoint those who read, understood and treasured the lonely tragedies of the books; treasured its inherent greatness. I believe that the comparative few who treasured *Arrowsmith* will resent the fact that it retains the outline and intention of the book, with a few minor alterations, and yet misses the novel's rich atmosphere, the power of its tragedies and its finely rebellious spirit; misses, too, the ringing drama of the essential conflict between the lonely, pure scientific spirit and the mercenary, relentless medical babbitry with which it comes in contact throughout its life time. The film will, as I say, disappoint the rabid followers of the novel.

Yet, as talkies go it is a good one. At least the film endeavors to strike Mr. Lewis's note.

John S. Cohen, Jr. *NYS*. Dec. 8, 1931

Edward G. Robinson, who has been suffering from a succession of weak roles, registers an impressive return to his old-time form in a brace of parts in an amusing combination of farce and melodrama called *The Whole Town's Talking*. In it Mr. Robinson appears as a mild and timid little clerk and as a notorious Public Enemy, who is his double. . . . *The Whole Town's Talking* certainly is not long on plausibility, and one is likely to have a frequent suspicion that the picture could have ended about a third of the way through its course if any of the characters had acted with just the slightest glimmering of intelligence. But the pace is fast, and the fun and thrills are reasonably frequent, and the photoplay becomes genuinely good fun.

"Argus." *Literary Digest*. March 16, 1935, p. 22

The picture that John Ford has made out of Liam O'Flaherty's *The Informer* opens a lot of new possibilities for Hollywood, tackles something that is really fine, and manages several memorable scenes. But because it deals with the sort of thing that must be handled adequately if it is to go over, its persistent inadequacies make it more disappointing than many pictures with less to recommend them.

The story gets off to a beautiful start, riding along on the unfamiliar color and excitement of the period when the Terror was in Ireland, tightening on the country and walking through its streets in armed squads. And it carries well through the early part of that evening when Frankie McPhillip (Wallace Ford is excellent in this part) came in from the hills, to slip home in the fog and be sold to his death, with the Tans piling out of their lorries to surround the house, and Gypo Nolan, the betrayer, watching the clock at headquarters in a cold sweat. For dramatic vigor and beauty of composition there have been few sequences to compare with the one that ends with the camera looking from behind Frankie down into the court where the Tans look up with their machine gun.

So far, the atmosphere and the sense of a tragic character have been well built. But shortly after Gypo has stumbled out with his blood money, there begins a train of happenings many of which hang fire altogether—the result partly of faulty casting, partly of bad plot treatment. . . .

Hollywood deserves a lot of credit for tackling such a job, and thereby opening a new field for pictures; but I do not feel that the film itself does right by a story so powerful and moving as that of a man who was driven by hunger and suspicion into the tragic foolishness of turning informer in the Irish Terror. [1935]

Otis Ferguson. *The Film Criticism of O.F.* (Temple, 1971), pp. 79–80

As cinema, that vague entity, the movie [*Mary of Scotland*] fails. John Ford, who, of all his Hollywood confreres, has the ability to give his work intensity, as witness *The Informer* and *The Prisoner of Shark Island*, is here mannered and stylized—a sure indication that he was not at ease in the play. His lighting effects seem forced and repetitious. The action is slow and segmented. Furthermore he leans on the work of other men. The court-room scene was obviously conceived with a long backward glance at Karl Dreyer's *The Passion of Joan of Arc*. The upward pan that concluded the film was borrowed from *A Tale of Two Cities*—the telepathic communion between Mary and Bothwell from *Dark Angel, Peter Ibbetson* and innumerable Hollywood essays in the mystical. The whole enterprise is a regrettable one and should serve as a warning against the indiscriminate taking over of unsuitable stage-successes to the screen.

Robert Stebbins. *New Theatre*. Sept. 1936, p. 21

Apart from scenario, the direction of [*The Plough and the Stars*] discloses certain fundamental weaknesses. In the main, these result from John Ford's reliance on excessive stylization—a tendency he first betrayed most noticeably in *Mary of Scotland*. The funeral procession of Mollser may be taken as a case in point. This took on almost the character of a slow dance, the three shawled women going through their paces as for a choreographer. Or consider his habit of fading out on a group of people frozen rigid—almost like architecture. Although Ford's desire to invest the character of James Connolly with great nobility was in evidence, his directives were so generalized that the great Irish leader took on the proportions of a stock character. The occupation of the postoffice, though more fully treated in the scenario, still emerged as a sequence of great expressiveness. The undeniably effective chase across the roofs was partly weakened in grip by the unrealistic character of the mise-en-scène. In this respect the choice seems to have been deliberate, for the scenario reads ". . . this roof is only an eerie impression of chimney pots, different roof levels, and smoke."

One might go on with an analysis of *The Plough and the Stars* if the thought that the film is really not the work of Ford and Nichols did not continually present itself. To all intents and purposes Ford and Nichols have yet to make *The Plough and the Stars.* No one in his senses, for example, could hold either one of them to account for the nauseating drool that splashes out of Barbara Stanwyck in the course of a performance as inept as any the screen has seen.

Robert Stebbins. *New Theatre.* April 1937, p. 27

Among newcomers it looked as though John Ford were one of the cleverest and one of the most dependable. In the same year as *The Whole Town's Talking*, with its deafening chatter and extraordinary misunderstandings, he also gave us *The Lost Patrol* and *The Informer.* The first of these, a simple film made without sets and avoiding all facile exoticism, was a finely heroic picture in praise of man, prey of hostile nature and of human enemies, yet it seemed a trifle deliberate and artificial, smelling somewhat of the workshop. *The Informer*, on the other hand, reminds one of von Sternberg at his best, as in *The Docks of New York.* That simple tale of shadowy houses and squalid streets, about a man who betrays another for money, is, despite an element of melodrama and an absurd ending, one of the most powerful talking films yet made. McLaglen gives an astonishing portrayal of a low brute, and we shall not soon forget his tearing down the poster which offers a reward of twenty pounds to anyone who will give up his friend, and which seems to pursue him and cling to him as though it were alive. Despite its rather studio-made air, it was as impressive as [Howard Hawks's] *Scarface*, or anything in the whole powerful literature redolent of fog and grime and dreariness which the Germans introduced to the Americans.

Maurice Bardèche and Robert Brasillach. *The History of Motion Pictures* (Norton and MOMA, 1938), p. 316

In one superbly expansive gesture, which we (and the Music Hall) can call *Stagecoach*, John Ford has swept aside ten years of artifice and talkie compromise and has made a motion picture that sings a song of camera. It moves, and how beautifully it moves, across the plains of Arizona, skirting the sky-reaching mesas of Monument Valley, beneath the piled-up cloud banks which every photographer dreams about, and through all the old-fashioned, but never really outdated, periods of prairie travel in the scalp-raising Seventies, when Geronimo's Apaches were on the warpath. Here, in a sentence, is a movie of the grand old school, a genuine rib-thumper and a beautiful sight to see.

Mr. Ford is not one of your subtle directors, suspending sequences on the wink of an eye or the precisely calculated gleam of a candle in a mirror. He prefers the broadest canvas, the brightest colors, the wildest brush and the boldest possible strokes. He hews to the straight narrative line with the well-reasoned confidence of a man who has seen that narrative succeed before. He takes no shadings from his characters: either they play it straight or they don't play at all. He likes his language simple and he doesn't want too much of it. When his Redskins bite the dust, he expects to hear the thud and see the dirt spurt up. Above all, he likes to have things happen out in the open, where his camera can keep them in view.

Frank S. Nugent. *NYT*. March 3, 1939, p. 21

Young Mr. Lincoln is another of the strangely honest movies that this year has produced, without producing much else: most of them have been unspectacular, though two have had real brilliance (*Wuthering Heights* and *Nazi Spy*). This one is good but, opening without expense or explosion, it may slip past all but its audiences without much notice. Outside of being better constructed than the year's Lincoln play, and less dependent on the business of make-up and excerpted speeches, it requires no comparison.

John Ford deliberately used a slow drawling tempo to fit the subject. And where Lincoln himself is not concerned, this has a clogging effect. With any ordinary trick actor the pauses, jew's-harping, and untangling of feet would have become a pure bore. But John Ford didn't have trick acting, and when he takes his time he never throws it away. The long sequence of fair-day in town is a fine example of the way he can make use of period color and scene and incident to give life to the story; he is a spendthrift with actual air and trees and water throughout. The trial scene is the big dramatic part, and comes over well as such; the best Ford manner shows in the dark and breathless struggle in the clearing at night; but the best things as a whole are the solid rightness of each thing used, and the shrewd way the main theme was given its head. [1939]

Otis Ferguson. *The Film Criticism of O.F.* (Temple, 1971), pp. 257–58

Suppose some truant Good Fairy were to ask me, "As I'm not employed just now, perhaps there's some small magic job I could do for you, Sergei Mikhailovich? Is there some American film that you'd like me to make you the author of—with a wave of my wand?"

I would not hesitate to accept the offer, and I would at once name the film that I wish I had made. It would be *Young Mr. Lincoln*, directed by John Ford. . . .

This film is distinguished by something more than its marvellous craftsmanship, where the rhythm of the montage corresponds to the timbre of the photography, and where the cries of the waxwings echo over the turbid flow of muddy water and through the steady gait of the little mule that lanky Abe rides along the Sangamon River. And there is something here more than the skill of filming in a stylized daguerreotype manner that is in unison with the moral character of Lincoln's sentences, or the eccentricity of Henry Fonda's performance that keeps the genuinely moving situation from sliding into sentimentality, and instead reaches a rare degree of pathos, as in the stunning departure of Lincon into the landscape at the end of the film.

There is a deeper thing here—in those fundamentals and premises from which craftsmanship and harmony grow. Its source is a womb of popular and national spirit—this could account for its unity, its artistry, its genuine beauty. [Original date unknown.]

Sergei Eisenstein. *Film Essays* (Praeger, 1970), pp. 193–41

Ford's work in *Grapes of Wrath* is outstanding again in terms of people. His sense of the value of a face, of a voice, of a posture, of clothing, has served him well in his excellent casting of the supporting players: the truckdrivers, migrants, deputies and vigilantes. And Ford has done more than to choose good examples of real people. He has come upon something that could never have been discovered in the studios: a realization of the highly-developed awareness which the common people of the world have of one another. He has used that knowledge in the memorable scenes of the picture: in the lunchroom where Pa Joad buys a loaf of bread; in the first migrant camp entered by the Joads, where we get a full and immediate understanding of their plight, not only from the wretched tents and pasteboard hovels and the litter, but also from the apathetic curiosity of the miserable squatters as silent notice of the new arrival runs intuitively through the camp; in the very first part of the scene where the kids of the same camp, attracted by Ma's stew, gather to beg silently, realizing the needlessness of words; in the masterful scene of the dance in the government camp where the direction measures up to Steinbeck's full meaning by a brilliant handling of mass and detail that would have been impossible if Ford had not understood the innate decency and joy of life and goodness which blooms in the lowliest people with the slightest encouragement. It is a pity that Ford's sense of environment has not come through as well as his sense of people. The opening of the picture is greatly weakened because he has given us no feeling of the country or of the people's background. Where are the vast stretches of the Dustbowl and the tiny houses as lonely as ships at sea? Where is the dust? It is hard to believe that Ford has ever seen *The Plow That Broke the Plains*. It is baffling to hear that a camera crew was sent into Oklahoma along Route 66; certainly but a few feet of their film was used. It is regrettable that the Joads were snatched across the beautiful and terrifying expanses of the country in a few pans and process shots; we could justly have expected more.

Edwin Locke. *Films*. Spring 1940, pp. 50–51

Looked at coldly—as coldly as one can with a picture so warm with humanness and its laughter and tears—the superlative thing about [*How Green Was My Valley*] is its technical style, the perfection of cinematic narrative that it achieves. In any such perfection it is impossible to know what the director and the script-writer individually contributed. Their work merges so successfully that it is one work, and masterly. It is surprising to look back on the film and realize how much of it is pure visual action, pictures powerfully composed, dramatically photographed, smoothly and eloquently put together. Dialogue is used most sparingly, and always for more reason than just to have some talk going on—always for carrying on the story, for illuminating character, for creating atmosphere and mood. The lilt of Welsh speech is predominant enough to give some unity to the various Irish, American and English dialects that must have been unavoidable with so international a cast. The soundtrack, with its voices, its noises from the mine, its music, is just what it should be—artfully contrived and always the helpful hand-maid of the camera.

James Shelley Hamilton. *NBR*. Nov. 1941, p. 11

The studio-made battle sequences [in *They Were Expendable*] convey a brilliant sense of the terror undergone by the men on their boats—things which must have seemed targets designed especially for drawing enemy-fire to the men themselves. The overall strategy of our retreat is not shown, into which a defeated force injected as much order as seems possible. Few moments are as despairing as this from the Allied point of view, yet in retrospect there is satisfaction in seeing imagination and inventiveness so well displayed in the use of these small craft, and as in most of our war films we have the rather special kind of brassy bravery which is typically American. All this is well done in *They Were Expendable*. In addition, there is the unique feature of Ford's direction which recommends the film beyond the simple fact that it is one of the best of the how-it-happened reconstructions.

Ford loves the seas in all moods and he loves the civilization that crops up where sea and land meet, as evidenced by the saturation of authentic mood in his *Long Voyage Home*. His joining the Navy during the war expresses this fondness of his. Ford also has a telling directorial style which relates the film images one to another in a way which heightens the dramatic elements and intensifies the mood. This enhanced such superior films of his as *The Grapes of Wrath* and *How Green Was My Valley*. Style and latent predilection are combined in this, his first industry-made film since the end of hostilities.

Stephen P. Belcher, Jr. *NBR*. Dec. 1945, pp. 4–5

Wagonmaster is the nearest any director has come to an *avant-garde* Western. To use this word of a film by Ford may sound strange; take it, though, not as implying an experiment in any new -ism, but in the sense in which it is the personal drama of the arrogant, self-deceiving Commander of the Post (see *Fort Apache*), and the tension between his Unionist troops and the squadron of Confederate prisoners of war who have won a half-liberty by volunteering for service against hostile Indians on the frontier. The indecisive scripting, and a lack of grasp and dynamism in the direction, prevent the story from working up any real tension, and the characters fail obstinately to impinge. Wise has, in fact, achieved little more than a series of effects; some of these are admittedly striking—disconnected glimpses of Fort Thorn, the Cavalry on patrol, a finely-staged Indian attack—but they fail to add up. We are left with some careful period reconstruction, and a visual style of constant accomplishment: Leon Shamroy's photography shows remarkable delicacy of tone and command of forceful, decorative compositions. These too, however, fail in the end to signify; a comparison of the images of *Wagonmaster* and *Two Flags West* points the difference between the expressive, poet's eye, and the elegant, superficial skill of the *decorateur*.

Lindsay Anderson. *Sight & Sound*.
Dec. 1950, pp. 333–34

Ford's art and artifice are used not only on behalf of the love story (it is the first he's filmed, though *The Quiet Man* is his 108th picture). They are also employed to reveal a way of life—stable, rooted, honorable, purposeful in nature's way, and thereby rhythmic. Everyone is an individual, yet everyone and everything has a place. Even "Squire" Danaher's egoism. . . .

The psychology of the characters is on a level much profounder than a generation debauched by psychoanalysis will recognize. When Sean drags Mary Kate up hill and down dale, feminist women will scowl and writhe (and invent reasons to damn Ford's film). But feminine women will know that it is the final act of the courtship, the means by which their wills are united, by which the woman has gotten her man and the man his mate. For Mary Kate will not have him truly until he fights her brother for her dowry, the symbol of her new allegiance. (When he gets the money she holds open a furnace door and Sean throws it in). Then as the fight is about to begin, she says triumphantly: "I'll be going home now, I'll have the supper ready."

The spell of *The Quiet Man* will stay with you. People may say that things are not thus in Ireland, that there a Catholic priest does not get his flock to cheer an Anglican bishop, that the IRA is not as genial as the representatives of it in this film, that the full-throated ballads sung in the pub are not so heartening, the "Squire" Danahers so tractable, the Mary Kates so beautiful, and the Michaeleen Flynns so wise.

Such cynicism will be in vain. John Ford has transmuted it all nearer to our heart's desire, and made us happy. We are obliged to him, and grateful for his art, and even for his artifice.

Henry Hart. *Films in Review*. Aug.-Sept. 1952, pp. 354–55

But there is . . . a different way of violating the Western form. This is to yield entirely to its static quality as legend and to the "cinematic" temptations of its landscape, the horses, the quiet men. John Ford's famous *Stagecoach* (1938) has much of this unhappy preoccupation with style, and the same director's *My Darling Clementine* (1946), a soft and beautiful movie about Wyatt Earp, goes further along the same path, offering indeed a superficial accuracy of historical reconstruction, but so loving in execution as to destroy the outlines of the Western legend, assimilating it to the more sentimental legend of rural America and making the hero a more dangerous Mr. Deeds. (*Powder River* [Lewis King], a recent "routine" Western shamelessly copied from *My Darling Clementine*, is in most ways a better film; lacking the benefit of a serious director, it is necessarily more concerned with drama than with style.) [1954]

Robert Warshow. *The Immediate Experience* (Atheneum, 1970), pp. 149–50

John Ford, for example, is one of the true veterans of Hollywood, still active, still productive. Not only his sound but even his widescreen films reveal his long experience, combining the visual continuity of silent editing technique with a perfect instinct for just how much each shot should tell. He is so certain of his effects that his editors claim he cuts his films himself within the camera, providing them with little more than they actually need to piece the scene together. His takes, generally shorter than most directors', move with incredible precision from point to point, always anticipating the audience's natural curiosity. Typical was the memorable fight scene in *Young Mr. Lincoln* (1939). It takes place at night in a forest, some distance from the festivities of a Fourth of July picnic. At first it is perceived only dimly—heard rather than seen through the trees, the brush and the darkness. Some women rush to the scene, and we see the fright on their faces. The moon appears from behind the clouds, and now we see the fight as the women see it, close, intense and deadly. The moon passes behind a cloud and a shot rings out. When the light returns we are watching from the edge of the scene. A dying man is dancing in agony while a puff of smoke mounts toward the sky, and a boy calls for his mother. Throughout this brief sequence, Ford's cutting and his choice of camera position alike have been dictated by the logic of the material, the flow of its emotion and by his superb instinct for what the audience will want to see from one moment to the next. Never one to cut for shock effect or to create an artificial sense of surprise or excitement, Ford's film demonstrates functional editing at it best—precise, unobtrusive and sure.

Arthur Knight. *The Liveliest Art*
(Macmillan, 1957), p. 190

The sound-track score [in *The Informer*] is carefully cued to emphasize the emotional tones of particular scenes. The themes of "the blind man and the minstrel boy," "the money," "the informer," and "Wearing the Green'" are woven together in a loose kind of medley which sounds at appropriate tempos. For example, at the court of inquiry, while Dan is adding up the money that Gypo has spent, the music builds to a crescendo and quickly breaks at the moment when Gypo, trapped by the evidence, drops all pretenses and breaks down.

More revealing than the musical accompaniment, however, is the way in which Ford finds visual and aural substitutes for Gypo's interior monologues. When Gypo, for example, first sees the (reward) poster we see, superimposed upon the screen, an image of Gypo and Frankie in a bar singing a soldier's song. When Gypo is met by the real Frankie at the Dunboy House, we see a different image superimposed. This time it is the poster which Gypo had seen a little while before. We know that his temptation has begun. Again, during Gypo's last escape toward Katie's room, the superimposed poster appears once more, like a misty dream, this time dark and glowering, full of accusation. At the brothel the despised woman, to whom Gypo later gives the money, dissolves for a moment, and Gypo thinks he is seeing Katie. Finally, after the betrayal, Gypo sits in a pub trying to formulate a plan. He seems to hear Frankie's mocking voice, "Ah, Gypo, I'm your brain. You're lost . . . You're lost. . . ."

Considering all these devices, it is surprising to find the *Christian Science Monitor* reporter explaining that Ford "rarely uses trick shots, but frames every take carefully from the straight-on angle." What Ford has really done here is neither to employ the trick shot nor the straight-on angle—it is hardly a question of that—but to use every resource of the camera to render the tortured consciousness of Gypo Nolan.

George Bluestone. *Novels into Film* (Johns Hopkins, 1957), p. 86

From a figurative point of view Ford can be compared with the paintings and drawings of Frederic Remington. . . . Actually even these elements come to the film across a long experience of western films born under the sign of Remington and something of a byproduct of the original narrative seam—Owen Wister's *The Virginian* was published in 1902, Porter's *The Great Train Robbery* reached the screen a year later. *Stagecoach* is therefore pure cinema and all discussions of it must begin with the tradition of horse opera. With a prediliction for hyperboles we might say that Ford's work comes in the wake of the minor westerns just as the Homeric poems come after the songs. In fact it represents the high point of a tendency that is among the oldest in cinema.

It might be added that the *Stagecoach*-western relationship is not an isolated example in the films of Ford. It has been pointed out that each type of film cycle, every cinematographic style in Hollywood bears as its seal a work by Ford. Let us, for example cite *Four Sons*, which came after the rage for war films; the satire *The Whole Town's Talking*, which is linked to the gangster films; *Mary of Scotland*, the typical biographical romance; *Hurricane*, which concluded a series on the south seas. Going backward one can also find in the history of the director traces of his ability to insert himself in the seam of commercially successful films. Think, for example of *The Girl in Number 29*, patterned on George M. Cohan's celebrated *Seven Keys to Baldpate*; *Little Miss Smiles*, which took advantage of Borzage's formula in *Humoresque*; *Silver Wings*, made in imitation of the Fox success *Over the Hill*; and even *The Iron Horse*, which came after Cruze's *The Covered Wagon*. In addition, there are the numerous remakes that make up the normal "routine" of the cinéast.

Tullio Kezich. *John Ford* (Guanda, 1958), pp. 11–13

It can be argued that *Wagonmaster* is John Ford's greatest film. If I choose not to argue the point at this time, it is because there are too many other candidates to consider, and these do not include *The Informer* and *The Grapes of Wrath*. . . . Ford does not waste any time over the subtleties of characterization and twists of plot. He strokes boldly across the canvas of the American past as he concentrates on the evocative images of a folk tradition of free adventure and compelling adaptability. There are no moral shadings. His villians are evil incarnate—whining, wheedling and uselessly destructive. The hero destroys them in the end as he would destroy a snake, and the sophisticated medicine-show girl smiles inscrutably as she realizes without an exchange of words that she is destined for this virile "rube." There are the Mormon square dances and the unforgettable circular stomp of friendly Indians. Above all, there are the wagons themselves, those symbolic vehicles that remind us that John Ford's *Stagecoach* initiated the modern American cinema. [1961]

Andrew Sarris. *Confessions of a Cultist* (S&S, 1970), pp. 41–42

In spite of these striking and sobering dramatic values, plus superb Technicolor photography (much of it in Ford's favorite locale, Monument Valley), [*Cheyenne Autumn*] is a great disappointment. Obviously, no amount of theorizing on my part is going to account adequately for its failure. However, one crucial defect is that, though it is a two-and-one-half-hours-plus epic supposedly dedicated to Indian courage and endurance, it is not really told from the Indians' point of view. The Cheyennes never emerge as much more than long-suffering puppets.

Besides, both the virtues and defects of Ford's movie-making techniques date from an earlier age. The kinds of clichés of characterization and incident that were probably a necessary compromise in, for example, *Stagecoach* in 1939 have a distractingly non-epic ring today in *Cheyenne Autumn*—especially in a totally irrelevant "cameo" episode, involving the Dodge City of Wyatt Earp (James Stewart) and Doc Holliday (Arthur Kennedy), and representing an embarrassing malfunction of Ford's overgrown adolescent notion of comedy relief.

All in all, though one would like to praise the film for its high-minded aims, it is hard to forget how ponderous and disjointed it is.

Moira Walsh. *America*. Jan. 16, 1965, p. 85

Cheyenne Autumn, which was "suggested" by Mari Sandoz's book, is despite its Technicolor and Panavision 70 a pallid and straitened version of the best Ford, with no new visual ideas and, what is perhaps worse, fumbling use of the old ones—with a few labored interludes in which Ford tries to intensify some facts of daily life and a few incomplete flourishes of action. The acting is bad, the dialogue trite and predictable, the pace funereal, the structure fragmented, the climaxes puny. [1965]

Stanley Kauffmann. *A World on Film* (Harper, 1966), p. 169

John Ford himself doesn't bother going outdoors much anymore. A few years back I dragged a painter-friend to see *The Man Who Shot Liberty Valance*; it was a John Ford Western, and though I dreaded an evening with James Stewart and John Wayne, I felt I *should* see it. My friend agreed because "the landscapes are always great"; but after about ten minutes of ugly studio sets, he wanted to leave. . . . What those who believe in the perennial greatness of the Western may not have caught on to is that the new big Western is, likely as not, a studio-set job. What makes it a "Western" is no longer the wide open spaces but the presence of men like John Wayne, James Stewart, Henry Fonda, Robert Mitchum, Kirk Douglas, and Burt Lancaster, grinning with their big new choppers, sucking their guts up into their chests, and hauling themselves onto horses. They are the heroes of a new Western mythology; stars who have aged in the business, who have survived and who go on dragging their world-famous, expensive carcasses through the same old motions. That is the essence of their heroism and their legend. The new Western is a joke and the stars play it for laughs and the young film enthusiasts react to the heroes not because they represent the mythological heroes of the Old West but because they are mythological movie stars. An actor in his forties would be a mere stripling in a Western these days. Nor would he *belong* in these movies which derive their small, broad humor from the fact that the actors have been doing what they're doing so long that they're professional Westerners. Like Queen Victoria, John Wayne has become lovable because he stayed in the saddle into a new era.

Pauline Kael. *Kiss Kiss Bang Bang* (Little, Brown, 1968), p. 42

Every Ford movie is filled with reverberations from another—which makes his use of the same players from year to year, decade to decade, so much more than just building "a stock company"—and one film of his cannot really be looked at as separate from the rest. What Ma Joad says of her life (in *The Grapes of Wrath*) is true also of Ford's work: ". . . it's all one flow, like a stream, little eddies, little waterfalls, but the river it goes right on." Ranse and Hallie Stoddard (James Stewart and Vera Miles) return to Shinbone for the funeral of Tom Doniphon (John Wayne) at the start of *The Man Who Shot Liberty Valance*, and Hallie visits the ruins of Doniphon's ranch-house, where she picks a cactus rose, a wild flower symbolizing Doniphon's old West, which is as dead as he is. A haunting musical theme is heard during this scene, and when one realizes it is the same music Ford used after the death of Ann Rutledge in *Young Mr. Lincoln*, its meaning in *Liberty Valance* is heightened. For Ann Rutledge was the lost love of Lincoln's youth, just as Tom Doniphon is Hallie's.

Peter Bogdanovich. *John Ford* (California, 1968), pp. 31–32

The Man Who Shot Liberty Valance is a fascinating film, but a film whose fascination lies less in what it is in itself than in what it reveals about the art of its maker, John Ford. In itself, it is a sporadically imagined work; passages which are fully realized artistically alternating with others which merely point sketchily to what they might have been, with another cast, perhaps, or another budget, or in another time. And yet, in a curious way, the sight of a barrel-bellied, fifty-five-year-old John Wayne heaving himself onto a horse, hopelessly destructive as it is of any suspension of disbelief, does nevertheless evoke feelings which no then thirty-five-year-old actor could summon. At moments such as these and others played out in obvious sets and against painted backdrops, the film as an artistic creation is scarcely even pretended at; rather, the effect is of a lecture-demonstration, or an essay on the Western; a summing up. And it is as this—as a self-exegetical essay—that the film takes on its peculiar but real excitement—even those sets and backdrops charged with their special significance. Despite its bearing on his films before, nothing in John Ford's previous work could have quite prepared one for it, and, faced with the fact of its existence, the stock figure of John Ford, notoriously taciturn interviewee and putative "folk artist," will hardly stand up to further perpetuation. [1970]

William S. Pechter. *Twenty-four Times a Second* (Harper, 1971), pp. 226–27

John Ford is The Compleat Director (*Arrowsmith*, *The Informer*, *Stagecoach*, *The Grapes of Wrath*, *The Long Voyage Home*, *How Green Was My Valley*, *The Quiet Man*), the dean of directors—undoubtedly the greatest and most versatile in films. A megaphone has been to John Ford what the chisel was to Michelangelo: his life, his passion, his cross.

Ford cannot be pinned down or analyzed. He is pure Ford—which means pure great. John is half-tyrant, half-revolutionary; half-saint, half-satan; half-possible, half-impossible; half-genius, half-Irish—but *all* director and *all* American.

Frank Capra. *The Name Above the Title* (Macmillan, 1971), p. 246

FRANKENHEIMER, JOHN (1930–)

John Frankenheimer is the current phenomenon in Hollywood. Actors who have worked with him claim that he is the most brilliant director they have worked with both in films and in particular in television where he has built up an enviable reputation. In his film work so far there has been much to justify this acclaim: his handling of the delicate sensitivity of adolescence in *The Young Stranger* brought the whole "rebel" phase into perspective with the emphasis thrown onto the feelings and development of one individual without striving for sensational cinematic effect. On the other hand, sheer technique transformed *The Young Savages* from a B-grade *West Side Story*-theme, into a powerful, hard-hitting account of brutality and ignorance in the New York slums, the photography and editing executed with the savageness of a Leonard Bernstein score.

Again *All Fall Down* is essentially outstanding because of Frankenheimer's direction. He aims at a very high standard and as such has constructed a film which artistically is the most important achievement from Hollywood for a long time, moreso than Rossen's *The Hustler*. But I can't help feeling that the film pays a little too much attention to how the story is presented (which is nevertheless brilliant) and not enough on the content. But this is Inge's fault and not the director's.

Robin Bean. *Films and Filming*. June 1962, p. 38

Birdman of Alcatraz . . . is a tribute to the iconoclastic courage needed to break the mold of the normal prison film dramas. As the dramatization of the record of an inmate rare, if not unique, in the annals of American penology, it leaves part of the picture in shadow, but it is, nevertheless, a thoughtful yet powerful portrait that cleaves to the heart and mind despite its omissions. Like Oscar Wilde's prisoner of Reading Gaol, this "Birdman" stirs the emotions and remains in memory. . . .

Mr. Frankenheimer's direction concentrates on the development of his hero, a glum, seemingly unregenerate lifer, saved from death by the pleas of his mother to Mrs. Woodrow Wilson, into a self-made scientific researcher and a man whose existence thereby took on meaning and substance. The direction and Mr. Lancaster's acting are notable for realism, nuance and restraint. A viewer is prone to believe that the fledgling sparrow he finds as he takes his lonely exercise will move this stony-hearted jailbird out of his despair.

A. H. Weiler. *NYT*. July 19, 1962, p. 19

Seven Days in May is like *Rigoletto* with Tucker, Merrill, and Peters; like a good, *early* Bernard Buffet; like an adequate red wine. It is to be enjoyed without feelings of guilt, there should be more movies like it, and it has nothing first-class about it.

Consider the scene at the beginning where a minor riot breaks out in front of the White House. Had it been directed by Otto Preminger (*vide The Cardinal*), it would have emerged prerehearsed, grandly violent but tidy: tourist-folder photography—if there were tourist folders inviting us to come to exotic Vietnam and see the glorious fighting. Had it been directed by Stanley Kubrick (*vide Dr. Strangelove*), it would have had a spontaneous, unnerving, newsreel quality, unspectacular but cruelly effective. It is, however, directed by John Frankenheimer and partakes of both modes.

True, it uses a hand camera; has movement that, though carefully calculated, seems random and disorganized; and, best of all, has a nice rhythm to it with just the right amount of gradual acceleration. Nonetheless, there are also slick camera angles, tricky panning shots, and rather sly cutting. Not that such devices are fundamentally wrong; they are merely out of place in such a nastily vulgar context.

Other virtues of the film are similarly ambiguous. This is the story of a military junta which is about to take over our government. An upstanding, sharp young colonel stumbles on the truth in the nick of time, tips off the aging and tired but able and right-thinking President and a band of his trusty aides, and together they foil the devilishly clever, Right-wing conspiracy. Its head is none other than the hero's venerated chief: a brilliant general, but, as it turns out, a fanatic. [1964]

John Simon. *Private Screenings* (Macmillan, 1967), p. 110

The film [*The Train*] that director John Frankenheimer has assembled around this [Resistance] incident is extraordinarily good in many of its parts but rather disappointing as a whole. Its greatest virtue is an almost overpowering physical realism. . . .

What the film does not seem to do is to get far enough back from its material so that we see it in perspective and react to it as a whole.

For example, we are frequently confused and left unconvinced by stratagems of the Resistance for which we were not given enough preparation. Then too, Paul Scofield, as the cultivated but inhuman Nazi colonel/art thief, is not an adequate personification of the adversary, though this is not the fault of his performance. . . .

Frankenheimer really does not have a sufficiently cohesive over-all esthetic. Hence we find him sometimes using his creative flair for cinema visuals to no good purpose. When the camera cuts from the good guys engaged in sabotage to the bad guys staring intently, the obvious implication is that the clandestine act is being detected. Frankenheimer employs this device several times simply as a suspense gimmick when the juxaposition has no integral justification.

When all this has been said, however, the film is worth seeing for its many incidental virtues, not the least of which is the awed honesty with which it asks, but does not answer, the question: was this sacrifice justified?

Moira Walsh. *America.* April 3, 1965, p. 466

Seconds is John Frankenheimer's eighth production and his seventh in six years. But the film does more than prove that he has been busy. It provides the most complete and effective definition of his recurrent themes and techniques and, I think, clearly establishes him (along with Stanley Kubrick) as the most important and distinctive of the new independent Hollywood directors who are trying to build their careers and art on the often shaky bridge between commercial success and personal, artistic statement. It is a work that once again reveals the basic problem of this development in the American film and goes further than any of Frankenheimer's others in solving it. . . .

The course, and results, of such internal warfare in a director's work can be traced (and with an encouraging sense of progress) in the eight films of Frankenheimer. The sequence of his films shows how even under varying commercial circumstances a director can still manage to choose materials that he can shape into a unified and developing set of personal themes and concerns and how he can also move toward a way of working with those materials and themes that is clearly his own.

Frankenheimer's chief thematic concerns are not, in themselves, unique; but he has done more with them than have his contemporaries. His point of departure is the kind of social criticism that is the common approach to meaning in the serious American film, but even here he has not been concerned with specific social problems only, but with the broader effects of social environment and values of the individual. His criticism of contemporary social values and structures involves the now traditional terms of the materialization of modern life, with its parallel mechanization in both technology and personality, the valuing of things by men who have become things themselves. But he has gone beyond the common oversimplications of the social problem film by dramatizing the personal side of the equation as well—what is involved in the loss of self that is not only a victimized stealing of self by the authoritarianisms of society, but a giving away of self (in various forms including fanaticism) by the individual.

Alan Casty. *Film Heritage.* Winter 1966–67, pp. 21, 23

Frankenheimer (known for the macabre *Manchurian Candidate*) is a master at controlling the explosive elements of an action film. In *The Train* he has done wonderful things with his main prop, the steam locomotive. He seems to have sensed the basic appeal that steam locomotives have for most people and he has exploited it superbly. The shots of trains rolling, blowing up or just lurking menacingly are intriguing. There is a distinct animism in his conception. Then, he has managed to give the entire film (in black and white) a kind of hard glint that is suggestive of a newsreel. The tints are so severe that the film looks more like documentary footage than a feature film during the action sequences. The effect is engrossing and contributes to the verisimilitude and dramatic intensity of the movie. If it lacks anything, it is a multi-level consideration of the men involved, such as we have in John Sturges' *The Great Escape*, but that obviously isn't Frankenheimer's immediate concern. The almost oppressive reality of all of the massive machinery may be the most accurate psychological commentary on the moods of war that we have ever had on the screen.

Leon Lewis and W. D. Sherman. *Landscape of Contemporary Cinema* (Buffalo Spectrum, 1967), pp. 51–52

The Fixer—or at least the hour and a half I could abide of it—is worse than ludicrous; it is repellent. It is odd that this should be so. Bernard Malamud's novel about the Jew falsely accused of ritual murder in imperial Russia was strong and serious. John Frankenheimer has shown brilliant narrative control and drive in other films. The cast (Alan Bates, Dirk Bogarde, Hugh Griffith, David Warner) is good. But everything has gone wrong. It was a mistake, I think, to shoot a sombre tale like this in cheerful colour; nor did making it in Hungary bring it closer to Kiev than if it had been made in Culver City. The medley of accents—Cockney, BBC, East Side New York, Eastern European—is distracting. The confusion of tone is even worse.

The film begins with a thunderous scene of a pogrom shot in

Frankenheimer's best bravura style. Suddenly the mood shifts to *Fiddler on the Roof*—gentle ghetto tailors uttering aphorisms; the hero speaking a Jacobowsky-like soliloquy while pondering whether or not to sleep with a Russian girl. Then a child is found murdered; the hero is arrested; and the rest of the film, as far as I could endure it, is beatings, torture, degradation, and fairly unrelieved sadism.

The Fixer is made with evident contempt for its audience. The screenplay, by that old Popular Front hack Dalton Trumbo, mingles sentimental cliché, sententious non-profundities, fake social concern, and a prurient relish in violence. This is a totally false film, devoid of a breath of human life or truth.

Arthur Schlesinger, Jr. *Vogue*. Dec. 1968, p. 180

Alan Bates deserves major credit [in *The Fixer*] for making this overpowering lead role believable. Yakov is a simple man without interest in religion or politics; but Bates succeeds in making him a man of some intelligence, a man of great spirit and will to survive. Director John Frankenheimer rates applause, too, for Bates' strong and sensitive performance and for many of the other good portraits done by the large cast. . . . The variety of English accents didn't bother me, but I do wish the script, written by Dalton Trumbo from Bernard Malamud's novel, were stronger and on a higher level for such worthy subject matter. . . .

My only real row with the picture is in the repeated scenes of the brutalities suffered by Yakov in prison. No doubt some of these are necessary to convey the man's determination to survive and prove his innocence. But director Frankenheimer and scriptwriter Trumbo seem to forget that our reading about man's inhumanity to man in Malamud is quite different from seeing it visualized in the realistic cinema medium. What *we* mustn't forget, however, is that *The Fixer* is based on an actual case from history. Perhaps if man is going to rise above his worst behavior, we must not avert our eyes from this behavior. As a hymn celebrating the survival of the human spirit, *The Fixer* is in a class by itself. It ends with: "The name is Yakov Bok, an innocent man, a Jew, also your brother."

Philip T. Hartung. *Commonweal*.
Dec. 27, 1968, p. 442

The Gypsy Moths represents a further development of Frankenheimer's thoughts and feelings about society and the individual, and once again he moves in an entirely different direction from his previous films. The outwardly slight story is a study in existential pessimism, of characters who deliberately challenge and play with death in the air and of those who live out the drab years of "the living death" on the ground. Taking the short, terse novel by James Drought as its basis, Frankenheimer and his writer followed the events and created the same characters as those in the book, but in the realisation of the screenplay in visual terms, the director has come closer than any other American film-maker to creating (without imitation) a Bergmanesque world of inner emotions and ambiguous means. . . .

Frankenheimer's technique, as expected, is superbly appropriate to his theme. He never coarsens his characters, no matter how low they fall in life. . . . These people are not monsters, and Frankenheimer's restraint is everywhere apparent: in the performances, in the love scenes, in the moment of violence, in Rettig's death . . . and his people are firmly rooted in their day-by-day existence, and not, as so often in Bergman, in places that seem to exist outside our known society. The location shooting around the town, at the air field, convey the very feel and smell and dust of the place, and his interiors once again, are masterly, with the sense of being lived in, and dark with the shadows of years. The colours are sombre inside, the right touch of brightness outside. As in many of Frankenheimer's films it rains, and the wind in the trees in the park and the sound of traffic all contribute to the realism that make his work, among other factors, so satisfying.

Gerald Pratley. *The Cinema of John Frankenheimer* (Barnes, 1969), pp. 193, 198

Competent, professional American directors are generally at their worst when they become serious and ambitious; when they reach for mighty themes, they fall for banalities. They become clods who think they can turn into important artists by the simple expedient of not being entertaining. John Frankenheimer's *The Fixer* crawls along on its intentions, and will no doubt be revered by those who believe that movies are being elevated when a picture is based on a prestige-laden prize-winning novel with a "universal" theme. Frankenheimer, who has demonstrated a talent for pace and pyrotechnics, for melodramatic suspense and showmanship (in *The Manchurian Candidate,* and even when working with less in *Seven Days in May*) abandons the skills he has, and trusts in his new nobility to carry him through. One would think that Frankenheimer, who was confined to a cell for *Bird Man of Alcatraz,* would avoid being trapped again, but he's more heavily shackled than his hero. He forgets how to stage the simplest actions. A book that won both the Pulitzer Prize and the National Book Award, that has a pre-revolutionary Russian setting and a Jewish hero falsely accused of crime, a man who refuses to confess and becomes a symbol of human dignity—what a set of chains! Do all the directors in Hollywood long to become respectable in the eyes of their old high-school English teachers? Does each have to make his own version of *The Life of Emile Zola*? Don't they know what a drag it was? . . .

Frankenheimer is apparently so sure that exaltation will take place that he doesn't cover his bets by developing any other possible sources of interest; the movie is unrelieved suffering. Borrowed grandeur can make a movie look awfully seedy (and in Malamud the grandeur was maybe already a little tattered). The movie of *The Fixer* flogs you—not because you're watching a man being beaten and tormented but because you're seeing an incompetent movie about a man being beaten and tormented. In the opening pogrom sequence—a try for power and intensity like Eisenstein's and Kurosawa's—when Frankenheimer does go in for pyrotechnics, he demonstrates only that his are inadequate for "serious," "epic" material. For the rest of the movie, his staging and handling of the actors are almost incomprehensibly solemn and inept, unless one recalls other Hollywood essays in sublimity. . . .

Pauline Kael. *Going Steady* (Little, Brown, 1970), pp. 209–10

GRIFFITH, D. W. (1875–1948)

Nursing a Viper (Biograph, Nov. 4).—The astonishing strength and power of this subject makes it one of the most notable ever produced by any company, American or foreign, although there are those who may hold that it is too powerful in some of its most gruesome details. Certain it is that a few feet of film at different points in the action might have been omitted without injury to the story, thus escaping possible complaint. The time of the story is placed at the opening of the first French revolution, when the half-starved peasantry broke out in indescribable savagery against the hated aristocrats. . . . Evidently the producer was fearful that he might not get his atmosphere of horror strong enough without showing many of the most brutal details, but in this he was mistaken. The actual murders and the carrying of a woman's head about on a pike pole might have been cut out and there would still have been ample atmosphere left for all necessary purposes. The dividing line where brutal details in a picture should cease is a difficult one to determine. A number of great pictures, such as Pathé's *La Tosca* have depicted scenes of horror with dangerous fidelity and have escaped without much, if any, complaint, it being held that the nature of the subjects warranted the extremity of realism. In the present subject it must be admitted that there is ample basis in history for all the details shown and much more, but at the same time it is *The Mirror*'s opinion that for general circulation in picture houses films depicting scenes of this character should be managed with careful discretion.

NYDM. Nov. 13, 1909, p. 16

The Birth of a Nation, an elaborate new motion picture taken on an ambitious scale, was presented for the first time last evening at the Liberty Theatre. With the addition of much preliminary historical matter, it is a film version of some of the melodramatic and inflammatory material contained in *The Clansman*, by Thomas Dixon.

A great deal might be said concerning the spirit revealed in Mr. Dixon's review of the unhappy chapter of Reconstruction and concerning the sorry service rendered by its plucking at old wounds. But of the film as a film, it may be reported simply that it is an impressive new illustration of the scope of the motion picture camera.

An extraordinarily large number of people enter into this historical pageant, and some of the scenes are most effective. The civil war battle pictures, taken in panorama, represent enormous effort and achieve a striking degree of success. One interesting scene stages a reproduction of the auditorium of Ford's Theatre in Washington, and shows on the screen the murder of Lincoln. In terms of purely pictorial value the best work is done in those stretches of the film that follow the night riding of the men of the Ku-Klux Klan, who look like a company of avenging spectral crusaders sweeping along the moonlit roads.

The Birth of a Nation, which was prepared for the screen under the direction of D. W. Griffith, takes a full evening for its unfolding and marks the advent of the two dollar movie. That is the price set for the more advantageous seats in the rear of the Liberty's auditorium.

It was at this same theatre that the stage version of *The Clansman* had a brief run a little more than nine years ago, as Mr. Dixon himself recalled in his curtain speech last evening in the interval between the two acts. Mr. Dixon also observed that he would have allowed none but the son of a Confederate soldier to direct the film version of *The Clansman*.

NYT. March 4, 1915, p. 9

People have spoken of Griffith's alleged "sheer sensationalism" in his plot [for *Intolerance*] in which he shows four periods of time conversing with one another. But jumping back and forth over barriers of time is the most accepted thing in the photoplay hurdle-race. You have seen films where the hero has visions of his childhood to urge him on to doughty deeds. Three scenes of the past alternate with three scenes of today in his thoughts, that the comparison may be rousing. The heroine has visions of her two possible futures if she chooses the prunes on the one hand or the peaches on the other. And as to jumping over geographical spaces, the photoplay dialogue that technically replaces the old stage interchange of words is a conversation between places, not individuals. In a moonshiner drama that I saw last week the director alternated between the cabin in the field, the revenue detectives on the road and the still on the hillside. We were given a conversation between these units. One picture, guns, horses, detectives and all seemed to be calling, "We are coming." Another picture, the still, the bushes and the hillside seemed to be answering: "We are hiding yet." The picture of the cabin, the field and the young moonshiners seemed to say: "We suspect nothing, but are on guard on general principals." Round and round this conversation progresses as the pictures alternate, till the still is finally destroyed, and the cabin besieged and taken.

The principle holds good, no matter how lofty the theme, or how far apart the places in the dialogue may be in time or geographical distance. In Griffith's *Intolerance*, Babylon is shown signalling across the ages to Judea, and there is many a message that is not printed out on the films or put into the apparently explicitly publicity matter. And in like manner the days of St. Bartholomew and of the crucifixion signal back to Babylon sharp or vague or subtle messages. The little factory couple in the modern street scene called The Dear One and The Boy, seem to wave their hands back to Babylon amid the orchestration of ancient memories. The ages make a resonance behind their simple plans and terrible perplexities. The usual shallowness of appeal of private griefs and loves as shown in the most painstaking intimate films, their inability to arouse complete responding passion in the audience, is thus remedied. The modern story is made vibrant by the power of whirling crowds from the streets of Time. The key hieroglyphic is the cradle of humanity, eternally rocking. This photoplay is given power not by straining for depth of passion, but depth of what might be called tableau-emotion, a much more elusive thing.

Vachel Lindsay. *The New Republic.*
Feb. 17, 1917, pp. 76–77

The punch of this latest David Griffith picture [*The Greatest Thing in Life*] seems to be in his ability to have Germans break down doors effectively, instead of using situations that break down the door of a person's heart. In producing another war picture Griffith does nothing big or unusual to justify our confidence in his being the greatest director. The most daring moment of this new production is when the white soldier and the negro soldier seek refuge in the same shell hole, showing the kindness of the negro and the breaking down of the white's prejudice. Little Lillian Gish is shown to beautiful advantage in three or four close-ups of a new type which idealize her expression. The rest of the time she jumps "ingenuishly" all over the place. The charm of Lillian is a very poignant thing and should not be tampered with in this manner, no matter how great the director. Fortunately we still have memories of her sanity and dignity in *The Lily and the Rose*. . . .

Hazel Simpson Naylor. *Motion Picture Magazine*. March 1919, p. 73

A time will come and that very soon, when tragedy and comedy alike will come to have to be specially constructed to suit the special needs of the screen, and in *Broken Blossoms* Mr. Griffith has given us an idea of the lines upon which film tragedy can properly be developed. There is no question here of happy endings or conventional situations. It is obvious that a note of sheer tragedy must be struck from part to part; if it is departed from for an instant the whole effect must be lost. And so there is not a moment of comedy or of laughter. It is the skill of Mr. Griffith that makes the gradual evolution of the tragedy inevitable. Readers of Mr. Thomas Burke's grim collection of stories *Limehouse Nights* will remember the tale of "The Chink and the Girl" . . . It is this story which Mr. Griffith has used as the basis of his film. He has developed it, of course, but in the main, it follows the original with commendable care. . . .

While he was making alterations we are surprised that Mr. Griffith did not also take his courage in his hands and eliminate the Limehouse note. For this is a Limehouse which neither Mr. Burke nor any other man who knows his East-end of London will be able to recognize. It may be a very good impression of an American producer's idea of Limehouse, but it is nothing more, and it might be well before the picture is publically shown to lay the action in an imaginary Chinatown concerning which an audience cannot be critical. . . . From an English point of view *Broken Blossoms* has its defects, but it is a genuine attempt to bring real tragedy on to the screen as apart from machine-made drama, and for that Mr. Griffith deserves the gratitude of all who are convinced of the potentialities of the film.

LT. Jan. 23, 1920

No great art, no healthy influence, no bright horizon, can ever be built on lies. Mack Sennett horseplay leads to oblivion.

I cannot bring myself to believe that Griffith doesn't know this. Hitherto, his greatest claim to real greatness has been the inherent *truth* of his work, the fidelity of his characters to life. But the grotesque caricatures that give "comic" relief to *Way Down East* can no more be compared to, for instance, The Little Disturber in *Hearts of the World*, than mud to marble. . . .

To tell a story *above the heads* of an average audience—as with *Intolerance*—may be part foolishness, but savors of nobility; to tell it *beneath* the intelligence of that same average is—unworthy of a real leader.

Be sure to see *Way Down East*. It has superlative artistry of scene and action. Lillian Gish never did finer work. New color effects continue the best Griffith traditions of continental innovation. And in the tense river scenes the great producer "pulls a Griffith" that probably out-ranks anything he has never done.

But prepare, even at that, to be disappointed. Griffith is grabbing for Mack Sennett's crown, and the whole movies world is the loser.

Myron M. Stearns. *Judge*. Oct. 2, 1920, p. 20

The story of *Way Down East* is too familiar to need complete retelling. It is, in its way, a classic of American rural life and is almost as widely known as *The Old Homestead* or *Uncle Tom's Cabin.* There is a real and unaffected poignancy about the betrayal of a young and ignorant girl by a sophisticated seducer which can easily be brought home to vast audiences. Here the moving picture has the advantage over the play. For photoplay art has resources which permit it to soften the crassness of melodrama and to disguise its shopworn qualities. The silent drama leaves our imagination more free, and the girl's misery, which is none the less real for being one of the oldest stories in the world, can still be brought to us with artistic freshness. . . .

Mr. Griffith could be depended upon for bringing out the full pathos of Anna's tragedy. His genius for this sort of thing has always been great. And, as usual, he has had the advantage of Miss Lillian Gish's unlimited cooperation. It is a truly astonishing thing about this young artist that one can always say that her latest work is her best. One wonders how high she can still climb on the ladder of superb screen acting. Or perhaps it is a question of how far Mr. Griffith and Miss Gish could go together, for it is often impossible to tell in their work where direction ends and interpretation begins. The rest of Mr. Griffith's cast is, as usual, well balanced, and shows some fine individual work.

NBR. Dec. 1920

Dream Street is no mythical locality but a portion of the Limehouse District of London, and the doings of the characters in this D. W. Griffith production are of the regulation every-day order that will hit the popular taste, in spite of the fact that the eminent producer has worked in considerable symbolism and an entirely unnecessary close-up of the mouth of hell. The story itself is as elemental and emotional as could well be imagined. It skirts the edge of tragedy, glides nimbly away and lands the hero and heroine in the lap of luxury, with fine clothes and star contracts and a baby daughter who will start the ohs and ahs and "Isn't she cute!" from every feminine patron in the audience.

Edward Weitzel. *Moving Picture World.*
April 23, 1921, p. 876

It is from the "whole" as signed by Griffith that comes the admiration he merits. There are scenarios of which the best that can be said is that "they contain some beautiful pictures." *Broken Blossoms* would have been acceptable if that was the only compliment one could give it! But in addition to all these skills, wasn't something else necessary to bring out the beauty of these cardboard characters? . . .

The childishness of the scene with the doll—the imagery is a dangerous one, given our blasé tastes—was bathed in reflections in which the real disappeared, in the idealism of a silvery halo swirling around people and things. Dazzled, we were obliged to put our hands before our eyes and veil our real sensibility; was it the light or the drama that made our eyes swell with tears? The magic that followed overcame our sneaky skepticism. . . .

Poem of silence and of light; nothing moved on the screen and all was understood—virginal, decent, human.

The same boldness is found in *True Heart Susie*; it would take too long to discuss it in detail; it is the same spirit that from one end to the other wrote the first cinematographic novel, that first picture book of which the screen can be proud.

There is so much gentleness and so little brutality in Griffith's talent that he made a very bad film on the war.

Cardboard bombs! Drunken Germans! the caricature of a tragedy whose only excuse is the brutally cruel touch of truth.

Griffith is a good storyteller who cannot use the sonorous adjectives of epics.

Intolerance was the most beautiful of his efforts, and the least successful because of this.

In him, cruelty is attenuated by taste. He portrays it without joy, without probing, making of it only what others could.

It is with a cradle, the prayer of a priest, that in one swift image redeems all that the noisy reconstitutions wasted in effort, in bad taste, and in errors.

Let Griffith leave all that to those who have only paroxysms with which to achieve an effect. His efforts most be more discreet, therefore more real.

It's childish to give him a medal, a title, a paper crown. He is one of those whose inner satisfaction is his reward.

Harry Baur. *Le Crapouillot.* March 16, 1922, pp. 19–20

The many fine things D. W. has done into celluloid, the mechanical and art improvements he has given the silent drama in years gone by, can never be taken from him, but I fear we must now look to other minds for the future advancement of the motion-play. It is not that his recent films such as *Way Down East*, *Orphans of the Storm* and *One Exciting Night* are not entertaining, but there is nothing about them to mark the producer as the leading light of the flicker art. Like Irving Cobb with his pen, Griffith still has genius to take a stale and ordinary tale and dress it up in such shape as to make it at least an interesting item.

D. W. cannot seem to get away from the situation of the attacking, raping or wronging of the defenseless girl. He places full reliance in this piece of mechanics as the most effective in existence, as is proven by the fact that he hardly ever attempts to make a screen story without it. *The Birth of A Nation*, *Intolerance*, *Scarlet Days*, *Orphans of the Storm*, *Hearts of the World*, *Way Down East*, *The Idol Dancer*, *The Great Question*, *Dream Street* all featured scenes of this nature. In fact, analyzation of almost any Griffith opus will show that it is composed for the most part of an appeal to the sensual instincts. He has also developed the tendency of many of the other big directors to exaggerate and over emphasize incidents to get them across to the spectator. Especially in comedy touches is this evident with the supervising fraternity. Working on the basis that every photoplay should have some comedy relief, many directors, unable to work it in smoothly and logically, drag far fetched bits of slapstick humor in by the heels. In this respect Griffith is one of the worst offenders, as witness his *Orphans of the Storm* wherein he had soldiers sticking swords into the rear end of fat women and another character wielding a comedy butcher's cleaver of which even Mack Sennett would think twice before using.

Tamar Lane. *What's Wrong with the Movies*
(Waverly, 1923), pp. 62–64

I am sure that I shall speak of an experience that came to a large number of Americans, who had given up the movies as hopeless, when I say that *The Birth of a Nation* revived in me the conviction that the screen has before it a great future, a splendid mission, a message to deliver to humanity that may atone eventually for its juvenile sins of omission and commission. For the first time, so far as I was concerned, the Griffith picture revealed to me a fact, of which I had been vaguely conscious, that the screen was not inherently a medium for pandering to the grossest passions in human nature, for visualizing merely the social phenomena that years ago gave to Jack Karkaway stories and the *Police Gazette* their vogue.

Edward S. Van Zile. *That Marvel—The Movie*
(Putnam, 1923), pp. 74–75

Every new production coming from the David Wark Griffith studios has unusual significance. One can never tell when Griffith may cast aside hokum and become the celluloid adventurer of old. The usual suspense preceded this new production, *The White Rose*, but disappointment was manifest. There is the usual wronged girl, moving through a maze of beautiful photography, awful comedy and absurd sub-titles. This time the wronged girl is superbly played by Mae Marsh —and here alone the production reaches its height. Miss Marsh has several moments when she comes close to silver screen greatness. We are not sure but that she touches it.

Say what one may about *The White Rose,* it is not possible honestly to suppress one's conviction that this sort of stuff is a complete waste of the genius of the man who could make *The Birth of a Nation, Intolerance,* and *Broken Blossoms.*

Photoplay. Aug. 1923, p. 64

It is a hard thing to say, but it is literally true that something in Mr Griffith has been corrupted and died—his imagination. *Broken Blossoms* was a last expiring flicker. Since then he has constructed well; I understand that his success has been great; I am not denying that Mr Griffith is the man to do *Ben-Hur*. But he has imagined nothing on a grand scale, nor has he created anything delicate or fine. People talk of *The Birth* as if the battle scenes were important; they were very good and a credit to Griffith, who directed, and to George Bitzer, who photographed them; the direction of the ride of the Klansmen was better, it had some imagination. And far better still was a moment earlier in the piece, when Walthall returned to the shattered Confederate home and Mae Marsh met him at the door, wearing raw cotton smudged to resemble ermine—brother and sister both pretending that they had forgotten their dead, that they didn't care what happened. And then—for the honours of the scene went to Griffith, not even to the exquisite Mae Marsh—then there appeared from within the doorway the arm of their mother and with a gesture of unutterable loveliness it enlaced the boy's shoulders and drew him tenderly into the house. To have omitted the tears, to have shown nothing but the arm in that single curve of beauty, required, in those days, high imagination. It was the emotional climax of the film; one felt from that moment that the rape and death of the little girl was already understood in the vast suffering sympathy of the mother. So much Mr Griffith never again accomplished; it was the one moment when he stood beside Chaplin as a creative artist—and it was ten years ago. [1924]

Gilbert Seldes. *The Seven Lively Arts*
(Sagamore, 1957, rev.), p. 283

His development has followed a peculiar line, which, it seems to me, is a line which all directors of personality and talent are likely to be forced to follow. Griffith, that is, was the great creative mind on the direction side of picture-making in the early days. He established himself in the public mind; he made great pictures such as *Judith of Bethulia*, *The Birth of a Nation*, *Broken Blossoms*, *Intolerance*. Then he began to repeat his faults, and not merely fail to acquire new virtues, but even to lose grasp on those which he had. He seemed to have been overcome by his own success: he seemed to have lost that aptitude for curiosity and for experiment which is the first necessity of the actual maker of films. He began making pictures which were worse and worse. His *America* and *Isn't Life Wonderful*? were not merely bad: they were boring. . . . Griffith, I feel sure, hadn't when he made *Isn't Life Wonderful*? seen any film for five or six years. That is to say, he may have physically seen them, but they had meant nothing to him. He knew he was a great director. He didn't think he had anything to learn from anyone. He didn't learn anything. He remained in technique, and in his judgment of what the public wanted, exactly where he had been at the moment of his greatest success (though one must admit in justice that *One Exciting Night*, a ghastly bad film, was, from a financial point of view, one of the most successful he ever made). It was not until he became the servant of others, it was not until he joined that unparalleled film organization on Long Island, not until he was given a story and told to make the best film he could out of it, that Griffith pulled himself together and made films as films are made today. It is true his *Sally of the Sawdust* was melodrama mingled with farce. It is true that it was a little crude in places and a little sloppy in others; but it was a picture that moved the audience, which made it laugh and cry, and, what is more, a picture which brought to the cinema a new and highly talented comedian in the person of W. C. Fields, long of the Ziegfeld Follies.

Iris Barry. *Let's Go to the Movies* (Payson & Clarke, 1926), pp. 223–24

In Griffith we see what Pudovkin might have been in America 1910–1930. In Pudovkin we see what Griffith might have been in the U.S.S.R. Griffith, possessing social sympathies, expressed these in platitudes on "tolerance" and "free speech," and read his American history in terms of *The Clansman* (the Ku Klux Klan and the Confederacy, in whose army his father was a General), and in the terms of the crudest Lincoln myths. His films in the past have been innocuous idylls and grandiose panoramas, allowing his distinction for his instincts of composition [*Abraham*] *Lincoln* has everything of the sentimentally idyllic, and nothing of the grandiose. It is an unintelligent Drinkwater chronicle-play on the screen, despite Stephen Vincent Benet's hand in the scenario (why "despite?"). The fact that it draws tears is rather against it than for it. The pathos of a tremendous social occurrence should not be refined or lachrymose, but revealing. The social occurrence seldom gets a chance here. Slogans of spurious manufacture explain the motivations of the Civil War.

Harry Alan Potamkin. *New Masses*. Oct. 1930, p. 16

In making *Abraham Lincoln* Mr. Griffith, a director whose excellencies have often been marred by his extravagances, was fortunately aware of the restrictions which his subject imposed upon him. He has gone back to the true and historical sources of the life of Lincoln, aided greatly by the vivid and gripping interpretation of Stephen Vincent Benet.

The early incidences of Lincoln's life and upbringing are truthfully portrayed and his pathetic romance with Ann Rutledge is sympathetically depicted. The debate with Douglas is emphasized with due regard to its historical importance and to the part it played in making Lincoln a presidential candidate. The major issues which this debate involved, the freeing of the slaves and the question of the inviolability of the Union, are skillfully stressed by Lincoln's well-pointed refutations of Douglas' arguments. The technical handling of this sequence is particularly noteworthy. . . .

It is only fair to say that the picture as a whole was made with a judicious regard for the susceptibilities of Southern audiences. General Lee is, of course, nobly portrayed by Mr. Hobart Bosworth and the stirring episode of Sheridan's ride is dramatically set forth. But none of the real horrors and deprivations of the war, the gradual wearing down of the South and its economic ruination are dwelt upon at all. Sherman's march to the sea is significantly omitted. As a matter of fact, the entire war is treated as a side light, it is the tragic background inevitable in a picturization of the President who remained unmoved in his determination to preserve the Union at all costs. This is in strange contrast to the present day realism which characterizes the depiction of the world war.

NBR. Oct. 1930, p. 10

Griffith has made *Abraham Lincoln*, with all he has in it, and it brings to us—with a curious finality of disappointment, a sentimental sense of the closing of a chapter—the impression of a director who has nowhere made a valid contact with the conditions of the screen today. There is nothing careless or haphazard about its construction; Griffith has laboured mightily, has worked for it, fought for it—indeed, the sense of tussle is still heavy in it—and brought to it every accent of his patriotic sincerity and every focus of his technical skill. *Lincoln* is the fruit of thought and endeavour; it recalls much of the faith of *The Birth of a Nation* and the eager search of *Intolerance* after pregnant device. But it is not a film. It has nothing in it of the creative cinema. Griffith, conscientiously discarding his silent method, has gone back to his technical beginnings and tried to re-create again with sound as an integral factor. But he has not gone back far enough, not right back into thought; he still conceives in silence while he executes in sound: the eye image comes first, the ear image seems a reluctant concession to the modern machine. The film falls into a series of disconnected dialogues, duplicating vision and heard through the missing fourth wall of the theatre; so fragmentary that the very disruption forms something in the nature of a unity. The scenes are unrounded and unresolved; the old parabola of moving image has gone, the old excitement of dovetailed sequences sacrificed to the formality of the sentence, but there has never been a thought of working *from* sound, shaping it, hammering its natural values to any desired end.

C. A. Lejeune. *Cinema* (Alexander Maclehose, 1931), pp. 40–41

If Griffith foreshadows the Russians in technique, he anticipates them even more strikingly in the subject matter he chooses and the way he treats it. His *Birth of a Nation* (1915) and *Intolerance* (1916) are the first movies to make use of the *extensive* powers of the cinema. They are the first movies conceived on such a scale that the individuals are less important than the vast background of time and space against which they move. Griffith treats his epic subjects as Eisenstein does, not as historical narratives running through time but as cinematizations in space of abstract themes. He shapes them primarily to express an *idea* ("War is terrible," "Through the ages love and intolerance have been at strife") to which the story is subordinated as a mere allegory. Hence the point of view of *The Birth of a Nation* is as one-sided as is that of *Ten Days That Shook the World*. Both films are propaganda, with Negroes as the villains and southerners as the heroes in one as against the same relationship between bourgeois and workers in the other. . . .

Griffith is a typically American product. He is to the cinema what Edison is to science: a practical genius who can make things work but who is not interested in "theory," i.e., the general laws that govern his achievements. Although his intuitive sense of cinema grasped the essentials of movie technique long before the Russians, he never really understood what he had discovered—which accounts for his not developing montage beyond the see-saw stage used in his finales, and for the fact that his latest picture, *Lincoln*, is less interesting technically than *The Birth of a Nation*. A few years of analysis, of comparing notes, of thinking about cinematic theory, and the Russians carried Griffith's discoveries far beyond anything he himself has done. During the past ten years Griffith has gone to seed with a thoroughness possible only to the American artist. . . . [1931]

Dwight Macdonald. *D. M. on Movies* (Prentice-Hall, 1969), pp. 70, 72

Griffith announced his film as "a drama of comparisons." And that is what *Intolerance* remains—a drama of comparisons, rather than *a unified, powerful, generalized image.*

Here is the same defect again: an inability to abstract a phenomenon, without which it cannot expand beyond the *narrowly representational.* For this reason we could not resolve any "*supra*-representational," "conveying" (metaphorical) tasks.

Only by dividing "hot" from a *thermometer reading* may one speak of "a sense of heat." Only by abstracting "deep" from *meters and fathoms* may one speak of "a sense of depth." Only by disengaging "falling" from *the formula of the accelerated speed of a falling body* ($mv^2/2$) may one speak of "a sensation of falling!"

However, the failure of *Intolerance* to achieve a true "mingling" lies also in another circumstance: the four episodes chosen by Griffith are actually un-collatable. The *formal failure* of their mingling in *a single image* of *Intolerance* is only *a reflection of a thematic and ideological error. . . .*

It is not that representation cannot be raised with correct presentation and treatment to the structure of metaphor, simile, image. Nor is it that Griffith here altered his method, or his professional craftsmanship. But that he made no attempt at a genuinely thoughtful abstraction of phenomena—at *an extraction of generalized conclusions* on historical phenomena from a wide variety of historical data; this is the core of the fault. [1944]

Sergei Eisenstein. *Film Form* (Harcourt, 1949), pp. 243–44

Again, *One Million B.C.* (1940), which was partly the work of D. W. Griffith, was almost laughed at by the critics who regarded it as being on the same level as a Buck Rogers fantasy. Yet it was distinguished by a serious anthropological approach and stunning cinematic craftsmanship. Two sequences in particular—the death of the dinosaur with the detail shots and the overlapping cutting showing the streams of blood flowing into the sunbaked earth and the labored breathing of the dying beast, and the climactic conflict between the cavemen and the prehistoric monster—are models of constructive editing, worthy of comparison with Griffith's best.

The tendency to condemn American films indiscriminately, and to regard European productions as superior *per se*, is the opposite of sound criticism. It is an approach based upon ignorance, and reveals the absence of true cinematic perception. The serious film-goer should approach movies free of the preconceptions which are akin to prejudice.

Joseph and Harry Feldman. *Films in Review.* April 1951, p. 22

D. W. Griffith made his first radical innovation in a now lost film, *For Love of Gold*, 1909, when he departed from the old "one scene—one shot" method by demanding a change of camera position in the middle of a scene. In moving the camera closer to the actors, he had invented the "full shot," in which only the upper half of the player's body was shown. Biograph was shocked; the studio managers believed people would think the camera work amateurish and that this scene had been included in the film by mistake. But audiences, pleased at being able to read the actors' thoughts in their expressions, unmistakably endorsed the new method. Despite studio opposition, in the next four years Griffith moved his camera nearer and nearer to the players. In this close approach to the action, the stereotyped gestures and "artistical attitudes" inherited from the theater were unnecessary. Moreover for this new kind of acting, stage training was not important and could even prove a handicap. The intense light needed for close-ups grew harder and harder on the human face, and Griffith began to gather round him young boys and girls on whose round cheeks time had not yet marked a single line. . . .

When Griffith began to take close-ups not only of his actors' faces but also of objects and other details of the scene, he demonstrated that it was the "shot" and not the actor which was the basic unit of expression of the motion picture. When to the full shot and the close-up he added the extreme long shots of *Ramona*, 1909, he had completed the "long shot—mid shot—close shot" combination which remains today the classic approach to the material in any motion-picture scene. When to these discoveries he added that of a method of assembly and composition of these lengths of film taken at varying distances from the action, the basis of modern technique had been established.

Richard Griffith and Arthur Mayer.
The Movies (S&S, 1957), p. 25

It is perhaps not too much to say that *The Birth of a Nation* was the last great work of art based on the old verities taken for granted by the worlds of Victoria and Edward. It was the last great work in the main line of nineteenth-century popular fiction, stoked by sentimentality and driven by simple conceptions of the nature of good, evil, innocence, and justice. But if in its philosophy the film looked backward, it presaged the future in its techniques. It was the first truly great motion picture, the first to realize all the potential of the long-dreamed-of machine that would record man in motion. In the driving rhythm of the film and in the quick, bold, impressionistic treatment of its theme, Griffith gave the world a powerful preview of the quality of the art which would follow the war.

Richard Schickel. *Movies* (Basic, 1964), p. 48

Griffith also towered over all his predecessors and contemporaries in the high purpose with which he approached film-making. In the earliest days, when nearly everyone else was grinding out low-grade melodrama and farce, he strove to make as many films of a higher type as was possible, drawing stories and themes from literary classics, biography, and history.

Inspired by the social criticism in the plays of Henrik Ibsen and the novels of Frank Norris and buttressed by his strong Christian outlook he lashed out against injustice, abuse, corruption, and other evils. A strong moral fervor, a sincere patriotism, and a high-minded idealism were almost constantly present in his work—occasionally, even to excess.

To the end, it was his aim to employ the new art-form, which he had done so much to develop, as an educative force within the frame of entertainment. Even the satanic presence in *The Birth of a Nation* was an effort to reveal what he felt to be the actual and insufficiently disclosed truth about his victimized Confederate ancestry.

In his idealism he was also a poet with a ceaseless passion to create cinematic beauty. From the first days he sought ideal locations, atmospheric lighting effects, and pulchritude in the persons of his actors. This endless quest for beautiful effects of every kind was a part of his romanticism and continued to increase as his style developed. He also delighted in depicting beauty of character as often as possible—glorifying nobility, moral purity, chivalry, maternal love, good breeding and graceful manners. Since the majority of these things are today largely out of fashion, they seem a quaint affectation to modern eyes.

It is true that he was sentimental to a great degree, but this was a radiation of his own loving-kindness—comparable to Albert Schweitzer's "reverence for life," Robert J. Flaherty's camera caressing the universe, and Walt Whitman's eternally embracing arms. D. W. was fond of idealized romantic love, handsome loving couples, attractive children, radiant family-groups, animal pets, roses, and glowing sweeps of landscape.

In the much harsher modern age this romanticism seems sugary and old-fashioned. Today the mode is rather for slum squalor, human bestiality, dull and literal depiction of the ordinary, every-day humdrum, and exploration of naked human flesh in search of erotic excitation. In his later years he detested the films then current for having lost the concept of the beautiful and the poetic.

But for all of his true sentiment he was fully aware of the savage nihilism rampant in life, the terror of tragedy, the wrack of human suffering, and he portrayed these with an honesty and courage that has not been surpassed or even equalled. Seeing the whole of existence, he sought to evoke joy and gratitude for the presence of so much beauty, continuing to repeat, "Isn't life wonderful?"

G. Charles Niemeyer. *Film Heritage.*
Fall 1965, pp. 20–21

Griffith was . . . fascinated by the work and even the personality of Edgar Allan Poe. In 1909, his first year as a director, Griffith made a film called *Edgar Allan Poe*, which romantically dramatized some of the legends about Poe's unhappy life, and later Griffith directed a film called *The Avenging Conscience*, which pulled material from "The Telltale Heart," "Annabel Lee," "The Black Cat," and "William Wilson." Griffith was attracted by Poe's theme of conscience and by the dark visions into which Poe wove the theme, but Griffith seems also to have picked up some of Poe's genius for rhythm, pace, and timing. Poe's better stories, like Griffith's better films, work on the principle of acceleration. Beginning slowly, the narrative gradually quickens, the focus narrows, the action speeds up, is pushed to a climax, and then abruptly halted. Griffith was the first film maker to discover that slow editing (shots which remain on the screen a long time, even if they are shots of violent and rapid action) will automatically slow the pace, while fast editing (the use of short shots, even if on static material) will quicken and speed the rhythm of the film. It is possible that Griffith's use of such devices came partly from his careful reading and filmic reworking of Poe's work.

Robert Richardson. *Literature and Film*
(Indiana, 1969), p. 39

Set in Paris in the time before and during the French Revolution, *Orphans of the Storm* resembles the historical epics of *Birth of a Nation* and *Intolerance* more than the elegiac melodramas of *Broken Blossoms*, *True Heart Susie*, and *Way Down East*. Yet beneath *Orphans*' epic surface lie the elements of pure melodrama (i.e., domestic tragedy). If this surface is stripped away, it becomes clear that *Orphans* is not really about the politics of the French Revolution but about the relationships of characters and families projected by Griffith upon that historical event. Griffith, for instance, develops historical figures like Danton and Robespierre not as political but as melodramatic characters: their historical significance becomes much less important than their moral relationship to the film's central characters. To Griffith, Robespierre is less of a power-hungry politician than a prude: Robespierre's remark that "France must be purged of all vice," characterizes his political acts (e.g. his persecution of Henriette) in purely moral terms and transforms him into a melodramatic character. Similarly, Danton, though he functions doubly as Henriette's and France's savior, draws more of his power in the film from the sad beauty of his frustrated love relationship with Henriette than his success as a leader of the revolution. . . .

Griffith's melodrama works in *Orphans* because of the directness with which it is told. Griffith has a way of animating his material, making it come alive that most directors lack; Griffith makes us feel the full impact of each melodramatic situation in a direct way, in contrast, say to the equally great indirectness of Sirk's and Mulligan's melodramas.

John Belton. *VV*. Oct. 7, 1971, p. 71

HATHAWAY, HENRY (1898–   )

Unnatural as it is, the color does no serious damage to the picture [*The Trail of the Lonesome Pine*]. This moldy bit of hokum, despite its willing actors and technically good direction, takes movies back to the days of their childhood. It combines all the features of the old-time serials and roaring Westerns. Filmed for the third time since its publication in 1908, John Fox Jr.'s novel of mountaineers and their feuds is as up-to-date as an heirloom.

For this recounting, Wanger studded his picture with stars under the direction of Henry Hathaway, who did commendable work on the *Lives of a Bengal Lancer*. Sylvia Sidney plays the dulcet heroine opposite virile Fred MacMurray. Supporting them—as effectively as the hackneyed story permits—are Fred Stone, Beulah Bondi, Henry Fonda, Nigel Bruce, and little Spanky McFarland.

Newsweek. Feb. 29, 1936, p. 32

Spawn of the North could be both praised and attacked from the documentary point of view—praised for its vivid and atmospheric presentation of the Alaskan seascapes and the men who dwell and work in them at the salmon fisheries, and blamed for hitching on to them an emotional and personal story about the stellar passions of its cast, which mostly hails from Sunny California. Personally speaking, I prefer to remember it only as one of the few occasions recently when I have felt a sense of real enjoyment (entertainment, too, if you will) in the vast temples of the West End. This film, in fact, has something which the cinema of bygone days (*O quam te memorem virgo*) used to supply as a matter of course—action and thrills, the quickened pulse and the lump in the throat. You remember *Way Down East* and the like? The heroine with the illegitimate baby thrust forth into the night, and into the ice floe rushing towards the falls? There must be many—I think I am one of them—who will never quite get the same thrill as they did when Barthelmess snatched Gish from the icy jaws at the last impossible moment. Sentimentality, passion, and a high wind over sea and land ought to be as popular now as they were then, and perhaps they would be if we had a few more films like *Spawn of the North*. . . .

All this brings us to the consideration of Henry Hathaway, the director. I am astonished to recall that he also made *Bengal Lancer*, but not even this fact will deter me from rating him very high—and that not because of Alaskan location work, but because of his sensibility and sensitiveness on the set. Observe carefully his direction of the scenes between Raft and Lamour. Note first the verisimilitude of the settings, second, the modest but unerring rightness of all his camera angles, and third, the sense of the ebb and flow of passion between two tough but inarticulate humans, which makes you forget to be superior even if hokum is at its height. He even gets away—triumphantly—with the Our-Dumb-Friend angle, supplied by Slicker, a fantastically intelligent performing seal. Fourthly and finally, though perhaps the very essence of the story may have done it for him, one may praise the fine timing, which more than once carries an emotional scene (twice as slow as even Hollywood plays them) on the backlash of a smashingly fast action-sequence. The script would indeed plot itself as an elegant and satisfying graph, and I rather think it would also have received a good mark from Aristotle. It is certainly the first time I have sat through a two-hour film and not found it a moment too long.

Basil Wright. *World Film News.* Oct. 1938, pp. 264–65

TAC tips its hat gently to *The Real Glory.* Samuel Goldwyn, Henry Hathaway, and Gary Cooper have combined here to make a melodrama of the old-fashioned kind, "of moving accidents by flood and field, of hair-breadth escape i' th' imminent deadly breach." It is unnecessary, of course, to add that it is Gary Cooper who, in the last reel, makes possible the independence of the Philippines, saves the life of the woman he loves, preserves the town from slaughter, upholds the honor of his commander, and raises the prestige of the American army. It is a good melodrama, tense and exciting, although it is a trifle disconcerting to see the principles of British and French colonization applied to a film about the United States Foreign Legion, suh. Still, who would want to stand in the way of Gary Cooper and a last-reel smash finish?

Gordon Sager. *TAC.* Oct. 1939, p. 28

[*Kiss of Death*] is an underworld film which does not depend on violence, gunplay or noise for intensity and excitement. It is, in fact, comparatively quiet except for a scene in which an invalid woman is tied fast to her wheelchair by a gangster and pushed down a steep flight of stairs to an agonized death: one of the most horrifying episodes ever seen in pictures. Even it is quiet, but for a scream.

Enormously effective in giving credence to the tale of its characters are authentic backgrounds of New York and vicinity. Thus the work achieves that semi-documentary quality which made *The House on 92nd Street* and *Boomerang!* noteworthy examples of a technique which dispenses with studio-built sets and backgrounds. At once this gives the characters a new dimension and fortunately removes any trace of production gloss and slickness. Terse dialogue is another aid to an understanding of the proceedings although complaint might be made that it does not round out the characters and establish their background as fully as in *Boomerang!* More than in any recent film this presupposes the spectator's familiarity with certain routine scenes by not showing them at all, but leaving them instead to the imagination. Scenes such as releasing a prisoner on parole, courtroom procedure, etc. This economy of narration enhances the compactness and tautness of the whole and achieves that rarity, a picture minus unnecessary footage.

NBR. Oct. 1947, p. 4

We learn only indirectly about Katie Elder's failure to influence her sons, as well as her success in hanging onto her integrity and self-respect: the movie opens with her funeral, and there are no flashbacks. This is too bad. An honest inquiry into the delinquency-producing influences on the frontier and a mother's inability to combat them might have been more interesting than anything the film actually presents, just as the process by which the father in *Shenandoah* instilled his principles into his sons would have been fascinating if it had been credibly dramatized instead of simply asserted.

Despite these intimations of significance, *The Sons of Katie Elder* turns out to be just an old-fashioned, routine Western. The three ne'er-do-well brothers (John Wayne, Dean Martin, Earl Holliman) team up with their not-quite-grown brother (Michael Anderson Jr.) to redeem themselves and avenge their mother according to a perfectly predictable formula. Their antagonist is that stock Western figure, the all-purpose "bad guy" (James Gregory), who, it turns out, not only swindled and murdered their father, thus nudging Katie toward a premature grave, but is also capable of devising the most improbably complicated skulduggery to eliminate the brothers before they can uncover the truth.

Routine though the film is, it is executed with some style and flourish, and is frequently quite entertaining.

Moira Walsh. *America*. Sept. 18, 1965, pp. 296–97

The Sons of Katie Elder bottles up its violence in the tough manner of action films Manny Farber used to honor for their Homeric virtues back in the late '40s and early '50s. The virtues of this kind of western are largely negative, that is anti-pop, anti-camp, and anti-pretentious. John Wayne is old and tough and implacable, but not entirely lacking in moral sensibility and emotional vulnerability. Henry Hathaway has directed Wayne as he has been directing him since *Shepherd of the Hills*, not with the classic force of John Ford and Howard Hawks, but with the serious craftsmanship one professional feels he owes another. Martha Hyer is more natural than I have ever seen her, and Dean Martin and James Gregory are okay as a black sheep and a black villain respectively. The big switch is George Kennedy's hired gunslinger, the first such character I have ever seen with a slight stammer combined with a fast draw. The spectacle of people in Hollywood trying to do something different in a western at this late date is curiously reassuring.

Andrew Sarris, *VV.* Oct. 9, 1965

Kiss of Death belongs to a genre that the French call *film noir*, an outgrowth of the gangster, topical, and sociological films of the previous decade. In brief, the "black film" is marked by a cold, detached, and brutal view of life, and frequently contains scenes of seemingly gratuitous violence and cruelty. . . .

Director Henry Hathaway came to make this kind of film by natural progression from his films *The House on 92nd Street* and *Call Northside 777*, films that employed an impersonal, documentary approach to contemporary subjects. Like those films, *Kiss of Death* was shot entirely on location. An introductory title states that every exterior *and* interior shot was made in the place it is represented to be, that is, in the municipal buildings, the rooming houses, and the streets of New York, with an excursion to Sing Sing up the river. The occasional narration, eventually revealed to be the voice of the girl who loves the protagonist, is a hangover from those same documentary techniques, and at times is at odds with what is on the screen. It is unlikely that Henry Hathaway had heard of *film noir* at the time he made this film, and yet to some degree he must have been under the influence of the films that composed the genre, or under the general influences of the wartime atmosphere that produced them. Whether the occasional ambivalence toward the subject matter is his own, the scriptwriters', or that imposed by the producers is one of those inside facts of production that is difficult to determine.

Eileen Bowser in *Film Notes*, edited by
Eileen Bowser (MOMA, 1969), p. 112

The success of the film [*True Grit*] . . . is based on its faithfulness to the author's intent and style. Screenwriter Marguerite Roberts has sensibly retained most of his best dialogue intact, and director Henry Hathaway has, in effect, used Wordsworth as his production designer:

"Every prospect pleases and only man is vile"—if comically so—in his visualization of the Indian Territory setting. Hathaway is seventy years old and has been making action films since 1933, so he knows instinctively, it seems, when he may invoke our laughter at the conventions of the western, when he must retain his seriousness about them. His visual style is as simple at Mattie's moral style (young Kim Darby is marvelous in the role) and as direct as Portis's prose style.

But perhaps the most important element in the film's triumph is John Wayne. He has discovered what's funny about the character he has always played (one has observed him working toward this knowledge in several recent movies), and now he gives us a rich double vision of it. He is himself, and he is himself playing himself—an exuberant put-on that seems to delight him as much as it does us. . . . [1969]

Richard Schickel. *Second Sight* (S&S, 1972), pp. 234–35

HAWKS, HOWARD (1896–   )

For some time now I have been drawing attention to Howard Hawks, to his simplifying style, to his way of putting together a film in violent segments, and the astonishing seduction of his images. Hawks executes everything given to him with the same simplicity, the same reassuring sureness. He is one of those who—without aging, helped by a set number of courageous collaborators who know and adore their craft and are becoming veritable magicians in their specialty—continue the good American tradition. Just about all of these films give me as much pleasure as satisfaction.

I hope that everybody has now seen *A Girl in Every Port*. Nevertheless, I will point out the beauty of the little Dutch girl, of the little Argentinian (Maria Alba), the athletic perfection of Louise Brooks, who is as attractive and slapable as ever. The wonderful consequences of MacLaglen's anger as he finds on each of his women the mark of his unknown predecessor—always the same. The perfect portrayal of the brutal encounters of the two friends with the Shore Patrols. And the friendly kidding of the scene in which Armstrong puts a piece of something on his shoulder to pretend to be an officer, or in which four times in a row he lets himself be fallen upon in four different ways, thereby obliging MacLaglen to come to his help and so interrupt a romance begun with a beautiful girl. And then at the end, the two friends fall into each other's arms after having battered away at one another.

And everything else. Yes! We watch everything that happens in this film as though we had been lucky enough to be hidden behind a fence and having a great time.

Jean George Auriol. *Revue du Cinéma.* Dec. 1928, unpaged

During the automobile races in *The Crowd Roars,* a picture which was offered last night at the Winter Garden, the throng (on the screen) cheers, and the attractive heroine expresses her anguish most satisfactorily, but, as invariably happens to a film narrative of which the director is author, the story is not precisely exciting—not nearly as effective as it is to the persons involved in the picture. . . . Nevertheless, those sequences devoted to the automobile racing are successfully portrayed, even though one more or less suspects what is going to happen. In fact, the closing episode in this production is far and away the best of all, for it reveals a certain originality in having the injured automobile racers eager to continue the race in ambulances on the way to the hospital.

Mordaunt Hall. *NYT.* March 23, 1932, p. 25

Without sharing the enthusiasm of critics who see in *Scarface* a masterpiece of American film-making, I am not one of those who say it is uninteresting. It is a completely successful film: excellent actors, good photography, irreprochable direction. It is a work of Howard Hawks, *auteur* of *A Girl in Every Port*, which is in itself a recommendation. But *Scarface* is a documentary and one doesn't become involved with its characters as one did with Bancroft in *Underworld*, Gary Cooper in *City Streets*, and Edmund Lowe in *Club 73*.

In *Scarface*, when you see a character appear you mechanically begin counting the moments he has to remain alive. Somebody else will soon pass, and a machinegunner is going to empty a clip.

The crimes that Capone was accused of committing or having committed were spread over years. In *Scarface* they are all grouped in an hour and a half of film projection. And that is the weak point of this technically successful film. The highpoints detract from one another. After a few minutes you are accustomed to the fusillades and the summary executions. They are too natural and suddenly too violent.

After such a spree of bullets and bodies one wonders what will become of the gangster film. Unless they make one "still stronger," and that doesn't seem possible, the exchanges of bullets will appear stale. Maybe gangsters will use cannons instead of machine guns? *Scarface* has exhausted the subject of Chicago gangsters, and perhaps this is just as well. Is there another kind of gangster film being readied, behind the scenes, of course, in which a clip of twenty-five bullets will be replaced by the small pearl-handled revolver, or some other lovable weapons which, who knows, will become the instruments of a new emotion, deeper, because closer to us?

Michel Vaucaire. *Le Crapouillot*. Nov. 1932, p. 73

Lacking even a journalistic, contemporary quality, *Today We Live* is a flimsy business. Mr. Faulkner is credited with having dramatized his own short story, but, unless they played him false on the coast, he evidently played an expensive practical joke on his employers, and tried successfully to outwrite the worst hacks in the business.

An amusing bit of Faulkner bravado originally, the story concerned an American flyer who condescends to heckle a youngster in the British naval service, whereupon the flyer has the pants scared off him in a mosquito launch manned by the youngster and his mate.

At best, it could have been turned into a good rough and tumble yarn, and, even in its present dreary state, Robert Young and Franchot Tone bring likeable qualities to the young officers.

However, Joan Crawford, in an odd collection of clothes, stupidly displayed off-key and out of date with the story, gives the show away by acting her head off in, as some one remarked in this magazine, the best tradition of the "Oh, the pain of it!" school. She manages, also, to appear completely detached from the three gentlemen in the cast. Thus, no censor could object to the fact that she sleeps out of wedlock because not even a censor could imagine from the writing, direction, or the attitude of the leading lady that she ever really was in love, or within two hundred miles of the young men.

Pare Lorentz. *Vanity Fair*. June 1933, p. 37

Viva Villa! is a glorified horse opera. It's a Western brought up to date. The story is woven around a historical, if legendary character; there aren't just a few hard riders, but hundreds and thousands of men always furiously riding, shooting, screaming, and at every opportunity singing *La Cucuracha*; there is sex of the frontier-saloon variety, mock marriages, polygamy, attempted rape and murder; there are ballroom and bedroom scenes; there are bank robberies and jailbreaks; there are vicious and false political insinuations; in fact the only thing that was left out was General Pershing and his army. . . .

In its technical aspects *Viva Villa!* shows the result of extended and troublesome production. The exterior sections (the mass scenes of fighting and riding) are far superior to the Hollywood portions: which are as phoney as the Hollywood portions of *Eskimo*. James Wong Howe, Hollywood's crack photographer, must have studied Tisse's work in

Thunder Over Mexico. For whatever cinematic quality it has is due to the contribution of the cameraman. As for the rest, the film is badly edited and clumsily constructed. A high pitch of dramatic excitement is reached much before the middle. The rest is anti-climax. The spectator's excitement is incited by the purely physical impact of the furious riding and war sequences, by the frequent sadism, and the lively musical score.

Irving Lerner. *New Masses.* June 12, 1934, pp. 29, 30

The story of *Road to Glory*, creditable as it is, does very little to distinguish the famous Napoleonic regiment of the French Army from any other regiment that reached the front lines during the World War. Against scenes of battle and trench life is told the story of three men and a girl—a captain, his father, a lieutenant, and a nurse—four people whose lives are hopelessly entangled until fate in the form of a German shell clears everything up. They are stock characters all of them, but delineated with such simplicity and quietness that their outlines never fail to be discernible. There is a disturbing note about this picture—that such excellent playing and directing have not resulted in tenser drama, that such incisive characterization is not moving through its own sharpness. Perhaps music would have given the film an overtone of emotionalism; perhaps we are not used to consultation and a sense of duty being the motivating forces in war drama. Whatever the reason for *Road to Glory's* failure to come off as an effective screenplay, it is an honest, straightforward photographic pattern.

Stage. Sept. 1936, p. 12

[*Scarface* is] a gangster picture which presents heroically the exploits of a criminal, showing him as rich, courageous and cunning against contrasting characteristics on the part of the guardians of the law. It glorifies crime, presents methods of crime and familiarizes the audience with them. Even though the criminal is brought to justice in the final scenes it is an influence against law and order and an incitement to impressionable minds to follow vicious practices.

Martin Quigley. *Decency in Motion Pictures* (Macmillan, 1937), p. 39

In view of the heavy thought that has recently gone into the question Is Humor Best for Us? I am happy to report that *Bringing Up Baby* is funny from the word go, that it has no other meaning to recommend it, nor therapeutic qualities, and that I wouldn't swap it for practically any three things of the current season. For comedy to be really good, of course, there is required something more in the way of total design than any random collection of hilarities. There must be point—not *a* point to be *made*, which is the easy goal of any literary tortoise, but a point from which to start, as implicit throughout as the center of a circle. *Bringing Up Baby* has something of the sort. The actual story goes into the troubles of a paleontologist who first offends a prospective angel for his museum, then his fiancée, and then gets into the wild-goose affairs of a girl and her leopard and terrier and other family members, ending up in jail and of course in love. That could be done in two reels. What puts the dramatic spirit into it is the character of the hare-brained young thing who gets him mixed up in all this. . . . The film holds together by virtue of constant invention and surprise in the situations; and Howard Hawks' direction, though it could have been less heavy and more supple, is essentially that of film comedy. All of which could be elaborated, techniques analyzed, points cited, etc. But why? *Bringing Up Baby* is hardly a departure; it settles nothing; it is full of an easy inviting humor. So do you want to go or don't you [1938]

Otis Ferguson. *The Film Criticism of O.F.* (Temple, 1971), pp. 215–16

Howard Hawks has had an uneven if successful career, but he directed the best of all airplane pictures, *Ceiling Zero*, and so it is too bad he and an above-average cast had to be wasted on the story of *Only Angels Have Wings*. With a good story, the swift suspense so naturally brought out in movies of pilots and their job would have become a terrific thing under its own power. But this was done in the run-of-the-mill Hollywood way: get something that will wow them, gag it up, bring the girls in, bring everything else in. . . .

Power dives are always ripping across a theater screen somewhere: but in this case more could have been done. The atmosphere was right to start with, the give-and-take among the men, the hard-pressed finances of the outfit, the dangers known and unknown, and the good likely people: Cary Grant, Jean Arthur, Thomas Mitchell, Richard Barthelmess, Allyn Joslyn, Siegfried Rumann. In the minor things, where the ridiculous or the stereotype didn't intrude, there was a swell realization of their personalities, of friendship and banter and weariness and trouble. Howard Hawks can be faultless in a sense of how to speed up a situation, or make it flexible and easy with the right emphasis, grouping, understatement. In fact, all these people did the best they could with what they were given—but look at it. The battle with mechanics and the elements, in this as in other air films, provides suspense all right; but so does hanging. [1939]

Otis Ferguson. *The Film Criticism of O.F.* (Temple, 1971), p. 256

Anita Loos' popular 20's satirical novel [*Gentlemen Prefer Blondes*] was turned more than 20 years later into a successful Broadway musical, where it retained its period costuming and background and, apparently, its satirical bite, and was fortunate in a brilliant comedienne, Carol Channing, to play Lorelei. One can see that as a fast, cynical and quite unromantic picture of two showgirls on the loose in Europe, it would be very entertaining; and one knows from Carol Channing's records of the numbers what she must have made of Lorelei. The film, unfortunately, is compromised from the start; compromised by the casting of Marilyn Monroe, by the abandonment of the 20's period and the incongruous up-to-date streamlining, by inflating some bright, witty songs into lavish production numbers, and by tamely ending the whole thing by letting two true loves conventionally come true. There is, too, a lack of grasp in Howard Hawks' handling, which is scrappy and uninventive. The plot and continuity of the second half is so disjointed that one feels it must, for some reason, have been decided to finish the film in a hurry. It just stops.

BFI Bulletin. Sept. 1953, p. 131

Rio Bravo . . . is a new film by Howard Hawks. I am beginning to like Hawks' films more and more. I have discovered him only through the untiring insistence of French film critics. To them—however strange it may seem to some of us here—Orson Welles, Hitchcock and Hawks happen to be the most interesting American film-makers today.

I am beginning to see why Hawks' films such as *The Big Sleep*, *Scarface*, *The Big Sky*, *Red River* and now *Rio Bravo* (less perfect than the other four) have the same flawless acting, the same minute characterizations that make his people alive—these details are often more important than the action itself—and a haunting, almost poetic, sense of local atmosphere. His films are so well integrated, so well put together, that they seem almost too simple. But there are no dull moments in them. They move. And his people are always interesting to watch. *Rio Bravo* is a very long film, but it succeeds in holding our attention completely. Unless you don't care about Westerns. As for me, the Western (more than the musical) is the only film form where the poetical feelings of America can still find some place. Give him a horse, a wagon, and boundless space, and an American begins to sing. Isn't this the same feeling and nostalgia that drives Kerouac's generation on the road? A man can not live without poetry.

Jonas Mekas. *VV*. April 1, 1959

Man's Favorite Sport? is just another movie in the preeminently commercial career of producer-director Howard Hawks, and the operative word here is "movie." For discriminating connoisseurs of the cinema as an art form—that is to say, for people with tastes too fastidious for exposure to more than a dozen films a year—*Man's Favorite Sport*? is a complete waste of time. After all, how much profundity can be derived in these perilous times from a plot concerning an Abercrombie & Fitch salesman trapped by an aggressive female into entering a fishing contest for which he is qualified more by literary reputation than by direct experience?

Somehow our woefully incompleat angler muddles through to victory despite his nearly drowning on those occasions when he is not about to be devoured by the nearest bear or woman. On the first viewing, this one basic joke of the phony painfully unmasked wears dangerously thin for a two-hour movie. Hawks's deadpan documentation of a physical gag is as effective as ever, but the over-all pace of his direction is curiously contemplative, as if he were savoring all his past jokes for the last time.

It seems unfortunate, at least on first viewing, that Rock Hudson and Paula Prentiss clearly lack a light touch for comedy, a fact of casting Hawks accepted gallantly and exploited skillfully when he was unable to land Cary Grant and Audrey Hepburn for his leads. The very clumsiness of the Hudson-Prentiss coupling is deftly integrated with the central parody of professionalism. Call it classic or archaic, but *Man's Favorite Sport?* harks back to the golden age of Cary Grant and Katharine Hepburn in *Bringing Up Baby*. The bitter spectacle of a man divested of his dignity, and the humor derived thereby, seem to apply to some pre-Feiffer species of male with dignity to spare. The only question in this age of anxiety is whether such a heroic creature has become extinct, like the dodo, or was always as mythical as the unicorn. [1964]

Andrew Sarris. *Confessions of a Cultist* (S&S, 1970), pp. 128–29

The vision of Howard Hawks is expressed in a classic way. In other words, he uses a quasi-inapparent style and he falls back on the tried and true. He has forged an esthetic that could be called neuter, at first glance invisible, designed to efficiently transmit to us facts that are intimately linked to the story. In fact, Hawks is a perfect storyteller formed by the American cinematographic tradition. . . .

Studied in detail, his direction reveals very important differences in his conception, use of the camera, and the quality of the photography. . . . When one thinks of the culminating scenes in Hawks' films one notices that the dramatic material is very varied and that the cutting innovations that underline it have little relation between them. Whether it is a question of the death of Paul Muni in *Scarface*, of the dialogue between Cary Grant and Thomas Mitchell in *Only*

Angels Have Wings, of the gasoline cans in *Air Force*, of the slap in *To Have and Have Not*, or the circular pan shot around John Wayne abandoned in *Red River*, one does not find in them the a priori means such as one finds, for example, in the lateral descriptive pans inevitably—in *Monument Valley*—found in the Fordian wild rides of "old troopers." Neither décors, landscapes, nor preferred figures of style, but only the sensibility of a prince. Howard Hawks is one of those rare men capable of dominating that division into "genres" that carves up American cinema; because of this he is able to reinvent each of them on the basis of original inspiration. The king of eclectics.

Jean-Claude Missiaen. *Howard Hawks*
(Editions Universitaires, 1966), pp. 164–66

The desire to entertain on Hawks's part, to share certain jokes, activities and people, is quite unalloyed by the sort of purpose Hitchcock's films contain. Hawks places much less reliance on the effects of the camera than Hitchcock, who deliberately uses it to create emotional response. Because of the nature of his friends Hawks's films are as recognizable as Hitchcock's, but Hawks himself is anonymous compared with the presence of Hitchcock one feels and, once ritually in every film, actually notices—a visual grotesque passing across the screen. If Hawks were to appear in his own films he would not stand out because the activities he records are his own. Hitchcock's physique compels him to meditation, but Hawks has been active. Before movies he built and raced cars and planes. He was brought up not in a city as dense as London, but in Goshen, Indiana, the sort of country Nick Adams grew up in. The associations with Hemingway emerge in respect for professionalism and personality and in a documentary celebration of some of man's most vigorous activities: flying planes in *Dawn Patrol, Only Angels* and *Air Force*; driving a herd of cattle in *Red River*; hunting big game in *Hatari!*; and in *To Have and Have Not* and *The Big Sleep* sitting out a tight spot and keeping the hand steady.

David Thomson. *Movie Man* (Stein & Day,
1967), p. 156

Red River is a magnificent horse opera—one of the more elaborate celebrations of those trail-blazing episodes that Hollywood loves to glorify as "historical events," i.e., the mid-nineteenth-century first cattle drive up the Chisholm Trail. . . . The director, Howard Hawks, makes the drive an exciting series of stampedes, Indian battles, and gunfights, with the fight between the two principals, John Wayne as the father and (Montgomery) Clift as the stepson, as the ferocious climax. *Red River* is not really so "great" as its devotees claim (what

Western is?), and a lot of it is just terrible, but Clift—in his most aggressively sexual screen performance—is angular and tense and audacious, and the other actors brawl amusingly in the strong-silent-man tradition. Russel Harlen's photography makes the rolling plains the true hero: the setting, if not the material, has epic grandeur. . . .

Pauline Kael. *Kiss Kiss Bang Bang* (Little, Brown, 1968), p. 338

El Dorado is not as great a film as *Rio Bravo*; indeed, considered in isolation from the rest of Hawks's work (an almost impossible thing to do), it is not a *great* film at all. The difficulty for the critic arises not only from the fact that the superficial resemblances to *Rio Bravo*, though so close, are misleading; there is also the fact that, although everything important in *El Dorado* is new, it is in many ways dependent on the earlier film for its significance. It is precisely our *awareness* of its differences from *Rio Bravo* that matters.

That it is not entirely satisfying considered as a self-sufficient entity is in various ways confirmed if we place it beside *Rio Bravo*: its relatively loose, and in some respects contrived, organisation becomes immediately apparent in relation to its great forerunner's tightness and naturalness. *Rio Bravo* grows organically out of Dude's alcoholism; the alcoholism of J. P. Harrah (Robert Mitchum) is brought in arbitrarily because Hawks lost faith in the script he started with and decided to do *Rio Bravo* again. One can only guess at the reasons for this decision. Both Hawks's own description of the original script (taken from Harry Brown's novel *The Stars in Their Courses*) as Greek tragedy, and the part of it that survives in the finished film (the episode of the boy's suicide) suggest that he was here toying with the idea of doing something (for him) completely new. One doesn't know to what extent commercial considerations influenced him, but the fact that both *Man's Favorite Sport?* and *Red Line 7000* (the latter of which, at least, broke new ground for Hawks) did badly at the box-office, whereas *Rio Bravo* has proved among his most popular films, may be significant. An artist, however firmly established, working in a commercial medium, can only allow himself a limited number of box-office disasters before it becomes difficult to find backing. . . . A Greek tragedy directed by Howard Hawks sounds a rather absurd contradiction in terms; yet the episode of the suicide and its aftermath is so poignant in its bareness and its stoical grief that one can't help regretting the film Hawks didn't make, and wondering what it might have been.

Robin Wood. *Howard Hawks* (Doubleday, 1968), pp. 152–53

Scarface (1932) is a passionate, strong, archaic photographic miracle: the rise and fall of an ignorant, blustery, pathetically childish punk (Paul Muni) in an avalanche of rich, dark-dark images. The people, Italian gangsters and their tough, wisecracking girls, are quite beautiful, as varied and shapely as those who parade through Piero's religious paintings. Few movies are better at nailing down singularity in a body or face, the effect of a strong outline cutting out impossibly singular shapes. Boris Karloff: long stove-pipe legs, large-boned and gaunt, an obsessive, wild face; Ann Dvorak: striking out blindly with the thinnest, sharpest elbows, shoving aside anyone who tries to keep her from the sex and excitement of a dance hall. Besides the sulphurous, extreme lighting and so many feverish, doomed types, like Osgood Perkins as Johnny Lovo, top hood on the South Side until his greedier right-hand man Tony Camonte takes over, the image seems unique because of its moody energy: it is a movie of quick-moving actions, inner tension, and more angularity per inch of screen than any street film in history.

Crisp and starched where *Scarface* is dark and moody, *His Girl Friday* (1940) is one of the fastest of all movies, from line to line and gag to gag. Besides the dynamic, highly assertive pace, this *Front Page* remake with Rosalind Russell playing Pat O'Brien's role is a tour de force of choreographed action: bravado posturings with body, lucid Cubistic composing with natty lapels and hat brims, as well as a very stylized discourse of short replies based on the idea of topping, outmaneuvering the other person with wit, cynicism, and verbal bravado. A line is never allowed to reverberate but is quickly attached to another, funnier line in a very underrated comedy that champions the sardonic and quick-witted over the plodding, sober citizens. [1969]

Manny Farber. *Negative Space* (Praeger, 1971), p. 25

There was always the impression with a Howard Hawks movie that what really mattered was the life going on behind the cameras, and that the movie which finally came out of it was an afterthought. Hawks was able to animate a sort of private island life within his company that made even a potboiler like *Hatari* seem credible. Hawks was taking his friends and cast and crew on a trip he wanted to make personally—and the film was both the incidental excuse for and the record of that experience.

Joseph Gelmis. *The Film Director as Superstar* (Doubleday, 1970), p. 266

Yet even in his best days Hawks was making "personal" films—the 1939 trash masterpiece, *Only Angels Have Wings*, made just before

His Girl Friday, is already a full-blown anticipation of the ethos of the boyish gang and of the dregs of *Hatari!*—and even in his best films there is the same insistent preoccupation with passive-aggressive sexual role-reversals and with such Hawksian motifs as the man-chasing woman (*Bringing Up Baby, The Big Sleep*) and tomboy heroine (*His Girl Friday*, in which *The Front Page* was rewritten to make a principal male character female). (Hawks, is, after all, the man who can claim credit for the discovery of Lauren Bacall, that most androgynous of screen sirens with her singing voice in *To Have and Have Not* dubbed by Andy Williams.) Not that such things appear only in his best films, as the great humor found in having Cary Grant in drag in WAC's uniform in *I Was a Male War Bride* can serve to remind one. And if one has one's doubts about the growing tendency to find humor in violence and killing in the later films, *The Big Sky* of 1952 certainly sets a clear precedent in its scene of an amputation without anesthetic played for comedy, as does much of *Scarface*. What is new, and *could* perhaps be considered variation and elaboration, is the way, in *Rio Lobo*, the violence has become increasingly kinky (a hornets' nest tossed like a hand grenade into a group of men, a young girl's face slashed, one of the villains set afire, another having a gun explode in his face) and is rather lovingly dwelt on; and the way the veteran sidekick of *Rio Bravo* and *El Dorado* has turned into Jack Elam's gleefully kill-crazy sinister old man.

Andrew Sarris has somewhere remarked (I think wrongly) on the loss of iconic stature suffered by Humphrey Bogart in the films of Huston compared with those Bogart made with Hawks; an observation which might well be turned around to apply to the diminished stature of John Wayne in Hawks's films compared with those Wayne made with Ford. What is, I think, embarrassingly clear, as increasingly younger girls pursue an increasingly aging, passive Wayne is the extent to which the star has become a stand-in in the fantasy life of the director, as the films themselves have come increasingly to offer a field day for clinicians. . . .

William S. Pechter. *Commentary*.
June 1971, p. 88

Action is as American as—as American as anything. To the cry of "lights, camera, action," directors like Howard Hawks responded with an emphasis on the latter—not only physical action, but verbal action as well. His films aim at a target and hit it right on. Hawks, who would probably say he made movies, not films, contributed enormously to the development of the American film as an electric, kinetic, crowd-pleasing spectacle—a mirror image—revved up and roaring —of America itself. . . .

Hawks has often been compared to John Ford. Their styles are similar. However, Hawks does not share Ford's more expansive historical vision, while Ford lacks the Hawks flare for dynamic, sophisticated comedy (*His Girl Friday, Twentieth Century*). Like Ford, though, Hawks is most successful when remaining within the American experience (*Scarface, Red River*) rather than venturing outside it (*Land of the Pharaohs*). At the 1970 Chicago International Film Festival, Hawks said that Ford "was a good director when I started, and I copied him every time I could." In fact, the Ford influence in *Only Angels Have Wings* can be traced to Ford's *Air Mail* (1932), in which the plot and characterizations are too close to be coincidental.

To the same audience Hawks revealed the philosophy intrinsic to all his films but one. On the advice of a friend who saw his first film (*The Road to Glory*, 1926) as catering to critics and not the public, his goals with every film since has been "to make entertainment" pure and, primarily, simple.

Tom Shales in *The American Film Heritage*,
edited by the American Film Institute
(Acropolis, 1972), pp. 98–99

HITCHCOCK, ALFRED (1899–)

In his treatment of men and women, Hitchcock is a born observer, a trustworthy chronicler of detail, but his observations have, as it were, no sequel in action, no real bearing on the course of motive and effect. He has not the warm humanity of a director like Griffith, nor the psychological insight of a director like Pabst. His figures are photographic records of synthetic men, not men of flesh-and-blood translated into the medium of the motion picture. Almost without exception his films move along their appointed theme by some forced action, some piece of incredible behaviour on the part of the people concerned. This is not, in itself, a direct obstacle to the achievement of a good film. There are many films, and good films, in which men and women act, not as men and women would, but as the director designed. But in these instances the film and its characters have been conceived deliberately outside realism—lifted from the practical world by some largeness, some generality, some symbolism of the scene. The fault with Hitchcock's unreality lies in the fact that he has been essentially a director of realistic films; his subjects have been intimate, detailed and individual. He has dealt with one man, not with men, and he cannot afford to play fast and loose with the facts of life. In this paradox of realism the technician in Hitchcock has always suffered from the material to which his technique was applied, and his development retarded by the very ease with which he can reproduce the outward characteristics of an unobserved inner life.

C. A. Lejeune. *Cinema* (Alexander Maclehose), 1931), pp. 11–12

Alfred Hitchcock, the English genius of melodrama, has made his first Hollywood picture, a brilliant screen dramatization of that highly popular novel *Rebecca*. Brilliant in the sense of keeping remarkable faith with the best-seller-readers of the novel by making the picture just what they hoped it would be. Perhaps that is due to Mr. Selznick. That astute producer, who had many good and often distinguished films to his credit before he became a news-headline figure through his long and finally triumphant bout with *Gone With the Wind*, has learned better than anyone else that a popular novel fares much better with movie audiences if it doesn't disappoint those who liked the book. . . .

Hitchcock fans will have to put up with a surprising lack of the characteristic Hitchcock improvisations in the way of salty minor personages and humorous interludes, and satisfy themselves with a masterly exhibition of the Hitchcock skill in creating suspense and shock with his action and his camera. Hitchcock has always had a way of being at his best three-quarters of the way through a picture and getting bored and careless toward the end—in *Rebecca* all his most effective efforts, those which have brought him his special fame, have been reserved for the last reels, in spite of a long stretch of talk necessary to explain the mystery.

NBR. April 1940, pp. 13–14

Alfred Hitchcock, of course, has always been a man of much more talent than taste, always a little awestruck in the presence of such terms as "psychological study" and "artistic novel," etcetera. I remember once spending an hour in an attempt to steer him, by elaborate, prepared questions, into the admission that his method itself, his practice in melodrama, was sounder drama than many upper-case dramatists; that such a method once extended to an essentially serious or purposeful subject would sweep the field. Mr. Hitchcock rubbed his stomach, beamed, and rumbled, but he wasn't having any. He talked nonsense about art but he was leery of it, somewhat as the grade-school man is forever reverent before the word university.

Rebecca is not really a bad picture, but it is a change in stride and not a healthy one. A wispy and overwrought femininity in it somehow. A boudoir. The first half of the picture just proves that a bright girl who is at home with such words as "lahst" and "conservtreh" could continue to be the lady of a house in which she tripped on every stair and bumped into every butler and slipped on every stretch of floor and dropped her gloves or coffee cup or otherwise made a frightful mess everytime a superior domestic appeared. Joan Fontaine, quite lovely as the bride, lived a minature hell every minute there, and so did I.

After that, things began to go (too late). All this absurd nightmare of helplessness turned out to be mere preparation for an unsuspected angle of murder and mystery and blackmail, and what things fermented beneath the surface of this proud estate in Cornwall. Then Hitchcock's infallible sense of timing and camera effect of suspense opened the window and let some fresh air in. [1940]

Otis Ferguson. *The Film Criticism of O.F.* (Temple, 1971), p. 295

Crocodile tears over the alleged decline of Alfred Hitchcock have for years been a favorite cocktail among those who take moving pictures seriously. That has always seemed to me an impatient and cheap attitude to take toward any kind of change, or disturbance, in the work of a good artist. It still does. Nevertheless, because my space is limited, I am going to use it almost exclusively to specify things which strike me as limiting, or disappointing, about *Lifeboat*. . . .

The handling of the cinematic problems is extremely astute, in spite of a smell of studio about most of it. But since too little was ventured of what followed as a logical obligation out of the root of the idea, it remains an interesting, disappointing demonstration of possibilities at a second or third remove. What disturbs me is the question whether Hitchcock recognizes this, as I would certainly be inclined to assume; or whether, like too many good but less gifted film artists, he has at last become so engrossed in the solution of pure problems of technique that he has lost some of his sensitiveness toward the purely human aspect of what he is doing. A friend of mine justly remarks that *Lifeboat* is more a Steinbeck picture than a Hitchcock. In *Shadow of a Doubt*, too, I felt that Hitchcock was dominated by his writers. In his finest films he has always shown, always cinematically, qualities of judgment and perception which to my mind bring him abreast of all but the few best writers of his time, and which set him far beyond the need, conscious or otherwise, of going to school to anyone. But too many people rock *Lifeboat*; and they lull what had every right and need, if it were undertaken at all, to be a great and terrifying film. [1944]

James Agee. *Agee on Film* (Beacon, 1964), pp. 71, 72

The numerous films produced under the banner of Selznick International have built for that firm a reputation for opulent production and lavish display of expensive talent. The numerous films produced by Alfred Hitchcock have won for this director top honors as a creator of tense, absorbing murder melodrama. It is curious, then, that the Selznick-Hitchcock collaboration, repeated for the fourth time in *The Paradine Case*, has not resulted in a more impressive film. Certainly Selznick has stinted neither on production values nor cast names, while Hitchcock reveals all his mature knowledge of filmcraft. The courtroom scene that comes as the picture's climax is by far the tightest, most realistic enactment of a trial that has ever been put on the screen. Time and again in the course of the film complicated psychological motivations are more clearly established by what Hitchcock's camera tells us than by what the sound-track says. But the sound track says too much. Because of it, somewhere along the line interest in the people themselves and what happens to them begins to diminish. Somewhere the things they say no longer come as drama but just as words.

NBR. Jan. 1948, p. 4

Hitchcock's American masterpiece was *Shadow of a Doubt*, a perfect stylistic morsel alongside of which the flourishes of *Citizen Kane* seem pathetic. The film was also a shaded portrait of a small American town. But the subject, compared with that of *Suspicion*, was weak and conventional.

Hitchcock's principal fault was to be content with too carefully worked out plots without always concerning himself with their human content. This base made it possible for him to embroider dazzling but sterile technical variations that quickly lose their force. This is evident in the childishly psychoanalytic *Spellbound* (1945) and even more so in *Notorious* (1946), a foolish story of atomic spies that in its artificiality almost equals Charles Vidor's grotesque *Gilda* (1946), that fetishistic hymn to the Pin-Up Girl Rita Hayworth.

Georges Sadoul. *Histoire d'un art: le cinéma* (Flammarion, 1949), p. 334

Hitchcock's long-planned *I Confess* marks a slight change of pace for the director. Based on a play of a solid, perhaps slightly old-fashioned, type, it develops its story mainly through scenes of dialogue (the flashback interludes, though well enough managed, have a little the air of padding), and, since the identity of the killer is revealed at the start, its suspense depends primarily on the priest's moral problem and on conflicts of motive and character. There are enough opportunities for tension, though, in such scenes as a cat-and-mouse interview between Larrue and Father Michael, Ruth Grandfort's confession, and the cold, authoritatively staged trial scene with its unexpected denouement. The final chase through the huge Chateau Frontenac seems a touch that Hitchcock could not resist: out of keeping with the generally sober tone of the film, it provides a showily melodramatic climax. The unresolved split between the straightforward thriller technique and the more penetrating psychological study of character, indeed, makes itself felt as a weakness at intervals throughout the film. . . .

I Confess is rather less successful than *Strangers on a Train* and a good deal more so than anything else Hitchcock has done since the ill-fated *Rope*. And, whatever its shortcomings, it has the professional concentration of effect, the narrative control, of a story teller who can still make most of his rivals in his chosen field of operations look like amateurs.

BFI Bulletin. May 1953, p. 67

Tension is almost non-existent in the first hour and a half of *Rear Window*, but the last twenty minutes are as exciting as anything Hitchcock has ever done. And what *Rear Window* lacks in suspense it more than makes up for in humor. Hitchcock's distinction as a director is not his ability to create suspense, as is commonly supposed. Other directors—Reed, Welles, Wilder—are equally adept with suspense. Hitchcock's brilliance is his wit, and his flawless technique for using that wit to support and counterpoint suspense. When his wit fails, his suspense fails (*I Confess, The Paradine Case, Under Capricorn, Rope*).

In *Rear Window* the dialogue is bright, but the direction is brighter still, as it needs to be, since so much of the action must be shown in half-seen half-heard vignettes at a distance, and the camera must always be brought back to the immobilized Stewart.

Hitchcock gives us the essentials of a dozen lives with deft cinematic sureness. In about 30 seconds of screen time, e.g., he shows us the evolution of a quiet cocktail party into a cackling mob where everyone is having a good time except the host. We see, as a reflection on a window pane, Grace Kelly searching the murderer's apartment as the murderer enters his front door. The climactic fight is filmed almost entirely in close-up, which magnifies our sense of the invalid hero's immobilization, and resultant desperation.

Steve Sondheim. *Films in Review*.
Oct. 1954, p. 427

Part of the trouble with Hitchcock is that he has seldom demonstrated a sense of milieu as opposed to an instinct for locale. He has been everywhere and nowhere. He went to Cannes for *To Catch a Thief* and captured only the stucco and the sea. He went to Vermont for *The Trouble With Harry* and returned with pretty shots of the autumn foliage.

On a technical level, Hitchcock is to be commended for getting away from studio sets. His finest film, *Shadow of a Doubt*, derived much of its power from the authenticity of the small town setting. This was one of the rare instances in his career when his locale was integrated thematically with his characters. For the most part, it has been a matter of big stars wandering over strange landscapes in contrived plots.

The main trouble with Hitchcock, however, is the trouble Grierson observed in 1931. A director of bits and parts can never become a first-rate comedy director. Comedy, or for that matter, serious drama, requires a continuity and development of character and idea. The longer Hitchcock remains with the tricks, twists, gimmicks, and charged props of melodrama, the less likely he is to ever graduate from a minor genre to a major theme. And that is not to say that Hitchcock does not deserve a great deal of credit for his restless spirit and his endless experiments with the tools of his art.

Andrew George Sarris. *Film Culture*.
Winter 1955, p. 32

Hitchcock thinks that *The Birds* is his most important film, and in a certain sense, if not with certainty, this is also my opinion. Beginning with a strong plastic idea, Hitch has understood that attention would have to be given to the plot so that it becomes more than a pretext for linking bravura or suspense scenes. He has created a very successful character, that of a young San Francisco woman, sophisticated and very snobbish, who will go through terrible trials and in this way discover simplicity, naturalness.

Of course, *The Birds* can be considered a film of trick photography, but of *realistic* tricks. Actually, Hitchcock, whose mastery increases from film to film, has a constant need to confront new difficulties: he's becoming a perfect cinema athlete.

François Truffaut. *Cahiers du Cinéma*.
Nov. 1962, p. 33

Over the years, Hitchcock has punched, kicked, thrown knives and fired guns at his audience; he has, in effect, loosed a virtual war of aggression through the inventions of his films, subjecting his audience as his protagonists to the terrors of paralysis, agoraphobia, confinement, vertiginous heights, impotence, and, above all, the unknown.

To do this, and make an audience pay for it, requires, at the least, a certain equanimity and poise, the kind of poise one finds splendidly evident in Hitchcock's earliest American films, *Rebecca* and *Foreign Correspondent*, which remain largely British in character, and still essentially intact as late as *Shadow of a Doubt*, his first distinctively American one. Yet increasingly the confidence crumbles, and the films veer schizophrenically toward empty entertainments on the one hand, and something like art on the other (with the self-conscious experiments of *Lifeboat* and *Rope*, two casualties of this latter front); for Hollywood is a place where one learns perforce to have a highly specialized preoccupation with an audience, and you're only as good as the box-office receipts of your last picture. I wouldn't want to distort particulars to convenience generalities; there are brilliantly successful things in a number of Hitchcock's films from the mid-forties through the fifties, and two of them, *Notorious* and *Strangers on a Train*, achieve a fair proximity to his best work; but, increasingly, the period is one of trying to recover lost composure. And, increasingly, the attempts grow more self-effacing: *I Confess* and *The Wrong Man*, aborted attempts to resuscitate the familiar materials in more serious form; *Dial M for Murder* and *The Man Who Knew Too Much*, the cautious reproduction of a proven theatrical hit and remaking of an earlier success of Hitchcock's own; *The Trouble with Harry*, vacuous reflection of the television personality public image; *To Catch a Thief* and *North by Northwest*, lobotomized commodity entertainments. [1963]

William S. Pechter. *Twenty-four Times a Second* (Harper, 1971), pp. 177–78

Hitchcock's last pure entertainment film to date, *North by Northwest* (1959) is his final say on the chase films. An extension of *The Thirty-Nine Steps* (1935) and *Saboteur*, this outrageous, continually delightful fantasy, is a kind of summation for Hitchcock on the virtues of the simple life—an uproarious and suspenseful comedy-thriller that seems to get better on every viewing; his imagination was given full rein and it produced perhaps his purest adventure into the abstract of excitement. He followed this with his first real "shocker," *Psycho* (1960), in which his ideas about montage come full circle and reach a culmination begun in 1926 with *The Lodger*. Probably the most visual, most cinematic picture he has ever made, it could be said that through the power of his consummate technique he directs not the actors, but the audience.

Hitchcock's newest film, *The Birds* (1963), is again a further development: it is his first "catastrophe picture" (as he calls it), his vision of Judgment Day and certainly among the most incisive and frightening movies he has made. *Psycho*, everyone was heard saying, couldn't be topped. He has topped it. *The Birds* is, in every way, a more serious, more thoroughly conceived film; an excellent blending of character and incident, of atmosphere and terror. If he had never made another motion picture in his life, *The Birds* would place him securely among the giants of the cinema.

And that is where he belongs.

Peter Bogdanovich. *The Cinema of Alfred Hitchcock* (MOMA, 1963), pp. 6–7

[*Psycho*] is third-rate Hitchcock, a Grand Guignol drama in which the customers hang around just for the tiny thrill at the end; like a strip tease; and one feels as one comes out, in both these cases, that one has been had; bad taste in the mouth. I think the film is a reflection of a most unpleasant mind, a mean, sly, sadistic little mind. But there used to be humor and romance in his films as well—I am thinking of *The Thirty-Nine Steps* and *The Lady Vanishes.* These larger qualities have been leached out by his years in Hollywood, and there now remains only the ingenuity and the meanness. [1960]

The old, or classic, Hitchcock followed Poe's recipes for the short tale: every sentence must contribute to the specific effect the writer wants to produce. This effect in Hitchcock's case as in Poe's —both are Pavlovian experimenters on the nerves of their audiences—is always the thrill, the Baudelairean *frisson.* In his better films the human aspect is sketched in only enough to engage the viewers' empathy and to lend plausibility to the unpleasant little surprises he has in store for them. But in *The Birds*, background has become foreground: we must sit through a half hour of pachydermous flirtation between Rod and Tippi before the sea gull attacks, and another fifteen minutes of tedium, mostly centering around Rod's old girl . . . before the birds get into action again. If one adds later interrelations between lovers, mother, girl friend and a particularly repulsive child actress, about two-thirds of the film is devoted to extraneous matters. Poe would have been appalled. [1963]

Dwight Macdonald. *D. M. on Movies* (Prentice-Hall, 1969), pp. 303–04

The Birds is here, and what a joy to behold a self-contained movie that does not feed parasitically on outside cultural references—Chekhov, Synge, O'Neill, Genet, Behan, Melville, or what have you. Drawing from the relatively invisible literary talents of Daphne du

Maurier and Evan Hunter, Alfred Hitchcock has fashioned a major work of cinematic art and "cinematic" is the operative term here, not "literary" or "sociological." There is one sequence, for example, where the heroine is in an outboard motorboat churning across the bay while the hero's car is racing around the shore road to intercept her on the other side. This race, in itself pure cinema, is seen entirely from the girl's point of view. We see only what she can see from the boat. Suddenly, near shore, the camera picks up a sea gull swooping down on our heroine. For just a second the point of view is shifted and we are permitted to see the bird before its victim does. The director has apparently broken an aesthetic rule for the sake of a shock effect—gull pecks girl. Yet this momentary incursion of the objective on the subjective is remarkably consistent with the meaning of the film. [1963]

Andrew Sarris. *Confessions of a Cultist* (S&S, 1970), p. 84

It is difficult to be level-headed about him. His films may not be mythological; yet the spies and the sinister nuns and the betrayals at the border of his English period are so essential to our thirties' mythology—part Greeneland, part *The Orators*—that we cannot separate them from a fuddle of affection. The cinema plays on our sympathy in a way no book does. The lights dim and we are back in the world of one-eyed conjurors, practical jokes, and Big Bad Wolves stealing behind the bedposts. . . .

His films, then, are like those children's games that adults want to play. They are made with a quality one associates with such pioneers as Méliès, Griffith, and Renoir—infectious enthusiasm. Hitchcock may well be the last commercial director to think of the cinema as a new medium and the camera as a fresh toy; and it is for this naïvety surely, and not for his so-called *métaphysique*, that the French *cinéastes* love him. He is an old man now; and yet in *The Birds*, and most movingly, he is able on at least three occasions to catch our breath at the sheer delight of his filming. It is remarkable, really, how Hitchcock has worked for forty years within the industry and yet been able to succeed on his own terms; how his exuberance and inventiveness have grown rather than diminished with the years. Because of this, Hitchcock's triumph is no small one; like all the great professionals he has managed, in spite of everything, to remain an amateur at heart.

Eric Rhode. *Encounter*. Oct. 1963, p. 44

Hitchcock's recent films have been concerned largely with compulsion and its consequences. The compulsion usually presents itself as a need to hold on to or restore the past (*Psycho, Marnie, Vertigo*); often coupled with an inability to live one's life except vicariously (*Psycho, Vertigo, Rear Window, Strangers on a Train*). Compulsion leads inevitably to violence: to psychotic murders, a fall from a tower, a mass attack by the world's birds. The birds, in the film under discussion, are but an analogue for those violent irrational forces that Hitchcock sees underlying our civilized world. In other films he has presented a "normal" violence which seems explicable to our common understanding, a violence that can be dismissed with the kind of pat explanation that closes *Psycho.* But the genius of *The Birds* is that its violence is totally irrational and thus totally inescapable. We can say that, in one sense, the birds attack *because* Suzanne Pleshette and Jessica Tandy are obsessed by their memory of men they have loved, and because the arrival of Tippi Hedren at Bodega Bay threatens the continuation of these obsessions. But of course there is no causal link in the "real" world, and this is why we are terrified. The birds are an eruption from the deepest levels of the unconscious, a visible manifestation of the capacity for irrational violence that we rarely acknowledge.

The film falls short of realizing many of its potentialities through a general sloppiness of execution that seems peculiar to Hitchcock's color films. Except for a few good moments (the gathering of the birds at the schoolground, a shot from the air with the town slashed by fire and the birds circling in) the film is largely devoid of those examples of "pure cinema" that Hitchcock claims as his only interest. It maintains its considerable power through the development of its theme alone.

John Thomas. *Film Society Review.*
Sept. 1965, pp. 13–14

With the possible exception of *The Birds* (1963), *Psycho* (1960) is the only Alfred Hitchcock film which qualifies for entry into the category of horror. In many others, however, there are moments when the atmosphere of suspense or excitement may suddenly darken, when chaos appears to take command, when we find ourselves looking down into the pit. It is interesting to note that as often as not these are moments selected as exemplifying "typical Hitchcock"; the "knife" episode in his first sound film, *Blackmail* (1929), horrible not so much for the distorted voices but for the muting away of other voices as we are drawn into the girl murderer's secret, closed, panicking mind; the moment in *The Lady Vanishes* when Margaret Lockwood, thinking she has at last found the missing old lady in the railway compartment, cries out in relief, "Miss Froy!"—and the hard, grim, strange face of the young German woman rises slowly into view beneath what has appeared to be a familiar hat. There is the organ note which goes on for too long in *The Secret Agent* (1936); the distant aeroplane sowing fertiliser where no crops are, in *North by Northwest* (1959)—Hitchcock well knows that the horror of a bright empty space can equal that of the dark enclosed room; the carousel out of control in *Strangers on a Train*. In *Rear Window* (1954) there is the sudden close-up of the murderer's face in the binoculars realising that he is being seen, and the extinguishing of the strip of light under the door which indicates that he is outside the room in which James Stewart is imprisoned by his broken leg. In *The Birds*, there is the silent gathering of the crows behind the girl waiting outside the school, and perhaps the most horrid moment in the entire film—the appearance of one little sparrow beneath the chimney and the heroine's warning "Mitch—look . . . !"

Ivan Butler. *Horror in the Cinema*
(Barnes, 1967–70), p. 113

North by Northwest. The title (from Hamlet's "I am but mad north-northwest: when the wind is southerly, I know a hawk from a handsaw") is the clue to the mad geography and improbable plot. The compass seems to be spinning as the action hops all over the country and the wrong people rush about in the wrong directions. It is an amusing Alfred Hitchcock thriller (the crop-dusting sequence ranks with classic early Hitchcock), though he persists in his new worst fault: he makes even a good thing last too long. . . .

Pauline Kael. *Kiss Kiss Bang Bang*
(Little, Brown, 1968), pp. 318–19

Torn Curtain is a remarkably rich film, yet one cannot escape, at the end, a certain sense of emptiness. This is partly due to what is in other ways so admirable—the undermining of the morality of what Michael is doing on a political level: we are left wondering what it has all been for, and not finding very much of an answer. Worse, Hitchcock this time seems not greatly inspired by his principals—especially Julie Andrews, who is never more than adequate. The richness of the film lies, in fact, to a somewhat disproportionate degree in the vividness and complexity of the subsidiary characters and the use to which Hitchcock puts them: especially true of the latter half of the film, where the lovers occupy remarkably little of the spectators' attention, becoming, indeed, little more than pretexts for the various episodes, themselves uneven in complexity and interest. This leaves the film curiously without a firm centre. . . . The chief source of dissatisfaction with the film is, I think, our sense that we are being discouraged (unsuccessfully) from feeling the character to be as nasty as he in fact is. Although it contains much that one values, *Torn Curtain* as a whole is notably less successful than any other of Hitchcock's recent films.

Robin Wood. *Hitchcock's Films* (Barnes, 1969), p. 189

But for all this talk—and good talk it is—about the primacy of images (and their sequence), for all his lifelong effort to refine his style, mostly by putting it under the intense pressure of severely limited subject matter and by restricting his physical freedom (all those closed-space films—*Lifeboat, Rope, Dial M for Murder, Rear Window*), the fact is that, whether he admits it or not, Hitchcock has been developing and quite coherently expressing a view of man in his films.

He chooses to believe that this view has grown out of the necessities of his art, and there may be a certain truth in that. There are two elements in this growth. From the beginning, he says, "it seemed natural for me to put the audience in the mind of a particular character," in other words to draw it into the work by inducing "subjective" identifications with his people. Obviously he uses an objective camera fairly often, the better to orient us, but, to take the most obvious recent example, the long tracking shot in *Frenzy* that sweeps from an aerial view of the city, along the Thames, under the Tower Bridge to deposit the viewer on the Embankment is a classic Hitchcock device, seeming to pull us almost literally into the life of London, compelling a surrender of our passivity as well as our objectivity.

But besides being an instinctive stylistic choice, it is a conscious one, since this kind of thing is better done with images than with words, which suits Hitchcock's strongly held belief that "the whole art of the cinema lies in its ability to appeal to a world audience in any language," meaning "that the stress on the pictorial enables you to reach the widest possible audience." Seeing a large number of his films in a short span, as I recently have, one is struck by how many of his best, most memorable sequences are essentially silent, how often dialogue is used to make an explicit equation between banality and rationality. This, in turn, means that his work more easily clears the subtitle and dubbing hurdles of the international market. All of which is a way of saying that built into Hitchcock's esthetic is the desire—to use a word he employs—to "nurse" the audience, soothing it with jokes, thrilling it with his elegantly conceived and carefully executed special effects, cajoling rather than bludgeoning it into the moods he wants to establish.

Richard Schickel. *NYT mag.* Oct. 29, 1972, p. 22

HUSTON, JOHN (1906–)

This is perhaps why I liked John Huston's direction of *The Maltese Falcon*. The son of a famous father—who incidentally plays a very small part in the film, for luck, perhaps—John Huston has used with effective moderation the idea of the camera seeking and emphasising some characteristic, mental or physical or both of its subject rather than its ordinary form. This approach has undoubtedly added to the strength of the very fine performance of Sidney Greenstreet as Kasper Gutman, the arch-crook, and Mr. Huston has been wise enough to confine the idea to one character only. His lighting and camera work is unusual in what would normally be unnoticed sequences. For example, a telephone on a bedside table with night-light upon it from the open window plus a side-lamp, the speaker being out of the picture, but the voice heard. In other words, the *picture* of a telephone *conversation*. The story is strong of itself with an unusual ending and fine acting, but it is the treatment which makes it the best thriller so far this year.

Evelyn Russell. *Sight & Sound*. Autumn 1942, p. 43

We have become so accustomed to motion pictures based upon the amatory emotions that whenever a film motivated by something other than sexual attractions and repulsions comes from Hollywood we are like a convict who, inured to the prison yard, is allowed an hour in the meadow of the prison farm. On such rare occasions gratitude often dissolves our discrimination, or our hats are in the air even before we have seen the brave new picture that is sans sex, sans glamour, sans everything b. o.

About twenty years ago one of the most curious writers of our day—he calls himself B. Traven—wrote a novel about an old gold prospector and two American derelicts in the mountains of Mexico which resembled, in theme, Frank Norris' *McTeague* from which Erich Von Stroheim had made the motion picture *Greed*. The theme: men can be so affected by the discovery of gold that they lose their souls and sometimes the gold as well. Traven called his novel *The Treasure of the Sierra Madre*, and Walter Huston's son John has made an exceptional photoplay out of it. Its action, like that of *Greed*, derives from actual human motivations, not the usual rationalized ones. . . .

This bitter fable is told with cinematic integrity and considerable skill. True, there is some unnecessary melodrama, for which Herr Traven is to blame. Occasionally there is Hollywood hyperbole, as when Mr. Huston assembles hundreds of Mexican Indians for an effect Sergei Eisenstein achieved with a few dozen. And Humphrey Bogart is miscast. Mr. Bogart can exhibit grace under pressure incomparably, but he cannot successfully be mean. Moreover, his part has atrocious lines. But these flaws are in the shadow of some outstanding virtues. First, the basic subject matter of this picture is valid, not synthetic. Second, the exposition of this subject matter is forthright, not bowdlerized, and it is possible to learn from the screen that morality is still skin deep. And third, Walter Huston portrays the old prospector with the creative élan that sometimes comes over actors who are truly great.

Henry Hart. *NBR*. Feb.-March 1948, p. 6

We Were Strangers, its own remarkable qualities apart, marks an important point in Huston's work. In the past, he has always concentrated on a group of people with conflicting motives and actions, telling the story through them, never really taking sides with any character; and this has set him apart from other Hollywood directors. In *The Maltese Falcon* the characters were brought together by greed and ambition; in *In This Our Life* the group was a rich disintegrating family, dominated by a predatory elder daughter: in *Treasure of Sierra Madre*, greed is again the motive—a film of brilliant passages and unrelieved, finally monotonous objectivity. *Key Largo* is unique for Huston in being a completely empty, synthetic work. It is academically interesting because Huston showed, for the first time, two characters of his own generation professing positive beliefs and some faith in human values: the soldier's widow and her dead husband's army friend, a cynic at first but regenerated at the close. They are as false as the others, but significant perhaps in the light of *We Were Strangers*, where the group of people is brought about for noble, unselfish reasons, motivated by common beliefs. Fenner already believes in the values to which Frank at the end of *Key Largo* was supposed to have been converted.

Huston, however, does not identify himself with Fenner, reserves his sympathy—he is too struck with the savage irony of the situation, the place of this desperate mission in the revolution as a whole. He has made a film about heroes, but it is not heroic; as an artist, he appears to appreciate intellectually the necessity of heroism, but to be more personally aware of the effectiveness of human weakness and viciousness; in some ways the portrait of Arliete, the police chief, is the most full-blooded in the picture. While Huston's sympathies are clear enough, he has held them back partially from the characters, and for this reason the personality behind the film remains at last elusive. [1950]

Gavin Lambert in *Shots in the Dark*, edited by E. C. Ansley and others (Allan Wingate, 1951), pp. 84–85

The Asphalt Jungle, directed for MGM with a surface vivacity and tricky hucksterish flash that earlier Huston doesn't have, sums up a great deal about his work and adds a freakishness that isn't far from Camp. Almost all of his traits, the strange spastic feeling for time, lunging at what he feels is the heart of a scene and letting everything else go, the idea that authority is inherent in a few and totally absent in everyone else, a ticlike need for posh and elegance, are funneled into this film, which describes the planning, organization, specialization, and cooperation surrounding a million-dollar jewel heist. . . .

Apparently influenced by French 1930's films like *Port of Shadows*, with their operatic underworld portraits getting lost in the gray trashiness of back rooms, *Asphalt Jungle* is just as inventive as Huston's other job-oriented films. . . . Few directors project so well the special Robinson Crusoe effect of man confronted by a job whose problems must be dealt with, point by point, with the combination of personal ingenuity and scientific know-how characterizing the man of action. Two exquisite cinematic moments: the safe-cracker, one hand already engaged, removing the cork from the nitro bottle with his teeth; the sharp, clean thrust of the chisel as it slices through the wooden strut.

Throughout this footage, Huston catches the mechanic's absorption with the sound and feel of the tools of his trade as they overcome steam tunnel, door locks, electric-eye burglar alarm, strongbox. It is appropriate that the robbers dramatically subordinate themselves to their instruments and the job at hand, move with the patient deadpan *éclat* of a surgical team drilled by Stroheim. [1950]

Manny Farber. *Negative Space* (Praeger, 1971), pp. 34–35

The African Queen is clearly a good picture; Bogart in particular is a pleasure to watch because, as in *The Treasure of the Sierra Madre*, he has put aside his screen "personality" and consented once more to interpret a part. His disreputable Charlie Allnut, a roaring, dirty, drunken river pirate hiding the soul of a suburban clerk, is an entertaining if not entirely plausible or original creation.

The whole picture, in fact, is entertaining but not entirely plausible or original. Miss Hepburn's prim missionary is too patly competent in adversity, the love affair is too predictable and too successful, the river cataracts are too tempestuous, the Germans are too stupid, and the destruction of the gun-boat is too unlikely and too inevitable. John Huston is an able, perceptive director and James Agee is a skilled and honorable writer; together they have brought a workmanlike adaptation of C. S. Forester's novel to the screen.

But there is no reason for making such a picture except the reason that pictures must be made. So, however excellent the technique, however painstaking the execution, however well timed the laughs, the thrills, and the embraces, one's judgment in the end is "So what?" *The African Queen* is a good picture in the sense that it will amuse almost anyone and irritate almost no one, but when you compare it with what has been done in Johannesburg you find that, in the sense of having a source or a purpose or a place in the records of our time, it is no picture at all.

Robert L. Hatch. *Reporter.* April 1, 1952, p. 38

If Melville's *Moby Dick* could ever be translated to another medium, it would no doubt be to the film. Its tragic grandeur, strange mysticism, dramatic rhetoric cannot be divorced from the realistic actualities of the sea, the life of ships and the hunt for the sperm whale, which the film alone can adequately represent. John Huston's film presents this surface of realism very well. The colour—a process devised by Huston himself with Oswald Morris—is remarkably fine; and the sea and the ship, the whaling village and the whale hunts are admirably realised. Huston has wonderfully controlled the tempi of the film, whose pace gathers into violence and then ebbs into a doldrum calm before the wild finale of storm and destruction and the quiet closing shots of Ishmael floating alone on his "soft and dirge-like main."

The physical excitements of the adventure story which is the superstructure of Melville's book are all admirably done. Where Huston has failed is in suggesting the mysticism of the book and the ominous influence of Moby Dick himself. The great white whale is no "portentous and mysterious monster . . . the gliding great demon of the seas of life"; he is often, only too clearly made of plastic and electronically controlled. Without this presence and motivation much of the story loses its significance: Ahab's strange rituals of preparation become absurd, and there is no explanation for the "evil magic" with which the crew's souls become possessed.

BFI Bulletin. Dec. 1956, p. 150

John Huston is a variable man who has let the world know it. He made *The Treasure of Sierra Madre*, a movie so dazzling that we thought for a moment we were witnessing the coming of a new art, and followed it with a half-arty, half-matured little job of his own, *We Were Strangers*, which might have ruined a less versatile director. The good picture had not made enough money to suit the Warners; the bad one was an independent production that should have bankrupted everyone concerned. Huston went back to Hollywood to make a bad picture that would make money. With *The African Queen* he gave notice that Hollywood was not going to make a martyr out of him, at least not so long as he had first call on the services of one of the most desirable properties in the business, Humphrey Bogart. In *The African Queen* he had also Katharine Hepburn and a good story, and out of these elements he made a picture in which two or three sequences were interesting and a few hundred feet were good color; all the rest was without taste and even without cinematic skill. In *Moulin Rouge* color was *used*, it was arbitrarily changed to create effects, it was taken away from realism, and the effect was pure magic; within this magic a cold, ferocious dislike of humanity suffused the screen, reflecting the hatred Toulouse-Lautrec might have felt for the world, preventing us from having the faintest sympathy with him. It was a masterpiece of sculpture at the top of a glacier, and the great popular success it achieved is a tribute to Huston's uncanny skill as much as to José Ferrer's technical brilliance in the lead. The odor of sexuality which occasionally came from the screen was a secondary item; the shooting of every scene to expose the vanity or the ugliness or the absurdity of the people involved was carried to the exact point at which a spectator might derive some pleasure from thinking himself superior to the unfortunates on the screen. The picture lacked all the elements of greatness—and was a triumph.

Gilbert Seldes. *The Public Arts* (S&S, 1956), pp. 29–30

On the face of it, *The Roots of Heaven* is promising Huston material. Like nearly every film he has ever made, it is concerned with a prodigious undertaking: sometimes it is the pursuit of wealth, sometimes it is an objective in war, or blowing up a ship or a politician, or killing a whale. Usually it involves a protracted physical ordeal of utmost realism; Huston's actors have been known to suffer a good deal. Then, of course, the assignment suits Huston's personal reputation as a globe-trotting director who works on the grand scale in the rough. The trouble with *The Roots of Heaven*, and with the last half-dozen or so of Huston's efforts, is that the virtues of this approach exist quite independently of the film itself. A style of *modus operandi*, elaborate with suggestions of integrity, perfectionism, devotion and marvelous temperament (e.g., his celebrated walkout on *A Farewell to Arms*), has come to be substituted for quality as an accomplished fact in work done. Huston's true style has evolved as a sort of behind-the-scenes swagger, which finds an exact correlation in the increasingly improvised and decorative nature of his films. All the energies of production are spent upon surface; in effects of color, lighting, and framing (usually provided by the Brilliant Oswald Morris); in an impressionistic gloss on costumes, scars, sweat, sand, and the precise entry of bullets into flesh. The appeal is to the eye, or as it were, to the eye-*cum*-guts. . . .

Huston's other current film, *The Barbarian and the Geisha*, finds the director on holiday in Japan, shooting from a script that contrives to blend "The Cavalcade of America" and "My True Story." . . . It marks, perhaps, the nadir in Huston's absorption with appearances, and it is saddening to think that the director of *The Asphalt Jungle*, made eight years ago on an MGM lot, has gained professional freedom and international celebrity in order to become, at 51, yet another taskmaster who goes out in the midday sun.

Arlene Croce. *Film Quarterly*. Winter 1958, pp. 43, 45

It has become almost a ghoulish task to comment on a new John Huston picture. The latest is called *The Unforgiven*, is set in the Texas Panhandle in 1871, and is, in a word, ludicrous. . . .

If one could take the film seriously, one would be disturbed by its curious race snobbism. (The plot hinges on whether or not an adopted daughter has Indian blood.) But it would be difficult to criticize this hodgepodge of crudely stitched sententiousness and lame story-conference inspirations, in which heavily emphasized early characters disappear and late entrants suddenly loom large. The direction shows a now-pathetic flash or two of old Huston quality, but for the most part it is feeble and disconcerted. That Huston could not get a good performance out of Lancaster cannot be held against him, but he has achieved what no other director has done: he has got a bad performance out of lovely, miscast Audrey Hepburn. [1960]

Stanley Kauffmann. *A World on Film* (Harper, 1966), p. 147

How much strain can a director's reputation take? Of late years, John Huston seems to have been trying to find out. I think he has carried the experiment too far with *The Unforgiven*. Some B pictures are good fun in their modest little way, but there is nothing worse than a big Hollywood film that goes wrong. *The Unforgiven* is a work of profound phoniness, part adult Western—I prefer Tom Mix—part that *Oklahoma!* kind of folksy Americana. It is limp as drama, every situation is built up until it soggily collapses, even the final Indian attack is tedious: can this be the man who gave us *The Maltese Falcon* and *Beat the Devil*? [1960]

Dwight Macdonald. *D. M. on Movies* (Prentice-Hall, 1969), p. 283

The last third of [*The Misfits*] is all Huston's and, working with Miller's ideas instead of his dialogue, he succeeds in partially fulfilling the enormous ambitiousness of the story. The mustang hunt itself is magnificent: Guido flies his ancient biplane into an immense valley where a small herd of wild horses are grazing, then drives them out of it toward the vast plains where Gay, Perce, and Roslyn await with lariats and a truck. Somehow Huston manages to work out most of the many dramatic themes simultaneously within this one long scene. There are so many epic conflicts being resolved that one is hardly aware of some of them: the archetypal struggle between man and beast, and, consequently, nature; the determination of justice in the wanton destruction of life; man's proud refusal to accept change on terms other than his own; and the closing of the frontier, bringing the "end of innocence"—an idea that has obsessed writers from Fenimore Cooper to Leslie Fiedler.

The obvious and serious flaws of *The Misfits* should not obscure the distinguished treatment of much of the material, a treatment so rare in American cinema that one is almost convinced this film is better than reason suggests. The long-shot of Roslyn alone out on a sand flat, writhing and stomping as she denounces her companions for their inhumanity, is cinematically perfect. Two fine scenes: one in a bar after the rodeo, where Roslyn hits a bolo ball 100 times consecutively as the cowboys are frantically passing bets on her and a small boy is becoming unintentionally plastered; the other, splendidly symbolic, where Guido is drunkenly trying to finish building his house in the middle of the night, though as he throws the boards up he steps on the heliotrope which Gay had tenderly planted when he and Roslyn were living there. The film is memorable for its characterization of the American cowboy, which is devoid of the conventional aggrandizements. . . .

Lawrence Grauman, Jr. *Film Quarterly*.
Spring 1961, p. 53

The greatest disappointment in the film [*The Misfits*] is director John Huston; he is the one who should have made the camera do its work. The bringing down of the stallion is effective enough, the visual analogy that the story intended it to be, but for the most part the running of the horses and the rodeo are conventionally filmed. Huston never manages to make us see Reno or Guido's house as they should be seen, the first an image of the rootlessness of the characters, the second a symbol of conventional living abandoned and then reaccepted. The most effective scene is the one featured in all the ads, in which Miss Monroe plays with a rubber ball and paddle. Here, Huston not only uses her body (comically, again) but catches the sense of spontaneous excitement and gaiety, the underlying hint of forlorn hysteria that the scene is supposed to represent. Through the film as a whole, it is almost as though Huston and Miller worked against one another: scene, dialogue, scene, dialogue—the film runs almost in labeled segments. But the scenes might have been shot by any Hollywood director, the dialogue written by any pseudo-serious script man.

Gerald Weales. *Reporter*. March 2, 1961, p. 47

Huston is a superior craftsman, and he revels in violence that is imaginitive and sinister—*The Asphalt Jungle*, for instance. When he attempts portrayals that require more depth of insight, he is more likely to falter. Although his *Moulin Rouge* was heralded at the time it appeared, largely because of its mellow (and Lautrec-like) color photography—for which a photography consultant, Eliot Elisofen must be given the main credit—it was an only dimly realized portrait of Toulouse-Lautrec. In fact, the movie threw Lautrec's life entirely out of focus, presenting him chiefly as a haunted, forlorn, lonely man, carrying a torch for a dismal prostitute and an immaculately dignified fashion model. The effect of the whole, after a spirited beginning that suggested the gaieties of the Moulin Rouge and the Moulin de la Galette, became soporific. . . .

Whether it is inability or laziness on Huston's part that prevents him from getting to the core of his subject, he seems particularly ill at ease when it comes to the statement of ideas. A George Stevens may make himself too clear, but Huston brings no ideological stamp at all to his films, contenting himself, one must assume, with the ideas already embodied in his properties. The adventurous aspects of his *The Roots of Heaven* he caught very well; he was on less familiar ground when it came to concretizing the ironic idealism of Morel, a mysterious figure in the movie (a good deal less so in the novel by Romain Gary) who devoted himself to protecting the race of elephants from extinction in Africa. Huston, a big-game hunter himself, had to swallow his own enthusiasm for killing game, and propound a thesis that was contrary to his own inclinations.

Hollis Alpert. *The Dream and the Dreamers* (Macmillan, 1962), pp. 148–49

It is impossible, I would think, for any educated person to sit through *Freud* without bursting into laughter at least once, and to some people it will seem excruciatingly funny. There are dozens of scenes where one seems to have strayed into a Mike Nichols-Elaine May parody: "*Try and remember, child*: What happened on that day of your sister's wedding?" Yet this grotesque side of the film, lamentable as it may be in a film devoted to one of our greatest men, was probably unavoidable, for it stems precisely from the widespread diffusion of Freudian ideas and their vulgarizations. An elementary explanation of a doctrine which is now so accepted as to offer material for nightclub comedy can hardly help seeming risible. And what John Huston has produced is a feature-length classroom film, even down to arty "think" titles, an intoning narrator, and the awkward mouthing of lines which clearly can never be properly spoken because they were written to be read. . . .

Ernest Callenbach. *Film Quarterly*. Summer 1963, p. 50

Reflections in a Golden Eye. John Huston has devised all sorts of visual equivalences to match the literary style of Carson McCullers. He has drained out all the color from the color film until the fatal climax, as if to fulfill Sergei Eisenstein's dictum on chromatic expressiveness found in the Russian director's overrated treatise, *The Film Sense*. (Eisenstein had criticized Alexander Korda for not varying the tonality of the film *Rembrandt* to correspond to the aging of the painter's palette.) Huston plays the horses for all they are worth, both symbolically and rhetorically, a bad habit he picked up from Arthur Miller in *The Misfits*. He succeeds in keeping a consistent distance from all his leading characters, and the ensemble playing of Brando, Taylor, Keith, and Harris cannot be faulted. Where Huston falters is in the atmosphere he provides for the action. Like Robert Wise with *The Haunting*, Huston overdirects *Reflections* for the sake of a mass audience in which he has little confidence. His film lacks the special stillness of the novel. . . . There is too much expressionistic foliage on the screen and too much declamatory thunder on the sound track. [1967]

Andrew Sarris. *Confessions of a Cultist* (S&S, 1970), pp. 323–24

A much more disheartening, in fact distasteful, movie is *Reflections in a Golden Eye*. Carson McCullers's vision was that of a world where aberration is the norm, where perversion is worn as a badge of genuineness if not of honor. But her quaint style—a kind of schoolgirl baroque laced with inversions (verbal as well as sexual), an innocent relish of unhealthiness couched in wobbly poeticisms—creates an atmosphere redolent with morbid fascination. Yet for all its superficial fidelity to the original, John Huston's film, with a script by Chapman Mortimer and Gladys Hill, is pedestrian, crass, and uninvolving to the point of repellence. Things are clumsily spelled out here. If, in the novel, Leonora threatens to horsewhip her officer husband, in the film she actually does it, and publicly, too. If, in the novel, the husband, consumed with love-hate for Private Williams, picks up the candy wrapper the soldier discards, in the film he is seen droolingly smoothing it out in the guilty privacy of his study.

Huston's direction is as literal-minded as can be, except for one far-fetched but abhorrent device. By some photographic process, the film emerges in one color, a kind of burnished gold (a top-heavy allusion to the already pretentious and meaningless title), but with one other color allowed to peep through: red, which comes out as a sickly rose madder in a piece of clothing or upholstery, and even more grotesquely in a woman's cheek. This envelops a painfully artless film in a painfully arty shell, and one feels trapped in a huge, overheated hothouse containing nothing but common snapdragons. [1967]

John Simon. *Movies into Film* (Dial, 1971), pp. 34–35

[In *The Bible*] Huston shoots arrows all over the place; he pushes himself too hard, he tries to do too many different things. The movie is episodic not merely because the original material is episodic but also because, like Griffith in *Intolerance*, he can find no way to rhythm together everything that he's trying to do. Yet the grandeur of this kind of crazy, sinfully extravagant movie-making is in trying to do too much. We tend, now, to think of the art of the film in terms of depth, but there has always been something about the eclectic medium of movies that, like opera, attracts artists of Promethean temperament who want to use the medium for scale, and for a scale that will appeal to multitudes. I don't mean men like DeMille who made small-minded pictures on a big scale—they're about as Promethean as a cash register. I mean men like Griffith and von Stroheim and Abel Gance and Eisenstein and Fritz Lang and Orson Welles who thought *big*, men whose prodigious failures could make other people's successes look puny. This is the tradition in which Huston's *The Bible* belongs. Huston's triumph is that despite the insanity of the attempt and the grandiosity of the project, the technology doesn't dominate the material: when you respond to the beauty of such scenes in *The Bible* as the dispersal of the animals after the landing of the Ark, it is not merely the beauty of photography but the beauty of conception.

Pauline Kael. *Kiss Kiss Bang Bang* (Little, Brown, 1968), p. 132

The Kremlin Letter is silly enough on its surface, with its *Mission Impossible* convolutions and its antiquated attempt to create an ambience of modern iniquity, that one may fail to notice underneath the classic Huston tale of the gathering together of a band of skilled professionals on a quest which fails. The spy-story twists and the depravity are *The Kremlin Letter*'s thinly spread surface chic; underneath—rather amazingly, given the duration of their absence—run the preoccupations of *The Maltese Falcon* and *The Asphalt Jungle*.

Of course, John Huston is in decline, and in itself, *The Kremlin Letter* is hardly substantial enough to alter the course or even cushion the fall. American directors are usually in and out of decline, but there are declines and declines, and Huston's is a prodigy: in the strict, classical purity of its prolonged downward movement, perhaps unrivaled even in the decline-crammed annals of the cinema. Yet it is still worth saying, and especially now that it is so much more difficult to say that, once, John Huston was good and sometimes much better than good. To attempt to fix the causes of so spectacular a squandering of talent would require more detail than I am able to offer here, but I would tentatively suggest that the deterioration has had much to do with Huston's growing self-consciousness of his reputation as a serious artist, and his increasingly desperate efforts to satisfy the demands thought to attend Artistic Seriousness. Once, Huston's films were alive with a certain hard if not deep intelligence, and an intense if narrow vision. Once, he took his stories from Dashiell Hammett and W. R. Burnett, and impressed his own dark meanings on them; now he takes his meanings from Arthur Miller and Tennessee Williams, and flounders helplessly in the absence of a story.

William S. Pechter. *Commentary*.
Nov. 1970, p. 91

INCE, THOMAS (1880–1924)

Evidently Thomas H. Ince and William Clifford, whose names are frequently bracketed under the titles of two-reel Western pictures, determined to give themselves a free rein in producing a typical Western subject on an extraordinarily large scale. It is as if they took the photoplay recipe that has been found adequate for shorter films and doubled, or tripled, all of the ingredients to make the biggest picture of its kind on record. The similarities and differences between this production and less pretentious Westerns, suggest the comparison of a circus in Madison Square Garden and one in a country village. Each adopts practically the same means to catch public fancy, and the difference lies in the degrees to which the means have been perfected. Instead of one ring, there are three rings; the menagerie is larger, the clowns and acrobats more proficient; still, a circus is a circus, and likewise a Western melodrama is just that.

But before considering the story that makes the classification so unmistakable, it is best to avoid the danger of seeming to dismiss *The Bargain* as a picture of small moment. On the contrary, it may be pointed to as a model of what can be accomplished in a popular field of photoplay work. The exteriors, photographed in the Arizona canyon, offer a sequence of glorious views in which the rugged wildness of a virgin country predominates. There is variety and a keen regard for a wise placing of the camera in gaining picturesque effects. Probably no preceding film has done such full justice to the scenic wonders of Arizona, which in itself is sufficient to give the picture a high recommendation. . . .

[To] compensate for somewhat elementary character drawing, the picture contains what many people prefer—a story replete with action and the suspense which an expert plot builder, such as Mr. Ince, seldom fails to create. . . . Altogether there need be no question about the wide popularity of this production.

NYDM. Nov. 18, 1914, p. 32

Civilization, Thomas H. Ince's effort to rival D. W. Griffith with a photo spectacle of the scale and scope of *The Birth of a Nation*, was displayed in New York for the first time last evening at the Criterion Theatre. It is an excellently elaborate photo pageant on the physical horrors of war, a big motion picture marked by lavishness in production and beauty in photography.

Civilization attempts to serve the pacifists as *The Battle Cry of Peace* tried to serve the cause of preparedness. Its argument is elementary, a leaf out of the pacifists' primer, a projection on the screen of something of that state of mind that was most in evidence in this neighborhood at the time the Ford expedition set forth from these shores. Its program describes it as a direct appeal to the "the mothers of men."

The hero of *Civilization* is the submarine commander who, secretly wearing the purple cross of the Mothers of Men Society, refuses to torpedo a defenseless passenger vessel. In the mutiny that follows the submarine is sunk. He is drowned and his spirit goes to an inferno inspired by Doré. There the Christ comes to him, receives him as a redeemed soul, returns among men in the discarded body of the dead man, and there takes the warring King on such a review of war's horrors as to make him cry for peace. The King then heeds the pleas of the Mothers of Men, and the last picture shows the soldiers returning jubilant to their peasant homes.

In the earlier part of this photoplay there are many stirring battle scenes, and the whole episode of the submarine and the sinking of another *Lusitania* is extraordinarily graphic—so graphic, indeed, that at this point in the unfolding of the spectacle last evening Billie Burke fainted.

Civilization was displayed last evening with a full orchestra in full blast with off-stage singing, both solo and choral, and with a preliminary corporeal pantomime of the sort employed in *Ramona* and always of doubtful value in the screen world.

NYT. June 3, 1916, p. 11

The greatest example of cinematographic art and truth is being offered to us this month. Two characteristic works of the American director Thomas Ince are being presented a few days apart. Last week it was *Despoiler*. Next week it will be *Civilization*. The public has been deeply impressed and its joy has been lively. I cannot say as much for the French cinema makers or merchants. They laughed at *Despoiler* and very few were present at the private premiere of *Civilization*. Too bad for them. They will learn to their sorrow what their negligence has cost them and their country. America is sending us admirable films that have enthused the crowd. Our artists have not deigned to study *The Cheat*. Nevertheless there were *Peggy, Molly, The Aryan, Honor's Altar* and several other magistral lessons of power and simplicity. But rest assured, the Parisian directors never go to see them. At most they pass their invitations on to the most sleepyheaded members of their family.

Thomas Ince would teach them a great deal. This director is an extraordinary case. He is neither a ham nor an obstinate literary type. He looks first and then he imagines according to what he has seen or could have seen.

His force, one of his forces, is that he begins with an idea and not with a laboriously constructed scenario. He has ideas worthy of the name. He sees as Wells does, and he achieves. He tries, at least, and this attempt is rich in lyricism and candor.

Beginning with an interior *élan*—poetic or human—to execute it he leans on precise details, of a living everyday nature that are intense precisely because they are ordinary. . . .

It is sure to take many years before a man like Thomas Ince is appreciated at his just value. For a long time to come he risks being known as a man who makes films that cost millions. He will be compared to the authors of *Christus*, which is irritating. These gigantic films of Thomas Ince's are not intentionally monstrous: the ideas dominate. The proof? He does not try for easy effects, he makes no use of Italianate picture postcard decors; he does not use illustrious actors or sensational actresses; each character is only a figure, each landscape only an accessory; what violence and what tranquillity!

May the categorical success of these works of high style decide the apprentices in our country to open their eyes. May they from time to time try to imitate nobody, not even nature. The *movement* of life, and if possible of *interior* life, that should be the goal of a true and captivating art. Don't try to make things big. Don't always be wanting to bring tears on or make only yourself cry before the screen. Listen to your sincerity. It speaks better than you do. But you have to recognize that it only speaks when it's in the mood to.

Louis Delluc. *Cinéma & Cie* (Grasset, 1919), pp. 24–26

Even such films as *The Fugitive*, produced in 1916 by Thomas H. Ince with William S. Hart . . . displayed distinctive creative merit. Ince's superb direction of the crowd of cowboys and entertainers at the bar puts to shame such recent attempts as *Rose of the Rancho*, for example. It was amazing to see how varied and yet well coordinated were the actions of each individual in the bar scenes.

Robert Stebbins. *New Theatre*. March 1936, p. 23

His appeal to that [pacifist] market was nicely calculated. On the one hand, the ambition of a ruler causing war, carnage, the starvation of civilians; on the other a secret army of women pledged to end the fighting. The leaders of the pacifist movement of the early twentieth century were quite willing to believe in miracles, especially when made real by the magic of the screen and *Civilization* is an apt rendering of the ideas and sentiments of most pacifists at the time. Its sources in the internationalist, humanitarian and religious movements of the preceding hundred years are clearly evident throughout.

Ince's editing has never been more economical or functional. "That universal appeal," said a contemporary review, "absolutely necessary to the success of any art work . . . is provided, not through the joys and sorrows of one little group of persons, but in a great series of bereavements and reunions." The skill with which these incidents are interwoven is striking even today, but the method itself proved to be the film's principal weakness. The "great series of bereavements and reunions" seems to take place in an emotional vacuum. Despite its fervid tone, *Civilization* is hollow, impersonal: in order to stress Christian internationalism, in order to apply to *all* wars, it had to remain allegorical, "What," the review continues, "keeps this from being a Master Film? Simply its absence of intimacy. These people are not our people, this king not our king, this war not our war, this flag not our flag. It is a myth of the imagination!"

Iris Barry in *Film Notes*, edited by Iris Barry
(MOMA, 1949), pp. 19–20

To this very day it is not uncommon to read that the Germans invented the moving camera between 1919 and 1925, even though it has been shown again and again that Griffith's *The Birth of a Nation* (1915) and *Intolerance* (1916) contained moving camera shots as spectacular as any to be found in a German film. Similarly, the Russians have been credited with startling innovations in editing techniques, even though these were derived from American productions. Not only D. W. Griffith, but Thomas H. Ince, that forgotten master of American cinematography, had discovered the secrets of editing at least ten years before Eisenstein and Pudovkin arrived on the scene. A glance at Ince's misunderstood and much neglected masterpiece, *Civilization* (1916) will reveal that Eisenstein, in particular, owed much to this great American director. For Ince possessed many of the stylistic mannerisms usually associated with Eisenstein. The violent movement, the swift tempo, the dynamic compositions, the emphasis upon crowds and abstract concepts, and the "collision" between shots—all these features of Eisenstein's style are also to be found in Ince. Indeed, it is possible to regard *Civilization*, with its striking representation of a mutiny at sea, as the precursor of *Potemkin*. And yet Ince has been reduced by the tendency to denigrate *all* American films, to the rank of a nonentity.

Joseph and Harry Feldman. *Films in Review*.
April 1951, pp. 21–22

If *The Battle of Gettysburg* is remarkable for its rhythmic qualities, *The Typhoon* for its editing, if even the social melodramas supervised by Ince remain in our memory thanks to his use of the close-up, it is assuredly in the Rio Jim cycle that that author gave his style both that lyric flight and that sense of true atmosphere that provoked the admiration of France after World War I. The attack on the stagecoach, the equivocal attraction of the saloon, the fight in the desert: all these darmatic elements of the western have already achieved in *The Aryan* an astonishing dignity. The man and the horse, the water and the rock, the heat of the day, and the night are the marks of this mythic grandeur that were to lift a commercial genre to the level of a great legendary tale. William Hart, regenerated, severe and vibrant adventurer, the ancestor of "the plainsman," "the man of the lost valleys," "the man without a star," rejoins in the mythology of the silent screen Mary Pickford, Douglas Fairbanks, and Chaplin. We now know that Ince did not direct but supervised these films (the direction was confided to talented men like Reginald Barker). But this is the point—he is grand in the measure that he was able to discipline an entire troupe and give the production he supervised that vigorous unity we feel in *The Italian* (neo-realist before there was such a word) and *Painted Souls*.

Henri Agel. *Les Grands Cinéasts* (Editions Universitaires, 1959), pp. 32–33

It was said that Ince never finished reading a property when he bought it for translation to the screen and had to be briefed by assistants so that he could talk intelligently to authors. Nevertheless, he was instrumental in setting the great American screen style, which is direct in its methods of story-telling and emphasizes fast, concrete action, tight dramatic construction, economy of statement, and a minimum of reflection and subtlety. He would work on a script until it was perfect, then stamp it "produce as written" and wait for the first "rough cut" of the finished film. These he worked on intensively, constantly trying to sharpen and simplify his films. His most devastating criticism was "it wanders" and when this judgment was passed, out would come the shears. In the trade he was known as the greatest film editor of his time; even in retrospect it is hard to name anyone who surpassed him, at least in the creation of a viable, commercial style.

Richard Schickel. *Movies* (Basic, 1964), p. 56

Thomas H. Ince did everything. He was so proficient of every aspect of filmmaking that even films he didn't direct have the Ince-print, because he exercised such tight control over his scripts and edited so mercilessly that he could delegate direction to others and still get what he wanted. Much of what Ince contributed to the American film took place off the screen; he established production conventions that persisted for years and, though his career in films lasted only fourteen years, his influence far outlived him.

Tom Shales in *The American Film Heritage*,
edited by the American Film Institute
(Acropolis, 1972), p. 43

INGRAM, REX (1892–1969)

It is as a work in kinetic photography that the screened *Four Horsemen* should first be considered, because its standing as a photoplay depends upon its pictorial properties and not upon its relation to a widely read novel. The most important fact about the production, then, is that, although it has a good deal of wordiness, erratic tempo and illogical emphasis common to screen adaptations of printed stories, it is nevertheless distinguished from many other works of its kind by genuine cinematographic qualities. It is made, if not entirely, at least in large part, of telling moving pictures. Many of its scenes are the result of fine photography, and, better still, fine cinematography. Rex Ingram, the director of the production, is among those who believe that principles of painting and sculpture should be applied to motion pictures, and scenes in *Four Horsemen* are concrete illustrations of what the application of these principles means. . . .

Mr. Ingram has made many eloquent motion pictures. This means that although the spectator now and then has the impression that the photoplay is simply the novel splendidly illustrated, this impression is dissipated as often as it is formed by scenes and successions of scenes which speak for themselves, tell their part of the narrative in their own language without the aid of words. The execution of the citizens of Villeblanche, for example, is done in pure cinematography, and is one of the most impressive incidents of the story. In bringing the symbolic Four Horsemen into the photoplay Mr. Ingram again has done his work cinematographically, and with such a discerning sense of the unreal in reality that what might easily have been banal or incongruous has become a pervading and leavening part of the picture.

NYT. March 7, 1921, p. 8

At the present time, Rex Ingram is one of the best directors. In America his name is cited immediately after Griffith's in terms of merit. Rex Ingram is still little known in France, but *The Four Horsemen of the Apocalypse* revealed him to the Paris public and was followed by *The Conquering Power*, *Black Orchids*, and *Hearts Are Trumps*.

Rex Ingram is above all an artist. His paintings and his sculptures are remarkable. Actually, he worked in these two fields for a long time before turning to the movies exclusively. . . .

The Conquering Power and *The Four Horsemen of the Apocalypse* contributed to an artistic reputation that was confirmed by *The Prisoner of Zenda*. . . .

In the evening I often visited this famous director, who did me the honor of consulting me on arranging the French atmosphere of *Black Orchids*. We spent long evenings together in his immense study and I was pleased to receive his confidences.

Rex Ingram adores France. When he finishes the film that is to follow *Black Orchids*, he will go to the Midi to make two films. . . .

One day I saw something strange:

Rex Ingram likes to make use of the law of contrasts in his films and he does not hesitate to follow a deliciously directed love scene with horrible phenomena whose ugliness is their sole reason for being in the movies.

One day Rex Ingram was filming a railway station scene for *The Prisoner of Zenda*. The station was in a German town and Ingram had chosen to play the stationmaster and a kind of spy, two terrible obese, misshapen gnomes, whose faces were terrifyingly ugly. . . . The director explained to the dwarfs the scene to be filmed and the impression made on us by the contrast of a handsome young man placed between two monsters was extraordinary . . . The immediate opposition of Beauty and Ugliness struck all those who saw the scene . . . Rex Ingram is destined to be one of the most famous directors in the world; we will soon see. . . .

Robert Florey. *Filmland* (Editions de Cinémagazine, 1923), pp. 90–91

The Prisoner of Zenda was Ingram's fourth production for Metro, following on the heels of *Turn to the Right*, his only ignoble effort since he was propelled through the portals of Universal City. Ingram realized that his artistic reputation had been seriously damaged by *Turn to the Right* (a cut-and-dried piece of hokum), and that he must do something sensational with Anthony Hope's story to regain control of his wabbling prestige.

Moreover, there were unfriendly rumors about Ingram going the Hollywood rounds. They said that the real credit for *The Four Horsemen of the Apocalypse* belonged to June Mathis—that Ingram had been no more than a mouthpiece, used to carry out her orders. Now June Mathis had left Metro to join the Paramount forces, and a dismally unintelligent picture like *Turn to the Right* was the result.

I heard this prediction over and over again from the chronic gossips of Hollywood Boulevard: "Ingram, without June Mathis, is just a poor third-rater. Watch him flop."

Rex Ingram himself probably heard echoes of this, for he set to work and made *The Prisoner of Zenda* into an exceptionally fine picture. He displayed the same fertile imagination that had distinguished *The Four Horsemen of the Apocalypse*, the same sensitive feeling for form, in composition and in rhythm, and the same intellectual alertness. If anything, he was a little too careful in this production—and herein lies the one criticism that may be made against *The Prisoner of Zenda.* In his desire to have everything perfect, every scene harmoniously composed, Ingram occasionally lost sight of the fact that a motion picture, and particularly a romantic one, should be more of an impressionistic painting than a steel engraving.

The glamourous romance and the hopeless tragedy of the South Sea islands were reproduced by Rex Ingram in *Where the Pavement Ends.* He made his picture reflect both these qualities, and did it in a legitimate way.

Where the Pavement Ends was too long for its substance—it exhausted several reels before it even scratched the surface of drama—but it was gorgeously beautiful, and it was dignified by intelligence and sincerity in its treatment. Harry Morey gave a vivid performance as a villainous trader, and Edward Connelly impersonated a benevolent but ineffectual missionary with genuine feeling.

Robert E. Sherwood. *The Best Moving Pictures of 1922–1923* (Small, Maynard, 1923), pp. 20–21, 105

The Four Horsemen of the Apocalypse was to the minds of many competent critics a much overrated novel. It displayed not only the merits of Ibanez as a story-teller but also his grave defects. His tale was rather clumsily developed, and its interest was not cumulative. It is hardly going too far to say that the author narrowly avoided handicapping his achievement by an anti-climax.

But the screen presentation of *The Four Horsemen* was absolutely free from the shortcomings ascribed to the novel. Not only was it marvellously effective in its appeal to the eye, but the logical and dramatic unfolding of the basic story was a striking revelation of the valuable service that an expert scenario-writer may render, now and then, to the professional writer of novels. For the many outrages that fictionists have received at the hands of the film-makers some atonement is offered at times, and *The Four Horsemen* as a photoplay proves that the pot may be unjust in calling the kettle black.

Edward S. Van Zile. *The Marvel—The Movie* (Putnam, 1923), pp. 79–80

If the art of the motion picture is the art of composition—of images arranged and photographed so as to create the impression of an atmospheric mood, or of dramatic forces in motion, or of background against which characters appear and make themselves known, and if the purpose of this art is to utilize any or blend all of these so as to help the visualization of life, time, circumstance in their true context—then the mechanics of effect must always be paramount in the use of the photoplay medium. Two American directors are preeminent in their understanding of these mechanics—Maurice Tourneur and Rex Ingram. And both at their most impressive moments have achieved intensity of action by producing "motion" in "stillness"—which is the exact reverse of what is commonly supposed to be the nature of pictures in motion. Thus, any criticism of Mr. Tourneur's or Mr. Ingram's contribution to the art of the photoplay falls into a discussion of technicalities—a point probably most distressing to the reader who wants to know what the story is about and who are the actors. . . .

In Mr. Ingram's *Scaramouche* Danton (most finely played by George Siegmann) turns upon the lords of the Assembly his pox-marked face and motionless, regards them and the power of the orator of liberty charges from the screen with a great dramatic force; the head of Robespierre, emerging from its ruff like that of a grotesque bird, casts its calm, strange eyes aloft—only the lips are permitted to move tirelessly—and a flood of droning sound descends from the picture, a cold, philosophic discourse that makes known the man. It does not matter that Mr. Ingram has gone to *All For A Woman* for his Danton and his Robespierre—to Emil Jannings and Werner Kraus; it is simply a proof of his good sense, his knowledge of how to render in pictures the meaning of these characters, which in a little footage are made to recreate great personal forces in the background of the story he is telling. The picture is full of such arresting pauses in movement which vibrate with "action." . . .

Of course, there are fine sequences of action in the accepted sense—continuous flows of movement passing from scene to scene always with the motive of balance in pictures. Scaramouche denounces the aristocrats in the public square and the windows of the palace shatter down before the brick-bats of the mob; Scaramouche meets the challenge of La Tour d'Azyr's retainer at the door of the Assembly (an exceedingly fine and dramatic sequence) and hurls his opponent to the floor; the crowds of the Revolution surge and march, singing the Marseillaise; at the last Scaramouche rescues his betrothed and his mother from the blood-lust of the mob where the movement is swift and direct. . . .

NBR. Fall-Summer 1923, pp. 1–2

It is nothing new to report that Rex Ingram has produced a beautiful film; this is expected of him by his admirers and he still persists in not disappointing them. The element of beauty is always the basis of his pictures' exceptionability. This beauty is both pictorial and physical—a correct richness of movement against a carefully chosen scenic splendour.

Having gone to the cities of the Mediterranean for the background of his latest film, he has come back with his reels of beautiful, delighting pictures. His screen version of Ibanez's *Mare Nostrum* photographically fills the eye and again satisfies us that Mr. Ingram knows how to point the camera at his scenic material. . . .

The story runs through in an entertaining way despite some sluggish spots, and achieves an effect of serious undertaking on the part of Mr. Ingram. A certain far-fetched mystery is added to the character of Freya by her close resemblance to a painting of Amphitrite, the sea-goddess, and gives excuse for a rather horrific scene in the Naples Aquarium—the one in which Freya, who is known to the attendants here, with an apparent fascination for death as it is associated in her subconscious with the destroying monsters of the deep, bribes the keeper to stir up a fight between two octopuses, and gazes greedily till the end when she falls upon Ulysses with a violent kiss. This is interesting as spectacle, of course; likewise it shows that Mr. Ingram has adhered closely to the Ibanez method of creating interest in some of his heroines by endowing them with the proper modern psycho-pathological tendencies. That the motion picture is beginning to recognize these in its character-treatments indicates that it is progressing in an interest in, and a technique to handle, situations in which subtle psychological values play a part, and is thus enlarging its discernment and scope.

NBR. March-April 1926, pp. 15–16

A stylist in the minor school of Maurice Tourneur, he achieved in his films an individuality and personal quality through his sensitivity to pictorial composition and atmosphere. Earlier, as an art student, he had studied sculpture at Yale. Partly for this reason, perhaps, as a director he depended upon light and shade rather than plot to create mood. A fertile imagination for the pictorial, an alertness for scene composition and the beauty of the shot, made his films striking, although they were often without dramatic form and devoid of solid film structure. . . .

. . . *Scaramouche* revealed Ingram's indebtedness to Griffith. Made after Griffith's *Orphans of the Storm*, *Scaramouche* showed many similarities in its crowd scenes, tableaux, and the use of significant detail for atmosphere. The colorful material of [his] films—the imaginary kingdom in *The Prisoner of Zenda*, the South Seas in *Where the Pavement Ends*, and the French Revolution in *Scaramouche*—gave Ingram full opportunity to exploit his flair for the pictorial. Whenever possible he high-lighted his films with interesting close-ups of eccentric types. This device, which gave a local-color touch to his stories, was to be adopted years later by von Sternberg. [1939]

Lewis Jacobs. *The Rise of the American Film* (Teachers College, 1968), pp. 379–81

KAZAN, ELIA (1909–)

For the first time in many a moon we are treated to a picture that gives a good example of a typical small American city—the people, their way of living, their mode of government, the petty politics practiced, the power of the press. Based on an actual incident that took place in Connecticut *Boomerang!* was produced by Louis de Rochemont and directed by Elia Kazan. His best to date, Mr. de Rochemont succeeds admirably in using the documentary technique and blending it with enacted material. So skillfully has he done this that it is difficult to recognize what is newsreel and what is enacted. The picture breathes authenticity, the people are real and you feel you have taken a trip through this Connecticut town and witnessed all the events. You feel you are not merely looking at a movie in a theatre, you feel you are a participant. To achieve such realism is the goal of every director and Elia Kazan, who directed *A Tree Grows in Brooklyn*, is to be congratulated on its realization here.

The picture has pace and movement and sustains interest throughout. For the information of the film industry this is accomplished without any "love interest," "glamor girls" or sex of any kind. Kazan goes into minute detail, using his camera to get inside the characters of the individuals, and he tells a maximum amount of story with a minimum of film. Little touches of humor and human understanding, which are the characteristics of a good director, crop up throughout the picture. Many lawyers could learn from some of the court scenes how a case should be presented with dignity and logic. . . .

Frank Ward. *NBR*. April-May 1947, pp. 4–6

Indeed, on the grounds of the original, every good and courageous thing has been done by Twentieth Century-Fox, the producer, to make *Gentleman's Agreement* a sizzling film. A fine cast, brilliant direction by Elia Kazan and intrepidity in citing such names as Bilbo, Rankin and Gerald L. K. Smith give it realism and authenticity. To millions of people throughout the country, it should bring an ugly and disturbing issue to light.

But the weaknesses of the original are also apparent in the film—the most obvious of which is the limited and specialized area observed. Although the hero of the story is apparently assigned to write a definitive article on anti-Semitism in the United States, it is evident that his explorations are narrowly confined to the upper-class social and professional level to which he is immediately exposed. And his discoveries are chiefly in the nature of petty bourgeois rebuffs, with no inquiry into the devious cultural mores from which they spring.

Likewise it is amazing that the writer who undertakes this probe should be so astonished to discover that anti-Semitism is cruel. Assuming that he is a journalist of some perception and scope, his imagination should have fathomed most of these sudden shocks long since. And although the role is crisply and agreeably played by Gregory Peck, it is, in a careful analysis, an extraordinarily naive role.

Bosley Crowther. *NYT*. Nov. 12, 1947, p. 36

Pinky's ordeal is brought home by the director, Elia Kazan, in vivid, compelling incidents—the instantaneous change from servility to savagery by the police when Pinky, involved (and out-acted) in a brawl with Nina Mae McKinney, tells them she is coloured; the scene in the store; her pursuit at night by two drunken white men.

But Pinky's dilemma—shall she forsake her race and become "white" or proclaim it and lose her lover?—is side-tracked into never-never-land. There is a dying, wise old *patronne* (Ethel Barrymore) to restore her to proper Negro pride, and leave her the family mansion. There is an upstanding Southern judge to uphold the will and flout a court seething with lynching fever. And a final celibate solace for Pinky—since the world's most polyglot Democracy cannot abide a hint of miscegenation—is running her mansion as a super clinic for Negro children, manned by a Negro staff.

All this apart, the cardinal crippling evasion of *Pinky* lies in the selection of an established white film actress to play the heroine. Thus is the audience insulated against the shock of seeing white and Negro embrace, against any effect of realism. I do not doubt that *Pinky* will leave Negro baiters comfortably purged and as rabid as ever, and I have even less doubts as to its effects on Negroes. As for average audiences; they will come from *Pinky*, touched, entertained and unperturbed by a well made and well acted film drama.

Richard Winnington. *Sight & Sound*.
Feb. 1950, p. 28

Panic in the Streets has all the action and drive of a good Western (in the days before Westerns were sicklied o'er with the pale cast of thought and lost the name of action). It is another on-the-spot collaboration of Elia Kazan and Richard Murphy, the director-and-writer team who gave us *Boomerang*; and if it is a curiously apt illusion of the defects of the fiction-cum-documentary form—and more specifically of Kazan's sophisticated and highly charged variation on the theme—it also exhibits its qualities in enough profusion to make this an absorbing and exciting drama of derring-do. . . .

It is a part of Kazan's technique to direct a scene with a sense that the relationships on display have gone on before the camera started grinding and will continue after it has stopped. At its best, this gives one a sense of life, not arbitrarily suspended and rearranged for the story, but sliced whole and served up that way, with its little tag-ends of past experience still showing, its suggestions of things still to come. For an actor this has a particular value, for instead of having to build his scene from the bottom up (like a dancer who jumps from a standing position) he starts with the relations to other players and to the setting already established, and the emotional content of the scene already charged. The danger of this method is that emotion sought for its own sake may be without validity for the story. This is what happens too frequently in *Panic in the Streets*, where all the players appear to be charged with a hostility for all the other players which is not always accountable. In an attempt to explain Mr. Widmark's congenital gloom, there is an excursion into the theme of frustration and guilt which, while it gives us a welcome chance to pass some time with the beguiling Miss Geddes puts an onerous burden of irrelevancy on the film as a whole.

Hermione Rich Isaacs. *Films in Review*.
July-Aug. 1950, pp. 17, 18–19

Panic in the Streets, the latest melodrama in this [semi-documentary] style, is directed by Elia Kazan, who four years ago made one of the first examples for de Rochemont, *Boomerang*. It turns out to be perhaps the best of the whole cycle, and at times it nearly breaks the bonds of its own conventions. For it has not only a particularly good story, but a sharpness and flexibility of observation in the writing and handling that occasionally makes it more than a melodrama about a city under the threat of plague—it promises to become a real account of people in this circumstance, instead of using the circumstance to heighten tension. . . .

Although the mainspring of the film is its physical tension, the search by the doctor and the police for the criminals, and the latter's manœuvres, the situation itself allows for a welcome variation of emphasis, of which the scriptwriter Richard Murphy (who wrote *Boomerang* and *Cry of the City*) and Kazan take full advantage. They touch on many aspects—rivalries and doubts within the city services (public health, city council, police), the stonewalling of an inquisitive reporter and the problem of what to do with him when he discovers the truth, the suspicion, hostility and fear of numerous people directly or indirectly involved in the case, the dangerous curiosity of bystanders. A brilliantly recreated cross-section of the New Orleans underworld moves across the screen. . . . The script is full of detail and shrewdness, and Kazan's handling of it often fascinating to watch—a brilliantly refined skill that is never ostentatious, and at the same time more personal than, for instance, the flashy strokes of Dassin.

Gavin Lambert. *Sight & Sound.* Aug. 1950, p. 242

Though the Zapata legend has little relation to the Zapata reality, it is the kind of tale of which John Steinbeck is fond, and the film script [*Viva Zapata!*] he has written around it is both poignant and oversimplified. The individual scenes are well constructed—dramatically and melodramatically. There are no allusions to massacres, to burnings of haciendas, to intrigues against fellow revolutionists who would share, or seize, his power. We are caught up in the wish that Zapata was as Steinbeck conceives him.

And that is the test of a creator's success.

Elia Kazan's direction of Steinbeck's salute to the revolutionary impulse is not always effective. Kazan is very clever in delineating small, highly dramatic and melodramatic situations. His forte is not the larger, the abstract, themes, and in this film he often evades the subtler, and sometimes the more important, scenes. . . .

But Kazan is very able whenever the drama involves action—as when the peasants appear, seemingly from nowhere, singly or in twos and threes, to walk by Zapata's side when the mounted Rurales half-lead, half-pull him along a road by a rope around his neck. And the final scene, of Zapata's assassination, is creatively dramatized. Zapata is alone in a courtyard and Carranza's troops fire down upon him from the roof. His body crouches on the ground, and, to protect itself from the hail of bullets, assumes the foetal position for maximum protection.

Henry Hart. *Films in Review.* March 1952, pp. 132–34

Leaning heavily on sensationalism, [*On the Waterfront*] is a medley of items from the Warner Brothers' gangland pictures of the '30s, brought up to date. Many ingredients of the classic pattern are present: 1) the individual (Marlon Brando) against the mob (Lee J. Cobb and Rod Steiger); 2) the understanding parish priest who smokes cigarettes and drinks beer (Karl Malden); 3) the wan, naïve daughter of the poor torn between her desires for revenge and for love (Eva Marie Saint);

4) the symbol of the tough guy's inner gentleness (it used to be violins, in this film it's pigeons); etc.

Yet, because of the inventive direction of Elia Kazan, the formula becomes fresh, the clichés become power, the expected becomes surprising. Never has Kazan's gift for handling actors been more evident, nowhere has his extreme individual style been more effective. Group scenes teem with movement and life; love scenes are presented in huge head-on close-ups and off-balance silhouettes. The tiny gesture, the pause and repetition in speech, the searching camera that misses nothing—Kazan uses these to illumine as well as to startle. His ability to dramatize subtle and intense relationships results in profoundly revealing scenes—e.g., the hesitant showdown between Brando and his brother in a taxicab and Brando's shy and embarrassed invitation to the girl to have a beer. The casting of Brando and Steiger as brothers is a stroke of genius, since Steiger, new to movies but familiar on TV, has for years been using many of Brando's mannerisms.

Steve Sondheim. *Films in Review*.
Aug.-Sept. 1954, pp. 360–61

East of Eden is in many ways a better film. Technically admirable, the film is the first distinguished production in Cinemascope, and will be remembered as such by future motion picture historians. Kazan used the wide screen functionally, panning horizontally, tilting to emphasize distorted relationships, experimenting with soft-focus lenses and unusual lighting and shadow effects, and constantly employing inventive devices to keep his camera moving and the viewer's attention directed to the appropriate section of the screen. The result is a wide-screen film which moves smoothly and dramatically, and expresses its symbolic theme in visual terms. Although the film is marred by Kazan's habit of over-statement and his exaggerated emphasis on violence, the extremes seem appropriate to the Cain-Abel conflict which motivates the plot. . . .

Kazan's style is based on theatrical timing and blocking, amplified by a corresponding application of camera technique. The visual style concentrates on continuous movement, with actors steadily in motion and a camera movement which is equally fluid, alternately panning and employing elliptical cross-cutting to keep the viewer's eyes in action. Distorted camera angles and varying ranges of view are clearly appropriate to a technique which emphasizes visual motion. The flow of movement is so regular that any sudden pause achieves the effect of an exclamation point, and Kazan employs this type of punctuation at frequent intervals. Occasionally he reverses the process, by keeping actors and camera in a stationary position which is eventually interrupted by a movement or gesture so unexpected that it immediately connotes violence. Kazan applies the same technique to his sound accompaniment, giving a punctuating effect to any sudden noise or silence. The Actors' Studio method, emphasizing intuitional playing with an emotional basis, is eminently suited to this directorial style. Audiences have come to anticipate the nervous gestures and unconventional diction of a Marlon Brando or a James Dean, and automatically identify them as a Kazan trademark.

Eugene Archer. *Film Culture*. Vol. 2,
No. 2 (8), 1955, p. 24

The advantages of Kazan's direction [in *On the Waterfront*] are in his fine eye for living detail (for example, in Terry's first interchange with the men from the crime commission); the disadvantages are that the best things are often overpowered by the emphasis given to the worst. Rod Steiger's fine performance as the brother stays within its own framework, while Malden's priest is so overburdened with reference and effect that it disintegrates. Though this priest is not cut from the same cloth as Paramount's priests, at times (and he has his coy moments) he adopts a similar protective coloration. The musical score is excellent; then at a crucial moment it stops, and the silence compels awareness of the music. There are a few places where Kazan's dexterity fails completely: moving the union men around as a herd is too "staged" to be convincing. And even "good theater" doesn't allow for elements that are tossed in without being thought out (the ship owner, an oddly ambiguous abstraction, possibly cartooned in obeisance to the labor-union audience) or tossed in without being felt (the complacent, smiling faces of the priest and the girl at the end—converted, by a deficiency of artistic sensibility, into pure plaster). Many weaknesses go back to the script, of course (for example, the failure to show the reasons for the union men's loyalty to the boss), but Kazan, by trying to make assets out of liabilities, forces consideration of his responsibility. [1955]

Pauline Kael. *I Lost It at the Movies*
(Little, Brown, 1965), p. 51

We must not be too hasty in applying the general rule that whenever Cardinal Spellman denounces a movie it is sure to be a first-rate work of art. If you find this hard to believe, consider the case of *Baby Doll*, which was written by Tennessee Williams and directed by Elia Kazan. His Eminence has declared that the picture will tempt those who see it into moral corruption; Mr. Kazan has drawn his cape about him and replied that all the picture does is tell the truth about life as it is lived. I found little temptation and less truth. . . .

The contrast between Sicilian vitality and Southern degeneracy is a familiar theme in Mr. Williams's plays, but this time the protagonists are such sketchy caricatures that the effect is one of farce rather than tragedy. They are puppets, not people. Whenever the Messrs. Kazan and Williams get together on a movie they don't seem able to resist any opportunity that presents itself to play for cheap laughs in the pit. Sometimes the clowning is effective, as I believe it was in *The Rose Tattoo,* and serves to reinforce the serious things they have on their minds. But in *Baby Doll* the result is largely ludicrous and ineffectual.

I suspect that if Cardinal Spellman had not seen fit to order Catholics to stay away, as he has every right to do, it would have been a good deal easier for the rest of us to judge *Baby Doll* for what it is—a picture that is several cuts above Elvis Presley's *Love Me Tender* but quite far below *A Streetcar Named Desire,* another Kazan-Williams collaboration, and not even to be compared with their *Rose Tattoo.*

Robert Bingham. *Reporter.* Jan. 24, 1957, p. 36

In tracing the rise and fall of a homespun television personality turned demagogue, *A Face in the Crowd* exhibits a tough-minded approach to the problems of mass culture and the facile manipulation of public opinion. Elia Kazan and Budd Schulberg employ both hilarious satire and bitter invective to dramatize their point. An orgiastic drum majorettes' contest in Arkansas ridicules the hypocritical exploitation of leg-bared adolescent girls for the nominal art of baton twirling. The absurdity of charity telethons, television weddings, soft-sell and hard-sell advertising techniques spills over into a broader indictment of susceptible audiences. If Kazan and Schulberg had been content to make their case by implication, *A Face in the Crowd* might have been a completely sophisticated piece of movie-making. Instead, every idea is completely spelled out, and the film degenerates into preposterous liberal propaganda. [1957]

Andrew Sarris. *Confessions of a Cultist*
(S&S, 1970), p. 21

The subject [of *Wild River*] is the Tennessee Valley Authority in its beginnings in the early 'thirties. The story of the taming of a river is such obvious dramatic material for film that the only wonder is it has not been used numbers of times since Pare Lorentz' *The River.* In Kazan's film the subject gives rise to a moral issue that is the surest stuff of tragedy: two rights clashing head on make a wrong. Here is the archetypal conflict of the state versus the individual that we find in *Antigone*: community need (the irresistible force) against personal conscience (the immovable object).

Kazan has a talent for achieving poetic statement from even the most accidental naturalistic detail. The idle, uncomprehending stare of an old woman in a cheap hotel lobby becomes a powerful image. Again, as in *Panic in the Streets*, *Baby Doll*, or *A Face in the Crowd*, the camera explores scenes in a wonderful old-fashioned way to provide a rich environment for the immediate drama. Kazan recalls the depression years with poetic swiftness through a fleeting look at a WPA sign, a picture of Roosevelt, or a group of hotel residents gathered in the lobby at night to listen to the radio. Scraps of songs from the 'thirties or a giggling desk clerk quoting the comic tags of the day—"Wanna buy a duck?" and "Vas you dere, Sharlie?"—are at once documentary and intensely theatrical in impact.

Finally, Kazan's pictorial sense is magical: fishermen at the river, golden sunlight on dark branches or dried stalks in the field, and mist over the water are among the fine things in this good film marred only by a misshapen story. The credits reveal that Paul Osborne's screenplay is based on *novels* by William Bradford Huie and Borden Deal, and Osborne may have provided additional material. This probably accounts for the story's lack of unity.

Henry Goodman. *Film Quarterly*. Summer 1960, pp. 50–51

More than other American directors, Kazan is able both to suggest and to assimilate reality. Those looking for thought content in his work, for ideas, will have to look long and far. He seems to have no consistent point of view of his own, and if it had been necessary for him to depend upon his own visions it would have been best for him to stay with melodrama, as in *Boomerang* and *Panic in the Streets*. It is with the visions of others that he is most at home, and he can fit himself neatly into the content of a Tennessee Williams, a lesser writer like Budd Schulberg, and even the facile slickness of a Laura Z. Hobson, who made the literary treatment of anti-Semitism less fashionable but more popular with *Gentleman's Agreement*.

Nevertheless, there is no better gilder of a lily than Kazan. He combines a good cinematic sense with a dependency upon the "method" approach to acting, using the latter system to excellent advantage. It is no accident that Actors Studio trainees have been frequently employed in his films, from Brando to Pat Hingle in the recent *Splendor in the Grass*. The "Studio" is written all over *Baby Doll*, for instance, and in the long run it may turn out to be his best film, for here acting and atmosphere combine to equate the private vision of the South that is peculiar to Tennessee Williams with what actually existed at the time the movie was made. Kazan managed in *Baby Doll* to come close to a point of view of his own, as he views southern pretensions with sardonic humor, and builds an essentially minor story into a magnificently humorous study of the grotesque and the decadent.

Hollis Alpert. *The Dream and the Dreamers* (Macmillan, 1962), p. 136

Elia Kazan, who has shuffled back and forth between Broadway and Hollywood for most of the decade, has made several important pictures, among them, *On the Waterfront*, which had a large number of beautiful performances by its actors, and which, on the whole, was a throwback to the thirties in theme and mood, but not in crispness and tightness. Technically, its trouble was an overabundance of fancy work, calling attention to Kazan's virtuosity, but detracting from the ultimate effect of the picture. The same might be said of all Kazan's showy Hollywood work, although *Baby Doll*, his controversial spoof of sensuality, was a tour de force, a vehicle for its director rather than its performers and which, considered in that way, was eminently satisfying.

Richard Schickel. *Movies* (Basic, 1964), p. 186

Elia Kazan's *America, America* manifests why he is an outstanding director and why he is not a first-rank artist. There are so many lovely and flavorful and dramatic moments that it is a small surprise at the end to realize that the film falls flat.

The chief flaw is a recurrent one in Kazan's work on film and stage: a defective sense of proportion. He does not know when to condense and move on; if he sinks his teeth in a scene or a sequence that he enjoys, the audience can just wait around and be damned to it until he has worried the material in every way his warm invention can think of. Conversely, and possibly in reaction to this, he is sometimes so skimpy that he is unclear. [1964]

Stanley Kauffmann. *A World on Film* (Harper, 1966), p. 155

Elia Kazan's *America, America* runs for three hours. It is a slow, a tedious picture. Partly the tedium results from Mr. Kazan's screen style. He works methodically, filling his scenes with factitious detail and apparently uninterested in the wit and allusiveness of which the camera is capable. Every episode, almost every shot, has its own beginning, middle, and end, and the numberless playlets are cemented together into a strip which, after the first two hours threatens to stretch grimly to eternity.

But the picture also seems endless because it has nothing very interesting to say. It is an account of how Mr. Kazan's uncle, a Greek boy living under the epicene cruelty of the Turks, made good his determination to reach this country . . . But dreams are moving or not according to the quality of the dreamer, and Mr. Kazan has portrayed his relative-hero (in the person of a singularly lumpish young actor) as unresponsive, irresponsible, gullible, dishonorable, slow-witted and very lucky—an unimaginative egoist who had heard that America was a fat land and who craved fat as a pig craves truffles. . . .

Robert Hatch. *Nation*. Feb. 3, 1964, p. 128

Kazan is not only vulgar in his effects ("forthright," wrote Dwight Macdonald, "the way a butcher is forthright when he slaps down a steak for the customer's inspection"), he also steals them from all over. From the New Wave he takes the *hommage* to a favorite director, and has the gall to insert a clip from his own wretched film, *America America*; from *Hamlet* (among other sources) he takes the conceit of a visible imaginary presence with whom one character converses to the bewilderment of others; from *Persona* he takes the arc lamp made suddenly visible inside the projector—but whereas in Bergman this means something, in Kazan it is a purely gratuitous piece of pilfering; from *Le Bonheur* he takes the device of a man's copulations with two women shown so that at first you cannot tell which one he is currently in bed with; from Fellini (if not from *Lady in the Dark*) he purloins an adult protagonist watching himself as a child, and even reenacting, in his adult body, scenes from his childhood; and so on.

It is all particularly heavy-handed when it reaches for symbols—as when the hero, [in *The Arrangement*] refusing to return to his job, watches a TV documentary in which wild dogs devour an antelope alive. Not only is this dragged out unconscionably, it is also intercut with the coming of his employers to reclaim him, and, on top of that, reiterated at a crucial point in the film. Kazan, moreover, cannot make human relationships come alive: we never understand what Eddie sees in Gwen, or Florence in Eddie. And Eddie's relations with his father, which are supposed to be shattering, are sagging, elongated commonplaces—compare the terseness and penetrancy with which a similar relation is portrayed in *Downhill Racer*. Add to this the final cop-out: the whole tangled and seemingly insoluble situation resolves itself handily to everyone's satisfaction. What, then, was all the fuss about? [1969]

John Simon. *Movies into Film* (Dial, 1971), p. 325

KEATON, BUSTER (1895–1966)

It is strange that the silent drama should have reached its highest level in the comic field. Here, and here alone, it is pre-eminent. Nothing that is being produced in literature or in the drama is as funny as a good Chaplin, Lloyd, or Keaton comedy. The efforts of these three young men approximate art more closely than anything else that the movies have offered.

They are slapstick, they are crude, they are indelicate, to be sure; but so was Aristophanes, so was Rabelais, so was Shakespeare. How many humorists who have outlived their own generations have been otherwise?

In *The Paleface*, Buster Keaton is captured by a tribe of Indians who have a grudge against the white men because some oil promoters have attempted to steal their lands. Buster is sentenced to death, but the fact that he wears an asbestos union suit saves him from considerable embarrassment when the Indians try to burn him at the stake. He is then made chief of the tribe, and he proceeds to outwit the oil sharks and save the reservation.

The Paleface is a veritable epic.

Robert E. Sherwood. *Life*. June 1, 1922

A Buster Keaton farce [*The Navigator*] in six reels—and funny practically every inch of the way. Which is an accomplishment, because it isn't easy to be laughable for six thousand feet of film. Buster plays the heroic Sap who finds himself with his sweetheart on an ocean liner cut adrift by enemies of the owner. The Sap becomes the captain, crew and cook until the vessel strands upon a cannibal isle. Then Buster dons a deep sea diver's suit and keeps the cannibals more or less at a distance until a submarine comes to the rescue. Of course, like all farces, this doesn't stand analysis, but the tale is studded with hilarious moments and a hundred and one adroit gags. Keaton was never funnier than in *The Navigator* and he has a pretty foil in Kathrine McGuire. It's a picture you'll enjoy.

Photoplay. Dec. 1924, p. 50

Buster Keaton has more of straight satire in him than the other two. *Sherlock Junior* was a funny dream about detectives, *Go West* a funny dream about cowboys, *The Navigator*, a comic nightmare about heroes and heroines marooned in the tropics. Keaton is much more purely fantastic than Chaplin or Lloyd, more like *Beggars on Horseback*—a comment on the ephemeral contemporary aspect of American and movie-American life. He derives from the cinema rather than contributes to it, and that is his limitation and his strength. *Electric House* was funny mechanically, the play of a disordered imagination with labour-saving contrivances, already familiar to us through scores of washing machines and lifts. As to the fact that Keaton never smiles, though this is an amusing characteristic, it is merely in excess the attribute of all clowns. Chaplin and Lloyd, too, have set funny faces, rendered funnier by deliberate or timid or artful smiles. On the whole they, too, are frozen-faced; it was mere cleverness on the part of Keaton's publicity agent to endow him with the distinctive appellation.

Iris Barry. *Let's Go to the Movies* (Payson & Clarke, 1926), p. 137

In spite of his bursts of speed and flashes of ingenuity, Johnnie Gray, the hero of *The General*, the new picture at the Capitol, is hardly the person who would be trusted with a locomotive. This role is played by Buster Keaton, who appears to have bitten off more than he can chew in this farcial affair concerned with the days of the Civil War. Mr. Keaton still preserves his inscrutable expression; he looks like a clergyman and acts like a vaudeville tumbler.

The production itself is singularly well mounted, but the fun is not exactly plentiful. Sometimes laughter yesterday afternoon was stirred up by the slapstick ideas, and at other junctures the mere stupidity of the principal character had the desired effect. . . .

This is by no means so good as Mr. Keaton's previous efforts. Here he is more the acrobat than the clown, and his vehicle might be described as a mixture of cast iron and jelly.

Mordaunt Hall. *NYT*. Feb. 8, 1927, p. 21

More original than Harold Lloyd, Buster Keaton, a music-hall actor, began as a partner of Fatty. He founded his comedy on impassibility. The-man-who-never-laughs engaged himself by contract never to laugh —neither in his films nor in any public place. His imperturbable *sang-froid* contrasted with the extravagant situations in which his teams of gagmen involved him. Weak and dependent on chance, like Charlie, an ingenious potterer, sad-looking, he seemed convinced of the absurdity of the world and life, ready to accept all and conquer all. In *Our Hospitality*, depending on how he passed the door the situation reversed itself and the coddled guest became fit to kill. Nevertheless he was less often the victim of the absurdity of situations than that of mechanisms amplifying the accessories of clowns: Keaton was in a struggle with trains and cannons in *The General*, with a transatlantic steamer in *The Navigator*, and with the cinema, its studios and its trick shots in *The Cameraman*. The gag, earthbound with Lloyd, expanded with Keaton to the limits of the crazily fantastic. . . .

Georges Sadoul. *Histoire d'un art: le cinéma* (Flammarion, 1949), pp. 206–07

For Keaton, then, the scenario is also a sort of "placement" of his character. Instead of imposing the pre-established yoke of a dramatic construction, he lets the action develop freely.

Where both scenario and direction are concerned, Keaton tries not to put showy elements between, on the one hand, his action in the world and the attitude it incarnates, and, on the other hand, the spectator; this is true whether these elements be dramatic threads or carefully selected angles and framing. On the contrary, all his art tends toward a maximum of simplicity. Though Keaton's simplicity in creation can be explained by the fact that he does not specifically set himself problems in expression but creates spontaneously, we should nevertheless not neglect the role played in his films by composition, which is evident both in the shot and in the construction of the film; it takes the form of a "geometrization" and in the final analysis leads to the simplicity and the limpidity of the "placement" of the Keaton character in cinematographic space and time.

There's no point in beating about the bush. The "virtuosity" of a Welles, a Resnais or a Ophüls is perfectly legitimate and admirable; but virtuosity in the manner of Welles, of Resnais, or of Ophüls is, in the measure that it is pure affectation of style and does not correspond to the personality or message of the director . . . perfectly contemptible. In wanting too desperately to "express" something one expresses nothing because one shouts and declaims.

Keaton (and Chaplin) provide us with an example of a direction of absolute simplicity which is nevertheless perfectly original and perfectly necessary.

It is in the luminous simplicity of this direction that Keaton is modern; it is for this reason that he continues the tradition of Griffith and that he imposes himself on us as one of the greatest creators of the seventh art.

J. P. Lebel. *Buster Keaton* (Editions Universitaires, 1964), pp. 71–72

Chaplin never really escaped from the music-hall tradition in which you wink at the audience as you trip your stooge. His sets and lighting remain those of the stage and look ugly on film. His set-ups are dullishly flat, as though the camera had been placed in the front row of the stalls, his editing perfunctory. In contrast, Keaton subordinates everything to the *mise-en-scène* and thinks first and foremost in terms of the total effect. He was probably the first comic to escape from the tyranny of the gag and to conceive of humour as arising from plot and from the play of character and environment.

Yet his talent is visual and entirely cinematic. No one studied *The Birth of a Nation* to better advantage. When asked why *The General* gave a more convincing picture of the Civil War than *Gone with the Wind*, Keaton replied, "Well, you see they based their film on the novel. I went back to the history books." This research was never pedantic. Keaton sought to understand the past as D. W. Griffith had done. He sought to create a mood, an ambience, a credible world in which imagination could find release. His choice of location, and of light and shade, is often ravishing, yet it is always in key with the action and in harmony with Keaton himself.

Eric Rhode. *Encounter*. Dec. 1967, pp. 35–36

That Buster Keaton had regained a certain critical eminence before his death is due largely to the tireless efforts of the film cultists in the little magazines. What the late James Agee described as the "Golden Age of Comedy" (and Silence) has been distilled into the precious essence of Chaplin and Keaton or Keaton and Chaplin. (By contrast the intermittent inspiration of Lloyd, Langdon, Arbuckle, Sennett, Laurel and Hardy, et al, seems relatively one-dimensional.) The difference between Keaton and Chaplin is the difference between poise and poetry, between the aristocrat and the tramp, between adaptability and dislocation, between the function of things and the meaning of things, between eccentricity and mysticism, between man as machine and man as angel, between the girl as a convention and the girl as an ideal, between the centripetal and the centrifugal tendencies of slapstick. Keaton is now generally acknowledged as the superior director and inventor of visual forms. There are those who would go further and claim Keaton as pure cinema as opposed to Chaplin's essentially theatrical cinema. Keaton's cerebral tradition of comedy was continued by Clair and Tati, but Keaton the actor, like Chaplin the actor, has proved to be inimitable. Ultimately, Keaton and Chaplin complement each other all the way down the line to that memorably ghostly moment in *Limelight* when they share the same tawdry dressing room as they prepare to face their lost audience.

Andrew Sarris. *The American Cinema* (Dutton, 1968), p. 62

In his previous films Keaton had revealed an ingenious talent for setting up gags in terms of the camera. [In *Our Hospitality*] however his highly developed gifts as a film-maker come into evidence. The exposition of the sequence is lucid and entirely pictorial (there are no titles whatsoever until the very end of the reel). The images are invariably correct and just and the rhythms impeccable. Keaton is not inclined to use the traditional post-Griffith techniques of cutting, which tended to a rather formal repetition of shots and set-ups; but prefers a freer style of *mise en scène* which is sometimes remarkably modern in feeling. This free style, owing nothing to contemporary conventions, contributes to the undated look of his film today.

. . . the final sequence reveals the economy and accuracy with which Keaton could develop a dramatic situation; and the deftness with which he can shift his mood from drama to comic bathos. It also includes one of the first examples of Keaton's Wellesian ability to use the screen three-dimensionally, setting off foreground action against action seen in the depth of the frame. . . .

. . . *Our Hospitality* shows Keaton in full possession of his mature gifts: as a film-maker he is as assured as a King or a Vidor; and certainly the superior of Chaplin, who at the time that Keaton was making *Our Hospitality* was preparing *The Gold Rush*—a beautiful film, but technically archaic and visually feeble when seen alongside the Keaton film.

David Robinson. *Buster Keaton* (Indiana, 1969), pp. 93–95

Keaton is considered today to be an artist of Chaplin's stature, yet, as we have seen, Chaplin was taken quite seriously from the start, and Keaton was not. Keaton was successful and got warmly reviewed, but nothing was written about him during his early careeer that compared with the analyses, encomiums, even poetry that were heaped on Chaplin. Gilbert Seldes, writing [in 1924] in *The Seven Lively Arts,* still was not "sure" about Keaton.

There are at least two possible speculations on this difference. First, in Chaplin's private life, he was much interested in intellectual matters and associated with intellectuals; Keaton was not and did not. So Chaplin became a pet of writers of all kinds. Second, the Tramp, Chaplin's character, was an outsider usually destined to stay outside, unsuccessful in jobs, usually in trouble with the police, vaguely anarchic. Keaton's character was usually a conformist whose troubles arose from trying to stay inside or else an outsider who quite genuinely wanted to get in. The Chaplin character was possibly more appealing, even flattering, to the intellectual's self-view.

Chaplin's praise was certainly merited and few would wish it had been less or had come later; but we can also wish that Keaton's had been more and sooner. [Robert] Sherwood was one of the early few who, most of the time, saw Keaton's quality.

Stanley Kauffmann. *American Film Criticism* (Liveright, 1972), p. 132

KING, HENRY (1888–   )

As if to show what may be done with stock stuff, Director Henry King and his associates have taken Joseph Hergesheimer's story *Tol'able David*, and, with a realistic cast headed by Richard Barthelmess, converted it into a generally persuasive and culminatingly exciting photoplay. . . . This is not to say that Mr. Hergesheimer's story was stock stuff, but that the basic material taken from it for the picture has been used time and time again on the screen and is familiar in the "fillum" world as homespun melodrama. Fundamentally that's all that *Tol'able David* is, rural romance, employing the usual properties, a young and intrepid hero, a generously built and generous-hearted mother, a sweet little country girl and an assortment of villains for the hero to overcome. How often it has been done, and how unconvincing it all is—usually.

But not this time. This time you believe it. It seems real. In most of the scenes it gets you. For Mr. King and those responsible with him have eliminated most of the slush: *Tol'able David* is sentimental in places, but not sloppy. It is bucolic, but its rusticity is not rubbed in. In all things, except, possibly, the fight between David and the three hyenish mountaineers, it is restrained, imaginatively suggestive when not briefly literal. For this reason it is stimulating. Dealing in well-known scenes and actions, it merely introduces them. As each appears the mind of the spectator takes it in and completes it, and the story moves on to the next detail, which the mind immediately picks up and carries on. Thus there is constant spontaneity of response on the part of the spectators. They are always telling part of the story to themselves, so they are always actively interested. Nothing is so tiresome as a story in which familiar details are dwelt upon and drawn out until there is nothing left for the spectator or the listener to imagine, and most motion picture directors seem to think they have a monopoly of the world's imagination, which shows they have no imagination at all. But Mr. King apparently has an imagination and has therefore left much for any one who sees *Tol'able David* to imagine. As a result, his photoplay is sharply pointed in its more intensified scenes, whether humorous, sentimental or dramatic, and continuously illuminating and promising, which means interesting in its more moderate intermediary scenes.

And Mr. King has accomplished this result in the only way in which it can be accomplished on the screen—that is by the medium of motion pictures. Not only did he and his company go to the Southern mountains where suitable natural settings abounded, but they took advantage of the ability of the camera to produce certain effects not inherent in any natural setting, and they applied principles of pictorial composition and cinematography to make their scenes expressive and pleasing to the eye. *Tol'able David* has vitality, therefore. It lives as a motion picture.

NYT. Jan. 2, 1922, p. 20

The fact that a bad play may be made into a good movie was forcibly demonstrated in the case of *Sonny*. As it appeared on the stage, it was incredibly awful, but when resolved into terms of pictures that move, "Sonny" appeared as an unusually dramatic story. Richard Barthelmess played the difficult dual rôle of two boys, one humble and one aristocratic, who met on the battlefields of France. The rich boy died and the other went home in his place.

Barthelmess gave a splendid account of himself in *Sonny*, and the direction of Henry King was remarkably good. Between them they managed to imbue the story with a spirit of sympathy, of humanity and of realism which it certainly lacked in its original form. . . .

Fury was a drama of the two-fisted, red-blooded variety, with the great grim sea as a background. In its flavor, it represented a mixture of Joseph Conrad and Thomas Burke. Richard Barthelmess, Patrick Hartigan and Dorothy Gish gave splendid performances as London waterfront types, and Henry King displayed the same directorial skill that made *Tol'able David* a great picture.

Robert E. Sherwood. *The Best Moving Pictures of 1922–23* (Small, Maynard, 1923), pp. 93–94, 100–01

How much can be expected of Henry King is difficult to say. His *Tol'able David* and *Sonny* were excellent pieces of celluloid, perfectly executed. *The Seventh Day* and *The Bond Boy* fell somewhat below the mark. Perhaps King is a prospect. At least, he seems to be endeavoring for plays of situation and not films of glamour and humbuggery.

Tamar Lane. *What's Wrong with the Movies* (Waverly, 1923), p. 68

Lillian Gish scores another personal triumph in her much heralded production of the popular Marion Crawford novel *The White Sister*. As a young girl, orphaned, turned out of her home by the cruel older sister, and finally bereft of her lover, she goes through every shade of emotion. When, after becoming a nun, the lover miraculously returns to her, the situation reaches an intensity, a passion, that calls for superb acting. The climax of the renunciation, and of the following volcanic eruption that gives the lover a chance to die as a hero, is well handled. Henry King's direction is good. Though Miss Gish may not reach the peaks of expression that she did under Griffith's supervision, her work is more evenly balanced and human. She is a woman, rather than a temperamentally high-strung girl.

Photoplay. Nov. 1923, p. 74

Henry King, the director of *The White Sister*, was the guiding spirit of [*Romola*]. He has a style of his own, and his artistic bent is apparent in most of the glorious scenes of this film. The settings are really something to marvel at, and no less impressive are the exteriors. There are white, winding roadways, flanked by sun-bleached stone walls, old gates that have stood the test of centuries of seasons, worm-eaten oaken doors, cobblestone squares and a glimpse of a lazily flowing river. Mr. King used Florence for all it was worth in this picture, and even if the story were not as good as it is, the scenes are so beautiful that they in themselves are worth every instant one spends viewing this picture. At times the photography is of such excellence that it appears to have depth. There are views in the sunshine and others tinted for moonlight which would awaken enthusiasm in the eyes of any artist.

NYT. Dec. 2, 1924, p. 13

In the interest of critical integrity the estimate of *Stella Dallas* will follow the method of the young pie eater who disposes of the crust first in order to begin undisturbed enjoyment of the luscious "filling." So, putting the worst first instead of the least good, the "severest critic" in us hastens to say that *Stella Dallas* might be described as a case where mother love is baked and done to a box-office turn.

But how superbly done! That is the whole point. And if you doubt whether this sort of thing is being done better and better compare *Stella Dallas* with *Over the Hill*, with which it has much in common. If *Over the Hill* "got you" while you were seeing it in the theatre and then made you slightly angry with yourself for having succumbed to its appeal, *Stella Dallas* will get you more and leave you less self-apologetic. . . .

But now for the filling of our pie. The picture is chuck full of purple berries of acting, of scenes sensitively felt and beautifully executed. . . . In telling the story, Henry King, the director, deserves praise for sticking consistently to his theme and having the courage to present an unrelieved tragic sequence without attempting to create diversion by jumping to a secondary plot or introducing inappropriate comic relief. This is especially true of the last three reels of the picture and the artistic unity thus achieved does much to make up for the emotional exaggeration already noted above.

NBR. Nov.-Dec. 1925, p. 3

A director who has just gone up to the top of the class is Henry King. It is a long time ago now that King made *Tol'able David*, a simple character study, extremely well managed and acted with Barthelmess as the hero. It was not a commercial success, though the more intelligent film fans still talk about it with affection. The succeeding films made by Mr. King were of no particular interest until he joined Mr. Goldwyn's organization and directed *Stella Dallas*, a picture fit to rank with any. One cannot but reflect that though a good director is essential for making a good picture, even a good director can only do so when he is given encouragement, latitude and good material. It would be untrue to say that any Henry King picture is worth seeing, though it is apt to be.

Iris Barry. *Let's Go to the Movies* (Payson & Clarke, 1926), p. 226

Henry King, I feel, is one of the most sincere of American directors, whose work seldom receives the attention it deserves. He is to be numbered among those directors in Hollywood who, if they were allowed the chance, would make a film to compare with the product of any of the better European *cinéastes*. All his productions contain points of definite interest, demanding a detailed examination for which there is not the space in these pages. To his credit must firstly be placed what was at its date the finest film America had produced, *Tol'able David* (1922), which was followed later by *Stella Dallas, Romola, The White Sister, The Winning of Barbara Worth* (a sophisticated western), *The Magic Flame*, and the better parts of *The Woman Disputed.* In *Tol'able David*, King expounded his theme with a delicate use of detail and a sympathetic employment of landscape for the emphasis of atmosphere. The material was distributed with a nicety of feeling rare in the American film; the continuity was balanced to perfection and flowed with admirable smoothness; and the characterisation, notably in the case of Richard Barthelmess in the name part, revealed a depth of character that has not been noticed in any later film by the same director. King robbed Griffith of all that was good, combining the spoil with his own filmic knowledge. The real value of *Stella Dallas*, a brilliant and deeply emotional film, was superficially destroyed in this country by the cheap and contemptible publicity that it received. It was diversely said to be "the greatest mother-love picture ever made," and that "Mr. King had focalised in it all the creative artistry of his great career," all of which was an attempt to put over Samuel Goldwyn's appreciation of the "art" of the cinema. It implied, on the contrary, not only the strangeness of Mr. Goldwyn's mind, but the negligible amount of appreciation he possessed for the work of his own directors. The story of *Stella Dallas* was not of unusual interest, but it gave scope for a consistent character development over a space of time, and lent itself to delicate touches of direction. Its lesson lay in the superb handling of acting material, notably in the cases of Belle

Bennett and Lois Moran, and also in Jean Hersholt's masterly rendering of the coarse riding-master. It was one of those rare films that rested on its treatment alone, a type of film not usually connected with America. Sympathy and delicacy are the two salient characteristics of Henry King's work, exemplified strongly in *Tol'able David* and *Stella Dallas*. He is a misunderstood and mishandled director; a man of deep cinematic mindedness, who struggles in vain against the overpowering and crippling demands of picture-sense.

Paul Rotha. *The Film Till Now* (Jonathan Cape, 1930), pp. 131–32

Most Hollywood movies are about the very poor or the very rich because social extremes are always dramatic. Such movies as do not fall into these categories—films about gangsters, for instance, or actresses—usually deal with some picturesque minor social group. The epic of the externally undramatic middle classes has yet to be screened. The nearest we have come to it is King's *Stella Dallas*. There is no question that *Tola'ble David* is a more successful work, is indeed one of the most *perfect* movies ever made. But *Stella Dallas,* in my opinion, was a more remarkable film. The theme was Mother Love, a temptation for any director. But King presented it not as shrilly sensational melodrama but as a deeply felt drama of a middle-class mother and her middle-class daughter. The mother (Belle Bennett) is just a bit "common" according to bourgeois standards, and the daughter (Lois Moran) realizes that her mother is the chief bar to her marrying the "nice" young man of her choice (Ronald Colman). This the mother learns by chance (for her daughter is too fond of her to say anything) and to insure her daughter's happiness, steps out of her life. For Hollywood this plot is a triumph of originality, for the castastrophe is precipitated by nothing more sensational than the bourgeois idea of some people being "nice" and others being "common." . . .

About King's latest work, *State Fair*, I find it hard to write with the proper critical restraint. I am not one who insists that a work of art shall be judged by its social implications, or lack of them. But there is a limit to the detachment of art from present-day realities. At a time when the American farmer is faced with ruin, when the whole Midwest is seething with bitterness and economic discontent, a movie like *State Fair* is an insulting "let them eat cake" gesture. [1933]

Dwight Macdonald. *D. M. on Movies* (Prentice-Hall, 1969), pp. 87, 88

A pungent, good-humored novel of Ioway, called *State Fair*, has been turned, almost miraculously, into a good-humored, pungent motion picture. The director, Henry King, has told a good story well; he has ably characterized some yeomen from the empire of tall corn; he has used music better than most American directors; and he made even Janet Gaynor fairly human at times.

The novel itself could have been used by Mr. King to make a distinguished esoteric name for himself if he had wanted to go to the trouble. It takes a wealthy farmer, his wife, and their two children to the state fair, and allows the children to have their first love affairs while the farmer is winning a prize for his Hampshire boar, and his wife is triumphing in the mince-meat arena.

When I saw how well Mr. King was doing the job I began to wish he had designed his picture after *Sunrise*, and had given us an impressionistic, kaleidoscopic, musical melodrama, rather than a straight narrative; but for years I have been lamenting the lack of Americana in motion picture plots, and now that I find genuine farm people on the screen I'm not going to complain.

Pare Lorentz. *Vanity Fair*. March 1933, p. 63

. . . It is the music which makes *Alexander's Ragtime Band* a show to be seen as well as heard. The nostalgia is gentle, and the humor is allowed to flow naturally from the incongruity of customs and costumes of a bygone day. Tyrone Power, Alice Faye, Ethel Merman, Jack Haley, and those innumerable singers who enter so gloriously in the spirit of the thing—these and Director Henry King are to be congratulated for sustaining a vitality that is not supplied in the sketchy plottings of the script.

Stage. Sept. 1938, p. 48

Tol'able David was what is known as a smash hit. Its subject matter—the tale of a poor mountain boy—was fresh and unstereotyped; its setting was real; its characterizations were honest and rounded; the narrative was simple and unmelodramatic; the whole picture was frank and pungent rather than sentimental. Years later the noted Russian director Pudovkin, in his book *Film Technique*, selected several sequences from *Tol'able David* as vivid examples of the correct use of plastic material. In the sequence in which a new character, a tramp who is a brutal escaped convict, comes into the action, King achieves characterization swiftly and entirely through the use of incident and shot arrangement, as the following summary from Pudovkin's book, [*Film Technique*] indicates:

1. The tramp—he is about to enter a house, but stops, his attention caught by something.
2. Close-up of the face of the watching tramp.

3. What the tramp sees—a tiny, fluffy kitten asleep in the sun.
4. The tramp again. He raises a heavy stone to kill the animal but is prevented from doing so only by the entrance of another character into the house.

Simply, pictorially, convincingly, the man's cruelty is depicted in four shots.

This scene, like King's technique throughout, stemmed from Griffith. Whether or not King was conscious of this influence is hard to say; but his leading man in *Tol'able David*, Richard Barthelmess, had been discovered by Griffith and used by him in *Broken Blossoms* and *Way Down East*. The Griffith influence was so marked, in fact, that Paul Rotha [in *The Film Til Now*] has declared, "King robbed Griffith of all that was good, combining the spoil with his own filmic knowledge." [1939]

Lewis Jacobs. *The Rise of the American Film* (Teachers College, 1968), p. 373

Since nothing is more repugnant to me than the pseudo-religious, I went to *The Song of Bernadette*, gritting my teeth against my advance loathing. But since, also, many of the deepest resonances of my childhood are Catholic; and since I intensely suspect and fear the implacable pieties of those who deny the rationally inexplicable even when they are being beaten over the head with it; and since, accordingly, I feel a triumphant pride in the work or mere existence of true artists and of the truly experienced in religion, I was unexpectedly and greatly moved by a great many things in the film. I owe this somewhat indecently subjective preface because I doubt that the film can be strongly recommended to anyone whose mind and emotions lack some similar shape. I can add that the picture is unusually well made—within limits.

The limits are those of middle-class twentieth-century genteelism, a fungus which by now all but chokes the life out of any hope from Hollywood and which threatens any vivid appetite in Hollywood's audience. In proportion to the excellence any given film achieves within these limits—which can be considerable—I suppose it is the more pernicious. If that is so, *Bernadette* is a champion enemy. For within those genteel limits I have seldom seen so tender and exact an attention to mood, to over-all tone, to cutting, to the edging of an emotion, and to giving vitality, sometimes radiance, in terms of the image and the sound more than of the character, the story, the line, the music. . . . [1944]

James Agee. *Agee on Film* (Beacon, 1964), pp. 72–73

And it seems that every one connected with the picture [*Twelve O'Clock High*] has added to his stature. Henry King's direction has something of the quality of military orders, terse, pared to necessity, forceful; something of the quality of precision bombing, deft, strategic, not a moment nor a movement wasted; something of the quality of group tactics which Savage so excellently sets forth in the Briefing and Interrogation Hut. Military experts may have sat in as technical advisers on flying procedure and protocol; certainly the large sections of army footage of actual air battles help to give the scenes in the air their lucid and convincing character; but the moving picture "know how" Henry King has furnished himself. It is a blend of his old silent *Tol'able David* and *The White Sister* with his new sound films, *The Song of Bernadette, Wilson* or *A Bell for Adano*, a fusion of the two techniques which is to be found in the work of John Ford or Clarence Brown, but rarely among those practitioners who have made their way to Hollywood via Broadway. . . .

Frances Taylor Patterson. *Films in Review*.
March 1950, p. 31

In *The Gunfighter*, a remarkable film of a couple of years ago, the landscape has virtually disappeared. Most of the action takes place indoors, in a cheerless saloon where a tired "bad man" (Gregory Peck) contemplates the waste of his life, to be senselessly killed at the end by a vicious youngster setting off on the same futile path. The movie is done in cold, quiet tones of gray, and every object in it—faces, clothing, a table, the hero's heavy mustache—is given an air of uncompromising authenticity, suggesting those dim photographs of the nineteenth-century West in which Wyatt Earp, say, turns out to be a blank untidy figure posing awkwardly before some uninteresting building. This "authenticity," to be sure, is only aesthetic; the chief fact about nineteenth-century photographs, to my eyes at any rate, is how stonily they refuse to yield up the truth. But that limitation is just what is needed: by preserving some hint of the rigidity of archaic photography (only in tone and décor, never in composition), *The Gunfighter* can permit us to feel that we are looking at a more "real" West than the one the movies have accustomed us to—harder, duller, less "romantic"—and yet without forcing us outside the boundaries which give the Western movie its validity. [1954]

Robert Warshow. *The Immediate Experience*
(Atheneum, 1970), p. 144

[In *The Sun Also Rises*] Henry King, a director of indifferent technique, has repeated some of the errors of his previous Hemingway production, *The Snows of Kilimanjaro*. Once more, he has misdirected his players into unduly expressive readings of the laconic Hemingway dialogue as if the ultimate meanings of the dialogue could be extracted from the dialogue itself rather than from the implications of understatement. The things that matter to Hemingway—love, sex, death and courage—are seldom expressed but always understood, never dramatized but always felt. By dramatizing talk which is only incidental to the emotions it conceals, King dissipates these emotions.

On the whole, *The Sun Also Rises* is an honorable failure. Credit must be given for attempting the project at all, and for boldly admitting the existence of impotence and nymphomania, although the groundwork was prepared by Joseph Mankiewicz' more tasteful treatment of the themes in *The Barefoot Contessa.* Except for the opening episode of *The Killers* and the middle section of *The Macomber Affair,* Hemingway is yet to be done full justice on the screen. It can be argued that genuinely great literature seldom is transformed into great cinema. Still it is difficult to understand why 20th Century-Fox intrusts *The Sun Also Rises* to a director like Henry King while they are wasting John Huston, a brilliant director with a Hemingway personality, on such drivel as *Heaven Knows, Mr. Allison.*

Peter Walsh. *Film Culture.* Nov. 1957, p. 17

Henry King, the most underpublicized filmmaker in Hollywood, belongs on anybody's "First Five" list. An inventory of his great pictures is the history of films—*Tol'able David, Fury, The White Sister, Stella Dallas, The Winning of Barbara Worth, Lightnin', Over the Hill, State Fair, Lloyd's of London, Alexander's Ragtime Band, Jesse James, Stanley and Livingstone, The Song of Bernadette, Wilson, A Bell for Adano.*

Still flying his own plane in his seventies, this lean, tall, handsome, urbane, but unflamboyant model of a corporation president makes film hits so easily, so efficiently, and so calmly that he is not news in a community of blaring trumpets, crashing cymbals, and screaming egos.

Frank Capra. *The Name Above the Title*
(Macmillan, 1971), p. 246

[*The Snows of Kilimanjaro*], unlike the original, is monotonously paced. Whereas Hemingway uses a variety of means for moving back and forth between the objective and subjective, the creators of the color movie eschew dissolves and rely exclusively on cuts. And in place of Hemingway's structure of rising tempo, the film—thanks to the need for a standard Hollywood happy ending—slows down painfully in order to allow sufficient time for Gregory Peck's miraculous recovery. After Susan Hayward dismisses a local witch doctor and "operates" on the hero herself, director Henry King clumsily crosscuts between Harry's bandaged leg and an obtrusively symbolic hyena prowling outside the tent. Once the contrived climax has passed, the dawn comes up like thunder and the rescue plane wings into view. The final image on the screen is of a huge tree which has replaced the hyena outside Harry's tent. No doubt, Robinson and King intend this image to symbolize "the tree of life." Hemingway's story, however, concerns "the snows of Kilimanjaro," or "the House of God"—which is not at all the same thing.

Edward Murray. *The Cinematic Imagination* (Ungar, 1972), p. 225

KRAMER, STANLEY (1913–)

One problem is that American directors, with a handful of exceptions, are not much interested in style; they are at heart didactic. Ask what they plan to do with their absolute freedom, with their chance to make a personal statement, and they will pick an "issue," a "problem." The "issues" they pick are generally no longer real issues, if indeed they ever were—but I think it a mistake to attribute this to any calculated venality, to any conscious playing it safe. (I am reminded of a screenwriter who just recently discovered dwarfs—although he, like the rest of us, must have lived through that period when dwarfs turned up on the fiction pages of the glossier magazines with the approximate frequency that Suzy Parker turned up on the advertising pages. This screenwriter sees dwarfs as symbols of modern man's crippling anomie. There is a certain cultural lag.) Call it instead —this apparent calculation about what "issues" are now safe—an absence of imagination, a sloppiness of mind in some ways encouraged by a comfortable feedback from the audience, from the bulk of the reviewers, and from some people who ought to know better. Stanley Kramer's *Judgment at Nuremberg*, made in 1961 was an intrepid indictment not of authoritarianism in the abstract, not of the trials themselves, not of the various moral and legal issues involved, but of Nazi war atrocities, about which there would have seemed already to be some consensus. (You may remember that *Judgment at Nuremberg* recieved an Academy Award, which the screenwriter Abby Mann accepted on behalf of "all intellectuals.") Later, Kramer and Abby Mann collaborated on *Ship of Fools*, into which they injected "a little more compassion and humor" and in which they advanced the action from 1931 to 1933—the better to register another defiant protest against the National Socialist Party. [1964]

Joan Didion. *Slouching Towards Bethlehem* (Dell, 1968), pp. 153–54

The Defiant Ones is probably Kramer's best picture: the subject matter is relatively simple, though "powerful"; the action is exciting; the acting is good. But the singleness of purpose behind it all is a little offensive. The theme is irrational hatred between two escaping convicts, a white man (Tony Curtis) and a Negro (Sidney Poitier); chained together, pursued by a bloodthirsty posse, they learn brotherhood. Q.E.D. If, instead of creating a false premise of incredible, primitive hatred between two very good men, Kramer showed some Negroes less attractive than Sidney Poitier, with less virtuous problems, some of the congratulations he got for daring would be deserved. The joker in *The Defiant Ones* was that although white liberals were pleased at the demonstration of solidarity, Negroes in theatres could be heard jeering at Poitier for sacrificing himself for his white "brother." Moviegoers with good memories amused themselves by pointing out that *The Defiant Ones* was *The Thirty-Nine Steps* in drag, and by noting that the episode about the farm woman was badly lifted from *La Grande Illusion*—with the convenient substitution of Negro for Jew (a familiar device in Kramer productions). [1965]

Pauline Kael. *Kiss Kiss Bang Bang*
(Little, Brown, 1968), pp. 205–06

Ship of Fools. Even if one has not read Katherine Anne Porter's best-selling novel, one can figure out, when confronted with a boatload of passengers en route from Vera Cruz to Bremerhaven on a German ship in the year 1933, that an allegorical exploration of the world that gave rise to Hitler is in the offing. The fact that Stanley Kramer produced and directed the film and that the script was written by Abby Mann provides a further advance tip-off. In case one might miss the message, one of the most interesting passengers, an urbane and sardonic dwarf (Michael Dunn), faces the camera at the opening and tells us that this is a ship of fools and that we may recognize people we know and even ourselves among the cast of characters. He tells us approximately the same thing again in the movie's final fade-out. . . .

. . . I doubt the didactic value of this kind of film, while at the same time I deplore the fact that didacticism somewhat dilutes its dramatic impact. Dilutes, not destroys. Fortunately, the picture is awash with interesting and believable—even if far from admirable—characters who possess independent vitality and are extremely well acted. . . . And director Kramer and scenarist Mann, while they have trouble with a few recalcitrant and labored plot strands, have generally managed to keep the proceedings tidily knit and absorbingly well-paced.

Moira Walsh. *America*. Aug. 14, 1965, p. 170

Stanley Kramer's attempt to revive slapstick in *Mad World* fails for every possible reason, but one is that it is more like the battle of the Somme than a Vietcong raid. To watch on a Cinerama screen in full color a small army of actors—105 speaking roles—inflict mayhem on each other with cars, planes, explosives, and other devices for more than three hours with stereophonic sound effects is simply too much for the human eye and ear to respond to, let alone the funny bone. The permutations and combinations of hard-core slapstick are as severely limited as those of hard-core pornography, and for the same reason: they are entirely physical. [1965]

Dwight Macdonald. *D. M. on Movies*
(Prentice-Hall, 1969), p. 425

I would have thought that in a year in which the Secretary of State's pretty young daughter is shown kissing her handsome Negro husband on the front page of the *Times* the subject of mixed marriage would hardly offer any more public surprises. But then I never imagined that Spencer Tracy's last movie with Katharine Hepburn would be a polemic on race relations, which is exactly and astonishingly what *Guess Who's Coming to Dinner* is, and a curious picture to watch. There they all are, everybody in his sweet accustomed place: father, a crusading publisher, home to play golf, mother snipping flowers on the terrace, beautiful daughter just back from a trip with a handsome fiancé. Except that *this* handsome fiancé is coloured, and suddenly everybody's caught up in a kind of integrated drawing-room comedy, and unable to decide whether there's anything funny about it or not. In fact, one of the few witty remarks in the script is Sidney Poitier's aside that his fiancée hasn't known him long enough to tell whether he's blushing.

Since Stanley Kramer's direction doesn't help much to resolve their dilemma, the actors are left looking wooden and uneasy. (The glorious exception is Spencer Tracy.) . . .

Ann Birstein. *Vogue*. Jan. 1968, p. 56

Stanley Kramer's *The Secret of Santa Vittoria* is a crude and conventional movie, but it isn't offensively bad in the grand Kramer manner. We don't sit there in agony, holding our heads and saying, "No, Stanley, no! Please, Stanley!" Kramer works the comic-Italian schtik, with the Italians so warm and fallible and "earthy" (so much earthier in our movies than in real life), as we've seen it in countless movies and television shows. Everything is geared to feelings and laughs we've already had; he doesn't even *try* to find anything new in the material. Robert Crichton's novel was only fair, but even mediocre best sellers deserve better than this. . . .

Kramer's ambitions and his failures have often been linked to a kind of muddled and opportunistic liberalism whose qualities in the arts can be indicated by a list of its compromises: it's quick and easy with judgments and moral categories but incapable of imagining the experience of evil, the contradictions of virtue, the dangers of the moral life in general; it sincerely dislikes prejudice but defends the victims of prejudice by cleaning and sprucing them to the point where their antagonists look reassuringly insane; it praises variety and diversity but feels comfortable only with an overall scaling down and flattening out of human strangeness, wildness, and complexity; it has explanations for everything but is constantly being surprised. This complex of attitudes was chased out of the older arts fifty years ago, and it's on the run in movies today. Look at the good American movies of 1969: they all have areas of blindness and confusion, and none of them is quite first-rate, but at least the directors and writers are trying to get some of the antagonisms and hang-ups of American life onto the screen without suggesting in the last reel that everything can be resolved with a little understanding and a show of goodwill.

David Denby. *The Atlantic Monthly*. Jan. 1970, pp. 101–02

Another distinguishing mark of top directors is the absence of camera moves. Undisguised camera tricks are the mark of the beginners who fall in love with bizarre camera angles and hand-held moving camera shots. Wrong. Fall in love with your actors. All else is machinery, and director's vanity. The audience must never become aware that there is a camera within a thousand miles of the scene. Mood scenes? Fine. Necessary. But establish moods subtly, suggestively. Don't let your cameras hang up figurative signposts giving mileage and directions. Audiences cannot both feel and think at the same time. If they notice your "show-off" camera, the mood goes out the window. Stanley Kramer's 360-degree pan shot in the courtroom of *Judgment at Nuremberg* served only to distract attention from his tense drama.

Frank Capra. *The Name Above the Title* (Macmillan, 1971), pp. 247–48

KUBRICK, STANLEY (1928–)

Stanley Kubrick's third feature film [*The Killing*] is an estimable entry into that small field of well-made crime films that expose the *modus operandi* of the colossal caper. Like *Rififi* and *The Asphalt Jungle* (after which it is principally patterned) its action is thickly and informatively plotted, possessed of that classic fatality that insures retribution, and dependent for its thrills upon a network of smooth calculation severed by fey circumstance and mislaid trusts. Inevitably all the effort comes to nothing; the returns are loss, seizure, death. But the particular glamour of this film lies in a signal absence of criminality as it is conventionally deployed. Unlike the gangsters in *The Maltese Falcon, Rififi* or *The Asphalt Jungle*, the chief characters of *The Killing* inhabit no underworld. . . .

His film lacks the pervasive knowledge and control of John Huston's masterwork, and although his material has absorbed him utterly, he has been wise to remain detached from it. His camera is relentlessly objective, cool, economically observant, and capable of an unusual rhetoric, as when, at the film's end, the hero's captors advance upon him and are framed to remind us of the menacing gunman targets that had filled the screen a few reels before. All the bizarre figments of the imaginative thriller are here (and it is to the director's credit that more often than not, they fall this side of pretentiousness): a high-powered rifle nestling in a flower box, a robber in a clown mask, an epitaph pronounced by a parrot. Excellent use is made of one of René Clair's headiest images—a suitcase full of stolen money yielding its contents to the winds. In fact, the visual authority of *The Killing* consistently dominates a flawed script. In a film that is largely a crescendo of detail and preparation, Kubrick has found it necessary, at the peak of tension, to resort to cutbacks in order to fill in information and set his sprawling scene. Thus the action at its climax knots and unravels, knots and unravels. This is done in the name of clarity, but a certain cumulative suspense is thereby sacrificed. Kubrick has also used an off-screen narrator where one would have preferred an absolutely cinematic exposition. The documented effect that is obtained invades the unique privacy of events and becomes negligible when we are told what we do not really need to know . . . and when we are *told* instead of shown. "It had been previously agreed upon that in case something should go wrong—" etc.

Arlene Croce. *Film Culture*. Vol. 2, No. 3 (9), 1956, p. 30

Kubrick stands much closer to his material than almost any other director currently working in Hollywood. In each of his films to date he has been the principal or sole author of the screenplay (he did the original draft of *Paths of Glory*, and Calder Willingham came in for the second), and he is at least the supervising if not the actual editor of his filmed material. On *Killer's Kiss* he carried credit for photography as well as direction, and he operated one of the cameras during the attack sequence in *Paths of Glory* (one fitted with a Zoomar lens). Thus it is not surprising that there should be a strong feeling of unity and single-mindedness in his films. Such a result is not guaranteed by one man's control of the material—he could be undecided about it. But it is rarely achieved in committee films. "A camel," as the recent proverb has it, "is a mule made by a committee."

There is an unconventionally intellectual air about Kubrick's films, but this may be more a by-product of style than an intentional ingredient. Certainly he does not mean his films to be intellectual in the sense of making a clear-cut statement about something. "I cannot give a precise *verbal* summary of the philosophical meaning of, for example, *Paths of Glory*. It is intended to involve the audience in an experience. Films deal with the emotions and reflect the fragmentation of experience. It is thus misleading to try to sum up the meaning of a film verbally." However, it is precisely his very evident style, praised by an eagerly perceptive band of professional film critics, which for some commentators (although not myself) prevents their involvement in Kubrick's characters and situations.

Kubrick has already given ample evidence of his strong grasp of *mise en scène* and the extension of character which an actor can be encouraged to bring to the pauses between lines of dialogue. On a second viewing of *Paths of Glory,* Douglas causes some uneasiness, but the film is otherwise beautifully performed, staged, photographed, cut, and scored—using, for example, a rasping, alarming staccato of drums during the battle scenes. It is a disappointment that Kubrick was not able to continue with Brando. Their relationship could not have been an easy one, but the result could have been fascinating.

Colin Young. *Film Quarterly*. Spring 1959, pp. 10–11

Of all the recent king-size spectacles, *Spartacus* is the least moving emotionally.

The reason is not recondite. It was written by Dalton Trumbo from the novel by Howard Fast and the breadth of vision on display is no wider than the Communist Party line Trumbo espouses and Fast now eschews. The Rome of 73 BC was a far more interesting place than Fast presented in his political tract and Trumbo presents in this 189-minute spectacle.

Everything is depicted with a lack of imagination that is truly Marxian. Our first sight of Spartacus—played with surly earnestness by Kirk Douglas—is on a stone pile in Libya where, of course, he is lashed by senselessly cruel Roman guards. Because of his fearless proletarian defiance, he is bought by a corrupt proprietor of a gladiatorial school at Capua (amusingly played by Peter Ustinov). The set for this school, and the training incidents depicted in it, are the only *distinctive* things in this film. . . .

The direction of young Stanley Kubrick is quite a feat for one of his years (31). He was aided, it is true, by a cast of talented and experienced players. Since Kirk Douglas was also the executive producer . . ., Kubrick undoubtedly had his troubles with him. But the other players greatly helped the young director. . . .

Anne Grayson. *Films in Review*. Nov. 1960, pp. 553–54

Most of the reviews of Stanley Kubrick's cinematic treatment of Vladimir Nabokov's *Lolita* emphasized the novel's awesome difficulties rather than its glorious opportunities. *Lolita* is, after all, a "road" novel. A director with a flair for cars and roadside Americana could have taken off with this material. As it is, Nabokov's literary wit has not been translated into visual wit, with the result that the film is leaden where it should be light. Kubrick has a fatal weakness for long scenes in which everything is explained and then explained again. Yet Nabokov's reverse-Jamesian conception of the European intellectual corrupted by American vitality is never adequately realized, and the sex is so discreetly handled that an unsophisticated spectator may be completely mystified. . . .

There is something to be said for the director's accepting Lionel Trilling's interpretation of *Lolita* as a love story concerned, like all great love stories, with forbidden love. However, I suspect that Kubrick lost his nerve and wound up underestimating his audience. People are not so easily shocked nowadays as they used to be. . . .

What *Lolita* needed more than anything else was a director in tune with Nabokov's delirious approach to his subject. We are never shown the inspiringly unconscious gestures and movements that transform the most emotionally impoverished nymphet into a creature of fantasy and desire. Kubrick goes through the motions with a hula hoop and the munching of potato chips, but there is nothing intuitive or abandoned about the man-nymphet relationship. The director's heart is apparently elsewhere. Consequently, we face the problem without the passion, the badness without the beauty, the agony without the ectasy. [1962]

Andrew Sarris. *Confessions of a Cultist* (S&S, 1970), pp. 60–61

Of the younger set of directors only Stanley Kubrick has shown genuine ability to learn from the American film tradition and to advance it. He gained attention with *The Killing*, a tough little crime film, went on to make a fine, serious antiwar movie, *Paths of Glory*, made *Spartacus* superior to its spectacular type, developed his sense of the absurd in his imperfect but daring *Lolita*, and now has given us *Dr. Strangelove*. Without the perspective of years it is easy to overestimate a good movie, but it does seem that this may be the best comedy since sound came to Hollywood, or, if not that, the best of the postwar years. More than that, in its utter anarchical irreverence, its complete ignoring of the moral shibboleths of the conventional wisdom of moviemaking in America, it is an epochal film. It is one of those rare, daring works of art which makes it a little bit easier for those who will follow to speak frankly. Respectable people have argued that it is an un-American film because of its refusal to accept at face value authority's claim to responsibility. But this is nonsense. In its rowdy questioning of verities it reasserts one of Americanism's oldest tenet—skepticism. That this virtue should receive its most vigorous airing in a movie, in that most timid of all our timid mass media, is the best sign that there may be some truth to the view that Hollywood is coming of age at last.

Richard Schickel. *Movies* (Basic, 1964), pp. 89–90

Stanley Kubrick's *Dr. Strangelove*, which did have a little style, was scarcely a picture of relentless originality; rarely have we seen so much made over so little. John Simon, in the *New Leader*, declared that the "altogether admirable thing" about *Dr. Strangelove* was that it managed to be "thoroughly irreverent about everything the Establishment takes seriously: atomic war, government, the army, international relations, heroism, sex, and what not." I don't know who John Simon thinks makes up the Establishment, but skimming back at random from "what not," sex is our most durable communal joke; Billy Wilder's *One, Two, Three* was a boffo (cf. *Variety*) spoof of international relations; the army as a laugh line has filtered down to Phil Silvers and "Sergeant Bilko"; and, if "government" is something about which the American Establishment is inflexibly reverent, I seem to have been catching some pretty underground material on prime television. And what not. *Dr. Strangelove* was essentially a one-line gag, having to do with the difference between all other wars and nuclear war. By the time George Scott had said "I think I'll mosey on over to the War Room" and Sterling Hayden had said "Looks like we got ourselves a shootin' war" and the SAC bomber had begun heading for its Soviet Targets to the tune of "When Johnny Comes Marching Home Again," Kubrick had already developed a full fugue upon the theme, and should have started counting the minutes until it would begin to pall. [1964]

Joan Didion. *Slouching Towards Bethlehem* (Dell, 1968), pp. 154–55

Kubrick's films up to now have given strong evidence of his incisiveness, his mordant humor, his felicitous eye, his cool maneuver of dramatic impact. The script of *Paths of Glory* (1957) had all the simplistic and banal antiwar propaganda that *Dr. Strangelove* transcends, but it was executed with ruthless, vivid immediacy. *Spartacus* (1960) was the best of the post-television film spectacles, an entertaining, if mindless, show with many well-done scenes, intimate and panoramic. *Lolita* (1962) was tantalizingly unsatisfactory, but in such sequences as the opening murder, it predicted the qualities that have now been suavely explored in his new film. *Dr. Strangelove* is, first and foremost, absolutely unflinching: relentlessly perceptive of human beings to the point of inhumanity. In technique, it understates provocatively and comments by apposition. Kubrick's precise use of camera angles, his uncanny sense of lighting, his punctuation with close-ups and occasionally with zoom shots, all galvanize the picture into macabre yet witty reality. [1964]

Stanley Kauffmann. *A World on Film*
(Harper, 1966), p. 17

There *is* a paradox involved in the film *Lolita.* Stanley Kubrick shows talents in new areas (theme and dialogue and comedy), and is at his worst at what he's famous for. *The Killing* was a simple-minded suspense film about a racetrack robbery, but he structured it brilliantly with each facet shining in place; *Paths of Glory* was a simple-minded pacifist film, but he gave it nervous rhythm and a sense of urgency. *Lolita* is so clumsily structured that you begin to wonder what was shot and then cut out, why other pieces were left in, and whether the beginning was intended to be the end; and it is edited in so dilatory a fashion that after the first hour, almost every scene seems to go on too long. It's as if Kubrick lost his nerve. If he did, it's no wonder; the wonder is, that with all the pressures on American movie-makers—the pressures to evade, to conceal, to compromise, and to explain everything for the literal-minded—he had the nerve to transform this satire on the myths of love into the medium that has become consecrated to the myths. *Lolita* is a wilder comedy for being, now, family entertainment. Movie theaters belong to the same world as the highways and motels: in first-run theaters, "for persons over 18 years of age" does not mean that children are prohibited but simply that there are no reduced prices for children. In second-run neighborhood theaters, "for persons over 18 years of age" is amended by "unless accomplained by a member of the family." That befits the story of Humbert Humbert.

Pauline Kael. *I Lost It at the Movies*
(Little, Brown, 1965), p. 209

[*2001: A Space Odyssey*] is so completely absorbed in its own problems, its use of color and space, its fanatical devotion to science-fiction detail, that it is somewhere between hypnotic and immensely boring. . . . Kubrick seems as occupied with the best use of the outer edge of the screen as any painter, and he is particularly fond of simultaneous rotations, revolving, and straight-forward motions—the visual equivalent of rubbing the stomach and patting the head. All kinds of minor touches are perfectly done. . . .

There is also a kind of fanaticism about other kinds of authenticity: Space travelers look as sickly and exhausted as travelers usually do; they are exposed in space stations to depressing canned music; the viewer is often made to feel that the screen is the window of a spacecraft, and as Kubrick introduces one piece of unfamiliar apparatus after another—a craft that looks, from one angle, like a plumber's helper with a fist on the end of it, a pod that resembles a limbed washing machine—the viewer is always made aware of exactly how it is used and where he is in it. [1968]

Renata Adler. *A Year in the Dark*
(Random, 1969), pp. 103–4

[In *2001: A Space Odyssey*]. Director Stanley Kubrick mesmerized me with his thoughtful, meticulous flight into the space age. But I am certain many will resist the hypnosis. In our year 1968, people demand to be electrified every minute and are attuned to the rapid pacing of such fine films as *The Graduate* and *Bonnie and Clyde*. Kubrick dares to move at an ultra-slow pace to create his very special atmosphere. This he overdoes with repetition, as if unable to edit the visually fabulous sequences. Nevertheless, in total it is a brilliantly conceived cosmic adventure. . . . The after-intermission half, by far the more gripping and complex, is climaxed by the ultimate put-down of Man as we conceitedly see ourselves. This being a wise-guy age, some will dismiss as pretentious Kubrick's grand cinematic design or his attribution of alternately playful and menacing human qualities to a villainous computer. At screenings I attended, some squirmed and left in mid-flight. Unable to get the film out of my mind, I wanted a *second* look and found both experiences spellbinding. I believe the unique odyssey will grow in stature on the list of Kubrick's films, as we move toward the 21st century.

William Wolf. *Cue*. April 13, 1968, p. 57

Stanley Kubrick always seemed a director who knew exactly what he was doing. In such films as *Lolita*, *Dr. Strangelove*, even *Spartacus*, he calculated his effects with masterful precision. But in *2001* one feels that this most deliberate of artists has lost control over his materials. It is morally pretentious, intellectually obscure, and inordinately long. Yet, though Mr. Kubrick may have lost his control, he has not lost his genius. *2001* is a movie in the grand style, intensely exciting visually, with that peculiar artistic power which comes from obsession. It is a film obsessed first with the gadgetry of space exploration and then, it becomes evident, with some personal Kubrickian mysticism about the cycle of life, death, and rebirth in the cosmos.

2001 is, I say, a film out of control, an infuriating combination of exactitude on small points and incoherence on large ones. It begins, for example, with a community of apes distracted by the mysterious appearance of a great black slab in their midst. Thereafter they learn to kill each other, presumably putting themselves on the road to being human. After half an hour or so of ape talk, one ape spins his club into the air; the camera transforms the club into a space ship; and we are in the year 2001 on the way to the moon. The black slab, after four million years, has been rediscovered, and it is emitting a signal, evidently beamed at Jupiter.

Mr. Kubrick has some nice satire about the squareness of interplanetary travel and travellers; and he offers some beautifully composed, whirling sequences of ships soaring through space to the tune of Strauss waltzes. But he has succumbed to technological fetishism. One noticed the first symptoms in *Dr. Strangelove.* In *2001* he has gone mad over electronic artifacts—flashing dials, rotating wheels, computer consoles, space stations. Alas, the technical detail is not only overwhelming but unclear. Obsession continues to outrun explanation, and this reviewer, at least, could not understand a good deal of what was going on.

Arthur Schlesinger, Jr. *Vogue.* June 1968, p. 76

Less than half [of *2001: A Space Odyssey*] had dialogue. It was a reorganization of the traditional dramatic structure. Process became more important than plot. The tedium was the message. It was a film not *about* space travel; it *was* space travel. "The truth of a thing is in the feel of it, not the think of it," Kubrick asserted.

Kubrick traces some of his fascination with the fluid camera back to Max Ophuls. His oeuvre, with the single exception of the optimistic transfiguration in *2001,* is a bleak skepticism and fatalism.

Joseph Gelmis. *The Film Director as Superstar* (Doubleday, 1970), p. 293

During the past twenty years, Stanley Kubrick has made a relatively small number of carefully constructed films, each of which has its own particular personality, each of which was an important stage in the development of Kubrick's highly useful analysis of contemporary social and psychological phenomena. All of his films are characterized by an objective logic which fits well with their basic analytical intentions. Kubrick's films comprise an important body of work which may be best described as contemporary anthropology. . . .

Ever since his earliest films, Kubrick's worldview has been informed by the proposition that contemporary alienation is best seen as the result of a dialectical tension between human beings and their inventions. The first corollary of this metaphysics of the machine has been the sense of violence and antagonism between individuals and groups which Kubrick explicitly outlines at the beginning of *2001* and which has fascinated him as a filmmaker in such varied films as *The Killing, Dr. Strangelove*, and *A Clockwork Orange*. These propositions by themselves make of Kubrick's work a fascinating course of study; they gain added interest when it is understood that Kubrick has stated them in thoroughly cinematic language. Along with Godard, Bergman, Lester and other important directors of the last twenty years, Kubrick has made it clear that the language of film is a flexible and subtle instrument for analysis of the way we live now.

James Monaco. *New School Bulletin.*
Summer 1973, pp. 75–76

LA CAVA, GREGORY (1892–1952)

Gabriel Over the White House offends no censors, even, because they take it for what it is meant to be: an opportunist, contemporary film which depends on its factual incidents rather than its dramatic veracity for its power. All the problems of the current administration are on view: the unemployed; the farm situation; war in Europe; the 18th amendment; but the film itself is full of long-winded, patriotic speeches which seem peculiarly false. No one set out to write a great drama about politics; the producers simply threw together an adaptation of a melodramatic novel, and if you find any drama in the contemporary incidents, it is because you write them in yourself; there is nothing in the structure or the dialogue of *Gabriel Over the White House* that doesn't seem obvious.

Pare Lorentz. *Vanity Fair.* June 1933, p. 37

This is the kind of picture which real showmen continually hope for but seldom get. *Private Worlds* is a drama of life—real, human, heart-touching. It is frank, delicate and certainly daring. Courage was required to attempt its production. Courage is the quality most required in its exploitation. In every way it calls for tactful selling that challenges any one's abilities to put over an unusual attraction in a manner to attract the greatest number. The rewards awaiting those who have the skill, ingenuity and desire to tackle such a proposition are most surely worth the effort. . . .

Because *Private Worlds* is so superbly portrayed and intelligently directed, it merits the highest praise. Fundamentally, as it reveals a deeper, truer understanding of the devotion and willingness to sacrifice that lies within a woman's heart, it is a woman's picture. Whether it proves the box office attraction which its entertainment and personnel values merit, is strictly up to those who play it. The producers have done their part faithfully and courageously. At this time, it does not seem otherwise but that *Private Worlds* will be one of the industry's most talked about pictures of this or any other year.

Motion Picture Herald. March 16, 1935, p. 38

Private Worlds is a surprisingly good thing for Hollywood to be making from a novel like Phyllis Bottome's, which is much too inward to be picked up by the cameras, and which might therefore have been replaced by some such convenient pattern as that of passions practiced between, say, Fredric March and Norma Shearer, the theme tune being, Private Worlds, I Love You. The original story has been simplified, heightened as to coloring, and made more compact; but it has been turned into a movie that runs off with less of flash than of dignity and honest intelligence.

Here and there in the film matters go noticeably wrong. The part of the matron is plugged too hard, and there are several spots where a patient is restored to calm in too much of a jiffy for total credence. Joel McCrea is miscast, and though Claudette Colbert is one of the few young women who could even be considered for the part, with brains and a good style of her own, she confuses a few basic meanings by sticking too close to herself—here she is to be found reading lines that would indicate a cold, controlled personality, and yet simply radiating her own charming come-ons from start to finish.

These things do not seem to be right, but in general the managment is so good as to cover up the fact that such a story—a combination of brash exterior action with extensive clinical explorations—is simply too complicated for the screen to handle properly. [1935]

Otis Ferguson. *The Film Criticism of O.F.* (Temple, 1971), p. 71

My Man Godfrey, for three-quarters of its way, is acutely funny. The adventure of a sane man among the witless wealthy, the story opens with a "scavenging party" at the Waldorf-Ritz to which competitors are expected to bring, besides such assorted objects as bowls of goldfish, goats and mangles, "a forgotten man." Mr. William Powell, unshaven and for once more bitter than bright, is secured by a lovely nitwit from a rubbish-dump under Brooklyn Bridge. The chaotic scene of the shrieking alcoholic rich, leading goats and waving mangles through the great chromium halls, is perhaps the wittiest, as well as the noisiest, sequence of the year, but the film does not maintain quite so high a standard . . . nor does "the social conscience" remain agreeably implicit. Mr. Powell is made to preach a sermon to the assembled family on social reform after saving them from bankruptcy by his knowledge of the stock markets and—curious moral—a huge luxury club rises on the site of the rubbish-dump in which his old down-and-out friends are given employment in elegant uniforms. But though "the social conscience" is a little confused, the film, in the earlier sequences, well conveys the atmosphere of an American Cherry Orchard, of a class with little of the grace and all the futility and some of the innocence of its Russian counterpart. Unfortunately, to these Americans prosperity returns, there is no dignified exit while the axes thud in the orchard, only the great glossy club rising over the wilderness of empty tins, and, last muddle and bewilderment, the marriage of the reformer and the brainless "lovely." [1936]

Graham Greene. *G.G. on Film* (S&S, 1972), pp. 105–06

One of the smartest, most amusing comedies of the season. If we may accept it as a sample of what we may expect from Universal's new management, we can look forward to getting some superlative entertainment when Charlie Rogers really gets under way. The picture is mounted handsomely and in his selection of the cast to support the stars the producer showed no disposition to squeeze pennies.

Gregory La Cava makes his director-producer debut with *My Man Godfrey*. I do not see how Greg has kept hidden so long his flair for the smartest kind of comedy. If he displayed it before it must have been in pictures I missed. Anyway, his direction is nothing less than brilliant. It is not obvious and reveals no striving to achieve results. He is not afraid to allow his characters to whisper when they should whisper and shout only when they should shout. Although he has a set of the most amusingly crazy characters ever assembled in a sophisticated comedy, he keeps them well in hand, blends the performances nicely and never resorts to farce.

Welford Beaton. *HS*. Aug. 15, 1936

Anyway, Shakespeare wrote his scripts a long time ago, and since his time the cinematograph was invented. It has been put to good use, this pleasing toy, on several occasions—as for instance, quite recently, when Frank Capra brought that shrewd provincial, *Mr. Deeds*, to town and Gregory La Cava recounted the fortunes of *My Man Godfrey*. Both are first-class comedies and whoever enjoys the one will like the other, though they are as dissimilar as pretty chalk and wholesome cheese. They must be classed in different categories because, being good films and dated 1936, both naturally play at sociology, but the one comes as near as no matter to meaning what it says and the other is an insincere, amusing gesture made in flippant salute to a serious problem; it is conscious of its inadequacy but content to be the funnier of the two. I am aware that Capra's is the better film, because it's honest rather than slick, places humour before farce, and is more human, more significant than its rival—which personally, I admit, I preferred. Gary Cooper has never given a performance to compare with his Mr. Deeds, that makes the Capra film a joy to watch; few actors have. Carole Lombard, supported by a brilliant cast, paints in *My Man Godfrey* an even wittier portrait of the clever female fool than she did in *Twentieth Century.* Capra's film is, we repeat, sympathetic and as near sincerity on the stark topic of undeserved poverty and undeserved wealth as capitalist Hollywood is likely to get; it is naturally and deliberately sentimental. In *My Man Godfrey* the underdogs are just a bunch of honest bank-presidents down on their luck, the altruistic butler is really a Harvard man, and the happy ending hands out luxury all round, spelling senseless security with a capital $; it is frankly just a flip and mannered comedy. The dialogue of either film is equally good, but in general the acting honours are with La Cava's team and, if you ask me, the direction of his picture is even surer and more successful.

John Marks. *Sight & Sound.* Autumn 1936, pp. 81–82

Stage Door is already booked by half a dozen critics as a masterpiece and it is certainly a remarkably directed description of a theatrical boarding house. Keeping a dozen young women flowing in a single stream for the best part of a film, and maintaining the while their separate little characters and stories is a very difficult feat in cinema. It means a huge ingenuity in the shaping of exits and entrances and the still more considerable business of holding the central necessarily fast narrative through the detail. Few films manage it. *Dead End*, for example, got the character detail but lost its narrative speed. Most films shy away from the detail. There is moveover, in *Stage Door* an interesting use of sound and particularly at the point in the story where the young girl who has lost her part in a play commits suicide. Add to this the excellent acting of Katharine Hepburn, Ginger Rogers, and quite a number of the smaller boarding house parts and the score might seem to be good for the masterpiece claimed.

Why is it not? The fact is there is something theatrical and light weight about the whole business. Here we have the story of youth, ambition, and disillusion in the great city. Evidently someone took it seriously for there is the sound band of suicide and there are the antics of tragedy. I don't know, but I wouldn't say there was real pity or that the tear was genuine.

John Grierson. *World Film News.* Feb. 1938, p. 30

Significantly, La Cava was most effective when he could work between the lines of his scenarios and against the conventions of his plots. W. C. Fields credited La Cava with the best comedy mind in Hollywood next to Fields's own, and *Life* magazine once reproduced La Cava's on-the-set sketches for the Billy Rose takeoff in *Unfinished*

Business. Of such trifles was the legend of La Cava fashioned. However, the La Cava touch never became as famous as the Lubistch touch even after the New York Film Critics Circle singled out La Cava's direction of *Stage Door* for an award in 1937. The La Cava touch was mainly touches, whereas the Lubitsch touch expressed a more distinctive vision of the world. La Cava's more solemn projects —*What Every Woman Knows, The Affairs of Cellini, Private Worlds* and *Primrose Path*—suffer from structural deficiences. He is remembered now for a few interludes of antic desperation in the midst of the Depression.

Andrew Sarris. *The American Cinema* (Dutton, 1968), p. 95

The meteor Gregory La Cava (*Symphony of Six Million, Stage Door, My Man Godfrey*) was an extreme proponent of inventing scenes on the set. Blessed with a brilliant, fertile mind and a flashing wit, he claimed he could make pictures without scripts. But without scripts the studio heads could make no accurate budgets, schedules, or time allowances for actors' commitments. Shooting off the cuff, executives said, was reckless gambling; film costs would be open-ended; no major company could afford such risks.

Films are a peculiar dichotomy of art and business, with executives emphasizing business. But not La Cava. He stuck to his off-the-cuff guns. Result: fewer and fewer film assignments for him—then none. The flashing rocket of his wit was denied a launching pad because he wouldn't, or couldn't, conform. So he mixed his exotic fuels with more mundane spirits, and brooded himself into oblivion—his rebel colors still flying. La Cava was a man out of his time—a precursor of the "new wave" directors of Europe. Pity he didn't live long enough to lead them.

Frank Capra. *The Name Above the Title* (Macmillan, 1971), pp. 245–46

LANG, FRITZ (1890–)

All of you movie hopheads taking the cure under Prof. Fearing, how many of you can remember as far back as *Fugitive from a Chain Gang*? It's not likely that many can. The cinema addict who can come out of his coma in front of the theater and remember how he got there, let alone recall the title and plot of the film that has been enthralling him for the last sixty minutes, really belongs in some other, less-serious ward, possibly the revolutionary dance. But if you do have a dim and confused recollection of *Fugitive from a Chain Gang*, MGM's current *Fury* is just like it, only better and it's a pretty good picture.

To be accurate, it's one top-notice picture with two or three mediocre ones tossed in on top of it just to make sure the basic story doesn't make too much sense. Nobody knows what we moviegoers would do if confronted with a film that took a substantial theme and followed it through to its logical end. Maybe we wouldn't know the difference. Or we might explode. There might even, as some say, be a revolution.

Lynching is the subject of *Fury*, and the first half of it is so realistic that when flames leap up in the old courthouse and encircle the caged victim, you actually smell the burning flesh. It's really as savage and convincing and as good as that. If you think of the story as ending there, where it always does end in fact, and if you also imagine the victim to be Negro, as he usually is and not white, then this is the film that will haunt your dreams for many a night and make the ordinary Hollywood thing seem tamer than a vacation postcard. . . .

Fury has . . . technical ingenuity, this time simply in the field of plotting. After the realism of the lynch scene has built up the picture's tension, the remaining half of it is kept going by a series of surprises —the victim's survival, his self-concealment that leads on to a trial of the lynchers, the seeming collapse of the case against the lynchers until the dramatic introduction of motion picture evidence, and so on —each improbable, but not impossible, event skillfully connected to the next. Nothing but good acting could put the latter half of the film across, and the cast was extremely good. It's amazing, seeing how much technical perfection alone can do for a picture.

But the real story lies wrapped up in the first part of it, and it's fine anti-lynch stuff, though not as pointed as it could have been—remember, we have to sell these pictures in the South. See the film, and imagine what might have been done with it.

Kenneth Fearing. *New Masses*. June 16, 1936

In the first week of the present quarter, *Fury* was presented at the Empire: Mr. Alistair Cooke in the last issue of *Sight and Sound* gave Hollywood and the American censor "irrevocable credit" for letting it be shown; prophesied that, "short of a miracle," it would remain the best film of the year. . . .

"The recurrent, long-drawn-out paroxysms of crowds are always provoked, encouraged and prolonged by stupidity and violence," Céline has said—and it is this foul phenomenon that Lang has expressed in moving pictures as profound as the best of the Russian cinema. One's principal criticism of *Fury* is that lengthy court-room scenes, even when sociologically interesting, are never good film material. The drama and dexterities of legal debate are a fad of the Americans and the movies; here it was essential to thrash the problem out verbally—and it might have been (but wasn't) done verbosely. Yet I should hazard that Lang had less say in these sequences of the film than in the action—the lynching itself and the vile contagion of frenzy which caused it. There was one shot—of the sheriff (Edward Ellis) grimly determined to defend his authority and his prisoner against the oncoming mob, with its growl of vengeance in our ears, and the camera steadily advancing, dragging us forward in the ranks of the unseen rioters, identified with their passion, cowardice and ferocity—that was magnificent, as fine a moment of vision as any so far achieved by the talkies. *Fury* had certain faults, but in my opinion, since the screen began to talk, no other serious film except *The Front Page* has so clearly shown that here is a new art and what this new art can do.

John Marks. *Sight & Sound.* Autumn 1936, pp. 78–79

March was a month of bounties, however mixed they proved on examination. Seldom has the moviegoer had the opportunity of observing within a limited period such varied productions as *You Only Live Once, The Plough and the Stars, Lost Horizon* and *The Good Earth* and the work of such distinctly divergent talents as Fritz Lang, John Ford, Frank Capra and Sidney Franklin.

Of the directors, Fritz Lang proved far and away the most individualized and absorbing. The scenario of *You Only Live Once*, which Gene Towne and Graham Baker banged out with brass knuckles, may have been bloated beyond decency by over-ripe coincidences, but the film from a directorial point of view provided an occasion of intense pleasure. All the mastery that went into *M* and *Fury* was in evidence, though sadly handicapped by a script that lacked social grounding and strained credulity to the breaking point. Nevertheless, the director, through a highly developed sense of social awareness, subtle implication and sheer drive managed to eke out a temporary victory over his material.

Instances of Lang's ingenuity abound throughout the film. We need but mention the newspaper office with the editor awaiting the verdict, or the use made of the rifle sight in the last sequence to create great tension. Lang's ability to achieve dramatic effectiveness by the use of objects, although this is but one of his methods, is possessed to equal degree by no director save possibly Alfred Hitchcock. There is this difference. In Hitchcock, this "Sachlichkeit" seldom justifies itself beyond pure virtuosity. What one gets in his case is almost always shock for shock's sake. We make this distinction only to point out a similar danger that lies before Fritz Lang in the event that the scripts available to him deteriorate even beyond *You Only Live Once*. We devoutly wish this eventuality never to become fact.

You Only Live Once was considerably marred by an unpleasant, mawkish last minute addition to the end of the film, probably through Hays' office insistence. Father Dolan, whom Eddie has murdered, appears from out of a misty heaven to open the gates of heaven for the slain couple.

Robert Stebbins. *New Theatre*. April 1937, p. 26

Fritz Lang must be a tremendous problem to producers as well as to himself. He can't be brought, and he can't bring himself, to do ordinary things in an ordinary way. Such gifts as went into the making of *M*, and *Fury*, aren't for the run-of-the-mill program picture, as *You and Me*, is convincing proof. Anybody might have done this story as well as it deserved to be done, a not particularly novel thing about a man and a girl on parole, the man's efforts to keep clear of the old gang, and his melodramatic resentment of the girl's keeping a secret from him. (her own criminal record.) The difference from other stories of the kind comes from avoiding the usual hostile attitude of society toward ex-convicts trying to go straight, and allowing some practical sympathizers to do something helpful for the unfortunates. In general, though, the story is not unusual, and Lang has tried to make up for that by unusual treatment. His individual touch is visible everywhere, in handling both characters and situations, but for the ordinary George Raft fan it will not only be unappreciated, it will be actually confusing. And the musical idiom of Kurt Weill, so heavily different from the incidental music of the usual movie, will not help. So the picture will appeal only to Fritz Lang specialists, and that is a pity, because, as he is one of the few really creative artists among directors, everything he does ought to be of a kind to attract big audiences. It is work like his that raises the level of production and appreciation, and he should be doing stories where his work counts for all it is worth.

NBR. June 1938, p. 17

In Germany Fritz Lang was already one of those directors whose very name guaranteed a film, and *Nibelungen*, for example, had even won the esteem of Goebbels. However, behind the facade, it was not always easy to devine the implied sense. Great problems were often touched upon and resolved in a way that was often too simplistic. Fritz Lang has finally blossomed in the United States. *Fury* was a large-scale attempt to attack the injustice of lynching and the film was an international success. *You and Me* is a step forward on new terrain. Kurt Weill, the composer of *The Threepenny Opera* has not only shown his understanding of a certain type of modern music, he has also been able to give it a Brechtian stamp. In part this is a true *Lehrfilm* like the *Lehrstucke* written by Brecht: simple and crammed with teaching. When Sylvia Sidney demonstrates on a blackboard that gangsters win nothing in relation to the risks they take, we have a perfect illustration of "crime does not pay."

. . . Fritz Lang has once more taken on an important human problem. The fact that he approaches it by means of a conflict of silence is probably a necessary concession to the public; it can be excused since a large accumulation of small details, analyses, and explanations would make his goal as a director too obvious.

You and Me begins with a cantata about how life has to be paid for; there is an explosion of images of all the beauties and necessities of life and the voice of the invisible speaker merely emphasizes the simple moral. Lang's tight rein on the large number of characters whom he conducts with a sure hand is the sign of a director who has made an international reputation with *M*. Kurt Weill has shown how *serious* music can be used in the cinema.

The film is evidence that a sufficiently strong personality can express what is unique about it in spite of the obstacles put in his way by the cinema industry. [Paul Marcus, *Pariser Tagezeitung*, June 1938]

In Alfred Eibel's *Fritz Lang* (Presence du Cinéma, 1964), pp. 125–26

Like the eminent contemporary English director, Alfred Hitchcock, Lang has a flair for dramatic intensity and terseness of rendition. Often his imagery and cutting, especially in his sound and dialogue, are so succinct that much of their brilliance is overlooked in a first viewing of the picture. His keen sense for fluidity of movement, apparent even in the longest of his scenes (he uses whatever elements there are in the shot to continue the flow), gives his cutting and sound a kinetic quality that is the envy and admiration of other directors. Also like Hitchcock he gets the maximum effect out of his materials. In Lang's films everything on the set—props, actors, background, sound—is utilized to enrich the scene, delineate character, heighten the mood. Such economy makes for simplicity of a high order. Perhaps more than any other man in Hollywood today Lang is the "director's director." . . .

Despite [a] final concession to the box office (for which Lang cannot be blamed) *Fury* was a memorable film, in theme as well as in rendering. Lang's acute direction built up a frightening tension. Everyday events and people suddenly took on tremendous and horrifying proportion; even the most insignificant details had a pointed meaning. All converged into a bitter denunciation of mob action. From the quiet beginning, when Joe Wilson is picked up on the road, to the scenes of the hysteria of the mob and the burning jail and to the trial of the hypocritical townspeople, Lang's camera piled detail upon detail from the point of view of the spectator, the victim, the community, and the law, making them an inspired commentary upon bigotry, provincialism, and intolerance. [1939]

Lewis Jacobs. *The Rise of the American Film*
(Teachers College, 1968), pp. 462–63

The Woman in the Window, Lang's latest, happens to be on the level of murder melodrama—which is all to the good so far as audiences are concerned because it will not disturb them with the kind of deeper meanings that made *M* so much more than a mere murder story and a man hunt. But it is a perfect specimen of its kind, and a very good kind, too.

Also, unfortunately for a reviewer, it is something it would be a shame to tip off a prospective audience about, except to sound an urgent warning not to walk in on the middle of it and miss seeing the beginning first and the ending last. Its punch—and it packs a big one—depends on being in your seat when the three old cronies, the professor of psychology, the doctor and the district attorney, chat over their drinks in the club and lay the foundations for the unexpected relationships that are going to disturb their friendship later; on sitting there as the story develops so beautifully one incident out of another; and on imbibing the tension minute by minute till the end—in its proper place—brings its vast relief like a drowning man getting finally to the surface and finding he can breathe again.

It is not giving away any plot to say that in this picture you find things you probably haven't suspected, unless you have dabbled in illegal doings yourself, about the devious but inevitable ways in which crime leads on to more crime, and about the inexorable fashion in which even the most trivial and apparently inconsequential actions fit into a pattern that a good policeman can put his nose to and follow to a sure arrest. In fact, if movies are a deterrent for anybody from anything, *The Woman in the Window* should be a very effective warning to anyone who thinks he could get away with murder.

Edward G. Robinson is no Little Caesar, or anything like it, in this.

Splendid actor that he is, he has created something fresh and new for his long gallery of excellent characterizations in the gentle cultured professor who couldn't stand more than two after-dinner brandies and looked once too often on the portrait in the art-gallery window. The rest of the cast is also up to what it needs to be. But the play's the thing, and Fritz Lang's handling.

James Shelley Hamilton. *NBR*. Nov. 1944, p. 9

What is Destiny? Fritz Lang shows us in *Woman in the Window*. A bourgeois who could as easily be you or me is innocently dragged into special circumstances that lead him to kill in self-defense. He is also forced to efface all traces of the crime, since the facts are such that he would be unable to justify himself. But following this action a net continually tightens and thickens about him until he is led to suicide; but by one of those sudden turns common to Destiny, all menace is suddenly swept aside.

The tragic intensity strikes us particularly hard since the events are situated in our everyday world and the adventure of Professor Wanley (Edward G. Robinson) can happen to any of us. And the anguish attains such a height that the scenario writer—evidently on instructions from the censor—has tried to calm us by bruskly breaking the charm with a banal epilogue: the professor awakes and the nightmare is unexpectedly shaken off. The real work, however, stops with the useless suicide; this is a tragedy in which Fritz Lang completely involves us after having made us stick a finger into the trap. His style has not weakened since *M*, and obviously the composition of the tragic with realistic elements leads to something that we find difficult to bear; the accumulation of tiny details enlarged as though under a district attorney's magnifying glass gives reality a fantastic and anguishing appearance. A footprint in the mud, a barbed fence, a pair of scissors, a moment of forgetfulness, a chance encounter, the most ordinary gestures and things become a trap, a threat, the proof of guilt, a weapon of pitiless Destiny.

Thus transposed the metaphysical tragedy is no longer a means of drawing off our passions harmlessly. On the contrary, it becomes a formidable test for the nerves. And it would seem that this is the goal of Fritz Lang; his art belongs to the pre-Nazi culture of post World War I, the culture of novelists like Ewers, for example, who searched above all to provoke strong emotion by brutalizing the reader under the guise of touching him more profoundly.

Jacques Bourgeois. *Revue du Cinéma*. Nov. 1946, p. 72

In 1943, the vogue of anti-Nazi films permitted him to make *Hangmen Also Die*, centering round the assassination of Heydrich, the Nazi "protector" of Czechoslovakia. Considering the elements—espionage and counter-espionage, the very stuff of Lang's best work—it was curiously uneven and unconvincing. Lang, working with American actors on an American theme, has produced *Fury*. Lang trying to recreate his own Central Europe on a Hollywood set, was completely at sea. This had been the experience of other important directors before him, and is an apparently inescapable dilemma. Perfunctorily praised for its patriotic intent, *Hangmen Also Die* hardly advanced Lang's career, or cast much light on the European underground. At the end of the war, he joined forces with Walter Wanger and Joan Bennett to form Diana Productions, his own unit. Presumably his purpose was to escape as much as possible from commercial restrictions, but the results so far hardly bear out these good intentions. *The Woman in the Window, Scarlet Street,* and *The Secret Beyond the Door* are acceptable thrillers in the style currently popular, but they might have been made by any of the studios and show only occasional signs of their director's technical inventiveness. [1949]

Paul Rotha. *The Film Till Now* (Spring Books, 1930, rev. 1949 and 1960), p. 481

Rancho Notorious is an extra plushy Western with scenery, songs and Marlene Dietrich in color. Every quality you might ask of a Western is in lavish supply at the Paramount—except entertainment value.

The characters of this film have a collection of the most gaudily lurid pasts ever to appear in flashback. At times the film becomes so preposterous it seems to be kidding. If the kidding is intentional, it is far too heavy-handed to draw much laughter beyond a derisive hoot or two. . . .

Along with all its stars, the film has Fritz Lang, no less, as director. It's like sending for a piledriver to crush an ant.

Alton Cook. *NYWTS*. May 15, 1952

Lumière's naturalism and Méliès' dreams are equal; to call one lie and the other truth is invalidated by their shared photographic existence. In Lang's *Beyond a Reasonable Doubt* the dialectic is such as to present the images alternately as truth and lies so that the ultimate effect is destructive of the whole criterion of truth and falsity. . . .

Compare this with *Toni*, made in 1934. Renoir read a newspaper report of a *crime passionnel*. It intrigued him and he decided to film it. The entire film was shot on location using as many non-professionals as possible. *Beyond a Reasonable Doubt* takes place on manufactured sets and employs professional actors in every part. The people and landscapes in *Toni* are free in a sense that does not apply in Lang's films. Renoir's characters aspire to the freedom of choice of real life and the action is apparently uninfluenced by the director's purpose. But the Renoir is as artificial as Lang in that he has set up the whole verisimilitudinous action for the cameras. From the outset Lang is franker in his use of contrivance. It is only as his film develops that the reality of the contrivance asserts a perspective in which physical reality—which is Renoir's goal—becomes an abstract, and epistemological reality undermines the spectator in the way Renoir's realism convinces him.

Both Lang and Renoir intend to film certain events as accurately as possible. Distortion is alien to both of them: for Lang it would pervert the functional cleanliness of the study and for Renoir it would elevate one aspect of atmosphere or personality above the others. The immense difference between the two directors is in their conceptions of visible society. Renoir's is particularized to infinity so that the complexity of motive and desire promotes a sense of phenomenology, while Lang conceives of an abstract society so simplified that every character possesses the whole range of archetype. Movement interests them both as it should film directors, but for Renoir the movement is physical and for Lang it is epic.

David Thomson. *Movie Man* (Stein & Day, 1967), pp. 26–27

In the first two American films, Lang clearly phrased his main themes, on which he was to play variations through most of the twenty other pictures he made here. *Fury* deals as much with the sickness of revenge, of hate, as it does with the iniquities of destiny—the mercilessness of which gives *You Only Live Once* (1937) its near-classical dimension: Eddie (Henry Fonda), the three-time loser, is as doomed from the start as Oedipus; but for Lang, it is not the outcome that matters in a struggle against fate, it is the fight itself. Long after the social aspects of these films—dangers of lynch mob mentality, society's injustice to exconvicts—are forgotten, the more universal qualities will continue to have strength and poignancy.

Their social commitment, however, is exactly what makes these two films so popular with Lambert and other Grierson-minded critics who will dismiss Sternberg as a "photographer," and discuss art in terms of "importance" and morality; the visual aspects tend to be ignored if there is—for them—no greater meaning attached. A film is not examined for how much of the artist is exposed, but for how much of society. Therefore—because it is a personal tragedy that does not in any way indict the world at large—*Scarlet Street* (1945), according to Lambert, is "only an exercise in low-life. Its texture is brilliant but no more than decorative in its significance; and for this reason its essential thinness becomes increasingly apparent," whereas *The Big Heat*—because it could be interpreted as a study of city corruption—"is a minor but frequently brilliant film that stands comparison with his best work." However, it could equally be argued that *Scarlet Street* is nearly flawless, whereas *The Big Heat* is marred by several "average family" scenes (Glenn Ford, his wife and child) that ring false because Lang has little interest in anything approaching normality—in fact, he denies its existence. On the other hand, all the characters in *Scarlet Street* are believable because each in his own way is warped by life, and the crippled—physically, emotionally—are Lang's true métier. The finest scenes in *The Big Heat*—in all his pictures—are the ones that deal with the insulted and injured.

Peter Bogdanovich. *Fritz Lang in America*
(Praeger, 1967), pp. 8–10

. . . *Man Hunt* is a tense and intriguing thriller that is both propaganda and exciting entertainment. Though the subject matter is distinctively and typically Lang's, it is taken almost entirely from the original novel [Geoffrey Household's *Rogue Male*], which patently expresses the themes already associated with Lang. Here is an excellent example of a director who does not write his own stories or scripts, and yet maintains the personal touch by selecting the material to be adapted. It is significant that this, his first war film, deals with a secret and silent struggle, not the overt one of John Wayne and Errol Flynn. . . .

Because he can be subjective about his motives, the book's narrator articulates what Lang often can only suggest. The character, for example, views himself as the unseen, unsuspected hunter who can strike without warning. . . . Though this feeling is implicit in the situation, only a line or two of dialogue point it out in the film. The plot's concluding revelation—that Thorndike had, after all, subconsciously intended to kill Hitler—is strongly hinted at near the beginning of the novel. . . . This revelation that there is a second, subsurface Thorndike remains in the film, but is more completely saved for the climax. The script, happily, plants an early suggestion of the change in the character without resorting to the facile method of narration; instead it is done in a more subtle and visual manner. The film opens with a close tracking shot that moves along a forest, revealing a man aiming his rifle at Hitler. He pulls the trigger, and we hear only the sound of a click. He smiles, starts to leave, pauses, places a bullet in the chamber, re-sights, brushes away a leaf that has just fallen, and is arrested by Nazi guards. As did the opening of *Das Testament des Dr. Mabuse*, this sequence starts the movie off *in medias res*, and thus maintains suspense by keeping the viewer unsure of exactly what is happening. Though the novel began with the same incident, it kept back a detailed description of the scene until later and so lost much of this effect. The film, working with visual details, reveals Thorndike's change of mind by having him insert the bullet, an action which the viewer recalls later when the facts are revealed. (The leaf is another added detail, a twist of fate not unlike the fall of the leaf in *Siegfrieds Tod*, for both are arbitrary events which reduce the hero's chances of success.)

Paul M. Jensen. *The Cinema of Fritz Lang* (Barnes, 1969), pp. 135–37

LE ROY, MERVYN (1900–)

We have heard—and this department in certain cases has agreed—that the Russian cinema has marked highwater in the creative achievement of motion pictures. If it has done this, it is because—granted that a properly conceived technique has fashioned it for extraordinary dynamic thrust and therefore effective compact—it has dealt intensely, imaginatively and provocatively with the material of human beings in relation to the social organism, with what happens to the souls of people, with what destroys or enlivens souls, with what society can do to souls through blindness or stupidity or selfishness or malice and sheer rage; it is because the Russian cinema, even when adulating and centering on a special cause, idea, or social scheme about which there is justifiable disagreement, has spurned the putty and paint, the prettiness and pretentiousness, preferred to follow uncompromisingly the bitter grain of life, and so remained authentic in theme and passionate in utterance. But with this film of bitter life before us, made in America, in Hollywood, praise be, there can be no hesitancy in saying that our picture producers, when they get the slant, the courage and the will, can turn out just as important films as can anyone, anywhere, in the world (as indeed—but often with too little proof—our producers have been contending all along). *I Am a Fugitive From a Chain Gang* proves the contention amply and is to be enthusiastically commended for its courage, artistic sincerity, dramatic vigor, high entertainment concept, and social message—the last a word we don't like, but have in all conscience to use.

NBR. Nov. 1932, p. 9

I Am A Fugitive.—There were two ways in which director LeRoy could have made this picture. He could have ripped the highlights from the startling novel, of the same name, written by a convict escaped from the chain-gang, and told in brief episodes the story of this man's life. As the story is a horrible one, he could have used the man as an instrument against his background and, like the Germans and Russians at their best, manipulated people as group actors, making the prison, and not the actors, the object of the film.

But unfortunately he had to expect a profit from his labor and try at once to tell a dramatic story and still to dramatize his prison. He managed to dramatize his hero, and he certainly did not soften the background, but in doing this he failed to characterize the brutal guards, the horrible complacency of state officials, their utter detachment from society.

I don't hold with the radical school of critics that indignation *per se* is art. However, I don't join hands with the arty boys, either, who maintain that all indignation is cheap, unartistic simply because it attempts to grind an axe. Actually, *I Am a Fugitive* is not a moralizing treatise. But you can't see it without feeling that it is a savage document against existing penal systems, nor can you ignore daily evidences that such systems are operating in our great commonwealths every day in the week.

I quarrel with the production not because it is savage and horrible, but because each step in an inevitable tragedy is taken clumsily, and because each character responsible for the hero's doom is shown more as a caricature than as a person. The men do not seem real. The chain-gang certainly does. You may very well say you want to go to the theatre to forget trouble. But *I Am a Fugitive* has no moral treatise. Personally I think you'll find it more dramatic than, say, a current play dealing with Chinese peasants, or Irish drunkards, or French maids, or middle class neurotics.

Pare Lorentz. *Vanity Fair*. Dec. 1932, pp. 46–47

I should not hesitate to call *Little Caesar* the most successful talkie that has yet been made in this country. The credit goes chiefly, though not entirely, to LeRoy. He gave it a dynamic driving pace which carried through to the very end. By skillful cutting he carried the rhythm of his episodes and related them so closely that, unlike most American talkies, *Little Caesar* seems to be an organic whole. He adroitly modulated the tone from tense melodrama (as in the gangsters' inner sanctum scenes) to satire (as in the superb banquet episode) to the bleakest realism (as in the last reel). And he precisely caught the atmosphere of his night club, of his cheap flophouse, of his lunch counters and hideaways. . . .

I have yet to see a dull movie by LeRoy. Whatever his movies fail to do they always *move*. He knows how to give speed and pace to a film. His recent picture, *Hard to Handle*, for example, is a commonplace affair as to plot and dialogue, just another press-agent story. But LeRoy keeps the mechanism purring along at such a smooth, swift pace that one is not bored—until after it is all over and one has time to reflect. He makes his actors talk and move rapidly. He gets impetus every now and then by a quick succession of short shots dissolving into each other every five seconds or so. Above all, he doesn't dot his i's. Once his point is made, he moves on at once. Essentially, it is the vaudeville black-out technique. [1933]

Dwight Macdonald. *D. M. on Movies*
(Prentice-Hall, 1969), pp. 98, 99

As a work of cinema, *I am a Fugitive from a (Georgia) Chain-Gang*, is superior to [Curtiz's] *The Cabin in the Cotton*. Its young director, Mervyn Le Roy, is as yet an eclectic of the second or third order. He has made as bad a film as *Numbered Men*, films as inflated for their tiny intelligence as *Big City Blues* and *Three on a Match*, and pictures as reputable as *Little Caesar*, *Five-Star Final* and *I am a Fugitive*. His career is an argument for the importance of content: the better the story, the better has been his direction! Le Roy is gifted in the American open-play tradition that has been deserted by von Sternberg, but which Milestone enlivened in *The Front Page*. His last films show Le Roy's indebtedness to Milestone, but he has not the older man's proficiency in timing. If the talkie has damaged anything in the American idiom, it is its metric. I do not lament this disturbance for it serves to break up the confounding of time with speed-uninterrupted action. In *I am a Fugitive* Le Roy shows skill in the alternations of speech and silence, but he fails to convey lapse of time, despite his use of the archaic calendar-leaves (an archaism improved somewhat by the coincidence of hammer-beat) and distance (which must be conveyed conjointly by space of time) by means of an inanimate, inexpressive map. Le Roy exhibits the Milestone weakness in his direction of women; he was successful with Aline MacMahon in *Five-Star Final* because she is a superior player with a masculine emphasis (her roles are "hard"). The young director was more successful in the sensational or spectacular scenes (although the second escape was, in its scenario, quite routine), and less successful in the scenes away from prison—as in the period of the fugitive's rise to success. This attests to the immaturity not alone of Le Roy, but also of the American movie-mind. Le Roy's faults are as much environmental as personal. They arise from the American aspiration to be momentarily effective, which coincides with the unwillingness to be thorough in the treatment of social material. *Five-Star Final* overpitched its tragedy—stretched it beyond the point of elasticity—neutralized the indictment with humor and terminated the drama with a cute remark. Of competence there was much, a competence of verve and of a quality superior to the blue-print workmanship of a Frank Capra, for instance. *I am a Fugitive* is too spectacular at times, the chain-gang is clustered in two sequences of the film to serve as a lavish background for the innocent prisoner played honorably by Paul Muni. By the end of the picture we are thinking not at all of the chain-gang but of the fugitive, and mainly because he has been made a man of the hour whose hour is destroyed by the vindictiveness of a state, which breaks the promise exacted by the insistence of the popular voice. It is in its characterization of the state (through governor et al) that the picture achieves its main importance. Were it not for the inspired conclusion, when the fugitive's agonized face disappears in the mist, I doubt that the antecedent action would be recalled.

H. A. Potamkin. *Close Up*. March 1933, pp. 36–38

Some of the most agile shilly-shallying of the season has found its way into the screen version of *Oil for the Lamps of China*. . . . Where Alice Tisdale Hobart described the impersonal ruthlessness of a great oil corporation, the photoplay becomes a confused effort to applaud the company for its paternal and affectionate attitude toward the men who dedicate their lives to its service. Where Mrs. Hobart told of the futility of trying to remake the Orient in terms of Western civilization, the photoplay tries to be a glowing tribute to the Atlantic Oil Company and its high-minded crusade to bring light to the Chinese barbarians.

The film goes further than that. It presents the Chinese Communist movement not as the struggle of a tragic people to find a path out of their degradation, but as a vulturous gangsterism preying on organizations like the Atlantic Oil Company, which stand for honor and decency in their relations with China's masses. Far from hinting that China may be a little less than enthusiastic about being exploited by foreign countries and bending the neck to the war lords of the counter-revolution, the photoplay affirms that China looks upon American commercial intercession with eagerness and hope. All in all, it is to be feared that Cosmopolitan Pictures have not been altogether pious in their treatment of the novel. . . . The tragedy of the film is that such splendid acting and technical skill could not have been devoted to making an honest screen version of Mrs. Hobart's novel.

André Sennwald. *NYT*. June 6, 1935, p. 25

Ever a prodigal house, Warner Brothers deliver *Anthony Adverse* to the screen . . . with their customary Midas touch. It is a lavish gold-leaf from Hervey Allen's book, an earnest cinema endeavor, taxing alike its studio's purse and artistry.

Whatever may be the lit'ry appraisals of Mr. Allen's period tale, it was humane—a sturdy document of drinking and loving and ambition thwarted by tragic retribution, and I salute Director Mervyn Le Roy's and Scenarist Sheridan Gibney's attempts to push all this past the censor.

If they are tardy about it, consider their task. *Anthony* is nearly $2,000,000 worth of property, a lot to jeopardize for emotional truth—without the ameliorating kudos. For if Mr. Hays looked the other way there are still forty-eight State snooperas as well as those in foreign fields to elude. And then you have the perfect let-down—the careless apathy of the average film fan to whom subtlety is spinach.

The burden of this is apparent in the picture's pedestrian direction. But Mr. LeRoy is adroit, he makes no more than the usual distortions from which all true tales suffer in their filmic rebirth and is admirably deft in his obeisance to mass morals.

Thus the "understanding" between Don Luis and Faith Paleologus carries no blush in his photography. Indeed so intense are these scenes and so significant that the villainous Don and his hellion all but walk away with the film. Here Mr. LeRoy has penetrated to some of the depth and sweep of the book; doubtless too, because of the fine portrayals of Claude Rains and Gale Sondergaard.

Douglas Gilbert. *NYWT*. Aug. 27, 1936

What with all we know of Hollywood idiocy, capitalism, plagiarism, fearsome-fascism (read all about it), we ought to have a neat pigeon-hole for the cycle of pictures with social teeth to them that the Warners have been releasing. If we are wise we won't, though: I never saw a good mouthful of dialectic yet that didn't prove any such thing impossible—they cannot be, hence they aren't, never were. And yet here currently is another, made from Ward Greene's novel on a case study of mob violence in the Deep South, directed and produced by Mervyn LeRoy, called *They Won't Forget*. Whatever is behind it, the fact is that in content and uncompromising treatment this film is just the blood-and-guts sort of thing we've been hollering for. I suspect it's more fun to demand when there is a pretty good assurance you won't get it, and so I imagine there will be a certain embarrassment at finding that here it is, and in the guise of nothing more than a pretty good movie. Pshaw. . . .

The film has an awful opening—six Civil War veterans lined up on a bench and speaking on cue for all the world like a Vitaphone short of Shep Fields and His Rippling Confederate Rhythm—but this is surely canceled by the handling of suspense in the schoolhouse; the powerful understatement in the fading out of the lynching sequence, where the camera doesn't follow the group away from the train but, as the other express comes through, raises the focus until the main object is the mail sack hanging from its patent gallows, seen for moments and then jerked out like a shot as the mail car passes, etc. For the most part, though, the story is told straightforwardly, the school, the home, the streets, the jail, first this, then that, one, two, three. And the general effect of day-by-day honesty is somehow helped out by a cast of unfamiliar faces, competent actors and not distinguished, altogether managing about the right air of candor, bewilderment, the good intentions and undistinguished state of actual life. . . .

This isn't one of the pinnacles of art; we aren't talking of that here. But those who remember the heightening of fascination and awe that Fritz Lang achieved by the magic of his craft in *Fury* will also remember that his story never squared itself with its ending. There are many different levels of creation and recreation, but what we will principally find in *They Won't Forget* is that the plain statement may tell more and remain longer than fragmentary eloquence, however high and handsome. [1937]

Otis Ferguson. *The Film Criticism of O.F.*
(Temple, 1971), pp. 185–87

. . . A grim and scathing portrayal of prejudice, intolerance, and mob fury in the deep South, [*They Won't Forget*] progresses with a newsreel objectivity that gives its incidents the reality if not the intensity of Lang's *Fury*. The depiction of Redwine, the terrified Negro janitor who discovers the body of the murdered girl in the school's elevator shaft, is one of the few instances in American films in which the fear and oppression that fill the life of the Southern Negro is strikingly told.

Other outstanding touches are the concluding scenes. Hale, the framed victim, is being rushed by train from the lynch mob in the Southern city to a place of safety. But a lynch posse board the train, overpower Hale's guards, and drag him to their waiting cronies. As he shrieks for help, another train speeds by, its rumble and roar drowning out Hale's cries.

This kidnapping scene is followed by one in which symbolism is used most expressively. The shot reveals a mailbag suspended from a crosstree beside the railroad tracks. At the moment of the lynching of Hale, a train roars by, emitting an unearthly shriek as a steel hook extended from the mail car catches the mail sack and whirls it away. So the unseen horrible deed is summed up far more tellingly than would be possible in an actual scene of lynching. Such imaginative touches reveal LeRoy at his best.

Never a strident director, always an efficient one, "as good as his script," Mervyn LeRoy can produce good films when he is given good stories. [1939]

Lewis Jacobs. *The Rise of the American Film* (Teachers College, 1968), pp. 486–87

There is positively nothing random about *Random Harvest.* It is shrewdly and meticulously dollar-crafted in every particular. Its British accent is as captivating as *Mrs. Miniver's.* It is cast with pearly players in every part. Its pedigreed plot is savored with just the right mixtures of ups and downs, ecstasy and well-bred anguish, implausibility and psyche. And it moves toward its climax with the measured tread and nicely-timed emotional bumps of a Hearst Cosmopolitan serial.

In short, *Random Harvest* is custom-built to evoke all the customary rave adjectives, yet not to stir any weighty ones. It is a super-colossal commonplace. . . .

Random Harvest probably cost upwards of $2,000,000, and it is perhaps the clearest example of the year of how a studio possessing lion's shares of movie-making capital and ingratiating talent can mate these two to synthesize a magnificent neuter, which will predictably bring in vast box office returns with which to produce more neuters.

John T. McManus. *PM*. Dec. 1942

Mervyn LeRoy, a Hollywood director whose best work was done during his long and successful association with Warner Brothers, demonstrates in his films a keen sense of sympathy with the Negro. One remembers his treatment of the Negro prisoner, played by Everett Brown, in that superb movie, *I Am A Fugitive From A Chain Gang,* dealing with Southern labour camps and produced in 1932. The Negro is shown in the early part of the film as one of Paul Muni's comrades. He reveals a good brain, a friendly nature and a clear philosophy. It is hinted that, like Muni, he also came into the chain gang as a result of circumstances almost amounting to a Southern States "frame up."

LeRoy's sympathetic handling of the Negro rôle reached its climax in the scene where Muni, rebelling at the injustices of the labour camp system and realising that the bigoted Southern warders will see that he never gets his long-promised reprieve, decides to make his escape. He is helped by his black friend, who with his great strength, patience and selfless bravery aids Muni to make a getaway by breaking his chains with his sledge-hammer. The feeling which remained after seeing *I Am A Fugitive* was that the Negro is an ordinary human being, capable of great friendship, loyalty and courage. [1948]

Peter Noble. *The Negro in Films* (Kennikat, 1969), p. 71

Louisa May Alcott's beloved classic [*Little Women*] is a bedazzling thing in Technicolor, handsomely set, beautifully costumed. As a result Marmee March's brave little alpaca-clad brood comes out looking like very flossy ladies of fashion. (Never mind that the Civil War is raging.) . . .

Mervyn LeRoy directed and managed to retain much of the original story's tearful tenderness. There's more to be said about and for this gentle offering, but perhaps you'd better see it for yourself.

Frankie McKee Robins. *McCall's.* May 1949, p. 7

I chose Mervyn LeRoy as a long-overdue subject to be honored with a tribute and film retrospective at the Gallery [of Modern Art] after re-screening his amazing output of 75 films. From such highlights as *Little Caesar* (1930) to *Gypsy* (1962), his range and diversity have seldom been equalled by any other producer-director. Beginning as an actor in 1923, with *Little Johnny Jones, Prodigal Daughters* and *Broadway After Dark*, LeRoy has developed his natural feeling for human emotion, his strong story-telling sense, and a great flair for imaginative invention into a flexible and thoroughly professional expertise in film production and direction. In addition, he is a completely delightful individual to work with, and I am grateful for his cooperation in making available his work for this tribute.

Raymond Rohauer in *A Tribute to Mervyn LeRoy* (Gallery of Modern Art, 1967), p. 5

This movie [*Gold Diggers of 1933*] sums up what is now meant by the phrase "pure thirties." It's a funny, good-natured backstage musical, and a Depression period piece as well. It was directed by the not conspicuously talented Mervyn LeRoy (the year after *I Am a Fugitive from a Chain Gang*), and it is memorable chiefly because the choreographer, Busby Berkeley, created a mad geometry of patterned chorines. . . . The innocent vulgarity of the big numbers is charming and uproarious, and aesthetically preferable to the pretentious ballet finales of fifties musicals like *An American in Paris*. Even those of us who were children at the time did not mistake *Gold Diggers* for art—and certainly no one took it for "life."

Pauline Kael. *Kiss Kiss Bang Bang*
(Little, Brown, 1968), p. 273

Mervyn LeRoy's classic study of chain gang life [*I Am a Fugitive from a Chain Gang*] was a transitional link from the prison film to the topical film. The motif of imprisonment and entrapment was a popular one in 1930 and 1931, and an entire cycle centering around prison life reached American screens in the post-Crash days: *The Big House* (1930), *Ladies of the Big House* (1931), *20,000 Years in Sing Sing* (1930), and *Convict's Code* (1930), to name a few, in rapid succession. . . .

LeRoy picked up on the persecution of innocents, but the means of entrapment he utilized reflected a social awareness, rather than the familiar plot device of the "frame up." *I Am a Fugitive* . . . was ostensibly an attack upon the chain gang system practiced in the South, but, despite the patent justice and necessity of that theme, its implications, in 1932, extended further. . . .

In the harsh and mindless world of the chain gang the imagery was all of confinement: the lock, the fence, the chain. And the camera lingered on prisoners' faces, all beaten in, devoid of hope or any sense of potentiality save the dull fears of beating and death. Black prisoners were segregated, and in an era when black people were depicted as having the emotional range of comic strip characters (on a continuum from "Lord have mercy" to a grinning "Yes, ma'am"), LeRoy presented them as suffering, trapped human beings. (In a contemporary chain gang exposé, Roland West's *Hell's Highway*, the black prisoners could usually be found singing cheerful ditties.) . . .

Andrew Bergman. *We're in the Money*
(NYU, 1971), pp. 93–95

LITVAK, ANATOLE (1902–   )

Persons familiar with the play [*Tovarich*] will discover some departures from original. Story changes are not radical (one or two modifications being prompted by censorship restrictions), but the overemphasis of the comedy side of the play, almost to the point of occasional slapstick, will be regarded generally as an unnecessary concession to film audiences. It is this aspect of Anatole Litvak's direction which makes the picture something less than superlative. . . .

Litvak seems imbued with the idea that he had to make *Tovarich* look like a big picture, whereas the story of the royal refugee couple, who enter domestic service in the household of a Paris banker, is a yarn of charming and finely shaded characterizations. Both humor and heart appeal spring from intimate acquaintance with the background and motives of each player. Litvak has improvised a confusing and noisy opening sequence of Parisians dancing in the streets in celebration of Bastille Day. This is followed by a farcial introduction of his principals. As a result, an understanding of the true predicament of the one-time members of the imperial household is not clearly revealed until the story has consumed considerable footage.

Variety. Dec. 19, 1937

The Amazing Dr. Clitterhouse. The elements of the strange and exciting are here, but there is a happy absence of that literal, unfilmic treatment which blunted and dragged down *A Slight Case of Murder* (you might have thought the crime-comedy style of *The Thin Man* would have taught a lesson on the difference between literary intentions and actual picture flow to the most literal bodies; but alas not yet). The story is ingenious, but Anatole Litvak and his producing-acting crew have so thoroughly kept the larky mood of it while setting up the necessary undercurrent of interest and suspense that it is hard to see where conception leaves off and the shaping of it into motion begins. . . .

In making use of both his actors and the situations of the story, the director has a fine organizational talent for keeping it good and clear in motion—for a good line, like a good idea for a sequence, is only half the battle, and the rest is planting it. Take Allen Jenkins' offside business: University? He had a brother in one, sure, it was his kid brother—what did they call the place . . . Harvard, that was it. Sure. What do you mean, how was he doing? It was legitimate, they had him in alcohol right there. He had two heads. Or the case of the Law whose name turned out to be Ethelbert. Then there was the neat idea of rigging up the mobsters as the Hudson River String Quartet and quartering them in the Carnegie Hall apartments, developed with many touches like that of having a Mozart serenade as background for talk about the split, the ice, and get this, mugs. And the reversal of usual trial stuff by throwing the decisive word to the human and baffled jury foreman—a fine sequence all around. But more than Algiers, this film shows evidence of our widening exploitation of the camera medium over here. Some of the pioneering in Alfred Hitchcock's approach seems to show through the dramatic irony of the gems in the doctor's bag, later under the pretzels, in the restrained burlesque of that complete and effortless opening sequence, in the inverted-telescope device of the dying gangster, in the shrewd use of music and sound as contrapuntal emphasis.

Many will enjoy the film without stopping to ask what makes the story run so lightly with such vivid effect—which is unfortunate as far as credits go but not wholly uncheerful: art is often most healthy when it does not stick out all over everything like a bagful of nails. [1938]

Otis Ferguson. *The Film Criticism of O.F.* (Temple, 1971), pp. 228–29

On the screen a ham story doesn't matter: *The Sisters*, too, is ham, and even more conventional—the girl who marries a hard-drinking journalist who loves her, but loves his freedom more. The pathos is very familiar—the husband returns drunk on the evening when his wife intends to tell him she is pregnant: they quarrel on Christmas Day beside the Christmas-tree. The San Francisco earthquake is thrown effectively in as makeweight, there is a tiny, timid sketch of a brothel which probably passed our universal aunts as a happy picture of family life, but the main situation is as old as the cinema—you remember it in *Cimarron*—the husband who rides away and goes on loving all the time. But, as I say, ham doesn't matter: *The Sisters* is worth seeing for the sake of the adroit period direction and the fragile, pop-eyed acting of Miss Bette Davis. [1939]

Graham Greene. *G.G. on Film* (S&S, 1972), p. 218

In *Confessions* [*of a Nazi Spy*], therefore, we do not have the characteristic twists and obscurities of the usual spy film. No one is playing a game with the audience. There are no properties like fine little revolvers in ladies' handbags, nor codes by means of music, nor expensive suppers where the hero and heroine confide, at last, that each is working for the other side. These properties are meant to increase the heart-beat and leave the spectator in that state of empty excitement proper before going to bed.

Confessions has a different aim—to depict truth. The writers, Milton Krims and John Wexley, and the director, Anatole Litvak, chose to utilize an indigenous and highly practical form: the combination of dramatized incidents connected and explained by a commentator. *Confessions* thus has a remarkable resemblance to an extended and full-length *Crime Does Not Pay*. It has the same general method, the same plain people and utilitarian dialogue, the same emphasis on clarity of situation. This form has grown up quietly in this country, but has been made little use of by documentary film-makers. It is a form capable of considerable force. In one of the final scenes—where the witness Westphal, ostensibly sick, is lying aboard a Nazi liner, and refuses to leave at the request of the U. S. consul, and says over and over again that he is ill, he is ill, while attending him, standing over his bed, is a Gestapo agent whose brutality we have witnessed earlier, dressed as a male nurse in a white uniform that is too tight for him—in this scene we have one of the most brilliant examples of the *Crime Does Not Pay* technique.

This sort of fictional exposition leaves you with the facts, and with the natural excitement of the facts, and provides you at the same time with an attitude toward them. It is a crusading picture, and an immensely successful one, for the audience invariably comes out of the theater discussing not the film as such, but its content, the Nazi Bunds, the system of espionage, the Gestapo in America,—i.e., the facts. Naturally, this form has its limits and its limitations. The characterizations, with the exception of the soldier Werner Renz (Joe Sawyer), and Schneider (Francis Lederer), are uniformly explanatory, rather than searching. Motivations are often weakly developed and abrupt: the confession of Dr. Kassel is based on the discovery of his illicit love affair, and that of Schneider on his psychopathic vanity; both these motives should take a long time to develop, yet they bring the confession in the course of a sentence or two of interrogation. Similarly, the dialogue tends to be schematic, the transitions clever, interesting, but not deepening in a psychological sense.

So the picture as a whole is straight-line, hard-hitting, expository, wasting time nowhere, rushing on as if it were a two-reel short which must hurry and tell you more and more facts. These facts are imbedded in each dramatic scene and in the commentary, and the whole film is entirely sharp and functional.

David Wolff. *Films*. Nov. 1939, pp. 82–83

It is extremely disconcerting to see how Hollywood affects the European historical film via its directors. Anatole Litvak's *Mayerling* has become a kind of standard for the romantic film in an historical setting. His comprehension of psychological nuance, his tactful and judicious recreation of the strict Hapsburg etiquette contrasted with free *Alt Wien*, sincerely indicated the course of liberal and conservative political conflicts which preceded the Triple Alliance. He was never afraid to use a range of emotion which to Hollywood might have seemed "unpopular." He contrived incidents full of petulance, adolescent shyness, boredom, hurt feelings, and family misunderstanding, on a scale which was as adult as it was intense. In Hollywood, Litvak has done *The Sisters* and *Confessons of a Nazi Spy.* In the first, Errol Flynn and Bette Davis were seduced from their normal pretentiousness into giving simple performances, although their script was uninteresting. The background of Western America ca. 1910 was tastefully revived, but where the Hofburg had seemed domestic in its magnificence, and hence, real—a political rally in a northwestern town now became inflated, and hence only decorative. Hollywood insists on such a change of scale and makes reality, or at least essential naturalism, commit suicide. *Confessions* was a kind of historical picture—only it happened to be our own period. It was unburdened by too much stardom, and the background, which we could think of as "documentary" rather than as "historical," read well.

Lincoln Kirstein. *Films.* Spring 1940

It is impossible to view *The Long Night* without it bringing back strong memories of the emotions associated with *Le Jour se lève*, and continually falling short of those memories because it dare not set out to be a film in the same class. The patrons of the American and British cinema would stand neither for the morals nor the sheer human tragedy of the French film. The strength of treatment in the French film is therefore emasculated in the new version, and the killing of the stuffed dummy of a villain has nothing of the urgency and human rightness when Gabin at last shoots Jules Berry and one cries out "Thank God," and feels the world a cleaner place. There is in both films the same satire against the police, the same excellent situation of a decent man hunted and isolated from the people who trust him and the women who love him. Although the shell of the place and the story is there, the open street thronged with workers and police-cars, the tall tenement block, the deep well of the staircase, the hunted man bemused and cornered in his room, the whistling bullets and the tear-gas, the richer feeling for human life and instinct and love always present in the French film is gone. Some of it had to go to satisfy the censor, some of it to match more closely the demands of adolescent patrons. Very well. But why should the rest of us be deprived of the right to see Carné's film in the specialised theatres and film societies?

Roger Manvell. *Sight & Sound.* Autumn 1947, p. 116

Everything has been put in [*The Snake Pit*] to shock or move or entertain an audience—and what there is of tracing thought-processes to their roots is so over-simplified that were it possible to cure its central character as patly as she is finally cured (apparently for good, as no mention is ever made of possible retrogression after she leaves the hospital) one would have to say she was treated barbarously by having had to undergo everything (even the homely, jealous nurse wasn't left out) but brain surgery (*there's* one thing they forgot). Withal, a film of superficial veracity (like the diagnoses of most psychiatrists themselves) of a subject that requires a bigger man than Litvak (*vide* Pabst's *Secrets of a Soul*); a good film with bad things (pat things, obvious things, clichés, false sentimentality versus unnatural unfeelingness, as in the husband's lack of real pain at his wife's plight, etc.). The late Paul Rosenfeld got into a half-dozen pages of his vignette, "The Hospital," the preface to his book, *Men Seen*, more of the "ordeal by fire" that is a hospital of any kind, and the jubilation of leaving a hospital cured—looking back at it as one leaves it, not as a house of horror, pain and death, but as a sylvan glade where one sojourned a while and was made well again—more of this, which can be the only valid purpose and meaning of such a painful subject, than all of *The Snake Pit* with its frightening *minutiae* like the rubbing of jelly on the patient's temples before the cathodes are applied in shock-therapy or the tearful singing of "Going Home" at the end. But the audience, hanging on to the *pipe*-smoking (naturally!) psychiatrist knows that everything will come out alright (otherwise why would they have chosen such a theme?) so even of suspense there is nothing.

Herman G. Weinberg. *Sight & Sound.*
Spring 1949, p. 18

Anatole Litvak's *The Journey* is supposed to be about the 1956 Hungarian revolt. It opens with some wide-screen color shots of Budapest airport, where Russian soldiers are standing about with Tommy guns and Russian jets are moaning overhead. The camera then enters the terminal, where we see a large, motley group of people, some sprawled across chairs or over baggage or on the floor, many on their feet just milling about. These, we understand, are foreigners, stranded in Budapest because of the uprising, and trying to get out. Ten seconds of this and we know where we are. We are back in the middle and late 1930's with Alfred Hitchcock and that glamorous band of international characters trapped in *Mitteleuropa*, whose interesting fates will be worked out in their efforts to escape the approaching holocaust. And we're right, for up to the terminal desk weaves Robert Morley, and in the most nasal and insular of English accents demands for the hundredth time immediate information about their flight, exactly as those two Hitchçock comedians used to demand, coolly, imperiously, in the midst of Hitler's Europe, the scores in the latest cricket match. We relax, we are on familiar ground. . . .

But all sorts of unpleasant things do keep happening on and off the screen (people are being hunted and shot), and someone is needed for the audience either to blame or dislike. The makers of the film find the answer to that in a rather recent addition to film conventions, the image of the American wife and mother abroad—by now as available an object for free-floating and generalized resentment as the American businessman of twenty years ago. This woman is yelling all the time (mostly at her two poor TV-stunned children); she is grossly pregnant, graceless, tasteless, and slovenly; she browbeats her mild and decent husband, is utterly selfish, hates sex, and demands that Deborah Kerr, a beautiful English aristocrat, prostitute herself to Brynner so that he will release them. Within the film's system of values she is certainly the chief moral delinquent, and although the audience can't blame her for all the dead Hungarians, it can dislike her actively and thoroughly enough to keep from considering that unpleasant subject. The curious effect of it all is to connect the agony of the Hungarian revolt with a wholly contemptible image of American society. The makers of *The Journey* may not have intended this, but this is what they have achieved, and it is the sort of thing that always happens when so many conventions are used so mindlessly.

Steven Marcus. *Reporter*. March 19, 1959, pp. 41–42

Five Miles to Midnight is one of those movies without a country that are becoming as fixed a part of the international scene as the Duke and Duchess of Windsor. A French-Italian coproduction manufactured in Paris, it was financed by U.S. money, directed by the Hungarian-American Anatole Litvak, and stars two world-travelers, Tony Perkins and Sophia Loren, supported by a largely Franco-American cast. If the pedigree of the film is confused, its artistic ancestry, on the other hand, is crystal clear. It is the immediate descendant of the slick, cynical French thrillers (*What Price Murder, Diabolique, Back to the Wall*) which occupy a permanent place on Gallic movie production schedules, and, until it grinds down to a clanking mock tragedy in the last reel, it is a well-ordered exercise in mechanical suspense.

Arthur Schlesinger, Jr. *Show*. April 1963, p. 39

However much the medical profession might criticize what [*The Snake Pit*] has to say, or how dated it now may be, for the time of viewing it is still convincing and deeply moving, thanks to an expert manipulation of film techniques. Olivia de Havilland's performance is brilliant: she evokes all the pity and terror of her situation. . . . In the main, however, the terrible isolation of the mentally ill is made felt by the camera placements and movements and the use of the nonsynchronous sound track.

The subjectivity derives only in part from camera angles. Sometimes the sound track contrasts with the objectivity of the camera, and we hear the patient narrating her thoughts or hear loud, discordant music at her greatest moments of panic. Objective and subjective angles alternate. The camera dwells on the patient's face, but when it cuts away, as often as not we are seeing from her viewpoint. In the opening sequence, there is a shot of trees and the sound of birds as she might see and hear them, but then a pan down that reveals her face is accompanied by the voice of the doctor who is unseen. We realize that she is not aware of him and confuses the voice with the patient sitting next to her on the bench. In subsequent scenes, the key turning in the lock and the bars are seen from a distorted angle as she imagines she is in prison. The various points of view are woven together very skillfully, without apparent discrepancy, comparable to the combined use of first and third person in a novel.

Eileen Bowser in *Film Notes,* edited by
Eileen Bowser (MOMA, 1969), p. 115

LLOYD, FRANK (1889–1960)

More pictures like *A Tale of Two Cities* and the millenium of the picture business would be near at hand. Charles Dickens' classic of the French Revolution, if one can be permitted to employ a bromide, might have been written specially for the screen. That is, judging from the manner in which Frank Lloyd has handled it. The picture is composed of virile elements in theme and in plot. . . .

Mr. Lloyd in the handling of the scenario and in the production of it has truly earned himself a place in the hall of fame of directors. Better than his masterly handling of the mob scenes, his delightful reproduction of the atmosphere of the period; better than his remarkable double exposure scenes and the selection of proper types, is the manner in which he has handled the plot itself. In so doing he has shown himself a master of picture craft. He has cut at just the right moment, has introduced the sub-plots at a time when their introduction is propitious, and has as a consequence derived from the story every possible atom of suspense. In fact, Mr. Lloyd has almost outdone Dickens. "Better than the book" is after all a silly cry, for a book and a picture are not comparable; but here we can say that Mr. Lloyd has translated the original work and endowed his translation with all the color and sentiment of its forerunner.

Peter Milne. *Motion Picture News.* March 31, 1917

All the parts in [*The Sin Flood*] are well played. Richard Dix as the young man, Helene Chadwick as the girl, James Kirkwood as the unfrocked preacher, Otto Hoffman as the actor, L. H. King as the bum and Ralph Lewis as one of the traders are especially good. And Frank Lloyd has done remarkably well as the director of the production. It's not his fault if the picture is not as strong as the [Henning Berger] play, for the action is essentially psychological; it goes on in the affected minds of the people present, and motion pictures, anyhow, cannot portray such action as effectively as it can be revealed through flesh-and-blood beings on a stage.

NYT. Oct. 30, 1922, p. 11

Oliver Twist, in its final form, was not a disappointment, either to the admirers of Jackie Coogan or to the admirers of Charles Dickens. Both of these distinguished collaborators came out well, with a sufficient amount of glory left over for Frank Lloyd.

Lloyd is an Englishman, and one who knows his Dickens well. He managed to retain the flavor of the novel, something which is not easy of accomplishment in the movies. Following the career of young Oliver through the poorhouse, through Mr. Sowerberry's funeral parlors, through the sordid filth of Fagin's quarters in the depths of London, and finally into the peaceful respectability of Mr. Brownlow's delightful home, Lloyd never lost sight of Dickens's scenes and Dickens's weird characters. . . .

Aside from his fine direction, Lloyd was responsible for the adaptation of the story. It was a terribly difficult task, in view of the fact that Dickens, in *Oliver Twist* as in all his novels, paid considerably more attention to his characters than he did to his narrative. He created his people and then permitted them to wander pretty much as they listed.

Oliver Twist was a coherent story on the screen, and this was entirely due to Frank Lloyd's deft weaving of the various strands of plot.

Robert E. Sherwood. *The Best Moving Pictures of 1922–23* (Small, Maynard, 1923), pp. 34–35

The Sea Hawk achieves its novelty through its maritime element. The hand-to-hand combats between the fighting ships of the day are done with spirit and skill by Director Frank Lloyd. These moments, in fact seem to be the best he has given the screen since he made *The Tale of Two Cities.*

These galley moments are remarkable. The huge battlecraft with their masses of almost naked humanity chained to the oars, sweltering under the hot Mediterranean sun, are graphic in their realism. . . .

The Sea Hawk has varying qualities. It is too long. The sea battles tend to lose through repetition. But the picture has strength and holds the interest. . . . There are times when Wallace Beery comes very close to stealing the picture in the serio-comic role of a freebooting scoundrel.

Photoplay. Aug. 1924, p. 48

In picture form, *Cavalcade* is a superlative newsreel, forcibly strengthened by factual scenes, good music, and wonderful photography. It is marred by pat and obvious dramatic climaxes, and by a conclusion which is anti-climactical and meaningless. And when one forgets the pace, the flow, and the really dignified and lovely quality of the picture—which is easier said than done—one can hear some very cheap theatrical observations from that choleric old empire-builder, Mr. Coward. . . .

As far as the subject matter was concerned I personally enjoyed the scene in *The Wet Parade* of a Tammany celebration in 1912 more than any of the chapters of English history dramatized in Mr. Coward's spectacle. Yet seldom has a movie company released a finer technical production than *Cavalcade*, and Mr. Lloyd, who once did a charming and unusual and really legitimate movie called *Young Nowheres*; and Mr. Menzies, who, since the beginning of Hollywood, has been the one man in the business who has brought imagination, skill, and a sense of beauty to the most neglected department in the industry—scenic-designing—deserve the highest praise for their work.

Mr. Lloyd might have spared us the broken hearted mother waving her little flag Armistice night, and he might have aided Mr. Coward if he had put the tinkly song, *Twentieth Century Blues*, in an earlier section of the picture. Furthermore, he might have greatly aided Mr. Coward if he had cut a shoddy bit of theatrical nobility and denied us the sophomoric toast, given in conclusion by the old father and mother, in which they hope "grace and dignity and peace" may be restored to old England. I can repeat, but not print, what the shade of Ben Jonson and his boys must have said to that.

Pare Lorentz. *Vanity Fair*. March 1933, p. 48

Mutiny on the Bounty is one of the best pictures that have been made, and this is largely due to the facts it was made from. More than most violent acts, a mutiny is a striking thing, requiring strong causes and breeding strong results. And more than most mutinies, that of H.M.S. *Bounty* was part of an incredible chain of events, logical developments and illogical strokes of chance, ill winds, bitter privations, the sweet land breezes off islands—and all anchored to a few powerful characters; heroes who were villains and villains who turned great.

The zest and careful research of Charles Nordhoff and James Norman Hall are responsible for the present version of the story: without their books Hollywood would never have come near this gold mine. But Nordhoff and Hall were not shrewd creators of fiction—their *Munity on the Bounty* was sometimes dull and frequently ineffectual, when you came to separate their handling of the story from the story itself, and their best passages were those where they were transcribing testimony, quoting from logs. It remained for the movies to give the thing a strong line of action and a fictional body.

The picture that Frank Lloyd has made wastes little time on preparations in England—the pressing of the crew, the signing on of Byam, etc.—and uses this time to best advantage in setting up the main currents of the story. They come over the side of H.M.S. *Bounty* and there is all the packed confusion and bustle of a ship, at the dead center of it the captain in his thundercloud; and before they leave there is a man flogged through the fleet, the flesh stripped from his bones in accordance with the printed word of Article XXI; and when they do leave there is a certain coordination of cameras, sound recordings, and cutting that makes something strange and beautiful out of an old hulk the movies bought up and glued their properties to.

The whole tone of the picture, in fact, is set by this beauty they have found in ships and described with the true care and knowledge of the craftsman.

The putting together of static fragments into a live story is what is most wonderful about this picture anyway. Just as the most striking aspects of ships getting under way and standing out in a line are sifted out and worked into a motion that is something more than the motion of vessels through water, so the details of various actions are made up into patterns and carried on from one to another. The action of the mutiny in particular has a brawling motion possible to no other art, with men pitched screaming out of the shrouds, blown down companionways, pinned to bulkheads, and just plain battered in a frenzy of released hatred. And the incidents leading up to the violent overthrow are made vivid in terms of the medium—the swish and pistol crack of the lash, the sweating, lean bodies, the terrible labor, and the ominous judgment from the quarterdeck. The ship and the ship's life open out here, but the film becomes grand by virtue of something more than quarterdecks and hurlyburly. It is the reworking of a large tragedy—men not only against the sea but against their own forces, both universal and particular. [1935]

Otis Ferguson. *The Film Criticism of O.F.* (Temple, 1971), pp. 103–04

[*Maid of Salem.*] A chilling and wrathful exposé of the old Salem ritual of witch-burning. It has been glamorized to the extent of dwelling for some luscious moments on the romance between Claudette Colbert as an innocent maid of the village and Fred MacMurray as a runaway Virginian, but these scenes have been so competently handled that they in no way detract from the fateful theme of the film. Once the panic of witchcraft starts (and you know what Director Frank Lloyd did with panic in *Cavalcade* and *Mutiny*), you are carried along on a vicious crescendo of madness and terror.

Stage. March 1937, p. 18

Wells Fargo is a prime example of the adaptability of the screen to the chronicle play. Aside from a few notable examples like *Abraham Lincoln* and *Murder in the Cathedral* the stage has never been really successful with this form even at the hands of Shakespeare, especially in the modern theatre. . . . The quick, shifting flexibility of the screen makes it a more suitable medium for such work than even the Elizabethan stage. The speed with which divergent locales can be interpolated and yet knit together offers the beholder an engrossing sense of variety. Such a panoramic scope gives great sweep to a historical subject like *Wells Fargo*. Yet though it covers a longer period than Drinkwater's play about the Great Emancipator it conveys less sense of sprawling development.

Frank Vreeland. *Foremost Films of 1938* (Pitman, 1939), pp. 46–47

For the period 1930–1940 Frank Lloyd remains one of the masters of adventure, one of those who introduced into the epic, the story of time past, the exocticism, that undefinable soft and trembling feeling that is the attribute of American cinema. Such is the common merit of *Cavalcade* (1933), featuring the sober and aristocratic Clive Brook; of *Mutiny on the Bounty* (1930), the cast of which remains one of the most dazzling in the history of the seventh art: Charles Laughton, Clark Gable, and Franchot Tone; and of *Welles Fargo* (1937), with Joel MacCrea and Frances Dee. It is often said that the charm of *Mutiny* is due in part to the novel by Nordhoff and Hall. But I would like to point out a moment that moves me after twenty years as it did when I first saw it. After a long stay on the Tahitian beaches—in a primitive Eden that evokes the novels of Herman Melville—the two heroes are about to separate. The one will return to England, the other has chosen henceforth to live among the "good savages." The moment of departure is at hand. It is the end of one of those beautiful, limpid and harmonious days that are common in that happy island all year long and that seem to make the place another Olympus. The slow and tender songs of the natives are mingled with the langorous sway of the tall trees. One of our heroes presses to him the woman who has been his smiling and docile companion. And slowly the sweetness of this pressure becomes one with the evening song and the movement of the palms. A mysterious unity joins the wondrous looks of the European to the amorous revery of the young woman and to the cosmic enchantment. The images modulate at a voluptuous cadence and the interpenetration communicates to us the vertigo that has for a moment taken hold of the voyager. If I evoke Rousseau or Chateaubriand it is not in an attempt to better define this impression. Actually it is in no way literary—it is halfway between an inebriating sensation, an anticipated regret, and an indefinitely prolonged dream. This accord between a moment of the story and a *mise en scène* so physically true is one of the great secrets of American films.

Henri Agel. *Romance Américaine* (Editions du Cerf, 1963), pp. 46–47

LORENTZ, PARE (1905–)

This film [*The Plough That Broke the Plains*] is remarkable less for itself than for what it represents; since in principle it is as closely allied to our own "documentary" ideal as any American non-fiction film hitherto produced. Fundamentally it is propaganda, organised by the Federal Government, in a non-political cause whose worthiness is not open to question; and it is actually one of the first screen-ventures to be undertaken with direct official backing in this way. The film has been written and directed by an officer of the Resettlement Administration. Ralph Steiner, who shares the camera-work, was previously an amateur.

The theme is the monstrous wasting of natural resources which has taken place on the Great Plains: arising out of cupidity and ignorance (though the former is little stressed) and leading finally, in the last decade, to widespread drought and starvation. Similar problems in relation to the despoiling of timber-land were touched on, but scamped, in the United Artists film *Come and Get It*. The present film traces the development of the soil from the days of the cattle-land and the pioneers to the wheat-boom of the Great War and the tremendous impetus which this gave to wheat-production. A few years later, as it goes on to show, the relentlessly plundered earth had crumbled to dust: now, faced by the spectacle of ruin and want, the Government urges support for its efforts at reconstruction.

The film's technique is documentary technique as we know it. Photographic quality is impeccable, viewpoints are carefully selected, commentary is used sparingly and helped out by sub-titles and by two excellent maps at beginning and end. The tempo is slow—so slow as to become rambling, for the implications of the climax are not sufficiently in keeping clear of the opposite trap, the conflict suggested in the building-up, and the final sequences accordingly descend upon us almost out of the blue. An American audience, already acquainted with the film's subject-matter, would no doubt find this easier to overlook; but it remains essentially a fault of structure, so that most of the vigour is in the beginning and end, with a noticeable sag in the middle. . . .

A. Vesselo. *Sight & Sound.* Winter 1936–37, pp. 146–47

Without benefit of Hollywood, Pare Lorentz has created in *The River* one of the splendors of the American film. He has done it in a field more cultivated by the Europeans than ourselves, that is the documentary film. He has taken as his theme the Mississippi River and its tributaries, the physical aspect of the great valley, its cities and its industries, the people who live in it, the crimes they have committed against "the richest free gift that was ever spread out before civilized man," the hopes for a decent life which that valley, in spite of human folly, still offers to humanity. That was the material with which he worked and over it has played so much intelligence and so much imagination that in about half the span of the usual feature picture he has managed to get everything in. . . .

The sense of something important going on is the essence of a good picture and *The River* has it to the highest degree. Inspired by it, Mr. Lorentz provided a text crammed with fact and uplifted by an unusual lyric quality which shows up in all their triviality the "narrations" of most nonfiction films. It is a little too cadenced in spots, but in the main the rhythm of the speech goes naturally with the rhythm of the picture; there is a list of names which makes you think of Homer's catalogue of the ships or of Scott Fitzgerald's guests at the house of the great Gatsby.

Gilbert Seldes. *Scribner's.* Jan. 1938, p. 67

No one has ever criticized Lorentz's first two films, *The Plow That Broke the Plains* and *The River*, on the ground that they were dull. . . . They "entertained" the spectator by making him a participant in what the film was about. By the use of familiar music, place names, and the American landscape itself, the memories and associations of audiences were stimulated toward identification with the people who faced the problems of erosion and flood control. The weak spot in both pictures was the fact that there really were very few people in them. Perhaps to fill this lack, Lorentz's new film is built round people almost entirely. And in order to focus sympathy and interest even more, the people are also professional actors, skilled in the eloquent expression of emotions which you and I ordinarily hide and only betray at moments when we are far from cameras and microphones. . . .

In short, the tendency of *The Fight For Life* is on the whole away from the present methods of documentary film. Mr. Lorentz seems to be going in the direction of such symbolic fictionizations of fact as *The Grapes of Wrath*, rather than following the down-to-brass tacks gambit of most documentaries, which are interested in facing up to a problem that has a local habitation and a name—and has, moreover, a tangible and possible solution. I rather doubt that the director intended to make this effect; he seems to have done it as an expedient to keep interest alive throughout a full-length film. And that he *does* succeed in doing, precisely in terms of the thinking of the largest film audience. There, possibly, is the justification for his method, or at least an explanation of it. Mr. Lorentz fictionizes and romanticizes real problems, but so do the people he is addressing. Actually his viewpoint represents very accurately the social conscience of the average moviegoer in its present phase of development. Many American documentaries have been more conscientious, specific, and practical than *The Fight For Life*. But the very confusion of this picture is akin to the attitude of the great audience, which has become conscious of basic social problems only in recent years, is still unaccustomed to carrying them in its mind, and hasn't the faintest idea of what to do about them. Because he feels with people like this, Mr. Lorentz is able to keep their interest alive, and sometimes he does it masterfully well. . . .

Richard Griffith. *NBR*. March 1940, pp. 12–13

Of all the medical pictures which have been presented in this or any other season, there are none which can fairly be said to rate with *The Fight For Life*, produced by Pare Lorentz from Paul De Kruif's book of the same name. If a better picture is made this year of grace 1940, this reviewer hopes to see it. . . .

Known for having written two of the best documentary films ever made, *The River* and *The Plough That Broke the Plains*, Pare Lorentz has surpassed himself in this picture. His restraint in portraying the methodic, efficiently routine, yet at all time tense fight for life against death by the hospital staff, is masterly. Above all he gets over the vigilant action of the scene when the real crisis comes, with a realism that jolts. You can fairly see death hovering over that bed as the doctors and nurses—seven people in all—move swiftly and silently to pit their knowledge against the grisly visitor. Louis Gruenberg's sound accompaniment builds up the suspense like the rising of a storm. Afterwards, when we hear the soliloquy of the young interne as he walks abroad past the lighted windows of a busy city street, it dribbles off into jazz and we hear a voice say: ". . . and now she is dead . . . now her striving body that brought a life into the world is cold and empty . . . now her blood that was bringing heat and life to them is turning from red to purple. . . ." This sequence alone would mark Pare Lorentz as one of the real geniuses of the screen.

TAC. March 15, 1940, p. 9

In the little sideplay of doctors graduating into their profession; in the purely tacked-on allusion to the hopelessness of slum conditions; in the lectures on the need of dispatch, decision, perfect sterilization; in the fight for life at the climax—in all these devices Pare Lorentz has borrowed just that many different techniques for only as long as they served his purpose, following no one through. That it is neither an inspiration to doctors (*Arrowsmith*) nor a caution or advice-chart to mothers (*Birth of a Baby*); neither a story of triumph over disease (*Yellow Jack*) and/or reaction (*Pasteur*) nor a story of a man's salvation (*The Citadel*). Its climax is thrilling but no true climax, for there is no dramatic reason why this woman should live or die, no true victory or defeat.

This kind of film above all others demands sincerity—and you know without asking that the sincerest purpose here was to get out sixty well-paced minutes of celluloid around a subject that had come up for filming. In that they did a fine job. The slums are as real as living there; the actors are restrained; the people are straight personal-appearance. The handling of the commentary is exceptional and Gruenberg's musical score is a rare blend of quiet effectiveness and original good sense. And the picture knows how to build silence into suspense.

We should not forget at any point that *The Fight for Life* is a groundbreaker in getting things that can't be spoken said well enough so that people will hear. But even with the best charity for those who have to fight for life in films every time they make another, we can realize the distinction: This is a good film; it is not such a good Pare Lorentz film. [1940]

Otis Ferguson. *The Film Criticism of O.F.* (Temple, 1971), p. 293

The two outstanding techniques for handling the content in the films are repetition and parallel structure. Both techniques contribute to the effectiveness of the messages conveyed by the films. There is little repetition of visual images in the four films. However, lines or phrases of dialogue are repeated, as are musical themes. Several key phrases are repeated in *The Plow That Broke the Plains*. For example, such lines as "High winds and sun, high winds and sun," "without rivers, without streams, with little rain"; "Wheat will win the war"; "Baked out, blown out, and broke"; are all repeated after other lines have intervened. The melodies of "Mademoiselle from Armentière" and "Old Hundred" are both repeated in Thomson's score; the second time each melody is used, it serves to make ironic comment on the pictures it accompanies.

Long portions of the sound track of *The River* are repeated: the roll call of rivers, the roll call of trees, the roll call of cities. The second time the sets of narration are used, they make ironic comment on the pictorial content. Lorentz even repeats the factory whistles for ironic effect. . . .

There is no use of repetition as a technique for handling content in [Joris Ivens's] *Power and the Land*. However, Charles Walker, the script writer on the film, used a technique that Lorentz developed to a high degree of perfection in *The River*—the technique of parallel structure. In *Power and the Land*, the problem and the solution are presented in parallel—that is, every task pictured in the first part of the film is repeated in the second half. In the first half, the tasks are difficult and often disappointing in their outcome, such as the spoiled milk being returned from the creamery. In the second half, the tasks are all done with the aid of electrical power. The tasks are easier to perform and bring obvious satisfaction and relief to the farmer and his family. The desire to make the structure as parallel as possible led to the criticism of the second half of the film referred to above.

Robert L. Snyder. *Pare Lorentz and the Documentary Film* (Oklahoma, 1968), pp. 192, 193

The social system was ignored, and we are left with films focussed exclusively and self-consciously on environment. Both films were like WPA murals—all cattle and horses and land, all rolling rivers and timber. The narration stressed a corporate, national "we," as if it were the Nation (and History) talking to itself. "Two hundred miles from water, two hundred miles from town, but the land is new," rumbled *The Plow That Broke the Plains*. From *The River*: "We built a hundred cities and a thousand towns, but at what a cost." It was that kind of naration. While the photography was often brilliant—there are shots of tenant farmers in *The River* that nearly match the photography of Walker Evans—it was somehow cold and self-serving, too concerned with becoming instant myth, too wrapped up with its role in an historical saga of the thirties. The same could be said for Virgil Thomson's folk-tune-filled musical score. When *The River* became obsessed with repeating place names (as if placing signposts on history)—"The Yazoo, the Monogahela"—its self-consciousness as a Document became very apparent.

Very few people were shown on the screen. The role of the citizen was that of the beneficiary of federal help. Except as victim—staring at mounds of dust nearly up to his windows, staring at floods—he had nothing to contribute to this saga. The reclaiming of the land and the re-channeling of river waters for public power were unimpeachable ends. But the nagging question remains: had the travail of the thirties produced no more compelling vision than that of environmental manipulation to serve a passive, stricken citizenry? "Blown out, blasted out," said *The Plow* of drought-wracked farmers, "nothing to stay for, nothing to hope for. . . . All they ask is a chance to start over, to have medical care." But how to start over? In the same competitive market that destroyed them in the first place?

Andrew Bergman. *We're in the Money*
(NYU, 1971), pp. 165–66

LUBITSCH, ERNST (1892–1947)

While *Passion* and *Deception* marked Lubitsch as a director of tremendous vitality and new ideas, this Teuton is in many respects an unknown quantity. Not until three or four more of his productions have been viewed can anything like a fair appraisal of his capabilities and possibilities be made. There is also the question as to what Lubitsch can do under certain handicaps which will be placed upon him in American studios. Given a free rein he would probably generate several worthwhile shadow plays.

Tamar Lane. *What's Wrong with the Movies*
(Waverly, 1923), p. 69

There has been a lot of worriment over the fact that Mary Pickford was going to grow up. Don't worry. Mary has grown up in *Rosita*, but she is just as charming, just as fascinating as ever and she does better acting than ever before in her career. There is probably no actress today who chould portray the gay, graceful, coquettish, little street singer of Seville who "vamps" a king, as she does. The production is incomparably beautiful. The sets seem, many of them, almost fairy-like in their loveliness. The production shows why Ernst Lubitsch holds his place among the leading directors of the world. Except in one or two minor details, the direction is flawless and the story moves with a smoothness that is most satisfying. No, don't worry about Mary growing up.

Photoplay. Nov. 1923, p. 74

So slim a plot, so hackneyed, if you will, is told with gaity and a wit that lift [*The Marriage Circle*] into the very first rank of screen comedy. Comparison with Chaplin's *A Woman of Paris* inevitably comes to the mind and eye. With all our admiration for Chaplin's remarkable advance in technique, his sure sense of picture value, and his artistic use of suggestion in telling his story, we cannot help sharing some of the regret which has been voiced that he had not chosen a worthier theme to illustrate his mastery of the art of directing. His picture inevitably involved a moral discussion instead of focusing attention upon its purely artistic qualities. *The Marriage Circle*, while still somewhat Continental in its flavor, avoids this ambiguity. It is more rounded and has a larger human interest. Technically it is the equal and in many respects the superior of the Chaplin picture.

The first and largest merit for the production goes, of course, to Ernst Lubitsch. Coming to us with one of the finest European reputations as a director, it looked at first as if Lubitsch had gone down before the cast-iron system of picture making with which the name of Hollywood is too often associated. Apparently his present employers realized that a European director could not function at his best with an American advisory committee of that's-the-way-it's-always-done wiseacres at his elbow. They seem to have had the courage to give him a free hand both in the choice and the treatment of his story. Result, a genuine Lubitsch picture which ranks with his best work abroad and takes equal rank with *A Woman of Paris* as a milestone in American picture-making.

NBR. Dec.-Jan. 1924, p. 1

The Marriage Circle may well silence those who claim that the film cannot compare as a dramatic form with the stageplay. For this is at once perfect cinematography and perfect conventional drama. Lubitsch, the producer of this delicious piece, has shown, not told, the story. Everything is visualized, all the comedy is in what the characters are seen or imagined to be thinking or feeling, in the interplay, never expressed in words, of wills and personalities. There is a minimum of subtitling, and the progress of the plot is not dependent on the letterpress. Gestures and situations, so lucidly presented that one is perfectly aware from the "pictures" alone of what is happening, give rise to other gestures and other situations which—because of the permanence of visual memory—one recognizes as the logical result of what has occurred before. There is a peculiar mental delight in watching a plot develop so. And with curious boldness Lubitsch has drawn on the minimum of the cinema's technical resources. Here are no magnificent halls, no costly crowds, no multiplicity of scene, no great bridgings of time or space. This deliberate limitation gives the film perfect unity. Lubitsch uses only one focus, brings the five characters up to us a little magnified and intimate, and, keeping them at that constant range, sets the action going simply, precisely, without hesitation. . . .

Now, while the scheme of this film is simple, the psychology of motive in it is enchantingly complex, and any attempt at a verbal description at once demonstrates the superiority of the pictorial over the verbal method of telling such a story. Henry James could, in a light mood, have told it as minutely as Lubitsch has in pictures: but at what a length.

Iris Barry. *Spectator* (Lon.). May 17, 1924, p. 788

While Ernst Lubitsch's screen translation of Oscar Wilde's play *Lady Windermere's Fan* is a worthy production rivaling most of the sophisticated subjects of its type, it shrinks in importance beside the original effort, for even though it is endowed with astute direction it lacks the Wildean wit and satire. Those who have seen or read the play will be disappointed in the pictorial result, for none of the players appears as one visualized them. Not only is the Wildian epigram blotted out, but Mr. Lubitsch frequently emphasizes the meaning of a situation. . . . Mr. Lubitsch said that he made up for the absence of Wilde's epigrams by the actions and expressions of the players. He has made the picture interesting, but this is far from giving it the sparkle of the author's words. . . .

There are artistry and inspiration about some of Mr. Lubitsch's direction. His idea to have heads popping up on the screen is only moderately effective, but that of having a pen wet with ink lying on the edge of an addressed envelope is excellent. It looks as if the missive really had been written in haste. Taking it all in all and it would seem that Mr. Lubitsch did not see eye to eye with Wilde in his portrayal of smart but blasé nobility, but he has nevertheless fashioned an entertaining picture which will probably be more popular in provincial communities—where Lubitsch is better known than Wilde—than a production that retained Wilde's nimble wit.

Mordaunt Hall. *NYT*. Dec. 28, 1925, p. 19

[*The Patriot.*] Paramount. Emil Jannings, Florence Vidor, Lewis Stone, Vera Voronina, Neil Hamilton, Harry Cording, 10 [reels]. A wonderfully made picture, but it did not draw. I believe this picture the most suggestive picture we ever ran. Just another reason why we need censorship. The small town exhibitors need clean pictures. (Lyric theatre, Wooster, Ohio—General patronage).

The Motion Picture Almanac—1929
(Quigley, 1929), p. 204

[*The Love Parade*]. Faced with the facts of sound, and more, of quite incidental and irrelevant musical sound, Lubitsch has invented for himself a curious hand-over-hand method of treating his visual and sound images; climbing, as it were, towards his conclusion with alternate grips of sight and voice, the two held firm together, but one always a handhold ahead. The songs, treated in this way, lose their fabric. Neither the eye nor the ear is ever bored, for behind the sound is a kaleidoscope of arranged images, behind the pantomime a commentary of composed sound. Lubitsch takes a sentimental lyric like "Dream Lovers," and arranges it with a changing pattern of women's figures to carry out its mood and comment on its rhythm; he sets the "Blue Horizon" song to the rushing images of the Riviera express, a chorus of peasants waving from the fields below, Jeannette MacDonald's edged voice matching the whistle and the wind and the speed of the steely rails. Our intellects may tell us that material like this is emotional clap-trap, but our senses will take it like an electric contact, sudden and sure. It is a bit of pure ciné-opera, in which every line advances the action, every chorus comments on the individual, every situation develops through song. The man who can create it, still unheard, is a master of his craft.

There may be directors on the screen who need not learn from Lubitsch; there are none, I think, who cannot. And the man who learns most of all from Lubitsch, is Lubitsch himself. In each successive production he comes to understand more fully the incessant movement forward of action and character-play, the use of third person commentary, the snap reference to an outside figure or object to focus an idea, and the deft reiteration of theme in another key.

C. A. Lejeune. *Cinema* (Alexander Maclehose, 1931), pp. 67–68

As long as we are to have polite comedies in the movies, a type of entertainment most unsuitable for celluloid, we are fortunate in having Lubitsch around to direct them. *Trouble in Paradise* is a pretty bit of frosting, so well-contrived that you barely mind the fact that there is no cake whatsoever under the tasty puff. . . . Unfortunately the playwrights did not give Mr. Lubitsch very much in the way of a drama to work with. After a pleasant prologue, the famous crook is employed by a wealthy, attractive widow; and of course they play hide and seek in and out the very attractive bedrooms in the house. But even with all the women in Paris pursuing him, one becomes a little bored with the proceedings and the protagonist, and one begins to look forward to the kill. . . .

Admitting the clever Lubitsch touches, one of two things should have been done with this stale bit of Hungarian pastry. Either the authors should have made the famous crook a thorough Raffles, giving him some action faster than a slow bedroom dogtrot, or they should have had him captured in the widow's bedroom and forced him to talk his way back to his pickpocket. As it is, Miriam Hopkins and Kay Francis ogle Herbert Marshall without much effect for the last part of the show; and although the clothes, the sets, and the atmosphere are in the usual tasteful Lubitsch manner, I did not find myself unduly concerned with Miss Francis' palpitations over Mr. Marshall (and, personable and amiable as he is, I have never found this English actor anything but a dreary performer.)

Pare Lorentz. *Vanity Fair*. Dec. 1932, p. 64

There are, in a sense, two Lubitsches. There is the Lubitsch who began as one of Germany's most popular screen comedians and who has developed as a highly individual director of boudoir comedies, with precisely the witty, sophisticated, deft, ironic touch needed for those delicious little affairs. And there is the Lubitsch who began as Reinhardt's assistant and who had always had a hankering for pretentious dramas with plenty of emotional fireworks and historical background. This second Lubitsch seems to me inferior to the first. A film like *The Patriot*, for all the impressive trappings of technique in which it is swathed, has something static, cumbersome and *dead* about it. As a "serious" artist, Lubitsch has nothing to say. The moral earnestness of a Griffith, the emotional drive of a Stroheim, Murnau's psychological insight, Sternberg's shadowy, somewhat "arty" lyricism with the camera—Lubitsch has none of these. His vital qualities are called into play only in comedy. When he takes himself seriously, it is as if an excellent vaudeville star should insist on appearing in Shakespearean tragedy. [1933]

Dwight Macdonald. *D. M. on Movies* (Prentice-Hall, 1969), p. 83

Ernst Lubitsch is at once a Hollywood tycoon and a has-been. And the very fact that a has-been is still a tycoon is a tragic commentary on the status of the contemporary American cinema. . . . He reached his peak in 1924 with an admirable satire on royalty and Hollywood called *Forbidden Paradise*. It was then that the *cinéasts* made a cult of him, and the Hollywood magnates honored him with the rank of Field General and built him an Ivory Tower. He crawled in and hasn't emerged. Once every season he produces the one Art movie and lets it go at that. He hasn't developed or grown. His castle, his insulation, and his contract keep him intact: the same in 1934 as he was in 1924. Even if we examine his latest opus, *The Merry Widow*, we find it merely a combination of his best and worst qualities. There are moments that are so dull that they recall the *Student Prince*. Others are bad enough to be compared with his first American film, *Rosita* (with Mary Pickford). The early sections of *The Merry Widow*, dealing with the widow's castle and the royal castle, recall the vast halls, the massive columns, the sweeping draperies, the uniformed officers, of *Forbidden Paradise*. There are a few fleeting moments when some of the so-called Lubitsch wit will bring a smile. But that is all. *The Merry Widow* is Lubitsch; it is also Hollywood; it is the cream of the American bourgeois film. It is a charlotte russe.

Peter Ellis. *New Masses*. Nov. 6, 1934, pp. 29–30

Mr. Lubitsch has been careful in his last three films to exercise his suavity in milieux where such dexterity would pass for wit. No director has been more apt to choose characters and situations at exactly the strength of his style. They are as glib, mischievous and amusing as he. But *The Merry Widow* is too good a book, its story takes uneasily to satirical turns, the nineties was an epoch to enjoy or despise, not to snigger at. And the Lubitsch box of tricks is trivially and self-consciously spilled. No conclusion could better reveal a manner outworn than the end of this film. The elegant jewel-box thrust desperately into a prison cell is as frantic an end as a romantic film could have. Here it is a sign that Mr. Lubitsch has exhausted one manner and must now choose—the dilemma was once Herr Lang's—to abandon his box of tricks and begin again with human beings, or else to fritter away an excellent small talent in more and more mechanical parodies of it. The fade-out was once Mr. Lubitsch's invitation to the audience to share his moue; it is now an interval between a jest and an episode.

Alistair Cooke, *Sight & Sound.*
Winter 1934–35, p. 166

[*Design for Living* is] a partial cleansing for the screen of a stage story notorious for its wealth and variety of moral code infractions. Even in its comparatively refined status it is an evil influence because it presents conduct on the part of attractive and likeable people which indicates denial and contempt of traditional moral standards, presenting, charmingly, wrong conduct as if it were right conduct.

Martin Quigley. *Decency in Motion Pictures*
(Macmillan, 1937), p. 34

All the American-made Lubitsch films have been distinguished by a personal style and craftsmanship. His flair for witty imagery gives his pictures a laconic and yet scintillating quality. His swift, deft plotting is enhanced by the rapierlike "comments" of his camera, which have become known as "the Lubitsch touch." Throughout his career he has displayed an uncanny ability to get the most out of his actors, too. His naturally sharp perception, made keener by the fact that he was working in a foreign land, gave him such insight into the traits and demands of America that his films, made with extraordinary technical skill, were often more penetrating than those of native directors in the twenties. With two exceptions his pictures have all been comedies of manners, centering entirely among well-bred, sophisticated, upper-class people. He delineates their fads and foibles with a Continental suavity that has made them fresh and fascinating to American moviegoers. His cultivation of this field may yet prove to be his downfall. . . .

Structurally as well as technically, Lubitsch's first sound films put their contemporaries in the shade. Faced with the problem of handling music, dialogue, and songs, he gave mobility to the until then static microphone, blending sound and image in a casual but extremely interesting fashion. The camera at that time was still imprisoned in a soundproof booth. But Lubitsch kept the camera moving freely and, with the same dexterity he had exhibited in making "silents," gave the images, dialogue, and songs a fluidity which kept both the eye and the ear amused. In these musical comedies there was little to remind one of the conventionalities of a *Broadway Melody* or

Paramount on Parade. The conception was rather on the plane of the stage operetta in which song and story move steadily along without the use of a chorus "leg line." [1939]

Lewis Jacobs. *The Rise of the American Film* (Teachers College, 1968), pp. 355, 358

Ernst Lubitsch has had his ups and downs, since long Before Capra; but there is a thing amateur critics like to call the Lubitsch touch, and whatever that is, he hasn't lost it. His new comedy, *Ninotchka*, started out with what any other comedy director would have ducked away from, a piece of light spoofing that starred Greta Garbo. Lubitsch never had the Capra magic of realizing every last detail as big and right as life; he goes more by steady competence and brilliant flashes. And so *Ninotchka* strikes a wrong note occasionally—nothing serious, but a thing for example like the movie-German accent of a Soviet envoy, or like the weight of too much stationary conversation. But the story gets there, its people are real enough, it has an overall radiance of pleasant but knowing wit. . . .

The humor is mostly in the meeting-of-East-and-West variety, no more harmful than Zostchenko, certainly as droll and possibly more up to date. It is the first movie with any airiness at all to discover that Communists are people and may be treated as such in a story. And Greta Garbo is the life of it. Barring the end—and no other was possible short of gloom—her confusion is human, her cause takes a salutary ribbing but is not disgraced. I found her more lovely in the straight-cut clothes of her first scenes than in the later "creations," for while I am strictly antinudist, I should say that a real and commanding beauty is clearest without clutter—all you need on the outside is a stretch of burlap and a bath. But this is comedy and good as such, Miss Garbo moving from the stern to the tipsy with no more effort and no less dignity than she ever showed. Compare hers with the strenuous if veteran performance of Ina Claire, and you will see by contrast something of a natural style in acting which may take hard work to perfect, but never looks like it.

Outside of Lubitsch with the no doubt coordinating touch, this is no one person's triumph—as no one picture should be. It is barbed wire on some aspects of modern life, sometimes with a dry point that is exquisite—the May Day marchers and the solid solemn ranks of Stalin posters. But it is mainly a gay affair, neither heavy with Thought nor absurd with venom; it is partly true and possibly beautiful, but it is certainly good. [1939]

Otis Ferguson. *The Film Criticism of O.F.* (Temple, 1971), pp. 274–75

The Shop Around the Corner may be slight, but though after a year it may be remembered vaguely it will be remembered pleasantly. It has those warm qualities that Lubitsch seems to have discovered within himself of late, not over-sentimentalized and presented with a humorous kindliness. It is romantic in a lively, almost jolly way, and its substance is no newer and more important than that familiar plot about a fellow and a girl who are in love with each other without knowing it. But it is housed in a charmingly foreign—but not too foreign—leather-goods shop in a Central European city, and peopled by such delightful players as Margaret Sullavan, James Stewart, Frank Morgan (not clowning) and Felix Bressart, being themselves as well as the parts they play with ingratiating excellence. It would be a shame to lay the praise on too thick; it's not pretentious but it's a beautiful job of picture-making, and the people who did it seem to have enjoyed doing it just as much as their audiences will enjoy seeing it.

James Shelley Hamilton. *NBR*. Feb. 1940, p. 22

The system that eliminated Stroheim caused the personality of another German director, Lubitsch, to blossom. His German successes won him the right to direct, on arriving in the United States, Mary Pickford in a pompous *Rosita*. But [Chaplin's] *A Woman of Paris* oriented him toward a new genre. He reworked Chaplin's masterpiece according to the proportions of sophisticated comedy. . . .

Lubitsch's master piece of that period was *Lady Windermere's Fan*, a brilliant, daring and skillful adaptation of Oscar Wilde's celebrated play. He achieved a tour de force with it by transcribing its psychological finesse without an over-use of subtitles. The film is, however, no more than a good job. Shortly before the introduction of sound, Lubitsch—that more cultivated, more intelligent, but less vigorous Cecil B. De Mille—returned to large-scale direction by filming two successful plays: *The Student Prince* and *The Patriot*, in which Jannings made use of sound effects. Commercial Hollywood owed a great deal to Lubitsch, who brought it a refinement for *nouveaux riches*. But his skills had little influence on the art of film.

Georges Sadoul. *Histoire d'un art: le cinéma* (Flammarion, 1949), p. 213

Prior to *The Marriage Circle*, almost any decoration would do—either wholly nondescript for a routine film or, for a more elaborate production, rooms choked with bric-a-brac and overstuffed chairs set off by loudly ornamental drapes and busy wallpaper. Lubitsch cleared away the clutter, providing clean playing areas for his action. The advantages were so immediately apparent that they were incorporated into the majority of pictures from that moment on. Few directors, however, have quite his ability to use settings to their fullest advantage. To Lubitsch, a door was always more than simply a way to get into or out of a room; it was a way to end an argument, to suggest pique or coquetry or even the sexual act itself. Corridors, stairways, windows—all had a dramatic function in the Lubitsch films. With his sparkling wit and polished technique, he soon became the leading exponent of the comedy of manners, inspiring and influencing a coterie of directors that came to include such talents as Mal St. Clair, Lewis Milestone, Wesley Ruggles and Frank Tuttle.

Arthur Knight. *The Liveliest Art* (Macmillan, 1957), pp. 134–35

It is not fair to leave the impression that Lubitsch devoted his Hollywood years wholly to sophisticated sex comedies like *The Marriage Circle* (1924) and, after the coming of sound, musicals like *Monte Carlo* (1930). He did a wide variety of things: the silent *Student Prince* in 1927, for example, with Ramon Novarro and Norma Shearer, and in 1932 (in sound) *The Man I Killed* (also known as *Broken Lullaby*), one of the most powerful of all antiwar films. . . . Taken as a whole, however, his American years were certainly not a climax, except perhaps in a commercial sense, to his years in Europe, and it seems to me that the same thing would have to be said, in different accents, for practically everybody who came over. . . .

Edward Wagenknecht. *The Movies in the Age of Innocence* (Oklahoma, 1962), p. 205

One fact is that films like his American sex comedies would never have been made in Europe—they were possible only with the "ooh-la-la" attitude toward sex in America—nor would they have been made by Lubitsch had he remained in Europe. He would have had little reason to make them. Indeed, this kind of film was not made by anyone else there after his departure. In short, the filmed "sex comedy" began as a distinctly American institution. Of course later on, much later on, it was to be taken up abroad, for a while in pre-Hitler Germany, but particularly in France and postwar Italy. Ado Kyrou mentions the pre-Hitler "l'esprit berlinois," and we have only to recall the effervescences of such heady concoctions as Ludwig Berger's *A Waltz Dream,* Erick Charell's *The Congress Dances*, Willi Forst's *Maskerade*, Walter Reisch's *Episode*, Geza von Bolvary's *Two Hearts in ¾ Time, The Merry Wives of Vienna, The Theft of the Mona Lisa,* and the Reinhold Schuenzel—Franz Doelle *Amphitryon* (French version, not the German original), to realize how much they had learned from the "American" Lubitsch, for they all possessed a lightness and verve astonishing for the usually heavy German film. France came out with Marcel Pagnol's *The Baker's Wife*, not to mention René Clair's works of pure joy and, of course, Sacha Guitry, "France's own Lubitsch." In Italy there were De Sica and Blasetti, among others; unforgettable is the pure gold of the former's *Gold of Naples*, particularly the "pizza" sequence, which is "pure Lubitsch."

Herman Weinberg. *The Lubitsch Touch* (Dutton, 1968), p. 58

Taken individually, Lubitsch's films are a mixed bag containing a number of high points, low points and curiously bland pieces. But looking over the entire panorama of his work as a giant canvas rather than as a chronological progression of hits and misses, an impressive image emerges. It is a vision of style and a key to human survival and enrichment of life . . . whether in the silent banter of his early films where comic romantics tusselled with promises of love, or Maurice Chevalier's boulevardier taking love where he found it, jocularly singing its praises, or Herbert Marshall's self-assured movements through an atmosphere charged with his urbanity and elegance, or Charles Boyer's suaveness and wisdom defying the grimness of a failing world.

A life-style for Lubitsch was a moral imperative, a necessity for defining man's sensibilities and fulfilling his potential. There is no doubt that his own was a particularly bourgeois wish-fulfillment, a glorification of life at once knowing and innocent as it could only exist in a kind of paradise. For the trouble with Lubitsch's paradise is the trouble with all visions of what life should be—a concept realized only in the mind and work of the artist . . . larger than life can ever be, transforming a darkened theater with its inimitable dream of perfection.

Calvin Green. *Film Society Review*. Jan. 1969, p. 34

Ernst Lubitsch (*Lady Windermere's Fan, The Student Prince, The Patriot, The Long Parade, If I Had a Million, Trouble in Paradise*) was the complete architect of his films. His scripts were detailed blueprints, replete with all the required sketches, drawings, and specifications. Every scene, every look, every camera angle, was designed in advance of photography and he seldom, if ever, deviated from his blueprints in the actual shooting.

His direction of his cast was strictly Lubitsch. Waving his ubiquitous cigar, this humorous, magnificent imp showed each actor exactly what to do and how to do it. His stamp was on every frame of film from conception to delivery. For high-styled romantic comedies and spicy musicals he set a standard that may never be equaled. The Lubitsch "touch" was unique.

Frank Capra. *The Name Above the Title* (Macmillan, 1971), p. 246

LUMET, SIDNEY (1924–)

Sidney Lumet, the director, is usually at least clever at least part of the time—an acquisitive magpie who has picked up, along with tinselly trash, a few small gems. This time [in *The Fugitive Kind*] he brings us nothing but bits of colored glass. The less-than-perfect mantle of Elia Kazan is here draped on considerably narrower shoulders. The finale: Miss Magnani, pregnant by Brando, is shot by her husband, who is dying of cancer. Meanwhile the new wing of the store—a pretty confectionary which she built to revive the spirit of her father's wine garden—is blazing furiously, deliberately fired by her husband. And while Miss Woodward stands on the sidelines screaming his name, Brando is forced back into the blaze by the streams of two fire hoses played on him by vindictive friends of the cuckold.

Let the description serve as its own comment. [1960]

Stanley Kauffmann. *A World on Film* (Harper, 1966), p. 85

B. If critics and audiences develop a resistance to stylistic conventions, the cinema may be shackled by the kind of pseudorealism that has virtually destroyed the theater as a creative arena.

A. This is all very abstract. How does it apply to *View from the Bridge?*

B. Well, Sidney Lumet has transformed Arthur Miller's choppy stab at Greek tragedy into a chillingly photographed slice of life, on the whole an intelligent process of draining off most of the pretentiousness into the gutter. An international cast has worked for once as an instrument of abstraction. Raf Vallone, Jean Sorel, Raymond Pellegrin, Maureen Stapleton, Carol Lawrence are so detached from any social context that they become relatively universal. Vallone is particularly inspired casting.

A. His virile force and subtle comedy style reminded me of Magnani in *The Rose Tattoo*.

B. True, but the film doesn't work because Miller's Freudian-

Stalinist determinism defrauds the street tragedy of any meaning. The idea of rationalizing Vallone's reactionary political act as the product of unconscious sexual repression is an example of muddled thinking. [1962]

Andrew Sarris. *Confessions of a Cultist* (S&S, 1970), p. 46

With Sidney Lumet's *Long Day's Journey Into Night* we are buffeted to the other end of the spectrum. Here a very great play has been not translated to the screen but reverently put behind glass—it matters little whether the plate glass around the stuffed fauna of museums or the glass of lenses encasing live theatre in inanimate images.

It is not that Lumet has done anything capriciously wrong—although a shot of Long Island Sound with anachronistic motorboats and yachts is disturbing, and a scene in which two men make drawing-room conversation while working on a car in the garage (Lumet's attempt to extend his range) without once referring to the work at hand is absurd. The problem is that a stage masterpiece can be put on the screen only if the author or some scenarist of genius recreates it in cinematic terms. Here, out of monumental but pedestrian veneration, we have characters and camera pacing restlessly around a small enclosure like so many caged panthers, or, in the case of Ralph Richardson, polar bears. This is stifling in its own right and quickly preempts the sense of confinement and frustration that should belong to the lives of the unhappy foursome.

When, at the very end, Lumet permits himself some fancy, though old-fashioned, camera movements, his endlessly receding camera, besides making the Tyrone family look like David Susskind's guests at the close of *Open End*, merely draws attention to unresolved incompatibilities between two art forms. The acting is adequate—in the case of Jason Robards, excellent—and André Previn's music trashy. But neither peripheral pluses nor minuses can much affect the respectful leadenness at the center. [1963]

John Simon. *Private Screenings* (Macmillan, 1967), pp. 41–42

Sidney Lumet, who scorns big, box-office movies and has directed such stimulating, but-not-always-successful films as *Long Day's Journey Into Night, Twelve Angry Men*, and last year's *The Hill* and *The Pawnbroker*, wrote an interesting article recently on why he prefers "films of conscience." For one thing, the movies, he says, "represent the last and only medium in which it is possible to tell a story of conscience, outside the printed word." He explains that Broadway has become "an economic battleground" and TV is limited by increased budgets and "the sponsors' need for happy endings and nice stories about nice people." In describing the "film of conscience," Lumet says the goal of all movies is to entertain, but that "kind of film goes one step further. It compels the spectator to examine one facet or another of his own conscience. It stimulates thought and sets the mental juices flowing."

Director Lumet's new film, *The Group*, fits the definition. Although it is a strange, all-inclusive, no-holds-barred movie that runs the gamut from scenes that are almost soap-operaish, to amusing scenes that are almost satire, to outrageously frank scenes that are almost voyeuristic, it is still greatly entertaining while it provokes thought and pushes the viewer into examining his own conscience. The viewer may not agree with a single one of the eight girls who make up The Group, but he is forced into considering the reality of their behavior and the irony of the story as a whole. It is not a pretty story, but at times it is very touching. . . .

Philip T. Hartung. *Commonweal.*
March 18, 1965, p. 698

Some of [*The Pawnbroker*'s] visual effects, of course, are not as successful: some camera movement and rapid cutting for the sake of movement and rapid cutting; the Kazan-like shots of running wildly through the streets of Harlem; the Antonioni-like walk through the streets at night, the vistas of cold, impersonal apartment houses; the glaring cut to a back-shot when the social worker futilely holds out her hand to the suffering Nazerman and he cannot take it; the street confusion of crowds, police car, ambulance, traffic that tends to disperse rather than intensify Nazerman's final crisis over the body of the boy. But on the whole the effects succeed with an impact that is both brutal and stirring, disruptive and cathartic. With them, Lumet has fulfilled the promise of the erratic technical displays of his earlier films. . . . It seems to me that the visual structure and effects of this film can be clearly traced as a final synthesis of the previously disparate elements of Sidney Lumet's films.

Alan Casty. *Film Heritage.* Spring 1966, p. 11

Lumet made his TV reputation in *live* TV. He's a live wire, he works best under pressure; when it isn't there, he invents it for himself, racing to be *ahead* of schedule. He is happy on the set when everything is going fast, even though the speed may be spurious because the work is slovenly. He isn't reflective, and he doesn't have more to give it if he takes longer. On the contrary, that just makes him impatient and irritable. When directing movies, he re-creates the conditions of live TV

—not going back. Other directors plead for retakes; the producer has to force him. He accepts the passable. The advantage is that he gets something live into movies and enjoys what he's doing because of the excitement of the high pressure, the sheer activity of it. Precision seems almost irrelevant to his methods. It's the spirit—or some spirit—that satisfies him, not the exact line of dialogue or careful emphasis on the words. He lets the words fall where they have been articulated so inaccurately. When you watch scenes being shot and see and hear what's the matter with them, you realize how much bad and negligent work that could be corrected is allowed to pass because of the mystique of movies being the editor's art. There are possibilities for long, fluid scenes in several places in *The Group*. Instead, the scenes will be chopped up with reaction shots and close-ups to conceal the static camera setups and the faults in timing, in acting, in rhythm of performances. Fast editing *can* be done for aesthetic purposes, but too much of it *is* done these days to cover up bad staging and shooting, and the effect is jerky and confusing. But, as it calls so much attention to itself, it is often taken to be brilliant technique. Explaining something he wants done, Lumet will say, "It can be very exciting"—which means what will *work*, not what may relate to any larger conception but simply something that will be effective here and now, in itself. The emphasis on immediate results may explain the almost total absence of nuance, subtlety, and even rhythmic and structural development in his work. [1966]

Pauline Kael. *Kiss Kiss Bang Bang*
(Little, Brown, 1968), pp. 84–85

It seems to me obtuse to knock *Fail Safe* because it deals with roughly the same subject as Stanley Kubrick's *Dr Strangelove*; after all, nobody holds it against Sophocles that he wrote about the same family as Aeschylus, and you could hardly maintain that thermonuclear war was a theme of less general interest than the misfortunes of the House of Atreus.

In any case, the two films differ markedly, not only in style but in basic postulates. *Dr Strangelove* was a nihilistic satire that demanded and got acting of outsize eccentricity: *Fail Safe* is a dramatised documentary in which understated acting is heightened and magnified—as in the early Orson Welles movies—by low-key camerawork and diamond-sharp sound editing.

Moreover, Kubrick's nuclear holocaust needed a madman to trigger it off, whereas in *Fail Safe* the crucial flaw is not human but mechanical: a minuscule error on the part of a computer creates a situation of irrevocable horror. Though I relished the wit and audacity of *Dr Strangelove*, I never felt personally threatened; *Fail Safe* (directed by Sidney Lumet from a script based on the novel by Eugene Burdick and Harvey Wheeler) makes the logic of catastrophe seem much more intimate and irrefutable. Step by plausible step, we are drawn into an apocalyptic experience.

Kenneth Tynan. *Tynan Left and Right* (Atheneum, 1968), p. 227

You don't have to be Jewish to love Sidney Lumet's *Bye Bye Braverman* but it helps a lot to be a New Yorker. I'm not certain why a picture set in one's own territory is so gratifying: perhaps it's the flattering implication that you live and work in places someone thinks interesting enough to put on film.

In this case, though, the city has been made the love interest of the picture. It is a great day in early summer, and from Sheridan Square to Far Rockaway the metropolis sparkles as though it were young and fresh from a bath. New York is no doubt the dirtiest, most crowded, most exhausting city on earth, but, as New Yorkers know, you also get Sundays in June.

For the rest, the movie is a stock item of folklore: the clowns in search of the funeral. Braverman has dropped dead, he is to be buried from a funeral home somewhere out in Brooklyn, and four of his friends set out to find the place. They are full of the memory of Braverman, but fuller yet of their own preoccupations, vanities, fears and needs. These four . . . play types, maybe stereotypes, so one must be on guard. However, I saw no offense, except perhaps in a tasteless scene with Godfrey Cambridge who plays a Negro convert to Judaism, and the worst of that passage was that it tried so hard and so unsuccessfully to be funny.

The picture is not exactly Sholem Aleichem, but neither is it mean. It doesn't make the mistake of patronizing these Jews by making them lovable, but it does just allow them to be likable; and I'm not going to let the Anti-Defamation League con me out of saying that modern urban Jewry has developed a gallery of personality styles that can be defined by fraternal caricature. *Bye Bye Braverman* is very slight, but it has a quota of gentle laughter. And the helicopter shots of bridges, elevated lines and expressways, the street-scene kaleidoscope of upper West Side, lower East Side, Bay Ridge, Flatbush and Prospect Park, give a hint of why John Lindsay ever wanted to be mayor of the place.

Robert Hatch. *Nation*. March 11, 1968, p. 358

My youngest son sometimes talks about "dignified-type movies." By this he means films which, with due reverence, copy a classic work or event already fully realized in another medium: a notable novel or play or historical event. *David Copperfield, Henry V, Wilson* were all dignified-type movies. Such movies rate little space in histories of the art. Often they are great bores.

Yet, every once in a while a dignified-type movie succeeds in evoking the quality of the work or event from which it is derived. Sidney Lumet did this in *Long Day's Journey Into Night*: he has now done it again with *The Sea Gull*. Lumet is a serious and gifted director of uneven taste. When he is on his own, as in *The Pawnbroker*, the results may be mixed. When he accepts the discipline of O'Neill or Chekhov, the result is likely to be more powerful than, say, the lastest *chef d'oeuvre* of Robert Aldrich. . . .

Chekhov requires ensemble acting; and here Sidney Lumet's touch falters. Vanessa Redgrave is a lovely, precise, and moving Nina; no actress around attains stunning effects with less apparent effort. Denholm Elliott and Harry Andrews are just right. But James Mason's Trigorin is a bit stagy and contrived (no doubt Trigorin was, too); and Simone Signoret, playing the actress as if out of Maupassant, and David Warner, playing the son as if out of John Osborne, are out of cadence with the rest.

"Shakespeare's plays are bad enough," Tolstoy once said to Chekhov, "but yours are even worse"—a salutary reminder of how foolish great men can be. Fortunately Chekhov persisted in doing this thing, and now Lumet has done well enough by Chekhov. For this reviewer, *The Sea Gull* seems likely to offer a far more satisfying aesthetic—if non-cinematic—experience than most other films of the month put together.

Arthur Schlesinger, Jr. *Vogue*.
Feb. 1969, p. 128

Chekhov was the musician of boredom. No one, not even Beckett, has drawn such recondite harmonies and such subtle discords from the motions, utterances, and silences of boredom. Frustrated lives palpitating in concert, hurling unsolicited gifts and demands at one another, misunderstanding or understanding one another too well, and hurting either way, they talk and live right past one another. Dialogues are not so much conversations as reciprocally embarrassing confessions colliding in mid-air, and the atmosphere is so smoky with frustration that joy cannot grow in it. Yet sapling joys do shoot up from time to time, only to wither swiftly and sheepishly.

That is the basic quality of *The Sea Gull*, and even if Sidney Lumet had captured it in his film version, it would probably have made for a cumbrous, oppressive film. But he captures nothing of the sort.

Lumet's boredom is one that settles viscously on the viewer who cares not a straw for Lument's straw men; whereas Chekhov's people, properly interpreted on the stage are as fascinating as a juggling act in which the balls are continually dropped until one hangs on every move of the bizarre, unhappy prestidigitators in the hope that one of their tricks might succeed.

Part of the trouble is the medium itself. The stage always affords full view of the arena of fumbles; every unsuccessful move can be seen in all its ramifications. Or, more precisely, the stage always shows you the space between the actors, the small but sufficient abyss into which their enterprises hurtle. The camera—except as handled by a master, which Lumet categorically is not—cannot capture the hollowness of space, the oppressive immovableness of a seemingly harmless enclosure, stasis settling on everything like a fine, corrosive dust. Then, again, a filmed play requires inventiveness in camera setups, a sharp feeling for montage, and self-effacing camera movements, lest, given the sparseness of action one become aware of technical overcompensation. But Lumet is either too dazzled or too crudely confident to be at home in art. [1969]

John Simon. *Movies into Film* (Dial, 1971), p. 44

At first glance, *Klute* looks like anything but a radical film, and indeed Robin Wood has contrasted it with *WR: Mysteries of the Organism*, characterizing them as, respectively, conservative and radical statements about sexuality. The bad girl "reforms" and goes to Pennsylvania with the good cop. Paul D. Zimmerman, writing in *Newsweek* (*Newsweek*!) praised the film "despite its fall into reformism," as though the truth necessarily will better be served if no one is ever saved from "La Dolce Vita." But surface appearances aside, I do not see how *Klute* can properly be termed conservative. . . .

What makes *Klute* a superior film is its understanding of the psychosexual basis of so much of the present unhappiness in America, and its insistence that there are still some normal people left. In this respect, it is significantly different from another recent film, *A Clockwork Orange*, which also sees psychopathology and disembodied sexuality rampant in the modern world. But Kubrick does not leave much hope—his most sympathetic character gains his sanity only through a rather feeble sell-out. . . .

Klute is neither a cop nor a private detective in the usual tradition. He is a factory guard with some knowledge of police methods who is looking for his best friend. . . . He is spectacularly ordinary. Roger Greenspun has written that Sutherland is "given precisely the latitude to evoke a romantic figure with all the mysterious intensity of a youthful Calvin Coolidge" and that the film should have been called *Bree*. But this is to miss the point. The meaning of *Klute* is that a true modern hero is not a sexually distorted character type (imagine Clint Eastwood or Dustin Hoffman in the role) but just a plain man who has not lost his ability to feel, to care, to love. Charisma is often based on an excess of tension. A romantic figure is usually enamored of his own sensitivity. [1972]

Jonathan Stutz. *The Velvet Light Trap.* No. 6, p. 37

Long Day's Journey Into Night is filled with talk. It is great talk; but it is talk for the stage, not for the screen. As a result, Lumet is obliged to move his camera meaninglessly around the performers as they discourse within the confinement of the original stage setting. When occasionally the director seems to strike at least a balance between word and picture—most notably at the end when, as Mary delivers the play's concluding lines, the camera slowly recedes, then bolts forward for tight close-ups of each of "the four haunted Tyrones," and pulls back again for a final long shot—the visual approach (in John Simon's words) "merely draws attention to unresolved incompatibilities between two art forms." In an interview, Lumet was quoted as saying: "For the benefit of those idiots who called *Long Day's Journey Into Night* a photographed stage play, every character had his own lens development. No two acts were shot alike" (*New York Times*, June 8, 1969). If the life of a play resides in its language, one will not make that play cinematic simply by finding "interesting ways to photograph actors while they incessantly *talk*. There is a basic problem here, but Lumet remains oblivious of it.

Edward Murray. *The Cinematic Imagination* (Ungar, 1972), p. 34

McCAREY, LEO (1898–1969)

The most heart-warming comedy of the season has been made from Harry Leon Wilson's celebrated *Ruggles of Red Gap*. Not only is it vastly and richly amusing in its account of the English man servant, who became valet to an American cattleman and learned the pioneer virtues, but there is about it a sympathetic and even patriotic quality which is touching.

Ruggle's astonishment and frequent consternation when faced with the rough-and-ready gusto of the 1908 frontier is delightful comedy, but Ruggle's discovery of the democratic spirit, and his development of his own manhood, make for really moving and poignant drama.

When told that the climax of the film consists simply of the Englishman's quiet recital of Lincoln's Gettysburg Address, one may not be altogether prepared for the discovery that it makes for a memorable and stirring dramatic power, as well as excellent patriotism. . . . The direction of Leo McCarey is admirable.

"Argus." *Literary Digest*. March 23, 1935, p. 28

Make Way for Tomorrow. Rugged simplicity marks this Leo McCarey production. It is a tearjerker, obviously grooved for femme fans, but the gripping manner in which it is told may overcome the sad theme and cause sufficient discussion at the box-office.

To get past the marquee weakness, title handicap and develop male patronage, the film will require a carefully prepared advance campaign, such as instituted at this house. Aside from taking full cognizance of Mother's Day and linking it to the picture's theme, management here plugged it in a novel fashion on the basis that it was a great heart drama of the present era. Even so, business is apt to be spotty where played solo.

McCarey, who also directed, has firmly etched the dilemma in which the elderly married couple find themselves when they lose their old dwelling place and their five grown-up children are non-receptive. He has kept audience interest focused on old Lucy Cooper and Pa Cooper as they are separated, each finding themselves in the way and not fitting in with the two households (one with a son and the other with a daughter).

However he might well have sacrificed the bitterly sad ending by following through with the happier motif he develops as the old pair are reunited for a few fleeting but joyous hours. That and the fact that this lighter mood is saved until the last seem to be weaknesses.

Variety. May 12, 1937

More important, there is Leo McCarey's film *Make Way for Tomorrow*—the most billiantly directed and acted film of the year. The story is the essentially sentimental one of an old couple who become a nuisance to their grown-up family; but so, for that matter, was *King Lear* sentimental. The great thing about the film is McCarey's handling of the players. We have not seen for a long time such a demonstration of what directorial control can mean to the art of acting. How much is McCarey will be revealed if you analyse any single situation; for example the old lady putting in a long-distance call to her husband. It is a difficult conversation for the sentiments of the old become, by emphasis, easily unreal. Yet McCarey gives delicacy and even something of tragedy to it, and it is done visually in the isolation he creates for the figure with his cameras. Robert Donat tells me that he was dumbfounded by the acting in this piece and I remember how a similar tribute was paid to McCarey by Charles Laughton after the production of *Ruggles of Red Gap*. My own view is that McCarey is a director's director, and the finest of all directorial craftsmen in Hollywood to-day. Like so many other able men, he derives from the school of Mack Sennett.

John Grierson. *World Film News*.
Aug. 1937, p. 10

Hollywood has developed the art of the domestic comedy to a high state of perfection. This type has its origin in slapstick but the weapons are words, not custard pies. They take a good deal of clever acting and clever direction and although they are unpretentious, to my mind they top most other Hollywood products barring Disney.

The latest is *The Awful Truth* with Irene Dunne and Cary Grant and, more important, directed by Leo McCarey. The plot is nothing and the situations are banal. It follows the course, quarrel, divorce, reconciliation. But among the ingredients the raising powder is the important thing and out of the oven comes a frothy bit of stuff that leaves no taste in the mouth and is easy on the stomach. . . .

The moral to this tale is that it seems the plot is not the important thing, it is the treatment, the twist or maybe just that the director and the players feel the same way about a script and the camera catches on. It is certainly not just luck for it has happened a number of times the past two years.

These films are not important but I think they are the sort of thing we go to the movies hoping to see. They offer a vision of release from the daily round and tempt one to believe that frivolity, zest, fun and clever repartee can be the body of life as it is lived (we hope).

Marion Fraser. *World Film News.* March 1938, p. 35

If ever there was a woman's picture then *Love Affair* is it. This brought together for the first time the elegant Irene Dunne and the "great French lover," Charles Boyer. And what a bringing together! Homeward bound from Naples they meet on a liner, where repressions are proverbially unknown and last flings *de rigueur*. They fall in love —indeed, it would have been a crime if they hadn't—they step off at Madeira to see his mother, covered in years and very old lace, and part when they get to New York with a date some months hence on top of the Empire State. He keeps the tryst, she would have done but is knocked down by a car at the last minute and paralysed. He doesn't know, she won't tell him. It is only in the last reel that he finds out and so, after an agony of suspense, true love triumphs. Sloppy, yes, but it gets you, because there is a lot of delightful humour cunningly mixed up with the sentiment and because Dunne and Boyer pour out such quantities of charm that it is impossible to resist them. As the child in *The Women* would say, a "lovey-dovey" film.

Alan Page. *Sight & Sound.* Summer 1939, p. 76

Leo McCarey, who directs so well it is almost anti-social of him not to direct more often, has created another extraordinary fine film in *Love Affair*. . . . Like other McCarey pictures, this one has the surface appearance of a comedy and the inner strength and poignance of a hauntingly sorrowful romance. It is a technique or a mood-creation developed, we expect, out of Mr. McCarey's past experiments, ranging from *Ruggles of Red Gap* through *Make Way for Tomorrow* to *The Awful Truth.* The formula would be comedy plus X (which is Mr. McCarey himself) equal such things as *Love Affair*.

The love affair Mr. McCarey and his company are considering is the unexpectedly idyllic romance between the jaded man of the world, Michel Marnay, and the younger, but almost equally skeptical Terry Mackay. Both of them were affianced elsewhere, not exactly for money (although that was part of the picture) but because they reasoned they might as well marry money if they had to marry at all. Then, suddenly, they met on shipboard, flirted since it amused them, parted unheroically when it occurred to them that news of an indiscretion might reach the ears of their respective future mates, and discovered, almost as surprisingly, that they were in love.

It is a discovery apt to alter the behavior of a couple of people who had been playing with life. Subtly, Mr. McCarey alters his style to meet the emergency. He finds it amusing that Michel should become a sign-painter, Terry a night club singer as they put themselves on probation for six months to determine whether they are worthy of marriage. But he finds it touching, too. And, although he keeps reminding himself (and his audience) that life is a comedian, he finds tragedy in the accident that overtakes Terry on her way to the marriage rendezvous and pity in the misunderstanding that keeps his lovers apart so long.

In a sense the film is a triumph of indirection, for it does one thing while seeming to do another. Its immediate effect is comedy; its afterglow is that of a bitter-sweet romance. A less capable director, with a less competent cast, must have erred one way or the other—either on the side of treacle or on that of whimsy. Mr. McCarey has balanced his ingredients skillfully and has merged them, as is clear in retrospect, into a glowing and memorable picture.

Frank S. Nugent. *NYT*. March 17, 1939, p. 25

The Warners' publicity department has *Juarez* billed as the film showing "how great the screen can be"; a few doors down Broadway the Warners' *Confessions of a Nazi Spy* is being run as a topical shocker. And just recently a little comedy piece passed through unobtrusively—though no one concerned with screen art could miss the beautiful assurance in the form with which its old statements, clichés of situation and attitude were lifted almost beyond recognition by a morning freshness of eye for each small thing around, and a way of expression as natural as singing in the shower. The movie (RKO) was *Love Affair*, still on view.

With Donald Ogden Stewart on the script, Charles Boyer and Irene Dunne for principals, Leo McCarey managed a happy command both of the complexities of his job and of the absurd, homely, garish, and touching things in ordinary life. The plot isn't worth recitation and so those interested in how art may be talked about even though cinematic, may skip it. Those excited over the mastery of form already achieved in pictures, and over what the screen can be, will like to follow this demonstration of the qualities of technique and imagination the films must always have and keep on recruiting to their service. [1939]

Otis Ferguson. *The Film Criticism of O.F.*
(Temple, 1971), pp. 254–55

Strictly speaking, [*Going My Way*] hardly has a right to pose as a religious film. There is no real contest with evil or with suffering, and the good itself loses half its force, because even the worst people . . . are as sugar-coated as *Mrs. Wiggs of the Cabbage Patch*. Yet it has, inadvertently, a good deal of genuine religious quality, and is often a beautiful piece of entertainment in spite of its Sunny-Jim story. Leo McCarey's leisured, limpid direction and Steven Seymour's splendid sets are partly responsible for this . . . but the best reasons are the loving attention to character. . . . [1944]

If only a half-dozen properly placed men in Hollywood knew how to apply the lessons in *Going My Way*, they might be assured of almost any number of hits, and we might be assured of an equal number of more or less good films. The lessons, if I read them right, are that leisureliness can be excellent, that if you take a genuine delight in character the universe is opened to you, and perhaps above all that a movie, like any other work of art, must be made for love. But I am ready to bet that the chief discernible result, if any, of *Going My Way* will be an anxiety-ridden set of vaudeville sketches about Pat and Mike in cassocks. . . . [1945]

James Agee. *Agee on Film* (Beacon, 1964), pp. 137–38, 347

Many Americans find themselves baffled and exasperated by that "anti-anti-Communism" which sees in overvigorous efforts to expose the Communist menace a growing threat to American freedom no less dangerous than Communism itself. Their bewilderment is understandable, for such an equation is clearly absurd and too often conceals a desire to remain "neutral" in the struggle against Soviet totalitarianism. But the fear of an irresponsible anti-Communism does not come entirely out of thin air; there *is* a wrong way, a dangerous way, to be anti-Communist. Those who do not believe this may find it illuminating to see Leo McCarey's new film, *My Son John*, an attack on Communism and an affirmation of "Americanism" that might legitimately alarm any thoughtful American, whether liberal or conservative. . . .

[R]eligion exists in this film only as a form of window-dressing, an essentially empty symbol to be counterposed occasionally to the symbols of Communism. Just as the elder Jefferson uses the family Bible to hit his son when he feels frustrated in argument, so the idea "religion" is used throughout the film as a kind of blunt instrument to settle every difficulty without resolving it. The film opens with the ringing of church bells, and it ends with John Jefferson's parents going into a chapel to pray for their dead son. But these elements are never realized in cinematic terms; they are presented so perfunctorily, so much as a matter of mere ideological decoration, that they have no strength as screen images—and, of course, in a movie it is not the intrinsic worth of an idea that counts, but the power with which it is made into an image; in the movie theater, we think with our eyes. [1952]

Robert Warshow. *The Immediate Experience* (Atheneum, 1970), pp. 163, 168–69

Leo McCarey. Some now put him in the ranks of the great and even the greatest. Prejudice or mystification? I cannot persuade myself that the very commercial and very conformist *auteur* of *The Kid from Spain* (1932), *The Awful Truth* (1937), which made its mark thanks to a dazzling twosome (Cary Grant-Irene Dunne), and *Going My Way* (which, alas, popularized a false and conformist idea of American niceness), is anything but a skillful craftsman. He was lucky enough to have met the Marx Brothers and made their best film: *Duck Soup* (1933). However, for the moment we are concerned with his sentimental aspect, which—dripping in *Going My Way* and *The Bells of St. Mary's*—was able in *Love Affair* (1939) to maintain an exceptional point of balance. It should, however, immediately be pointed out that this balance is always at the level of a very pretty picture postcard and not of just and nuanced sensibility such as one admires, for example, in Borzage. . . .

Henri Agel. *Romance Américaine* (Editions du Cerf, 1963), p. 47

Jean Renoir once remarked that Leo McCarey understood people better than any other Hollywood director. McCarey's moments may outlive his movies, be it Charles Laughton reciting the Gettysburg Address in *Ruggles of Red Gap* or, even more memorably from the same film, Binnie Barnes teaching Roland Young to play the drums; or Victor Moore saying goodbye to Beulah Bondi in *Make Way for Tomorrow* or Irene Dunne speaking to Maria Ouspenskaya in *Love Affair* or Barry Fitzgerald embracing his mother in *Going My Way* or Cary Grant and Irene Dunne reminiscing about their lost marriage in *The Awful Truth.* After enough great moments are assembled, however, a personal style must be assumed even though it is difficult to describe.

McCarey and Capra seem to go together like ham and eggs. They both started at about the same time in the twenties with the same kind of gag training. They both slipped unobtrusively into the sound era, and didn't hit their stride until the mid-thirties. Both declined in the late forties, virtually faded away in the early fifties, and returned in the late fifties. . . .

Andrew Sarris. *The American Cinema* (Dutton, 1968), p. 100

However, about two-thirds of the way through [*Ruggles of Red Gap*], the tone suddenly changes, the reversal taking place in a dangerous scene that miraculously succeeds. Ruggles, living in Red Gap, has been learning to admire the rough-and-ready ways of American democracy. In the saloon he recites the Gettysburg Address in its entirety to a ragged gang of illiterate Westerners. What might have been embarrassing or awkward is extremely convincing and moving. Much is due not only to Laughton's recitative powers but even more to the excellent direction of the sequence, consisting of a less than profile reverse angle shot, up close, as Laughton speaks the opening lines to himself; reaction shots; Laughton rising full view as he gains confidence; the long shots of the barroom and the men's backs as they move away from the camera and toward the speaker; and the slow pans of serious faces, all combining to produce a model of leisurely and accurate pacing. . . .

No matter how cheap the material or poor the direction handed to Laughton in his long film career, he never walked through any role. . . . When he encountered directors as capable as Leo McCarey, he could give great performances, and, despite his singular appearance, could submerge his personality in the character, a rare ability in screen acting.

Eileen Bowser in *Film Notes*, edited by
Eileen Bowser (MOMA, 1969), p. 95

At comedy, no one was better than Leo McCarey (*Laurel and Hardy, Love Affair, Going My Way, The Bells of St. Mary's*).

Leo would at times play the piano for hours during filming—noodling or trying to compose tunes. Yet while he played he pondered, reviewed, analyzed, invented, just as Stevens did while walking and smoking.

All directors must ponder and meditate in their own way. For they all have this common problem: keeping each day's work in correct relationship to the story as a whole. Scenes shot out of time and context must fit into their exact spot in the mosaic of the finished film, with their exact shadings in mood, suspense, and growing relationships of love or conflict. This is, as one can imagine, the most important and most difficult part of directing, and the main reason why films, perforce are the director's "business."

Frank Capra. *The Name Above the Title*
(Macmillan, 1971), p. 245

MAMOULIAN, ROUBEN (1897–)

There's Rouben Mamoulian of the Theatre Guild. He made a first film at the Astoria Studios of the Paramount. He put his camera on rubber wheels and glided it to look upon the players from this angle and that. He was given a typical Hollywood story—no more trashy than the others—and a maudlin heroine, annoyingly reminsiscent of Pauline Lord and Gladys Brockwell, and one of those mother-themes (my burlesque, good-bad mammy) . . . you know the ingredients—a whore, a pimp, a convent daughter, devoted nuns, a genteel sailor-boy looking for a little wife and a Wisconsin dairy, bichloride of mercury . . . another version of *Stella Dallas.* Given these millstones Mamoulian looked for sympathy to his camera. He proved himself more facile, more competent than Hollywood. But the film *Applause* remains sick stuff. Applause for Mr. Mamoulian must be modified by a censure of him for accepting the theme and the players. A movie, like water, never rises above its source. . . . We need philosophers who seek great themes told with insight and ultimate import. We need artists who build structure. That Mr. Mamoulian has used his camera as a mobile instrument is O.K. But moving a camera, getting angles, weaving together a couple of different sounds—the mother's chant, the daughter's prayer (what a banal sentimentalism!)—do not build a structure.

H. A. Potamkin. *New Masses.* Dec. 1929, p. 14

[I]t is interesting to note how one director has succeeded to an unusual degree in freeing himself from the fetters of sound recording. The picture is *Applause*, the first starring vehicle of Miss Helen Morgan, and the director is Rouben Mamoulian. . . .

The fact that he had dialogue to deal with didn't disturb him at all. Instead of allowing the dialogue to intrude itself in the story or even to take a respectable place alongside of it, Mamoulian has used his camera for all it was worth and made *it* tell the story.

The result is that *Applause* exists—to me, at any rate—as a cohesive, well integrated series of pictures. Its intensity, its sharp projection of tragedy, emerge from the eye of the camera; an omniscient, omnipresent eye that slides easily over the links of the story and emphasizes only the true and the relevant. . . .

Always there are artful touches, designed to illuminate the characters or to indicate the humors of the story. The opening sequence is deadly eloquent in its simplicity. There is a deserted street of a small town. Scattered bits of newspapers and bill posters are blown about by the wind. That is all. But you can feel the bleakness of the day, the chill November winds that sweep through the vacant street. And then one of the bill posters is flattened momentarily against the side of a building. It is the advertisement of Kitty Darling and the burlesque troupe coming to town. You hear the music of a cheap band, growing louder as it approaches, and then the shouts and laughter of people. Around the corner the crowd sweeps into view. There is Kitty herself, sitting majestically in her faded brougham, lavishing bows right and left, while the crowd swirls around her.

Certainly the mood of the picture is imparted without any waste of time and, I might add, without any waste of words. Taking a leaf from Mr. Mamoulian's book a rule for directors might be adduced to the effect that when you want to get a point over quickly to the audience, don't say it with words. As a matter of fact, the most telling sequences in *Applause* are done in pantomime. The dialogue is held to the subservient function of framing the story and heightening the characterizations.

Thorton Delahanty. *The Arts.* Dec. 1929, pp. 240–41

In spirit and form it owes much to René Clair and F. W. Murnau, the only movie directors who ever properly blended music and pictures. However, unlike his contemporaries, Rouben Mamoulian, who made *Love Me Tonight*, was not content to imitate the Europeans. He simply applied the fundamental principle used by them and, with the aid of a pleasant story, a good musician, a talented cast and about a million dollars, he has done what some one in Hollywood should have done long ago: he has illustrated a musical score.

From the opening scene, there are at least a dozen times when you are almost convinced that here is just another musical production brightened with some clever lines and some pleasant acting. You are quickly disillusioned. . . .

You see, as of yore, the chimneys swept with morning mist. A bell tolls the hour. A workman appears, throws his pick to the ground and starts to work. A chambermaid appears, glances at the sky, and sweeps her doorstep. You hear the bang of the pick, the swish of the broom. A cobbler sets up his last and pegs at his shoes. Bang, swish, crack—and then the music fades in and gradually the city wakes up in the orchestra until, finally, with chimneys smoking, hucksters crying their goods, cabs cawing at one another, the orchestra in a loud crash provides a raucous, lively entrance for M. Chevalier, who gets out of bed, opens the window and sings a little chorus to the city.

This opening scene is carried on too long, and the singers force their gaiety, but it is thoroughly done and it is an indication of the good sweep of the show. Once under way, Mamoulian never lets go, and after this opening chorus he presents his songs in better order and balance. Long before the pleasant finale, you realize that suddenly the former stage director has hit his stride; that once rid of his marble busts, his symbolic nonsense and his amateur preoccupation with camera angles, he has conceived and produced a fortunate, charming musical picture.

Pare Lorentz. *Vanity Fair*. Oct. 1932, p. 44

Like Michael Arlen, Mamoulian is a bright young Armenian. Also similarly, his productions are glib, imitative, chic, with a fake elegance, a pseudo-wit and a suggestion of Oriental greasiness. They are marked with that vulgarity which is continually straining for effect, which cannot express a simple thing simply. A Mamoulian production can be depended on to overstress the note, whether pitched to lyricism, melodrama, fantasy. Thus his *City Streets*, a gangster melodrama is directed as heavily and pretentiously as if it were *Greed* or *Sunrise*. There are brooding shadows, shots of pigeons flying beyond prison bars (freedom—get it?), weird angle shots of sculpture. Thus, too, in *Applause*, a sentimental little backstage tragedy, he puts Helen Morgan through her extremely limited paces with all the solemnity due a Sarah Bernhardt. The trashy emotionalism of the story, which a more honest director would have restrained, Mamoulian plays up for all it is worth. His *Dr. Jekyll and Mr. Hyde* is a cheaply sensational affair compared to the more silent Barrymore version. The brutal exaggeration of Hyde's makeup, physically so much more revolting than Barrymore's, spiritually so much less so, is a typical Mamoulian touch. [1933]

Dwight Macdonald. *D. M. on Movies*
(Prentice-Hall, 1969), p. 81

Queen Christina follows quite closely the career of Sweden's notorious seventeenth century queen as it was known to most of her contemporaries, without benefit of modern pathological psychology. The one serious concession it makes to presumed movie demands is in giving Christina an abiding passionate love for the Spanish ambassador, whereas the rumors of the time credited her with no more than a passing affair of scandal. That concession is understandable—what would a Garbo film be without passionate love? Where the film falls down as an historical picture is chiefly in its failure to suggest the cold and rugged Sweden of those rough days when the warrior sons of the Vikings took up the Protestant banner and made such a stir in Europe. Mamoulian's silken direction has a strangely softening effect on the scenes he is depicting, which distorts history far more than mere departures from recorded fact.

But the film gives Garbo space—and magnificent space—for the loveliest characterization she has yet offered. With beauty, with dignity, with deeply moving poignancy and a wise, serene humor, she lifts a rather shallow story into something beyond the dimensions of the scenario. Never, with perhaps the exception of *As You Desire Me,* has Garbo been given a story worthy of her fine spirit and beautiful art, but here she has been given a part in which she can create illimitably beyond the bounds set by the plot craftsmen. The only assistance she has is from the dialogue provided by S. N. Behrman, who has written words fitting the extraordinary queen for whom they were composed.

James Shelley Hamilton. *NBR*. Feb. 1934, pp. 11–12

Whether we will ever be able to put music in a picture and still have any picture left remains a question, but Hollywood is getting a little quicker with answers and the true solution may come someday. I'm afraid that *The Gay Desperado* is stiff and slow and wears pretty thin. But it has the right idea—the comic-opera idea with its face lifted, brought near enough to life so that it is not merely making fun but poking it, at the intolerable solemnities and at itself a little. . . .

Mr. Rouben Mamoulian's finished show favors effects over effectiveness and cardboard over character. The girl's fiancé, apart from being a pest by type, is nothing more than a few hasty lines; Harold Huber, usually a very good type, is miscast as the Leo Carrillo of *Viva Villa*; Leo Carrillo himself is more sketchy and unconvincing than I recall seeing him; and anybody who gives Ida Lupino this much rope deserves the consequences. The show cries out for more care, in handling actors and in planning situations; it seems the right sort of thing but is definitely under the wrong auspices. And I should be more reluctant to hang this on Mr. Mamoulian if it weren't for his performance in movies so far. He is no doubt an artist at something, but one picture after another shows him as having no flair for the medium, so that among all active film makers he stands apart, definitely in the company of those intellectual types who are always standing on the outside looking elsewhere, who can talk art right out of the movies into cinematographics as quick as look at you, and wouldn't know a good picture if somebody came along with one and set it off under them like a bonfire. [1936]

Otis Ferguson. *The Film Criticism of O.F.* (Temple, 1971), pp. 157, 158

[*Queen Christina* is] a re-writing of history that transcends dramatic license, presenting among other objectionable incidents a bedroom sequence which registers with voluminous and unnecessary detail the fact of a sex affair. The sequence is emphasized and dwelt upon beyond all purposes legitimate to the telling of the story, thereby assuming a pornographic character. Its portrayal of the queen is dangerous because queens have authority, acceptance.

Martin Quigley. *Decency in Motion Pictures* (Macmillan, 1937), p. 37

Intelligence, an experimental willingness and aptitude, and an understanding of pictorial and sound effects (which springs both from his operatic experience and from his studies of other craftsmen) have raised Mamoulian into the first rank of directors. His awareness of pace, rhythm, movement, and music has made his musical films his best; in these more than in his dramatic pictures he has blended the cinematic elements into an excellent whole. . . . Mamoulian's use of mobile sound was then novel: for instance, a chorus starting a song is left by the camera for a second scene, and the music continues through this second scene, being modulated so that a conversation can be heard above it. The camera moved freely, daringly, and even enthusiastically—sometimes, in fact, too much for the spectator's comfort. . . .

In *Applause* Mamoulian endeavored to blend light, shadow, and sound imaginatively and dramatically, and whenever possible he introduced nature to heighten the mood. His love scenes were exquisitely lyrical, presaging those in all his later works. His young lovers on top of a skyscraper were played against the sky and the wind; later, in *City Streets*, his lovers were placed in a setting against the sea; many of his later films show them in the rain. Such scenes, stemming from his thorough knowledge of the stage, are indicative of Mamoulian's forethought and awareness of the dramatic elements at the disposal of a director.

Mamoulian's daring and perspicacity in moving the camera, while other directors' cameras were literally hand-tied, contributed much at the psychological moment to the mutual adaptation of sound and camera. Although *Applause* was a sensitive venture in the right direction, however, the lack of restraint in Mamoulian's use of the camera suggested immaturity, defective discrimination, a lack of understanding of filmic continuity. Harry Alan Potamkin later cautioned Mamoulian against allowing his ingenuity to "become a routine of excess mobility and other fallacious devices."

Mamoulian's second undertaking, a melodramatic gangster film, *City Streets* (1931), displayed a firmer control of the medium. The film demonstrated Mamoulian's awareness of sound's possibilities and his intelligent application of the contributions of other directors (traits he has manifested ever since). [1939]

Lewis Jacobs. *The Rise of the American Film* (Teachers College, 1968), pp. 469, 470

Given a phony happy ending which nullifies Odets' idea, a star without depth, inexpert direction by Rouben Mamoulian, *Golden Boy* is a slick, swift, exciting but insensitive movie. The best parts—the savage photography in the fight sequences (by Musuraca and Frend) and the sympathetic treatment of the family of the Negro fighter who is killed —were not part of the play at all, which should prove something about the cinema art.

Gordon Sager. *TAC*. Oct. 1939, p. 28

Few plays get transferred from the stage to the screen so directly and straightforwardly as *Golden Boy* has been. Some tough words which the sound track is never allowed to utter have been dropped, some highfallutin speeches about their souls which the two main characters gave vent to on the stage to give the play its spurious air of being a tragedy (as well as their quite unnecessary killing off at the end), and a minor character whose function was not so much dramatic as to provide a bit of tossed-in social significance. Otherwise the translation has been faithful and complete, even to implications, a proof that Clifford Odets wrote a good movie to begin with, which needed only screen treatment to round it out to its proper dimensions. . . .

The movie people have had the right instinct about these things, and have known how to handle them. They keep the Odets that is genuine and toss out the uncertainties. So we have on the screen two definite and vivid backgrounds: the Bonaparte home . . . and the world of the prize-ring, crafty, wisecracking, impinging closely on gangsterdom. . . . The climax expands to an extent that the stage could not supply in the fight scenes, where the passions of the fight game spread out from the ring and the actual battle to the roaring crowd with terrifically eloquent pictorial comment, and there is an added scene in the dressing room of the dead negro fighter (trailing clouds of *Porgy*) that does more than pages of the most ambitious Odets dialogue to show how the Golden Boy saw the end of his get-rich-quick road.

Rouben Mamoulian has done one of his best jobs of directing and cast-picking.

James Shelley Hamilton. *NBR*. Oct. 1939, p. 11

From 1930 to 1935 it was thought that Rouben Mamoulian would be one of the masters of Hollywood production. To his credit were a film about music halls, *Applause* (1939), and the most spectacularly dramatic of the gangster films, *City Streets* (1931), with a magnificently contrasted couple (the giant Gary Cooper and the tiny Sylvia Sidney). He is an hallucinating director of actors, as is shown in *Dr. Jekyll and Mr. Hyde* (1932), featuring Federic March. He was also the first one to make good use of technicolor, *Becky Sharp* (1935). But Mamoulian quickly ran out of steam, in spite of several returns of the flame—such as the boxing scene in *Golden Boy* (1939), with William Holden, or the suavely indecent scene in *Queen Christina* (1934), in which Garbo piously touches the furnishings and the objects in the room in which she has spent the night with John Gilbert, and finally that attack (better than in a De Mille film) of a gang of itinerant circus workers in *High, Wide and Handsome* (1937). There is perhaps a touch of something really Spanish in *Blood and Sand* (1941), with Tyrone Power. Mention should also be made of his direction of Marlene Dietrich, the seraphic painter's model in *Song of Songs* (1933)—an intermezzo in a career which under Sternberg was of a Baudelaire-ish perversity.

Henri Agel. *Romance Américaine* (Editions du Cerf, 1963), p. 48

Rouben Mamoulian, an Armenian who came to America in his twenties at the invitation of George Eastman, had already demonstrated his flair for cinema in *Applause* and *Dr. Jekyll and Mr. Hyde* when he directed *Love Me Tonight*. The opening, as Paris shuffles rhythmically into wakefulness, is beautifully modulated and sophisticated in its use of sound effects. And Maurice Chevalier is immediately likeable as the cheerful tailor who is driven to masquerade as a baron in order to get his rightful money from the Vicomte de Varèze. In the ensuing gambols at a French château, one can detect the influence of many tastes, from Clair's (in the marriage of fragile sentiment and winning verve) to Lubitsch's (the crisp patter and wickedness of the dialogue). But even though his style is eclectic, and even though the Rodgers and Hart numbers are a massive asset to him, Mamoulian is constantly ready to stamp his own imaginative signature on the film. His experiments with overlapping sound are amusing in the context of the plot and also advanced for the period; his visual capers are never gratuitous (e.g. the speeded-up action as Chevalier gallops away on a rebellious horse is balanced neatly a few minutes later by the slow-motion as the hunt leaves the deer in peace and "tiptoes" home). *Love Me Tonight* has that infectious spontaneity that distinguishes the American musical at its best, and rarely makes the mistake of taking its romantic setting too seriously. "The son of a gun is nothing but a tailor" resounds through the château, and Jeanette MacDonald rides wildly, unforgettably, after her bourgeois hero.

Peter Cowie. *Seventy Years of Cinema* (Barnes, 1969), p. 104

Rouben Mamoulian's is not a name which springs naturally to mind as a director of horror films. . . . However, his one essay in the genre, *Dr. Jekyll and Mr. Hyde* (1932), is not only the most horrific but also much the best of the various versions of Stevenson's over-adapted classic. . . .

Mamoulian's gift for beautifully lit and composed camerawork is frequently in evidence, notably in this opening sequence in Jekyll's house, and also later in the same setting when, assured of his engagement to Muriel Carew, he runs to the organ and pours out his exultation in music. Such a scene could easily topple over into the ridiculous, but Mamoulian manages to create such a joyous radiance in a succession of brief shots (particuarly telling is a large close-up of the wrinkled, devoted, smiling face of the old servant), that we are wholly attracted into sharing it. There are few occasions when sheer happiness has been so successfully and yet so simply captured on the screen.

Anyone watching *Dr. Jekyll and Mr. Hyde* is, of course, waiting for "the change." Even by today's standards, Mamoulian's contrivance is masterly. The camera, becoming briefly subjective again, slowly approaches a mirror on the Doctor's laboratory. The potion is drunk, to the expected, but discreetly restrained, choking and gasping. Then, with no cuts, no dissolves, the transformation begins. lines and shadows etch themselves into Jekyll's face. . . . Almost immediately the camera turns from the mirror and starts to revolve—slowly at first then with increasing speed until it is spinning round the room and everything becomes a blur. Simultaneously the famous sound effects begin. Mamoulian's own heartbeats, a struck gong with the moment of impact cut off and the vibrations reversed, light frequencies photographed on to the soundtrack. For all the ingenious noises which have been created in films since, it is doubtful if this effect has ever been surpassed in hypnotic menace. An extraordinary sense of claustrophobic muffledness was felt, as if indeed our ears had been stuffed with cotton wool so that we heard the thumps of our own heart, the singing in our own brain. Gradually the rotary movement slows down, the sound quietens. The camera stops, not looking into the mirror. We are looking at the laboratory—just as it was—nothing, apparently changed. But we ourselves? There is no sound, except for Jekyll's (our) laboured breathing. Slowly the camera approaches the mirror. It is a magnificent build-up, and it speaks well for March's make-up and performance that the first revelation of Hyde is not a disappointment.

Ivan Butler. *Horror in the Cinema* (Barnes, 1967–70), pp. 59, 60–62

MANKIEWICZ, JOSEPH L. (1909–)

The cause of good race relations in this country has not been served by Joseph L. Mankiewicz's *No Way Out*. Nor has any other cause been served except the one that wishes to divide us, that denies that Americans strive toward democracy, that repudiates democracy itself.

The title of this picture asserts that in the United States the American Negro can find no way out, and the wholly synthetic story of this picture propagandizes for that demagogic fallacy. The corollary of such a contention is race war, and this picture advocates and depicts it.

To what end?

Would Mr. Mankiewicz, who directed and (with Lester Samuels) wrote this picture, really like to see Americans abandon their efforts to evolve a way for the races to live together? Does he *really* believe these efforts to be hypocritical and futile? Does he *really* want to abandon law and let mobs of whites and blacks settle the race problem once and for all?

If not, what did he intend to do when he made this picture? To make the Negro unhappier, as those on the Right will say? To make the Negro revolt, as those on the Left desire? (Incidentally, the Communist press has attacked this picture because it does not develop more extensively its theme of race war.) Or has Mr. Mankiewicz irresponsibly undertaken to make a quickie for the Negro movie theatres, believing bemused esthetes and liberals will applaud it because Negroes are in it? Or is Mr. Mankiewicz tortured by some gix of his own?

These queries are all political, for it is unnecessary to review this picture except politically. Essentially, *No Way Out* is what Communists used to call agit-prop, that is, a production designed solely for purposes of agitation and propaganda. It is unworthy of literary or cinematic consideration: its story is too contrived, its direction too melodramatic.

Henry Hart. *Films in Review*. Oct. 1950, pp. 24–25

20th Century's *A Letter to Three Wives* was the début of Joseph L. Mankiewicz as writer-director, and the best American comedy of 1949. It was a mere shadow of those acid Hollywood comedies of the thirties, but it had a supply of ironies and made a certain alkaline comment on present-day American customs and manners. It was in general over-written and under-directed—the laughs being predominantly verbal and the structure literary.

Mankiewicz's new film *All About Eve* makes a grandiose effect of being very cynical and very sophisticated about the New York stage, and it has been accepted at its face value by a large part of the American press and the American public. (Its chances at the British box-offices are perhaps not so good.) *All About Eve* cannot truly be compared with *Sunset Boulevard*, which looked detachedly at a tragedy of a silent film star who has outlived her fame, and wrung from it an acrid pictorial sort of poetry. Mankiewicz's film is an emotional backstage drama from within, studded with glib Coward-Arlen epigrams and so starved of visual substance that nearly the whole weight of its 2 hours 18 minutes falls on the shoulders of one player—Bette Davis. It will leave nobody any wiser (or sadder) about the New York or any other stage.

Richard Winnington. *Sight & Sound.*
Jan. 1951, p. 373

In short, what really interests Mankiewicz in *All About Eve* as well as in most of his other films are the women, and through them the permanence of a certain femininity, the archetype of a certain way of being female and in consequence not a man. And it is the woman who wins on all counts, as does a certain form of civilization that is manifestly feminine and sometimes American. A civilization whose best daughters are the Daughters of the Revolution. You know them very well: those who did more than anybody for the fame of MacArthur and would place him in power if God (Lord, make the blood of men run; we don't care about the rest), if God gives them life and a bit of power. Mankiewicz only pretends to attack the theater and its milieux, but it's really a lovers' quarrel. . . .

Jacques Doniol-Valcroze. *Cahiers du Cinéma.*
May 1951, p. 27

As a director, he has always shown a marked feeling for characterization and an ability to extract rounded, perceptive performances from his actors. As a producer, his capacity is tremendous; as a writer, he is facile, witty and urbane. But as the writer-director-producer of the recent *People Will Talk*, he disastrously permitted his dialogue to run on at the expense of tight plot development, chose to hedge his writing and direction with assured box-office personalities. Now, happily, in *Five Fingers* (20th Century-Fox) he has thrown the reins of production one way, the pride of authorship another, and as director alone has fashioned out of L. C. Moyzisch's novel, *Operation Cicero,* one of the tightest, fastest and most absorbing spy melodramas since Hitchcock crossed the Atlantic.

Arthur Knight. *Theatre Arts.* April 1952, p. 41

Eyebrows raised and tongues clicked when Mankiewicz first tested Marlon Brando for Antony. Those who saw Brando on the stage before *Streetcar* were somewhat more optimistic. And it turns out that Brando *can* speak without a mouthful of mush. Physically, he is ideal for Antony—his face is properly animalistic, his mouth hard, his eyes crafty. He is at his best in the scene directly following the assassination when, kneeling beside the body of Caesar, he vows vengeance on the conspirators. This scene, incidentally, is effective cinema. The camera tracks to a long shot to underline the feeling of Antony's isolation as he mourns alone in the enormous senate chamber, and then comes in quickly to focus on Brando's face and speech.

Since Houseman has left the script intact and the arrangement of scenes close to the original, the only movie technique in his *Julius Caesar* is the way the camera comes in for close-ups whenever the narrative requires them. The other camera work is confined largely to sharp blacks and whites which emphasize the stark, relentless action. Mankiewicz, like Houseman a man of the theatre, has a keen eye for grouping, and his crowd scenes—the triumphal procession in the early sequences, the assassination of Caesar, the funeral oration in the square—are both utilitarian and pictorially beautiful. The battle scenes, always offstage in Shakespeare, have not been expanded. They are meager, but they serve.

On the whole, *Julius Caesar* is a splendid achievement. But, in the last analysis, one cannot have both pure Shakespeare and pure film. The cinema should, because of its nature, give *visual* interpretation to what Shakespeare's poetic imagery verbally suggests. But Shakespeare is too traditional to be tampered with, and so his plays cannot be re-fitted to the screen in the same way contemporary stage dramas can. But when all is said and done, Houseman's *Julius Caesar* is cinema Shakespeare at its most sincere, its most distinguished, and its most polished.

Robert Kass. *Films in Review.* May 1953, pp. 238–39

The problem of transferring Shakespeare to film has rightly daunted Hollywood, and in the case of *Julius Caesar*, it has daunted Metro-

Goldwyn-Mayer into downright mediocrity. Something like the paralysis of fear sets in on such occasions so that elaborate preparations are made to counteract it. The method employed by John Houseman, who produced the present work, and Joseph L. Mankiewicz, who directed it, has been not to get excited and to avoid the effect of a costume drama or a DeMille spectacle. They have succeeded, perhaps, beyond their hopes as the concrete result is a film without heroic proportions—and if one thing is essential to the general success of Shakespeare's historical drama, it is heroic proportions. Overwhelming material means, truly, are not necessary to such proportions; art, however, is.

In structure and character motivation, *Julius Caesar*, as plays go, is not very strong. Little is done here to bolster it. The action continues well past the catastrophe and reveals that neither of its more "colorful" characters, Antony or Caesar himself, is the protagonist but Brutus, in whom is lodged (with Cassius as his alter ego) the key political temperament of the drama. On the stage about fifteen years ago, Orson Welles solved the problems of form and motivation by making the play a parable of Fascism, something to which his directorial talents were well suited. At least this made perfectly clear, if rather brutal, sense; the present film comes through only on the level of common sense. But common sense cannot specifically reveal a work of art in realization; only a particular and lucid idea of it can do so. No such idea was anywhere on the studio lot when this production was filmed.

Parker Tyler. *Theatre Arts*. June 1953, p. 84

It's possible that at some time during the long existence of the Italian nobility there has been a barefooted contessa, but it's more probable that such a creature is merely a conceit of 19th century melodrama. Joseph L. Mankiewicz, who wrote and directed *The Barefoot Contessa*, likes to get hold of an old piece of ham and spice it with wisecracking dialogue—which is his forte. His *People Will Talk* was a re-do of a German B picture called *Dr. Praetorius*, and there is interior evidence in the present film that the germinal idea of a barefoot contessa is from the paperbacks beloved of Europe's chambermaids. . . .

Of what value is all this stupidity? At least it provides a glimpse into Mankiewicz's curious psyche. What do we see? An ambivalent hatred and envy for the aristocracy; an ambivalent distaste for and truckling to the proletariat; a surprising amount of Hollywood and Vine vulgarity and irresponsibility. In short, a confusion so great that Mankiewicz sometimes changes his mind in the same scene. Thus, though one of the Riviera spongers derided in this film, who is a pretender to a throne, is at first presented as a feeble-minded lush, he is suddenly allowed to pay a noble tribute to the count who rescues Ava from the South American. And the count, whom the pretender calls "a king among counts as I am a clown among kings," is then shown to be so ignoble that he marries the woman he loves without telling her he is no longer a man.

Henry Hart. *Films in Review*. Oct. 1954, p. 430–32

Stylization is the key to the success of any musical, but it is peculiarly indispensable to *Guys and Dolls*, a Broadway show that came over as a clever, tuneful musical. Hollywood's dismal past is filled with the corpses of clever, tuneful Broadway musicals. Aside from vulgarities of taste, the disastrous film versions of *Oklahoma*, *Brigadoon*, and *Kiss Me Kate* suffered mainly from the camera's tendency to stare coldly at the musical conceits of fanciful characters. Joseph Mankiewicz and Michael Kidd are therefore to be congratulated for demonstrating in *Guys and Dolls* that the camera can wink, as well as stare, at the improbable.

It is difficult to determine where Joseph Mankiewicz' direction leaves off and Michael Kidd's choreography beings. Theirs is a collective effort of taste, verve and pacing. The choreography is particularly brilliant in the opening scene in Times Square that sets the lighthearted, low-life tone of the entire film. Mankiewicz has wisely employed a stylized set of the Square, combining a painted backdrop with such realistic props of the city as cars, newsstands, and subway entrances. The Damon Runyon world of softhearted hoodlums and beautiful Salvation Army dolls would have been grotesque in documentary process shots of real New York. [1955]

Andrew Sarris. *Confessions of a Cultist* (S&S, 1970), p. 17

In *The Barefoot Contessa* Humphrey Bogart has a role very different from those he is usually given to play. Instead of the usual sympathetic tough guy we have an intellectual, no less sympathetic, but whose only violences—with rare exceptions—are spiritual. Joseph L. Mankiewicz has given him the job of representing him: like him, he is a film director; like him, he writes his own films. He is a cinéast in the way that one is a writer: it is no accident that I looked for my points of reference in novelistic creation. The grandeur and servitude of the cinema has an important place in the action: we are concerned not only with heavy economic implications that deny the liberty and dignity of *auteurs*, but also with the honor and joy of the craft. The films made by Harry Dawes-Humphrey Bogart are one of the subjects of this film. The circle is closed; the cinematographic serpent bites its tail. It is a perfect—and living—circle.

Claude Mauriac. *Petite Littérature du Cinéma* (Editions du Cerf, 1957), pp. 114–15

It is certain that *Suddenly, Last Summer* is a controversial film in the sense that people will discuss its meaning on so many levels that the intention of the film may be entirely overlooked. The film leaves audiences in mute astonishment, with their senses stunned; this is its intention, and *Suddenly, Last Summer* is directly provocative and unusual enough to grasp the viewer's total involvement, no matter how much one may resist. The jolting climax is out of Williams' nightmare world of exotic make-believe—it is unreal, vaguely symbolic of primitive rituals, a wildly *American* evocation of mysterious Spanish motives and hatreds, and above all, it is an extremely moral film. Despite the story's somewhat enthusiastic preoccupation with evil, the immoralists are thoroughly punished, and the excitements of the plot are neither half as brutal nor as realistically compelling as Buñuel's *macabres mexiques.*

The film also causes one to believe that the *dénouement* is somehow a matter of exquisite intellectual imagination—a tendency of certain writers to illustrate, with ingenious diversity, the emotional and sexual destruction of expatriate Americans or Anglo-Saxon Europeans trapped under another, more disturbingly erotic sky. This is a cliché regarding Latin, Asian or African atmospheres that thrives because of its infinite theatrical possibilities. Apparently, sex is always more sinister in the warmer climes.

A filmed play, *Suddenly, Last Summer* may seem a trifle talky at times, but then, no one should expect less from either Williams or the director concerned here, Joseph L. Mankiewicz. The latter has long been associated with uncontrollably verbal films (*People Will Talk, The Quiet American*), although in this case, the long monologues seem to be more controlled so that nonlistening cinemagoers may be kept in suspense while awaiting the major piece of visual excitement.

Albert Johnson. *Film Quarterly*. Spring 1960, p. 40

All about Eve was a handsomely mounted Darryl F. Zanuck production. It reeked with glamour, and so lavish were the décor and the trappings that "the bitter comedy" was handicapped in its satirical purpose. Mankiewicz was himself theatrical in his attempt to dissect the

Broadway concept of the theater, and, in a sense, paid homage to it. There was overstatement in the film, but there were also subtle wit and a good deal of perception. The stage would have been lucky to have some of the bright lines sprinkled through *All about Eve*. . . .

The style of the picture was all Mankiewicz. It would not have required his own admission to see that the documentary approach was not for him. His purpose was to fictionalize unashamedly. If the story absorbs, if the people are exciting to watch and listen to, the audience will inevitably remain in the realm of illusion. His pace and his rhythms were kept relatively slow; each of the scenes was allowed to create its own tensions, stretched about as far they would go. And, unfortunately, at times farther. The picture seemed long—although it was not by today's standards of length—and the crispness of the dialogue was not matched by equally crisp editing. Mankiewicz seemed to have such respect for his own screenplay that he allowed himself to savor each of its moments.

Hollis Alpert. *The Dream and the Dreamers* (Macmillan, 1962), pp. 151–52

A nondaily reviewer inevitably finds it necessary to bypass discussion of certain films for the sake of others, but the film scene, no less inevitably, sooner or later gets becalmed, enabling him to profit of the doldrums for a little corrective retrospection.

What, at this late date, has not yet been said against *Cleopatra*? This perhaps: that it manages to be a *total* disappointment. Whatever was interesting about it clearly ended up somewhere else: on the cutting-room floor, in various hotel rooms, in the newspaper columns. The range of the film extends from the expensively vulgar to the expensively ordinary; it lacks not only the intelligent spectacle of a *Lawrence of Arabia* but even the spectacular unintelligence of a C. B. DeMille product. . . .

Mankiewicz, as writer or director, has no genuine flair for the action-crammed historic canvas; his gift, such as it is, is for brisk comedy, which is of small avail here, and for witty repartee, which will not be squeezed from stones like Elizabeth Taylor. Nor does Richard Burton offer much more than craggy grimaces and rocky mouthings. [1963]

John Simon. *Private Screenings* (Macmillan, 1967), pp. 78–79

Virtuosity of another sort was demonstrated by Joseph Mankiewicz, who made three notable experiments with film as a medium for sound rather than sight. He avoided (just barely) criticism for doing photographed plays. But the real glory of his best pictures, *Five Fingers, Letters to Three Wives, People Will Talk*, and, finest of all, *All About Eve*, was the dialogue, which reached for—and sometimes attained—Wildean heights of epigramatic wit. These were the apotheosis of Hollywood's attempts to needle naturalistic dialogue almost to the level of poetry, and the pictures did indeed flash by, carried along by the flow of the writer-director's pen rather than with his camera. Only when Mankiewicz reached desperately for importance (as in *The Barefoot Contessa*) did the technique fail him. Of course, *Cleopatra* should not be held against him. Indeed, he probably did as much as any man could to save a job well botched before he arrived on the scene.

Richard Schickel. *Movies* (Basic, 1964), pp. 186–87

It depends, I suppose, on what you like. Movie goers who enjoy well-acted, handsome, somewhat sophisticated films should swarm around *The Honey Pot*. Directed and written by Joseph L. Mankiewicz, it has many of his usual touches: some slick cinema, some bright, witty dialogue nicely put over by his good cast, and a loopholey plot that doesn't bear too close scrutiny.

The story starts as a present-day version of *Volpone*. In fact, the movie itself begins with a scene from the Ben Jonson play on the stage of a beautiful Venice theater where fabulously wealthy Cecil Fox (Rex Harrison) is the sole spectator. . . .

By now *The Honey Pot* is half over and, although you may be admiring the stunning color photography of Venice and the interiors, and the fine performances of this cast, you suddenly realize this is one of the talkiest pictures ever made. Very good talk it is with plenty of snappy repartee; even though the Volpone situation is quite obvious, it plays a double purpose in revealing character. But then Mankiewicz, who is full of surprises, switches from this stagey, theatrical technique and swings into action. One of the "girls" is found dead, and the next morning her body is moved into a gondola on the canal. And later another dead body is transfered to another gondola on the canal. And so, is *The Honey Pot* a murder mystery? Not really. But the last part of the film is so entertaining I wish Mankiewicz had either made the first half move faster or had later cut some of its static scenes. But I wouldn't have anything cut from the last part —when the story's ironies are underlined; when Harrison's Fox, whose secret ambition is to be a ballet dancer, does his stuff to the "Dance of the Hours"; when Maggie Smith steps out of her drab role and steals the whole picture; and when Adolfo Celi comes on as an Italian police inspector who is not a caricature but a wise, thoughtful man. Even though its plot cannot bear minute analysis, *The Honey Pot* has enough bitter-sweet satire and chi-chi to draw customers.

Philip T. Hartung. *Commonweal.* June 2, 1967, p. 323

The Honey Pot, Joseph L. Mankiewicz's free variation on *Volpone*, gives the critics a chance to congratulate themselves on their liberal education. Most of them haven't bothered to review the film but have been satisfied to ask, smugly, how a Hollywood entertainment could possibly compare with a seventeenth-century classic. It compares favorably, I'm afraid. I agree that the opening scenes of the film, the introduction of the three greedy ladies who hope for the "dying" Cecil Fox's fortune, are not as imaginatively varied and succinct as the comparable scenes in Volpone; Mankiewicz does better when he isn't staying so close to the text. His satiric dialogue is often very good, and although everyone has been outraged when the movie abandons Jonson for murder mystery halfway through, I'm more interested in praising the mystery plot as the only recent one with any suspense and ingenuity. The major characters are intriguingly difficult to evaluate, because they have a dimension beyond the cardboard figures we're used to seeing in American comedies. And two scenes between the cynical Mr. Fox and the relatively innocent nurse of one of the rich ladies are as masterful examples of high comic writing as we can hope to see in movies; in their subtle dramatization of the attraction of opposites, in their psychological acuteness and extemely complex manipulation of sympathies, they probably surpass what Ben Jonson wrote. (Okay, the comparison isn't fair—Jonson wasn't interested in psychological complexity—but I resent the way in which pompous reverence for the classics has hurt appreciation of this film.) . . . The mixture of satire, farce, and thriller works unusually well, but it does lead to a preposterous ending—funny enough, but without any relationship to the film's rather human concerns. *The Honey Pot* is too larky to be art, too talky to be great cinema, but it's delightful entertainment, with a sophistication, for a change, that you *won't* find on television.

Stephen Farber. *Film Quarterly.* Fall 1967, pp. 60–61

The Barefoot Contessa. Insiders' exposés usually tell little that isn't known, but they are great for exposing the intellectual pretensions of the insider. And those pretensions are sometimes very appealing to movie fans. . . .

In the forties Ben Hecht impressed some people with a whoppingly ludicrous movie called *Specter of the Rose* (sample dialogue: "My heart is dancing a minuet in the ashcan.") Joseph L. Mankiewicz had apparently been concealing *his* load of florid deep thoughts, and in 1954 he unburdened himself, telling All about Hollywood—where the men aren't men and the women are magnificent, frustrated animals. Flamenco dancer Ava Gardner is discovered in the slums of Madrid by a millionaire movie producer (Warren Stevens), a gutless, sycophantic press agent (Edmond O'Brien), and an alcoholic, broken-down director (Humphrey Bogart). She becomes a glamorous star but only feels at home with her feet in the dirt (symbolized by a guitar player, a chauffeur, and a gypsy dancer—one played by Riccardo Rioli). The movie, absurdly garrulous about telling the dirty truth, is so ornate and so acidulous that a lot of people took it very seriously. *Contessa* is a trash masterpiece: a Cinderella story in which the prince turns out to be impotent. It's hard to believe Mankiewicz ever spent an hour in Hollywood; the alternative supposition is that he spent too may hours there. . . .

Pauline Kael. *Kiss Kiss Bang Bang*
(Little, Brown, 1968), pp. 234–35

In "The Novelist and the Cinema—A Personal Experience," Graham Greene complains that the 1958 film treatment of *The Quiet American* was the worst perversion yet perpetrated on one of his serious novels. The screenplay, written and directed by Joseph L. Mankiewicz, certainly reveals important thematic alterations. Pyle . . . remains guiltless in the movie, while Fowler . . . is duped by the Communists (the latter, of course, are the real villains of the piece). In short, Greene's criticism of America disappears from view. . . . Although *The Quiet American* on the screen is considerably diminished in scope and complexity, enough of the original conception nevertheless remains to make Mankiewicz's film a distinguished achievement. . . .

It must be owned, though, that the flashback structure is not handled by the film-maker with complete success. The reader of the novel can easily accept the convention of a first-person narrator writing down his reflections of events occurring in the past. It is much more difficult for the viewer to accept Michael Redgrave standing before the body of Audie Murphy as he remembers out loud all the happenings of the past—only to discover the actor more than ninety minutes later still standing in the same position! Like *The End of the Affair, The Quiet American* on film employs the narrator for transitions between scenes; and like the earlier movie (though not to the same extent . . .)

there is an inevitable reduction in reflective significance in the translation from page to screen.

Edward Murray. *The Cinematic Imagination* (Ungar, 1972), pp. 258–60

MILESTONE, LEWIS (1895–)

A rollicking farce-comedy, fashioned from a story by Gelett Burgess and entitled *The Cave Man*, is the highlight on the Rialto program this week. Here is a mile of mirth filled with unusually clever situations that have been handled most adroitly by Lewis Milestone, who also directed *Seven Sinners*. Not a little of the merriment that was aroused in the theatre yesterday was due to the witty subtitles by that imaginative writer, Benjamin de Casseres.

Mordaunt Hall. *NYT*. March 1, 1926, p. 17

Two Arabian Knights. This is real comedy. "Gags" to be sure, but new ones—and spicy!

Although the action starts in the trenches, it is not just "another war story." A hard-boiled army sergeant and one of his men are gassed, recuperate to go into a fistic encounter and be captured by the Germans. They escape, in the stolen white uniforms of two Arabic prisoners. Past watch dogs, beneath electrified wires, into the arms of more prisoners. They land on a ship bound for Arabic cities, where they encounter one of the harem-variety beauties. Naturally, both fall for the veiled, mystic woman.

How to outrival one another? The sergeant soaks the clothes of his private, who retaliates by stealing the pants of his superior. Then the Turkish rival and the plot for the doughboy's extermination. A duel—but you must see it.

The clever titles add materially to the picture, even though they are a bit risque in places. Louis Wolheim, the new screen-actor with a face so homely that it requires no make-up, will make a hit in this picture. . . . William Boyd rises to new comedy heights. He is funny, yet sympathetic. Mary Astor sparkles by her dashing young beauty.

To Lewis Milestone, the twenty-nine-year-old director, goes the credit for the production. He started with a drama script, threw it away and created a comedy. Over the heads of the children, but lively entertainment for the rest of the family.

Photoplay. Nov. 1927, p. 53

All Quiet on the Western Front is certainly the finest of all the Great War pictures, and the outstanding film made with speech and sound.

No other scenes of battle like these have been thrown on the screen, nor such imagination in projecting what human beings, simple everyday human beings, are called upon to endure in circumstance that defies and upsets men's reason. And faithful it remains in feeling and narrative to Remarque's original. Mr. Anderson and Mr. Abbott doubtless saw to this. But to Mr. Milestone goes the credit of effecting the similitude in united and dynamic picture terms. He has used his camera to form a cinematic pattern and so has created a true motion picture first of all. Behind this pattern he has utilized another, that of sound and dialogue, so perfectly fitted to the first that the two move together without blur or intrusion upon each other. *All Quiet* is not a photographed and phonographed narrative. The sound and image mediums blend as one, as a form of artistic expression that only the motion screen can give; the essential structure of images in motion to create the visual effect is never marred by the recording "mike." So much, briefly, for the technical achievement which the film represents in adapting sound to pictures so as to preserve the form. It may only be added that after seeing this film no one can deny the potency of sound effect to heighten the power of the motion picture. Here men talk and laugh and cry out in agony against the terrible background monotony of machine gun sputter and crashing shells forever shifting back and forth across the grey front from far off to blinding nearness, until there is created in the audience out of the continuous presence of the nightmare the feeling of the not unusual, the acceptance of the awful reality, which it was necessary for the soldier to feel and accept before he could endure the thing he had to face and exist or die in.

NBR. May-June, 1930, p. 5

Films, like other works of art, convey experiences as well sensations. The final experience of a film is determined by the temper of the presentation. And that is where war-films fail. Either in the temper of the particular story of the human relationships involved, or in the temper of the treatment. . . . The failure of *All Quiet on the Western Front* is that of the temper of the treatment. . . .

All Quiet on the Western Front, directed by Lewis Milestone, is competent work. There are splendid scenes of the charging soldiers, leaping soldiers, men caught in the barbed wires. There is a good moment of rapid flashes of faces in bold. Unlike the dialogue of *Journey's End*, the speech of *All Quiet* is constructed with some attention to intervals, to time and even emotional quality. But directorial competence is not enough. The temper is lacking.

Lacking the informing temper, the film lacks the structure it demands, the heroic structure. The succession of episodes defeat any possibility of a pervasive experience. A sequence of agony is followed by a sequence of comedy trying to be sardonic—the Maxwell Anderson *What Price Glory*! influence. The agony and the "relief" are discharged with equal force and reach the same pitch, so that the experience is neutralized. The final experience is one of no experience.

Harry Alan Potamkin. *New Masses.* June 1930, p. 14

Battle scenes have been represented in many a picture, but *All Quiet* surpasses them all in the stark horror and madness of the business of fighting. Although the picture is not devoid of gentler moods, and is sprinkled generously with captivating humor, the predominant impression is that of life in the raw, of existence stripped of all adornments and bared to the bone. For this reason the total effect produced is not so much the tragedy of war as its callous bestiality. One is staggered, and shaken, and almost ready to sob, but one is not really thrilled. It is probably because of the elemental quality of its material that *All Quiet* is not so good a drama as *Journey's End*: but its appeal is more immediate, and technically it is a superior piece of cinematic craftsmanship, for which achievement Mr. Milestone, who directed the picture, deserves unstinted praise.

Alexander Bakshy. *Nation.* June 11, 1930, p. 7

But there has been no really great film of the war, either with or without dialogue, with the exception of a few Soviet productions, which take in the war as a parallel to their main theme, rather than as the main theme itself. There has been no document of the war purely and beautifully expressed in terms of cinema, nothing to build a permanent memorial, as the literature and sculpture and painting of every country has done, to these four years of international chaos. *All Quiet on the Western Front* is perhaps of all the productions derived from the war theme the one which I should choose to have the final word. I do not consider it in the round a finely made picture. It suffers from the conflict of its cast with its ideas, its purely American technique with the problems of a youth essentially European. It has no complete unity, thinking and acting in different hemispheres; but it is almost always cinema, and at moments, as in the scene of the boy running from the hospital with the boots in his hand, very fine cinema; and towering above the sentiment of the stock presentation of the studios is the one great elemental virtue—that this film does show, without compromise, and in its own medium, the complete futility and waste and bestiality of war.

C. A. Lejeune. *Cinema* (Alexander Maclehose, 1931), pp. 221–22

Nearly all [*The Front Page's*] action happens in the reporters' room of the criminal courts building in what is called a "Mythical Kingdom" —a locale easily recognizable to anyone at all aware of conditions in a certain mid-Western city whose name is spelled with seven letters of which the first is C. This action centers about the hanging of a man, and is principally concerned with the value of that hanging as news to the readers of modern metropolitan newspapers. Other aspects of the fate of the condemned man are touched upon forcibly but incidentally: its aspect as an example of justice administered in the interest of politics, for instance, and its aspect as an example of predatory victimizing. But the main emphasis of the motion picture is put on the loyalty of newspaper men to their profession—or, to say it another way, the hold the newspaper profession gets on its members. The "plot" interest lies in whether Hildy Johnson will be able to escape from the reporting business and get married—for it is made obvious that if he does not escape, marriage will be a quite secondary thing in his life: he will always be a slave so long as he works for Walter Burns and his paper.

In spite of so much of the action being confined to a single set Mr. Milestone has contrived to get outside often enough to create a sense of the life of a city rushing madly along providing "news." Of course it is a hectic life he pictures, drastically ignoring everything quiet and sane and normal, and he has done it at a reckless pace that gives the audience no time to reflect on what it is seeing. He has, and probably quite wisely, gone in for entertainment above everything—if he had handled his material with a solemn regard for its significance in American life the result would have been shocking and almost unbearable.

James Shelley Hamilton. *NBR*. April 1931, p. 15

Rain is the most interesting of the pictures prayerfully shipped eastward this month. Milestone has compressed Maxwell Anderson's neat version of Sadie Thompson's wrestling with that ole devil Davidson into a dignified, smooth picture. For the second time he has experimented with a rigid dramatic structure and, again, has expanded it enough with camera tricks and atmospheric scenes to allow an even photographic flavour.

He has concentrated his circuitous but steady action upon the long-harrassed Sadie, and Joan Crawford gives an amiable and shrewd characterization: a performance, in fact, which is not so much deep or tender as it is a facile demonstration of how to work before a camera. . . . It is an interesting, pleasant exhibition on the part of a skillful director and a very competent cast. . . . But we have had *Bride of the*

Lamb, Salvation, Revolt, Rape and many versions of *Rain* since Sadie first discovered that life was a quaint gift from some one; so no matter how good the job, the simple question remains: why do it at all?

Pare Lorentz. *Vanity Fair.* Nov. 1932, p. 58

An enormous amount of praise has been heaped on *All Quiet on the Western Front*—more, I suspect, for its obvious sincerity and emotional integrity than for its cinematic qualities. It is a very fine movie, but I am inclined to think it has been overestimated. There is much talk of the picture's realism, but I found the sets extremely artificial and the lighting very much in the overdramatic, glossy slick Hollywood manner. The French cottage had a property cow and a property cart posed in just the right place before it, the whole forming a composition reminiscent of a Royal Academy landscape. The daylit battle scenes were reeking with California sunlight (compare the grim gray tone of Russian war films), and the night tableaux were full of calcium star shells, melodramatic shadows, and fake moonlight. There were too many dugout scenes, and they were too full of confusion and squalor. Hollywood dugouts are always phony looking, anyway. Furthermore the film is monotonous. Milestone is said to have cut it from 18,000 to 12,000 feet, but another 2,000 feet could easily have been taken out. . . . Milestone's use of the close-up seemed to me excessive. His trick of showing five or six faces in rhythmical succession, while effective as a means of presenting the boy soldiers as a group of individuals, became an annoying mannerism. He has a way of shoving his camera into the face of the speaker—a trick he repeats in *The Front Page.* This gives a powerful drive to the spoken lines, but it gets tiresome. Also the lines aren't worth so much emphasis most of the time. [1933]

Dwight Macdonald. *D. M. on Movies*
(Prentice-Hall, 1969), pp. 102–3

The first few silent sequences of Mr. Lewis Milestone's *The General Died at Dawn* are as good as anything to be seen on the screen in London: the dead Chinese village with the kites circling down toward the corpses, the long pale grasses shivering aside as the troops trample through, The General with the scarred satisfied face riding away along the rough road in the slick American car. After that it becomes a melodrama, though a melodrama of more than usual skill, about an American with a social conscience (Mr. Clifford Odets has written the dialogue) who tries to run a beltful of gold through to Shanghai with which arms may be bought to overthrow the local war-lord. . . . If it were not for a rather ludicrous ending, this would be one of the best "thrillers" for some years. [1936]

Graham Greene. *G.G. on Film* (S&S, 1972), pp. 112–13

Now while the general excitement of picking the one, the ten, the how-many-hundred best pictures is still hot upon us, I wish to urge the case of the absolutely best negelected picture of two years, *The Captain Hates the Sea.* After having made it boldly, the film's producers (Columbia) lost heart very early, the rumor got around that it was a flop before the print arrived, the bookers booked half-heartedly, the exhibitors exhibited even less so, the press quite naturally assumed that nothing so modestly presented could be at all funny, and that was that. The best reports made it show so poorly that I never bothered with it until it was too old for review, over which I have been uneasy ever since and in expiation of which I hereby establish something like Malcolm Cowley's conscience fund for book reviewers. . . .

The people are natural, the situations they get into proceed naturally from them and from each other, and are carried out with an ease of direction that is as simple and right as the principle of cantilever, so that everything matches with the dominant mood of good temper, gentle mockery, droll high spirits, and edge. Practically everything, that is: there is in the picture's disfavor a queer confusion that shows from time to time, and strikes a particularly jarring note in the firing-squad business, the pitiful case of a man's having married below him and going practically crazy.

Well, it is past recalling now, or at least—in the event that neighborhood exhibitors could be persuaded to revive it sometime—it has gone underground. But in support of its right to a better life I submit that, after more than a year, I can recall with affection and recite to the extreme irritation of friends entire sequences, almost by the dozen, about the captain and the steward and the bird and the whiskers, the flatfoot, the smooth gentleman, the whiskey-sodas and pretty moll. [1936]

Otis Ferguson. *The Film Criticism of O.F.* (Temple, 1971), pp. 112, 114

. . . Lewis Milestone, director of *All Quiet on the Western Front*, was in the early days as potentially great as Eisenstein. Though he is today a highly successful commercial director, his apparent artistic decline has come about through cynicism and materialism. The giant has been fitted by the studio tailor.

Jim Tully. *Cinema Arts*. June 1937, p. 42

The film appeared at a time when sound was still new and film makers were groping for a correct application of the added element. It is to the credit of Milestone that he conceived *All Quiet on the Western Front* on a visual basis; he subordinated dialogue to the image and used sound effects simply, fluently and realistically. A flair for cutting that he was later to exploit more cunningly, was also apparent in the film, especially in the machine-gun episode. Here Milestone intercut moving shots (taken from a crane) of soldiers being shot down as they run across a field, with still shots of the machine gunners. The repetition of moving and still shots created a rhythmic visual pattern which, when combined with the rhythmic rat-tat-tat of the guns, made for an intensity of effect.

The vital theme and impressive technical range of the film overwhelmed critics of the day: contemporary movies were for the most part vapid in content and static in treatment. Not as great as many claimed it to be, *All Quiet on the Western Front* stands out as a noteworthy achievement in the roster of more serious Hollywood efforts.

Previously to this sound film, Milestone's picaresque *Two Arabian Knights* (1927–1928) and his bootlegging exposé *The Racket* (1928) had called attention to him as a competent and resourceful director with a penchant for acid, realistic touches and rowdy characterizations. All these qualities came to the fore in 1931 in his second sound film, the rapid-fire newspaper melodrama, *The Front Page*. This, like *All Quiet on the Western Front*, was one of the first talkies to recapture the spirit and movement of the silent film. So artfully paced was its dialogue, so swift were its cuts, that Harry Alan Potamkin declared [in *Vanity Fair*, March 1932] that with this film Milestone became "the second American director since Griffith to advance a major strategy." Exaggerated though the tribute was, it nevertheless indicated Milestone's directorial abilities. A robust film if not a great one, *The Front Page* excelled most of the talkies of its day by sheer treatment. The speedy delivery of lines and business and the reemphasis upon cutting as a prime structural element—dialogue is clipped, curt, direct, faster than normal, as are the players' gestures and movements—made the film a model of mobility for confused directors who did not know yet how to handle sound. [1939]

Lewis Jacobs. *The Rise of the American Film*
(Teachers College, 1968), pp. 488–89

There is some shrewd observation and invention in Mr. Steinbeck's opus, and this is quite evident in the movie, but, like so much popular fiction (and I include the more serious variety), it is the interpretation of the material in terms of concepts that invalidates the realism—or, since *Of Mice and Men* has so many realistic devices that, largely for cinematic reasons, succeed, perhaps I should say *spoils the reality.* The finally disastrous element of the movie is its effect of a "realistic" Frankenstein-monster in Lennie, the huge cretin. His normal pal, George, is at pains to reveal to society that he alone is responsible for saving Lennie from the authorities, and thus is as morally responsible for the girl's murder as Frankenstein's creator for the deeds of his monster. Why hedge? Lennie is George's *thing.* There is no other force that motivates the cretin other than a pitiful kind of animal intelligence; in Lennie, in fact, we get full-fledged just the ambiguity I mentioned above: a crossbreeding of the two antithetical schemes: man-animal and machine-human. In the movie, the ostensible truth is that George is a boon to Lennie, that he checks, soothes, and consoles him, as well as manages him; in short, that he is the civilizing force in the brute's nature.

Parker Tyler. *The Hollywood Hallucination*
(Creative Age, 1944), pp. 144–45

The fact that Milestone chose to make this picture represents the abandonment of earlier positions that found him along with many other disillusioned liberals in the pacifist camp. . . .

In the matter of form the comparison between *All Quiet* and *A Walk in the Sun* is equally striking. The earlier film was laid out on fairly conventional lines. Since it came early in the history of talking pictures mechanics were sometimes clumsy, photographic reproduction still crude in the light of today's sleek standards. At the same time the director's work was informed and enriched with pure cinema techniques which hung over from silent days but would soon be temporarily by-passed in the heat of experimentation with sound. Today, the cycle is rounding out. Dialogue and sound effects begin to be placed in proper prospective. The director's palette, instead of being constricted, is now immeasurably broadened by the addition of the new dimension. Lewis Milestone remains among the most knowledgeable and adept of Hollywood's directors, and in *A Walk in the Sun* he has fashioned an intricate web of words and pictures, mounted on a highly provocative time-scheme.

The story of how a platoon in the Texas Division landed at Salerno and made its way inland to take a farmhouse and destroy a strategic bridge is told in a series of alternate conversations and action sequences leading into tableaux. In this the director takes his cue from the novelist. . . . If the film has a major fault it is that the opening half bogs down in static literary patterns. The written words, stretched out in spoken dialogue, seem at once too many and too much the same.

Hermione R. Isaacs. *Theatre Arts*.
January 1946, pp. 45–46

It was not the aim of [*Pork Chop Hill*] to do the job of recording the battle. Milestone appears to have been intrigued by something to which Marshall makes only passing reference. The battle being fought was as bloody and as difficult as any in the Korean campaign. And dramatically, dialectically, it was the most absurd. Seventy miles away truce talks were in progress, which soon would decide where and when to end the war. The film brings these talks and the battle closer together in time. Although in fact three months passed before the Americans gave Pork Chop Hill back to the Chinese, "feeling it was no longer worth the price of a squad or a man," Milestone wished to make a sharper, more general point, than that made in the book, or in the film as it is now being seen. At present the film ends with Clemons leading his survivors down the hill in a series of long slow shots, through the subsiding smoke of battle, and we are reminded of the earlier stages when their direction had been up the hill against the enemy's guns. Over this is cast the voice of Clemons. "So Pork Chop Hill was held, bought, and paid for at the same price we commemorate in monuments at Bunker Hill and Gettysburg. Yet you will find no monuments on Pork Chop. Victory is a fragile thing and history does not linger long in our time. But those who fought there, know what they did . . . and the meaning of it. Millions live in freedom today because of what they did."

Quite apart from wondering what the third sentence means, we have no conviction at all that the *last* sentence has been proven. It seemed when I saw the film to have been tacked on as a last desperate attempt to give some final (and acceptably "patriotic") point to the undertaking. (In fact, it appears, it *was* added.) What the rest of the film has tried to say is that the hill was useful to both sides as a bargaining point in the truce talks, permitting whoever had it to speak from a position of comparative strength. But this is hardly saving millions from a fate worse than death.

Milestone wished to have an additional sequence, which would add to the irony of a more continued cross-reference between Panmunjom and the hill, not simply ending on the achievement of a band of men, but with the statement that their achievement in the end was not merely heroic. In this version, four days after the men walk down the hill, the truce talks would end. The hill is neutralized, given the status of a no man's land. Low fog and smoke blow across the deserted, abandoned battlefield. "The men who fought there know what they did, and the meaning of it."

This ending would have had very much more force than the existing one, and since the material which preceded it would have supported such a conclusion, it would have given point and substance to a film which for all its gritty, shell-shot realism lacks final conviction.

Colin Young. *Film Quarterly*. Fall 1959, pp. 12–13

After *All Quiet on the Western Front* Milestone directed films of various kinds and often had to submit to hard commercial necessities, but the great theme of war remained his predominant interest. . . . In each case it was a film stripped of the usual redundant rhetoric which, with rare exceptions, American films of this type were unable to avoid. Milestone's films, however, are characterized by a tone that sincerely tends toward reportage, even if on a practical level they had to compromise with the nationalistic goal that had determined their production.

Such compromises now appear more evident, for example in the film about the 1953 Korean War (*Pork Chop Hill*, 1959), that concludes with the usual off-screen voice saying that millions of men live in freedom today thanks to what American soldiers accomplished; in other words, it is not possible to misunderstand that the film is saying that war may not only be necessary but also sacrosanct, like those in which Americans fought "for the freedom of nations."

The fact that Milestone was, however, not convinced (and it would now be difficult for him to become so), at least inside himself, by Hollywood's bellicose ideology can be seen not only from a close general analysis of the film but also of the dialogue; American producers well knew that the public neither wanted to nor could make such analyses.

We remember that the "great" mission spoken of in the film has as its goal the conquest of a small hill which the assault commander, Lt. Joe Clemons—not excessively patriotic and lacking in excessive respect for his superiors who ordered the hill to be taken—calls a stinking heap.

We remember that the director insists in intercutting scenes of bloody battle with the scene in which the Chinese enemy use a loudspeaker to invite American soldiers to leave off the futile struggle. Among other things, the voice keeps saying: "We want peace, we want peace. Why do you want to die before you have begun to live?" In other forms we see here concepts about the uselessness and absurdity of war that we have already seen in *All Quiet on the Western Front*.

Lino Lionello Ghirardini. *Il cinema e la guerra* (Maccari, 1965), pp. 264–65

MINNELLI, VINCENTE (1902–)

The Clock did not please me, even if its story was simple, even if its action went from left to right, and from right to left. The emotion may have been honest, but the method was too rich for my eyes, and the writing as finally used on the screen too weak for my mind. I tasted again the hopeless mediocrity, the spiritual indolence of the thousand pictures I have reviewed.

A simple boy meets a simple girl, and they move through not so simple scenes, and simply nothing much happens all the time. The fault is with a man called Vincente Minnelli, who comes from Mr. Rockefeller's Radio City Hall—where he once a week thought up songs of sentimentality, chinchilla routines, colorful artilleries of naked legs—and filled a huge stage with more color and movement than is found in the entire French Revolution. A born bourgeois, I, no less than anyone, could swill myself to stupefaction on all this staged opulence.

Boldly and with great honesty, I'm sure, Mr. Minnelli has moved his box of tricks to Metro-Goldwyn-Mayer, and now given more space, more people, and more sets, he has buried a small story in a great clutter of production, so that his central characters find themselves in the position of the feeble, posed tenors that filled the stage (it goes up and down like a lift to Hell) of the Music Hall. It would take a Newtonian intellect to follow his camera angles. If there ever was a story, it dies in the cruel embrace of the production department; if there was any emotion in it that could have lived up to its huge sets it is drowned in a sea of extras and railroad terminals, and process shots to end all process shots. At first it is momentarily diverting—then your eyes become fixed in vacancy.

Stephen Longstreet. *The Screen Writer.*
Aug. 1945, pp. 9–10

The picture strives so hard to impress with its color harmonies and to sock the senses with its camera effects that those who are not hoggish about the sort of thing purveyed by *Ziegfeld Follies* run the risk of becoming a bit cloyed by the time the over-long film reaches its finale. Between opening and closing is packed a prodigious amount of material, some of which frankly is not deserving of the lavish treatment accorded it. The weight of the talent carries the film over some of its weaker moments. Time and again the picture depends upon the trouping of its performers to sustain audience interest.

Film Daily. Jan. 11, 1946, p. 6

Cabin In The Sky was excellent entertainment, and certainly gave some parts of prominence to a number of Hollywood's coloured actors. Nevertheless, like all exclusively Negro movies, it suffered from the same defects: complete unreality and relentless continuance of the stereotypes, such as the dice-throwing, razor-carrying, good-for-nothing, jazz-playing, gambling "darkies." It had a fair success, though not, of course, in the Southern States, where all films featuring coloured actors in any degree of prominence are subject to a virtual boycott. [1948]

Peter Noble. *The Negro in Films* (Kennikat, 1969), p. 201

[*The Bad and the Beautiful.*] This is a Hollywood story, set for the most part in the studios, bound up with the whole business of making pictures. Clever, sharply observed little scenes reflect the Hollywood surface: the egotistic babble at a party, the affectations of European directors, the sneak preview, the trying on of suits for cat-men in a B picture. If these sidelights sometimes appear conventionally romanticised or caricatured, they are none the less intriguingly staged. Less has been made of the central story. The part of Shields gives Kirk Douglas the chance for yet another display of dynamic, driving forcefulness, expertly presented. But the other characters are in effect dummies to be maneuvered into convenient situations. . . .

Minnelli's direction of a script which tries a little too hard for bright sophistication, with some lapses into glossy convention, is brilliantly assured, clever and ingenious. Paradoxically, this ingenuity, with the deliberate pursuit of effects, seems to impose rather too much strain on the material; a story already involved becomes fragmentary and superficial. The Hollywood picture entertains, there are some highly effective scenes, such as Georgia's hysterical drive after Shields has thrown her out, but in the long run the film leaves a curiously negative impression. For all the cleverness of the apparatus, it lacks a central point of focus.

BFI Bulletin. Feb. 1953, p. 18

Tea and Sympathy (MGM). Ever since its first appearance on Broadway, I have thought it a pity that Robert Anderson climaxed his drama about cruelty and prejudice in a boys' school with a sentimentalized adultery. The outrageous spectacle of the housemaster's wife (Deborah Kerr) giving herself, for the most selfless and highminded of motives, to the persecuted schoolboy (John Kerr) is likely to obscure the fact that the play says a great deal that is valid about the cruelty of the mob toward the non-typical individual, and also about the deplorable moral standards that are to be found in fashionable boys' schools.

Whatever my feelings about the matter, however, the adultery is still the main event in the film version. To achieve some sort of moral balance at the urgent request of the Production Code Administration, the whole story has been enclosed in a flashback which establishes 1) that the deed was wrong and 2) that it had serious consequences. (The flashback, incidentally, upsets the play's timetable and implies, for anyone who bothers to do a little simple mathematics, that the heroine's taste for younger men started with her deceased first husband.)

As a further concession to screen regulations, the false accusation which nearly ruins the boy's life has been softened from a charge of homosexuality to the more general charge of being a "sissy." Nevertheless, the most remarkable thing about the film is how little Mr. Anderson has changed, in adapting it for the screen, what was supposed to be hopeless material that the censors would never pass.

Moira Walsh. *America.* Oct. 27, 1956, p. 112

The film-maker, then, who would bring *Madame Bovary* to the screen must begin from the premise that, for him, Flaubert will split in two. One part the film-maker will find useful for visual mounting; the other he must inevitably discard. He will recognize that he may be discarding the most characteristic part of Flaubert himself—his language. He will recreate in his own style the verbal style which he reluctantly abandons. He will keep the officious voice of Flaubert off his sound track, and strive to refine himself out of his film as Flaubert strove to refine himself out of his book. He will alternate between seeing Emma in her environment and seeing the environment through Emma's eyes. He will mount his images, shot by shot, with at least as much care as Flaubert mounted his phrases. He will be prepared to suffer the same agony of composition in heightening pictorial values as Flaubert suffered in shaping his words. He will instill his presence into the frame, but only by his use of the camera, only by the way he handles his pieces of physical reality—the wedding table, the cigar case, the broken statuette, the withered bouquet. Treating it only as raw material, he will in a sense destroy his model and create thereby a new cinematic entity. In short, to criticize Vincente Minnelli's production of *Madame Bovary* is to write a new scenario.

George Bluestone. *Novels into Film*
(Johns Hopkins, 1957), p. 212

[Minnelli] quoted the following lines from Somerset Maugham to sum up his own attitude to film making: "I have been called cynical. I have been accused of making men out worse than they are. I do not think I have done this. All I have done is to bring into prominence certain traits that many writers shut their eyes to. I think that what has chiefly struck me in human beings is their lack of consistency. I have never seen people all of a piece. It has amazed me that the most incongruous traits should exist in the same person and for all that yield a plausible harmony." This attitude emerges more or less strongly in all Minnelli's films, most strikingly, perhaps, in *The Cobweb*. It is expressed in his flair for surreal and impressionist imagery and for throwing oblique rays of illumination upon the human panorama, such as the New York bar scene in *Brigadoon* or the Washington reception in *Undercurrent*, which momentarily reveal people caught unawares, as it were, by the passing camera.

In his work, Vincente Minnelli is an observer, an open-minded explorer, rather than a philosopher. He once said that art is shaped by popular opinion more than popular opinion is shaped by art. His own pictures certainly reveal his acute awareness of popular myth and idiom. He uses them for satire and comedy, for fantasy or serious portraiture and sometimes for poetic expression. For all his sophistication he has always preserved the common touch. It is combined with fastidious taste, love of elegance and an indefinable magical power to conjure forth haunting visions: he can cast a spell. Underlying these qualities are the warmth and humanism which distinguish *Cabin in the Sky*, *The Clock* and parts of *The Cobweb*, but which have had little place in the subjects of his other pictures.

Catherine de la Roche. *Vincente Minnelli*
(New Zealand Film Institute, 1959), p. 4

If a director's interests in the art of the film are identified with a particular genre, it is extremely difficult for critics to accept his experiments with other material. Vincente Minnelli's tendency to creatively indulge his curiosity about the special challenges of light comedy and drama has only brought taunts from his critical detractors, who are inclined to dismiss his failures with little insight into the most inescapable hazard of directing, either on stage or screen—the inept script. Minnelli is the only director in Hollywood at present who is not primarily devoted to the fashionably squalid school of cinema, and the worlds that his films create upon the screen are never completely real because they are always environments in which art is too omnipresent. Minnelli seems old-fashioned to the contemporary converts to neorealism, because he adheres to a belief that the foremost duty of the cinema is to astonish. . . . Besides such newcomers as Kubrick, Lumet, Delbert Mann, and Ritt, Minnelli's work often appears needlessly commercial. But none of these younger men would be interested in handling the subject matter of Minnelli's films unless they had control of the script. . . . No matter how labored the script, Minnelli's film images always suddenly burst into life at certain points, and one senses that his material ceases to interest him before and after these moments. To those who had discerned this same trait in the latest films of such directors as Renoir, Huston, Wyler, and Ford, it may be conjectured that the atmosphere of improvisation—of on-the-spot changes of business and characterizations preferred by these veteran film directors while shooting a film—may account for the peculiarly uneven quality of the completed film as a whole. Minnelli is equally inclined to prefer the spontaneous, unexpected revelation about some aspect of personality, or the visually striking image which may occur to him in the middle of his tasks, and besides, his flair for décor and costume arrangement has not diminished. The backgrounds in Minnelli's films always seem about to reveal a wall inscribed with "Vermeer was here"; he cannot leave life as it is—he is a rearranger of the out-of-place, as he sees it, in décor as well as in characterization: *intensifying* the commonplace is his forte.

Albert Johnson. *Film Quartely*. Spring 1959, pp. 32–33

[*Four Horsemen of the Apocalypse*.] It is forty years since the Four Horsemen rode out of the storms across a Europe prostrate from war, famine, and disease, Conquest on his white horse, War a horseman in flames, Pestilence on a black charger, Death riding on the pale horse. The earlier film was probably Rex Ingram's most distinguished work in the cinema, the pronounced pictorialism which later degenerated into a mere prettiness was here at its most controlled and concise; now another director renowned for his pictorial flair, but one with a stronger and richer imagination than Ingram, has reworked the theme. Minnelli still uses the elaborate pictorial symbolism of the four horsemen riding through the clouds—rather more frequently, if I remember, than Ingram did—but this refurbishing and updating can hardly be numbered amongst its distinguished director's major successes, at best a half-success, but a half-success which gives a great deal of pleasure. . . .

No one knows better than Minnelli that each film has its own style and mood. "It is our search for these," he once said, "that is one of our most exciting tasks and the key to what results we may achieve." Ibanez' torrent of rhetorical prose is matched by Minnelli's superb rhetorical pictorialism—his groupings, use of colour, elaboration of decor in the dramatic scenes, with the superb sweep and evocative power of the crowd scenes, carry the eye effortlessly through this frenzied panorama of the years 1938–44, often using the colour to unify the loose construction of the screenplay.

Richard Whitehall. *Films and Filming*. May 1962, p. 32

For Minnelli, the cinema is a mirror game that definitively established his universe: one in which appearance (image, film) is the only possible reality. The cinema consecrates the life of Art, since for Minnelli life is the cinema and the cinema is life. "The artist lives as he creates," he lives by his creations and not by himself. The passage from illusion (decors, film) to reality is constant, the game provokes a transfer between reality and the imaginary, pulling the spectator into a potential reflection that must in the final analysis be considered as the only truth. The characters are possessed, bewitched by their art, just as Kirk Douglas lives for his films in *The Bad and the Beautiful* and *Two Weeks in Another Town*: a tyrannical producer or actor he finishes a great director's film; he has the faith that permits him to live entirely in his art. Kirk Douglas, in these two films (and in *Van Gogh*) represents the first aspect of the Minnelli character, *active*, one that constructs his world by crushing others or making use of them to attain his goals. Douglas, Robert Mitchum, Frank Sinatra, concretize their dreams and impose them. The second aspect of the Minnelli character is *contemplative*. Examples are Glenn Ford, Richard Burton, Gene Kelly (and all the musical comedy characters). They regard the world as aesthetes do and contemplate the beauty and spectacle of life.

François Truchaud. *Vincente Minnelli* (Editions Universitaires, 1966), pp. 146–47

Yet perhaps the saddest thing about the film [*On a Clear Day You Can See Forever*] is Yves Montand in his first English-singing role. Montand was once a singer but never a linguist, and he performs here as one who has forgotten singing and not yet learned English. Vincente Minnelli, the *auteur* critics to the contrary notwithstanding, was always a mediocre director with some flair for tear-jerking, as in *The Clock*; his alleged talent for directing film musicals never registered on me. In the present case, only one musical number, "Come Back to Me," can be said to come off, but only at the cost of desperate trickery. Thus, to put Dr. Chabot not into his office but on top of the Pan Am building when he is trying to will Daisy back to his experiments and his arms, means preferring visual flashiness to emotional validity. As for the film's last hope, the legendary Cecil Beaton's costumes, I can only quote an actor friend: "Even poor Cecil was asleep at the swatch."

John Simon. *Movies into Film* (Dial, 1971), p. 335

In *Meet Me in St Louis* we can for the first time see Minnelli's talents whole, or nearly whole (there is still almost no real dance for him to cope with). And it is here that we begin to appreciate the secret of his special way with musicals. It is that while phenomenally sensitive to music (he is a pianist himself) and to the subtlest variations of pacing and rhythm within a scene, a movement, and possessed of a great visual flair, the consequence no doubt of his having begun his professional life as a painter and designer, he is fundamentally a *dramatic* director. *Meet Me in St Louis* is conceived and directed as a coherent drama, a story about believable people in a believable situation. The musical episodes are all judged from the outset according to their power to advance the story, epitomize a situation, intensify a mood; they all have to have their dramatic *raison d'être*.

But music and choreographed movement are not confined to the obviously musical episodes, the outbursts of sheer *joie de vivre* like the "Trolley song" or the moments of intense introspection like "Have yourself a merry little Christmas," music and drama interpenetrate each other. The sequence in which the youngest daughter, Tootie (Margaret O'Brien), is dared into playing a Hallow-e'en joke on a frightening neighbour, scared out of her wits but too inflexibly proud to admit it, is handled with choreographic precision as the camera tracks away in front of her, holding her face in centre frame as she leaves the light and warmth of the bonfire for the menacing, dangerous dark. And the principal dance episode, the cakewalk Esther (Judy Garland) and Tootie dance for their family to "Under the bamboo tree," is given just the right fragile charm by Minnelli and his choreographer Charles Walters. The collaboration, under Arthur Freed's watchful eye, is incomparable in other respects, the casting down to the smallest roles is just right, and how beautifully the scene of father and mother (Leon Ames and Mary Astor) singing "You and I" at the piano catches the required Victorian familial warmth and intimacy—not only because of the performances, but because of the impeccable re-creation by designers Lemuel Ayers and Jack Martin Smith of a turn-of-the-century middle-class domestic environment. *Meet Me in St Louis* is one of those films where just everything goes right, seemingly effortlessly, by chance. But chance, one may guess, like goodness, had nothing to do with it.

John Russell Taylor and Arthur Jackson.
The Hollywood Musical (McGraw-Hill,
1971), p. 82

Tea and Sympathy is strictly for those sentimentalists instantly persuaded by the fable that unusual sensitivity in a schoolboy, existing in a total society of young brutes, gets him falsely branded as a homosexual. Even as a dated myth, the thing is questionable. The young hero's consequent agony and the way it is soothed by tea and sympathy (administered by Deborah Kerr as the headmaster's wife) was mounted for the screen as if it were a precious objet-d'art in danger from rioting but miraculously saved. Besides being archaic, the film is a prodigiously silly fable, pulling the realities with which it deals dishonestly, systematically out of whack. For all that I and those on the set know—or for that matter, that the author knows—the persecuted youth is really heterosexual and his victimization by his schoolmates and his headmaster is a simple outrage. Of course, it would be just as much an outrage if he *were* the "sister boy" the others call him—but the last is a point, presumably, that occurs to nobody.

As always in works so superficially contrived, it is not an individual or an idea that is libeled in *Tea and Sympathy*, but reality itself. One is saddened to think so, but it seems most unlikely that the play or the film would have attained its passing eminence had there not been a ready-made public of unthinking observers to react to it. The chief stupidity involved is that the homosexuality of the occasion, far from being the archaic sister-boy myth, is the sadism of the schoolboy rabble that tears off the distraught youth's pajamas during a "bonfire ritual." A good-looking young actor named John Kerr adequately plays the part of the victim as a fleeing, toothsomely fleshed he-virgin altogether worthy of the statutory ambisexed sadism of the schoolboys. What is an old-fashioned academic institution, in other words, is made to appear in *Tea and Sympathy* as a baseless "criminal conspiracy."

Parker Tyler. *Screening the Sexes*
(Holt, 1972), pp. 249–50

MURNAU, F. W. (1889–1931)

Sunrise was adapted from Hermann Sudermann's story *A Trip to Tilsit,* and although Tilsit is actually a town in East Prussia, it is set forth in one of the very few subtitles that the locale of this story might be in any country. As it threads its way across the screen this narrative gathers impetus. It is filled with intense feeling and in it is embodied an underlying subtlety. Mr. Murnau shows himself to be an artist in camera studies, bringing forth marvelous results from lights, shadows and settings. He also proves himself to be a true story teller, and, incidentally, here is a narrative wherein the happy ending is welcome. . . .

In a remarkable series of scenes one is taken through the city on a tram car, and then follows the adventures in an amusement park, in which a straying pig affords some of the comedy. Mr. Murnau does all his work quite differently from any other and when he stoops to somewhat hilarious fun it does not matter, for it is filmed with astuteness and originality.

In an early chapter there are a flood of flashes concerned with people going on a holiday, and you perceive a steamboat's nose shot up mystically on the sands of the seashore. To show the city, an immense set was constructed, and on it there were two surface-car lines and countless vehicles. You perceive a whirling disk and then this gradually dissolves into the joyous sight of the amusement park.

Mr. Murnau uses a moon, and he evidently likes its reflection on the water. He fashions a storm on a lake, and keeps the spectators on the edge of their seats until the finale of the production. He makes you hope that the characters won't do such a thing, and you trust that the Man and his Wife will get back safely to their picturesque little farmhouse.

This picture is exotic in many ways for it is a mixture of Russian gloom and Berlin brightness.

Mordaunt Hall. *NYT*. Sept. 24, 1927, p. 15

Not since the earliest, simplest moving pictures, when locomotives, fire-engines, and crowds in streets were transposed to the screen artlessly and endearingly, when the entranced eye was rushed through tunnels and over precipices on runaway trains, has there been such joy in motion as under Murnau's direction [in *Sunrise*]. He slaps down the cramping cubes of sets and makes, whenever possible, walls of glass and steel that imprison in their clear geometry the intersection of long smooth lines of traffic, people walking, trains gathering speed. When the rare shot shows human gesture against a static background, the stillness is an accent, after the rush of a full and moving screen. He knows every complication and subtlety of his method—his people walk over uneven rather than level ground, along paths always devious. The earth has mist over it, and breath comes visibly from nostrils. Distortion he uses but rarely, and then only as the object naturally might be distorted against the eye. . . .

The last half of the picture moves more heavily. It has less freshness and more obvious invention. The episodes of the photographer's studio and the barber's shop are ordinary in conception and detail. Fortunately, however, here the emphasis is laid upon the young peasant couple, and the energy and youth of George O'Brien and Janet Gaynor make even the duller moments come alive. Muranu's imagination is whetted by speed and confusion; his camera should always be taxed to its capacity. His real power comes through when, at the end of their day, the young pair are set against every conceivable effect of light on darkness. Rockets leap upward; bonfires burn on the water's edge; there is monstrous lightning; and, at the last, a crowd of lanterns is held up over the still black water. Night and storm revolve behind the frightened man and woman, and the picture springs back to an intensity hardly to be believed.

Louise Bogan. *The New Republic.* Oct. 26, 1927, p. 263

A song of two humans. Heads or hearts? Neither—hands made this. It is very elaborate. There is no psychology, no insight, nothing we have been waiting for. The technique—Oh, damn technique. London twitters because a picture had been made perfectly using the medium. "At last." But at last belongs to them, there have been plenty, in the days when we were trying to get room for the movies in columns devoted to repertory theatres, hunt balls, and motoring notes. *Sunrise* tries very hard and succeeds in providing A Happy Hour For Housemaids. Which is all to the good and it is good of Mr. Fox to spend so much on them. It may accustom housemaids, among whom mentally are most of those who employ them, to the films' particular methods: but the films' material it does not give them. The cinema should be the means of this age to express what this age feels and there is nothing of this age in *Sunrise*. *Sunrise* takes us back and makes us unlearn. It is pre-Morris and mock-Morris. The point is that literature did its job very well and the cinema is not doing its own by repeating the process. There is a great deal to be unloosed here, in each of us, and we wait and wait and sometimes a film comes along, and sometimes *Sunrise*. Trying as it sets out to do to be of no place and every place, of all time and no time, it succeeds quite elaborately in repeating the superficialities of every age whilst giving expression to none of the complexities of this.

Robert Herring. *Close Up.* March 1928, pp. 44–45

The Four Devils, directed by Murnau is *Variety*, swiped, denatured and lollypopped. The grim strength of *Variety* is turned to Hollywood mush. The leading characters are prettified and as barren of character as a *Saturday Evening Post* cover. Let's not talk about the story—or any more about this picture. It's soothing syrup.

New Masses. Jan. 1929, p. 15

Sunrise throughout was built by moods. Lighting, pace, the carriage and movement of actors, and the camera were all applied to create the dominant mood of each sequence. The opening sequence of multiple exposures presented holiday excitement in terms that were, in that day, fresh and dazzling. Trains and steamboats loomed up and disappeared in flashes, suggesting the journeys being taken by the many vacationists. In sharp contrast was the quiet sensuality of the seduction scene. The overhanging mists, the dew, the full moon, the sinuous and constant movement of the camera—all combined to create a dark, somnolent mood. Again, the trolley car bumping along through the countryside into the city expressed vividly the high excitement of the two frightened country people riding on it. The amusement-park sequence was another instance of glittering dissolves and "gliding" cameras that reproduced all the color and feeling of the place.

Cinematic skill was further revealed in the editing. Details were combined to communicate an idea, an action, a sound. For example, at one point we see a huge shot of a horn and then a large close-up of a woman shouting through cupped hands; thus the effect of a sound is given. This was expressive of Murnau's conviction—he was a staunch advocate of titleless and silent films—that symbols are the best means of obviating the need of literary devices. This synthesis of all factors to create a particular mood for a scene or a sequence imbued *Sunrise* with a psychological intensity and a rare style. [1939]

Lewis Jacobs. *The Rise of the American Film*
(Teachers College, 1968), p. 363

Thus far we have put forward the view that expressionism of montage and image constitute the essence of cinema. And it is precisely on this generally accepted notion that directors from silent days, such as Erich von Stroheim, F. W. Murnau, and Robert Flaherty, have by implication cast a doubt. In their films, montage plays no part, unless it be the negative one of inevitable elimination where reality superabounds. The camera cannot see everything at once but it makes sure not to lose any part of what it chooses to see. . . .

Murnau is interested not so much in times as in the reality of dramatic space. Montage plays no more of a decisive part in *Nosferatu* than in *Sunrise*. One might be inclined to think that the plastics of his image are impressionistic. But this would be a superficial view. The composition of his image is in no sense pictorial. It adds nothing to the reality, it does not deform it, it forces it to reveal its structural depth, to bring out the preexisting relations which become constitutive of the drama. For example, in *Tabu*, the arrival of a ship from left screen gives an immediate sense of destiny at work so that Murnau has no need to cheat in any way on the uncompromising realism of a film whose settings are completely natural. [1958–1965]

André Bazin. *What Is Cinema?* (California,
1967), pp. 26–27

We must consider *Tabu* an American film in that it was financed by and released by an American company, Paramount. But in that it had no stars (American or otherwise) and was the work of one man, Murnau (assisted by that fine American cameraman, Floyd Crosby), it could with some justification, also be considered a German film. But whatever its nationality . . . *Tabu* was undoubtedly the greatest poetic-documentary that the American cinema ever produced, certainly a finer film even than *Nanook of the North*, which takes its place as the leader of the realist-documentary school.

Tabu, which started as a simple picturization of the life of Polynesians, somewhat on the order of Flaherty's *Moana*, was transformed into something quite different when Murnau took over the reins. There was documentary coverage of South Sea life and customs; there were the expected vistas of palm trees and rolling surf, but these were merely the backgrounds to a story as mystical as Murnau's old German fantasies . . . Murnau imbued it all with his own particular poetry and that romantic fatalism so beloved of German directors after World War I.

Joe Franklin. *Classics of the Silent Screen*
(Citadel, 1959), pp. 116–17

NICHOLS, MIKE (1931–)

First things first. The most pressing question—since we already know a great deal about the play and the two stars [of *Who's Afraid of Virginia Woolf?*]—is the direction. Mike Nichols, after a brilliant and too-brief career as a satirist, proved to be a brilliant theatrical director of comedy. This is his debut as a film director, and it is a successful Houdini feat.

Houdini, you remember, was the magician who was chained hand and foot, bound in a sack, dumped in a river, and then appeared some minutes later on the surface. You do not expect Olympic swimming form in a Houdini; the triumph is just to come out alive.

Which Mr. Nichols has done. He was given two world-shaking stars, the play of the decade and the auspices of a large looming studio. What more inhibiting conditions could be imagined for a first film, if the director is a man of talent? But Mr. Nichols has at least survived. The form is not Olympic, but he lives.

Any transference of a good play to film is a battle. (Which is why the best film directors rarely deal with good plays.) The better the play, the harder it struggles against leaving its natural habitat, and Mr. Albee's extraordinary comedy-drama has put up a stiff fight.

Ernest Lehman, the screen adapter, has broken the play out of its one living-room setting into various rooms in the house and onto the lawn, which the play accepts well enough. He has also placed one scene in a roadhouse which is a patently forced move for visual variety. These changes and some minor cuts, including a little inconsequential blue-penciling, are about the sum of his efforts. The real job of "filmizing" was left to the director.

With no possible chance to cut loose cinematically (as, for example, Richard Lester did in his film of the stage comedy *The Knack*), Mr. Nichols has made the most of two elements that were left to him—intimacy and acting.

He has gone to school to several film masters (Kurosawa among them, I would guess) in the skills of keeping the camera close, indecently prying; giving us a sense of his characters' very breath; tracking a face—in the rhythm of the scene—as the actor moves, to take us to other faces; punctuating with sudden withdrawals to give us a brief, almost dispassionate respite; then plunging us in close again to one or two faces, for lots of pores and bile.

There is not much that is original in Mr. Nichols's camerawork, no sense of the personality that we got in his stage direction. In fact, the direction is weakest when he gets a bit arty: electric signs flashing behind heads or tilted shots from below to show passion and abandon (both of them hallmarks of the college cinema virtuouso). But he has minimized the "stage" feeling, and he has given the film an insistent presence, good phrasing and a nervous drive. It sags toward the end, but this is because the third act of the play sags.

Stanley Kauffmann. *NYT*. June 30, 1966, p. 28

The emotional elevation of the film [*The Graduate*] is due in no small measure to the extraordinarily engaging performances of Anne Bancroft as the wife-mother-mistress, Dustin Hoffman as the lumbering Lancelot, and Katharine Ross as his fair Elaine. Nichols is at his best in getting new readings out of old lines and thus lightening potentially heavy scenes. The director is at his worst when the eclecticism of his visual style gets out of hand. The opening sequence of bobbing, tracking, lurching heads in nightmarishly mobile close-ups looks like an "hommage" to Fellini's *8½*. A rain-drenched Anne Bancroft splattered against a starkly white wall evokes images in *La Notte*. The languorous lyricism of Ben at Berkeley seems derivative of Varda's *Le Bonheur* and even some of John Korty's landscape work in the same region. Unfortunately, the cultural climate is such that the intelligent prose cinema of Mike Nichols tries to become the intellectual-poetic cinema of Michelangelo Nichols. Still, I was with *The Graduate* all the way because I responded fully to its romantic feelings, and my afterthoughts are even kinder to a movie that, unlike *Morgan*, didn't cop out in the name of "sanity." [1967]

Andrew Sarris. *Confessions of a Cultist* (S&S, 1970), p. 327

The roaring success of Mike Nichols' *The Graduate* is hardly surprising —he has built it on the dependable formula of Restoration comedy. I would not raise hopes too high: this Way of the Affluent World, to a script by Calder Willingham and Buck Henry, is consistently funny and frequently ironic, but it quite lacks the aphoristic wit of Sheridan or Congreve, and as it wears on it forsakes cynicism for chase and begins to resemble more Harold Lloyd than Mayfair dandy. Still, the spice of the piece, the source of its tension and laughter, is the confrontation of jaded maturity with the demanding innocence of youth. "Never trust anyone over 30" is a slogan that could have served the Restoration as well as it does our own time, and Nichols makes the old formula seem as topical as mini-skirts. Youth wins because its nerves are stronger and its needs simpler; it is not really a moral victory, but it serves that purpose.

If Nichols grasps but cannot hold the style of his model, it is because his older actors let him down. Dustin Hoffman has the right manner as the highly moral and readily seducible Graduate; he is at once gauche, disconcertingly direct and well armed by incredulity against the ploys of his elders. And Katherine Ross, as his destined sweetheart, is properly flouncy in a somewhat dim-witted righteousness. But Anne Bancroft, the seductress, invests a little too heavily in her lechery, and in general the attendant parents, spouses and family friends put too much heartfelt venom into what is essentially a masque of animal spirits. As a result, the film keeps threatening to turn the corner from Belgrave Square into Peyton Place.

Of course, I may be saddling Mr. Nichols with my own concept of his purpose; it is quite possible that he gave no thought at all to the 18th century and had in view no more than a cautionary tale for the 1960s. In that case, though, it is odd that his picture is so much more effective when it is outrageous than when it is outraged.

Robert Hatch. *Nation*. Jan. 15, 1968, p. 94

Catch-22. Mike Nichols's movie version of the novel is, in tone, as hot and heavy as the original was cool and light. Indeed, I think it fair to say that he and writer Buck Henry have mislaid every bit of humor that made the novel not only emotionally bearable but aesthetically memorable, replacing it with desperately earnest proof that they hate war. Part of their adaptive failure was probably inevitable. So much of the book's effectiveness stemmed from the rich matrix of relationships between its characters, the wide, in fact endless, range of their responses to the situation they shared. In the compressive process of screen adaptation a good deal was bound to be lost. Even so, these movie people seem to me only the ghosts of their former selves, more evidence of Nichols's desire to conspicuously consume acting talent than of a gift for skillfully employing it in larger numbers than he has heretofore attempted.

But the key to the film's almost total failure lies in its restructuring of the novel. It is shot as if it were a single hallucinatory flashback suffered by Yossarian, Heller's Everyman-turned-Bombardier. This gives Nicholas several advantages. It conveniently focuses a sprawling book in which Yossarian, though central, was not really dominant. It allows him to jumble the time sequence, which in practical terms allows a director to throw in shockers—a nude here, a gush of blood there, a slight gag anywhere at all—whenever the pace lags. It also allows him to mix style with some impunity—a bit of Bergman, a little filch from Fellini, some mocking references to the epic manner of our old war movies, a lot of theatrical expressionism, just plain pretty shooting when all else fails. It also excuses the lack of depth in all the characters that swim through his bad dream; after all, a man hallucinating doesn't see people in novelistic dimensions, does he? [7/3/70]

Richard Schickel. *Second Sight* (S&S, 1972), p. 310

Joseph Heller achieved an extraordinary tension between horror and farce. The film is too often heavy-handed. Take the elaborate over-emphasis in the chaplain's reaction to Colonel Catheart on the toilet, for example; or the ponderous irony of a scene where two characters, walking a landing strip and discussing a business deal, remain oblivious to the plane skidding by them and exploding into flames. The movie *Catch-22* lacks the poise and control necessary to walk its high wire.

This may derive in part from the difficulty of compressing a long, perhaps overlong, novel, with a complex structure and a mob of characters, into a two-hour movie. The screenplay skims so many episodes so quickly that the dramatis personae are, in many cases, inadequately established and the pattern of the film is hard to follow. Among the actors, Alan Arkin seems an unduly passive and even somnambulistic Yossarian. Perhaps Anthony Perkins as the chaplain and Orson Wells as General Dreedle come off best; but the kaleidoscopic style of the film makes it hard to judge performance.

Can one's disappointment come from having expected too much? Certainly the film has its lovely moments, both visually (a squadron of planes taking off in a shimmering dawn) and dramatically (Yossarian in the hospital). But I can not resist the feeling that a much less pretentious, polished, and worked-up film—I mean, of course, *M*A*S*H*—comes closer to catching the gay and savage anarchy of Joseph Heller's novel.

Arthur Schlesinger, Jr. *Vogue*. Aug. 1970, p. 40

As the film's [*Carnal Knowledge*] director, Mike Nichols accepts Feiffer's characters on Feiffer's terms, which sometimes means miming the way the cartoons present characters. More than once in the film, abrupt editing brings us face to face with a character who is talking about himself and, it seems, talking to no one in particular—a character who fills the screen the way the line-drawn figure fills the cartoon frame. But this time Feiffer has tried to break through the isolation of his characters. To make his cerebral humor dramatic, he's tried to put his characters in touch with each other and, thus, with the audience.

Nichols has done his best to help out too, although the attempt is doomed. Among the close-ups of deadpan monologues, for instance, Nichols slips in one where Miss Bergen giggles uncontrollably. Acting for the moment without self-consciousness, she becomes that antithesis of a Feiffer character which Feiffer himself seems to have hoped for. But Nichols has had to improvise this vignette outside the confines of the script. Only in one or two clashes between Jonathan and Bobbie (Ann-Margret), the "Ballbuster" of record, does Nichols get from the script the humanity Feiffer wanted to put in it.

Of course it isn't Feiffer who's selling tickets to this film. It's Nichols. He's the only American director getting his name above the title on the marquee these days. He's even described as an Orson Welles who's made it commercially. Yet Nichols' films still don't have the one thing Welles' did right from the start: a style of their own. Publicity has made the Nichols name readily identifiable, while his films remain, if not anonymous, at least non-descript and eclectic. I assume Feiffer would praise Nichols as profusely as Edward Albee and Joseph Heller did when Nichols directed their material. But being congratulated by the writer isn't the highest accolade a director can receive. Nichols' most serious limitation so far is that he's too much of a writer's director. His work has acquired a chameleon quality, always hiding against the background of the script.

Colin Westerbeck, Jr. *Commonweal.*
Sept. 3, 1971, p. 453

Carnal Knowledge gives us games, anxieties, hypocrisy, perversions, and traumas; it revolves around sex, but avoids a presentation of true sexuality. Instead, it is concerned with the politics of sex, the manipulations by arid, sterilized people of their imaginary wantonness. As in *The Graduate*, Mike Nichols is able to squeeze quite a few laughs from the mechanics of sexual jockeying, observed dispassionately. Nichols, and scenarist Jules Feiffer, both possess that cold sentimentality of the innocent who has learned how to market and mock his own naïveté. They idealize the sexual huckster and pragmatist at the same time that they are, apparently, tearing him down. But he is their first love, this robot Don Juan; and like all masturbating idealists, they are faithful to the end. . . .

Nichols is a brilliant director of actors. The seduction scenes in *The Graduate* have some of the mordant high style of *Bringing up Baby*; and some of its lucid precision. But Nichols works in a highly limited and stylized mode in which, unlike Hawks, he seems to take little joy. Like many another "theatrical" director—Cukor, Welles, Ophuls, Bergman—he usually keeps his characters in the same frame and rarely resorts to a cut. Occasionally, this is used to devastating effect: the first scene of the film, Sandy picking up Susan at a fraternity mixer, is done in a pair of shots that are as smooth and exact and locked together as greased cogs. Occasionally, he does it to oppress the audience. *Carnal Knowledge* is basically a horror film without suspense. [1972]

Mike Wilmington. *The Velvet Light Trap*.
No. 6, pp. 31–32

PENN, ARTHUR (1922–)

Mickey One, in Arthur Penn's film of that name, is K from Hamtramck—a young stand-up comic of Polish extraction on the run from a trial to which he has not been summoned, for a crime at which he can only guess, presided over by judges he cannot identify. Is it real or in his mind? Given the flare and cut, wipe and jump style of slightly portentous photography, I believe we are meant to understand that, as for him, it may be largely in his mind, but for the rest of us it is real enough. Mickey is on the lam from the gangsters who hunt us all for the sins we forget having committed. And at the end comes an apocalyptic moment when, it seems, K at last meets Godot.

This is a very heady metaphysics that Penn has framed in slightly quaint Prohibition-era gangland. . . . His camera work and editing have a slapdash energy that is invigorating. I enjoyed watching it—enjoyed particularly Beatty being as emotionally hair-trigger as Marlon Brando, and Hatfield engaging with Jeff Corey (who plays his partner) in fragments of Ionesco absurdity. Afterwards, though, *Mickey One* seemed to me less an organized creation than a quick run through of all the "in" devices of contemporary letters—the idea being that if you spin enough of them, and make it fast and noisy, *something* is bound to happen.

The picture sums itself up in a night scene wherein a mad artisan cavorts in front of a huge outdoor mobile that is engaged in destroying itself, to the delight of its creator and an attending crowd, when the process of pyrotechnic entropy is interrupted by the arrival of an indignant fire department. If this means that Penn sees himself as firing off in all directions for the innocent pleasure of lighting up the sky, it is a disarming admission. It would have been still more disarming if he had found a way to give Jean Tinguely credit for the self-immolating mobile, and had otherwise acknowledged that he was making sport with a vaudeville of borrowed ideas and techniques.

Robert Hatch. *Nation*. Oct. 18, 1965, p. 259

The film makers recently released a trio of films that looked without much success *Inside Daisy Clover* and at other Hollywood folk and folkways in *The Oscar* and *Lord Love a Duck*. Now they're looking inside Americans and some international characters here and abroad. What they find in a Texas town in *The Chase* is no better than what they found in Hollywood. . . .

The Texas town, which should have been called Gomorrah, is boiling over with adultery, alcoholism, intolerance, greed, violence, and various other illnesses and evils—all soundly railed at by the local religious fanatic. Since she's a nut, the citizens pay her no heed but go their merry way—with orgies, beatings (during the worst of which they almost kill the sheriff, who is determined to save the convict) and an utterly senseless, viciously portrayed lynching bee. Considering all the talent connected with *The Chase*, it is hard to figure out how the film went so haywire. Director Arthur Penn, who has *The Miracle Worker* and *Mickey One* among his credits, allowed everything to be overdone. Even the good performances by Marlon Brando, as a fair-minded, *High Noon* kind of sheriff, Angie Dickinson as his wife, Robert Redford as the convict, and E. G. Marshall, Janice Rule, James Fox, Jane Fonda, among the sinners, cannot save *The Chase*. Hardest of all to figure out is what a first-rate producer like Sam Spiegel was trying to do in this ill-considered extravaganza.

Philip T. Hartung. *Commonweal*.
April 1, 1966, p. 55

During the first part of the picture, a woman in my row was gleefully assuring her companions, "It's a comedy. It's a comedy." After a while, she didn't say anything. Instead of the movie spoof, which tells the audience that it doesn't need to feel or care, that it's all just in fun, that "we were only kidding," *Bonnie and Clyde* disrupts us with "And you thought we were only kidding."

. . . Penn is a remarkable director when he has something to work with. His most interesting previous work was in his first film, *The Left Handed Gun* (and a few bits of *The Miracle Worker*, a good movie version of the William Gibson play, which he had also directed on the stage and on television). *The Left Handed Gun*, with Paul Newman as an ignorant Billy the Kid in the sex-starved, male-dominated Old West, has the same kind of violent, legendary, nostalgic material as *Bonnie and Clyde*; its script, a rather startling one, was adapted by Leslie Stevens from a Gore Vidal television play. In interviews, Penn makes high, dull sounds—more like a politician than a movie director. But he has a gift for violence, and, despite all the violence in movies, a gift for it is rare. (Eisenstein had it, and Dovzhenko, and Buñuel, but not many others.) There are few memorable violent moments in American movies, but there is one in Penn's first film: Billy's shotgun blasts a man right out of one of his boots; the man falls in the street, but his boot remains upright; a little girl's giggle at the boot is interrupted by her mother's slapping her. The mother's slap—

the seal of the awareness of horror—says that even children must learn that some things that look funny are not only funny. That slap, saying that only idiots would laugh at pain and death, that a child must develop sensibility, is the same slap that *Bonnie and Clyde* delivers to the woman saying "It's a comedy." In *The Left Handed Gun*, the slap is itself funny, and yet we suck in our breath; we do not dare to laugh. [1967]

Pauline Kael. *Kiss Kiss Bang Bang* (Little, Brown, 1968), pp. 49, 60

There is much in *Bonnie and Clyde* which one can legitimately praise. Director Arthur Penn has caught, without seeming to strain, the aridity and emptiness of the countryside through which Bonnie, Clyde and the rest of their addled and unbright mob rattled at dangerous speeds in a succession of comically antique stolen cars to pull their undistinguished jobs, and in the process he has created an arresting visual equivalent of their blank, bleak inner lives. . . .

What emerges from these good aspects of the film is a comment on the quality of some American lives. Bonnie and Clyde are the products of the rootlessness and aimlessness of morally and intellectually ill-educated youth responding to the problem of growing up absurd in a period of historical transition (the parallel between the middle 1930s and the middle 1960s obviously never being far from the minds of the movie's creators). They, like so many youths today, seek and fail to find fulfillment in momentary thrills and momentary notoriety; and by stressing the ordinariness of the landscape and society that nurtured them, by making them comical rubes instead of glamorous jet-setters, the writers and director often manage to hit us more stingingly where we live than others who have attempted to make an essentially similar—indeed, familiar—message.

What, then, is responsible for the vague feeling of dissatisfaction with which the film leaves one? Partly it is the thumping emphasis on period costume, décor and music. It is all awfully cute and cutely awful, and it surely enhances the movie's appeal to those who seek only idle entertainment when they venture forth to the local Bijou. But it irreparably dulls the film's cutting edge; what might have been a purgingly savage satire on a watershed period in American life all too often degenerates into an arch, trivializing attempt to get us to giggle-along with the gang. [1967]

Richard Schickel. *Second Sight* (S&S, 1972), pp. 141–42

Mickey One, an exceptional film because it dares to bring innovation and experimentalism into the Establishment of Hollywood finances, is not a flawless one, but it deserves the support of all who care about the future of new ideas and approaches in American motion pictures. It is hoped that Penn and his associates are not discouraged by what has happened to *Mickey One* so far, because as it is seen more often by the audience it deserves, it will be discussed, remembered, and respected.

Alan Surgal's script has some of the patterns of classical Greek tragedy within it, but these are steadfastly remolded into a modern setting (Chicago), and the nameless young hero (Warren Beatty) is a successful nightclub comedian. The traditional fall in status and flight from retribution are recognizable influences in the film, but unlike the Greek heroes, the comedian neither knows the nature of his transgression, nor the identity of his pursuers. There are other imaginative borrowings: from the literature of Kafka, Ionesco, and Beckett; from the cinematic nighttowns of every American gangster-film ever made; the carnival art of George Grosz and Paul Cadmus; the sculpture of Tingueley; the comic artistry of mime, and the artistic utilization of rubble in the tradition of von Sternberg's *The Salvation Hunters*, Kershner's *Stake-Out on Dope Street*; and (although made later) Penn's own *The Chase*. Add to all of these a sense of excitement and joy and there is *Mickey One*.

Albert Johnson. *Film Quarterly*.
Winter 1967–68, p. 42

What immediately strikes one in the films of Arthur Penn may appear at first glance a superficial feature, but it leads right to the essence of his art: an intense awareness of, and emphasis on, physical expression. Physical sensation (often, but not necessarily, violent) is perhaps more consistently vivid in his films than in those of any other director. Again and again he finds an action—often in itself unusual, hence striking, action—likely to communicate a physical "feel" to the spectator, and devotes all his resources—direction of the actors, camera position and movement, editing—to making that "feel" as immediate as possible, arousing a vividly emphathic response. Here, as illustration, are five examples, one from each of Penn's films:

1. *The Left-Handed Gun*: As the McSweens' home is burned, Mrs. McSween, distraught, struggles helplessly to check the chaos around her. The sackers unwind reels of printed fabric which brushes and almost entangles her. She collapses, despairing, on the steps of the shed, clutching handfuls of the contents of an overturned barrel (which, overturning, nearly hits her), holding them to her forehead, rubbing them in her hair.

2. *The Miracle Worker*: Annie Sullivan introduces herself to the blind and deaf Helen Keller by thudding down her trunk on the step

on which Helen is sitting. The child senses the vibration, feels with her hand. Penn cuts to a close-up of the hands as Helen's feels Annie's, the delicacy of contact suggesting that the fingers are the child's ears and eyes. Helen raises Annie's fingers to her nose and smells them.

3. *Mickey One*: During the credit sequence a girl sprawled across the bonnet of the car Mickey is driving, presses her lips to the windscreen. The camera is positioned inside, so that we see the flattening of her lips, the misting of the glass by her breath. Mickey turns on the windscreen wiper, which rises up to touch the girl's open mouth.

4. *The Chase*: At the height of the climactic riot, Mary Fuller, drunk and hysterical, suddenly stuffs part of the pearl necklace she is wearing into her mouth and bites. The necklace bursts. Some of the pearls stay in her mouth, others scatter on the ground amid car tyres, etc.

5. *Bonnie and Clyde*: C. W. Moss's "Daddy," infuriated by the sight of his son's tattooed chest, suddenly flicks hot thick soup (or pease pudding) across it from a saucepan with a large spoon. C. W. is in the right foreground of the screen, so that the soup is flicked towards the spectator. [1969]

Robin Wood. *Arthur Penn* (Praeger, 1970), pp. 6–7

Alice's Restaurant. Arlo Guthrie's song of "The Alice's Restaurant Massacre" is an anecdotal, humorous, artfully exaggerated account of some of his own adventures with his friends, a picaresque story set to music. There isn't much of a formal plot, things just seem to happen. . . .

That's what the movie's all about, too, and director Arthur Penn had the good sense to try to make it in the anecdotal, rambling style of the song, and had the considerable ability to bring it off. There are more things added to the story told in the song, like Arlo visiting his dying father, Woody, in the hospital in New York, and he and Pete Seeger singing for him. Other people and trips and encounters are added, but everything happens casually and without any forcing for a standard plot.

The last quarter of the movie becomes terribly morose, with Woody dying and a young junkie friend of Alice and Ray's getting killed, and a colorful but somehow strained and joyless "remarriage" ceremony Alice and Ray hold in their church-house, after which Arlo and most of their friends leave them for other travels and adventures. There is a last long shot of Alice standing at the church door, not looking very happy. I can't tell whether this last part was added for "significance," or perhaps because some things like that really happened and Arlo wanted them in the movie, or what. Though the ending makes the whole thing heavier, it doesn't basically violate the spirit and style of the song or of most of the movie. Arlo is relaxed and charming and funny playing himself, and Pat Quinn is a tough and tender, sharp and impetuous, sad-eyed, marvelous Alice. The movie is never dull, and moves along at its own informal, quirky, personal pace. It is as likable as Arlo himself.

Dan Wakefield. *The Atlantic Monthly.*
Nov. 1969, pp. 170–71

Though there are brilliant action sequences in each of his films, it used to be argued that Penn was an "arty" director influenced by the Italians. *Mickey One* was dismissed by many critics as pretentious and Penn himself is overly modest about the film despite the fact that it holds up as a strikingly original experiment. . . .

The world-wide reaction to *Bonnie and Clyde*, especially among those under twenty-five, indicated that the film touched some sort of psychic nerve. It made schizophrenics of critics, who couldn't decide how they really felt about it. It appealed to the intelligentsia and to the yahoos.

Joseph Gelmis, *The Film Director as Superstar*
(Doubleday, 1970), p. 193

Like *Easy Rider* and *Medium Cool, Alice's Restaurant* is a difficult film to dislike, but by the time I saw it I was starting to dislike films that were difficult to dislike. The most salient feature of *Alice's Restaurant*, however, is how little there is in it either to like, dislike, or otherwise hold onto. If there is anything interesting about the film it is that somewhere in its meandering progress from start to finish it changes course, and what starts looking like another celebration of the new tribal rites finishes as an elegy to "aging children" and the poignancy of parenthood. Yet the most interesting thing about this is just how little interest it sustains. Somewhere along the way (or so it would seem from the film's seesawing uncertainties of tone), Arthur Penn appears to have sensed that all this is not really heaven, and that flower children, too, can be up-tight, have problems, destroy themselves, or reach thirty. This is the news that *Alice's Restaurant* brings, to which at least one possible response might be: So what? . . .

As for the film's fragility, let me offer one possible (if, admittedly, less charitable) alternative view. Somewhere along the assembly line on which a catchy tune is converted into Kentucky Fried Chicken for the now generation, Arthur Penn has made a film, a kind of updated *Jolson Story* refurbished with lots of the new candor ("candor": our currently favored form of dishonesty). In it, Arlo Guthrie, a modestly talented young man with a voice the surefire blend of Dylan's sourness and Donovan's sweetness, a cherubic simpleton's face sometimes startlingly reminiscent of Harry Langdon's, and a screen presence registration of zero, gets to repeat his big success while Arthur Penn, a director whose films have yet to betray evidence that an original thought has ever crossed his mind, feels his way toward some groping realization that there is trouble in paradise. Our tenderness toward this enterprise is solicited; it is a personal film; it is hard to dislike. I believe, however, that it may be worth making the effort. . . .

William S. Pechter. *Commentary*. Feb. 1970, pp. 79–80

Since it seems to be customary to have second thoughts on *Bonnie and Clyde*, here are mine. They are in no way a palinode, only an amplification of what, I feel, I originally stated with excessive laconism.

What is basically wrong with the film is not so much violence as hero worship. The point at which the disaffected intellectual and the foot-loose lowbrow meet is their shared love for the outlaw. Arthur Penn and his scenarists combine the sentimentality of the second-rate intellectual with a first-rate roustabout's amorality, and out come a Bonnie and Clyde who are all bumbling charm, naïve cleverness, derailed ingenuity. Critics who have seen them as bunglers are myopic; for all their limitations, imposed on them by an unjust society exacerbated by the Depression (here immature sociology joins hands with amateur psychiatry), they are witty, inventive, fun-loving, and alive—which is more than you can say for any of the other characters in the film. The policemen are faceless nonentities; the sheriff and the self-righteous father, downright repulsive. Bonnie and Clyde, moreover, are even physically beautiful—star children among the toadstools.

The message is that in a capitalist society, and a bankrupt one at that, the outlaw is a far finer fellow than the inane solid citizen who plays into the hands of the exploiters on top, quietly tightens his belt, and even rats on the guys who rob the rich man's banks. The robbers don't exactly turn the loot over to the poor—even this fanciful hagiography daren't go that far—but they do make a few Robin Hoodish gestures that ring even falser than their specious context.

John Simon. *Movies into Film* (Dial, 1971), p. 169

In late 1967, when the federal government was farther removed from popular affectons than at any time since 1932, *Bonnie and Clyde* arrived to engage public interest in a very significant way. Suddenly, people were fascinated by the thirties—clothing, hair styles, lingo—and once again attracted to outlaws. As before, when the state appeared to be willfully presiding over social collapse, the outlaw became a dynamic and tragic figure, one filled with contemporary meaning. No economic loss to breed a *Little Caesar* rags-to-riches saga in 1967: the problems of that year were subtle, varied, and more explosive than the simple, if awful, breakdown of the Great Depression. The apathy and melancholy of a people struck by economic helplessness was replaced by the anguish and activism of those struck by national ruthlessness. *Bonnie and Clyde* was relased a scant two months before the anti-war march on the Pentagon in October of 1967, and its distance from *Caesar* described the spectacular jolts to our sensibilities during the decades since Rico had soared to the top.

Director Arthur Penn's vision of the outlaw fit the sixties as exactly as Rico fit the thirties. Clyde had more roots in Freud than in Carnegie: sexually impotent and violent, his portrait brought together socio-psychological strains of the fifties and sixties. Rootless, homeless, anomic, Clyde is going toward nothing; he is just running from. "You better keep running, Clyde Barrow," says Bonnie's wizened mother. But where? Clyde aspires to no gang leadership: the cut and dried dynamics of the early thirties are replaced by a hodge-podge of sociological loose ends. It was Clyde's lack of focus as an outlaw that made him the darling of 1967, the bloodiness of his demise that made audiences somehow reach to him, puzzled at their reasons for doing so. If the Johnson government was the law, then increasing numbers of people knew they were outside it: outside its draft laws, outside the drug laws. For thousands, 1967 marked a watershed, marked their deepening sense of becoming outlaws.

Andrew Bergman. *We're in the Money*
(NYU, 1971), pp. 170–71

Penn is an iconoclast, a bushwhacker of American archetypes and sterotypes. He lies in wait for our most cherished legends, and drops them in their tracks. Thus, when we get to his movie, we too—we most of all—must expect to be ambushed. In catching our folk heroes off-guard, he also hopes to catch us. He wants to take everyone in the theater by surprise—the people in the seats as well as the people on the screen.

Custer's Last Stand is the ambush to which Penn's latest film, *Little Big Man*, eventually leads. . . .

When he was interviewed by the student audience at a preview of *Little Big Man*, Penn was harshly criticized for such comic treatment of Indians, especially Cheyenne women and homosexuals. . . . They were clearly disappointed because his film doesn't idolize the Indian as a culture hero. And their New Left image of the Indian is just as clearly something Penn's film avoids on purpose. The ending of Berger's novel fits that currently popular image better, as Berger lets Lodge Skins die on the hilltop to symbolize the extinction of his people. Penn has seen that such melodrama pleases us too much. It fulfills our most predictable expectations: it is just our new reading for the old proverb that says the only good Indian is a dead Indian.

Penn doesn't mind offending some of us in order to stop the propagation of dead Indians. The Indians in *Little Big Man* are neither murderous savages in the old style nor noble savages in the new style. Early in the narrative Jack explains that the name Cheyenne means "human being," and from then on the Cheyenne refer to themselves as "human beings" in the dialogue. Penn thinks the Cheyenne are human beings too: he makes them a part of the human comedy.

Colin Westerbeck, Jr. *Commonweal.*
Jan. 22, 1971, pp. 397–98

In *Little Big Man*, Arthur Penn uses the mode of comic elegy in order to sustain a reverent feeling for the American past without falling into sentimentality (his *Alice's Restaurant* was an elegy for the present, or at least for certain ideals of the present destroyed by madness and violence). Penn's version of the Old West . . . is bathed in legend, exaggeration, and nonsense; it is the past transfigured in the telling, made accessible to the present through comic stylization and an ambigous, partly farcial treatment of violence that is purely contemporary. If, at the same time, Penn had been able to resist imposing certain ideologies of the present onto the past, he might have made a great movie. . . .

The two scenes of Indians being massacred are staged straight for terror and horror, rather than in the farcially scary style of the rest of the movie's violence (when the Indians themselves attack a stagecoach, for instance, it tips over going around a bend like an automobile in a Sennett two-reeler). The slaughter of the Cheyenne is particularly horrible, since we've come to know this community from the inside, but I don't suppose Penn trusted either himself or the audience sufficiently to do it any other way. . . . There's no doubt that the scenes are intended to build up rage against the whites, and they had that audible effect on other people in the theatre. How can this rage be released? By another slaughter, of course, slaughter of Custer and his men, which is the climax of the movie, and again we are back to farce, with Custer ranting and staggering about until he falls flat on his face. . . .

Leaving aside the question of Penn's altering the tone of the movie according to who is being slaughtered, I question the artistic and political ethics of building up the desire for revenge in the audience. Not only does it place the audience in a poor moral position, not only does it weaken the sense of outrage that the rest of the movie establishes, but it also contrasts badly with Crabb's narrative tone, which dwells on the sense of loss and is free of the ideology of hate. What starts as an elegy for lost values winds up as an exercise in white self-hatred, and although it may seem incongruous to say so, I can't help feeling that Penn's movie is another victim of the war in Vietnam.

David Denby, *The Atlantic Monthly*. March 1971, pp. 1–6, 8

PORTER, EDWIN S. (1870–1941)

If George Melies was the first to "push the cinema toward the theatrical way," as he claimed, then Edwin S. Porter was the first to push the cinema toward the cinematic way. Generally acknowledged today as the father of the story film, he made more than ficitional contributions to movie tradition. It was Porter who discovered that the art of motion pictures depends on the continuity of shots, not on the shots alone. Not content with Melies' artificially arranged scenes, Porter distinguished the movies from other theatrical forms and gave them the invention of editing. Almost all motion picture developments since Porter's discovery spring from the principle of editing, which is the basis of motion picture artistry.

Significant for his genius for structural technique, Porter is equally noteworthy for his eye for content. Unlike Melies, who made fantasies, Porter turned to the real world for subject matter. He dramatized what he saw, reflected and commented on contemporary American life, illuminated many of the issues and interests of his time. His efforts to make real occurrences dramatic by means of editing widened the scope of movies, educated its technique, and through the introduction of the story film made the industry boom. . . .

Porter's career in motion pictures lasted seventeen years. It was within four years that he transformed motion picture art. During the years 1902 to 1906, he discovered the principle of editing (*The Life of an American Fireman*) and developed its methods to include direct story construction (*The Great Train Robbery*), contrast construction (*The Ex-Convict*), and parallel construction (*The Kleptomaniac*). In these years also he reached out daringly for new social subject matter (*White Caps, The Miller's Daughter*), explored more carefully the use of camera devices (*Dream of a Rarebit Fiend*), and enlarged the scale of production (*Uncle Tom's Cabin*).

Superseding Melies with these innovations, Porter became the dominant figure in the industry. Film makers imitated him zealously until 1908, when D. W. Griffith, bringing still greater talent to filmdom, became the most admired of movie celebrities. [1939]

Lewis Jacobs. *The Rise of the American Film* (Teachers College, 1968), pp. 35–36

As early as 1909, a film had been made of Harriet Beecher Stowe's famous novel *Uncle Tom's Cabin*, directed by Edwin S. Porter . . . with, of course, a white actor playing the part of Uncle Tom. Originally a stern and sincere indictment of slavery, the novel was altered so much in its filmic transcription that the original theme became confused. The resultant movie was a sentimental tale, mostly concerned with the faithful, dog-like devotion of Uncle Tom for Little Eva, the daughter of his white master. And as this film, which was the first full-length production to exploit the theme of Negro subservience, dealt with the slave in "his proper place," it had a wide success. [1948]

Peter Noble. *The Negro in Films* (Kennikat, 1969), p. 31

Till Edwin S. Porter's *Life of an American Fireman*, U.S. movies still consisted of "topical views"—tidbits of nature study, brief comic interludes, and nearly as brief scenes from stage successes (Joseph Jefferson as Rip Van Winkle, Sarah Bernhardt enacting the duel scene from *Hamlet*). But, taking his cue from Méliès, Porter captured the popular imagination by introducing narrative and thus gave the movies a fresh lease on life. Georges Méliès had told stories on the screen in the manner of the theater, but an Edison film by Edwin S. Porter was the first to arrive at a cinematic form of narration. It shows a fire chief sitting in his office dreaming (in what was then called a "dream balloon") of his wife at home. We cut to a close shot (the first known) of a street-corner fire alarm and to another of a hand setting off the alarm. We cut again to another distant scene, that of the firemen jumping from bed, sliding down the firehouse pole, and starting toward the fire. The remaining frames of this short film detail the rescue of a woman and child from a burning home. Today, film scholars dispute the order and meaning of these frames, the argument turning on whether Porter merely anticipated or actually invented the principal device of screen narrative, cross-cutting, which enables the director to annihilate space and time.

Richard Griffith and Arthur Mayer. *The Movies* (S&S, 1957), p. 9

Apparently Porter himself only dimly understood at first the full implications of *The Great Train Robbery*. Soon after, in bringing *Uncle Tom's Cabin* (1903) to the screen, he reverted to the theatrical style of animated tableaux set against painted, two-dimensional settings. It suggests how forcibly the director had been carried along by the logic of his story in *The Great Train Robbery*—and by the fact that he was working out of doors. But the success of this film was too overwhelming to be long ignored. It established the single reel as the standard length for American films (between eight and twelve minutes of film). It set both the fashion and the pattern for Western films. And it inspired other directors to join Porter in exploring the implications of his disjunctive style of editing, his free juggling of time and space. Their cameras were no longer confined to the studio: scenes taken on location were combined with shots staged against painted sets. And all were assembled and given their final form at the cutting bench, generally by the director himself. As these little stories began to reach the screen, interest in the movies revived throughout the world. In this country, nickelodeons and store shows sprang up in almost every neighborhood. Overnight the movies became the poor man's theater.

Arthur Knight. *The Liveliest Art* (Macmillan, 1957), pp. 17–18

Porter's great work [*The Great Train Robbery*], complete on about ten minutes of film, was almost done. Held by Edison to the formula he had created, he ground out hundreds of imitations while others moved past him. Despite restrictions, however, he managed to experiment with contrasting construction, a way of pointing the ironic difference between situations confronted by similar characters from differing classes, and parallel construction, as in *The Kleptomaniac*, a story of two shoplifters, one rich, the other poor. In these, as in many other pictures, Porter grounded his art solidly in realism, setting the visual tone for nearly all the good American pictures to follow (however romantic their plots, characters, and viewpoints). His pictures also carried a strong undertow of social protest, or, at least comment. Working in the Edison atelier, it is remarkable that he got away with it. Apparently he sensed what many have since discovered—that there is no more successful medium for didacticism (or propaganda) than the movies. Despite the industry's distrust of "messages" nearly all of the artists who have worked in films have tried to make pictures in this vein and, as we shall see, more of them have succeeded—at least partially—than Hollywood's critics have conceded.

Richard Schickel. *Movies* (Basic, 1964), p. 26

Some of [*The Great Train Robbery*] is quite ordinary. The interior scenes are shot in conventional stage fashion. The actors move right to left or left to right. Their gestures are theatrical. But once Porter is out of doors, we are almost in a modern picture. People move toward the camera and away from it. The camera itself rides on the top of a train as the bandits fight for control of the engine. When the train is stopped, and the passengers pile out and line up to be robbed, one man makes a break—directly toward the camera—and is shot dead. Through the window of the railroad station, Porter managed to create the illusion of a train coming to a stop, and, through the open door of the express car, a moving landscape. In two pan shots, he carried his bandits down off the engine and across the woods. For a fillip of excitement after the last scene of the story, Porter added a close-up of a bandit who aimed his pistol at the camera and pulled the trigger.

The important point about *The Great Train Robbery* is that Porter built up what was, for those days, an effective continuity of action through a dozen scenes. But he never used two different camera angles in any one setting. He cut back only once to an earlier locale—the station. He didn't intercut as he might have done quite often; in the chase of the bandits by the posse both groups rode by in the same shot. Yet the total effect was of true and mounting excitement—in terms of those days.

Kenneth Macgowan. *Behind the Screen*
(Delacorte, 1965), pp. 114–16

In 1919, while shooting an Elsi Ferguson picture that Hugh Ford was directing, Ford, knowing that I had worked for Porter, remarked that Porter could have been at the top of whatever branch of making motion pictures he chose if he had concentrated on that branch alone. Ford had helped direct Pauline Frederick in Rome in 1914 in *The Eternal City*, the last motion picture Porter made. For Edwin S. Porter sticking to one phase of moving pictures was impossible. His inventive urge finally took him out of the production end of motion pictures and brought him into the business of manufacturing Simplex motion picture projectors. The man who began moving pictures as entertainment for the masses abandoned everything he had done to those who followed him.

Fred J. Balshofer and Arthur C. Miller.
One Reel a Week (California, 1967), pp. 49, 51

Trick films were popular everywhere during the first decade of the motion picture; the French were particularly prolific in the genre. Porter had begun making them at least as early as 1900. *The Dream of a Rarebit Fiend* makes use of stop-motion photography, painted backgrounds, double exposure, and miniatures. The exuberant inventiveness of the early film-makers provided a rich store from which masters of comedy such as Mack Sennet would draw the elements of a surrealistic world and playfully transform reality itself.

Eileen Bowser in *Film Notes,* edited by Eileen Bowser (MOMA, 1969), p. 4

PREMINGER, OTTO (1906–)

First thing everyone will ask concerning the film, *Margin for Error,* will be whether it is as good as the stage play was. And that is not an easy question to answer. Nor is it too fair a question to ask. . . . Little, in moviemaking, is left to the imagination of the audience: on the stage much is left to the imagination, necessarily and sometimes fortunately. Behind the footlights, a player can refer in a few words to some off-stage happening; each in the audience mentally visualizes the scene as he or she wishes to, moulding it to acceptance. On the screen these "off-stage" happenings are carefully portrayed: these are the things, often, that make an otherwise ordinary film into a great one. And vice-versa.

There are many other differences. So it is just not fair to compare. If a good stage play is made into a good movie, that's close enough. And *Margin for Error* is a good movie—entertaining, amusing and sufficiently melodramatic in its melodramatic moments. Mr. Preminger has brought the full flavor of the stage play to the screen and the hundreds of thousands who see the film and who never saw the play are not going to suffer at all from not having seen the stage production. That's comparison enough.

G. E. Blackford. *NYJA*. Jan. 25, 1943

Once and only once in the uninspired hour and a half of *A Royal Scandal* is there any promise of suiting action to the words. That is when the Empress Catherine promises to take her current palace favorite, Alexei, for a drive in the country. But this happens off-screen somewhere. On-screen, the film is a succession of Ernst Lubitsch gab-fests in gilded chambers and gaudy boudoirs, starting off with a coterie of whiskery generals straining for laughs with a patter composed mainly of *inskis* and *ovitches*; and finally settling down to a series of imperious twosomes involving Catherine (Tallulah Bankhead), her favorite (William Eythe), and the Chancellor (Charles Coburn) and poor, miscast Anne Baxter in a pattern of intrigues and *rouble-entendres* which might, for want of a worse term, be referred to as Lubitschkis.

Setting aside for now the question of whether the saucy Lubitsch touch was ever all it was cracked up to be, the way it is soup-ladled out by director Otto Preminger in *A Royal Scandal* is certainly more noxious than naughty.

John T. McManus. *PM*. April 12, 1945, p. 16

It was with surprise that young old Parisians like us received from Hollywood, some years ago, the recipe for light film comedy. It is with the same surprise that we learn from the same American film-makers the way to make, in so-called commercial films, an intellectual point and how to treat a subject from the inside. This lesson will have the evolutionary importance of several other inventions such as the western, the cream pie, Mickey Mouse, etc.

Laura is no doubt a better example than the films of Orson Welles or Preston Sturges to support our theory with, because the latter are too flagrantly intellectual in the very manner in which they choose and treat their stories. *Laura*, however, is a simple detective story. The new style we want to talk of is therefore not in its plot: it comes from a general trend, from a desire to enrich and every day spread a little farther the domains of cinema; it shows that these intellectual privileges are not, as is believed in Europe, the exclusive property of esthetes and that they are not appreciated only by the film clubs. . . .

The characters in *Laura*—the situation is rare—have a real existence. As soon as they appear, we see them with their real ambiance, their real character, and the way they have to dress. The existence of Laura Hunt, a young woman of the type of a hundred out of a thousand in New York, is shown in a way that allows for no cuts or additions. In the final analysis it matters little that the story is a detective story. Laura could also be put in a family or love story without in any way altering her destiny as an attractive and troubling girl who does nothing to either provoke or retain men and who only very soberly profits from her gift to protect herself. Indifferent and scarcely bothered, she slips among the corpses that are not obstacles. The miracle is to have brought her to life.

This miracle has been accomplished by a director whose technique is a smooth, almost automatic instrument, a director who simultaneously puts into relief all the characters in a well-stocked scenario, and who is able to persuade his actors that they are in on the game. Of course, this is not the first time that spectators have been led to believe that the heroine is dead only to find her ravishing and alive in the midst of the film. The miracle desired by the public is initially wished for unconsciously and without hope by the hero—who we forget is only a "cop." We even sympathize with him doubly when, during one of the most brilliant dolly shots—and one the most successful in recent years—the fellow tries to calm his haunted head by the thought of Laura and her portrait on the wall. . . .

When Laura opens the door and enters in the flesh, without malice, without remorse, and without plans—satisfied to simply be Laura—we are convinced that the cinema is really a fine invention.

Revue du Cinéma. Nov. 1946, pp. 72–74

Without doubt, the Production Code, with its many rules of do's and don'ts, has fenced in the movies so that they have not attained their rightful stature; and no doubt the Code, which was drawn up in the early thirties when the motion picture industry decided they preferred self-regulation to censorship by a wide variety of governmental and other organizations, needs revision. But I'm sorry to see the issue brought to a head by an inferior film like *The Moon Is Blue*. Audiences who have been clamoring for adult films (and have been blaming the Production Code, when most of the blame should go to the studios who insist on making movies for the twelve-year-old mind) won't find what they have been looking for in F. Hugh Herbert's shallow comedy. . . .

Although Preminger's direction is static, the film does have a couple of good performances. . . . But for all its good cast and fancy setting, *The Moon* adds nothing to the art of cinema and it certainly does not deserve the attention it will get for flouting the Production Code.

Philip T. Hartung. *Commonweal.*
July 17, 1953, p. 369

The plain truth is *The Man With the Golden Arm* is a very inferior film—as film. The script is inexcusably clumsy, the sets are unbelievable, and the casting is ridiculous. I do not see how Preminger will ever live down casting Eleanor Parker as the malingering wife. His extenuation, probably, is that the story is so sordid—no one will deny it—that he had to do something to lighten things up. But did he? The theme is of the darkest and should not have been lightened. Moreover, he had cast Sinatra as the addict, which is lightening things plenty, and distorting them too much. Did this film not deal with drug addiction no one would pay any attention to it, least of all the intelligentsia, who have taken up cudgels on its behalf, for vague anti-censorship reasons.

While it's true no normal person would be enticed into taking dope by seeing this picture, I am not so sure abnormal people may not have come away sub-consciously and very complicatedly intrigued. After all, the addict, as played by Sinatra, is not made unattractive, and his self-excuses are condemned only once, in two lines of dialogue indistinctly spoken by Kim Novak in one of her histrionically less capable moments. Otherwise, the addict is presented as the victim of his environment, which is never categorized, one way or the other.

As for the happy ending—in the book the addict commits suicide—Sinatra cures himself in a factually impossible way. And there should at least have been mention of the terrible truth that less than two per cent of those "cured," even with medical help, stay that way.

Diana Willing. *Films in Review.*
Jan. 1956, pp. 34–35

The Man with the Golden Arm is fashioned by a cunning and assured hand which has, in this instance, overreached itself. For the primary aim of those who deal in such sophisticated and insidious mixtures (with very stylish photography and a classy refinement of cliché in the writing) is to be consistently entertaining. And this, after the opening sequences, the film fails to be. Perhaps from the all too predictable one-step-forward-and-two-steps-back of the drug addict's progress it looks for a greater fascination than in fact exists. And without this fascination one has ample leisure to realise that, in spite of some clever observation, there is about the film's setting and characters something consciously picturesque, something at once calculating, immoral and cheap.

BFI Bulletin. Feb. 1956, p. 16

It is difficult to figure out why producer-director Otto Preminger chose to film George Bernard Shaw's *Saint Joan.* Perhaps after making money and controversy with such sensational movies as *The Moon Is Blue* and *The Man with the Golden Arm,* he wanted to show he could do something of a classical nature completely without censorship problems. Joan is a good subject for cinema, but Shaw's thoughtful and often witty chronicle play, in six scenes and an epilogue, is not. Though brilliantly written, it is extremely talky; and once script-writer Graham Greene started cutting, as he had to do because of the play's length, and started adding scenes, as he had to do to lessen the static effects and make the movie move, he ran into trouble.

. . . Preminger's second mistake, after deciding to film Shaw's play, was in selecting an inexperienced, unknown, high school graduate, Jean Seburg, to play the difficult lead role. . . .

Strangely enough, Miss Seburg, who looks embarrassed in some of the episodes, is at her best in the trial scene. It is in this scene, expertly written by Shaw to show that both the Church and the trial itself were fair, that director Preminger shows himself at best too. Much of the movie is staged as if it were a high school pageant, but Preminger realizes the core of the play is in the trial, and he and his cast take full advantage of Shaw's dialogue. Although this *Saint Joan* leaves much to be desired, it is still a provocative movie that is worth seeing.

Philip T. Hartung. *Commonweal.* July 19, 1957, pp. 400–401

Exodus (and, I presume, the book by Leon Uris from which it derives) is not, in fact, any of the things the public has taken it for. It distorts facts; the actual event upon which its title is based occurred in 1947, and the result of world-wide attempts to force the British to let the refugees into Palestine was that they were, instead, shipped back to Germany to another detention camp. Other "facts" about—the whole atmosphere of underground activity in pre-Israel Palestine is treated by Preminger in a shallow cat-chase-dog international espionage style, whereas in reality it constitutes, of course, one of the most outstanding achievements of the human spirit in our age. For one who has lived through that period and that time in that place, *Exodus* is sacrilege.

But let us not be sticklers for truth. I suppose it's understandable that one doesn't want one's work cluttered up with a lot of facts, and one's images with a lot of comparisons to what actually happened. In many ways, in fact, this may well be a defendable position, what with *creative liberty*, *dramatic transposition*, *audience identification*, and other strictures applied to movie-making by contemporary "independent" Hollywoodites. It is also conceivable, finally, that a good film could be made of something that never happened at all. The problem here then, is not so much one of reality as one of truth. And we are emphatically asked to believe that the "inner truth," at least, of *Exodus*, is the story of the birth of Israel.

A film-maker in tackling a historical subject, contemporary or otherwise, faces no less of a responsibility to his viewers than other artists tackling "reality." Certainly we expect no historical treatise, but even a sham concoction like *Ben-Hur* pays at least lip service to factual, historical occurrences. Certainly a film which uses the emotional entanglement of millions with its subject can be expected to have some form of reverence for both that subject and for those millions. Preminger—abstractly—could perhaps find some excuses for distorting the *reality* of Israel, but he seriously offends the intelligence of his paying public by distorting its truth.

Gideon Bachmann. *Film Quarterly.* Spring 1961, pp. 56–57

Better than *Bonjour Tristesse* and *Exodus*, *Advise and Consent* continues a difficult task, the more and more rigorous synthesis of two essential currents in the work of Preminger. They may once have seemed contradictory, but they are now shown as complementary.

A being (*Laura*), a will (*Whirlpool*), a passion (*Billy Mitchell*, *The Man with the Golden Arm*), fascinated and took possession of the characters to lead them simultaneously to their destruction and the awareness of themselves (*Anatomy of a Murder*, *Bonjour Tristesse*). But this possessive force manifested itself under *two forms*, according to two modes of existence that referred to visions of different worlds. These two forms, these two representations of a power, would seem contradictory if they weren't shown in *Advise and Consent* as opposed but necessarily complementary aspects of a single force: death, simultaneously fixation and destruction, corpse and fermentation.

On the one hand, a being or an idea of being was *external* to those it fascinated and determined (*Whirlpool*, *Anatomy of a Murder*). On the other hand, the same idea, the same conflict developed in the *interior* of the characters to destroy them, to live off them (*The Man with the Golden Arm*, *Bonjour Tristesse*, *Exodus*). Thus there was the presence, the force and the action of a will or an idea (the presence of death), sometimes external to the characters, paralyzing and freezing them, sometimes within them, initially latent, insinuating itself and animating them until their end.

The synthesis begins with *Bonjour Tristesse*: Cécile is fascinated by what she is not (Anne) and it is her passion, her inner struggle, that destroys her. In *Exodus*, the English are fascinated by an ideal they cannot understand, whereas the Jews are inwardly animated by this same ideal. It is from the relationship between the paralysis of those who experience this force from the outside, and the explosion of those who live it inwardly that is born the conflict which is both constructive and destructive.

In *Advise and Consent*, the idea is initially external to all, except the President and Seab Cooley, each a different kind of incarnation of death. But then the idea insinuates itself in all of them, it is interiorized by all who come in contact with it, it lives in them and on them until they are destroyed.

Jean-Louis Comolli. *Cahiers du Cinéma.*
Nov. 1962, pp. 45–46

Like most of Preminger's films, *The Cardinal* is better seen than heard. As his camera sweeps across the ecclesiastical canvas represented by Rome, New England, Georgia, and Vienna, Preminger's meaning comes through more strongly in his feeling for architecture than in his feeling for drama. It is significant that the opening credit sequence depicting Father Stephen Femoyle ascending an endless series of steps lingers in the mind long after the same character's final speech has been completely forgotten. One visual ascension is not necessarily worth a thousand verbal summations. It is just that Preminger is much better with images than with actors. . . .

The Cardinal is an uneven film, whatever one's frame of reference. The primarily visual critics will hail it, and the primarily literary critics will deplore it. This is as it should be with a director whose talent is more expansive than incisive. If I side with the visual critics on Preminger, it is because I believe we are in the midst of a visual revolution, which the literary establishment is apparently ignoring if not actively resisting. . . . [1963]

Andrew Sarris. *Confessions of a Cultist* (S&S, 1970), pp. 110–111

. . . Otto Preminger is legally and fervently American but is still atmospherically European. Several other contraditions apply to him and his career. His professional record is both vastly overrated and incompletely known. He is increasingly adored by certain film cults, who devote whole issues of journals to him, while other critics, at least equally serious, view his work with steadily decreasing interest. He has a reputation—deserved—for intelligence and cultivation, and another reputation—equally deserved—for shrewd exploitation of mass tastes. He has fought courageously for the liberalization of constricting film production codes, and he has fought his good fight with an eye and a half on the box office. . . .

His latest films, *The Cardinal* and *In Harm's Way*, have summoned most of these contradictions to particular inspection. In the past, much of what he has done has had a gloss of art, but these most recent films seem to have puzzled many because they have no such gloss. *The Cardinal* is a polychrome heartstring-tugger, nothing else; *In Harm's Way* is one more guts-and-glory naval saga complete with John Wayne as a crusty commander and an ensign son who finally does him proud. Those who have thought of Preminger as a man who managed to smuggle sophisticated work past the Hollywood sentries have been going about with slightly bewildered, hurt looks. This present inquiry hopes to explain why their disappointment is not justified.

Preminger is an outstanding example of the paradox constructed principally by popular imagination. In addition to giving him success, the public has insisted on accrediting him with a stature to which, in fact, he has never asserted title. . . . But Preminger is cannily innocent. He has never claimed to be a great artist nor, so far as I know, allowed that claim to be made directly for him. It is the American public —stimulated by the fastidious worldliness, the accent, the Erich von Stroheim pate, the air of arrogant and nonchalant candor—who have insisted that the director of *Under Your Spell* (Hollywood, 1936) and *Beverly Hills* (Broadway, 1940) has a special aura of fine artistry. In his newspaper interview, radio and television appearances, Preminger has done little to discourage the idea that the mantle of Max Reinhardt rests upon him, but it is only his personality, not any specific claims of his, that have encouraged the idea. [1965]

Stanley Kauffmann. *A World on Film* (Harper, 1966), pp. 170–71

Advise and Consent illustrates a trend in Preminger's work: it is a thoroughly practical film about an abstract subject. The quality of justice in *Anatomy of a Murder*, the saintliness of *St. Joan*, the nature of faith in *The Cardinal* and the validity of nationalism in *Exodus* all share in this paradox. In contrast to the definition of romanticism, Preminger is one of the most unatmospheric directors. So intent is he on the shifting movements of the characters that his Israel in *Exodus* and his small town in *Anatomy* seem as neutral as if in a newsreel. That sweeping pan over the landscape of Cyprus at the beginning of *Exodus* is not a pastoral movement; significantly it ends on Eva Marie Saint's eyes. The human perception and understanding of an event are more important to Preminger than the event itself. Thus his St. Joan is not a saint but a girl some think a saint and others scorn. Her miracles are accomplished not with dramatic cuts or effects but during level and controlled shots. Similarly, the cynical are no more condemned than the charitable are elevated. Even though the Archbishop in *St. Joan* mouths many of Shaw's sharpest comments on faith, Joan kneels before him and the camera rises above him in a complementary and ambivalent movement.

David Thomson. *Movie Man* (Stein & Day, 1967), p. 168

Bunny Lake Is Missing, despite the emphasis on textbook Freud, incest, and sado-masochism, is not a bad film. The central action centers around the supposed kidnapping of a child. The pace of the film, for the first hour, is relaxed, and the contrast between tone and subject matter maintains the suspense and tension. Sir Laurence Olivier's portrayal of the police inspector is flawless, and the rest of the cast acquit themselves admirably.

The underlying theme of the film is the old philosophic problem of whether "to be is to be perceived." To develop the theme, Preminger uses a tape recording of children telling about their dreams, and television shows; the first of which the characters listen to, the second of which they watch, as structural metaphors. In terms of image, shadow and light are constantly juxtaposed as physical correlatives to mental states of mind. Unfortunately, there is more shadow than substance given to this part of the film. This is undoubtedly because Preminger felt he would lose the mass audience interested only in a good mystery yarn (which it is) if he were to develop the problem fully. So instead of grappling with the issue, he ties it up in the end with an obvious and artificial conclusion, ties a ribbon around the package, and waits for the dollars to roll in.

Leon Lewis and W. D. Sherman. *Landscape of Contemporary Cinema* (Buffalo Spectrum, 1967), p. 68

Those who dig Younguns should love *Skidoo*, and indeed the audience laughed and cheered in all the right places when I saw it at a screening at Paramount at the invitation of Mr. Preminger, who was appropriately clad for the occasion in one of his Nehru suits. It must be noted, however, that the audience was stacked, consisting almost entirely of young people and their fellow travelers; there were probably more men with beads than at any event since Vatican II. Like Western-lovers grooving on scalping scenes and shoot-outs and rustlers crashing the old corral, this audience was digging the Youngun equivalents: acid trips, nude body paintings, pot smoking, anti-Establishment jokes, cop-baiting, lots of capital-letter LOVE Talk—the works, man. . . .

For those who can't just get their kicks by watching other people turn on in a film, *Skidoo* offers plenty of good old-fashioned titillation passing as the latest thing in fun and games: in the course of it all we get to see Alexandra Hay, the latest thing in beautiful blond teeny-boppers, undress in order to have her body painted, get fondled and unbuttoned by Groucho, and caught in a shower with Frankie Avalon; for those who still have a thing about older women (over eighteen) there is Carol Channing stripping down to her bra and panties and yellow vinyl boots; the black model, Luna, in a gown that is almost entirely backless even at the bottom, gets out of that and into bed with Alexandra Hay's hippie boyfriend; there is something for everyone. Mr. Preminger is really in there swinging, and I wouldn't be surprised if he next produced the Timothy Leary Story, a sort of inspirational film along the lines of *The Cardinal*.

Dan Wakefield. *The Atlantic Monthly*. Dec. 1968, pp. 146–47

ROSSEN, ROBERT (1908–1966)

The more or less standard fight film has added stature in its 1947 version. It's still the little guy forsaking education for the prize ring and, Cinderella-like, reaching the top. The girl wavers between love for him and distaste for boxing. The climax comes within seconds of the big fight's final gong when the gamblers lose and the pug wins crown and girl. But *Body and Soul* is written with more integrity than usual, the sequence of events accents telling sidelights, and James Wong Howe's shrewd camera elicits more frenzy from the championship bout than newsreels draw from the real thing.

Body and Soul is also more than a fight film. As latest example of the influence of Broadway's more serious talents on Hollywood it provides an excuse to reconsider that migration of the mid-thirties. Remember Odets and Irwin Shaw taking their rough talk to Hollywood, Orson Welles turning from experiments on stage and radio to the screen? Remember the excitement of seeing emigrants from the Mercury, Federal and Group theatres in films—Agnes Moorehead, Joseph Cotten, Ruth Warrick, Franchot Tone, John Garfield? They were New Yorkers who went to Hollywood with something to say.

By now their contributions to filmdom are variously assimilated indeed. Cotten wears expensive chaps while Tone runs to silk pajamas. Orson Welles is deep in Shakespeare and Miss Moorehead dabbles in murder. Only the Dead End Kids and Garfield are readily recognizable, or the infrequent film which bears direct traces of the old school. *Body and Soul* is such a film, its sternness mellowed by reminder. Here are the gin and tinsel, squalor and sables of the depression era, less daring than when first revealed in *Dead End* or *Golden Boy* but more valid and mature because shown without sentiment or blur. The old tenement films with "social significance" had general reform in mind. They represented a native protest of our social fabric. But *Body and Soul* gets deeper into its milieu, makes specific the blame, and tightens up the conflicts of its cast with logic.

NBR. Nov. 1947, p. 9

Out of Robert Penn Warren's prize novel, *All the King's Men*, which was obviously based on the familiar rise and fall of the late Huey Long, Robert Rossen has written and directed, as well as personally produced, a rip-roaring film of the same title. It opened at the Victoria yesterday.

We have carefully used that descriptive as the tag for this new Columbia film because a quality of turbulence and vitality is the one thing that it most fully demonstrates. In telling a complicated story of a self-made and self-styled "red-necked hick" who batters his way to political kingdom in an unspecified southern state, the picture bounces from raw-boned melodrama into dark psychological depths and thrashes around in those regions until it claws back to violence again. Consistency of structure—or of character revelation—is not in it. But it has a superb pictorialism which perpetually crackles and explodes.

And because of this rich pictorialism, which embraces a wide and fluid scene, it gathers a frightening comprehension of the potential of demagoguery in this land. From ugly illustrations of back-room spittoon politics to wild illuminations of howling political mobs, it catches the dim but dreadful aspect of ignorance and greed when played upon by theatrics, eloquence and bluff. It visions the vulgar spellbinders and political hypocrites for what they are and it looks on extreme provincialism with a candid and pessimistic eye.

In short, Mr. Rossen has assembled in this starkly unprettified film a piece of pictorial journalism that is remarkable for its brilliant parts. It clearly observes the beginnings of a Huey Long type of demagogue in an humble and honest lawyer fighting the "bosses" in a sleepy dirt-road town. It follows this disillusioned fellow as he gets the hang of politics and discovers the strange intoxication of his own unprincipled charm. And it wallows with him in egoism, corruption and dictatorial power until he is finally shot down by an assassin when his triumphs appear uncontrolled.

All of these things, Mr. Rossen, as director, has pictured stunningly. His final episode of personal violence and mob hysteria is superb for savagery. But in his parallel endeavors to transfer from Mr. Warren's book some real understanding of the character, he has met with much less success. In fact, the whole middle section of the film, which is deeply concerned with the brutal impact of the fellow upon his wife, son, mistress and friends, is a heavy confusion of dense dramatics that is saved from being downright dull only by the variety and vigor of pictorial detail.

Bosley Crowther. *NYT*. Nov. 9, 1949, p. 37

Robert Rossen's career as a Hollywood script writer began in a distinguished way with *They Won't Forget* for Warner's in 1937 and tailed down into the mediocre levels of competent success until he again asserted himself as an individualistic writer-director with *Body and Soul* and as a creative producer with *Undercover Man*, both in their way more satisfactory than *All the King's Men.* His penchant for candid camera characterisation and newsreel effects was given play in those films and in *Johnny O'Clock.*

It has been applied exhaustively in *All the King's Men* but unfortunately without the discretion that can co-ordinate fact with fiction. The backgrounds dramatically angled and grouped by photographer Burnett Guffey in the Californian towns of Suisun, Fairfield and Stockton, and peopled by the actual inhabitants of those places, run away with the story.

The film has two separate textures and conflicting rhythms though some of the earlier sequences do admirably fuse the naturalistic and fictional, notably the hangover prelude to the barbecue speech. It is easy to understand why Rossen, in revolt (like so many in Hollywood) against the lacquered studio conventions, sees in the realism of the Italians a shining light. But realism comes from within as well as from without and the core of meaning that might have made this film a step forward from *Boomerang* (if not an Oscar winner) does not exist amid all the courageous camera-work.

This, it is worth noting, is given an exceptional visual brilliance by the lowering weather—unusual in California or at least not advertised on the screen—in which much of the film had to be shot in order to make the schedule. And the sound track crowns these adventitious effects of realism by vivid crowd noises, overlapping dialogues, carefully handled acoustics and a restriction of music.

Rossen, canonised and protected by Oscars, can well go on to exploit the double escape—from studio and from sunshine. And simultaneously he can well be caught on another success wagon as the brilliant writer-director and practitioner of facile realism before he has time to marshal the talents that, confusedly still, exist in him.

Richard Winnington. *Sight & Sound.*
June 1950, p. 168

Robert Rossen has aimed for greatness in *Alexander the Great* and has missed honorably. His literate script strives for the genuine historical issues with minimal concessions to the popular image of pagan lust and violence. His direction is consistently effective without attaining any climactic summation. Script, acting, and direction fall into place in the narrative without rising to any heights. In many respects, however, *Alexander the Great* stands closer to *Richard III* and *Henry V* than to the traditional Hollywood spectales. . . .

The martial scenes are designed to make Alexander's victories seem tactically plausible. The Macedonian phalanx is shown in some detail, although generally the battle charges deteriorate into a confused jumble of shields and aggressive postures. Sharp-eyed connoisseurs of spectacle may detect some doubling up of extras for mass effects.

The film is least successful when it attempts to be conventional. The tepid orgies are inadequate. More successful is a staged battle between a Persian armed with a club and a Macedonian equipped with shield and spear.

Despite the film's documentary credentials, some of Rossen's motivations for Alexander seem questionable. Alexander's retreat from India seems less the consequence of the death of his best friend than the necessity of ending the film. Despite its weaknesses, however, *Alexander the Great* is a creditable achievement in a genre that has flourished for so long without intellectual distinction. That this film can be discussed at all on the level of art and history rather than production statistics suggests that *Alexander the Great* points to the proper direction, though not the ultimate destination, of the historical epic.

Andrew Sarris. *Film Culture*. Vol. 2, No. 2 (8), 1956, pp. 29–30

Robert Rossen made one very extraordinarily fine picture, *All The King's Men*, a hard-hitting, muscular study of the rise of a demagogue that achieved its power through blunt statement and technical means that reveal him for what he was—another graduate of the Warner Brothers academy. His other good pictures of the postwar years, *Body and Soul*, *The Brave Bulls*, and *The Hustler*, were all studies in the decline and fall of the professional, who through mastery of his art almost achieves the stature of a hero, only to be laid low by a combination of inner flaws and flaws in the system. By demonstrating the interaction of these factors Rossen was able to retain a basically humanistic approach to his people without sacrificing his ability to air his cynical view of the outer forces that distort the individual. An underrated movie-maker who fell from favor in the late fifties, Rossen stands now on the brink of new recognition.

Richard Schickel. *Movies* (Basic, 1964), p. 187

A film that moves beyond the boundaries of realism in a more unified manner is Robert Rossen's *The Hustler* (and his unfairly maligned *Lilith* could be cited as well). Here, many of the critics sensed something beyond—and complained. They wanted nothing to get in the way to blur the realistic depiction of the milieu of the pool player and pool hall. Almost all saw the film as a conflict between the old pool player and the young: old doctor and young, old gangster and young, old lawyer and young, old cowboy and young—who's going to win? It is about more than that. It is for one thing (as are a number of Rossen's films) about power—its lure and its destructiveness. Its figure of the gambler takes the stock material of so many realist films and gives him both intensity and complexity. Power, sadism, lust, greed, sexual perversion and the crippling of love, the corruption of money—these are part of his complexity and part of his struggle (against the girl who is physically crippled but not yet destroyed) for the unformed soul and unshaped energies of the pool playing young American, the wanderer, skilled, but isolated, without mission, purpose or connection. The climax of the struggle is the sequence of Derby Week in Louisville, which itself culminates in the defeat of the pool player while he triumphs over the rich homosexual—perspiring in the ardor of his loss—in the swank basement pool hall of hell. This whole sequence, I believe, is one of the most memorable and significant—visually, dramatically, symbolically—in the American film. True, Rossen softens the film's ending, but maybe we can't have everything yet.

Alan Casty. *Film Heritage*. Spring 1966, p. 6

At 58, three years before being carried away by sickness, Robert Rossen delivers in extremis, with *Lilith*, his incontestable masterpiece—which serves as well to wipe out past errors (*An Island in the Sun*, *Mambo*) as to relegate success (*All the King's Men*, *The Hustler*) to the second rank. This man, said to be rough, grumpy, gauche, and preoccupied with pounding first truths without much nuance, came, against all expectation and thanks to a single film, to confuse the more or less vague ideas that critics maintained about him. In retrospect, certain precautions assert themselves. Lately a new viewing of *They Came to Cordura (film manqué*, certainly, out of balance and confused, but attaching) and of *The Hustler* has established the mapping points that were missing, corrected false perspectives, and inevitably caused new attention to be paid to some formal or thematic indications that a casual approach could in the past cause to be neglected. Thus we must agree that the manifestly ultra-classical skill of *The Hustler* has too often masked the very real originality of the thesis that the film supported, that developed as if underground a fragile network of hauntings and obsessions that the efficacy of spectacle and suspense seemed to indicate as secondary, when they were probably the first cause of the work and its stay. . . .

The cinema obeys laws too obscure for there not to be some presumption in attempting to codify the uncodifiable; we must confess that in spite of the beauties of *The Hustler*, nothing could let us suppose that Rossen carried in him a diamond as brilliant and as cutting as *Lilith*. Yet one masterpiece is enough to change the face of a man: just as *Night of the Hunter* abruptly revealed to us that we ignored everything of the monstrous genius who hid his torments behind the picturesque grimaces of a good humored ogre, in the same way *Lilith* imposes on us the manifestness of a universe until then hidden and which, suddenly offers to broad daylight its true nature and its true depth. *Night of the Hunter*, *Lilith* are unique films, the first because no doubt it sums up in its duration the obsessions of an entire life; the second because it drives off roughly to a distance from it the marking points that preceded it, those nine other films whose qualities or defects interest henceforth in so far as they prepare or foretell the achievement of the ultimate work that an admirable struggle tore away from death and madness. The purity of the meeting point of themes and forms excludes the possibility of a happy chance; everything leads one to believe that after *Lilith*, Rossen, withdrawn from the world, waited for the same terrible gentleness that he had tamed to carry him off silently. He worked no longer and practiced, he said, the tête-à-tête with the sun; this nonchalance finally won, after what detours, heightens the pathos of the last shot of *Lilith*, of the last shot of Rossen's work. Vincent Bruce advances toward the camera, ravaged, destroyed, broken, to murmur facing the audience the two syllables of despair: "Help me. . . ." This cry of distress definitively closes the work on the bankruptcy of illusion; the threshold is reached where the cinema confesses and goes beyond its original sin. Beyond this confession, reigns silence.

André Fieschi. *Cahiers du Cinéma in English.*
Jan. 1967 (7), p. 32

SEASTROM, VICTOR (1879–1960)

At the Capitol this week there is a picture which defies one to write about it without indulging in superlatives. It is a shadow drama so beautifully told, so flawlessly directed that we imagine that it will be held up as a model by all producers. Throughout its length there is not an instant of ennui, not a second one wants to lose; it held the spectators spellbound yesterday afternoon, the last fade-out being the signal for a hearty round of applause. This celluloid masterpiece is Victor Seastrom's picturization of Leonid Andreyev's play, *He Who Gets Slapped*. . . .

The first flash on the screen shows a clown twisting a colored ball, which gradually fades out into the figure of Beaumont, the scientist, gazing upon a revolving globe. There are many such clever touches in different chapters of this absorbing narrative which deals with the ultimate revenge of the scientist-clown, merely known as "He Who Gets Slapped," on the man who stole the glory for his work and also his wife. You see the student arguing with Baron Regnard before a gallery of aged notables, and suddenly the nobleman slaps the scientist's face. The old men rock in their mirth, and this, coupled with the loss of his wife, spurs the student to become a clown with a small traveling French circus. . . .

Mr. Seastrom has directed this dramatic story with all the genius of a Chaplin or a Lubitsch, and he has accomplished more than they have in their respective works, *A Woman of Paris* and *The Marriage Circle,* as he had what they did not have, a stirring dramatic story to put into pictures. . . .

For dramatic value and a faultless adaptation of the play, this is the finest production we have yet seen.

NYT. Nov. 10, 1924, p. 20

What would be your anticipation if you were told in advance that the heroine of a picture falls from grace in an attempt to raise the money for a mortgage and that her downfall determines the fate of all the other characters in the story? Wouldn't you expect either a jazz picture with lots of cabaret scenes or else an out and out melodrama of the old school? And wouldn't you count upon seeing the girl's adventures and all the details of her seduction as far as current censorships permit? And mightn't you just possibly decide to keep away from "just another picture" of this obvious sort?

That would be an excellent reason for going to see *The Tower of Lies.* Provided, of course, that you are sincerely interested in the progress of picture making and experimentation. For this picture is different. It is an attempt to tell a story largely through the powers of suggestion and calls upon the audience to use its imagination instead of anticipating the obvious. The heroine simply leaves for the city and we know absolutely nothing about her until she returns in her finery, almost three reels later. But meanwhile the tragic effect of her fall has been mirrored tellingly in the mind and heart of her father, who cannot grasp the reality and entertains an insane delusion in which he plays at being king and queen with his daughter as in a fairy tale which he used to tell her in the nursery.

The net effect of this treatment is to raise the seduction from a banal adventure to a tragedy with fresh human values. The old father, insane and stumbling blindly into the river, becomes the symbol of faith breaking itself against sordidness, of a precious ideal shattered.

NBR. Nov.-Dec. 1925, p. 4

Seastrom, the Swedish director, is a man whom America has nearly ruined. In Sweden, one cannot help feeling, the cinema has steered its own sweet course irrespective of a desire to please the people at all costs. Therefore, it has been possible for men in Sweden to experiment, to try to get thought, imagination, fancy, emotion-provoking scenes on the screen. There has been much poetry and a great deal of fancy in Swedish films.

Seastrom became famous even among those who had never seen his pictures and eventually he hired himself out to America. There this perhaps rather too artistic person was given stories by Hall Caine to direct, stories which should have been handled by a man like Rex Ingram who understands the handling of crowds, understands the kind of climaxes which popular stories need. Seastrom showed no peculiar ability at all; he has always been given the wrong kind of work (*Confessions of a Queen* and *Name the Man*), and I feel sure had he been allowed to handle any one of the many films portraying country life in America, films about pioneers or about small towns or about farmers: if he had been given something like *Wanderer of the Waste Land* or *So Big* to direct, he would have done very much better than he has with the material given to him. He has a genius for the rural. In *The Tower of Lies* he has redeemed himself on exactly these lines. Also witness the love scene in *He Who Gets Slapped*, the only really attractive part in that tedious picture.

Iris Barry. *Let's Go to the Movies* (Payson & Clarke, 1926), pp. 229–30

The prudery of the ignoble bigots in Puritanical days is adroitly put forth in the picturization of Nathaniel Hawthorne's story, *The Scarlet Letter*, which was presented at the Central Theatre last night. No attempt has been made to render this a movie, for it is as faithful a transcription of the narrative as one could well imagine. The producer has not sparred for a happy ending, and in portraying the conduct of the scandalmongers he has found a way to include a little comedy here and there without exaggerating the characters. . . .

Louis B. Mayer, head of the Metro-Goldwyn-Mayer studio, could not have chosen a better director than Seastrom for Nathaniel Hawthorne's narrative. He is painstaking in studying his characters, and it was to his advantage to have Lillian Gish in the principal role, that of Hester Prynne. Miss Gish has a strong inclination for such parts, and in this vehicle she gives an excellent conception of the courage of a young woman in the face of sneering, scorn and tittle-tattle. It causes one to contrast those days with the present time; the fashions of the past with the feminine creations of our generation. . . .

After the preliminary scenes near Boston, the director loses no time in depicting the shameless bigotry of the people, by first showing Hester Prynne's canary escaping from its cage and then having the young woman locked in the stocks for unseemly merriment and prancing through the lanes on the Sabbath. Actually she had only run after her bird, and this caused her to be late for the church service. A splendid idea of the little it took to start wagging tongues is obtained through the glimpses one has of the congregation, who look at Hester with the eyes of Pharisees eager to be present at her punishment. . . .

There are some cleverly pictured scenes in the church and the sights of crowds betray imaginative direction, both in the handling of the players and in their arrangement according to the shades of their costumes.

Mordaunt Hall. *NYT*. Aug. 10, 1926, p. 19

Gloomy and even morbid, *The Wind*, Lillian Gish's final picture for Metro-Goldwyn, is nevertheless a fine and dignified achievement. Its lack of lightness will stand in the way of its success with many, but the enjoyment of the few—presuming that serious moviegoers are in the minority—is assured.

It is a study of the dramatic effect of climate on character, better portrayed than in *Sadie Thompson*, as a matter of fact; but there the comparison ends. Miss Gish's heroine is no flamboyant creature, but a timid girl from Virginia, who comes to live on her cousin's ranch in Texas, which she fondly believes to be another Garden of Eden. Instead Letty finds herself in a barren, sand-swept country, where human existence is forever at the mercy of the devouring elements. When life is not imperiled by the violence of the wind, morale is undermined and sanity threatened by the monotony of it. This is portrayed as only the screen can portray an atmospheric condition. . . .

Unrelieved by the ghost of a smile, the picture is a somber cross-section of a life that is little known to those who prefer to see conventional heroines in the routine of familiar romances. But its relentlessness is gripping. Sound effects are justified here, for they are concerned with the wind, which dominates the picture and every character in it.

Picture Play. Feb. 1929

Like Murnau, Victor Seastrom, the Swedish director, aimed to express a universality in films, and to do it with simplicity and sincerity. He, too, depended upon the creation of mood. In approach, however, these men were widely different. Murnau was subjective, interested mainly with the camera eye; Seastrom, more objective, concerned himself with characterization through acting and with the forces of nature. In Seastrom's pictures, as in von Stroheim's, the work of the camera is not particularly noticeable; the cutting is academic. It is the relevant details placed within the scene as a whole that makes the film significant. Watching a Murnau picture, one is always aware of the amazing technique involved; it is only after seeing a Seastrom film that one becomes fully aware of its power. . . . Although achieving little public renown in the United States, he made a number of notable productions, of which one in particular—*The Wind*—is one of the finest achievements among silent American films. In technique, Seastrom was a director of distinguished talent; in subject matter, a man of keen social outlook. Though perhaps only *The Wind* was fully representative of him, all his pictures had a lyrical approach, the strength of honest characterization, and social awareness. The theme of his films was always man in conflict with society and nature; it dealt in the larger emotions, and the whole was rendered simply and lyrically. The titles of his efforts indicate Seastrom's concern with man's struggle with man and natural forces: *Name the Man* (1923), *He Who Gets Slapped* (1924), *Confessions of a Queen* (1924), *The Tower of Lies* (1924), *The Scarlet Letter* (1926), *The Wind* (1928). Never spectacular or sensational, his films did not get the attention they deserved. [1939]

Lewis Jacobs. *The Rise of the American Film*
(Teachers College, 1968), pp. 365–66

"I wanted to make a film of *The Scarlet Letter* . . . I was asked which director I would like, and I chose Victor Sjostrom, who had arrived at

MGM some years earlier from Sweden. I felt that the Swedes were closer to the feelings of New England Puritans than modern Americans." With historic simplicity, Lillian Gish described the background to this 1926 film. She leaves it for us to explain her extraordinary taste and judgment—her acting genius. Her Hester Prynne is one of the most beautifully sustained performances in screen history—mercurial, delicate, passionate. . . . Sjostrom chose the Swedish actor Lars Hanson for Arthur Dimmesdale . . . The photography is by Hendrik Sartov, who had earlier worked with Griffith; the adaptation—or diminution—of Hawthorne is by Frances Marion. Sjostrom presents a heroine struggling against moralistic conventions; his conception is so strong that the coy elements in the scenario and the cloying titles almost disappear from consciousness. He stages Lars Hanson's final revelation scene with a power and conviction that justifies Lillian Gish's hunch: these two Swedes understand Hawthorne's guilt and suffering.

Pauline Kael. *Kiss Kiss Bang Bang*
(Little, Brown, 1968), p. 345

SENNETT, MACK (1880–1960)

Cohen Collects A Debt (Keystone, September, 23).—As one sits through this eight or ten minutes of senseless, idiotic horseplay he wonders what it is all about. Never once is the spectator allowed to grasp the thread of the story, if there is a thread, and all he is treated to is a continuous show of waving arms and prancing feet. . . .

NYDM. Feb. 27, 1909, p. 13

His Favorite Pastime (Keystone) March 16.—One of the few farcial comedies in photoplays that gets continuous laughter. The comedian [Chaplin] whose favorite pastime is drinking highballs, is clever, in fact, the best one Mack Sennett has sprung on the public. He is a new one and deserves mention. The situations in this comedy are finely handled. This is a real comedy.

Moving Picture World. March 21, 1914, p. 1526

There is no use talking about situations. In *Tillie's Punctured Romance* there are nothing but situations. There's a story, of course, and it is sufficient. It shows how Tillie is wooed by Charlie and is given the mitten in favor of Mabel. When Charlie reads that through the death of the uncle Tillie is heir to three millions, he encompasses a hasty marriage before Tillie gets the news. Of course, it afterward develops uncle is not dead, but very, very much alive. Tillie, however, is pretty near dead by the time she has removed from her expansive chest several matters that weigh heavily upon it. Before the battle is over the Keystone "cops" have the riot of their tempestuous, catlike lives, an automobile takes a plunge into the Pacific—the only calm element in the show—and Tillie, after several tedious lifts and sudden immersions is finally landed on the pier. Mabel falls in the arms of Tillie. Charlie is "jugged."

Mack Sennett has done well.

George Blaidell. *Moving Picture World.* Nov. 14, 1914

Mack Sennett, great comic director, is a discreetly audacious man. The recent buffoonery that he has had made "under his direction" had an instructive luster. From a practical point of view, he makes masterful use of all the achievements of our art. Artistically, he shows a very marked personality. In France, we still don't really know what a comic director is. The vaudevilles or farces of our screen are only somewhat funny because of the verve of the actor. Max Linder and Lévesque spend their energies in nonfilms. Everybody keeps talking of the techniques of American cinematography.

Gratuitous nastiness, since I don't think that Mack Sennett is more mechanical or traditional than Griffith, Ince and DeMille. Like them, he obeys the laws of current technical perfection—unless he commands them. But this is only to provide a base for his imagination and even his sensibility. He is pictorial. Is that a technique? If so, prove to me that Devambez, Marcel Capy, Forain are all technique. Mack Sennett, very close to these powerful ironists, with the comfortable sharpness of humorists born in the home of humor, is a very spontaneous modern caricaturist. Does he know it? It doesn't really matter. Those who are most great are not necessarily those who think they are great.

Louis Delluc. *Cinéma & Cie* (Grasset, 1919), pp. 158–59

There is one serious point which a good critic (Aristotle, for example) would have discovered when he regarded the screen as long ago as 1914 and became aware of the superiority of the comic films. He would have seen at once while Mr. Griffith and Mr. Ince were both developing the technique of the moving picture, they were exploiting their discoveries with materials equally or better suited to another medium: the stage or the dime novel or whatever. Whereas Mr. Sennett was already so enamoured of his craft that he was doing with the instruments of the moving picture precisely those things which were best suited to it—those things which could not be done with any instrument but the camera, and could appear nowhere if not on the screen.

This does not mean that nothing but slap-stick comedy is proper to the cinema; it means only that everything in slap-stick *is* cinematographic; and since perceiving a delicate adjustment of means to end, or a proper relation between method and material, is a source of pleasure, Mr. Sennett's developments were more capable of pleasing the judicious than those of either of his two fellow-workers. The highly logical humanist critic of the films could have foreseen in 1914—without the decade of trial and error which has intervened—what we see now: that the one field in which the picture would most notably declare itself a failure would be that of the drama (Elinor Glyn-Cecil De Mille-Gilbert Parker, in short). Without a moment's hesitation he would have put his finger on those two elements in the cinema which, being theoretically sound, had a chance of practical success: the spectacle (including the spectacular melodrama) and the grotesque comedy. Several years later he would have added one word more, that grotesque tragedy might conceivably succeed. For it is not only the fun in the Keystones which makes them successful: it is the method of presentation. [1924]

Gilbert Seldes. *The Seven Lively Arts.*
(Sagamore, 1957 [rev.]), pp. 15–16

My admiration for Mack Sennett is temperamental and chronic. I think it dates from that long ago when he played the moony, semi-conscious farm hand, forsaken by the sweetly pretty little milkmaid for some burlesque city slicker, with oiled hair and a bushy mustache. And it endures today when he is a multi-millionaire, the owner of a moving picture studio with some twenty-two or twenty-four stages, and an established reputation as the producer of comedy of a burlesque type. For to me his is a real creative force in the cinema world—a master at interpreting the crude primary impulses of the dub, the numbskull, the weakling, failure, clown, boor, coward, bully. The interpretive burlesque he achieves is no different from that of Shakespeare, Voltaire, Shaw or Dickens, when they are out to achieve humorous effects by burlesquing humanity. To be sure, these others move away from burlesque to greater ends. It is merely an incident in a great canvas. With Sennett it is quite the whole canvas. But within his range, what a master! He is Rabelaisian, he is Voltairish. He has characteristics in common with Sterne, Swift, Shaw, Dickens—where they seek to catch the very things which he catches. Positively, if any writer of this age had brought together in literary form—and in readable English—instead of upon the screen as has Sennett—the pie-throwers, soup-spillers, bomb-tossers, hot-stove stealers, and what not else of Mr. Sennett's grotesqueries—what a reputation! The respect! The reclaim! As it is, there exists today among the most knowing of those who seek a picture of life as it is—or might be were it not for these inherent human buffooneries which Mr. Sennett so clearly recognizes and captures—a happy and sane tendency to evaluate him properly.

Theodore Dreiser. *Photoplay*. August 1928, p. 32

Every month now brings us some new Sennett talkie, and nearly all are good. Not quite all. Sennett is not a genius; he has his dull, his very dull moments. We never feel, watching his work, that we are on the brink of some fine imaginative adventure, some excursion into an achievement beyond good craftsmanship. Once, long ago, he had his adventure in *Susanna*—a fairy-tale bit of pantomime, beautifully massed, fantastically lighted, and richly played by Mabel Normand, but indeterminate in its goal, and missing success by just that extra spark of fire that warms and illuminates the poet's creation. *Susanna* is Sennett's one essay beyond fine craft. I do not think we shall experience another. But even if *The Lion's Roar, The Hollywood Theme Song* and *Dance-hall Marge* are to be taken as types of the best in Sennett's modern work, we need hardly repine. The point is that this tough old teacher of pantomime should be still at work, turning his experience and intelligence into new channels, knocking into shape another generation of pupils, roughing his material of laughter into fresh forms for a fresh decade.

With the entrance of Sennett into the field of talking pictures, the wheel has come full circle. We find ourselves back at the beginning of things, in a cinema that is rough and joyous, incidental and without subtlety; a cinema bound by no traditions, no refinements, and no fashions; a cinema that has never known a Wiene, or a Pabst, or a Pudovkin, but is ripe to give a Chaplin to the world.

C. A. Lejeune. *Cinema* (Alexander Maclehose, 1931), pp. 48–49

The advent of sound and the collapse of the world's economic structure found Sennett with his back to the wall, but still full of fight. Then came a thrust from nowhere, a sudden and unexpected stab which Sennett, like Caesar in the Forum, accepted as the unkindest cut of all.

The animated cartoon was a new and popular toy—especially to a world in despair. It preserved and accentuated a thousand-fold all the illusions of slap-stick. The pen was mightier than the bed-slat. By the exercise of a few thousand strokes of a cartoonist's quill, a whole animal kingdom of stars came into being and had an immortal existence in an inkwell. . . .

A nimble rodent has become the world's hero. In the eyes of Mack Sennett, he must always remain a scaggly mustachioed villain whose mischief will never be undone.

Who killed Cock Robin? "I did," said Mickey Mouse.

Gene Fowler. *Father Goose* (Covici-Friede, 1934), pp. 406–07

In the last few years it must have been evident to the most pessimistic-minded that motion pictures have been steadily moving toward that bourne of all good literature and the graphic arts—*satire*.

Not that pictures will not continue to serve good old vegetable soup, Boston baked beans, homemade pie and plenty of lobscouse, with a lavish sprinkle of bullets; but the general tendency has been toward that solid form of creative brainwork which is the essence of High Humor.

The evolution of Fun in pictures has been from slapstick and pie-throwing to the more familiar forms of humor typified in homely household scenes and Gargantuan spaghetti-eaters in cock-eyed restaurants up to those fine satiric plays and isolated scenes that I shall specify later on.

As the progenitors on the American-speaking stage of all our native satire today were Charley Hoyt's and Harrigan & Hart's social satires in the nineties, so the present movement in pictures to the realm of the brain-chuckle stems from the Mack Sennett and old Keystone comedies.

These latter comedies have never got their full share of appreciation. The "Intelligentsia" always gave them a snooty look and condemned them to the limbo of idiocy.

As a matter of fact, the Sennett and Keystone comedies were among the first burlesques (a burlesque always precedes the coming of legitimate satire) on our American everyday life that the present century has given us.

Everything was caricatured and ridiculed in these uproarious funfests. It is true the technique was at times crude, but the main impression left on me after seeing hundreds of these "comedies" was that of truth in a concave mirror.

I heard it said by a picture director in those days that "humor in the movies will never go beyond Sennett. The public doesn't and never will get satire."

This director made the mistake of believing that there is "a general public."

There are *publics*—hundreds of different kinds of publics.

The pictures in the past have made the mistake of believing that there was only *one kind* of public—and that public was always measured by the mental calibre, the personal likes and dislikes of producers.

Benjamin de Casseres. *Cinema Arts*.
June 1937, p. 80

Ince and Tourneur, both film dramatists, dealt exclusively with the feature film; Mack Sennett specialized in the production of comedies rarely more than one or two reels long. He was the first of America's comedy directors to develop a distinct film style: slapstick. With its burlesque satire, with its action and fantasy achieved through the use of camera trickery, his method was the fruition of some fifteen years of experiment with the humorous incident and the chase situation. For a decade this type of comedy had been developing in form and broadening in content. Sennett consolidated its traits, added new ones, and gave it a unique and inimitable flavor of his own. He was the first to perceive that if a chase is funny, a riot is funnier; if a pretty girl is pleasant, a dozen pretty girls are delightful; if a cop is comic, a gross of cops are hilarious; if an action—such as a fight or a man running—when photographed at normal speed is interesting, the same action photographed at sub-normal speed or high speed (creating the effect of extra-fast motion or slow motion) is exciting. But more than this, Sennett had a feeling for pace and unity in scene progression—even though the events were in themselves mad and were improvised as the action developed—which distinguished his films from all other comedies of the day.

Years of work with Griffith as an actor at Biograph gave Sennett the conviction that, above all, movies must move, and it was this attitude applied to his own pictures that created a unique comedy style. In full command of his own studio in 1912, he made his pet subject, the vaudeville cop, a national figure. With his patrol wagons flying down the street, custard pies encountering various faces, never-ending chases, and bathing beauties swirling about the Keystone cop, Sennett created a world of absurdity which in two years made him the top comedy director. In 1916 his success and fame had become so pronounced that he became the third producer of the Triangle Corporation, sharing honors with Griffith and Ince. [1939]

Lewis Jacobs. *The Rise of the American Film*
(Teachers College, 1968), pp. 209–10

The Sennett world is inaccurately remembered today. Slapstick is in a decline, and the antics of the Three Stooges bear little relation to the ordered madness and harmless violence which Sennett made so funny.

The principal feature of this master comedian's world was that nothing in it had normal consequences. Frenzied beatings caused the pain of a pinprick, hundreds of bullets produced no fatalities. In this slightly off-center caricature of the world of ordinary experience, people could do things that in real life would have the most catastrophic effects. They are the things we all wish to do, without daring to—hence the primary appeal of Sennett's work.

Nothing was sacred to Sennett and his studioful of irreverent comedians. To the primitive humors of undress and obesity he added wild ridicule of virtue, authority, romantic love, religion itself. In Sennett's world all lawyers were shysters, all pious people hypocrites, all sheriffs both stupid and venal, and in that world everybody was caught with his pants down. His mysterious knack, and it remains a mystery, was that of creating satire as sharp as a needle while simultaneously extracting the sting.

Richard Griffith and Arthur Mayer.
The Movies (S&S, 1957), p. 71

In the United States thousands of commercial organizations had launched the slogan "Time Is Money," and Americans cottoned to the idea that high pressure signified efficiency. But the hilarious "mile a minute" chases in Sennett's comic films clearly indicated that the faster you go the less you accomplish. During that time the nation was beginning to exalt the importance of pure quantity. . . . Sennett outrageously multiplied everything: policemen, bullets, projectiles, criminals, pretty girls. The result was wild confusion. The Model T Fords that Sennett has conquering all sorts of obstacles, crossing rivers and lakes, crashing into houses and cars only to finally burst in sulferous explosions were a sardonic commentary to a people who were beginning to persuade themselves that the possession of an automobile was a matter of great importance. Contemporaries saw with less evidence than later critics did the fact that the magnificent and audacious "nonsense" of Sennett's films reflected a skeptical vision of national life. The fact that the king of laughter is a penetrating and cruel judge of American customs is obvious if we consider his definition of the comic film. The pretext for a comic film will be found, he told an interviewer, either in sex or crime. For him, these two ideas constituted the essential base from which comic ideas spring. For level-headed citizens observing with a certain apprehension the tendencies of American life, the significance of this new doctrine must have been less than reassuring. [1961]

David Turconi. *Mack Sennett* (Editions Seghers, 1966), pp. 86–87

Sennett films were compounded of attractively diverse elements. There was a slight touch of madness about them—they defied both logic and gravity and hovered on the edge of fantasy—yet down to earth as they were, the girls who appeared in them glorified them with a touch of beauty. The result should have been a hodgepodge, but it was not, somehow; it was a world. How this was achieved was Sennett's secret, and this constitutes his final claim as an artist, for nobody else has ever been able to do it so well. The terrible punishments which his characters received and inflicted, for example, were saved from sadism by the exhilaration they exuded; you felt that the people on the screen —and you, for the moment—were superior to the hazards of life.

Edward Wagenknecht. *The Movies in the Age of Innocence* (Oklahoma, 1962), p. 41

If there is one symbol of the art of Sennett, it is of the Kops, mounted on a decrepit flivver, their blue-clad arms and legs protruding in wild tangles, their faces set in masks of stolid dignity, pursuing a miscreant through the wastelands of southern California, on which the outlines of the megapolis to come were barely sketched in. . . .

What did it all mean? The chase offered a dozen possibilities of interpretation: it was a comment on all who pursued goals with too much zeal and not enough sense, it was a dramatization of the individual's struggle against society or organization, it was a grand thumb in the eye of authority. But most of all it was good, clean fun. And it is one of the things for which our movie-makers have lost the knack, one of the things about which nostalgia plays us no tricks. The chases (and comedies in general) were better and funnier in the old days than they are now. And Mack Sennett was one of the very, very few who made genuine folk art while working in a mass medium.

Richard Schickel. *Movies* (Basic, 1964), p. 59

Comrades is about the adventure of a couple of tramps when one of them decides to impersonate Marmaduke Bracegirdle, a British Member of Parliament scheduled to pay a visit to an American family. In this representative of Sennett's Biograph comedies there are few signs of the special elements he was to incorporate in the slapstick comedy; however, it is evident that he had grasped the principles of dynamic film-making which D. W. Griffith was exploring at this time. Sennett composed this one-reel film out of about thirty-five short scenes and cut freely back and forth between the interior and exterior for purposes of comic contrast.

Eileen Bowser in *Film Notes*, edited by Eileen Bowser (MOMA, 1969), p. 8

The Sennett contribution to the world of screen comedy—and ultimately to the language of a nation—was a study in organized madness. As we have seen, much of the heritage of Keystone was that of the early French comedies, and the American screen was waiting for someone to point the way. Mack's raucous combination of French fantasy with the ludicrousness of American burlesque produced slapstick, an offspring that, although Gallic in nature, was purely American in spirit. Keystone was one man's unique opportunity to remake the world as his own logic told him it really was, and Sennett made the most of it! We may occasionally reflect upon the capricious nature of life today, but the vehicle that Keystone afforded Mack Sennett is not within our reach; we cannot reconstruct the whole thing to suit ourselves as Mack did.

Sennett's world of Keystone was fundamentally one of absurdity, in which dignity and refinement were revealed as a sham and replaced by vulgarity and ridicule. His comedians thumbed their noses at convention, and life on the Keystone screen was stripped of the masks society had imposed upon human behavior. Impulse and emotion replaced reason and rationality as the motivators of human action, and the hypocrisy of society's sacred institutions was laid bare for all to see. Married men flirted with other women while their spouses sought the attentions of other men; any criminal fresh from prison could easily pass as a pious clergyman (and did) with as much authority as the real article could command; the human frailties that cause us to hire police for protection from ourselves and our fellow men were just as much a part of their nature; the badge and uniform didn't really change the man in Keystone's view.

Kalton C. Lahue. *Mack Sennett's Keystone*
(Barnes, 1971), p. 277

It has been often said that Hollywood had produced only three true geniuses: Chaplin, Disney, and Thalberg. Well, in my estimation Dick Jones was the Irving Thalberg of Sennett Comedies. Each was a supreme creative catalyst, adored and admired by writers, directors, and actors. Each insisted on anonymity—no credits on screen or in publicity. Each functioned as production head of his studio.

Both started in pictures at sixteen, skyrocketed to the top, made a million dollars before they were thirty, and both died in their thirties—killed by the pressure of their jobs.

There was one major difference between them: Thalberg and his superior, Louis B. Mayer, had a passionate hatred for each other—my wife and I saw Mayer dance publicly all night at a cabaret on the Strip the day Thalberg died. Dick Jones admired and praised Sennett's uncanny sense of comedy and graciously gave him all the credit. "Without the Old Man's genius," Jones used to say, "there'd be no Mack Sennett Comedies and no Dick Jones."

However, the writers and directors knew that while Sennett was the heart, the body, and the name of the studio, Dick Jones was the brains. He assigned writers and directors, cast the parts, thought up and listened to story ideas, supervised the editing. Then, without appearing to do so, he had everything tried out on the Old Man. Although Sennett had no great sense of humor—as most of us commonly know it—his reaction to comedy was an infallible audience-barometer. If Sennett laughed, audiences would laugh. If Sennett *didn't* laugh—well, rewrite it or reshoot it, said Dick Jones.

Frank Capra. *The Name Above the Title*
(Macmillan, 1971), p. 51

STERNBERG, JOSEF VON (1894–1969)

Although there are several episodes in [*Underworld*] that could have been improved upon by a little more thought and study, it is a compelling subject, one that has a distinctly original vein. It was directed by Josef von Sternberg, who gained notoriety by his work on that disagreeable production *The Salvation Hunters*. Here, however, largely through the competent work of Mssrs. Bancroft and Brook, Mr. von Sternberg gives a better idea of his powers as a director. While Mr. Bancroft's acting is possibly not quite as intriguing as it was in James Cruze's film *The Pony Express*, this stalwart player is nevertheless so well suited to his part that one does not care so much about his guffawing when a smile would be more effective. . . .

Evelyn Brent is very attractive and she gives a capable performance as "Feathers." Sometimes Mr. von Sternberg shows that he is too fond of posing her looking away from the persons with whom she is supposed to be conversing, but that is his fault.

Mordaunt Hall, *NYT*. Aug. 22, 1927, p. 21

But it is doubtful whether any film before *The Salvation Hunters* showed a conscious effort made to set up a continuous rhythmic feeling; and there it only persisted strongly through the first half of the film, the scene of which was laid on a mud-dredger. This dredger worked continuously, either the claw-bucket travelling up and down dribbling filth, or the crane-neck swinging out over the mud-barge and back. This was movement in three dimensions of a slow but regular kind, and it proved to be soothing and not distracting. Other shots had the usual fixed backgrounds of walls, doors, etc. And these two series of scenes were alternated in certain simple ratios, according to the demands of the action as it moved through one scene to another. Here, at first, it is difficult to say whether we have an example of simple or counterpoint rhythm in its truest sense; whether the regularly recurring movements of the dredger, or the simple permutations and combinations of the scenes with moving and fixed backgrounds, provide the metre.

This film, made at a negligible cost by an enterprising group of Hollywood unemployed, came in for some curious treatment at the hands of the critics. Iris Barry in her disappointing book, *Let's Go to the Pictures* [sic], speaks of it as follows: "Chaplin, one heard, hailed the picture as a masterpiece. When Chaplin opens his mouth, all the critics yap in unison. *The Salvation Hunters* was acclaimed throughout the world. It was a dismal failure. When it had gone its rounds, Chaplin said that he had thought he would see whether the cinema audiences had any sense. He thought he would praise a bad picture and see how many would swallow what he said." This little trick of Chaplin's lacks confirmation: let it suffice to point out that on the strength of this picture alone he took Georgia Hale and starred her in *The Gold Rush* in the place of Lita Grey. Iris Barry was not the only critic who misunderstood the importance of *The Salvation Hunters*. Other critics made the same mistake, probably because they were unused to any sensible handling of rhythm in films, and distrusted the term itself on account of its misuse by directors of the so-called absolute or abstract films that hail from Paris.

Eric Walter White. *Parnassus to Let*
(Hogarth, 1928), pp. 25–28

A quick comparison with *The Way of All Flesh* might be in order. That picture, as a picture, swung up to a higher curve—reaching its apex in the ruin of the amiably vain bank cashier—and then dropped almost below the endurance of the sensitive movie goer. The curve of *The Last Command* perhaps never climbed so high but never fell so low, travelling along at a consistent level both in story value and in character portrayal. The climax came at the end, so that there was no time for falling off whereas in *The Way of All Flesh* the climax came just after the middle of the picture and almost broke it in two. . . .

In what it tries to do this is certainly a powerful story sinuously told and ably directed—certainly a better than the average Hollywood plot. Yet, in its very finish and in its sometimes not altogether honest treatment of the issues involved in the story, it has something of the Hollywood flavor. This feeling grows when one considers some of the extravagances of treatment notably in the coal tender scene, in the theatrical parody of the revolution, and in the Hollywood studio scenes. But Emil Jannings is still powerful enough to be able to counteract the Hollywood virus. For that, everyone will be very thankful.

NBR. Feb. 1928, pp. 7–8

In this film [*The Docks of New York*] as in *Underworld*, and I hope in those that will follow, Joseph von Sternberg shows genius and lifts himself to a rank which one should not hesitate to identify as that of the leading director in the world. Nobody, not even Pudovkin, whose power he has, nor Murnau, from whom he borrows his mastery of lighting, nor any of the many American directors to whom he owes his technique of forceful details, no other man of the cinema puts us into a state of such excitement and forces our attention so. . . .

. . . The subject of *The Docks of New York* is of primordial importance. The title (*Les Damnés de l'océan*) leads one to expect a description of the hellish life of stokers, but there are only a few shots of this. Dudule and Bancroft, exhausted stokers of an unidentified ship, go ashore to spend the night and one expects the heroic-comic adventures of international ports; but the idea, once lightly sketched in, disappears completely. Bancroft flexes his terrible muscles, he fights and goes through terrible scuffles, but soon we have left behind the now classic subject of Bancroft's violence. At every instant Sternberg ignores the themes that his colleagues have made a style of. He even deprives himself of Bancroft's formidable laugh, and all through the film the actor remains astonishingly calm. . . . One overseas film writer says that the best film would be one in which one believed until the end that the hero would not marry the heroine. Stripped of its vulgarity, this sally expresses the impression one gets all during *The Docks of New York*. But one comes away with the memory of a film impregnated with a life whose essential is in its energy and force.

Louis Chavance. *Revue du Cinéma*.
May 1929, unpaged

Everybody knows our admiration for Sternberg. With some very few others he has given the cinema a means of containing within it certain hard moral realities, certain emphasized reactions of misfortune and of love that will be the real test of its intellectual power. That's why I think it is important, in order to safeguard the purity of his first films, to react strongly against his last production: *The Drag Net* . . . everything in it is false, completely false, and morally disgusting. Some scenes from *Underworld*, chosen among the most sublime, reappear almost image for image. . . . If the so-called adventure film has come to this imitation, to this stereotype, it might just as well stop now. If the drama of a fatality as poignant as that of *Underworld* is to parody itself in combinations of this kind, it had better be ignored.

André Delons. *Revue du Cinéma.*
May 1929, unpaged

There was distinctly a new emotional effect in that interesting film [*Thunderbolt*]. In the opening sequence two lovers on a park bench are about to part forever. The girl at last tears herself away and the picture holds attention pitilessly on the agonized young man while the crunching of the girl's feet on the gravel dies away into the night. This sound was so different from anything yet heard on an audible screen that it became a text for critical attacks on talkies in general; but it should have been hailed as a keynote of a fine new art, for it was employed with the rare discernment of a true artist. In the raid on "The Black Cat," that constitutes another sequence, somebody pulls the lights, and the voice of the chief detective is heard in the darkness telling everybody to keep perfectly still, telling "Thunderbolt" to put up his hands—he's under arrest. Then lo, the lights are switched on again—and Thunderbolt has escaped. When Thunderbolt is finally captured in a tenement hallway, all idea of the escape of so resourceful a man is put at rest by the approaching siren of the police patrol that is never seen.

Arthur Edwin Krows. *The Talkies*
(Holt, 1930), pp. 112–13

Morocco sets its sound in the background. Its speech is purely that of pictures, except where the pictures can be told more effectively by sound. For example: the Legionnaire is sent forward to capture a machine gun nest. You hear the put-put-put of the gun, at first in the distance, then nearer, nearer, as the soldier, whom you always see, creeps closer to it. The effect is wonderfully heightened, partakes of reality itself, gives the immediacy of self-experience. The capture of the gun is left in the air with a fading screen, and the suspense is kept like a bridge over the following sequence of events. This sort of thing is unfailingly terse, cinematically economic, a cunning grasp of the power of suggestion as made possible by the image in motion and the sound that in the context of that image, and in association with it, you see and know. The artist gives his engagement supper to his can make another image of its own. It is the sort of thing that points the way to the method of the motion picture of tomorrow, and makes of *Morocco* a stimulating forerunner.

And again with the use of dialogue in this film: when a character speaks it is merely in substantiation of the thing the action has made

friends. All is sumptuous, splendid, covered with light, gaiety and tender feeling. The tragic past of his fiancée is gone. Then the drums of the returning Legionnaires are faintly heard. You get the sensation of the stirring city in the warm night outside. And Jolly must tear herself away, must go to find her lover. There is no word spoken. Eloquently the silent screen speaks to us as of old. And when she is gone, you get the shot of the long, richly laden table with its startled, embarrassed guests, and its host at the head, left to his contemplation of the situation. He rises, for he must follow Jolly, just as she must follow the soldier, Tom Brown. Then Menjou, who plays the artist lover, says, and from the screen emanates not a mechanical voice out of the flat middle of a shadow, but living words from the human lips, quiet, moving and immensely real: "You see—I love her." How terse and how explanatory—yet it is the picture, the cinema, the parade of images, convoluting yet always leading to that moment, and not the sound device, that makes the simple utterance so effective. One could go on finding in this film a text book and finding in the firm and sinewy grasp of its director the resolve to bring the motion picture, with the new powers that science has given it, back to its own.

NBR. Nov. 1930, pp. 4–5

The Blue Angel is notable from the directing angle on account of von Sternberg's clever combination of talking and silent film technique. He uses dialogue sparingly and climactically and employs long sequences of purely cinematic story telling. In other words, he allows the camera to tell the story whenever possible rather than letting the actor tell it vocally. That, in a nutshell, is the goal of good talking pictures today, now that the ghost of the all-talking picture has been laid.

Certain talking sequences, or sometimes merely single phrases, are in German. This in no way detracts from our understanding of the action. For they are used purely for atmosphere, at times when the action fully conveys the meaning. Thus, for instance, the Professor's housekeeper addresses him in German through the door of his bedroom. But her manner and the breakfast tray in her hands plainly shows that she is telling him that it is time for him to get up and have his breakfast. . . . Intrinsically these German sequences have the same effect which silent sequences would have. It is unnecessary to make them vocal except for atmospheric effect. But the atmospheric excuse is sufficient, for though the hero is a professor of English, teaching English to his pupils and succumbing to an English traveling cabaret entertainer, he moves in an environment of German speech. As long as pictures have become lingual there is no reason why they should not also become polylingual when the story logically calls for it.

Occasionally Mr. von Sternberg's directorial style leads him into slow tempo as if building up for a dramatic suspense which never quite comes off. This is all the more noticeable in a picture which has a minimum of action and a surplusage of characterization and atmosphere. These defects were perhaps abetted by Jannings. One sometimes wonders whether Jannings, especially since he became an undisputed star, has not always set the tempo of his pictures, however his director might cry for speed. His slow, deliberate method of acting and gesticulating at times anticipated the talking picture while he was still acting on the silent screen.

NBR. Jan. 1931, pp. 10–12

In the early days of his career, Sternberg presented, in films of simple climactic progression, the honest American idiom of the open attack. But soon he was cultivated by cult. For a time he appeared out of the reach of the sycophants. To resist cult, however, requires stamina; Sternberg yielded. He traded his open style for fancy play, chiefly upon the legs in silk, and buttocks in lace, of Dietrich, of whom he has made a paramount slut. Sternberg is, by his own tokens, a man of meditation as well as action; but instead of contemplating the navel of Buddha his umbilical perseverance is fixed on the navel of Venus. His diligence was frustrated when he met the innate sobriety of *An American Tragedy*. The result is an aimless, lugubrious mess. As for his direction of melodrama, there is more honest stuff in John S. Robertson's *The Phantom of Paris* than in *Dishonored*—more honest because less egregious. The fireworks may dazzle the schoolboys of criticism, but they will contribute no permanent color to the motion picture. Whether Sternberg is a man of ability or not, I place him on less honest a level than even George Fitzmaurice who made *The Unholy Garden*.

Harry Alan Potamkin. *Vanity Fair.*
March 1932, p. 52

There is no possible excuse for *Blonde Venus*, except that it supports the incredibly accurate prediction made in this department some months ago that Marlene Dietrich was due to explode with a loud hollow pop. The story has all the dramatic integrity of a sash-weight murderer's tabloid autobiography; and Miss Dietrich, as usual, smiles serenely, crosses her legs, lights cigarettes, and waits for Sternberg to make her exciting. In a perspiring effort to do so, he starts with her in the raw, then puts his star in all the old clothes he could find around the lot, makes her first wife, then mother, then mistress, then tramp, and asks her to do everything but skin a cat to amuse the customers. For all these antics she remains unexciting. The explanation is near at hand.

Mr. Sternberg's employers, despite repeated warnings, allowed their erratic cameraman to write his own scenario; and not all the directors in the world could have taken such a dramatic curiosity and made Miss Dietrich, or anyone else, exciting. Miss Dietrich, of course, seems utterly disinterested in the difficult business at hand and ignores poor Herbert Marshall, a child actor, and the world in general in as complete an exhibition of somnambulance as any actress ever gave an enthusiastic, if misled, public.

Pare Lorentz. *Vanity Fair*. Nov. 1932, p. 58

In his silent films Sternberg was as interesting a director as Hollywood had to offer. They were cut so smoothly, with such a delicate sense of rhythm, that they had that finished, complete quality which few American films possess. Their photography was the best in Hollywood: luminous gray tones, rich dramatic chiaroscuro, with each shot a well-thought-out composition in itself. A scenarist himself, Sternberg knew how to tell a story, how to keep it moving and give it suspense. His films moved along smoothly and swiftly, with the minimum of wasted motion. Skillfully he kaleidoscoped the narrative so as to get pace and avoid wearisome exposition, as in *Underworld* when the murder is followed immediately by the judge pronouncing sentence of death.

All of these gifts Sternberg had—and still has. But they have degenerated into the hollowest, most patent kind of technical trickery. His latest movie, *The Blonde Venus*, is perhaps the worst ever made. In it all Sternberg's gifts have turned sour. The photography is definitely "arty"—a nauseating blend of hazy light, soft focus, over-blacks and over-whites, with each shot so obviously "composed" as to be painful. Sternberg's rhythm has declined to a senseless, see-saw pattern. And his kaleidoscopic cutting has reached such a point that the film is all pace and nothing else. The scene changes often, simply because Sternberg didn't have the vitality to get anything much out of any one scene. [1933]

Dwight Macdonald. *D. M. on Movies*
(Prentice-Hall, 1969), pp. 96–97

Arty, abstruse symbolism qualifying its action, dialogue, musical accompaniment, production features in backgrounds and crowd groupings and even the manner in which the camera is used, the story [*The Devil Is a Woman*] is interpreted in a way that is probably understandable, and thus appealing to more intellectually inclined drama students. The masses—preview audience being the measuring gauge—just as probably will find it difficult to comprehend.

Motion Picture Herald. March 2, 1935, p. 55

It was *The Docks of New York* . . . which put von Sternberg in the front rank. Just as [Karl Junghans'] *Such Is Life* was the swan song of the silent film in Europe, so did *The Docks of New York* represent the logical conclusion of a whole range of technique in which American skill was combined for the first and last time with the pictorial perfection of the Germans. In this gripping tale, the characters were brought to life with rugged truthfulness. . . . *The Docks of New York* was notable because of its photography. Seldom have we seen anything more beautiful than the scenes with which the film opens, the glistening bodies of the stokers in the oily steam, the smoky port with its fog, or than the low bar where, as a joke, Bancroft decides to marry his drowned woman and, in the midst of an incredible uproar, sends for the clergyman. As in *Underworld*, American vitality is added to the beauty of misty outlines and of faces half-hidden in shadow. In *The Docks of New York* the silent film reached a kind of perfection evermore to be regretted, which gave hope that through this German [sic] the American film was about to become humanized. He created two or three stirring and powerful films and provided a dramatic model full of verve and vigor.

Maurice Bardèche and Robert Brasillach.
The History of Motion Pictures (Norton and
MOMA, 1938), pp. 209–300

The most conspicuous attempt to turn the movie camera on everyday life was a true experiment, conducted outside the industry. Josef von Sternberg, a film editor, produced with little capital and unknown actors *The Salvation Hunters*, 1925, which Fairbanks bought for United Artists release and which Chaplin proclaimed a masterpiece. But it did little to endear the idea of screen realism to audiences. It was the dreariest picture on record. Silent pictures were usually full of ceaseless activity: things had to be kept moving at all costs. Sternberg decided to explore the contrasting effect of complete immobility. *The Salvation Hunters* consisted of a series of scenes in which groups of characters stood or sat around without moving a muscle, looking extremely depressed and not even blinking their eyes. From time to time Sternberg cut in a shot of the real star of the picture, a symbolic dredger which dipped into a harbor and brought up a load of slime. All this to express the idea that nothing ever happens in the lives of ordinary people. Audience reaction was, in substance: even *our* lives are not so drab as this, and if they are we don't want to know about it. Asked to comment on the failure of a film he had praised so highly, Chaplin said, "Well, you know I was only kidding. They all take everything I say so seriously I thought I'd praise a bad picture and see what happened."

Richard Griffith and Arthur Mayer.
The Movies (S&S, 1957), p. 216

Without question, von Sternberg's *The Devil Is A Woman* is one of the crowning masterpieces of the American Cinema. It was extremely unpopular with audiences and critics when it was released, but over the years its reputation has grown, due largely to special showings in Europe. . . .

It is impossible here to review the beauties of individual scenes, but one or two are particularly unforgettable. One shot has Antonio in pursuit of Concha running down an enormous baroque stairway which is covered in so much serpentine and confetti that it resembles the interior of some cave. The duel sequence in the pouring rain, seems almost out of Goya. And, again, the entrance of Don Pasqual, when he surprises the lovers in their tryst by opening two great doors and framing himself in a huge painting of death in the bull ring, is splendidly theatrical. . . .

We are left with the practical problem of audience reception to the film today. And it is a problem. Some viewers are bored stiff by the whole thing, others are completely fascinated. It is visually one of the greatest films of all time, but not all of your audience will care for it.

David Stewart Hull. *Film Society Review*.
Nov. 1964, pp. 12–13

Everyday life, as such, seldom appears in Sternberg's cinema. His characters generally make their first entrance at a moment in their lives when there is no tomorrow. Knowingly or unknowingly, they have reached the end or the bottom, but they will struggle a short time longer, about ninety minutes of screen time, to discover the truth about themselves and those they love. Although there is much violence and death in Sternberg's world, there is relatively little action. The various murders, duels, executions, suicides, and assaults serve merely as poetic punctuation for lives drifting to their destinations in reflective repose. Death in this context is less a conclusion than a termination. The paradox of violence without action is supplemented by the paradox of virtue without morality. There are no codes or systems in these dream worlds; the characters retain their civilized graces despite the most desperate struggles for psychic survival, and it is their poise under pressure, their style under stress, that grants them a measure of heroic stature and stoic calm.

Sternberg's films are poetic without being symbolic. We need not search for slumbering allegories of Man and God and Life, but rather for a continuous stream of emotional autobiography. Sternberg's exoticism is then less a pretense than a pretext for objectifying personal fantasies. His equivalent literary genre is not the novel, nor the short story, nor the theatrical spectacle, but the closet drama unplayable but for the meaningful grace of gesture and movement. There persists an erroneous impression that the art of a *Morocco* or a *Shanghai Express* consists of the magnifying of trivialities. Yet there is nothing trivial about the size of Sternberg's emotions, and nothing disproportionate in the means employed to express them, critics from John Grierson to Susan Sontag notwithstanding. Also there is conscious humor in the director's awareness of his own absurdity though some spectators still imagine they are laughing *at* Sternberg when they are actually laughing *with* him. The colorful costumes, the dazzling décors, the marble-pillared palaces merely underscore by ironic contrast the painfully acquired wisdom of the all too human prisoners of grandiose illusions. The limitations of this aesthetic are self-evident. An insufficient grasp of one's time and place is hardly a positive virtue even for the most lyrical poet. It is only when we look around at the allegedly significant cinema of Sternberg's contemporaries that we recognize the relative stature of a director who chose to write with a camera in the first person long before Alexandre Astruc's "*caméra-stylo*" made such impious subjectivity fashionable and such personal poetry comprehensible.

Andrew Sarris. *The Films of Josef von Sternberg* (MOMA, 1966), p. 8

It was von Sternberg's ambition to make a film in which everything photographed was artificial and his closest approach to this was his last film, *The Saga of Anatahan*, which, though made under great limitations and without the quality of playing he had in America, has a completeness that summarizes his work and a simplicity that denotes full maturity—the restrictions imposed by finance stimulated a purer abstraction. The subject is archetypal: fifteen men and one woman marooned on a volcanic island for seven years; but the film is utterly abstract: the set is a man-made jungle that shines in the light and throws a lattice of shadow on the action. The Japanese faces seem devoid of expression. To possess the woman, the men proceed to kill each other off in dynastic struggles as absurd as those in *Scarlet Empress*. The same pendulum motif of destiny taunts them: the waves that advance on and recede from the island; the swinging hammock occupied by different men in succession; the lost movements of men wandering in the jungle, and the swaying woman as she dances for the men. The narrative of *Anatahan* describes the men searching in vain for meaning on the island. Von Sternberg's world is pessimistic because it mocks the idea of meaning. Its constants are the two sexes, the patterns of their movements and the light that exposes and confuses them.

David Thomson. *Movie Man* (Stein & Day, 1967), pp. 47–48

Sternberg evoked for *The Scarlet Empress* a Peterhof Palace such as never was and yet was never anything else but Russian, eighteenth-century Byzantine Russian. The twisted, anguished sculptures of saints and martyrs were gargoyles sprung, like Athena from the head of Zeus, from the unending fecund imagination of the director and masterfully executed under his supervision by the Swiss sculptor Peter Balbusch, a long-time Sternberg devotee. Similarly, Richard Kollorsz, a German painter, executed ikons and portraits more Byzantine than any real ikons of the Russian Orthodox Church. Just as Eisenstein a decade later was to heighten the Kremlin palace of Ivan the Terrible with poetic realism, Sternberg heightened the Peterhof Palace the same way—and not only the décor but the very characters themselves—but Sternberg did it first. In the same way, the elaborate ritual of the wedding of Catherine and Peter in the Cathedral of Kazan in Sternberg's film antedates the elaborate ritual of the coronation of Ivan IV in the Ouspensky cathedral in Eisenstein's. It was this that caused Henri Langlois, curator of the Cinémathèque Française (and an avowed admirer of Eisenstein) to cable Sternberg, after he had belatedly seen *The Scarlet Empress* in March, 1964: "Have just seen marvelous *Scarlet Empress*. Stop. All *Ivan Grozhny* comes from your film. Stop. All my respect and admiration."

Herman G. Weinberg. *Josef von Sternberg* (Dutton, 1967), p. 62

Sternberg's alternative to the Hollywood style of film-making was a synthetic language of personal statement. Story was unimportant, elapsed time insignificant; most of his films leap years in the telling, charting an emotional relationship or moral decline without respect for chronology. Imitating *Kammerspiel*, he used lighting, *décor* and minutely observed gestures to entice from nature and the human face their hidden "spiritual power," and his development became a search for new elements that would allow him to distil in greater purity this inner essence. Themes from German and Austrian plays were absorbed, and, though repelled by the over-bearing German film dramas, he admired the style of its stage directors. In film, his main influences were Austrian or French. Like Max Ophüls, another Viennese, he adopted instinctively a fluid style of tracks and dissolves, and from playwright Arthur Schnitzler, also revered by Ophüls, a liking for acid and satirical dialogue. Jean Perrier, pioneer of *le grand décor*, suggested to him the emotional and dramatic possibilities of design, which Sternberg was later to explore with Perrier's pupil, Hans Dreier.

John Baxter. *The Cinema of Josef von Sternberg* (Barnes, 1971), pp. 14, 16–17

STEVENS, GEORGE (1905–)

Alice Adams is a picture that will be remembered longer than it deserves, and all because it is designed not so much as a show as for purposes of elevation. It is the kind of picture that takes up a subject. What is more, it takes up a subject that a lot of people are very close to, because a lot of people have had doors slammed in their faces, usually when they were too young to know how to put their feet in them; and because they have practiced in private all these pitiful little artifices, now made public.

The Adams girl lived on the wrong side of town. She didn't get to parties, pretended that she simply couldn't stand going; she pretended that holes in stockings were a perfectly delightful eccentricity, that she was having a perfectly ducky time. And she was completely miserable.

Now, such painful subjects demand a great deal of delicacy and restraint in the treatment. And quite apart from delicacy of any sort, *Alice Adams* goes about slugging its points home by means of an assortment of devices that are only described with the beautiful economy of one word, which word is hokum. Take the dinner scene, where she has the boy in to meet the folks on a sweltering night: detail piling on detail, everything going wrong in the most stock manner, until the audience is all set for the shot where the old man's galluses drop his dress trousers down clear to the floor, revealing a pair of bright polka-dot drawers. The actual treatment, that is, seems a cross between harrowing tragedy and the honeymoon-breakfast routine in a Charley Chase. [1935]

Otis Ferguson. *The Film Criticism of O.F.* (Temple, 1971), pp. 89–90

Talk of the Town is a totally unexpected and therefore particularly rewarding experience, something like, say, finding a pearl in a clam. It is a rip-roaring, knock-down-and-drag-out comedy about civil liberties. And not only is it as right as Rightist Hollywood can be in its conclusions, but it is practically epoch-making in that its hero is a millhand named Dilg, a soap-boxer whose chief passion, aside from the rights of man, is *borscht*. . . .

So, as Hollywood movies go, *Talk of the Town* is really something. It puts the charm and persuasiveness and reckless humor of *Mr. Deeds* earnestly and constructively to work on the side of fuller understanding of the men who take to soapboxes on behalf of human causes, and also of the forces which operate to knock them down and out. After seeing the how, if not the why, of anti-labor skulduggery in *Talk of the Town*, John Doe, American, may very well take home with him from his neighborhood theater a new and healthy skepticism toward the propaganda of the National Association of Manufacturers as reflected on his radio and his daily paper . . .

Talk of the Town is chiefly the work of two of Hollywood's more responsible writers—Sidney Buchman, who wrote *Here Comes Mr. Jordan*, and Irwin Shaw, the one-time boy dramatist who conquered Broadway with his *Bury the Dead*, a half dozen years ago. . . . It is also resourcefully directed by George Stevens, the man who made *Woman of the Year*, and if you are the sort who watches for such things, you can see how nicely Stevens fashions light comedy out of the heavy responsibility of teaching a Supreme Court Judge the meaning of plain ordinary justice.

John T. McManus. *PM*. Aug. 28, 1942

George Stevens's last film as a civilian [*The More the Merrier*] is partly nice and partly disappointing. The chiseling, cringing sex and claustrophobia of war-torn Washington might have delivered a really original, really native comedy, and the types set up to carry this comedy are not bad in conception; they are spoiled in execution. Stevens has a free, pretty feeling for business (like Jean Arthur's awkwardness after the love scene on the steps), for special colorations of talk (there is some good adlibbing), and for gratuitious satire (a poke at the G-men and a snort at the surplus of women in Washington). Yet the film as a whole is a tired soufflé, for unfortunately Stevens doesn't know where to stop. Farce, like melodrama, offers very special chances for accurate observation, but here accuracy is avoided ten times to one in favor of easy burlesque or the easier idealization which drops the bottom out of farce. Every good moment frazzles or drowns. The most flagrant example is Jean Arthur, whose mugging and whinnying seemed to me as redundant and, at length, as uningratiating, as if a particularly cute monkey, instead of merely holding out his hat for a penny which I might gladly have made a quarter, insisted that he was working his way through Harvard. [1943]

James Agee. *Agee on Film* (Beacon, 1964), p. 42

It is not the plot, but its incidental material, that gives this picture [*Shane*] its distinction and reveals George Stevens' directing virtuosity. A shot of a group of little girls watching, with feminine involvement, a sow suckling her young, quickly intimates the simplicity and directness of the community's life. A close-up of Joey biting down on a peppermint stick each time Shane gets hit in a fight with the rangers, dramatically communicates how intensely Joey identifies with Shane. A variety of folk episodes and frontier customs enrich the action and the characterizations—a town meeting in the Starrett kitchen, Fourth of July festivity with quaint music and dances, a stark burial on a barren hill with a man playing "Dixie" and "Taps" on a mouth organ. The color photography of mountain, valley, sky and storm is occasionally breath taking.

Stevens' skillful direction is also shown in the excellent characterizations of almost all the parts. The rangers are stereotypes, including their gunman (Jack Palance, who overacts), but the homesteaders are individualized. . . .

It is too bad that some of the characterization so carefully bestowed on Shane and Starrett is nullified by a senseless hand-to-hand fight between them, and that Shane's development from outcast-killer to a constructive member of the community is inconsistent with his becoming a killer again in order to save Starrett. Had his having fallen in love with Starrett's wife been used to motivate his departure, his characterization would have remained intact, and Joey's call "come back," echoing so dramatically from the Wyoming mountains, would have quickened an echo in the hearts of the valley's homesteaders.

Nina Weiss Stern. *Films in Review*.
April 1953, pp. 196–97

Shane stands apart from most Westerns of recent years—even such superior ones as *Red River*, *The Gunfighter*, *High Noon*—mainly by virtue of George Stevens' unromantic and entirely convincing evocation of the period. The horse opera ingredients of the *genre*—the girls in the saloon bar, the chases on horseback—are missing, and the values of the film are those of a serious dramatic work—a killing, for instance, is shown as a sordid and brutal affair and the dead man is mourned. Stevens does not, like John Ford, use the formula elements of the Western for his own purposes; he largely discards them. What emerges is a kind of dramatic documentary of the pioneering days of the West. One says emerges, because the film was perhaps intended to be something more than this. The figure of Shane, romantic, isolated, with great reserves of strength which he is now only prepared to apply in a righteous cause, was perhaps intended as a kind of symbolic heroic figure of the pioneering spirit of the time. An empty performance by

Alan Ladd, however—his casting seems to have been the only box-office concession in an otherwise exceptionally single-minded film—fails to convey this and robs the film of a real centre. In the event, it is the scenes without him—particularly a beautifully directed and played burial sequence—which are most successful and give an impression of the director's quality.

BFI Bulletin. Sept. 1953, p. 132

Formerly a cameraman, he shares with Wyler a strong feeling for the dynamics possible within the frame, an ability to shift the dramatic emphasis within a shot without recourse to unnecessary editing. In *Shane* (1953), a "big Western" built around the hackneyed theme of farmers versus cattle ranchers. Stevens managed to infuse a new vitality, a new sense of realism into the time-worn story through the strength and freshness of his visuals. In one incredibly protracted long-shot Alan Ladd and Brandon de Wilde are speaking in the foreground while, from the distant hills, a horse and wagon approach the camera, drawing nearer and nearer until the riders dash into screen center with their important news. By this device Stevens has been able to prepare the audience for their arrival while still concentrating attention on the dialogue between his principals. Stevens habitually spends a long time on his picture—a year on *Place in the Sun* (1951), two years on *Shane*, even longer on *Giant* (1956). A meticulous craftsman, he has been known to take days lining up a single exterior shot, then months on the final editing and shaping of his film. But out of it come the tremendous compression and richness that typify his best work, the ability to encompass dramatic overtones of atmosphere and characterization within a single shot.

Arthur Knight. *The Liveliest Art* (Macmillan, 1957), p. 198

Constantly turning the spectator back and forth from this secret annex to the world outside, this film would be triumphant simply as a piece of visual art alone, for William Mellor's black and white CinemaScope photography is extraordinary. An air raid is excitingly re-created by sound and camera; in a dream sequence Anne's slumber is tortured by a symphony of Hitlerian cries and faces of the doomed; and a grunting, nocturnal burglar is symbolically presented as a shadowy phantom of death. The Amsterdam exteriors were directed by George Stevens, Jr. and photographed by Jack Cardiff. One's glimpses of a German band marching briskly past the canals, the soldiers patroling the streets with boredom or violence, and once, through the Franks' embroidered curtains, a grim processional of Jews moving to wintry death—all come together to form a pattern of sorrow and despair.

To George Stevens, the story of Anne Frank is not only an indictment but a revelation of the gentler side of the human spirit. If his film at times hovers dangerously on the edge of sentimentality, it is because he suspects that many may not wish to be reminded of the grimmer side of Anne's story. (One is never told in the film *how* Anne died.)

As a whole, *The Diary of Anne Frank* is an uneven, massive work, with more excellences than flaws, but the latter are irritating. The first half of the film is the best, although it begins shakily: the initial sound of an American-accented voice, an unsubtle and intrusive musical score and the flashback, bringing Anne's voice to our ears too quickly and harshly, somehow tends to break the magic of one's earlier response to the striking images of Otto Frank's dispirited figure musing dazedly among remnants of the past. The immediate presentation of reality (in the shots of the Prinsengracht canal, with lazy seagulls fluttering above the waters) is lost for quite a few scenes as one gradually gets acquainted with the characters. What finally restores total involvement with the film are two sequences of suspense emphasizing the presence of fear: an emotion established and held throughout the remainder of the work. . . .

Albert Johnson. *Film Quarterly*. Summer 1959, pp. 42–43

George Stevens is preeminently the stylist of the American motion picture. By the mid-1950's he had reached a towering position in Hollywood, the result of a series of critical and financial successes. If any picture can be said to have made him, it is *A Place in the Sun* (1951), which won him the Academy Award against the strong competition of Kazan's *A Streetcar Named Desire*. Until then, Stevens had swung, with equal facility, between comedy and the serious dramatic film. His comedies—*Woman of the Year*, *The Talk of the Town*, *The More the Merrier*—were bright, reasonably sophisticated, and uncommonly well made, although the earlier *Vivacious Lady* probably represents the high point of this direction, abandoned in recent years. *I Remember Mama* and *Alice Adams* prepared audiences to a degree for *A Place in the Sun*, but not entirely, for with the latter he took his major step forward.

It was a taxing job to boil down the 840-page bulk of Dreiser's *An American Tragedy* to two hours on film, and Stevens boldly, and perhaps rightly, decided to give its plot a contemporary setting. . . . Dreiser's view of his characters had some substantiality, but he was mainly concerned with revealing a villainous society whose forces were responsible for Clyde Griffiths' dilemma. The Stevens film softened and humanized this view, made Dreiser's class demarcation less rigid, and placed emphasis on psychological factors as well as on the societal, a point of view that became characteristic of serious films made in the following decade.

In *A Place in the Sun* George Eastman (changed from the original Clyde Griffiths) responds to the countless proddings from his environment (the billboards with their pictures of indolent girls in bathing suits, the obscenely yellow Cadillacs, the all too obvious difference between being a bellhop and a member of a wealthy and prominent family), and begins his pathetic climb toward his flimsy dream of success. Stevens also finds a gnawing loneliness in him, and suggests the hidden, psychopathic streak in his nature. Remembering Clyde in the novel, we see how important to the film this character change is. Presented in Dreiser's terms, he would have seemed, for the purposes of drama, utterly weak and mooning, not worth the bother of being re-created for another time. As representative of a psychological problem, and thus society's problem, too, he becomes understandable, even representative, important to Stevens, since his tendency is to build toward the archtype.

Hollis Alpert. *The Dream and the Dreamers* (Macmillan, 1962), pp. 137–39

George Stevens, one of the overrated, has made a number of very important pictures, among them *A Place in the Sun, Shane, Giant*, and *The Diary of Anne Frank*. A former cameraman, his pictures are excellent visually and often have the most adroit and understated editing touches. But somehow all of them have failed to be totally satisfying. Stevens has sight without insight, a talent for the big picture that works hard to say not very much. There is a vagueness, a diffuseness about his finished products that leaves the viewer restless and dissatisfied, despite the obvious good intentions of the director. In the end, the picture seems to be an object lesson in the dangers of form without function, or, at least, without a content sufficient for the sumptuous visual passages Stevens usually provides. . . .

Richard Schickel. *Movies* (Basic, 1964), p. 187

[In *The Greatest Story Ever Told*] George Stevens' direction is plodding and repetitious: whenever he has what he thinks is a fine shot, he is sure to repeat it several times; his groupings are studiedly picturesque, and a sequence like Christ's temptation in the wilderness is ludicrous throughout. Or take the scene in which the evils of everyday life are depicted in newsreel style with grainy photography, absurd in cinerama and color. Here a robbery, there a rape, yonder a murder—all taking place side by side along the main street, for Christ to look at, suffer, and do nothing about. It is sheer nonsense. As for pacing, the picture does not let you forget a single one of its four hours for a moment.

The whole conception is oh, so discreet, so defensively inoffensive. If this Christ says, "O ye men of little faith!" the apostles chuckle—it is all so pleasantly jocular. The stuff about rich men's difficulties in entering heaven, or the business of the money-lenders in the Temple—how painlessly it is all presented as if we had been given local anaesthesia first. Unlike Pasolini, who can make his Christ in *The Gospel According to Matthew* at least partly compelling through complexity, sternness, and a quality of fiery aliveness, Stevens gives us a milky, homogenized Jesus: no mention of his having come to bring the sword or to break up family ties, of barren fig trees, or of anything else troubling. Even the Lord's Prayer appears in the popular Protestant version! [1965]

John Simon. *Private Screenings* (Macmillan, 1967), pp. 151–52

Many years, and, of course, many millions went into this latest opus [*The Greatest Story Ever Told*]. George Stevens, "in creative association with Carl Sandburg," produced and directed and was coauthor of the screenplay. In my view, Stevens is the most overrated craftsman in American film history, but some of his pictures have been competent entertainments—*Shane*, for example. No more than three minutes of this new film have elaspsed before we suspect that Stevens' name and fame have been purchased by the Hallmark Greeting Card Company and that what we are looking at is really a lengthy catalogue of Christmas cards for 1965—for those Who Care enough to Send the Very Best. All the side lighting (dawn or sunset), back lighting (halo effects), picturesque groupings, and soda-fountain colors seem inspired by the soggiest nineteenth-century religious chromos; any self-respecting Victorian household would have been proud, sir, to hang any still from this film in its parlor. [1965]

Stanley Kauffmann. *A World on Film* (Harper, 1966), p. 28

Perhaps the greatest story ever told cannot be told in the cinema medium. Certainly the moviemakers have tried often enough and even ran out of titles when they named two very different versions *King of Kings*, but most of their efforts left much to be desired along religious lines or cinematic lines or both. The latest attempt, producer-director George Stevens's *The Greatest Story Ever Told*, is by far the best, although even it is meeting with such a divergence of reviews that one wonders if the critics saw the same film. . . . Director Stevens curiously underplays some of the episodes which tends to make the film rather dull at times and too slow moving; but the technique also tends to give momentum to the big scenes: the Sermon on the Mount, the events of Holy Week and the Passion, and, strangely enough since it comes in the middle of the picture just before the intermission, the most exciting sequence of all, Christ's raising of Lazarus from the dead, which quivers with tension both visually and on the sound track with shouts of "The Messiah has come" and the music of Handel's "Hallelujah" chorus.

Producer Stevens has used color well, contrasting the vivid scenes with others that concentrate on whites and grays. The color photography of Utah's rugged buttes and desert landscapes is striking in Ultra Panavision 70 and the one-lens Cinerama process. At times the scenery takes over and dwarfs the figures, but the panoramas are stunning. Perhaps Stevens was over-awed by his subject matter. His film is of excessive length—four hours including the intermission. And some of his commercial touches were entirely unnecessary, particularly the use of name stars . . . in small roles that could almost have been played by extras. . . .

Philip T. Hartung. *Commonweal.*
March 12, 1965, p. 765

A Place in the Sun. George Stevens's most highly respected work is an almost incredibly painstaking movie derived from Dreiser's *An American Tragedy.* Perhaps because Stevens's methods here are studied, slow, and accumulative (which does suggest a parallel with Dreiser), the work was acclaimed as "realistic" which it most certainly is not. It is full of meaning-charged details, murky psychological overtones, darkening landscapes, the eerie sounds of a loon, and overlapping dissolves designed to affect you emotionally without your conscious awareness. It is mannered enough for a very fancy Gothic murder mystery, while its sleek capitalists and oppressed workers seem to come out of a Depression cartoon. This version gives the story a modern setting, but the town is an arrangement of symbols of wealth, glamour, and power versus symbols of poor, drab helplessness—an arrangement far more appropriate to the thirties than to the fifties. Stevens and his scriptwriters (Michael Wilson and Harry Brown) pre-interpret everything, turning the rather simple story into something portentous and "deep."

Having expressed rather major reservations, I should point out that this is definitely not the accepted view, and that the movie is almost universally honored as an example of adult cinema, one critic having gone so far as to say: "It will bankrupt the emotions." Whatever one thinks about it, it is a famous and impressive film. . . .

Pauline Kael. *Kiss Kiss Bang Bang*
(Little, Brown, 1968), pp. 331–32

As a director, probably as a man as well, he has always cared. The difference is that now he knows what he is doing when he cares. Earlier, this undifferentiated caring was responsible for some of his worst excesses. His musical comedies are leaden. Such films are supposed to be free, irresponsible. Stevens always cared too much. He draws closer to the caperings of Astaire and Rogers in the same way as he later draws close to the Crucifixion, hovering, caring. . . . He sits and watches one of Katharine Hepburn's finest performances, on the edge of his seat, as it were, watching, hoping, caring. His comedies are unsuccessful because, caring, he made very slow and careful films. The fact that Stevens could never not care is why he was unable to make light, spontaneous-appearing pictures. When he understood himself well enough to know not to try, he began making those films—those he made after the war—which were his best, those in which he truly expressed himself.

So strong is the character forming these pictures that even had Stevens been allowed to make those he most wanted to—*Paths of Glory*, *The Naked and the Dead*, *Winterset*, among them—one doubts that his career would have been any different, that the body of his films would contribute any knowledge or feeling we do not have from the films he actually did make.

Stevens' slowness, his carefulness, his ability to watch, his extraordinary craftsmanship, the fact that he—the least cynical of all motion-picture directors—has always been able to care: these qualities fused to create a series of motion pictures which are much more meaningful to us and our times than is generally admitted.

His attitude is often dismissed as sentimental. Certainly his excesses are often sentimental enough, but his attitude is not invariably so. The attitude, as revealed in the later films is, rather, suprisingly rigorous.

Donald Richie. *George Stevens: An American Romantic* (MOMA, 1970), pp. 71–72

George Stevens will photograph the same scene from many *different* angles—another method of shooting several takes of the same scene. But, in addition, Stevens's method gives him the option of using the best parts of different angles of the same scene. In the cutting room he cannily integrates the bits and pieces.

Wyler is at his best when he films a script or play that has been completely worked out by someone else. To make sure actors fully understand the nature and character of their parts, Wyler digs and probes into their minds, using the gibe, needle, or compliment with equal versatility.

On the other hand Stevens, having learned his ABC's in the inventive school of slapstick comedy, works hard and long with his writers on story and script. He is not averse to making script changes during the shooting. In contrast to Wyler, he is inarticulate; at times, it is difficult for actors to understand what he is after. . . .

Well, what *was* George Stevens thinking about, walking alone and smoking his pipe for an hour? As a fellow director I think I know. He was mentally reviewing his whole picture—scene by scene—from beginning to end; analyzing the characters, their growth, their degradation, their effect on each other. Did the preceding scene (shot or unshot) logically build to the one at hand? And would the present scene lead logically to the ones that followed? Was the scene he was shooting necessary? Why? Which character (or characters) should it most affect? Did it ring true? Did he believe it? If not, why? Should he pitch the girl's emotions higher? Could the leading man's reaction be more effective if played silently, or should he make more of his spoken lines? All gut decisions the director must make for himself.

Having concluded he should make no changes, he must take another look at the scene to check his gut decision. So, "Let's take it again." This, too, is directing—à la George Stevens. And his batting average is very high (*The More the Merrier*, *A Place in the Sun*, *Shane*, *Giant*).

Frank Capra. *The Name Above the Title*
(Macmillan, 1971), pp. 244–45

In *Fun in a Chinese Laundry*, Josef von Sternberg defends his treatment of Dreiser's novel by saying: "I eliminated the sociological elements which, in my opinion, were far from being responsible for the dramatic accident with which Dreiser concerned himself." George Stevens, who directed *A Place in the Sun*, is not (so far as I know) on record as saying the same thing, but his film is similarly lacking in social criticism.

Neither picture shows a willingness to criticize American society as Dreiser does in the novel. In 1931, with a depression throughout the land, sympathy was for the underdog—even if society itself went uncriticized; in 1951, with affluence and McCarthyism everywhere, poor girls were unfashionable and the values of American society were even more sacrosanct. Andrew Sarris is probably right, though, when he says that von Sternberg's technique is closer to Dreiser's own objective method than Stevens's arty, romantic and subjective pictures. What would Dreiser have thought of Clyde . . . going to the electric chair to the accompaniment of romantic background music and with a superimposed shot of Elizabeth Taylor's face in soft-focus floating above his head? In Dreiser's uncompromisingly realistic novel, Clyde has other things on his mind. . . .

Edward Murray. *The Cinematic Imagination*
(Ungar, 1972), pp. 122–23

STROHEIM, ERICH VON (1885–1957)

It is as a cinematician, a worker with moving pictures which are inherently and independently dramatic, that Mr. von Stroheim is chiefly distinguished. His two productions, in many particulars, resemble the usual screen offerings. They are, to outward appearances and in general structure, photoplays such as are commonly known. They have plot, and people, and subtitles, action and scenery and settings similar in the main to other dramatic and narrative motion pictures. Mr. von Stroheim has not departed completely from the path the many follow. He cannot be said to have introduced something entirely new and different.

Nevertheless, his work in many of its details is different and new, if compared with that of the great majority of directors, for he has realized that the substance of the photoplay is the dramatic motion picture, not the subtitle, nor the spectacular scene, nor the beauty of the tricks of any star, nor the sentiment or surprises of any story, but moving pictures that have meaning, that are where they are in a photoplay because they are an integral part of it, telling in themselves some essential incident of the story, exposing, suddenly some unexpected but consistent, or anticipated, but not obvious, side of the character of one of the people in the moving pictures, therefore that his story is unfolded forcefully and his characters are definite and comprehensible individuals.

When Mr. von Stroheim uses a closeup, for example, it is because at that particular moment spectators are naturally straining to see some character or detail of action more closely, and when he suspends the story's action to introduce what is known as "atmosphere," it is because at the particular moment there is dramatic significance between the relation of the action and its environment. The scene of *The Devil's Pass Key* is Paris, and views of the city and its life are shown throughout the photoplay as they heighten its successive crises. Furthermore, in the pantomime of his players, Mr. von Stroheim's direction is evident. Of course, ability on the part of the actors is necessary, but many of the eloquent little things they do, and things they effectively refrain from doing, seem the result of his skillful guidance. Altogether, *The Devil's Pass Key* is a photoplay which is chiefly and most importantly a work in moving pictures—and this is its distinction.

NYT. Aug. 9, 1920, p. 6

This picture [*Foolish Wives*], which has been advertised, actually, as "a one hundred per cent American" enterprise, is an insult to every

American in the audience. Consider: an American, of sufficient prestige and importance to be selected by the President of the United States as a special envoy in charge of a vitally important mission to the Prince of Monaco, is depicted as a man who does not know how to enter a room or wear a formal dress!

His wife is represented as the type of woman who strikes up a terrace flirtation with a Russian count who accepts money from a serving maid! To say nothing of the continual innuendos to American ideals; the little sly thrusts at our traditions and our sentiments. . . . Von Stroheim, who is a competent actor at all times, projects himself into too many scenes.

He has abused his directional privileges.

This film may make money. That is a question. It is not a picture that will do you any good. It is not good, wholesome entertainment. It is not artistically great. It is real nothing.

Photoplay. March 1922, p. 70

From von Stroheim great things can be expected, or nothing. In the few films he has offered to date he has done more to get the business of directing out of mechanical ruts than any other four men. His *Foolish Wives*, which bored the mobocracy and brought ridicule from the brilliant critical brethren, was in reality a very superior piece of photoplay craftsmanship, original in ideas and treatment and deserving of higher rating than *Orphans of the Storm*, *Loves of Pharaoh*, *The Storm* and other second-class material which however brought forth applause and bravos from both screen public and scribes. This Teuton cares nothing at all for the time-worn directorial technique and conventional stage mechanics which even the masters practice. He moves his characters and plays his scenes just as he chooses and with pleasing originality and logic. Von Stroheim, above all, has the courage to do as he chooses. Some very fine photoplays should come from this megaphone wielder provided he can overcome his desire for pretentiousness and is not altogether offset by the scissors of the censorious clique.

Tamar Lane. *What's Wrong with the Movies*
(Waverly, 1923), p. 67

Von Stroheim started out with an ordinary story, but he invested it with symbolism and more than one touch of the mellow old-world cynicism of Molnar and Schnitzler. In the hands of [Rupert] Julian the opus lost some of its Continental gloss. It became an *Affairs of Anatol*. Yet, with all this *Merry-Go-Round* is decidedly different. It is permeated with the flashing, decadent atmosphere of Vienna in the gay days before the world war put its crushing boot upon the capital of the tottering empire.

A lieutenant of the royal court of Franz Joseph is fascinated by a little organ grinder of the Prater, the Coney Island of Vienna. At first only a passing fancy of a cynical young boulevardier, the girl becomes the dominating force in his life. He is forced into a court-made marriage, but the war comes to liberate him and make him realize the essentials of life stripped to its realities. Von Stroheim, we suspect, started out to show that life is a merry-go-round rolling pleasantly in a circle. In its present form, *Merry-Go-Round* shows that life, after all, leads right up to the conventional sunset fadeout, with the usual clutch, the usual back lighting and the usual garden. . . . For the sophisticated only.

Photoplay. Sept. 1923, p. 64

Ferocity, brutality, muscle, vulgarity, cruelty, naked realism and sheer genius are to be found—great hunks of them—in Von Stroheim's production, *Greed*. It is a terribly powerful picture—and an important one.

When Von Stroheim essayed to convert Frank Norris's *McTeague* into a movie, he assumed what is technically known as a man-sized job. There was absolutely nothing in this novel of entertainment value, heart interest or box-office appeal—none of the qualities that are calculated to attract the shrewd eyes of the movie mogul.

Nevertheless, there were the elements of fierce drama in *McTeague*, and these have been taken by Von Stroheim and turned loose on the screen. He has followed copy with such extraordinary fidelity that there is no scene in the picture, hardly a detail, that is not recognizable to those who have read the book. . . .

There are two defects in *Greed*—one of which is almost fatal.

In the first place, Von Stroheim has chosen to be symbolic at intervals, and has inserted some very bad handcoloring to emphasize the goldenness of gold. This detracts greatly from the realism of the picture.

In the second place, Von Stroheim has been, as usual, so extravagant with his footage that *Greed* in its final form is merely a series of remnants. It has been cut to pieces—so that entire sequences and important characters have been left out. Thus the story has a choppy quality; many of its developments are abrupt. We see Trina in one instant the tremulous young bride, and in the next the hard, haggard, scheming shrew of several years later. The intervening stages in her spiritual decay are not shown, although Von Stroheim undoubtedly included them originally.

This is Von Stroheim's own fault. He must learn to acquire some regard for the limitations of space. *Greed*, I understand, was produced in forty reels, which would take eight hours to unwind; and the eight-hour day for movie fans has not yet dawned—thank God!

Von Stroheim is a genius—*Greed* established that beyond all doubt —but he is badly in need of a stopwatch.

Robert E. Sherwood. *Life*. Jan. 1, 1925

Stroheim is often called depraved because he uses a certain amount of imagination in depicting attempted seductions. Yet never did any film-director mete out more awful retribution to his villains than Stroheim. The crafty Lothario of *Blind Husbands* falls from a high place and is killed horribly. In *Foolish Wives* his corpse is thrown down a manhole, in *Greed* the murderer dies of thirst in the desert, and in *The Merry Widow* the wicked Crown Prince is assassinated and dies in a dirty puddle in the street. If this is not moral, what is? And if his true lovers, and Mrs. Elinor Glyn's, show some skill in caresses this is all to the good, for nice people do not make love nastily and a little education in the art of wooing is badly needed, particularly by the conventional Anglo-Saxon races. To show the wicked characters as repulsive and the good ones as attractive is very highly moral, and when this is done nothing is left to be desired.

Iris Barry. *Let's Go to the Movies* (Payson & Clarke, 1926), p. 154

Here is the long heralded von Stroheim production [*The Wedding March*] at last unfurled with a flourish. It is a story of court life in Vienna before the War. A young prince, lieutenant in the Royal Guard, is urged by his mercenary parents to marry for money. They select the daughter of an immensely rich corn plaster king but meanwhile he starts a flirtation with a winsome young harpist at a country inn, which soon develops into a serious love affair. A none too prepossessing butcher has been anxious to marry this girl and threatens to kill the prince. The terrified girl promises to become his wife in order to save her lover, although he has abandoned her and goes through with the marriage that has been arranged for him. The picture contains a great deal of spectacular military pageantry done in color against the background of famous St. Stephans in Vienna, and Fay Wray stands out in some poetic love scenes. This is a picture which will probably interest all but some may like it and others not. There is in places too much of the von Stroheim realism and also there is an unevenness in story apparently caused in the cutting of the picture to prescribed feature length.

For the mature audience.

NBR. Nov. 1928, p. 9

Von Stroheim always has a good story to tell: Stroheim is a good story.

In his first picture, *Blind Husbands*, his cigarettes are not so long and exotic, nor his uniforms as upholstered; but Stroheim's atmosphere of condescending to appear in the flicks, his wonderfully kept-up Court-of-the-Emperor bearing, proves itself an enduring receipt.

The public has to tire of seductions by moonlight, of Stroheimesque seductions in orchards laden with blossoms or in palatial chambers, before a Stroheim picture can be sent to the destructor.

Scenes in the Tyrolean Alps are quite thrilling. We know, more or less, what will happen; that never was any argument against a movie situation.

A pretty wife who is neglected by her noble, honourable, (what do you know about that?) upright husband; an old friend of the husband, with unshaven face, carved German pipe, and a habit of spitting each time the scenario calls for atmosphere; and Stroheim *personally* appearing in the picture and *personally* directing it. Stroheim putting the scent behind his ears, kicking a dog which gets in his way (or perhaps not in this one), and watching a religious demonstration. Then Stroheim, the wife, the husband, the faithful friend, all on the mountain. And what more could you want? or rather, what more could Stroheim want? Not, I hope, the titles about mountains, and men's souls, and the purity under the beast's clothing.

In ten years' time the Shaftesbury Avenue Pavilion might revive it again: the years will certainly add to its value as history.

Oswell Blakeston. *Close Up*. Nov. 1929, p. 424

Whether von Stroheim will ever equal or excell his two fine silent films [*Foolish Wives* and *Greed*] is a matter more of doubt than of conjecture. His clear movie intelligence has never progressed with the body of modern thought. He has little social sense; his problems belong to a generation and a world that is fast becoming legendary. Hollywood pampers him; his worst faults—his sentimental and sometimes vulgar texture of photography, his extravagance, his splashes of vile colour—are never likely to trouble the sensibilities of American studio supervisors. The best thing that could happen to von Stroheim would be a sudden jolt into a cinema that is, like the cinema of the Soviets, alive and urgent, with no traditions either of technique or of social convention. In Europe von Stroheim would be forced to find himself, to turn that really grand talent of his to valid achievement. But the tragedy of von Stroheim is that America, the worst country in the world to succour his brain, is the only country in the world capable of supporting his body. To work freely, he must have the scope, the prodigality, the license, that only America can give him; to be himself, he must sell his chances of spiritual and mental quickening for the conditions that only Hollywood can afford to provide.

C. A. Lejeune. *Cinema* (Alexander Maclehose, 1931), pp. 76–77

. . . With the flexibility and resource of a virtuoso, Von Stroheim adapts his style [in *The Wedding March*] to the particular mood or emotion he wants to convey. His love scenes are lyrical with moonlight, apple blossoms and soft-focus effects. His butcher shop and brother are presented with the most realistic insistence on the sordid and physical. The beginning of the film is in still another key: it is cool, deft analysis of social situations—a prodigal son asking his parents for money, a flirtation in a crowd. This flirtation is a lengthy episode in which, by a directorial *tour de force*, one's interest is held with only the slightest instruments of expression—a raising of the eyebrow, a glance, a discreet smile. To heighten the effect of this scene Von Stroheim places it against a background of an entirely different tone: the pomp and circumstance of the Corpus Christi procession. This same principle of dramatic counterpoint is followed in the treatment of the characters. The minor actors are not suppressed to form a neutral background to the "stars" as in most American movies, but on the contrary their personalities are strongly underlined. Thus when they come into contact with the principals or with each other, situations are created that are rich in the complexity of varying motives and emotions. The final wedding sequence, which assembles all the characters of the film, is built up wholly on this sort of counterpoint. *The Wedding March* is a most ambitious picture, as vast in emotional scope as *The Birth of a Nation* is vast in physical scope. Its greatness rests in the fact that it is ambitious without being heavy, serious without being dull, at once deeply felt and expressed in effective cinematic terms. [1933]

Dwight Macdonald. *D. M. on Movies*
(Prentice-Hall, 1969), pp. 91–92

Stroheim's uncompromising realism struck a sympathetic chord with Eisenstein and it is natural that the two should have admired each other's work. But whereas Eisenstein was working in a Socialistic state, where the movie was regarded as something more than an innocuous diversion, Stroheim worked in the hot-house atmosphere of that great citadel of reaction—Hollywood. Eisenstein shelled a decadent capitalistic society from the vast plains of the USSR, which served as a stand from which he could hurl those projectiles—*Potemkin* and *Ten Days*—shattering the hypocritical complacency of a Europe which confused its death rattle with the crunch of tanks, the thud of regimented hordes and the megalomaniacal screeching of dictators. Stroheim bored from within, and while Eisenstein knocked off Europe's armor plate, he dissected an aristocracy in its last stages of sophisticated decay with the precision and effectiveness of a surgeon's scalpel.

Stroheim revealed the great festering wound which was eating away the heart of this society. *Foolish Wives*, *The Merry Widow* and *The Wedding March*—not projectiles, surely, but subtle and insinuating cups of poison. Kings, queens, princes, great barons, wealthy industrialists, the glittering haut-monde—locomotorataxia, haemophilia, nymphomania, satyriasis, perversions, gluttony, rape. This was Stroheim's "High-world." His brief war scenes in the lamentably unfinished *Merry-Go-Round* had all the terrible indictment of those in *The End of St. Petersburg.* In *Greed* he ripped the last shreds of respectability off the body of man as an animal and cried: "For shame!" The spectacle he revealed was shameful enough, but the disclosure only made him enemies and his eventual social ostracism was sealed with the mutilation of this film—a mutilation that endeavored to lessen the shock of this whining, pitiful creature that God was supposed to have created in His own image, and which Stroheim revealed so mercilessly under his microscope. But Stroheim disowned the adulterated version of his masterpiece (as he had disowned every one of his preceding and succeeding works, all of which were similarly mutilated) just as Eisenstein, years later, was to disown the adulterated and perverted version of his great epic of the Mexican people, *Que Viva Mexico!* [1936]

Herman G. Weinberg. *Saint Cinema*
(DBS, 1970), p. 68

If Cecil B. DeMille dominated the movie in its post-war period, Erich von Stroheim was its most inspiring force. Von Stroheim emerges as one of the most important directors in American film history not only for what he accomplished himself but for his stimulation of other directors and for his artistic integrity. No director since D. W. Griffith had so fired the motion picture world. Praised, condemned, finally outlawed, he was the most discussed and respected director during those years when DeMille, at his peak, was the commercial model for the industry. While the rest of the movie makers tried to simulate DeMille, von Stroheim was acknowledged as inimitable, a "genius." If the industry envied and valued DeMille, it was von Stroheim of whom they stood in awe. Von Stroheim was on another plane, not perhaps so dexterous a commercial technician as DeMille but more truly the artist. In this Viennese movie people saw a man with a creative passion, whose will could not be broken and whose integrity could not be compromised. . . .

That von Stroheim had been a careful student of Griffith is evident throughout [*Greed*]. The use of large close-ups, details, camera angles, dramatic lighting and composition, the iris-out, the mask-in—all stemmed from Griffith. Even more suggestive of the Griffith influence were the symbolism, the style of acting, the characterizations themselves. A person's rough treatment of a bird or cat, so familiar in

Griffith's films, was used here to indicate that person's character. At the wedding we see a large close-up of Jean Hersholt's hands, clasped behind his back in jealousy. This was reminiscent of Griffith's close-up of hands clasped in anguish at the trial in *Intolerance*. The fragility and innocence of Zasu Pitts, her fluttering delicacy, were all very close to the traits of the Griffith heroines in the Lillian Gish school.

Whatever else *Greed* may have been, it had the virtue of being unforgettable down to the last moment, when the two men are dying in the desert. The constant repetition of the theme, the hammering away at the idea, may have been burdensome to the watching spectator, but it produced an after-effect, rare in films. [1939]

Lewis Jacobs. *The Rise of the American Film*
(Teachers College, 1968), pp. 343, 349

Stroheim considers humanity with a bitter pessimism. But he is indignant rather than disdainful in his passionate criticism, which especially strikes at the upper classes, the decadent nobility, and the rich industrialists. This criticism is tinctured with pity, almost with sentimentality: a mutilation, an infirmity, a great love, a seduced girl, ugliness itself, make touching blue flowers bloom in this Stroheim hell. This is what distinguishes Stroheim's humanity from the negative and supercilious anarchism that was soon to be propagated by von Sternberg.

Georges Sadoul. *L'histoire d'un art: le cinéma*
(Flammarion, 1949), pp. 210–11

With the mighty triumverate of Griffith, Thomas Ince and Mack Sennett, the era of the mastermind director took hold of the industry in the ten opulent years that preceeded the Armistice. . . . Thoroughly integrated in the prevailing American traditions of gentility, puritanism and revolt, their pictures document the actual life of their contemporaries. With courageous artistic imagination that today seems as archaic as do many of their films to present-day audiences, they pushed back the frontier of cinema technique, the mechanics of the camera, and even moral standards.

In such a lively, dynamic atmosphere of work and competitive spirit, von Stroheim surged to the front of social realism, beyond the limits realized by his predecessors. Rising through the rough and hostile battle for recognition, social status and acceptability, approval as an artist in an alien land meant a great deal to him. He yearned for success, but on his own terms only. Von Stroheim saw life slightly askew; he demanded that the film inform and educate, not merely entertain the public with frothy vacuous romances. With an instinct for the subtle, poignant and caustic impression of a class, a morality, an individual eccentricity, he allied his art with the other creative film pioneers of the social scene: Eisenstein in the Soviet, Pabst and Murnau in Germany, and Renoir in France.

Jules V. Schwerin. *Films in Review*. April 1950, p. 4

Perhaps the full measure of the greatness of *Greed* is to be found only by comparing what remains with the original novel. So faithful was von Stroheim to the text that his intentions are clear in every scene, even though the structure of the story and the development of its characters were destroyed in the course of re-editing his footage. Such minor characters as the swaggering, cigar-smoking charwoman, or the stooped, evil-looking old junkman, for example, seem much too strongly drawn for the insignificant roles they play in the film, unless one remembers that originally they were the principals in an important subplot, the story of a mysterious treasure to which the charwoman holds the key. Similarly, the strange, symbolic inserts of hands caressing golden cups and fingering sparkling jewels which seem so out of keeping with the rest of the picture were actually salvaged from the avaricious dreams of the old junk dealer. Occasionally in the lengthy subtitles used to supplant eliminated action, abrupt references are made to ideas and incidents for which there is no longer any visual preparation. Worst of all, the McTeagues' descent from middle-class respectability to the direst poverty and Trina's disintegration from a gentle, loving wife to a slovenly, penny-pinching shrew takes place so quickly, so baldly as to tax one's credibility. Small wonder that *Greed* remains one of Metro's most expensive flops. It confused and bewildered audiences through what it didn't show—what it did show is mighty strong meat even for audiences today.

Arthur Knight. *The Liveliest Art* (Macmillan, 1957), p. 140

Somehow [Stroheim] persuaded Carl Laemmle to permit him to star in and direct his own story, *Blind Husbands*, 1919. It was at once apparent that an important talent had arrived. Stroheim's handling of his actors, his camera placement and cutting derived from Griffith, but here was an insistence and intensity which bespoke an individual vision of the world. That vision was certainly a novelty to movie audiences. They were familiar enough with the wickedness of Paris, the desperations of Monte Carlo, and the infidelities of *Alt Wien* as routinely portrayed by Hollywood, but Stroheim's versions of these worlds had a detailed, firsthand intimacy which carried new conviction. This was obviously the straight dope on European decadence. His films portrayed successsively the prewar world dancing heedlessly on the volcano; the blindness and confusion of wartime society; and finally, pleasure and post-war Europe in full disintegration.

Richard Griffith and Arthur Mayer.
The Movies (S&S, 1970), p. 213

What an abyss between Stroheim and Lubitsch! One has only to compare *The Merry Widow* of Stroheim with the talking version made by Lubitsch where he returns to the vaudeville of the operetta.

Stroheim has said that the difference between him and Lubitsch is that Lubitsch shows us a king on his throne before showing him in his bedroom, whereas Stroheim shows him first in his bedroom, so that when we see him on his throne we have no more illusions about him.

Vast shiny parquets, majestic staircases, high columns, ornaments carved in stone or elegant wood, the glittering folds of draperies—all that magnificence of a vanished world, created out of nostalgic desire, always has the look of authenticity in Stroheim, who knew how to use ceilings long before Orson Welles. The circumspect eye of Lubitsch, the ex-shopkeeper, contemplates all this sumptuousness with the self-satisfaction of the nouveau-riche; he seems to stand there with his mouth open, not very sure of his footing on the slippery floor, for he might trip over the fold of some brocade curtain.

The difference between Lubitsch and Stroheim is most striking when we see them approach similar situations. In *Old Heidelberg*, the abandoned girl encounters the landau where the prince has taken his place beside the princess: Lubitsch shows only the prince, deliberately omitting the girl he has been forced to marry. Stroheim has no need for such an ellipse to sum up a tragic situation when, in *The Wedding March*, Mitzi follows the princely carriage with tearful eyes.

Like Chaplin, Stroheim disdains pretentiously audacious shots and unusual angles. He uses such shots only when he must make a situation immediately apparent, or place a character. Thus, at the start of *Queen Kelly* he shows us the moral baseness of the prince by shooting him, ignobly sprawled on the pavement, across the bellies and feet of his coach horses.

Nowhere in the work of Stroheim is the sumptuousness of great residences shown to us only for themselves. If, as in *Queen Kelly*, he shows us a marble staircase behind a foreground of glistening tiles in the immense vestibule of the castle, he evokes this splendor only to make us feel the violent contrast between this majestic decor and the piddling humanity that profanes it: the little group of lackeys and boisterous officers who are dragging the drunk prince upstairs to bed.

Lotte H. Eisner. *Film Culture*. April 1958,
pp. 16–17

But it is most of all Stroheim who rejects photographic expressionism and the tricks of montage. In his films reality lays itself bare like a suspect confessing under the relentless examination of the commissioner of police. He has one simple rule for direction. Take a close look at the world, keep on doing so, and in the end it will lay bare for you all its cruelty and its ugliness. One could easily imagine as a matter of fact a film by Stroheim composed of a single shot as long-lasting and as close-up as you like.

André Bazin. *What Is Cinema?* (California, 1967), p. 27

. . . Stroheim is also a romantic like Griffith, to whom he is greatly indebted. The heroines of his later films, with their pale faces framed by long hair and romantically photographed in soft focus and close-up, recall the innocent girls in Griffith's films. A Griffith villain, like the sadistic Battling Burrows in *Broken Blossoms*, is an antecedent for such Stroheim characters as Kallafati [*Merry-Go-Round*] and Schani [*The Wedding March*].

The difference between the directors is more one of attitude than of subject. Griffith's films are warm and sentimental while the coldly sophisticated Stroheim tempers his romanticism with cynicism.

Griffith's films often end happily with the last-minute rescue, like the Modern Story of *Intolerance*. The lack of happy endings in Stroheim shows that his heroes and heroines rarely emerge from their experiences unscathed. A Griffith heroine like the Dear One in *Intolerance* lives in a single bare room decorated with one flower in a pot, a statuette of the Madonna and a single crucifix or a religious painting on the wall. Contrasting with it is the fancy apartment of the Musketeer of the slums, which is filled with erotic statues and pictures of naked women. This great contrast in decor related to character is used in a very similar way by Stroheim in every film from *Merry-Go-Round* to *Queen Kelly* with the exception of *Greed*. . . . Just as the Boy in *Intolerance* attempts to break away from the evil Musketeer when he falls in love with the Dear One, so Stroheim's aristocratic heroes rebel against their luxurious backgrounds because of their new-found love.

Joel W. Finler. *Stroheim* (California, 1968), p. 130

Queen Kelly as it can be seen today is even further from Stroheim's intentions than his earlier films were, since he did not even begin to complete its shooting. Nevertheless, his presence is strongly felt. He was again portraying, with his usual ironic tone, the decayed aristocracy of a bygone Europe before World War I. The film exhibits his characteristic predilection for the bizarre and the exotic, for voluptuous images, for rich details. The portrait of Kitty Kelly doubtless needs the ironic contrast of the "royal" madam of the African brothel to fulfill Stroheim's conception of Gloria Swanson's role. However, as the picture stands, Seena Owen's Queen is so extravagently drawn as to tend to overshadow the producer-star. The Queen's character is first suggested in a series of close-ups of the contents of her bedside table, which include a rosary, a copy of Boccaccio's *Decameron*, a bottle of champagne standing in ice, an ash tray overflowing with cigar butts, and a package of Veronal: she wanders from her bath naked, clutching her long-furred white cat to her bosom; in a sudden rage, she quite literally foams at the mouth; when she whips Kitty Kelly down the palace staircase, it is with evident sadistic enjoyment. She is the female counterpart of the roles Stroheim earlier created for himself.

Richard Griffith in *Film Notes*, edited by Eileen Bowser (MOMA, 1969), p. 73

It is, I think, the hallucinated fantasy of Stroheim's films that remains their chief fascination for us today, the meticulous detail only the means by which these fantasies could be embodied, and I think it is this that Stroheim shares with Griffith. In both Griffith, the Southerner, with his morbid sentimentality, his fixation on suffering, his obsession-horror with miscegenation, and Stroheim, the self-invented quasi-nobleman, one sees an extraordinary genius for neurotic self-dramatization, and a genius equally for the dramatic projection of their fantasies on a gigantic scale. I use the word "genius" without irony; it is one thing to be neurotic and quite another to externalize one's neuroses into a *Broken Blossoms*. And I find that, despite the foreground trashiness of *Broken Blossoms*, the world in which it is placed, the tormented Limehouse streets, exists for me with a nightmare persistency which is testimony to the force of its realization. But, though the genius of these film-makers *is* extraordinary, at least as extraordinary is the receptivity of the silent film medium to what they made of it. It was a medium which used to attract epithets like "Magic Shadows," and I submit that the extent to which it became this in the hands of a Griffith or Stroheim has yet to be sufficiently considered.

William S. Pechter. *Twenty-four Times a Second* (Harper, 1971), p. 300

STURGES, JOHN (1911–)

The chief merit of this Civil War western [*Escape from Fort Bravo*] lies in the skill with which a number of familiar situations have been re-created and developed. The place and atmosphere are quickly sketched in: the lonely fort with its cantonment of surly Confederate soldiers; the grim and rocky desert lands surrounding it (the locations were shot in the Death Valley National Monument); and the ever-present Mescalero Indians waiting to attack. The long, final battle against the Indians is most skilfully handled and generates a real tension and sense of involvement with the participants. The characterisation, though, does not equal the care expended on the action scenes and the triangle situation is not explored with any great insight. The conception of Bailey, the cowardly "poet," in particular, is banal.

BFI Bulletin. April 1954, p. 52

[*Bad Day at Black Rock*] will be compared to *High Noon*—an honor in itself—for many reasons. It is not a traditional "head 'em off at the pass" Western, but a study of people caught in the grip of fear. The arrival of the stranger sends a tremor of panic through every man in town and each reacts in his own impulsive way.

Also, the movie takes place within twenty-four hours. It has a dramatic unity, an economy of word and action, that is admirable in an age of flabby Hollywood epics that maunder on forever.

Director John Sturges has arranged his scenes so that faces often tell the whole story. Nobody has to look frightened and then say, "I'm afraid," as is the prevailing custom. When a man looks frightened you know it, and you know why. Sturges has used the screen medium exactly as it should be used.

Every scene is like a painting composed for best dramatic effect. The wide CinemaScope screen, for instance, is not used to accommodate 500 extras but to get the strongest impact where only a few people are involved.

Six men stand in a tight circle on railroad tracks that stretch out to infinity, and plot how to erase the stranger. Or they sprawl over a dingy hotel lobby and taunt him, their cruel faces a mocking background while Tracy's face—in the foreground on one side of the screen —reflects his growing concern over the jam he is in.

William K. Zinsser. *NYHT*. Feb. 2, 1955, p. 16

[*Bad Day at Black Rock* is] a very refreshing and most unusual experience by John Sturges. The Western theme shown in this picture provides an interesting display of cinematic techniques proffered by this director. For once we had the pleasure to witness the efforts of a man who has seriously approached the problem of the wide screen not with a "fill it up" mentality, but with a genuine endeavor to express the feelings of the hero within the framework of time and space through an able use of the camera, thus establishing a most enlightening point-counterpoint.

The skill of some sequences, the mood and symbiosis between man and nature makes this film sometimes superior to *High Noon* by Fred Zinnemann.

G. N. Fenin. *Film Culture.* May-June 1955, p. 27

The Hallelujah Trail (*Sur la piste de la grande caravane*), film in cinerama and in color of John Sturges, with Burt Lancaster, Lee Remick, Pamela Tiffin, Jim Hutton, Donald Pleasance, Brian Keith.—Even the worst enemies of John Sturges would not wish him such an end. The pseudo-talent of the Clausewitz of westerns endlessly draws out a battle—not for women, *misogynie oblige*, misogyny imposes obligation!—but for a convoy of whiskey. Imbecilic and crude parody of a style already parodic. Note the scene of "massage" that rivals the famed session of masturbation Jane Fonda-Jean-Claude Brialy in *La Ronde* (*Circle of Love*) of Vadim, less unexpected than one might believe in this hypocritical farce.

M. M. *Cahiers du Cinéma in English.* 1966 (3), p. 64

The Old Man and the Sea. James Wong Howe's color photography of the sea is excellent; outstanding among numerous beautiful scenes is one of a fleet of small fishing boats starting out just before dawn, each with a lantern on its mast. Some of the special effects are poor; it is obvious when a studio close-up has been superimposed on a location shot. Sturges' direction is only fair. Perhaps no director could have much effect on Tracy, but Sturges has contributed a few heavy-handed touches of his own. The dream scenes of the African coast are needlessly literal, and a really egregious blunder is the moment when the weary Old Man, bearing his mast on his shoulder, trudges up the street and stumbles to his knees before a church door. I almost heard a voice whisper: "Get it? Station of the Cross!" [1958]

Stanley Kauffmann. *A World on Film* (Harper, 1966), pp. 89–90

This is a very curious film. In a sense it is quite ambitious, although it comes from Hollywood in an era of cautious blockbusters and indeed cost some millions of dollars to produce. The theme it takes from the Hemingway story is nothing less than that of human failure and death, or more precisely, of the manner in which men meet them; "man can be destroyed but not defeated." It attempts an unusual type of narrative for a film, half visual and half verbal. And also, by following the simple Hemingway story without adding plot complications, it faces Spencer Tracy with the challenge of a *tour de force* of unassisted acting. . . .

In structure *The Old Man and the Sea* attempts to approximate the effect of the Hemingway story by utilizing vast stretches of narration (spoken by Tracy, and woven quite neatly into the words he speaks on the screen). For a film of this sort, we may be prepared to accept devices which would in an ordinary story film seem merely ridiculous; but on the whole, the experiment cannot be considered very successful. The old demon of redundancy rears his head as persistently as in any Shakespeare film. "He smiled," says the narration; and a faint smile crosses Tracy's face . . . John Sturges, the director, told me that both Tracy and editor Arthur P. Schmidt wanted to use less narration, but he looked at the film without it and decided to keep it all; so the blame must fall squarely upon him. It was, no doubt, a tempting solution: while the old man sits in the skiff, waiting for the fish to do something new, let us have the narration keep things going by telling of past or imminent events, or explaining things that might not be understood. But the incessant talk weighs heavily upon the pace of the film, which is by the nature of the action none too sprightly at best. . . .

As a whole, *The Old Man and the Sea* is a strange amalgam of practically unassisted acting, good camerawork and editing, and a lot of special effects. It is a goodly distance from the razor-sharp suspense of Sturges' *Bad Day at Black Rock* or *Gunfight at the OK Corral*. But it is in many ways an encouraging film, though seriously flawed, and we can certainly continue to look to Sturges for interesting work.

Ernest Callenbach. *Film Quarterly*.
Winter 1958, pp. 45–46

Because of the box-office success of a series of nine westerns done between 1949 and 1961, John Sturges can justly be considered as a solid specialist of the genre. This is true first because of the fidelity which he has shown it and second because of the care with which he surrounded it, at least during the first part of his work. Since *The Walking Hill* and *Escape from Fort Bravo*, he has not been afraid to disappoint his most ardent admirers by giving them films in which they saw signs of carelessness in both subject and style. What, in effect, is there in common between those previous to 1958 (*Fort Bravo*, 1954; *Backlash* and *Bad Day at Black Rock*, 1955; *Gunfight at the O.K. Corral*, 1956; *The Law and Jake Wade*, 1958); and more recent films such as *Last Train from Gun Hill*, 1958, *The Magnificent Seven*, 1960, *Sergeants Three*, 1961? The first group wanted to infuse new blood—

or at least richer blood—into the western by showing a real interest in the special story of people defined by their character and behavior. The second group made use of proven themes that no longer needed to exert effort to have both their subject and their dramatic value accepted. All that had been gained in the human richness of the hero, in his perfect identification with the environment and with the situations proposed, is suddenly lost in 1958 when *The Law and Jake Wade*, a relatively original work, was followed by *Last Train from Gun Hill*, a heavy-handed copy of Delmer Daves' *Three: Ten to Yuma.* Afterward the process continued with the transposition of Kurosawa's Japan into a Mexican village to give us *The Magnificent Seven* (1960), and in making Rudyard Kipling's *Gunga Din* via George Stevens into *Sergeants Three* (1961), an amiable joke for the four-man "rat pack": Frank Sinatra, Dean Martin, Peter Lawford, and Sammy Davis, Jr.

J-L. Rieupeyrout. *La grande aventure du western* (Editions du Cerf, 1964), pp. 382–83

The Great Escape is not quite as vivid in its conception of mechanistic horrors run amok, but it presents a picture of men in an almost Arthurian Idyll (as Jonathan Miller points out) that is equally interesting and eventually more appealing. In a sense, it looks backward since it is not touched by the popular themes of the Sixties—angst, alienation, malaise or anomie to name a few—but its universality makes it more timely than the work of hangers-on turning out feeble copies of Godard, and just as timeless as the best work of Godard himself. Basically . . . it is an adventure story on a grand scale. The film is based on a book by Paul Brickhill (1950) which describes the escape of more than 250 British and American airforce officers from a prison camp in Germany run by the Luftwaffe. The meticulous planning of the men, their flight through the German countryside and their eventual fate make up the substance of the film. The utter fascination which attends the adventure stems from the juxtaposition of the differing personalities of the men as the plot progresses, and from the almost dreamlike beauty of many of the scenes themselves. . . .

Leon Lewis and W. D. Sherman. *Landscape of Contemporary Cinema* (Buffalo Spectrum, 1967), pp. 52–53

Ice Station Zebra. The submarine commander (Rock Hudson) is given his top-secret special assignment by his superior, who asks, "Jim, just how much do you know about Ice Station Zebra?" We're in purest old Hollywood with such exquisite locutions as "Something's gone wrong up there, that's for sure." . . . I wanted to leave, but it was icy outside, too, so inertia kept me, and after a while I had invested so much time I thought I might as well try to figure out what the devil was supposed to be going on. It was obvious that the movie hadn't been made to exhibit the wit and wisdom of Mr. [Douglas] Heyes (screenwriter); perhaps there was a good spy-adventure story buried in the verbal muck and the director, John Sturges, would dig it out. . . . Sturges's direction is as dull as in *The Satan Bug*, but after a while you don't expect it to be good, the way it was in *Escape from Fort Bravo*, or *Bad Day at Black Rock* or *The Great Escape*, and so you adjust to this and don't mind it very much. Your expectations get scaled down in everything else, too. *Ice Station Zebra* is terrible in such a familiar way that at some level it's *pleasant*. We learn to settle for so little, we moviegoers. [1968]

Pauline Kael. *Going Steady* (Little, Brown, 1970), pp. 222–23

STURGES, PRESTON (1898–1959)

It may have been Shrove Tuesday in November for some folks yesterday, but it was *Christmas in July* for those who caught the new picture at the Rivoli. And a joyous occasion it was, too. For this tricky and wrily titled film, which is another of those one-man creations by Preston Sturges for Paramount, is just about as cunning and carefree a comedy as any one could possibly preordain—the perfect restorative, in fact, for battered humors and jangled nerves. As a post-election jog to national sanity, we recommend *Christmas in July*.

Maybe you already know Mr. Sturges from *The Great McGinty* and *Remember the Night*. If so, you are aware of how he can take a thin idea—a trite idea, even—and elaborate upon it with such fresh and elliptical fun that it suddenly seems important. Thus, when we tell you that his hero in the present instance is a $20-a-week clerk who hopes to win a slogan contest paying $25,000, that the whole story has to do with nothing more than the things he does when he is deluded into thinking that he has won it, then you'll appreciate the wonder of the Sturges sleight-of-hand. Out of such gossamer, really, he weaves a delightful comic fabric before your eyes.

How does he do it? Well, through the creation of solid comic characters, for one. His hero—and inevitable heroine—are just nice, honest youngsters, that's all. They want a break, so they can get married. But against them are arrayed such a scatter-brained lot of practical jokers, business tycoons and slightly off-center store clerks that the attainment of the break becomes a gantlet. Then Mr. Sturges contrives some wholly bewitching surprises. Details are worked out with elaborate ingenuity. Things pop when you least expect them. He keeps you laughing with, not at, his youngsters.

Bosley Crowther. *NYT*. Nov. 6, 1940, p. 35

Preston Sturges sky-rocketed into Broadway fame some years ago with *Strictly Dishonorable* on the stage; in the last year he has soared to an even higher fame in Hollywood by following the example of Chaplin and the early Griffith, and embodying the writer-director combination in his own person. The striking part of it, of course, is that he has turned out three sizable hits in quick succession, and that they all have an individuality which makes them definitely Preston Sturges products and which someone will pretty soon be calling the Sturges "touch."

Strictly speaking, the story of *The Lady Eve* isn't something that Sturges wrote all brand new for himself—it goes back to something by Monckton Hoffe or even farther, but Sturges has trimmed it and refashioned it to his own style. . . . The taste of a cocktail, however, isn't so much in its basic ingredients as in the proportions and finesse with which they are shaken together. *The Lady Eve* has the fantastic, the high comic, the satiric, the farcial and out-and-out slapstick all mixed up in it, and the result can't be labelled anything else but a laugh show. The whole theme, with all its variations of keys, is played to one end, to get laughs, and at several different levels it gets them.

Mr. Sturges seems to be a dashing kind of worker—he dashes things off without much apparent care for polish and inner harmony. He goes at it hit or miss, and luckily—whether through accident or great talent—it turns out mostly hit. He hasn't yet reached the level of Lubitsch or René Clair or Capra at their best, but when he does it will be in a spot all his own. His gusto sweeps merrily over the pitfalls he creates for himself, and over-doing is probably a better thing than under-doing.

NBR. March 1941, p. 14

Preston Sturges, if you are driven to giving serious thought to him, is an astonishing and rather bewildering figure in the set-up of movie esthetics. Maybe he's just having his idea of fun, and hoping to make an honest million by giving fun to others. Maybe he's carefully creating an individual cinematic form of his own. Whichever it is, there's an excellent chance to look it over and, if possible, size it up, in *The Miracle of Morgan's Creek*.

This film moves in a fantastic and irreverent whirl of slapstick, nonsense, farce, sentiment, satire, romance, melodrama—is there any ingredient of dramatic entertainment except maybe tragedy and grand opera that hasn't been tossed into it? But with a swift nonchalance so pointedly deft that it leaves a persistent impression the whole thing was contrived with the shrewdest kind of deliberation, up to the point where it gets so dizzy with its own whirling that it reels and tumbles in a heap. Whence it staggers to its feet for a final gesture of frantic fantasy.

The picture goes back to a kind of thing we almost never see any more and haven't seen in full flower since the free and easy days of Keystone, when Mack Sennett rough-housed such matters as sex and marriage and maternity so thoroughly that nobody could possibly look at them as realities of human behavior. It isn't likely that this flight of the Sturges comic spirit will bring that giddy springtime back again, but there's a breath of it in the central situation: finding a father for the unborn child of a girl who is either an unmarried mother or a bigamist, which is such a preposterous business that it's got to be funny or outrageous.

NBR. Feb. 1944, pp. 6–7

The Miracle of Morgan's Creek, the new Preston Sturges film, seems to me funnier, more adventurous, more abundant, more intelligent, and more encouraging than anything that has been made in Hollywood for years. . . .

Yet the more I think about the film, the less I like it. There are too many things that Sturges, once he had won all the victories and set all the things moving which he managed to here, should have achieved unhindered, purely as a good artist; and he had not even attempted them. He is a great broken-field runner; once the field is clear he sits down and laughs. The whole tone of the dialogue, funny and bright as it often is, rests too safely within the pseudo-cute, pseudo-authentic, patronizing diction perfected by Booth Tarkington. And in the stylization of actions as well as language it seems to me clear that Sturges holds his characters, and the people they comically represent, and their predicament, and his audience, and the best potentialities of his own work, essentially in contempt. His emotions, his intelligence, his aesthetic ability never fully commit themselves; all the playfulness becomes rather an avoidance of commitment than an extension of means for it. Cynicism, which gives the film much of its virtue, also has it by the throat; the nihilism, the humaneness, even the gaiety become, in the light, mere postures and tones of voices; and whereas nearly all the mischief is successful, nearly every central and final responsibility is shirked. Of course there is always the danger, in trying to meet those ultimate human and aesthetic responsibilities, of losing your gaiety; but that never happened to Mozart—or to René Clair at his best. [1944]

James Agee. *Agee on Film* (Beacon, 1964), pp. 73, 75–76

Harold Lloyd's return to films in *The Sin of Harold Diddlebock* [*Mad Wednesday*] is eased in with a clip from one of his silent successes, *The Freshman* (1923). In this manner the producer-writer-director Preston Sturges sought to establish that Lloyd was once an extremely comical man, a fact that is less in evidence in the ensuing sequences of the current film. It is curious that Sturges, who has not been averse to low comedy in the past, should contrive for one of Hollywood's most inveterate slapstick comedians a work more given to bombast than to pratfalls and custard pies. True there is a short chase scene and a ledge scene hilariously staged in the ancient tradition, but Mr. Lloyd is chiefly assigned to lengthy measures of flowery discourse most of which he delivers in a voice pitched monotonously to the level of a shout.

That the film is nevertheless entertaining is chiefly due to the comic dependability of the notion of a middle-aged timid soul who comes into money and simultaneously discovers the pleasures of wine, women and horseracing. Sturges is at his happiest in the conceits of several incidental characters: the inspired bar-tender dreaming up Diddlebock's first drink; the elderly lady who takes hungry cats to her heart; Jack the lion whom Diddlebock buys along with a circus in a moment of alcoholic aberration; a whole slate of misanthropic bankers. . . . There is a fair complement of the director's accustomed shrewd comment on the current scene, though not sufficiently weighted and pointed to warrant his claim to the title of social satirist.

Hermione R. Isaacs. *NBR*. April-May, 1947, p. 7

Preston Sturges' last film, *Unfaithfully Yours*, was an acid and fantastic comedy generally underestimated and neglected here; there is little risk, unfortunately, of the same fate overtaking *The Beautiful Blonde from Bashful Bend*—which is an almost incontestable disappointment. Sturges' attempt at harnessing his talents to a Betty Grable vehicle seems no more successful than that of the late Ernst Lubitsch.

The story, though it starts unpromisingly, is in fact promising. A voluptuous saloon entertainer in the Wild West, trained in childhood by her grandfather as an expert crackswoman, has the habit of drawing a gun whenever she loses her temper: which is frequently. After accidentally shooting the local sheriff in his posterior, she is obliged to flee the town, and is mistaken for the new schoolmistress at Bashful Bend, a remote settlement peopled with typical Sturges eccentrics—petty pompous dignitaries, ineffectual hayseeds, crazed cowboys, infantilist idiots and formidable matrons. The middle sequences, dealing with her impersonation and the consequences of it, are the best, and contain a measure of fun: but the climax—a prolonged slapstick gun-battle, followed by a courtroom scene in which the Blonde again plugs the sheriff's posterior during a *mêlée*—is much too heavy-handed, littered with ancient and repetitive gags.

Somehow the ramshackle air of Bashful Bend itself seems to have permeated the whole film, which lacks the dexterity, invention and lightness one expects from the maker of *The Lady Eve* and *The Palm Beach Story*. . . .

BFI Bulletin. Dec. 31, 1949, p. 211

The death of Preston Sturges . . . leaves us with several brilliant satires. Although he started out as a brilliant script-writer and his films have affinities with other American comedies, his work has a surpassing distinction. One is conscious at the end of each film of that rare cinematic phenomenon—a supremely fit intelligence successfully at work. Comedies these days tend to be built upon one good idea which remains undeveloped but is externally linked to anything else vaguely funny. With Sturges ideas and situations are developed internally with a brilliant inventiveness. His assurance allows him to pull out his comedy simultaneously in several emotional dimensions and he has the confidence to pull switches on the audience that would be disastrous in other hands. . . . His treatment of patriotic hysteria in *Hail* was courageous in 1944, and taking his films as a whole, his satire missed none of the important American political and social values. Taken as seriously as it deserves, *Sullivan's Travels*, the story of a conscience-stricken Hollywood director in search of real life anguish, entitles Sturges to be ranked as a great humanist director. The finest tribute to him is his films, and simply thinking about them makes one want to see them all again.

Film (Eng.). Sept.-Oct. 1959, p. 32

There doesn't seem much doubt today that Preston Sturges (1898–1959) was God's Gift to American Comedy. Unfortunately little remembered today by the mass audience, his films were among the biggest box-office draws of the early 'forties. Although he worked for almost every big studio during his short career, his best films were made at Paramount and have, until now, been absolutely unavailable.

If your society is crying for a comedy, you can't go wrong with any of the four listed above. The best, of course, is *Sullivan's Travels*, the most witty and knowing spoof of Hollywood movie-making of all time. A film director (Joel McCrea) goes out into the world with a beautiful young extra (Veronica Lake) to find out material for a socially conscious feature. His efforts end him a place on a chain-gang. Like all of the Sturges' comedies, there is an underlying strain of bitterness at the bottom which gives all of his work a maturity his plot lines would not normally suggest. Beautifully scripted, directed and acted, *Sullivan's Travels* made numerous "ten best" lists of a few years back. And we mean ten best films of all time. Don't overlook this film!

Film Society Review. Oct. 1964, p. 12

Sturges's first film, *The Great McGinty*, might be described as Capra with the gloves off. McGinty (Brian Donlevy) begins by beating up pluckily independent shopkeepers on behalf of a party machine boss, becomes a corrupt politician in his turn, and is broken only when he decides to go straight. A scene contrasting his pro-public spending platform with the class-conscious Senator Honeywell—as well as the contrast of names—leaves little doubt that McGinty is a Democrat. No doubt studio chiefs saw this study in Democrat corruption as useful Republican propaganda. But with that artistic cunning which can triple- or quadruple-cross any censorship, the film, in fact, sweeps the snooty Honeywells contemptuously aside, and poses the real alternatives as either utter cynicism or the Democratic ethos. But since the former is a popular, and respected, American attitude, Sturges has McGinty get away—helped by, appropriately, a disillusioned cop—and end his days, not too uncongenially, as a bartender down South America way.

Sturges's tact matches Capra's, point for point, as is evidenced by a very difficult scene where our hero, as Mister Big's strong-arm man, beats a toughly individualistic bartender to make him pay protection. If the scene is morally explosive as it is, it is because Donlevy retains our human sympathy despite his classic villain behaviour. The reasons are: (*a*) we've seen Donlevy on his uppers and like him as an underdog, (*b*) his victim has a bully physiognomy, (*c*) he's so confident in his own toughness that he starts the fight, which (*d*) we don't see, instead it is (e) reflected on the face of a comic little man who (*f*) thinks about joining in with a bottle but can't bring himself to. The (*a*) to (*e*) points may be classic examples of entertainment tact, but (f) is more challenging. That little man is, and is felt to be, 'the little man', the American conscience which, in historical fact, has so rarely made up its mind to interfere in cases of political bribery and corruption.

Raymond Durgnat. *The Crazy Mirror*
(Horizon, 1969), p. 166

Reflecting to perfection the mood of wartime Hollywood, *Sullivan's Travels* danced on the grave of the thirties social cinema. The plot device is a movie director's urge to make films "of social significance," and his eventual conclusion that the highest function of the medium is not to portray a sordid reality, but to entertain. Such a theme also reflects in an obvious way the interests of writer-director Preston Sturges, creator of comedy, whose energies were devoted to deflating pomposity and pretension. "Raised to be a genius" by a culture-hungry mother, unlike that similarly trained prodigy, Orson Welles, Sturges maintained in later life a stubborn pretense to philistinism. . . .

Time has worked its changes on our reactions to this group of comedies. When they appeared, critics hailed Sturges' rediscovery of slapstick which had almost disappeared from the scene. Of them all, the rowdy, noisy *The Miracle of Morgan's Creek* and *Hail the Conquering Hero* were generally thought to be the funniest. Seen at a greater distance, Sturges appears to have been more a writer's director—full of clever plot ideas and witty dialogue—rather than some intuitive Mack Sennett revival. A new generation's favorities are *The Lady Eve*, *The Palm Beach Story,* and *Sullivan's Travels.* It may be that Sturges' sense of comic timing, which failed him in later years, was gradually slipping from him. Perhaps it is only that the timely topics of the two later films, *The Miracle of Morgan's Creek* and *Hail the Conquering Hero*, now seem dated.

Sturges' comedies were never all slapstick, but each contained one or more deftly inserted slapstick sequences, one of the best occurring in *Sullivan's Travels:* after John L. Sullivan has thumbed a ride with a youthful hot rod enthusiast, a wild ride of the caravan ensues, a sequence which recovers the pure delirium of Keystone as the action goes far beyond the bounds of the real world and all dignity is upset. At regular intervals in the film, the characters are dumped in a swimming pool or involved in chases. Surprise is another essential ingredient in the success of *Sullivan's Travels.* The director manipulates his audience, letting us assume a reality which he abruptly pulls away.

Eileen Bowser in *Film Notes*, edited by
Eileen Bowser (MOMA, 1969), pp. 107–08

To the end of his days Preston Sturges described himself as a writer rather than a director, and he would have been the first to admit that the films he directed through the forties and fifties relied more on verbal wit than visual style. Still, all his screenwriting efforts in the thirties would now be of only the most esoteric concern if he had not made the decisive leap from the writer's cubicle to the director's chair with *The Great McGinty* in 1940, followed by *Christmas in July* that same year. *The Lady Eve* and *Sullivan's Travels* (1941), *The Palm Beach Story* (1942), *The Miracle of Morgan's Creek, Hail the Conquering Hero* and *The Great Moment* (1944) *Mad Wednesday* (1947), and, somewhat anticlimactically, *Unfaithfully Yours* (1948) *The Beautiful Blonde from Bashful Bend* (1949), and *The French They Are a Funny*

Race (1957). Although it is relatively common for writers to become directors nowadays, the switch was somewhat unusual in the craft-conditioned thirties when it was not unknown for producers to fire directors who had the temerity to take up typing. As it was, the successful accession of Sturges sparked a writer-director movement involving John Huston, Billy Wilder, Joseph L. Mankiewicz, Dudley Nichols, Clifford Odets, Nunnally Johnson, Robert Rossen, Samuel Fuller, Frank Tashlin, Richard Brooks and Blake Edwards, among others.

Andrew Sarris. *Film Comment*.
Winter 1970–71, p. 81

TOURNEUR, MAURICE (1876–1961)

Few motion picture directors equal, and fewer surpass, Maurice Tourneur in the art of making scenes for the screen. By his work he stands out prominently, even among that small group of exceptional men who appreciate the peculiar powers of the camera and know how to employ them in the production of a photoplay. Once more, and in some ways more than ever, he has revealed his creative genius in *Sporting Life*, the featured film at the Rivoli this week.

The play is a melodrama, based upon the well-known Drury Lane product, and, as many will remember, it has to do chiefly with a young English Lord and his desperate efforts to re-establish himself financially through the successes of a pugilist in the ring and a racehorse, the phenomenal Lady Love, in the Derby. There are abundant opportunities in the play for exciting scenes.

Mr. Tourneur has not faltered before any of the big, comprehensive scenes, such as those of the prizefight and the Derby race, while in little incidents also he has done not only the obvious and expected, but the surprising. The spectators who viewed the picture yesterday afternoon were drawn into the excitement of the play's episodes, applauding and exclaiming at the succession of climaxes as people do only when they are thrilled by a sense of participation in what they see or hear.

At one point, as Lady Love dashed forward to the race, some one in the orchestra shouted "Go!" and many of the spectators literally started forward from their seats. It all seemed real. But this effect was accomplished by the climax of an episode, and each effect of the photoplay was similarly accomplished.

As a whole, *Sporting Life* is a series of stirring episodes linked together—or, rather, separated—by the obtruding incoherencies of one of the most loosely constructed stories. Even Mr. Tourneur's scenes are marred by impossibilities of his story. The spectator may concede much to melodrama, expecting things that could never happen to happen realistically, even willing to endure the cheap heroics that seem to be inseparable from the old-fashioned thriller; but he has a right to demand consistency within the liberal limits allowed, and *Sporting Life* does not meet this demand. One is continually asking, Why? What? How? and receiving no plausible answer. It is a pity that, in making such a remarkable picture, Mr. Tourneur did not insist upon a better built vehicle.

NYT. Sept. 16, 1918, p. 9

Yet, as a whole, *The Last of the Mohicans* is a truly exceptional picture—in many ways a magnificent, a very wonderful picture. It has been far easier to record what we conceive to be its flaws than it will be even briefly and vaguely to indicate its perfections.

To begin with, it is probably the first really adequate photodramatizing of a period in our own history which is epic and of which much has been written and documented away and now resides in libraries and museums where the present generation is not likely to look for it. Thus, that which is rich and native to our origin is likely to pass from our mind and imagination and from those of our children. Mr. Tourneur's picture is therefore opportune—it should serve the purpose of helping to call back to us through the powerful visualizing medium of the screen that which we otherwise are in the way of losing. His picture gives to us not only an entertainment, a thrill, in the truest, most direct sense; it gives to us a fine bit of history and picture interpretation as well, such as should print its colors and movements on the minds of old and young alike. These colors are from a design which Mr. Tourneur, above all directors for the screen today, understands how to execute in the manner of an artist.

The composition of *The Last of the Mohicans* is superb. It ranges in almost exact impression from that of the color sketches of Remington to that of the drawings of Doré. Here are color, tone, line, sky, cliff, forest and human figures at their most impressive in motion-photography. It is the forerunner of that impressionism which the future of the motion picture holds perhaps beyond that of all other arts. Much is being written of foreign pictures that attempt the expression of space, the exact picturing of atmosphere in cubistic terms, such as will supplant the need for mannikin action of characters through plot as the means of creating the illusion of life and the play of emotions. Mr. Tourneur's shots with the camera are dramatic in themselves, his lights and shadows strike back on the nerves and make pictures beyond the picture on the screen, create moods and bring the onlooker into understanding with the feeling of the actors in the given situation of which the composition of the picture is an analysis in terms of line, light and shadow.

NBR. Dec. 1920, pp. 2, 5

We wish that all those who delight in sneering at the movies could be compelled by act of Congress to see Maurice Tourneur's production, *The Last of the Mohicans*. They would undergo what is generally known as a rude awakening. For here is a photoplay that combines magnificent pictorial beauty with real dramatic power—one that can hold the spectator's attention without insulting his intelligence, or that quality which he likes to think is his intelligence.

The fact that Cooper's famous novel has been rather badly mauled in the course of adaptation had little effect upon our enjoyment of the picture. We could not help feeling, a trifle timidly, perhaps, that the mauling process had rather tended to improve the original; but of course we wouldn't want to say that out loud.

Robert E. Sherwood. *Life*. Feb. 3, 1921, p. 177

If we had a National Cinematographic library, as we should have, into the archives of which each year were placed the best pictures and finest examples of the cinematographic art achieved during that year, and I were on the board that voted upon the admission or rejection of submitted films, I certainly should include *The Last of the Mohicans* in my list of eligible exhibits. There is, to me, an impressive effort made in this fine picture of Maurice Tourneur's to treat a big subject with dignity and a certain reverence to which its traditions entitle it, and yet to do so without losing sight for an instant of its picture possibilities. Uncas, the Indian, is neither a handsome thing to look upon, nor yet a romantically fascinating hero. But Uncas is real, and the adventures through which he leads the trusting Munros are thrillingly true to the spirit of the story. Tourneur differs from most of the directors in his class in that he can achieve great beauty of background without sacrifice of story value, and while he does permit a certain repetition of his favorite shots, the views from a darkened cave through to the blazing firelight or sunlight or moonlight beyond, for example, with silhouetted figures against the light, they seldom interfere with the spectator's interest in the tale. There is more good melodrama in *The Last of the Mohicans* than in a half dozen crook plays; more fine, hair-raising fights, and one supreme climax in the leap from the cliff that has not been equalled for several seasons. There is a nice sense of delicacy in the treatment of the romance, and there is as fine an effect in the panoramic close-up of the escaping villagers as I ever have seen screened.

Burns Mantle. *Photoplay*. April 1921, p. 78

The Foolish Matrons is exceptional chiefly for its cinematography—that cumbrous and inexpressive word must do till we get a better one for the characteristic and most important element in the technique of motion pictures: the power to evoke emotion and understanding through visualized action. This power has been used with masterly skill to tell a story that needed masterly treatment to save it from being merely an illustrated novel.

Though it escapes being that, it is still hardly more than a novel told in pictures. Which is not the belittling statement it sounds like; for why should a motion picture not use the structure of a novel as well as that of a drama, so long as it builds with its own material and tools? It means only that this story is not essentially dramatic. It couldn't be, dealing as it does with three almost separate sets of characters, which make dramatic concentration in the usual sense impossible. But the weaving together of the three strands is remarkably well managed, as a matter both of continuity and writing and direction.

The whole thing is in the nature of a tour de force for Mr. Tourneur, for it is not at all the kind of thing his fame as a director has been built on. It is as far removed as possible from *Woman*, *The Blue Bird*, and *Victory*, or even *The Last of the Mohicans* and the picturesque old English melodramas he used to do. It is what might be called a problem picture, and the problem is no less a one than marriage: why is it a success or a failure?—the sort of thing one would expect, done in a different way, from Von Stroheim or DeMille.

NBR. June 1921, p. 5

Maurice Tourneur again comes to the front as a maker of motion pictures in the screen version of *Lorna Doone*, at the Strand this week.

The outlaws attack the carriage in which little Lorna and her mother, the Countess, are riding. There is a struggle. The outlaws ride off with the child and leave the mother where she has been thrown to the ground, stretching out her arms helplessly, reaching for her child, her partly raised figure reflected brokenly in the glistening wet sand on which she lies. Then a flash of the carriage, abandoned by horses and men, standing hub-deep in water, the waves licking its decorated sides and soaking its soft cushions. These are pictures.

And it is largely in pictures that Mr. Tourneur has told the old story, pictures composed with a keen eye for effects, and sharp, therefore, with meaning, pictures in soft tones and striking contrasts, all related by the action of an appropriately speeded story, each occupying its proportionate space in the whole. For Mr. Tourneur is a storyteller as well as a maker of motion pictures, and he knows the value of restraint as well as that of emphasis. He knows, rather, the part that restraint plays in emphasis, and so does not too heavily underscore any incident for the sake of the unrelated and independent effect he might obtain with it. For instance, the mother does not wallow on the sand in a prolonged closeup. She does not cry out, with the aid of a subtitle, "My child! My child!" or anything else. A flash of the figures on the sand, a gesture, the intensifying reflection—and that is all. But one sees everything, the imagination is started—and more of the scene or anything added to it would only dissipate the illusion of reality which the spectator helps to create for himself and reduce the individual in the threatre seat to some such observation as "The woman's a good actress, isn't she?" Yet how many directors would have measured the power of this little scene by its footage?

The scene is little and of comparatively slight importance. It is chosen here merely to illustrate Mr. Tourneur's vivifying treatment of the story, which is familiar to you, of course.

NYT. Dec. 4, 1922, p. 20

Tourneur is the leader of the artistic school of directors and in many respects is five years ahead of the rest of the pack. He has some ideals and attempts to put them into practice at every opportunity. Huge sets, mob scenes or any of the other forms of lavishness mean little or nothing to Tourneur. He likes a colorful story which lends itself to interesting backgrounds and artistic treatment, but he can get more drama and beauty out of a small two-walled set representing an underworld den or a close-up of a small Mexican hut, than other studio skippers can get through the burning of Rome or replicas of Fifth Avenue mansions which occupy the full length of the stage. Tourneur's scenes are often exquisite compositions of light and shade painted with photoplay ingredients.

Tamar Lane. *What's Wrong with the Movies* (Waverly, 1923), pp. 67–68

Although Tourneur was an impressive pictorialist and director of talent in his day, his films did not stand the wear of time. Griffith's films, dated in sentiment, had a solid cinematic structure that gave them permanent importance and still inspires respect. Their content, moreover, was taken from life; it dealt with real problems. Tourneur's scenes of visual beauty, on the other hand, while often compensating for structural weakness, failed to cover the vast stretches of mere grandiosity and emptiness in his work. Vivid in light, shadow, composition, his films were devoid both of inner integrity and significant content. When his imagery was not over-wrought, however, Tourneur did bring to the camera a splendor that affected later pictorial techniques. His importance in the history of American films, like the importance of some other pioneers, lies not so much in the work he left but in his suggestiveness to the industry. Much of the atmosphere, design, and pictorial beauty of pictures today are due indirectly to Tourneur's influence. [1939]

Lewis Jacobs. *The Rise of the American Film* (Teachers College, 1968), p. 209

Maurice Tourneur's place in film history is a secure one and is the result of his highly developed esthetic ease.

He was the first director to *insist* that each individual shot be so composed as to produce a beautiful, as well as a dramatic, effect, and the first to use dark masses in the foreground to dramatize the action beyond. He was one of the few directors who have really wanted "to do something" with the motion picture. . . .

While at the Lycée Condorcet the young Maurice became friends with François Jourdain, a painter of some note, and, through him, met Leon-Paul Laforgue, the poet and writer. It was these associations which led him, after graduation at 18 from the Lycée, into illustrating magazines and books and designing posters and fabrics, and into interior decoration. Then he became an assistant of Auguste Rodin, and of Puvis de Chavannes, and worked on the latter's sketches for the decoration of the grand staircase in the Boston Public Library.

Such work, and such associations, fixed in Tourneur's psyche the conviction that the esthetical should be part of whatever one does. And it was this mental attitude which later led Tourneur to try to make the esthetical a part of the motion picture.

George Geltzer. *Films in Review*. April 1961, p. 193

The Wishing Ring turned out to be an enchanting, will-o'-the-wisp comedy-drama; the lightness of touch, however, concealed a sophisticated knowledge of filmmaking. Modern audiences may notice nothing unusual about the film. They enjoy its freshness and impish vitality, but since there are no striking innovations or dramatic effects, they don't regard it as an important picture. Yet pictorially, and from the editing point of view, *The Wishing Ring* is sprinkled with surprises.

Tourneur's method of cutting swiftly between various elements within a scene became common with certain directors later in the silent period. The technique of time-cutting, linking two shots separated by time without using a time-lapse device such as a fade or dissolve, did not become common, or even acceptable, until the early sixties. *The Wishing Ring* contains only a few such technical flourishes, but it is a most accomplished production for 1914. Pictorially exquisite (cameraman John van den Broek was an essential ally for Tourneur's pictorial eye), it proves that Tourneur was one of the men who introduced visual beauty to the American screen. American pictures of 1914 were often well photographed, but I have seen few to compare for sheer visual elegance with Tourneur's.

Keven Brownlow in *The American Film Heritage*, edited by the American Film Institute (Acropolis, 1972), p. 146

VAN DYKE, W. S. (1899–1944)

It becomes increasingly difficult, with the growth of extreme specialization, to praise any specific person for the excellence of some feature of a film. Here is a nice problem in concerted effort: who should receive credit for making *White Shadows in the South Seas* a criticism of the white man's ruthless business of civilizing primitive races? Did the director, W. S. Van Dyke, plead with the producers to retain some elements of intelligence, that the highly romantic and incredible love story might not merely be another contribution to the delectation of half-wits? Did Ray Doyle, the adaptor, realize the worth of an idea to a scenario and slip it in surreptitiously? Or perhaps Frederick O'Brian himself insisted upon the preservation of that critical quality and stipulated its retention in his contract. . . .

It is just because *White Shadows* is a film adaptation that it falls short of being a significant motion picture. By its insistence upon a trivial and improbable romance it vitiates the importance of the central motive, which recounts the deleterious effect of white traders upon a native tribe of the Marquesas Islands. But what is important about the film is the fact that it actually dared to handle a problem of adult proportions. The cycle of events attendant upon the unscrupulous and heartless exploitation of the natives by white pearl traders is dramatically indicated by the opening and closing shots of two ramshackle cabarets; the tragic consequence of the advent of the traders to the hitherto unexplored island is closed by the picture of Fayaway, no longer in her native costume of rushes, but dressed in a cheap calico, mourning for her husband, who has been murdered by one of his own race. . . .

White Shadows in the South Seas is not a film to cause undue elation among those who conceive the cinema to be more than simple entertainment, but at the present state of affairs must be greeted with generosity and accepted with gratification as a serious and sensitive effort in the right direction.

C. Adolph Glassgold. *The Arts.* Sept. 1928, pp. 166–67

A happy beginning for Metro Movietone sound films, *White Shadows* once more takes us back to the paradisiacal island of a South Seas forever lost, where admirable and fleeting creatures live among enormous and dramatic tropical plants and under a warm, slow wind that brings attractive clouds.

Flaherty has contributed—I don't know to what extent—to the making of these *White Shadows in the South Seas* in which one rediscovers the enchantment of the water, of the fishing, of the cooking, of all the principal charms of *Moana*, as well as that healthy admiration of physical joy. There is also the deep and tragic dives of the pearl fishers—into a crystal and fantastically peopled sea.

The synchronized electric music is agreeable; it allows us to hear an excellent and discreet musical accompaniment that popularizes the American manner of leitmotiv. In addition there is good use made of the multiple shouts, the calls, the sound of the wind, of weeping, and of exotic songs. The scene in which Mount Blue learns to whistle at a girl is properly reinforced by the sound of whistling—sometimes skillful, sometimes timid—that accompanies the images.

Jean George Auriol. *Revue du Cinéma.*
Dec. 1928, unpaged

Flaherty's *Nanook of the North* was truer, its Eskimos purer in strain. One feels here, without knowing, that in *Eskimo* Hollywood has somewhere diluted the blood. Yet in Flaherty's film there was no excitement, no impact of race and the predatory civilization that lays its ways upon the native. *Nanook* was a half truth, an isolated record in pictures, incomplete, unrelated. *Eskimo* is a half truth, too, but in a different way. It gives one a sense of living, of alien feeling, of momentary beauty in barrenness. Then it adulterates all this with natives that are not Eskimos, and an undue accent on sex.

It is for its details, its individual scenes, that one considers *Eskimo*, not as a whole. It is for the fight to the death of the two locking bucks of the caribou herd, the magnificence of the stampede across the wastes of snow, animals plunging into the river with the small band of men down upon them with spears and imprecations, fighting death in hunger. There is the harpooning of the whale, the landing of the walrus, incidents in a hunting life, with the men, alert and sure leaping about in their reversible kayaks, all of them moving to a certain basic rhythm.

But the love scenes on which the fiction depends, the Eskimo way of lending a wife to a friend who is without one, but not to a white man, without his consent, do not feel true. I do not mean that this is not the custom, but that the emphasis in filming these scenes is wrong, and the manner too close to that of the studios to seem born in the wastes of the Arctic. There is rape, and consequent murder of the white trader who causes the death of the Eskimo woman; the hunt is now on, with the Northwest Royal Mounted in possession of the field. The film begins to lag, the narrative grows pedestrian here, and there is interpolated a comic interlude with the subtlety of *What Price Glory*.

W. S. Van Dyke did this before, in *White Shadows of the South Seas*, commenced by Flaherty. He did it again in *Trader Horn*. As a director, he lacks sincerity, and a sense of style, that can transmit honestly and with simplicity the content of his film. So *Eskimo* is half true and half Hollywood. The two will always lie, like palimpsests, unmerged. In *Eskimo* one resents this; because it is so close to beauty, its adulteration is the more disastrous.

NBR. Feb. 1934, pp. 12–14

An amusing, exciting, and generally satisfying motion-picture has been made out of the popular Dashiel Hammett's febrile detective story, *The Thin Man*. Altho the screen usually is at its best in the manipulation of mystery narratives, its propensity for mixing comedy with murder frequently has unfortunate results. The efforts to be comical about a corpse usually are not quite as uproarious as the producers seem to anticipate, and there still are squeamish souls who recall with something less than side-splitting mirth an episode in a film called *Guilty as Hell*, wherein a merry newspaper man gaily flicked cigarette ashes on the body of a murdered woman as he debonairly went about the job of solving the mystery. It might, therefore, seem less than enthusiastic praise to say of *The Thin Man* that its mood essentially is one of gaiety. Yet so skilful is the amalgamation of the qualities of comedy and melodrama that the possibly warring elements fit together beautifully. Thanks to some excellent direction by the expert W. S. Van Dyke, and two striking performances by William Powell and Myrna Loy, the new film is excellent entertainment.

Readers of the book will remember it as a successful example of the "hard-boiled" school of detective-story writing, with the characters consuming vast quantities of alcoholic liquors, and indulging in vigorous language as they went about the comparatively minor business of murdering and solving murders.

The photoplay leaves out the violent talk, keeps in most of the drinking, and brings the mystery section of the novel out of the background right to the front of the proceedings. There is an occasional trace of whimsy in the comedy which the author might not enjoy thoroughly, but, on the whole, the humor is shrewdly and not too ostentatiously managed, while the plot seems definitely more sturdy than it was in the book. . . .

"Argus." *Literary Digest*. July 14, 1934, p. 29

. . . W. S. Van Dyke, the director of *Hideout*, is obviously profiting from *It Happened One Night* and from his success, *The Thin Man*, which was also a copy of the Capra production. At the risk of boring you with it, I will say again that nobody can approach the Americans in humor and they are very good in the cinema generally when they avoid ideas. What they thrive on are notions and conceits, which pass in Beverly Hills as ideas. In any event *Hideout* was amusing and both [Robert] Montgomery and Maureen O'Sullivan were excellent in their parts. It told of a gangster who was taken in by [a] farmer family and falls in love with the daughter. The cops finally come for him but she promises to wait until he has finished his term. The farm stuff is good and Van Dyke handles it well, even to the dinner table scene which is a replica of the dinner table scene in *The Thin Man*. If you will observe closely, you will see my barriers are breaking down one by one. Essentially what I am saying is that seeing *Hideout* is preferable to walking around outside in the rain.

Robert Forsythe. *New Masses*. Sept. 25, 1934, p. 29

Out of the gusty, brawling, catastrophic history of the Barbary Coast early in the century, Metro-Goldwyn-Mayer has fashioned a prodigally generous and completely satisfying photoplay. *San Francisco* is less a single motion picture than an anthology. During its two-hour course on the Capitol's screen it manages to encompass most of the virtues of the operatic film, the romantic, the biographical, the dramatic and the documentary. Astonishingly, it serves all of them abundantly well, truly meriting commendation as a near-perfect illustration of the cinema's inherent and acquired ability to absorb and digest other art forms and convert them into its own sinews. . . . The plot attains an impasse which might well be broken only by some such cataclysmic force as an earthquake. And *San Francisco's* earthquake comes. It is a shattering spectacle, one of the truly great cinematic illusions; a monstrous, hideous, thrilling débâcle with great fissures opening in the earth, buildings crumbling, men and women apparently being buried beneath showers of stone and plaster, gargoyles lurching from rooftops, watermains bursting, live wires flaring, flame, panic and terror. Out of it, inevitably, comes the regeneration of Blackie Norton, the happy ending of the love story and a new San Francisco.

Frank S. Nugent. *NYT*. June 27, 1936, p. 21

. . . Van Dyke was to make a beautiful film called *Eskimo* which again used the methods indicated in *White Shadows*. The film is not without faults; it continually throws the natives and white men into contrast, though less harshly. A tale of murder and of race antagonism, it contains scenes like those of the walrus hunt and the attack on the caribou which are as touching as the finest things in the *Georgics.* Under a pallid sky each man or animal stands out in sharp silhouette against the great expanses of white snow. The actors speak Eskimo, which does not disturb us in the least, for the dialogue is not meant to be understood but, like the music of *White Shadows*, blends with the images. The important thing about the film is the way in which sounds and images are thus blended and combine to create a definite rhythm. Right at the start of the talkie era, Benjamin Fondane wrote in *Bifur*: "Dialogue and sound should be content to fulfill the function formerly entrusted to double-exposure and to take its place." With Van Dyke this is what happened.

Maurice Bardèche and Robert Brasillach. *The History of Motion Pictures* (Norton and MOMA, 1938), p. 311

Lest there be misgivings about the quality of this historical spectacle, we hasten to assure you that the screenplay of *Marie Antoinette* is one of the most brilliant ever to be concocted. Rich, emotional dialogue with a clarity and dignity of words that comes as close to literature as anything ever written for the soundtrack. The settings—the Tuileries, the court at Versailles, Paris—are lavish, formidable and regal. The cast is composed of one hundred and fifty-two players whose ability and standards are unquestioned. . . . Lest there be misgivings about the quality of this spectacle, we hasten to assure you that something happened during the execution of this fabulous enterprise and *Marie Antoinette* is a mammoth bore. *Somebody forgot to light the fire.*

Stage. Sept. 1938, p. 48

. . . *The Thin Man* (1934), directed by W. S. Van Dyke, set a high mark in realism with the ease, spontaneity, and intimacy of the actors' speeches and the flow of images and talk generally. The camera did not wait on the sound, and the conversation did not seem to be aware of the microphone's presence. In the house-party scene the informality and realism were heightened by the subdued snatches of conversation, the mingling of voices, and the occasional high-lighting of some "wisecrack." The whole scene was maintained at a natural pitch and tone without any "microphone consciousness." [1939]

Lewis Jacobs. *The Rise of the American Film* (Teachers College, 1968), p. 441

It's a Wonderful World is, despite the title, one of the few genuinely comic pieces in a dog's age (direction of W. S. Van Dyke). It occasionally gets too loud and raucous for my taste, but it has a lot of funny people and funny situations, and it clips right along. Much as I do not admire Mr. Ben Hecht, I must insist that he is one of the most brilliant writers in pictures—even among the few who know what pictures are all about he is at the top—and has been proving it for years. His script, like that of the aviation movie, is frankly designed for box-office success. The difference is that it's all of a piece; it hangs together and moves smartly without confusion. It is the familiar compound of the romantic comedy and the detective thriller. Beyond the fact that it brings a shady private detective and a caricatured lady poet unwillingly (at first) together as fellow fugitives and at the same time investigators of some excessively criminal manipulations, the plot is too complex and unimportant to go into. Its virtue is that it does not make you think of plot: suspense holds like a cable, the interest keeps jumping, and there's a pretty good laugh around every corner. (Hecht knows slapstick, but he has a lively imagination that has gone to schools more subtle than Keystone Academy, and he is none the worse for either.) [1939]

Otis Ferguson. *The Film Criticism of O.F.* (Temple, 1971), pp. 256–57

This former assistant of Griffith has had great historical importance. He pioneered all the paths of escape and adventure: the South Seas (*White Shadows*, in 1928), the horror of the Pole (*Eskimo*, in 1931), *Trader Horn* (1930) which is to black Africa what *Stagecoach* is to the western, the imagery of the jungle dominated by the superman (*The Adventures of Tarzan*). It is often said that Van Dyke was the artisan-type of MGM, the good (or good enough) craftsman who furnished a not too spicy diet, comfortable suspense for everybody (though *Eskimo* is well above this level. . . .)

Henri Agel. *Romance Américaine* (Editions du Cerf, 1963), pp. 51–52

In 1936, MGM's half-hearted *The Devil Is a Sissy* moved partially towards the environmental preoccupation of *Dead End*. Its urban neighborhood spawned bullies such as Mickey Rooney and Jackie Cooper. But when Freddie Bartholemew's father declared "The next generation is finding itself out there . . . on the street," he missed the environmental point that the next generation was losing itself in that very place. *The Devil Is a Sissy* had no idea of what to make of the streets, and its potential delinquents, Cooper and Rooney, were better suited to small-town pranks—ducking away from the school road to go fishing, attaching a funny horn to the old jalopy—than to slum jungles.

Louis B. Mayer's heart was ever with Andy Hardy, and Freddie Bartholemew wraps up *The Devil Is a Sissy* by teaching his new-found friends, Jackie and Mickey, to be obedient to probation officers.

Andrew Bergman. *We're in the Money* (NYU, 1971), p. 154

VIDOR, KING (1894–)

The most serious fault to be found in the photoplay [*The Turn in the Road*] is emphasized by its most prominent virtue. Mr. Vidor shows that he has a grasp upon the fundamentals of pictorial composition and the techniques of making pictures dramatic and meaningful. Yet he does not depend upon pictures to tell his story. He relies upon uninspired subtitles at points where the full force of moving pictures is essential for strength. Because he sometimes uses pictures so effectively, one is disappointed when he leans on the broken crutch of words.

An illustration may serve to suggest Mr. Vidor's power with pictures. One of the characters in the story is a little boy who is the personification of confident love. Another is a man chiefly distinguished by his money and his meanness. They are in their separate homes when a furious storm breaks. The child is shown in his bed, half sitting, looking out of a window on the storm. He is interested, and, apparently, it does not occur to him to be afraid. Each flash of lightning illuminates his radiant, innocent face. The man is shown sitting in his luxurious library. At each flash of lightning and instinctively imagined crash of thunder, he winces, shies, as it were, in fear of forces which his money and power cannot overcome. This is a simple contrast, but it is effective. . . .

Apparently, Mr. Vidor was anxious to make *The Turn in the Road* proclaim his belief that God is Love and Light and his production brings something of this message, but it cannot be denied that it also has something of the shortcomings common to most photoplays with a purpose. How much of the message is brought, how much of it is lost and the effect upon the story of its moral burden, will depend, in the case of each spectator, upon individual reactions.

NYT. March 30, 1919, Section IV, p. 6

No matinee idol! No Young Love. No conventional Romance. Likewise —let it be regretfully remarked—no audience to speak of [for *The Jack-Knife Man*]. But artistry. A comfortingly high degree of most acceptable artistry. King Vidor, who made the picture, steps with it (and his few that have preceded it) into the small circle of real screen storytellers. . . .

Humor, pathos, and a large degree of the convincingness that comes from attention to the realities—*The Jack-Knife Man* has these.

It is lacking, however, in drama. Perhaps that is why it is not drawing better. Perhaps it is this lack, also, that makes the picture merely very good, instead of exceptionally good.

Instinctively, with work as good as this, that is *not* getting over particularly well, one searches for its defects.

But to-be-sure, the picture is ahead of its time. The picture audiences have been educated down to a low level of appreciation; a host of immaterial conventions are accepted as part of the necessary equipment of any story. Young Love, for instance. Who can blame a picture-patron for feeling cheated when he is shown a photoplay without a pure and beautiful actress, as heroine, when he has been led for studio generations to believe that all good pictures have 'em?

Myron M. Stearns. *Judge*. Sept. 4, 1920, p. 22

In praising Laurette Taylor's performance, sufficient credit cannot be given to King Vidor, who directed her. After the work of production was all over, Miss Taylor confessed that she could not have done it without the intelligent advice of Mr. Vidor. When the first screen tests of her were made, he didn't say a word—but allowed her to romp about and grimace in any way she chose. Then he showed her the results in the cold gloom of a projection room, and after seeing these, she submitted to his direction without a whimper.

Mr. Vidor did not display the best possible judgment in the selection of a supporting cast for Miss Taylor. Aside from Russell Simpson, who appeared as Peg's father, there was scarcely a single performance in *Peg O' My Heart* that deserved even so puny an adjective as "adequate." It was a singularly mediocre troupe.

However, Laurette Taylor was the whole picture—and Laurette Taylor, as I have taken pains to point out, was extraordinarily good.

Robert E. Sherwood. *The Best Moving Pictures of 1922–23* (Small, Maynard, 1923), p. 48

The Big Parade is not properly to be compared with most other motion pictures, it is related to the very best that the theatre, legitimate or cinema, can offer as drama of a moving and important kind. Yet it is as a motion picture that it is astounding, that it renews faith in the cinema form and creates an enthusiasm for its destiny. For *The Big Parade* has unchained the movie, has freed the prisoner from the house of hokum and delivered it from the wardenship of "the masses," for whose appeasement supposedly it has been incarcerated. And oh, believe us, "the masses" will acclaim this prodigy that has been liberated to them—even though they may not analyse the reason.

Why this has happened, multitudinous reasons will be advanced—by the public, the producers, the sharps of the sales forces, and the discerning critics. The answer, perchance, is this: once again among the very few times it has happened, a writer of imagination and a director gifted to reflect that imagination have been permitted—to a very measurable extent, at least—to produce an *original screen story*, not a scenario that substitutes for a written fiction, holy or profane, popular or classic. *The Big Parade* is a cinegraphically visualized result of a cinegraphically imagined thing, not a book in pictures or the picture of a book; the story and the picture are one and the same thing—a motion picture, namely, something conceived in terms of a medium and expressed by that medium as only that medium could properly express it. A writer thinks of the thing he will write on paper with ink, by using a typewriter or a pen; Mr. Stallings and Mr. Vidor have thought of the thing they would compose together on film with a camera, by using a mechanism that moves the film so as to create the illusion of a moving object—or of life.

NBR. Nov.-Dec. 1925, p. 2

After seeing the picture seven times, the first impression remains that the greatness of *The Big Parade* was in the early opening scenes, the sweeping of everyone into something that they did not clearly understand, the enlistment through sheer mass hypnotism, the unthinking but definite cruelty of many women seeing war as romance instead of reality—the best lesson to those with eyes to read of the necessity of real education of people, instead of a standard fitting of a few facts and no real thought to hundreds of schoolchildren.

Beyond this there was the clear photography, the authentic feel of the film, the extraordinary impression of the rush of lorries, the queer terror of the woods. It was amazing how much fear could be suggested in the mere continuous pace of movement.

I felt in the English version that the transition from the lorries rushing up the French cobbles to the plunge into the woods was almost too abrupt. In the French version the journey up was longer, and there was more of the fight in the forest. On the other hand, there was an extremely stupid and sentimental episode added at the end, of Jim's return to the farm wounded, which considerably detracted from the authentic atmosphere of the picture. It is curious to surmise how the film could be so well cut and so badly cut at the same time.

The French version had however a few metres of a raving shell shocked soldier in the hospital scene which fitted into the epic picture, but was presumably judged too realistic for English eyes.

As for the rubbish circulated in England that *The Big Parade* showed how America won the war, did we, in any of our English war films, show the Americans, the Belgians, the French, the Serbians and Russians, marching to victory beside us? It was comment of a particularly stupid and humiliating kind, quite unworthy of the tradition of an English sense of justice.

Bryher. *Close Up*. July 1927, pp. 17–18

[*The Crowd*.] Here you have Life. Life as it is lived by millions in New York and other big cities where the crowd walks, pushes, tramples each individual member.

A tremendous production; a powerful story of a man who was born to be "something big" but has a furious fight for mere existence.

Cocky, self-confident, blind to his own failures, James Murray, as John Sims holds the love and the sympathy of his audience from beginning to end just as he holds the sympathy and love of his frail, self-sacrificing wife, Eleanor Boardman.

You have lived the same experiences as this simple, devoted couple. You have suffered and struggled, laughed and rejoiced, worried and fretted in the same manner.

No picture is perfect, but this comes as near to reproducing reality as anything you have ever witnessed. Yet it loses none of the suspense and thrills of a great picture because it is a real-life story.

The photography is splendid, the titles are as heart-yearning as the picture. . . .

Take several handkerchiefs, because you will cry with laughter and weep with sympathy while viewing this unusual King Vidor production. Don't miss it.

Photoplay. Dec. 1927, p. 52

The young Americans do not want to let themselves be suffocated by the fanciful, by the sumptuosities of the Italian Renaissance, by pink, purple, or golden adventures—not even by their own optimism. They want to see reality, to see today's America.

But, out of pride and fear, the American people have a horror of being revealed to themselves; they neither like nor tolerate anything but their legend. It is impossible to know what fate they have reserved for the young cinema. The American people have recognized themselves in the unmysterious and terribly clear images of *The Crowd*; they have reacted with gravity and seriousness, but they nevertheless bear King Vidor ill will for having chosen New York on which to exercise his powerful talents as a "revealer." . . .

King Vidor's style as well as his spirit has displeased many. Certainly, *The Crowd* contains many useless, ugly, and heavy repetitions;

Vidor cannot decide to choose; he puts everything in and no doubt he feels the need to explain, to clarify, to feel that everybody understands what he is showing. He piles detail upon detail, which crush by their weight and reality. It can be objected that his images are exaggeratedly true, but let no one complain of the romanticism of the gigantesque, of the taste for social drama, of vain opulence—you wanted to spend two hours in New York, and so too bad for you. The direction of *The Crowd* is perfect and full of breathtaking surprises; it is neither discreet, nor elegant; often it attacks and overwhelms you.

Jean George Auriol. *Revue du Cinéma.*
Feb. 1929, unpaged

Having but recently emerged from a defensive war with the dramatic critics I had hoped that my first assignment as a movie reporter would give me an opportunity to praise, laud and otherwise demonstrate to all concerned that fortunately I had not yet drunk at the fountain of invective, bitterness, mudslinging and egoism. Still innocent and sober I considered myself very likely when tickets for *Hallelujah* were offered to me. Certainly an auspicious beginning; praised by most critics, an all-Negro cast, a year's labor, directed by one of Hollywood's hopefuls . . . "all talking, singing, dancing."

First shot: dusk . . . cotton pickers going home, happy, gay, full of song in praise of . . . "Cotton, cotton, cotton." Picnic? Well—looks like it. Clean, rested, full-bellied. No, they did not work all day trying to pick enough cotton to fill the big wagon. Yes, they were costumed and some even looked as if they could pick cotton and others seemed to have suffered at the hands of the make-up expert who had never heard of sweat, of sticky clothes, of lint sticking in nostrils, ears, eyes and . . . but powder and grease paint belong in the movies. So be it. But it's a nice scene . . .

Chain gang for the poor hero. But he sings, which is all right. . . . The innocent girl he loved before he saw the tart before he killed the villain before he got religion before he ran away with the little bad girl before he killed the villain before he was sentenced to the chain gang where he sang a heartbreaking song. The end.

Oh, we're a hard gang to please. We are un-American, anti-Hollywood, we are the damned.

Em Jo Basshe. *New Masses.* Oct. 1929, p. 15

The picturization of *Street Scene*, Elmer Rice's Pulitzer Prize play, brings up again, this time with some new angles, the familiar questions of stage and screen: the tendency of the films to rely upon the play producers for their material whenever possible, even when that material is not suited to the films, the difficulty of translating a creation in one medium into another, the relative merits of stage and screen as artistic forces and so on. Photographed stage plays are no novelty to movie audiences any more. Scores of them have been adapted, with more or less success, to the films. *Street Scene*, however, is probably the first one to present considerable difficulty and to bring out a rarely-met cleavage between stage and screen.

To illustrate this cleavage, consider the title: what was a simple and appropriate name for the stage play is a misnomer for the motion picture. Whatever else King Vidor's skillful product may be, it is not a street scene. Accustomed to presenting, with little or no difficulty, the drawing-room comedies and melodramas of the stage, the films have found a problem of a different sort in this segment of city life, which depends for its effect upon your constant recognition of the fact that here is but one section of a whole, one part of a street, into which other and irrelevant characters are continually wandering. While the turgid drama of Mr. Rice is mounting toward its dramatic climax in front of you, Life, as the writers put it, is going on in other forms to right and left of you. Battle, murder and sudden death may, for all you know, be lurking quiescent behind those other brownstone fronts.

This is something the camera fails to catch. Often victor in its hand to hand conflicts with the stage, the motion picture is here torn between close-ups and long shots, and the overwhelming preponderance of the former converts what was once a panoramic bit of realism into the equivalent of a drawing-room triangle. When the camera starts to focus upon one or two or three characters, the plot thickens and *Street Scene* flies out of the window; petty domestic tragedy supplants the original "slice of life" conception.

NBR. Sept. 1931, p. 9

Between the self-consciousness of a Sternberg and that of a Vidor—who is also cult—there is a great difference. Sternberg's has the smoke, but not the flame of battle. Vidor's preoccupations merely bespeak the innocent; King Vidor aspires to an important expression he cannot achieve. He has more zeal than intelligence. *The Big Parade* remains his best film, because it is a chronology, and Vidor is a chronologist. *The Crowd*, which reduced a large, if debatable, theme to an arbitrary pamphlet, was further confused by a mismating between a simple sequence and expressionistic symbolism. Similarly, the conflict between ability and aspiration was present even in the sincere *Street Scene*. This film again reveals Vidor's immaturity. He is obsessed with details remembered from other pictures; they explode as spontaneous combustion—that is his method, which is no method at all. The cult-

position Vidor holds distracts him from his logical field of action—matter like *Billy the Kid*, which he directed diffidently. The result is inevitably the setup of the tear-jerker and descent to the level of a Frank Borzage. Only Vidor's innocence and goodwill—and Beery's acting—preserved *The Champ* from the cheapest properties of the subject matter.

Harry Alan Potamkin. *Vanity Fair.*
March 1932, p. 52

Off on the wrong foot, Vidor seemingly could do nothing right. The cast is incompetent and would be in any production. The photography makes some of the picture seem like an ancient Cecil B. De Mille print that had gone through a fire, and the music evidently is furnished by two worn phonograph records made by the Six Hawaiian Guitar Kings. The film also is intolerably long. I understand the company has two or three conclusions to tack onto the picture, according to the size of the town in which it is shown. In the version I saw, brave Luana jumps into bad ole volcano.

I would not have mentioned *Bird of Paradise* at all, in fact, except that King Vidor was once the most promising director in Hollywood. He had an unfortunate experience with *Hallelujah*, a picture he conceived himself. The picture received nothing like the credit it deserved, and so many theatre owners were afraid of it. I believe Vidor lost some money for his trouble.

Whatever the reason, since he has done nothing but re-make stage plays and turn his hand to routine productions. He might ponder over [Mamoulian's] *Love Me Tonight* and consider that the lowest common denominator is not always the most successful.

Pare Lorentz. *Vanity Fair.* Oct. 1932, pp. 44, 69

"Solid" people began to know that King Vidor had made a film that . . . a film which . . . People "solider" still appeared who had seen the film in New York, and there were others who had managed to see "a reel or two" in secret. *Halleluhah!* a name just made to be whispered, began to surface. Those who had seen *Hallelujah!* would chew the ears off those who hadn't seen seen *Hallelujah!* but who pretended to have so that they could seem in the know and so that they could take the wind out of the sails of those in the first category. In short, the situation became intolerable. Half of Paris humiliated the other half; and everybody wanted to join the first half. . . .

Finally, one managed to see *Hallelujah!* at two in the morning in a cellar into which you entered like a conspirator after your identity and your fingerprints had been checked. It must be admitted that one left *boulversé* (the word was still in fashion) and that one did not regret the experience.

But what happened?

What happened was that as a result of the secrecy about this film which was kept underground too long, when the public finally saw it they were sometimes disappointed. First, because those who had seen it in secret had, as always happens, exaggerated its beauties; but above all, because after three years of talkies this film had lost much of the force of novelty and exploration that it had had, and so supremely, at the time King Vidor had made it. I know no example of a director working so well against his own interests.

Pierre Bost. *Le Crapouillot*. Nov. 1932, pp. 43–44

Director King Vidor's gift for injecting genuine human emotions, credible characterization, and an authentic feeling for the soil into his photoplays results in transforming *The Wedding Night* into a fine, mature, and poignant motion-picture. Beautifully played by Anna Sten, Gary Cooper, and Helen Vinson, the new film manages, without any show of sensationalism, to be real and honestly moving.

Its story is based on one of those plots in which the actual events of a novelist's life parallel the book he is writing. It is a device which has been used so often that it has ceased to have any novelty, but *The Wedding Night* does not depend on any such qualities. . . .

Of such simple material Mr. Vidor has made his photoplay. Altho the ending is forced and unnecessary, the entire mood of the work is handled with such delicate, honest feeling; the people are so real, and their emotions so believable, that the picture becomes curiously stirring in drama.

Under the director's skilful guidance, the players give striking performances. Miss Sten offers the best portrayal she has yet made for American films, and Mr. Cooper is even better than he was amid the romantics of *The Lives of a Bengal Lancer*.

"Argus." *Literary Digest*. March 30, 1935, p. 32

The picture [*So Red the Rose*] tells the story of an old feudal Southern family during the Civil War. Its treatment of its slaves is humane, understanding from the "white God" point of view. At no place in the story is hinted the encroachment of the industrialists who turned feudal plantation life into the "outdoor factory." Such a picture might have shown the speed-up, beatings, starvation of the slaves, might have given American audiences an honest clue into the "revolt of the slaves" that took place during the Civil War. Thus, when the slaves on the Bedford plantation revolt, there is no sympathetic basis upon which they may turn against their white masters. One sees only crazed Negroes turning against the gentle hand that has cared for them so many years. . . .

It would be manifestly unfair to King Vidor to ignore some of the splendid directorial touches upon which his reputation is based. One of the most amusing scenes in the picture is the satire on Southern pride marching off to war, personified by Walter Connolly, as head of the Bedfords, who doesn't believe in the South's cause until he is wakened one night by the flat of a Union sabre on his broad posterior. Then, suddenly, the cause becomes alive and he turns the house out to find the beautiful uniform he once wore to a Governor's reception. For Marse Bedford is going off to war, attired as a Southern gentleman.

On the other hand it would constitute a negligence not to point out to Mr. Vidor that if *So Red the Rose* succeeds at the box office in the South it will be at the cost once again of provoking even sharper racial lines than exist in these states at the present time, of provoking an even greater hatred by the whites for the Negroes, of breaking the solidarity between workers of all races that is today beginning to change the Old South of infamous reputation into a New South built on workers' pride.

Arthur Draper. *New Theatre*. Jan. 1936, p. 31

The best news of the month, next to *Mamlock*, was King Vidor's film, *The Citadel*. Even bearing in mind the many excellences of *Wedding Night* and *The Crowd*, certain passages in *Hallelujah*, *Our Daily Bread*, and the man hunt in *Texas Ranger*, *The Citadel* is far and away his best film. In it he appears to have found a theme—the socializing and humanization of the medical profession—that has permitted a better coalescence of his gifts than previously. At present writing no 1938 domestic film suggests itself as even the tentative peer of *The Citadel*, pervaded as it is by an atmosphere of mature adult thought all too infrequently encountered in run-of-the-year production. We are grateful that a worthy idea has been handled with intelligence and imagination, that Vidor has shown respect both for his talent and the sensibilities of his audience. Most of all, that he has found himself after the almost self-imposed trivialities of straight commercial production.

We have always held that the touchstone of ability in any art is the use made of its basic stuff. In *Citadel's* concluding passages—from Denny's death on—Vidor amply proves his right to rank among the field's chosen. Here is a simple, direct use of sound, image and cutting that achieves genuine impact in a manner strictly and classically filmic. We look forward to the time when Vidor shall shape an entire film with the passion and clarity of this section. Mind you, we do not wish to detract from the remainder of *Citadel* but it must appear obvious that not all of the film is equally as well thought out.

Robert Stebbins. *TAC*. Dec. 1938, p. 7

King Vidor has stature not so much for his brilliancy of rendition or profundity of filmic conception as for a certain sincerity and viewpoint that has, time and again, lifted his films out of the regular run of entertainment trivialities and make him a notable director in the late twenties of the silent era when von Stroheim, Seastrom and Lubitsch were the American screen's major figures. A social conscience, a mind quick to absorb advanced ideas, and a belief in honesty and realism have repeatedly brought him to the forefront during the past fifteen years after long intervals of semiobscurity as a director of "pot-boilers." When Vidor's efforts have been motivated by his beliefs, they have been uncommonly good; when the reverse is true, his films have been marked by a plodding if intelligent cinematic style. Significantly his last effort, *The Citadel*, has once more given him prominence and reveals him not as a man who has seen his day but as a director who will continue in the forefront of his contemporaries by the earnestness of his social outlook. . . .

Vidor has believed from the first that a picture must have something of social import to say. His earliest obscure efforts in the early twenties were colored by this interest; they comprised most of the few realistic films about the common man and his struggles during the post-war deluge of "sex" and "jazz" movies. *The Turn of the Road*, *Better Times*, *Poor Relations*, *The Other Half*, *The Family Honor*, *The Jack-Knife Man*, and *Dusk to Dawn* stressed characterization, local problems, economic issues, relation of capital to labor, social conditions generally—elements Vidor was to employ again and again and to make his own. These pictures won regard for him as a sincere and promising talent but no one thought when he directed *Proud Flesh*, an unusually deft satirical comedy, that his next film would lift him to fame and prove to be the biggest box-office sensation since *The Covered Wagon*. That next film was *The Big Parade* (1925). . . .

The phenomenal success this film enjoyed brought forth exaggerated praise; the picture was hardly as worthy or artistically significant as it was declared to be. A romantic depiction of America's part in the World War, *The Big Parade* was on the whole a superficial, if impressively executed, production. . . .[1939]

Lewis Jacobs. *The Rise of the American Film*
(Teachers College, 1968), pp. 454–55

. . . Metro-Goldwyn-Mayer assigned King Vidor to direct *Hallelujah*, which, to quote a 1929 publicity blurb—"will be the ace of the all-Negro talking pictures." If it was hoped that a director as intelligent as Vidor, and Negro actors like Daniel Haynes and Nina Mae McKinney, would make *Hallelujah* memorable, then expectations were short-lived. The slight story, of a country boy who temporarily succumbs to the wiles of a bad woman, probably seemed at first to possess some dramatic power . . . But the central theme became swamped, inevitably perhaps, by the forty or so singing sequences of folk songs, spirituals, baptism wails, work songs and blues. *Hallelujah*, written by novelist Wanda Tuchock, was, however, an interesting film, and certain parts of it indicated the undeniable power of the director. But how much King Vidor was influenced by Hollywood's attitude to Negroes generally, and how much the film was altered in the cutting room are questions which must forever remain unanswered. Suffice to say that, in spite of all its promise, M.-G.-M's "all-Negro epic" made only a minor contribution to the Negro struggle for recognition on the screen. [1948]

Peter Noble. *The Negro in Films* (Kennikat, 1969), pp. 51–52

While the film [*War and Peace*] always holds one's interest, it seldom involves the audience in the action. We are touched when the Rostovs, Natasha's family, who are likened to a family of gay, healthy, happy animals, suddenly take themselves seriously and decide to rescue wounded soldiers instead of their furniture. We are touched when Natasha goes to her first ball (beautifully staged) and discovers first love. We are touched when a simple peasant (John Mills) expresses his strong faith in God and has no fear of death. We are stirred when the great Napoleon (Herbert Lom) behaves like a petulant child when he finds there are no Russians in Moscow to surrender to him.

But as a whole, *War and Peace* is a cold and handsomely made epic that one watches from a comfortable distance without projecting oneself into the story. The characters in *Gone with the Wind*, the American-made epic, also concerned with the effects of war upon society, compelled our attention whether we liked them or not. Tolstoy's affection for his characters shines through *War and Peace*, but unfortunately they fail to hold us. The splendid Technicolor photography of scenes like the duel between Fonda and Helmut Dantine (as a dissolute Russian officer), or the hunt on the Rostov estate, is exciting beyond compare, and the panoramas in VistaVision are first-rate; but the film has no more warmth than pictures in an art gallery. *War and Peace* is still a film to be seen, however, for its top-notch production, even though it excites little emotion as its asks: "What difference does it make if part of Poland is lost, or a piece of Austria changes hands?"

Philip T. Hartung. *Commonweal.*
Sept. 14, 1956, pp. 587–88

There is a moment at the end of King Vidor's little-known film *The Stranger's Return* that precisely sums up the essence of his vision. The heroine, a city girl, has just seen her grandfather, patriarch of a rural community, die in his great old age. She walks out of the house with tears blinding her eyes; suddenly she sees the garden, the whirling butterflies, the sun glittering on the leaves of the family orchard. She goes towards the plough that rolls slowly across the fields and her step quickens to a run. Now she is walking proudly beside it. She has renounced urban living for good: she has accepted the soil.

In the handful of films in which he has been free to express himself, King Vidor has asserted the values of an America almost everyone else seems to have forgotten: the America of the backwoods. As romantic as Thoreau, as intoxicated by the forests and lakes of the wilderness as Fenimore Cooper, Vidor has savaged the city's destructive power in his masterpiece, *The Crowd.* His images evoke landscape as no other director can, not even Ford; there are shots in *North-West Passage*, *Duel in the Sun*, *Beyond the Forest*, *Hallelujah*, *Billy the Kid* and *The Stranger's Return* which almost let one breathe the scent of the soil.

We live in an unromantic age, and King Vidor is a romantic poet who celebrates the beauty of nature, and of natural man. His genius expresses a philosophy of moral purity which would provoke jibes from most audiences today. Yet I believe that his work will live long after the experiments of the Sixties look jaded; lyrics always outlive acrostics. His traditional art may have left new frontiers unexplored—he is not a von Sternberg or a Welles, an inventor of forms—but almost single handedly he carried into the sound era the grassroots-America cinema of Griffith and Maurice Tourneur. For that we must always be grateful.

Of Vidor's silent films only two are important: *The Big Parade* (1925) and *The Crowd* (1928). *The Big Parade* stands outside the mainstream of his work, and does not wear well: the first half is heavily sentimental, showing the enlisting of sympathy of the American people for war; the second half, staged on the Western Front, lacks the intensity of feeling that inspired Milestone's *All Quiet on the Western Front.* This remains an impressive spectacle to which Vidor brought little save his showman's skill.

Charles Higham. *Film Heritage.*
Summer 1966, p. 15

A number of documentary techniques were employed in making *Our Daily Bread*, some of them no doubt dictated by economy. Vidor had no studio resources behind him. . . .

With the arrival of the ditchdigging sequence, all that has gone before seems but buildup for this compelling climax. Inconsistencies are forgotten as Vidor sweeps the spectator with emotion by means which, on paper, sound incredibly mechanical. As he did in the famous advance through the woods in *The Big Parade*, Vidor used the metronome to time the movements of the actors as precisely as in a ballet. The sequence was shot without sound recording equipment: the metronome and a drum directed the action. As Vidor describes it, "The picks came down on the counts of one and three, the shovels scooped dirt on count two and tossed it on count four. Each scene was enacted in strict 4/4 time with the metronome's speed gradually increasing on each cut. When the increased speed of the metronome resounding through the bass drum had driven the diggers to their most feverish pitch, we then resorted to decreasing the camera speed gradually, which in turn further increased the tempo of the workers."

Skillful and varied camera placements make important contributions to the total effect. The workers appear in long shot over the horizon; they approach the camera; their backs retreat from it; they disappear in clouds of dust. There is no music under the sequence: instead the track bears the clink of the picks and shovels in an insistent beat, up to the point where the water breaks through. Here the music swells with the triumph of the workers. The shots become shorter, the action more frenzied, the spectator is deluged with images.

Even on repeated viewing and after technical analysis, this sequence continues to cast a romantic spell. In it, we, like the men we watch, are physically reunited with the earth from which we came. It is a cardinal example of that movie phenomenon in which the breaking up and rearranging of photographed events somehow result in an intensification of the experience being recorded. An interesting comparison might be made between this sequence and the cream separator sequence in Eisenstein's *Old and New*, in which something of the same exultation is evoked by quite different methods.

Eileen Bowser in *Film Notes*, edited by
Eileen Bowser (MOMA, 1969), p. 92

The epic westerns . . . were totally imbedded in themes of thirties film: the personification of evil, the saliency of corruption, the gang values of revenge, the emphasis on unified nationhood. Vidor's *The Texas Rangers* is a shocker, coming from so sensitive a moviemaker. Uncomfortable with myth, Vidor struggled through a hopeless attempt to make western types of Fred MacMurray, Lloyd Nolan, and Jack Oakie. Oakie and MacMurray are outlaws who join the Rangers as a lark. After gazing upon some Indian atrocities, they are socialized into defenders of the law. Their gangster values cause MacMurray to refuse to arrest his friend Nolan (as opposed to the Virginian's [in *The Virginian*] solemn lynching of his closest friend) and MacMurray to kill Nolan, after the latter has rubbed out Oakie.

Around these basic gangland premises was built a tale of the civilizing of the West and the cleansing of Texas. Vidor began with a kind of *March of Time* narration over shots of roaming cowboys and cattle: "to insure prosperity and progress, the Texas Rangers were formed." The head Ranger (Edward Ellis) tells recruits that Texas Rangers die "for an ideal . . . so that Texas may be a civilized place." Civilization, progress, and prosperity lie just ahead—the perfect functioning of society hampered only by an "external" threat in the presence of red men. That "civilization" meant "prosperity" was made very clear when Ellis declares, after the Indians have been massacred, "Now that we've placed the Indians on the reservation, we can be prosperous." As always in the thirties, only external threats blocked prosperity.

When a final stumbling block to the conversion of "frontier into civilized land" is encountered, small wonder that it is corruption. Fred MacMurray is sent to clean up a town run by a corrupt boss and is warned "no gunplay, unless absolutely necessary." The shysters are, after all, white men. In exorcising external threats to national wealth and chasing after corruption, *The Texas Rangers* showed how time-bound it was. . . .

Andrew Bergman. *We're in the Money*
(NYU, 1971), pp. 89–90

WALSH, RAOUL (1892–   )

Fred Niblo, John Robertson, Frank Lloyd, R. A. Walsh, Emmett Flynn, and Reginald Barker can be classed among the "they might but won't" crew. They are men of some out-of-the-ordinary talents who now make a very laudable film and then a very poor one. Intermittently good photoplays may be expected of these supervisors but as leaders of a new school of directors they cannot be relied upon.

Tamar Lane. *What's Wrong with the Movies* (Waverly, 1923), p. 69

Often humorous, sometimes grim, with a sentimental strain here and there, the film translation of *What Price Glory*, the play by Maxwell Anderson and Laurence Stallings, which was presented last night at the Sam H. Harris Theatre, is a powerful screen effort. The blazing jealousy of Captain Flagg and Sergeant Quirt is vividly pictured in those scenes behind the lines, and these same soldiers are depicted as brothers in arms, as marines who forget everything in loyalty to their flag, once they step out of their billets to fight. Both are shown to be men who under fire are touched by the very weakness of others that they sneered at back of the trenches. . . .

Taking advantage of the scope offered by the screen, the bickering and recriminations between Flagg and Quirt are first shown in China, where a Sadie Thompson type of girl—described as having divorced one regiment to be married to the Marines—first steps in between the two professional soldiers. How Quirt outwits Flagg is brought out in these scenes, as it is later in others in the Philippines and in France. So successfully has this been accomplished by Raoul Walsh, the director, that not only were there many an explosion of laughter last night, but two or three times the audience reached such a high pitch of enthusiasm that they applauded loudly. . . .

There are some very realistic fighting scenes in this production, with cannon booming, Very lights tearing through the air and poison gas being wafted from the enemy lines. These periods are thrilling, being pictured with an unusually faithful conception of war as it was in France. The "Trench of Death," a short scene, is one of the tragic notes. Here a whole line of men is buried through the explosion of a mine and after the disaster the bayonet points are beheld sticking up through the earth.

Mordaunt Hall, *NYT*. Nov. 24, 1926, p. 26

Loves of Carmen is an embroidered picture, and fortunately much of it is cinematic embroidery in the sense that it is said with pictures. Carmen, like a kind of butterfly with a sting, hovering around the neck of the ponderous, ever hungry, rather messy Escamillo of Don Victor McLaglen, more good-natured than bull-fighters, we believe, are generally reputed to be; Carmen sidling toward and dancing away from her Don Jose—a somewhat anemic, sobbingly despondent Don Jose in the hands of Don Alvarado. Carmen stinging the cigarette girls to anger and, when she has won Escamillo, whirling past the cigarette factory on her way to the bull fight in Escamillo's resplendent carriage to flaunt her conquest in their faces; and best of all the Carmen that must ever remove her newly acquired and very ladylike high-heeled Spanish slippers to cool and free her brown gypsy feet, are matters that have been put vividly into pictures to create a swiftly changing but continuously patterned image. For reasons like this, though the caged full-grown tiger Carmen of the opera has been largely abandoned for a screen-liberated, lithesome, tiger-kittenish Carmen not too far removed from the Hollywood mould, this Carmen and the story of Carmen as told by this picture, have acquired new life and fresh interest.

It is a long film, yet its continuity is excellent and there is economy of narrative, the elaboration occurring in the incidents where action concentrates. It is also a frank film, one in which the producers and Raoul Walsh, its director, have not minced matters. In watching this picture one might do well to remember that Carmen, the true Carmen of Merimée, was not a person preoccupied with morals, but that in fact she didn't know what they were. . . .

NBR. Sept. 1927, p. 5

How Gloria Swanson beat the censors is being demonstrated in her newest and raciest picture. For *Rain* has come to the screen almost intact. Those portions objectionable to the purity leagues have been glossed over, but all the implications of the story are the same. And it is a great story. All normal people should be able to work up at least a mild frenzy over the battle between Sadie and the fanatical reformer of the South Seas. Raoul Walsh directs with speed and vigor, and acts very capably as Handsome, the marine. And Lionel Barrymore is almost perfect. But Gloria Swanson dominates the picture, with a flashing performance. You will like *Sadie Thompson*. It's stirring and ironic and funny. You couldn't ask more.

Photoplay. April 1928, p. 52

Raoul Walsh has made a curious assortment of films, showing at rare intervals a feeling for cinema and always a strong motive of picture-sense. Chief among his work ranks *Sadie Thompson*, an adaption of Somerset Maugham's brilliant short story and play, *Rain*. In this film, some three years ago, Gloria Swanson made her come-back to the screen and Lionel Barrymore acted with distinction. Walsh did his best to tell the story of the fugitive from San Francisco and the professional reformer who persecutes her until he himself is obsessed with sexual desire; but the contrived happy ending, which may have fitted in with United Artists' idea of picture-sense, was mediocre. Nevertheless, Gloria Swanson's performance was remarkable, and succeeded in placing her as an actress of talent far above the usual Hollywood standard. Walsh's second best picture was one of the war films so prevalent a few years ago, and as such was singularly unsuccessful. Despite its mock-heroic character, *What Price Glory*? was directed with some degree of vigour, and was, of course, satisfactory from a commercial point of view. Like the other American war films, it said nothing of the war itself except for a few sequences of blood and thunder. At an earlier date than this, Raoul Walsh had revelled in attempted fantasy, for he was responsible for the ice-cream mixture of *The Thief of Bagdad*, and others of an Eastern texture, such as *The Lady of the Harem*. To his credit, also, are to be placed the Negri film, *East of Suez*, *The Wanderer*, *The Loves of Carmen*, and *The Monkey Talks*.

Paul Rotha. *The Film Till Now* (Jonathan Cape, 1930), pp. 209–10

Millions of Americans who still cherish fond recollections of *The Covered Wagon* are going to be grateful for Raoul Walsh's masterful production, *The Big Trail*, which will lamentably find itself called *The Second Covered Wagon*. Printed upon the new wide film and projected upon the vastly large "Grandeur" screen, the landscapes, wagon trains, distant vistas and camp scenes achieve an incredibly greater sweep. Yet the story is weaker, and there is a certain lack of primitive sincerity and honesty that made *The Covered Wagon* a sublime epic of human struggle and hope. *The Big Trail* is often stagey, melodramatic, ranty. It was the total absence of these qualities that was the greatness of the earlier picture. . . .

However, the picture is brilliantly photographed and expertly directed. Some of the views are extraordinary. It was for such shots as this that wide-film, in whatever form, was created.

Theatre Magazine. Jan. 1931

Cock-Eyed World. This story seeks to present attempted seduction as legitimate comedy material, a procedure which is wholly offensive to decency. It tends to lower moral standards of impressionable people by confusing lust with legitimate adventure. It is crowded with leers and vulgarities.

Martin Quigley. *Decency in Motion Pictures* (Macmillan, 1937), p. 34

They Died with Their Boots On is the Custer story, full of action, Indians and anachronisms. . . . In his direction, Walsh prepared for the all-out encounter by a series of incidents that led logically to the famous massacre. In semi-darkness the 7th Cavalry, with the gallant Custer at its head, moves from Fort Lincoln to join the forces of General Terry. Few films have matched the succeeding scenes in building suspense. Actual combat with the Indian hordes is realistic. Custer fell with his men, having been trapped before he reached Terry. . . . *Boots* is a surefire western, an escape from bombers, tanks and Gestapo. It's American to the last man.

Variety. Nov. 19, 1941

Although some ten minutes have been cut from its original running time, *Battle Cry* remains a very long film. And for the most part a very unsatisfactory one. One of its chief faults lies in its failure to recreate the spirit of the early war years. Lacking this urgency, the business of training, which so largely occupies the film, seems unrooted in the needs of the times, and uninteresting enough on its own account. For the same reason the shallow slogans of patriotism and war-needs, unendorsed by the febrile tension which lent them their cogency and drama, appear trite. (Not, it should be added, through a deliberate artistic representation, but, negatively, through the lack of any clear sense of involvement.) The film's other major drawback is a rambling formlessness in construction which is vertiginous in its onslaught on one's senses of space and time. Unconnected good things remain. In the various love stories, involving a rich, bored service wife who temporarily scores a sophisticated victory over the simple girl back home, a sincere war-widow, and a mixed-up girl gone wrong, Anne Francis as the latter gives an excellent performance until thrown by the script's banal development. There is a good rough-house scene, some well-photographed battle episodes, Aldo Ray's easy sincerity and excellence of playing wherever possible, and various other well-observed, if familiar, types. But the film's most completely "felt" force is summed up by an extra who is required, on witnessing a waitress in a bar turn to fix her stocking, practically to rupture himself in his rush to peer over the counter.

BFI Bulletin. June 1955, p. 82

Sometimes a great deal of corn must be husked to yield a few kernels of internal meaning. I recently saw *Every Night at Eight*, one of the many maddeningly routine films Raoul Walsh has directed in his long career. This 1935 effort featured George Raft, Alice Faye, Frances Langford and Patsy Kelly in one of those familiar plots about radio shows of the period. The film keeps moving along in the pleasantly unpretentious manner one would expect of Walsh until one incongruously intense scene with George Raft thrashing about in his sleep, revealing his inner fears in mumbling dream talk. The girl he loves comes into the room in the midst of his unconscious avowals of feeling, and listens sympathetically. This unusual scene was later amplified in *High Sierra* with Humphrey Bogart and Ida Lupino. The point is that one of the screen's most virile directors employed an essentially feminine narrative device to dramatize the emotional vulnerability of his heroes. If I had not been aware of Walsh in *Every Night at Eight*, the crucial link to *High Sierra* would have passed unnoticed. Such are the joys of the *auteur* theory.

Andrew Sarris. *Film Culture.*
Winter 1962–1963

A climb-to-success story in the great American tradition—the carnage piling up at the bottom of the ladder—*White Heat* is also genuine black comedy as are few other films (Buñuel's *El* is another) which lay claim to the title. Black comedy will not come of "irreverent" spoofs on "taboo" subjects (like *The Trouble with Harry* or *The Loved One*), but rather from a vision so outrageously terrible that one has to laugh at its very extremity: one must laugh in order to bear it. *White Heat* commands such a vision and does so with such absolute integrity that (because it's not by Buñuel or someone of similar intellectual repute) one can never be sure the the film's makers even know what they're doing. Unlike *Bonnie and Clyde*, no one nudges you in the ribs.

I don't know where on earth one can get to see *White Heat* now off of Forty-second Street; probably, its violence would proscribe it even from television, where most of what was great in the American film now writhes under the cutter's knife. And yet it is among the best films made in this country, and one with much to tell us about the kind of country—its marriages, family life, and corrupting aspirations —in which it was made. This it does with so utter a lack of pretension that its casual brilliance almost seems accidental—surely, since the film was made in Hollywood and doesn't have subtitles, they couldn't have known what they were doing, could they? [1967]

William S. Pechter. *Twenty-four Times a Second* (Harper, 1971), p. 90

Today, *What Price Glory* remains the archetypal celebration of war as a game played by roistering comrades. In its time, however, it was also a step toward a more realistic treatment of war. . . .

Raoul Walsh's direction is expert, fast-paced, and moves with sureness from shot to shot, with a frequent use of close-ups of significant details, often to introduce a scene, and a wide variety of camera positions. No doubt he had seen the much-praised battle sequences of *The Big Parade*; some years earlier he had been trained in the D. W. Griffith school of film-making. At any rate, his battle sequences are excitingly mounted and dramatically photographed, with extreme contrast in lighting effects, such as the quick repeated flares of light in the darkness revealing impressive long shots of men advancing and falling, and emotionally they are quite effective. For the most part, *What Price Glory* lacks the really great moments of *The Big Parade*, and yet there is one scene presented in so masterly a fashion that it is unforgettable: it is the scene of the dying Mother's Boy stumbling down the steps of the field dressing-station and crying out to Captain Flagg to "stop the blood." In other serious scenes of this comedy, the speeches made in titles seem stilted and ludicrous today, but here the horror of war is fully felt for a brief moment.

Eileen Bowser in *Film Notes*, edited by
Eileen Bowser (MOMA, 1969), p. 62

As a silent director, Raoul Walsh made the classic *What Price Glory?* in 1926 and other features like *Evangeline* (1919) and *Sadie Thompson* (1928) in which he appeared with Gloria Swanson. But even when he went on to sound film, his greatest successes, Walsh remained a silent director to many. His rough-tough, speeded-up pragmatic artfulness was perhaps thought too commercially proficient to qualify as art. Now, through a reappraisal of Walsh works like *White Heat*, *The Roaring Twenties*, and *High Sierra*, the vigor of his vivid cinema is being recognized.

Humphrey Bogart gets the respectful star treatment on his first appearance in *High Sierra*. First we see his legs as he walks out of a prison gate, then his arms as he gives a farewell handshake, then his back as he looks at the prison he's leaving, and then, finally, his face as he looks at the prison he's entering.

Director Raoul Walsh probably used the approach for more than homage, because when we first see Bogart we are slightly stunned; he looks old. His hair has been tinted grey along the sides, and the prison haircut, high above the ears, makes him look even older. This is not to be, one could safely then assume, quite the romantic odyssey other gangster pictures were. For Roy Earle (Bogart), almost everything is going to be downhill—even when he climbs to the top of a mountain. It is there that he makes his final stand, holding out for hopeless hours like the resisting anachronism that he is. Walsh is mourning, to some extent, the waning of a genre. Certainly gangsters did not disappear from the screen. But they belonged to the thirties, and the Walsh film, in 1941, seemed to know it.

Tom Shales in *The American Film Heritage*, edited by the American Film Institute (Acropolis, 1972), p. 100

WARHOL, ANDY (1930–)

Well, Andy Warhol's *The Chelsea Girls* is full-length with a vengeance. It goes on for about 3½ hours on two separate but equally dismal screens, thus really lasting seven hours. But because a minute of Warhol's brand of boredom is easily the equivalent of an hour of the Hollywood kind, the actual duration is 17½ days.

Ostensibly intending to show how the decadent tenants of the Hotel Chelsea live, Warhol has merely invited his various friends, followers, and freaks to disport themselves *ad libitum* and *ad nauseam*, while his no less freakish camera either just lies there chewing the crud [sic], or jiggles around as if palsied, or zooms in and out compulsively, for no reason except that the zoom lens is a gadget, and Warhol's birdbrain is enamored of gadgets. Indeed, I think it *is* one. We get narcissists, pederasts, lesbians, transvestites, drug addicts, sadists, hustlers supposedly revealing the shabbiness of it all, but actually reveling in the exhibitionism of it. If, for example, Nico, who is a genuine narcissist all right, primps and preens for the camera for a minor eternity, that still does not yield any revelation. Either the girl or the camera would have to be a little more than an idiot. As it is, no comment on narcissism emerges, no point of view, not even anything like the beginning of a conspectus. And when the subject is more ticklish, say, homosexuality or sadism, the "exposé" becomes even more coyly truncated: suggestions, titters, token gestures. Not even the courage of scabrous convictions.

One character, the self-styled Pope of Greenwich Village, does reel off a few funny remarks along with endless trashy farrago. But it is all too stagey to be *cinéma-vérité*, too stupid to be cinema. *The Chelsea Girls* is a testimonial to what happens when a camera falls into the hands of an aesthetic, moral, and intellectual bankrupt. [1966]

John Simon. *Private Screenings* (Macmillan, 1967), pp. 261–62

The authenticity of this filmmaker, Andy Warhol, is evinced in the unflagging interest of this film. It is himself. It is impossible to imagine anyone else succeeding in a project like this. Witness the unedited

Queen of Sheba Meets the Atom Man: no noted routine of its remarkable players, no pornographic trick in the Lower East Side bag, was overlooked, and yet this effort is tiresome from beginning to end. What then is the secret to the endless absorption of *Harlot*, as well as Warhol's other movies? Simply, that every moment is invested with the actual reality of its creator, the turning of business into art, of publicity into poetry, of mass media into human meaningfulness. He protests, he testifies that his films are boring, that he loves the emptiness of their endless hours, that he has never bothered to sit through most of them. But our attention is riveted to the apparent vacuum, to the inventory of vacuum and such an inventory extends into timelessness. The harlot and her company of the couch pose on forever, just as when we first see them, they seem to have been even so situated since the orientation of their possibilities.

Warhol's art of his inattention to significance carries, just that, the significance itself. He would claim to want, with his special and extreme handling of Pop Art, to lobotomize the public. Yet this operation-theatre he brings us to and in which we at first resentfully feel ourselves to be the patient, suddenly actualizes as the real and traditional theatre; we are audience as always, suddenly alive and watching, horrified after amused, scholarly after ennuied. And alarmed. The "destructive" artist proves again the prophet and makes of his life a stunning cry, withal keeping his mask-distance of laughter and contempt. He emerges gentle from a warehouse of Brillo boxes, having stated his bleak vision, as social an artist as any '30's fiend could ask for.

Ronald Tavel. *Film Culture*. Spring 1966 (No. 40), p. 51

Some of the more sophisticated Establishment reviewers write as if everything that happens south of Fourteenth Street comes out of Dante's *Inferno*. Warhol is not bosh, but neither is he Bosch. The Chelsea Hotel is not hell. It is an earthly, earthy place like any other, where even fags, dykes, and junkies have to go on living twenty-four hours a day. This is where Warhol has been heading through the somnambulism of *Sleep* and the egregiousness of *Empire*—toward an existential realism beyond the dimensions of the cinema. Warhol disdains the conventional view of film as a thing of bits and pieces. Perhaps "disdains" is too strong a term for an attitude that is at best instinctive, at worst indifferent. As his scene segments unreel, the footage is finally punctuated by telltale leaders and then kaplunk blankness on the screen. This indicates that each scene runs out of film before it runs out of talk. If there were more film, there would be more talk. If there were less film, there would be less talk. How much more gratuitous and imprecise can cinema be? Goodbye Sergei Eisenstein. Hello Eastman Kodak. Besides, what with the problems of projection and the personalities of projectionists, each showing of *The Chelsea Girls* may qualify as a distinctly unique happening. [1966]

Andrew Sarris. *Confessions of a Cultist* (S&S, 1970), p. 275

Technical gimmicks continue throughout the film [*The Chelsea Girls*]. Apart from the two reels, Warhol has other ways of abusing the camera. There are moments when he zooms in and others when, arbitrarily, he zooms out! The sound does the same. Sometimes it is clear and sometimes it is garbled. The colors are sometimes interesting, though again, after *Red Desert*, it is difficult for an amateur to excell in the use of that color either symbolically or esthetically. The LSD sequence may be red but there is no justification for that color other than the pleasure of Warhol's group. The point that one has to make, when appreciating the technical efforts in this film, is that it is very difficult to succeed using a medium which is mocked by the user.

There are nevertheless a number of qualities that need to be mentioned. The first is the feeling of truth that one receives from this odyssey into boredom. Far from revealing, as would a nudie picture, erotic sequences, Warhol is terribly close to the prudish when he allows his performers to act out their homosexual loves. Their existence is deadening. Their lives are not one long orgy. It is a penis and a quarter in close to four hours of film and the rest is lolling about doing nothing, nothing, pawing a little, all with evident hesitation, without harmony or desire. Was it the camera's eyes that forbade them to act as they normally would? I doubt it. It is true that there are no actors in the film. That these people have not the slightest idea of what acting means. . . . There is no pretense (save the fooling around with the above-mentioned technical child's play) to fabricate something that does not exist; to illustrate the depth of degeneracy. In this artless film that really parallels the rhythmic modes of existence of a certain group of people, thought, touch, love are all expressed in a minor key. The truth of the tedium is thus the initial paradoxical quality.

Serge Gavronsky. *Cahiers du Cinéma in English*. May 1967 (10), p. 46

It is interesting that so many of the critics praised Miss [Shirley] Clarke for her outstanding achievement in *Jason*, the same critics who scolded Andy Warhol for his peep-show pictures like *The Chelsea Girls*, and *I, a Man*. I have just seen the new Warhol *Bike Boy*, which in spite of its vulgar dialogue (complete with *the* four-letter word again and length-of-erection discussion) and a peeping camera that concentrates on nudity, particularly male, does succeed in making some pungent statements about the motorcycle gangs and the lives they lead. Its opening scenes satirizing homosexuals is very funny, although too long. Perhaps if Warhol could keep his busy camera from peeping so much and devote his film making to some serious study, he too could come up with a *Jason*.

Philip T. Hartung. *Commonweal*. Oct. 27, 1967, p. 120

Warhol . . . is defiant and aggressive. In *Harlot* the camera remains fixed for forty minutes on exactly the same scene, a splendidly sinister group of four people, two men standing behind a sofa and a woman with a cat and a female impersonator sitting on it. We don't know what they are waiting for, and their pregnant silence has the intensity of a group portrait by some painter, such as Goya, with a sense of the macabre. While, on the sound-track, Warhol's voice carries on a more or less irrelevant conversation with an unknown individual who appears to be one of his boyfriends, the female impersonator eats several bananas with voluptuous and exasperating slowness, and finally makes the gesture of masturbating with a whole banana. Those bourgeois who could stand the monotony were no doubt well and truly *épatés* before they got to the bitter end. The film would have been worthwhile, I suppose, had the remorselessly unchanging image been accompanied by a brilliant dialogue which wove an intellectual and emotional pattern around it; however, Mr. Warhol and his friend just sounded slightly high on pot or whatever, and in a mood to enjoy their own feeble puns. If that is the level of conversation in the advanced homosexual underground, one might even prefer Mrs. Caudle's Curtain Lectures.

John Weightman. *Encounter*. July 1968, p. 55

. . . The media regularly give us the gist of a past event in the world the gist of its human consciousness, without regard to the physical quantity of experience that is literally measured by the clock, and no matter what aspect or aspects of it are handled or for what purpose (documentary or imaginative). This technique results from the *device* of compressing action of diverse kinds, spread through lengthy clock time perhaps, into a conveniently communicative form (narrative, expository, etc.). Life in Warhol films (as he likes them to remain, unedited, with nothing whatever on the cutting-room floor) is a sort of dead-eye dick when it comes to such accepted formal transmutation. Values, take note, are *not* involved; that is, even here in *Fuck* [released as *Blue Movie*], the process of fucking is not calculated to depict sexual sensations in a way to illustrate what supposedly is their chief charm: a real excitement, mounting steadily to orgasmic climax. What we know as "blue films," however much faked or however real the feelings of those sexually involved, would normally seek to represent a certain palpable excitement, to grow "hot," to mount tantalizingly to the climax. If the result be hollow or obviously phony, it is the fault of carelessness or ineptitude or some "plausible" sort of faking. But all this is not at all the point in Warhol's (actually cool) *Fuck*.

This film is not meant to *represent*; it is meant *to be*. And therein, like it or leave it, lies its great, really cool distinction. . . .

. . . *Fuck* is definitely not as exciting as possible to the emotions. Which is the sole reason why it is so exciting to the intelligence. . . . It just won't pretend that fucking is Heaven—or Hell.

Parker Tyler. *Sex Psyche Etcetera in the Film*
(Horizon, 1969), pp. 15–17

In America, sex is a humorous but not very erotic pastime for homosexuals as well as their straight countrymen, as the moviegoer can see from Andy Warhol's *Lonesome Cowboys*. Uneven and rough in the Warhol style, this camp Western is nonetheless an interesting film with some high-comic scenes. Most of the explicit sex turns out to involve a handsome young cowboy seduced away from his fellows by a brazen hussy, and is just the same old hip movement thing we have seen in the other movies cited. But the interplay—the jealousies, rivalries, and jokes, sexual and social, among the gang of cowboys—shifts from the put-on to the weird sort of sudden reality that can come in this sort of improvisational filming when people are reacting to and off one another. Sometimes the camera frames a face for what seems like a sort of TV man-in-the-street monologue about Great Issues, and one cowboy tells how the gang should really settle down and try to build a home—then build a town, and build a city, "and then we'll be ready for World War I."

In this, as in the other American films mentioned, viewers hoping for a dirty movie will probably be disappointed by finding a lot of laughs and hardly any thrills, cheap or otherwise.

Dan Wakefield. *The Atlantic Monthly*.
April 1969, p. 141

The cinema of Brakhage or the cinema of Markopoulos or the cinema of Michael Snow has nothing to do with the entertainment film. They are clearly working in another, non-narrative, non-entertainment area, as in a classical way and meaning we say all poetry is in a different area. But the cinema of Warhol, *The Chelsea Girls*, *The Nude Restaurant*,

The Imitation of Christ [a segment of *Four Stars*], is part of the narrative cinema, is within the field of cinema that is called "movies," it deals with "people," is part of it. Is part of it, but is of a totally different ilk. That's why the movies of Andy Warhol cannot be ignored by commercial exhibitors. At the same time, once they are in, and they are In, they are undermining, or rather transforming, or still more precisely, *transporting* the entertainment, the narrative film to an entirely different plane of experience. From the plane of purely sensational, emotional and kinesthetic entertainment, the film is transported to a plane that is outside the suspense, outside the plot, outside the climaxes—to a plane where we find *Tom Jones* and *Moby Dick*, and Joyce, and also Dreyer, Dovzhenko, and Bresson. That is, it becomes an entertainment of a more subtle, more eternal kind, where we are not hypnotized into something but where we sort of study, watch, contemplate, listen—not so much for the "big actions" but for the small words, intonations, colors of voices, colors of words, projections of the voices; the content that is the quality and movements of the voices and expressions (in the Hitchcock or Nichols movies the voices are purposeful, theatrical monotones)—a content of a much more complex, finer and rarer kind is revealed through them. And these faces and these words and these movements are not *bridges* for something else, for other actions; no: they are themselves the *actions*.

Jonas Mekas in John Coplan's *Andy Warhol*
(New York Graphic Society, 1970), pp. 141–42

Warhol's first film *Tarzan and Jane Regained . . . Sort of* (1963), was shot in Hollywood and was a loosely-constructed, rambling, two-hour movie in the informal style of [Ron] Rice and [Vernon] Zimmerman, but Warhol established his static aesthetic immediately afterwards with *Sleep* (1963/64), *Eat* (1963), *Haircut* (1964), *Blow Job* (1964), *Empire* (1964) and so on. The formal statement in these silent films is everything: the confrontation of the audience with an image that changed in conventional terms only marginally and only over a long period of time; once again, audiences were outraged. It was, however, an affirmation of the principle of nonactivity and his faith in the superficial aspect of seen objects that closely parallels his silk-screen paintings. In the Tavel scripted works, *Harlot*, *Screen Test*, *The Life of Juanita Castro*, *Horse*, *Vinyl*, *Kitchen* (all 1965) and *Hedy* (*The Shopper*, 1966), the action became more probing. Travel, as a homage to Warhol, constructed his plots as a series of *tableaux vivants*, but created dramatic conflict through the confrontation of the "actors" with their script or a prearranged environment. Invariably, there is some sexual ambiguity to resolve: in *Screen Test*, Mario Montez, posing as a star auditioning for a part, is made to face the fact of his masculinity in the simplest possible (physical) way; in *Hedy* (supposedly inspired by Miss Lamarr's alleged shop-lifting court case) the star (Mario again) is confronted with the decline of her screen career and the unsatisfactory conclusion of her five marriages. But the real conflict is of the actors with their roles. Neither Tavel nor Warhol provides enough information to allow a "routine" performance; the relentless presence of the camera demands that the actors complete the role themselves; the result is a transparent fluctuation between total absorption in the myth (role playing) and a state of very vulnerable self-revelation.

David Curtis. *Experimental Cinema*
(Universe, 1971), pp. 152–53

WELLES, ORSON (1915–)

In a season that has had no startling surprises among its movies, *Citizen Kane* has struck most of the reviewers like a revelation and sent them hunting up all the dynamite adjectives in the dictionary. A revelation the picture is, as a matter of fact, a revelation to those who have forgotten, or who have never known, of what a motion picture can do technically. Welles is a smart young man and a clever one, with all his huffing and puffing, and he has had practical experience of both the stage and the radio, and has done highly effective things in both those forms. He knows what can be usefully carried over from the theatre and from the air-waves to the screen. Moreover, he has obviously, and with intelligence, studied the motion picture medium in its masterpieces, particularly some of the silent films made in Germany and Russia in their great creative days: it is with these that some of his most striking effects of camera angles and composition awake comparison. . . .

Welles must be the first director to bring something important and valuable from the radio to the screen. He knows how to build dramatic effects through the ear alone from having done it so often on the air, and from that knowledge he gives sound on the screen an extended dimension, with echoes and reverberations, with orchestrations of voices, that deepen and vivify his scenes for the hearing in much the same way some of his sets do for the eye.

There's a lot to study in the way Welles has made his picture, much more than can be taken in all at once. Some of it is obvious but mighty little of it is crude or unskillful, and it is subtle where subtlety counts most powerfully. Above everything else it is full of young and vigorous energy. That must be why some people find it exhausting—some even tiresome. . . .

What does it all add up to—what does it prove? Mostly that Mr. Welles can write, produce, direct and act a remarkable motion picture. That Mr. Welles is a dynamo, which isn't news. At times he is masterly —in the swift way, for instance, he covers the years of Kane's first marriage, packing everything essential into a few sequences. Also masterly, and curiously so in a man so stentorian in other ways, is his gift for dramatic reticence when the lack of reticence (which most directors would have been tempted to lest the public miss what they were driving at) would have thrown the subtle build-up of his characterization out of balance. He has brought something to the motion picture that is partly his own personality and the Mercury Theatre players who are fresh and welcome people on the screen, and partly a craftsmanship that adds elements from radio and stage to cinematic technique it did not have before. Most of all, probably, he has invigorated the movies with a kind of vitality that is sure to have effect on other movie makers. Whether *Citizen Kane* will have a big appeal in its own right, without benefit of publicity, remains to be seen. People who like a straightforward story with likable people in it may find this picture confusing and unsympathetic, even cold and unpleasant. A psychological study of a very complicated man, told without signposts for the slow-witted or inattentive, is pretty much of a gamble. How it will fare will come out when the picture leaves the haunts of the highbrows and starts jogging through the second and third runs.

At any rate Orson Welles has landed in the movies, with a splash and a loud yell.

James Shelley Hamilton. *NBR*. May 1941, pp. 7, 8, 9

Anticipating everybody's first question about Orson Welles's second movie, the answer is yes and no. The story, or that part which Welles has retained of *The Magnificent Ambersons*, is not a patch on *Citizen Kane*; in fact it is little more than a carry-all for the 1942 cinema surprises of the movies' latest and likeliest revoltist. Cinematically, however, *The Magnificent Ambersons* is more seasoned, more satisfying and yet more revolutionary than *Citizen Kane*.

It may not make much money, because in presenting this dated story of the decay of a landed American family Welles has observed virtually none of the copybook maxims of movie money-making, and this is a current sore point between him and RKO. But whatever else may be said of young Orson Welles, the movie upstart, it is certain that his experimenting with camera, light and sound is the most provocative and stimulating to reach our entertainment screen since sound cinema broke with the old silent forms. Welles has been good medicine for movies. He is still a theatrical playboy monkeying with a new medium, but even his most theatrical trickery is slicker than many directors' most serious efforts.

Here are some effects to watch for:

Sound: So that the camera need not rush around eavesdropping, Welles simply disembodies voices at times, making it possible for a voice from the far end of the room to supersede voices near at hand, and permitting "sound montage" in which two or three conversations may interlace each other, cutting in order of their importance to the story. Sometimes voices are deadened as if in a soundproof room; but in the staircase picture . . . Agnes Morehead's whisper from the top landing seems to drown out Tim Holt's shout from below. It seems a bit eerie at first, as the famous asides did in Eugene O'Neill's *Strange Interlude*.

Light and Shadow: The same staircase picture . . . illustrates how Welles's tricky lighting techniques, developed from his bare-stage *Julius Caesar* of four years ago, are used to envelop the Amberson dynasty in the twilight of its magnificence. In the '90s the Amberson house was light and gay. Now, 1914, the elegance of the past clings only in heavy, somber shadows. Watch, too, for the swan song of old Major Amberson, during which the shadows close in to encircle his face like a deathmask.

The camera really works overtime to make this movie legible for you. One sparkling example is the scene in which you realize the encroachment of the automobile age on the horse-and-buggy Ambersons during a sidewalk conversation. Out of the corner of its eye the camera catches, reflected in shop windows, glimpses of passing carriages and autos to overtones of clopping hooves and chugging engines.

L. L. and J. T. M. *PM*. Aug. 14, 1942

Previously, the camera "analyzed" a scene and broke it up into a certain number of "shots" that it offered to the sympathetic attention, the *Einfühlungsvermögen*, of the spectator; the labor of perception and aesthetic identification was done in advance for the spectator by those responsible for the cutting and editing. Without the spectator being aware of it, his interest was automatically caught by the significant details. When Orson Welles films a dramatic scene, he lays its elements before us *simultaneously* and makes *us* do the work of breaking up the scene—work that previously the director had obligingly spared us. When Kane's wife tries to commit suicide, we see (or we should be seeing, for the director works for the ideal spectator just as the author writes for the perfect reader) all the composite parts of the scene, from the glass and spoon in the foreground to the sound in the extreme background of Kane vainly calling out and hitting the door with his shoulder. In *The Magnificent Ambersons*, when Mary breaks with George Amberson, the street in which the scene takes place is completely visible at every moment because of the extreme clarity with which the background is photographed, and this street is as important as the actual byplay of the actors. What Orson Welles places before us at every moment is a complete fragment of the universe, a microcosm in which all the elements are equally necessary, equally important, and in which each one derives an added intensity from the presence of all the others. Welles's *synthesizing* point of view restores to us a world of density, in which each object is indispensable and has its own function and meaning. [1948]

Claude-Edmonde Magny. *The Age of the American Novel* (Ungar, 1972), pp. 27–28

For a fellow who has as much talent with a camera as Orson Welles and whose powers of pictorial invention are as fluid and as forcible as his, this gentleman certainly has a strange way of marring his films with sloppiness which he seems to assume that his dazzling exhibitions of skill will camouflage.

Take *The Lady From Shanghai*, for instance, which came to Loew's Criterion yesterday: it could have been a terrific piece of melodramatic romance. For the idea, at least, is a corker and the Wellesian ability to direct a good cast against fascinating backgrounds has never been better displayed. It's the story of a roving merchant seaman who falls in with some over-rich worldlings and who almost becomes the innocent victim of their murderous hates and jealousies. And for its sheer visual modeling of burning passions in faces, forms and attitudes, galvanized within picturesque surroundings, it might almost match *Citizen Kane*.

The build-up, for instance, of the tensions among four people, in particular, aboard a yacht sailing from New York to San Francisco is tremendously captivating. In the group are the mesmerized sailor, his enchantress who is a sleek, seductive thing, her husband who is a famous criminal lawyer and his partner, a wild-eyed maniac. And in the subtle suggestion of corruption, of selfishness and violence in this group, intermingled with haunting wisps of pathos, Mr. Welles could not have done a better job. . . .

But no sooner has Mr. Welles, director, deposited this supercharged group in literal San Francisco after a particularly vivid voyage up the Mexican Coast than Mr. Welles, the author, goes sloppy and leaves him in the lurch. For the protean gentleman's arrangement of triple-cross murder plot designed to entrap the sailor is a thoroughly confused and baffling thing. Tension is recklessly permitted to drain off in a sieve of tangled plot and in a lengthy court-room argument which has little save a few visual stunts. As producer of the picture, Mr. Welles might better have fired himself—as author, that is—and hired somebody to give Mr. Welles, director, a better script.

And he certainly could have done much better than use himself in the key role of the guileless merchant sailor who is taken in by a woman's winning charm. For no matter how much you dress him in rakish yachting caps and open shirts, Mr. Welles simply hasn't the capacity to cut a romantic swath. And when he adorns his characterization with a poetic air and an Irish brogue, which is painfully artificial, he makes himself—and the film—ridiculous.

Indeed, his performance in the picture—and his exhibitionistic cover-ups of the story's general untidiness—give ironic point to his first line: "When I start out to make a fool of myself, there's very little can stop me."

Bosley Crowther. *NYT*. June 10, 1948, p. 28

Macbeth, à la Orson Welles, is a dish that you will either like or dislike, depending on your attitude to Orson Welles. Mine's favourable, as it happens; I find everything he does interesting and, in varying degrees, above average. So, by my own premise (with which I am stuck, at least for the duration of this article), *Macbeth* is a good film with bad things in it . . . among said bad things being a Scotch burr that no more fits the characters than a bottle of Johnny Walker Black Label before Macbeth would have suited him, or before Lady Macbeth would have suited *her* . . . an obvious attempt to duplicate the effectiveness of the battle scenes of *Alexander Nevsky* in the same pictorial manner but which doesn't come off because, after all, Welles, though he goes to good sources, is apparently no source himself . . . a picturesque but incredible castle of the Scottish kings that stems awkwardly out of the stylized sets of the German silent historical films (*Nibelungenlied*, *Treasure*, etc.) . . . and things like that. But the opening witches' scene is fine and eerie, and I liked Lady Macbeth's believable passion, while the fight at the end is first-class blood and thunder, far more believable than the technicoloured clashing of sticks in *Joan of Arc*. I'm sure no one else would professionally have dared to film *Macbeth* so we should be grateful to have it, if only as a contribution to Shakespeare on the screen. It has not the polish of Olivier's *Hamlet* (and it is, of course, not nearly so great a play) but since when is polish the measure of Shakespeare? Passion is, and there's enough of it in Welles' *Macbeth* to suit all but the most finicky students of the bard's every word.

Herman G. Weinberg. *Sight & Sound*.
Spring 1949, p. 18

For reasons which escape this reviewer, Orson Welles's *Macbeth* had a very bad press. New York cineasts, lavender leftists, feminists, and movie esthetes of all varieties, as well as serious critics, united in putting it on the pan.

Why? Their European counterparts thought Welles' *Macbeth* wonderful.

I understand that the original version which Orson Welles handed over to Republic—after shooting the whole thing in 13 weeks—had an incomprehensible sound track as well as excessive footage of the absurd miscast who plays Lady Macbeth, and excess footage of other Wellesian mistakes. Perhaps everyone remembers this version. But for anyone who did not come into contact with such early douleur, the present version seems worthy of something more than dismissal.

For a definite mood is created. Some intimation of tenth century Scotland is insinuated. Something of that century's primitivism is retrieved. In short, a little of the spirit of Shakespeare's poetical reconstruction reaches the motion picture screen.

This is a wonderful thing. And all the critics who call out detractions from their tower of Babel, should say a word in favor of it. Little enough Shakespeare gets on the screen. And the little which does should be encouraged.

It is true that the sets are monotonous; that the casting must have been done by a blind man (especially for the roles of Lady Macbeth, Malcolm and Macduff); that Welles himself would rather be theatrical than work hard for a subtlety; that Shakespeare's text has been yanked and bent and beaten. All this is true. But there is a further truth. This film is recognizable Shakespeare. It is an adequate *Macbeth*—on the screen, where the masses can see it.

Henry Hart. *Films in Review*. Feb. 1951, p. 35

For some reason, Orson Welles has seen fit to make some fundamental rearrangements in the construction of Shakespeare's most tightly constructed play. The total effect of the sceneshifting and abridgments made by Mr. Welles the director is to provide almost a monopoly of the screen to Mr. Welles the actor. I am sure that this was done out of a mistaken desire to streamline the story rather than vanity, but the result actually undermines the effectiveness of the *Othello* Mr. Welles has created with his imposing stature and his magnificent voice and diction. The only other living actor I can think of offhand who could surpass Mr. Welles's bearing and resonance as Othello is Paul Robeson, who isn't being asked to appear in movies currently.

The play is not, as Mr. Welles has tended to make it, simply the story of an intrigue against Othello, any more than *Hamlet* is simply the case history of a sensitive young man with an Oedipus complex. "Iago's plot is Iago's character in action," as A. C. Bradley said, "and it is built on his knowledge of Othello's character." To reduce Iago to a mere schemer, as Mr. Welles has done, is thus to reduce Othello to a mere gull.

Robert Bingham. *Reporter*. Nov. 17, 1955, p. 36

Although Orson Welles' *Othello* is a very uneven film, and on the whole less original than his *Macbeth*, it is to his disputable credit that he had the courage to attempt this kind of adaptation. As far as I can see, he has, here as in *Macbeth*, tried, not to make his film an accompaniment to Shakespeare's writing . . . but to use the writing—whatever he saw fit to retain of it—as an accompaniment to the feeling of excited surprise with which Shakespeare apparently inspired him. . . .

In *Othello*, the use of extreme camera angles (the successive towering shots of Welles in his dark robes stalking through the corridors of his apartment), of bizarre compostions (the nightmarish sequence of Roderigo's death, with the lap-dissolved shots of stinging white lines against blackness, suggesting Silbey Watson's work in *Lot in Sodom*) and especially the distorted treatment of space—the alternation of looming close-ups with fly-like long shots of the same figure, the successions of extreme camera angles with no reversion to normal perspective —which suggests the Elizabethans' use of spatial relationship on their stage, all have been called superficial. But this, precisely, is the point: Welles is concentrating on the *surface* of his film, like the showman he is: on jolting the audience so often and so sharply that its interest and attention will never flag. He uses a gigantic view of his open-mouthed face—followed by a distant view of sniggering faces crazily suspended over a parapet—in the same way and to the same purpose that the Surrealists used their unnatural juxtapositions of familiar objects.

Unlike other film esthetes, Welles does not employ these angles and compositions to clarify their context, but to abolish any context. Whereas in *Citizen Kane*, he used it (in my opinion) to inflate the real significance of his subject, and distort its inherent dramatic values, here, in Shakespeare, he has a partner worthy of his talents. The result of such attempts throughout the film, although never as exciing as the best of *Citizen Kane*, is more mature for it shows a greater depth of intent.

Donald Phelps. *Film Culture*. Winter 1955, p. 32

Probably for years Welles was collecting ideas, angles, gags, stunts, and brainwaves with a view to using them all in his first film. The array was indeed formidable; and *Citizen Kane* has ever since been a reservoir of new filmic devices for directors. It is the life-story of an American newspaper magnate (W. R. Hearst is probably the model), and opens with news-reel editors compiling an obituary of him. A reporter is put on the track, and the jigsaw puzzle of the man's life is assembled in interviews with his friends, his enemies, his collaborators. Through their eyes, making lavish use of the "flashback" device, Welles shows us every side of the hero's personality: the young man who wants to clean up the town through the medium of his newspaper, the forsaken husband who smashes his wife's room to pieces, the ambitious politician, the sentimental lover, the eccentric millionaire, the stubborn little boy. All these various aspects of Kane's life are treated in as many different styles. The sound-track conveys acoustically the impression of the millionaire's vast, echoing hall. The "old" news-reel of Kane's early career is actually shot with sixteen frames to the second, as it was done in the silent film days. It is a fascinating picture; but because of its congestion of technical stunts, if fails to move us.

Egon Larsen. *Spotlight on Films*
(Max Parrish, 1956), p. 112

Our admiration for Orson Welles had faded with the memory of his films. *Othello*, his last work, filled with sometimes farfetched beauties, was in 1952. It was time for a new film to make us once more directly confront the art of this visionary. Yes, beginning with the first shots [of *Mr. Arkadin*] we ask ourselves how we could have for so long done without this kind of cinema, a cinema that more than others is charged with novelties and riches.

Each shot is so full that we are sorry not to have more time to exhaust scarcely glimpsed indications. But our enchantment is for a great part made up of the rapidity of the mixes. It is the rhythm of the tale rather than its texture that keeps us breathless. The sumptuousness and the resonances of the visual harmonies were not conceived to be experienced separately. The only thing that matters is the symphonic swell in which an ensemble of new notes destroys a previous ensemble that had made it necessary before it too disappears. The way in which the shots are joined shows such virtuosity that we don't even get the feeling of a break when the images placed side by side are very different from one another. . . .

I would have felt only admiration if I hadn't reseen the film. The second showing surprised me. The images that I now had time to study more closely—since I no longer was held up by the need to follow the plot—struck me as unusually thin. It was as though surprise was necessary to stir wonder. It was as though the story, which I considered unimportant, was more so than I thought. Of course some scenes (the Goya ball, etc.) remained astonishing. But the intermediary sequences seemed unenchanted, frames empty of their substance.

All cinematographic criticism is impressionistic. It is in multiplying these impressions, in seeing the film several times, that we can hope to reach a certain objectivity. I will return to *Mr. Arkadin.* A third, a fourth viewing will perhaps make me rediscover my initial sense of being dazzled. Then I will again be able to taste in Orson Welles' champagne something other than flat foam.

Claude Mauriac. *Petite Littérature du Cinéma* (Editions du Cerf, 1957), pp. 137, 139

Narration—the voice of an all-seeing, all-knowing commentator who sets the scene, threads the story together and, from time to time offers his special insight into the motivations and thoughts of the characters —was common enough in radio. Films, on the other hand, except for newsreels and documentaries, were still using subtitles for introductions, place names and dates until Welles introduced the narration technique in *Citizen Kane* (1941) and *The Magnificent Ambersons* (1942). . . . Although *The Magnificent Ambersons* may look like a more conventional film than *Citizen Kane*, actually it is a good deal more inventive—but in subtler, more cinematic ways. . . .

The picture opens with an adroit sequence designed to establish the period and to introduce the leading characters of the film. Over Welles's witty narration we see, almost cartoon-fashion, the styles, the customs, the way of life in a small town at the turn of the century. He refers to "that prettiest of all vanished customs—the serenade," and we see a slightly intoxicated Eugene Morgan (Joseph Cotten) with a group of musicians courting Isabel Amberson (Dolores Costello)—and awkwardly falling into his own bass viol. Next, Welles talks about the stovepipe hats then in fashion, and shows another suitor, Wilbur Miniffer, wearing one as he rows Isabel on a quiet lake. And a moment later we learn from the narration that Isabel is going to marry Wilbur even though she really loves Eugene. Thus, within three minutes of film the background, the principals and the central situation have all been brought before the audience, presented with the unique economy made possible by the narration technique. Welles used it at several points in the picture to give insight into character, to comment upon the changing social scene or upon the action itself.

Arthur Knight. *The Liveliest Art* (Macmillan, 1957), pp. 186–88

The long descent from *Citizen Kane* goes on, and yet *Touch of Evil* need not have been treated so shabbily. I cannot pretend that Welles's new film is a good one. It is not. It is often laughably bad, often pompously bad. Yet it has virtues. For one thing, it is not dull; and that, in a decade of big-budget, wide-screen, many-starred extravaganzas, is a pleasant surprise. It also makes an attempt—a fruitless one as it turns out—to deal with a serious theme.

In *Touch of Evil*, as in *The Lady from Shanghai*, Welles is concerned with power and corruption. The film is about Hank Quinlan (played grossly by Welles, who has broadened physically if not as an artist since *Citizen Kane*), a police captain whose compulsion to punish thieves and murderers is so strong that he plants evidence to ensure convictions. *Touch of Evil* is pure Orson Welles and impure balderdash, which may be the same thing. It shows, as all Welles's films do, that he is a man who understands the ways in which a camera can be used, and that he will sacrifice plot and verisimilitude for an attempt at a consistent mood—in this case an almost tangible sense of corruption. Unfortunately, the line between the corrupt and the comic is a thin one, and Welles keeps slipping over. *Touch of Evil* may not be much of a film, but it was made by a man who has a genuine and personal movie style. As a result, it is much more interesting than, say, the witless *Witness for the Prosecution*, which also has a collection of stereotypes and Dietrich in a black fright wig. *Touch of Evil* is not a good movie, but it is a good bad movie, which is more fun to see than the mediocre or even the adequate.

Gerald Weales. *Reporter*. June 26, 1958, p. 33

Mr. Arkadin. Like any modern artist worth his salt, Welles has thrust his abstractions closer to the surface. To the deep focus of the late Gregg Toland and the cosmic camera angles inherited from Murnau, Welles has added a fluent tracking style with the visual controls of remembered meaning. For example, the vertical camera movement down a tower after Arkadin's death supersedes the script and quite naturally escapes the attention of our literary film critics. Similarly, to express any enthusiasm for the prodigality of Welles's lateral tracks is to violate the guide rules of the exalted criticism that insists that after *Citizen Kane* Orson Welles was obliged to deal with Big Themes, at least as big as Hearst, perhaps "Citizen Schiff" or "Citizen Sulzberger." Fortunately Welles has gone his own way, and what a dazzling spectacle he provides here for those discerning moviegoers who have outgrown the tedious affections of realism. For the others I can think of nothing more fitting than to be shipwrecked on *The Island*, that Japanese regression to the anachronistic anonymity of the silent-screen characters. [1962]

Andrew Sarris. *Confessions of a Cultist*
(S&S, 1970), pp. 64–65

Welles's style has never been more baroque than in *The Trial*, his lighting and camera angles never more picturesquely exaggerated, his piling up of material detail (those toppling drifts of lawbooks, that forest of half-naked old men outside the court) never more excessive, his scale never more grandiose. But, as it is the loser of an argument who shouts, so this visual braggadocio is to conceal the fact that our director hasn't the foggiest notion of what *The Trial* is about. Expanding the normal-size bank in which Kafka's hero worked into the Gare de Lyon—literally: Welles rented the abandoned station—still doesn't put any meaning into the film. Those acres of desks are, of course, intended to suggest that Modern Man is Lost in the Conformist Mass—King Vidor did it better forty years ago in *The Crowd*—just as the last shot, when the smoke from an explosion takes on a mushroom form, is supposed to induce solemn reflections. The elaboration of scale and decor is as boring as in any Biblical spectacular and for the same reason: because it is used without mind or feeling, not to bring out meaning but to distract us from asking for it. [1963]

Dwight Macdonald. *D. M. on Movies*
(Prentice-Hall, 1969), pp. 298–99

The sad thing about Orson Welles is that he has consistently put his very real talent to the task of glorifying his imaginary genius. Now one of the few definable traits of a genius is that no matter how much he loves himself, he loves something beyond himself more. There is nothing about the work of Orson Welles to convince us that he has ever felt humility or love anywhere except in front of a mirror. The success of *Citizen Kane*, Welles's only unassailable achievement, stems in large part from the fact that the protagonist elicits mingled contempt and envy, feelings that Welles is perfectly equipped to dispense. The sentimental note in *Kane*, the quest for Rosebud, is much more of a useful narrative device than a convincing expression of fellow feeling.

But if Welles's solipsism vitiates his bid for genius, his colossal lack of taste tends to mar even his talent. True, when he adapts or concocts entertainments such as *Journey into Fear*, *The Lady from Shanghai*, or *Touch of Evil*, or when he broadcasts an invasion from Mars, there is little or nothing for his proliferating showmanship to smother, but in such cases the audience cannot be quite sure that a really good three-ring circus wouldn't be closer to art. In his attempts at great works, however—and he is fatally drawn to them—Welles's tastelessness becomes a nagging pain in the discriminating spectator's stomach. *Macbeth*, *Lear*, *Othello*, *Moby Dick*, *Danton's Death*—all these were approached by Welles as though they were no different from something by Jules Verne or Eric Ambler, and, by the time Welles got through with them, they weren't. [1963]

John Simon. *Private Screenings* (Macmillan, 1967), p. 56

Orson Welles's screen version of [*The Trial*] ends in a way that I understand very well, though how he fancies that the tale leads up to his moral I cannot even guess. The picture closes with a mushroom cloud and we all agree that mankind cannot be too often enjoined against global self-destruction (the usefulness of clichés in this context, however, becomes increasingly dubious); but what concerned Kafka was the degradation of the individual spirit, not the incineration of the universal gene. And despite very real nuclear terrors, I suspect that his foretaste of hell will prove to be the more real.

Welles has always had a weakness for pinning contemporary symbols of doom on to classic moralities—setting brown shirts loose in Caesar's forum, causing swastika and hammer and sickle to flicker balefully above Bosworth Field. The preacher in him gets the better of the magician and he lapses into banality. In the case of *The Trial*, moreover, I suspect that Welles has also been unable to find an exit from the enigma, and has therefore blasted his way clear. It is not an elegant solution.

However, there is merit in the bulk of the picture. Welles, as I said, is a magician; he is exceedingly adept at enforcing the reality of illusion, and he creates the world of K's torment with a brilliant grasp of erotic absurdity and visual *non sequitur*. *The Trial*, he asserts almost belligerently, is a dream, and it may well be so. Like Joyce's Earwicker, K appears to sleep at different levels, and the deeper his slumber the more dilapidated, ornate, repetitive and labyrinthine become his movie surroundings. When he rises toward wakefulness—and he may even wake at moments—his neighborhood becomes more functional and utterly bleak. Welles over-seasons his stew with Freud—levitation, pursuit and the ascent of circular staircases tap out a Viennese Morse code at the spectator—but he did convince me that I was watching the dream obverse of reality. And visually his effects are often stunning (I mean like a box on the ear).

Robert Hatch. *Nation*. March 9, 1963, pp. 215–16

Welles was ahead of his time. He insisted on making movies which called attention to the fact that they were, indeed, movies. In his bravura use of film all pretense of artlessness, all the subtle techniques developed by earlier masters to give the illusion of the realistic point of view were abandoned. Welles compelled the attention to film *as film*, as something unique unto itself, something limitless in its possibilities. It is only in recent years, in the hands of the young European directors, that the technique has been widely used and accepted by audiences. "The cinema," Welles summed up, "has no boundary; it is a ribbon of dream."

Richard Schickel. *Movies* (Basic, 1964), p. 136

It is a classic solution of movies to declare that the sequence of events just witnessed was only a dream of one of the film's characters. It is possible to think of many more films as dreams than simply those admitting it. The whole of *Citizen Kane* might be Kane's own dreamed recollections in the last moments before his death. The fact that the film takes the form of investigations carried out by a representative of a newsreel company could be interpreted as showing the degree to which Kane's own publicity has conditioned his attitude to himself. Like newsreel and the sort of popular journalism Kane's own newspaper purveys, the visual context of *Citizen Kane* has a constant sense of factual escape which is typical of dream experience. What determines *Citizen Kane*, in scene after scene, is the general preconception, rather than the actual realization. In other words, the events are predominantly in the past tense, and it is a characteristic of Welles's film that it ignores much of a movie's present-tense powers. What carries *Citizen Kane* along is not the physical realization but the affectionate nostalgia beneath the investigative structure. The early scene at the boy Kane's prairie home when his parents sign him away to the bank is rare for its sense of actuality. At this stage the film's perspective is still within the bounds of naturalism and the shot of Kane's parents and the representative of the bank in the house, with young Kane seen through the window throwing snowballs, involves a directly meaningful spatial relationship which is enhanced by the sequence having opened with a shot from outside the window of the mother looking out at her son.

As the film progresses—and it has a generally chronological sequence—the perspective becomes more distorted. The wide-angle lenses exceed the eye's angle of vision and distend the depth of focus, both of which are refinements of the camera's recording function, and serve to separate the area near the camera from the distance. That is, the middle distance becomes expanded and a character will appear to move from long-shot into close-up unnaturally quickly. In Xanadu, at the end of his life, Kane's world has become one of gross close-ups and huge panoramic shots in which the human scale is so dwarfed as to be close to absurdity. *Kane* is often no more than a variety of striking still photographs, in which the control of the camera is heavy with intended meaning.

David Thomson. *Movie Man* (Stein & Day, 1967), pp. 33–34

One of the most brilliant directors in film history has produced another disappointment in an increasingly disappointing career. Orson Welles's *Falstaff* is a talented disaster. Certainly it is not without the dazzling directorial touches that are in everything he does (particularly the battle scenes), but most of those touches (excepting the battle scenes) are quite of the wrong, tristful, sere-and-yellow-leaf variety.

Welles's failure here as director derives, I believe, from his laziness *as actor*. In his films of *Othello* and *Macbeth*, apart from their other inadequacies, he refused the major challenges in the title roles. He fudged the big moments, found clever ways around them, gave us glimpses instead of confrontations, skimpy modern understatement instead of full-throated classical technique. In *Falstaff*, with a script puréed from both parts of *Henry IV* and from *Henry V*, Welles is simply too lazy—or perhaps by now too frightened—to take on the role as Shakespeare wrote it, not a jolly saloon-mural fat man but a giant of slyness, wit, guile, and vitality. W. H. Auden writes that Falstaff says, in effect, "I am I. Whatever I do, however outrageous, is of infinite importance because I do it."

But this ebullience, this radiant self-confident energy, would be too much work for Welles, who has let the muscles of his talent get flabby, so again he devises a way *around* the part. He erects a theory of Falstaff as sinning saint or somnolent pseudo-Hamlet, which makes the character very much less trouble for him to play. . . .

. . . The story of Welles's career begins to look like one of the great wastes of talent in our time. His films now give off a whiff of surly wrongheadedness, perhaps as his anger at self-wastage and at wastage by others begins to harden into an intricate but poorly reasoned *position*. [1967, WNDT-TV]

Stanley Kauffmann. *Figures of Light* (Harper, 1971), pp. 4–5

The struggle between tradition and progress, old and new, order and disorder is one of the most powerful forces behind Welles's work. It is reflected in his American background and his love of Europe, and in his film-making that embraces both Shakespeare and modern American thrillers.

This drive to reconcile the irreconcilable goes beyond the subjects and themes of his films. In his European-made films it is at work even in the casting, which almost seems to be done on the assumption that Europe is a single country. The entire shaping of each film from *Kane* through *Falstaff* shows a desire to burst out of commonly accepted limitations. Welles is not content with a single viewpoint—in *Kane* there are at least seven different ones (the reminiscences of the five people interviewed by the reporter, the newsreel, and the God's-eye-view opening and closing scenes), while in all his films he alternates between the detachment of stationary long shots and the involvement of wide-angle close-ups or of dolly shots that stalk the action like a hungry leopard. He is not content with the straight-forward flow of time—four of his films (*Kane*, *Othello*, *Arkadin*, *Falstaff*) begin with the end of the action before leaping to the beginning, and *Kane* continues leaping throughout; *Ambersons* frequently skips across the years with the most laconic of vignettes. In *Touch of Evil* and *The Trial* the leaps are not so much in time as in space. . . .

Welles's persistent attempts to harness opposites and contradictions generate a tremendous potential energy in his films. Usually this energy is released little by little, like a controlled nuclear reaction, maintaining a steady urgency that compels attention. But even his most controlled films are often on the verge of exploding. . . .

The two biggest casualties of Welles's explosive pressure are *Arkadin* and *The Trial*. *Arkadin* is like a grenade that flies apart chiefly along its groovings: each episode holds together fairly well, but fails to connect with the others. *The Trial* is more like the nuclear explosion with which it ends: nearly everything in it disintegrates.

William Johnson. *Film Quarterly*. Fall 1967, p. 19

Yeats said "Rhetoric is heard, poetry overheard," and though I don't agree, I think I see what he means, and I think this assumption is involved in much of the rejection of a talent like Welles'. His work is often referred to as flashy and spectacular as if this also meant cheap and counterfeit. Welles is unabashedly theatrical in a period when much of the educated audience thinks theatrical flair vulgar, artistry intellectually respectable only when subtle, hidden. Welles has the approach of a popular artist: he glories in both verbal and visual rhetoric. He uses film *theatrically*—not stagily, but with theatrical bravado. He makes a show of the mechanics of film. He doesn't, if I may be forgiven the pun, hide his tracks. Movies gave him the world for a stage, and his is not the art that conceals art, but the showman's delight in the flourishes with which he pulls the rabbit from the hat. (This is why he was the wrong director for *The Trial*, where the poetry needed to be overheard.) I think that many people who enjoy those flourishes, who really love them—as I do—are so fearfully educated that they feel they must put them down. It's as if people said he's a mountebank, an actor showing off. But there's life in that kind of display: it's part of an earlier theatrical tradition that Welles carries over into film, it's what the theatre has lost, and it's what brought people to the movies.

Welles might have done for American talkies what D. W. Griffith did for the silent film. But when he lost his sound and his original, verbal wit, he seemed to lose his brashness, his youth, and some of his vitality. And he lost his American-ness; in Europe he had to learn a different, more exclusively visual language of film. . . .

Pauline Kael. *Kiss Kiss Bang Bang* (Little, Brown, 1968), pp. 199–200

Orson Welles's sixty-three-minute *The Immortal Story* which takes place in Macao is also a handsome sight. In it Jeanne Moreau, recumbent to receive a passing bedmate supposedly 17—although he looks 35—is rendered more sensuously appealing than ever. The picture is based on one of Isak Dinesen's Gothic tales. It indicates once more Welles's penchant for the mysterious macabre. A program note declares that it is about "the artist playing God" and "that life imitates art with ironic consequences." But the total effect is inconsequential, despite its suggestion of even more portentous meanings.

Harold Clurman. *Nation*. Oct. 7, 1968, p. 348

Like so many of his films, *Chimes at Midnight* [*Falstaff*] asserts Welles's emphasis on the mortality of human beings, on their essential fragility. While Falstaff carouses in the tavern with Prince Hal, we already see that ahead of them both lie two deaths; for Hal the death of his youth, killed by his assumption of power; for Falstaff the death of his friendship with Hal, and the death of his spirit—goodness crushed by high office. And the film powerfully reminds us of the horror and loneliness of power, as witnessed before in *Kane* and in other Shakespearian adaptations; no more shattering sequence exists in Welles than the still, cold, and beautiful episodes of Henry IV's "Uneasy lies the head" speech, delivered with agonizing magnificence by John Gielgud.

This is a film that has a predominating mood of pain, of suffering, which makes it perhaps the most deeply felt of all Welles's works; a film that is the product of pain itself, of Welles coming to grips with the realities of middle age, old age, and death. If *Kane* was more dazzling and *Ambersons* more richly poetic, if *The Lady from Shanghai* emerges as a more striking *tour de force* of technique, then we must still reserve for *Chimes at Midnight* the special place in an artist's history we keep for the simple and profound, the momentary humble distillation of genius. Many of Welles's films have been showier; none has been nobler.

Charles Higham. *The Films of Orson Welles* (California, 1970), p. 170

. . . *The Trial*, boredom and all, is finally, not without meaning, though not so much one it contains as one which contains it. In an idiom which appears to be narrative or dramatic, Welles has actually given us an instance of pure *mise en scène, mise en scène* freed of all necessity, concerned solely with independent visual effects. Perhaps a director of greater genius than Welles could do this and make it continuously interesting; but I doubt it. For I think that, with something like the regularity of a law, any attempt to make pure cinema, or, for that matter, pure poetry, out of the materials of narrative or drama, materials whose natural end is in the discovery of meaning, results in something neither meaningful nor good cinema nor good poetry. Were *The Trial* visually beautiful to see, there would be no boredom, but the fact is that, for all the attention lavished on the refinement of the film's surface, that surface is one of an almost unrelieved ugliness; to John Grierson's famous dictum—when a director dies, he becomes a photographer—one feels compelled, on such evidence as *The Trial*, to add the corollary that, when the photographer is a dead director, he will be a bad photographer. How to begin to do justice to what is projected on the screen: that incoherent litter of bric-a-brac which passes for its composition; the crude contrastiness of its lighting; those graceless movements of actors and camera; that spastic cutting; those static setups, and takes which seem to last forever? For anyone familiar with Orson Welles' talents at their peak, even more shocking than how bad *The Trial* is, is how bad it looks: it looks like the dregs of Cinema 16. And, like every message from the avant-garde, species Cinema 16, from three minutes in length on up, it closes with the Bomb, that all-purpose, photogenic emblem of deep meaning and universal significance. Only never before has that well-known mushroom cloud been so unphotogenic; never so meaningless.

William S. Pechter. *Twenty-four Times a Second* (Harper, 1971), pp. 173–74

WELLMAN, WILLIAM (1896–)

Amazing air duels and an impressive study of aviators are depicted in *Wings*, Paramount's epic of the flying fighters of the World War. . . . After the exhibition of the first half of this absorbing subject, Commander Richard E. Byrd was noticed in the lobby talking to Jesse L. Lasky and the words of the hero of the North Pole and transatlantic flights evidently pleased the producer. As the Commander turned to re-enter the theatre he remarked:

"And I wouldn't say so if I didn't think it."

And there were scores of others who found the realism of the episodes highly exciting, not excepting a young officer of Uncle Sam's flying force who declared loudly:

"That crash in No Man's Land was a real bust-up."

If the audience was thrilled by some of the scenes in the first part of the production, the subsequent chapters must have proved even more stimulating for in the course of these sequences William A. Wellman, the director, has adroitly spliced actual war scenes with those filmed in this country specially for the production. There is an underlying idea throughout some of the episodes that the motto of the gallant warriors of the clouds was:

"Let us eat, drink and be merry, for tomorrow we (may) die."

This feature gives one an unforgetable idea of the existence of these daring fighters—how they were called upon at all hours of the day and night to soar into the skies and give battle to enemy planes; their lighthearted eagerness to enter the fray and also their reckless conduct once they set foot on earth for a time in the dazzling life of the French capital.

The glimpses of the young uniformed men in the Folies-Bergere and other places are pictured as they often happened to the fighters of the allied nations. . . .

Each time an airplance hurtled in flames to the earth there was a doleful hooting behind the screen. When the aviators are about to take-off and the propellers are set in motion, the sound of whirring motors makes these stretches all the more vivid. . . .

The Magnascope, which gives a picture twice the usual size, is used to a great extent in this film.

Mordaunt Hall. *NYT*. Aug. 13, 1927, p. 10

The exceptional quality of *Wings* lies in its appeal as a spectacle and as a picture of at least some of the actualities of flying under war time conditions. If you are interested at all in aviation, and, who in these days of breathless flights is not, you will get much enjoyment out of *Wings*. In the course of the story the maximum activity of the American aeroplane force is given an opportunity for display. A series of remarkable engagements is shown from individual air duels to mass attacks and daring sorties to attack enemy troups at close quarters.

Here there is, of course, an unlimited opportunity for many remarkable shots. Air battles are photographed from every conceivable angle, producing many bold cinematic effects. The conflagration and demolition of two enemy observation balloons is particularly effective. So much, in fact, happens in the air that it is almost impossible to take it all in. . . . William A. Wellman, the director, is . . . worthy of praise for directing a picture in which the patriotic appeal not infrequently overrides artistic considerations. *Wings* undoubtedly has its thrills.

NBR. Sept. 1927, p. 7

[*Wings*.] A great war spectacle of the air. Thrilling airplane fights and manoeuvers in and above the clouds. Unfortunately the story is weakly built and, with the exception of several touching scenes, misses conviction.

Two youngsters, both loving the same girl, quarrel over her just before battle. One lad is brought down within German lines and is lost in the marshes. He steals an enemy plane and makes his escape toward the Allied front. His pal goes on a lone hunt for him, sights the German plane and blazes away at it. The other boy is shot to pieces and, dying, is recognized by his friend.

The two lads are splendidly played by Buddy Rogers and Richard Arlen. Clara Bow, as the girl, is too sophisticated for the part. By all means see *Wings*.

Photoplay. Sept. 1927, p. 52

The Public Enemy. Roughest, toughest and best of the gang films to date. It's so strong that full-throated protests across the country are either apt to smother or enhance its natural box office capabilities. . . .

Bill Wellmen sent this one across and has continuously built it up to a peak with his direction. It's low-brow material given such workmanship as to make it high-brow. Maybe Wellman's still sore because they wouldn't let him do his balloon corp picture, and so the resultant venom went into this effort. To square everything there's a foreword and postscript moralizing on the gangster as a menace to the public welfare. That possibly will see it through but the yelp about this one from the smaller communities seems as certain as the flood of attendance it's going to get anywhere. There are also two offsets in the dialog. One supposedly is an "out" for two boys living with their girls. The other infers that the same duo's original desire was to be on the level.

Wellman hasn't glossed his version of the modern bad man with any heroic attributes or anecdotes other than with an abundance of physical courage. This boy is a bully behind his gun with men and the same with his fist toward his women. Cagney makes it an ungrammatical and powerful performance realizing upon everything and a little more than he flashed in *Doorway* [*to Hell*].

Variety. April 29, 1931

. . . *The President Vanishes* is an example of the slickest form of demagogy that has ever been produced. It doesn't possess the crudity or the obviousness, or the Hearst-stink of *Gabriel*. This new film is well acted, superbly cast, produced with skill and exciting as a good mystery film. Wanger has utilized the highly developed mystery film technique to create a most important piece of publicity for Roosevelt, the New Deal and the Roosevelt war policy. The film shouts "left" phrases; on the surface the munition makers are castigated. Smedley Butler's revelations are made valid and realistic and it is seemingly anti-fascist, anti-war, anti-everything. . . . [But] wipe the superficial film of demagogy away and you will clearly see its anti-working-class character.

Peter Ellis. *New Masses*. Dec. 18, 1934, p. 29

A Star Is Born is a good picture and the first color job that gets close to what screen color must eventually come to: it keeps the thing in its place, underlining the mood and situation of the story rather than dimming everything else out in an iridescent razzle-dazzle. The boardinghouse is drab and the sanitarium is severe and quiet, and when it comes to the splendors of Hollywood money, the sets have a rich but subdued luster (done, I suspect, by featuring natural-wood finishes and dull metals and by having a pretty good taste in browns and pastels). And if the outdoors looks a little parky, that is not a fault but Beverly Hills—though it is still true that where outdoors is not landscaped, the color cameras still need adjustment to make up for the sensitive compensating apparatus of the human retina: they are still too bold and brilliant. . . .

For about the first time, the mechanics of the industry are worked in with thorough coverage: fan-magazine gossips, preemeers, the struggle of extras, the splendid pampered way of stars, the shot-in-the-dark making of a star with cosmetics and lighting and gowning and naming and shameless press agents. And all done with a sense of the actual hardness and fabulous confusion—as for example in the mild burlesque of the screen-test scene, which is a little orchestra of strange hustling sounds and motions in itself. But this is more in the way of the story's atmosphere than of its point. Hollywood only forms the background for the familiar picture of a man on the skids—not demoralized by anything peculiar to the industry, but by himself and a public captiousness and careless cruelty that is as old as old. With the exception of

Lionel Stander, who is made to carry all the personal opprobrium, everybody has a heart of gold. [1937]

Otis Ferguson. *The Film Criticism of O.F.* (Temple, 1971), pp. 176–77

The response of my immediate neighbours to *A Star is Born* may be worth recording. Len Lye describes its colour as "technically a terrific job," and on these matters Lye is, of course, an authority. He has thought more about colour possibilities, and certainly realised more of them, than anyone in the country.

From other than a laboratory point of view—and all honour to the Technicolor people for their progress—I find the colour of *A Star is Born* no great shakes in excitement. Lye's own recent work in *Trade Tattoo* is a generation ahead when it comes to mobilising colour to the point of sensation. In the Hollywood article, it is still, for the most part, a mere decorative addition to the story.

Yet it is worth a critic's while to examine this film very closely, and distinguish those points where colour steps in to help up the description. The simple fact emerges, for example, that black has curious dramatic powers in a colour film. There are moments in *A Star is Born* which stay in the head—the shadow of a train falling across a woman's face; the eyes of a girl when she is kissed in the dark; the eyes of a man watching in the dark. These moments are all of a kind, and very simple, but they seem to indicate that in colour we may achieve a new and useful sense of intimacy. On the other hand, overlighting has been a deplorable convention in film studios, and few directors have tried to find what black and white might do in the same direction. The ironic situation has, perhaps, arisen, that it has taken colour to discover for us the powers of black and white. After all, the most intimate dramatic appearance of eyes that ever occurred in a film was in *M*.

In the abstractions of its musical comedy values, the almost classical conventions of its hokum, Hollywood is, as ever, a thousand times surer of its ground; and these fine little aids to intimate and dramatic statement which colour is bringing, are, I fear, incidental only. But, as it happens, *A Star is Born* is excellent good hokum. The detail of the acting "business" is particularly good, and the film is finely directed. The less said about its story of rising and waning star values, and all the vanities and ambitions which are the life stream of Hollywood, the better.

John Grierson. *World Film News.* Oct. 1937, p. 20

Men with Wings. The thrilling saga of aviation, the struggle of man to conquer the air, told from its infancy to its established place in the world of today, is presented brilliantly by Paramount. Truly a cavalcade of aviation, the film should appeal strongly to every type of audience. Dramatic and powerful, there is also a warmly human story that brings laughs and tears, as well as thrills and suspense. Heartbreak and applause go hand in hand with progress, and a magnificiently written script moves the story faithfully from one year to another in the progress of aviation, and the men and women who made planes. . . . The direction of William A. Wellman is superb. He paces the story well, achieves tremendous drama and warm emotion, without at any time letting the story become uninteresting or unwieldy. Wellman also gets credit for the production value, which is top notch.

Film Daily. Oct. 24, 1938, p. 7

One of the most difficult of all literary problems in the materialistic twentieth century is to make the supernatural credible. William Wellman almost succeeds in *The Next Voice You Hear*.

The voice is the voice of God warning mankind to repent over all the radios of the world at the same time (in the U.S., 8:30 P.M.). The effect of this divine intervention upon the lives of an aircraft worker, his family, neighbors and fellow workers, provides the action and the story. The effects are meager, and in this mediocrity lies the flaw which precludes complete success. The sins of the American working man are singularly uninteresting and their obliteration seems scarcely to require the very voice of God.

Had Mr. Wellman pitched his problem higher, amid lives more godless, he might have compelled more people to suspend disbelief for greater lengths of time. His fundamental device of using the radio has contemporaneous efficacy and he skillfully employs other touches to lull skepticism and entice belief. One of these is the statement that various nationalities simultaneously hear God speaking in their own languages. And too much thanks cannot be heaped on Mr. Wellman for never reproducing the voice of God. People repeat what He said.

But to seduce belief Mr. Wellman relied too heavily on the homely routine of an American working class family—its hopes, prides, squabbles, pretensions and fears. All these are portrayed in such detail that everybody *has* to believe in that family and therefore, Mr. Wellman hopes, in the assertion that that family heard the voice of God. It's a well tried device. In this case it bears the load of the supernatural less than it bores.

Henry Hart. *Films in Review*. Sept. 1950, p. 31

There is a sort of bitter, shimmering poetry in the first version of *A Star Is Born* that will unjustly cause one to forget the very beautiful film that Cukor made with Judy Garland in 1954. The 1937 cast included Janet Gaynor, Frederic March, and Adolphe Menjou. The satire against the prefabricated and inhumane world of entertainment and publicity was softened by a virile and heightened sense of modern fatality. The technicolor was no doubt still rudimentary; however, effects such as the seaside sunset magnifying the suicide of one of the protagonists have remained in the minds of those who saw the film at the time. This bitter poetry, this stringency that was nuanced with tenderness, was to be rediscovered again in one of the most *intimist* war films of the following decade, *The Story of G.I. Joe*. Wellman's handicap is that he has no doubt made too many films—considerably more than a hundred. He will have to be patiently rediscovered.

Henri Agel. *Romance Américaine* (Editions du Cerf, 1963), p. 53

The Ox-Bow Incident. This Western is an attempt at a poetic tragedy of mob violence. It is set in Nevada in 1885; two cowboys (Henry Fonda and Harry Morgan) ride into a small, lonely cattle town and become involved in the hysteria of a lynch mob. Three innocent men (Dana Andrews, Anthony Quinn, and Francis Ford) are hanged, while we see not only their fear and despair, but the varied motives of the members of the posse who take justice into their hands and are left to suffer for their injustice. If you expect too much of this film you may reject it all together: it's easy to be put off by the studio sets and lighting and the forties approach to a "serious" subject. But William Wellman, a good, under-rated director, has made the characters so vivid that after many years people may still recall Frank Conroy as the sadistic Southern major and the rapid changes of expression of William Eythe as his son. . . .

Pauline Kael. *Kiss Kiss Bang Bang* (Little, Brown, 1968), p. 328

Director William Wellman, whose credits include *Wings*, *Public Enemy*, *A Star Is Born*, *Nothing Sacred*, and *The Ox-Bow Incident*, among many others, has made of this fantasy material [in *The President Vanishes*] a taut, tough, action-filled mystery melodrama. Although the film mounts a scathing attack on the munitions industry, international bankers, and demagoguery, it spends little time pamphleteering: it illustrates, and moves on. It makes its points in crackling bursts, montages, and special effects, in a shorthand style. Wellman gives us the full terror of the fanatics in a single image: we see, through a shop window, a wide street on which the Gray Shirts run swiftly and silently into view, unseen by the object of their attack inside the shop until they burst noisily through the glass. Simple objects help carry the burden of meaning. The President's wristwatch has at least three functions: first, through dialogue, we see the human side of the dignified holder of America's highest office when he whispers to his wife, in the midst of formal ceremonies, that he has "forgotten to wear it again"; second, his secretary becomes involved in the plot when she finds the watch on the floor of her apartment; third, it bears the emotion of the final scene when the President gives it to his loyal supporter. In another case, an ash tray has significance: the warmongers plot at the dinner table; the camera moves down to a close-up of the ash tray heaped with cigars, which smolder, burst into flame, and dissolve in an explosion that leads into a montage sequence illustrating the carrying out of their plans (such sequences were common in Hollywood at this time, many of them the work of the montage expert, Slavko Vorkapich). These touches would be clichés in other hands, but terse and dynamic solutions to the problems of film narrative when employed here by William Wellman. His direction is characteristic of the hard-edged, swift, and confident style of the topical and gangster film of the thirties.

Eileen Bowser in *Film Notes*, edited by Eileen Bowser (MOMA, 1969), p. 93

When James Cagney, playing a young hoodlum, smashed half a grapefruit into the face of Mae Clarke, his moll, history was made on two counts. First, the screen acquired an important new male star. Second, female characters were in for much rougher treatment from males on the screen than they had ever had before. Equality for women was now recognized in more than one sense!

The gangster cycle had been started by Warner Bros. the year before with *Little Caesar*. Now *The Public Enemy* pushed it even further in several directions, especially in the depiction of violence. Nothing in the previous picture had quite the same shattering (some said nauseating) impact as the final scene in *The Public Enemy* in which Cagney, kidnapped from a hospital bed, is delivered dead, plaster cast and all, to his family with the corpse toppling into the camera lens.

A postscript to *The Public Enemy* said the producers wanted to "depict honestly an environment that exists today in certain strata of American life, rather than glorify the hoodlum or the criminal." The film had a different effect: Cagney was playful and dynamic, and so much more appealing than the characters opposed to him that audiences rooted for him in spite of themselves.

Martin Quigley, Jr. and Richard Gertner. *Films in America 1929–1969* (Golden Press, 1970), p. 36

WILDER, BILLY (1906–)

A Foreign Affair. Taking as their point of observation an American Congresswoman in Berlin, accompanying a Congressional committee sent to investigate the morale of American troops, the Messrs. Brackett and Wilder have looked realistically upon the obvious temptations and reactions of healthy soldiers far from home. They have wisely observed that black markets are not repugnant to boys with stuff to trade and that frauleins are simply bobby-soxers with a weakness for candy-bars. They have slyly remarked that Russian soldiers like to sing gymnastic songs and that Americans are nothing loath to join them of a quiet night in a smoky cafe. And especially have they noted that an American captain may actually fall in love with a svelte German night-club singer and take her beneath his protective custody, even though she may have been the mistress of a former Nazi trump.

Of course, they have made these observations in a spirit of fun and romance. And the shame of the captain's indiscretion is honorably white-washed in the end. But there is bite, nonetheless, in the comment which the whole picture has to make upon the irony of big-state restrictions on the level of individual give-and-take.

Under less clever presentation this sort of traffic with big stuff in the current events department might be offensive to reason and taste. But as handled by the Messrs. Brackett and Wilder as producer and director of this film—and also as its principal writers—it has wit, worldliness and charm. It also has serious implications, via some actuality scenes in bombed Berlin, of the wretched and terrifying problem of repairing the ravages of war. Indeed, there are moments when the picture becomes downright cynical in tone, but it is always artfully salvaged by a hasty nip-up of the yarn.

Bosley Crowther. *NYT*. July 1, 1948, p. 19

The relative failure of the ending [of *Ace in the Hole*] is an illustration of Wilder's limitations. His is a talent which one respects rather than likes. This is not the result of his choice of subject, nor of his occasional tendency to vulgarity (*A Foreign Affair*) or to sensationalism for its own sake (*The Lost Weekend*); it is because he seems to lack the powers of analysis which his cold, observant style demands. It is the technique of a reporter, brilliantly conveying the immediate impact of a character or situation, less successful in developing it. A more human director, or a more skilful analyst, could have made more out of Tatum's clash of conscience; Wilder is content to report it, as he reported Norma Desmond's tragedy, and Tatum is credible as a character in the sense that Norma Desmond is credible—a gigantic figure who catches the imagination, so that one accepts him at his own valuation. But as writer (*Ace in the Hole* is scripted by Wilder, Lesser Samuels and Walter Newman) and director Wilder has developed an exact, sardonic, objective style whose technical assurance carries him over passages where the quality of thought is unduly superficial. In *Ace in the Hole* style and purpose achieve for the most part a fusion more impressive even than in *Sunset Boulevard*, and the result is perhaps his most remarkable film.

Penelope Houston. *Sight & Sound*. June 1951, p. 45

The half-burlesque, half deadly earnest spirit of the stag play *Stalag 17* has been uproariously and tensely preserved by Billy Wilder in the screen version. A mixture of joke and conspiracy in a story of American enlisted men behind German barbed wire, the movie rushes from situation to situation in a bubbling stream of entertainment at the Astor.

The film version expands from the one-set barracks of the Donald Vevan-Edmund Trzcinski play to take in the whole compound of German prison camp Stalag 17, but the scenes added in the Billy Wilder-Edwin Blum script are integrated perfectly with the ones from the theater. . . .

Wilder piles the visual jokes one on top of another in his picture of men making shift under the watchful eyes of the guards. How they distill booze, have horse races, rig a radio, hold a dance, smuggle Christmas trees and arrange a peep show is as important to the peculiar delightful bittersweet quality of *Stalag 17* as digging escape tunnels or smelling out a traitor. . . .

When it opened on Broadway, *Stalag 17* was described by this reviewer as having a style "as facile as a routine movie." Wilder has given it facility, all right, a facility for continuous rapid-fire action which alternately brings forth the laughs and tingles the spine. His movie has turned out to be far better than routine, and it is one of the treats of summer moviegoing.

Otis L. Guernsey, Jr. *NYHT*. July 2, 1953, p. 18

No one should expect anyone so cynical as Billy Wilder to tell a simple Cinderella story straight, and he has not done so in *Sabrina*, which doesn't much resemble *Sabrina Fair*, despite Samuel Taylor, who wrote that play, having collaborated with Wilder and Ernest Lehman on the screenscript.

Sabrina has everything light entertainment requires: a pleasant story gently mocking of the rich, whose customs and appurtenances are put opulently on view; bright dialogue; a cast of popular and competent actors; directorial savvy and chi-chi. There isn't much in *Sabrina* that is related to reality, but there are occasional bits of social satire, and one line of realistic dialogue satirizing the Cinderella theme itself: "Nobody poor has ever been called democratic for marrying somebody rich." . . .

As for Billy Wilder, there is considerable evidence in *Sabrina* that when he is not hard boiled he is hard put to it. He resorts to farce a little oftener than skill requires; borrows from other directors a little too brazenly (he even lifts the gurgle from *The Man in the White Suit*); and in his satire does not always distinguish between the truly powerful and the merely rich.

Henry Hart. *Films in Review*. Aug.-Sept. 1954, p. 361

From the study of human psychology and cruelty in *The Lost Weekend* and *Sunset Boulevard*, his most remarkable achievements, Billy Wilder switched to the Freudian experiments of *The Big Carnival* and *Stalag 17*, reaching dissimilar effects. A subsequent excursion into light comedy brought us *Sabrina*, a commercially efficient rendition of a Long Island version of the Cinderella story, in which the original satirical context of the Broadway play was completely ignored. The fairy tale eliminated the allegedly "dangerous" implications of the character of Sabrina's father,—the chauffeur who had grown rich on his employer's time by investing wisely at the bull market, the symbolic funeral mania of the half-imbecilic Larrabee senior, the atmosphere and behaviour of the big business species.

The Seven Year Itch is another step down in the career of the talented director. The Broadway play deals with the adventure of a married man approaching middle-age who is left alone in his Manhattan apartment, while his wife and child go on vacation to the country. . . .

It was a simple sometimes funny comedy enriched by nuances and subtle insights into the American "psychological" approach to the battle of the sexes.

The screen version cannot advertise the same quality. From the very beginning Marilyn Monroe is exhibited as an exasperatingly sensuous woman, whose sultry assets—strictly on the physical side—are photographed from almost every possible angle. She was apparently forbidden to make the slightest attempt at acting; she has been built into the film as a symbol of sex, in a definite geometry of solids, the display reaching a paroxysm that leads us to suspect a streak of sadistic satire in Wilder's direction.

George N. Fenin. *Film Culture*. Summer 1955, pp. 22–23

Among the most spectacular declines of recent years has been that of Billy Wilder. Until *Stalag 17* (1953), his record had been an extraordinary one; his films of the forties produced and co-scripted by Charles Brackett were comparable only with those of Sturges in the consistency with which they presented a recognizably personal point of view. Bitterness, disenchantment, a dry brittle humour—these served to conceal the ruthless cynicism of *A Foreign Affair* and the profound misanthropy of *The Big Carnival*. . . . Or perhaps it would be more accurate to say that Wilder's contempt was reserved for the human flotsam that his outsize central characters—anti-social, egoistic, neurotic—had to contend with. For his heroes and heroines Wilder chose "outsiders," individuals shut off from society by lust (*Double Indemnity*), alcohol (*Lost Weekend*), vanity (*Sunset Boulevard*) or ambition (*Big Carnival*). His attitude toward Norma Desmond and Chuck Tatum is a mere pretence at detached, analytic observation; the very fact that they are chosen as protagonists betrays a certain indulgence toward them. It is always the *others* whose behavior is more despicable—the people in the restaurant in *Lost Weekend*, the tailor's assistant in *Sunset Boulevard*, the husband in *Double Indemnity*, above all the sensation-seeking crowds of *The Big Carnival*. In *A Foreign Affair* the only two characters in the entire film for whom the director shows the slightest shred of respect are Dietrich's opportunistic ex-Nazi and the hard-boiled general played by Millard Mitchell; everyone else—Congress member, soldier or German civilian—is caricatured or shown as selfish or heartless. Wilder's outlook, as demonstrated in all these films, is depressing, but at least it has what in the commercial cinema is the rare merit of being completely self-sufficient.

The Lost Weekend (1945) is the director's first study in moral deformity, and, all things considered, probably his finest achievement. It is free alike from his habitual melodramatic contrivance and excess, and from a masochistic immersion in the hero's weakness. It approaches as close as Wilder has ever come to compassion; that is to say the method of external observation is here legitimately and appropriately used as an end in itself. There are some inevitable box-office concessions, but they do not seriously impair a film that is supremely honest in the true sense of the much-abused term of film criticism.

Joel Greenberg. *Film Journal* (Australia).
March-April 1957, p. 11

In *Some Like It Hot*, which returns Marilyn Monroe to the pleasure domes after three years' absence, United Artists has managed to avoid turning out a routine potboiler but has certainly cooked up a queer kettle of fish.

In the picture's opening scene, which is set in Chicago in pre-crash 1929, a hearse that is hauling bootleg booze leads a magnificent vintage prowl car a splendid chase, in the course of which a couple of tin lizzies are demolished. This is followed by a raid of a "coffee house" *qua* mortuary (the bereaved are lugubriously ushered into a rear room where "we have Scotch coffee, Canadian coffee, and sour-mash coffee." The situations, the Volstead-era gorillas, the comic lushes, the dialogue and sight gags (gin spurting from a bullet-riddled coffin, etc.) are all of ancient formula, but director Billy Wilder piles them up so thickly and so artfully that the whole atmosphere is one of amiable caricature. The predictability of the gags heightens rather than diminishes the enjoyment of what promises to be a nostalgic *tour de force,* and one settles back in happy anticipation of an old-fashioned spoof of both the 1920's themselves and the gaudy celluloid myth to which they gave rise.

But then the picture abruptly slides out of focus. The hundred-proof flavor of the jazz era is rapidly diluted in a series of watery jokes in which the events and the vernacular of the 1950's are prefigured: groping for improbabilities, the hero-heroine (played by Tony Curtis—that locution will be explained later on) says, "Suppose the Dodgers leave Brooklyn!"; a tough cop (Pat O'Brien), waiting for his colleagues to burst into the afore-mentioned speak-easy, indulges in an atomic-age countdown: "You flipped your wig," Mr. Curtis tells his crony Jack Lemmon.

Jay Jacobs. *Reporter*. April 16, 1959, p. 35

I think Billy Wilder is the most talented producer-director-writer combination now operating in and out of Hollywood, and I'm even willing to go along with those who say his heart's in the right place. But I don't think much of *The Apartment*.

The flacks hired to promote this 124-minute, black-&-white film, say it isn't just comedy, or romantic comedy, or near-tragedy, or "mordant yet compassionate" satire of US business, but a bit of them all. If so, it's a bit of too much of too many antithetical things.

I suppose a young clerk in a large insurance company *might* advance himself by lending his apartment to *five* of his superiors for their adulterous "quickies," but I don't think the idea is really very funny, or even interesting. Especially since the men in this film who hustle dumb floozies in and out of the young man's apartment, are such insensitive boors! As for the young man himself, and his falling in love with an elevator girl who's had an affair with his boss *in his own apartment*, well, young American males of today may be that stupid, but I doubt it. . . .

No script even partially by Billy Wilder can be altogether devoid of wit, and there are touches, here and there throughout *The Apartment*, that make one remember the Wilder of *Sabrina*, *Sunset Boulevard*, *The Major and the Minor*, *Ninotchka* and *Bluebeard's Eighth Wife*.

To say nothing of *The Spirit of St. Louis*, *Stalag 17*, *The Big Carnival*, *A Foreign Affair*, *The Lost Weekend* and *Double Indemnity*.

Ellen Fitzpatrick. *Films in Review*.
Aug.-Sept. 1960, p. 428

. . . Mr. Billy Wilder has made in *One*, *Two*, *Three* a film of no usefulness at all. Despite an air of almost hysterical exuberance, it is not even vulgarly funny. Of course, Berlin divided is not the most risible of topics, but geography is not the problem—it is a matter of imagination and taste. James Cagney does not strike me as the sort of man who embarrasses easily, but he looked out of countenance in his role of star (and West Berlin's representative of Coca-Cola), in this dirty show for family entertainment. Its sex, concocted of sordid boastfulness and impotent leering, is the worst kind of obscenity—and the most immune from censorship.

The plot involves the idiot sexpot daughter of a Coca-Cola high executive (which one, I wonder), an East German activist, some Russian purchasing agents and a series of gags that Laurel and Hardy would have scorned to pull down from the dust. Mr. Wilder was getting a reputation for satiric humor with *Some Like it Hot* and *The Apartment*—*One*, *Two*, *Three* is about as sharp as the soda pop it advertises.

Robert Hatch. *Nation*. Jan. 6, 1962, p. 20

One, *Two*, *Three*. In Hollywood it is now common to hear Billy Wilder called the world's greatest movie director. This judgment tells us a lot about Hollywood: Wilder hits his effects hard and sure; he's a clever, lively director whose work lacks feeling or passion or grace or beauty or elegance. His eye is on the dollar, or rather on success, on the entertainment values that bring in dollars. But he has never before, except perhaps in a different way in *Ace in the Hole*, exhibited such a brazen contempt for people. Is it possibly life in Hollywood that is so conducive to this extreme materialist position—a view of the world in which human experience is reduced to a need for sex and gadgets (with even sex turned into a gadget), a view in which people sell out their souls and their convictions for a pair of silk stockings, in which Americans, Russians, and Germans—all men—are brothers in petty corruption and lasciviousness? Hollywood may see itself as a microcosm of America, and may consider that its shoddy values are the American way of life that the rest of the world aspires to, but is this degraded view of political conflicts and human values really supposed to be funny? It would have to be relevant to something first. Surely satire must have some closer relationship to its targets than those cheap "topical" jokes which were dated decades before Berlin was divided. Is *One, Two, Three* really the irreverent political satire the critics have called it, or is it just a lot of scattershot and noise and simulated action —*Hellzapoppin*' in Berlin?

Pauline Kael. *I Lost It at the Movies* (Little, Brown, 1965), p. 153

There is nothing sweet about *The Fortune Cookie*—the image it leaves with you has nothing to do with desserts, Chinese or otherwise. It is, instead, a jackhammer of a film savagely applied to those concrete areas of the human spirit where cupidity and stupidity have been so long entrenched. It has all the defects of a power tool—it is crude and noisy and nervewracking. But it has a virtue that cancels out these faults; it is a bitterly, often excruciatingly, funny movie.

Directing from a script he co-authored with his faithful screenwriter companion I. A. L. Diamond, Billy Wilder has returned to the kind of relentless hard-eyed social and moral observation that has marked his best work from *Double Indemnity* through *Sunset Boulevard* to *The Apartment*. . . . At the top of his form, Wilder never tries to woo the audience's consent to his sardonic vision of man; he simply overpowers its resistance with an endless salvo of first-class one-line gags, the prodigal introduction of grotesquely distorted comic characters, as if he were some latter-day Ben Jonson. He mounts the whole gaudy high-pressure display against a background that seems to include every monstrous mistake ever made in the arts of architecture, home furnishing and dress. I would never claim that Wilder's is a total or even balanced vision of our world. But the landscape he presents is familiar enough to make one uncomfortably aware of the fact that there is an irreducible minimum of dreadfulness in any human society and that its contemporary manifestations are very much as he presents them. [1966]

Richard Schickel. *Second Sight* (S&S, 1972), pp. 87–88

Irma La Douce is, for Wilder, a watershed film. After *Irma La Douce* the team of Wilder and I. A. L. Diamond explode into a vision of man as grotesque and nihilistic. In *Kiss Me, Stupid* and *The Fortune Cookie*, the "good man" is pictured as a fool and a hoople; the social community is pictured as a collection of nasty bastards; and the Hollywood happy endings cannot negate the fact that the power of the films lies in their Swiftian vulgarity and misanthropy.

Obviously, this theme was always latent in Wilder's other work (especially when he collaborated with Diamond). But in his best early work (*Sunset Boulevard*, for example), the misanthropy was held-in-check by the hard-line irony and the drama of the plot. But that horridly beautiful image of Gloria Swanson at the end of the film, inviolate in her madness, walking down the stairs directed by Von Stroheim in an absurd parody of *Queen Kelly*, is, finally, the type of image which dominates Wilder's latest work. *Kiss Me, Stupid* and *The Fortune Cookie* (more successfully in the latter), are examples of Black Humor. Like the novels of Barth, Donleavy, Heller, Pynchon, Vonnegut, and others, the screenplays of Wilder/Diamond offer laughter as the only possible response to the horror of the human condition.

In films like *Some Like It Hot*, *The Apartment*, *Stalag 17*, and *One, Two, Three*, the laughter was offered to the viewer as an alternative to the horror. Instead of confronting transvestitism, suicide, genocide or the cold war, we could laugh. And laugh we did. Those four films were, in my opinion, successful comedies. In *Irma La Douce*, Wilder forces us to confront the fact that innocence is only a dream. Yet, he does it lightly, softly, almost nostalgically, as if to say: "After this, dear viewer, your laughter at my films will be of a different nature. Enjoy Shirley MacLaine while you can." Like Jack Lemmon, who arises from the Seine fully clothed as a British gentleman in a reference satire to Botticelli's *Venus*, Wilder will arise after *Irma La Douce* as a new man, but he will not be naked, and his garments will be black, like Lemmon's business suit.

Leon Lewis and W. D. Sherman. *Landscape of Contemporary Cinema* (Buffalo Spectrum, 1967), p. 39

In the short history of film, Wilder is the screen's equivalent of Guy de Maupassant, an author of grand pessimism, sarcastic excess and sense for his time. Wilder's downcast point of view adds up to a human tableau that is both moral and cosmic, personal and traditional. His vision of the world can be both grandiose and shattering, but its ferocity too often reflects search for artistic effect, rather than expression of true anguish. And the limits of his talent lie here. Wilder creates films of a kind that force respect rather than affection. Too often, he will manipulate his audience and when the laughs threaten to dry up, throw in little sops of sentiment or go for the yocks with bubonic plague.

Enough has been said about his proverbial bad taste, and also about his origins in the Habsburg Vienna when it earned the title of "gay" and launched a thousand musical comedies. His humour is Jewish and *saftig*, hard-sold and therapeutic—the little guy's self-defense against adversity and piled-up injustice and the big guy's safety-valve. Of film-makers, only Wilder could have planted in James Cagney's mouth, when Communists hijack his Coca-Cola, the line ". . . and they don't even return the empties!" Only he could have made *Sunset Boulevard, Ace in the Hole* and, probably, *The Apartment*—highwire acts that break the rules with style, brilliance and corrosive thrills.

At their best, Wilder's movies sparkle with gross reality and risky propositions, cold wit and sardonic pathos. Now and then, among belly laughs or grins that don't know which way to turn, they say something serious and sad about the struggle for success. They often skirt disaster, and usually bring their points home with minimum pontification and maximum intelligence per square inch of film.

Axel Madsen. *Billy Wilder* (Indiana, 1969), pp. 146–47

Billy Wilder, content to let the spectator chuckle privately at the sly innuendoes of *Sunset Boulevard* . . ., sharpens his comic genius to the point of burlesque in *Some Like it Hot*, giving the film an outrageous, hectic tone admirably suited to the period—1929, with jazz and boot-legging in full swing. Joe (Tony Curtis) and Jerry (Jack Lemmon) are unemployed musicians who just happen to witness the St. Valentine's Day massacre and must flee for their lives. They dress up as girls and join a female jazz band en route for Miami Beach—with all the hilarious and often satirical results that the imagination of Billy Wilder and I. A. L. Diamond can conjure up. The gags progress with a smoothness that masks the iron discipline Wilder wields over the film. The female impersonation is exploited for all it is worth, and takes on an extra dimension of wit when Joe "changes back" into a playboy yachtsman, explaining to a wide-eyed Marilyn Monroe in an impossible Cockney accent how girls leave him frigid. Wilder's utterly shameless attitude toward sex is, appropriately, geared to the final line, as Joe E. Brown, the polygamous millionaire who has been courting Jerry, replies, "Well, nobody's perfect!" to his "bride's" desperate admission that he is a man. In these grotesque circumstances, even the cold-blooded slaying of George Raft and his henchmen at the dinner table exudes a certain sardonic humor. *Some Like it Hot* belongs to the handful of really memorable American comedies.

Peter Cowie. *Seventy Years of Cinema* (Barnes, 1969), p. 229

One of three novels by James M. Cain to be made into films in the forties (the others: *The Postman Always Rings Twice* and *Mildred*

Pierce), *Double Indemnity* comes closest to the unvarnished spirit of the original work, because it was co-written (with Raymond Chandler) and directed by Billy Wilder, whose pictures have never been exactly tolerant of human foibles.

There are no appealing characters in this melodrama in which a California femme fatale seduces an insurance salesman into helping her murder her older husband so she can collect on a double indemnity policy. Not ever the murder victim or the insurance agent working to solve the case arouses any strong feelings of sympathy.

The public went to see it anyhow back in wartime 1944, and it still holds up well today, when its coldly analytical approach is even more widely appreciated.

The lack of passion extends to every element of the picture, including the love scenes between murder conspirators Barbara Stanwyck and Fred MacMurray, which are downright frosty.

The screenplay has been much praised for the terseness and wit of its dialogue.

Martin Quigley, Jr. and Richard Gertner.
Films in America 1929–1969 (Golden, 1970), pp. 138–39

WYLER, WILLIAM (1902–)

There was one film which compared with the quarter's best, was much too near the stage. But since the stage play was *The Children's Hour*, practically any movie adaptation was bound to keep the adult pity and astringency of the original. Lillian Hellman, who wrote the play and was sensibly lifted to Hollywood for the adaptation, gave to the appalling [Sidney Franklin] *The Dark Angel* its four minutes of life, a fragment of children's dialogue which reminded you of the refinements of half-calculated cruelty that toddlers use for humour. In *These Three* this reminder was expanded into a whole movie and deepened into a genuine tragedy. Of course, since the original pathos was based on a charge of Lesbianism, Hollywood saw to it that Joel McCrea was introduced as a go-between so that none of us 200,000,000 little ones should suffer pain or shock. This fatuous concession (McCrea's all right, but I mean the gesture of including him made him look like a bishop) dissipated the tension between the two girls which was the chief dramatic element of the play. But for all that, *These Three* kept its dialogue and gained a terrified, brilliant performance by Bonita Granville. And William Wyler's direction used the distance between us and the characters for the most effective and bloodless Aristotelian purposes, tracking the camera relentlessly up to their faces when we would rather have escaped from the problem, scuttling pitifully away from them when we ached to give them a warm embrace.

Alistair Cooke. *Sight & Sound*. Summer 1936, p. 24

There are inherent weaknesses in *Come and Get it*, weaknesses which Mr. Goldwyn and Directors Hawks and Wyler (the fact that *two* directors had a hand in this film proves, more conclusively than anything we know, that the producer is a responsible party) overcome with nothing more startling than a change of pace. Edna Ferber's novel tells the story of a rough, ruthless logger named Barney Glasgow. Glasgow has his own ideas about all that beautiful lumber going to waste in the Wisconsin hills, and sets a record of cubic-feet-of-lumber-cut or something, and wins for himself a position of prominence, and a wife. . . . A short and tragic denouement shows him as an old man, making love to the daughter of his early sweetheart. Barney's early disposition, and the bawdy days of nineteenth century Wisconsin make much more effective cinema than the luxury-toned mannerisms of the later period. The logging scenes are masterpieces of photographic crescendo, and we feel sure that the cabaret sequence, wherein Barney and Lotta, the dance hall girl, twirl trays at the mirrors, will go down in picture history as a *tour de force* of silent comedy. . . . The remainder of the story is told by personality, of which he has plenty, and domestic relationship. There is such a care of detail, and such richness of incident from here on, though, that the only lack may be put down under the head, panorama. There are no more spacious scenes of unkempt country, or of bawdy camaraderie. The sequences during the latter three-quarters are quiet significant ones of personal triumph and personal tragedy.

Stage. Dec. 1936, p. 14

Dead End was a serious and successful play on Broadway. It is equally serious and successful as a film. It is beautifully directed by William Wyler, who is not only one of the great directors, but one of the rare two or three whose sense of drama is as adult as his skill. It is profuse in human sympathy as it dives down into the tenements of East Side New York and discovers the teeming tragedy of the poor. What more can we ask? We have challenged the cinema to grow up and take stock of society and here it does both. We have cursed its dream life and sugar-stick endings. Here is real life and—as one gangster generation dies of its own evil and a new generation is marched off to the reformatory—here is the spondaic ending of honest observation.

Yet, and in spite of watching the film with eagerness and respect, I dislike it intensely and it won't do at all. It is acquarium stuff. It looks at people distantly, like fish, and its sympathy is cold with distance. The poor, poor beggars, are poor; they are uncomfortable; they breed thieves and gangsters and a curse on the conditions that breed them; they struggle against overwhelming odds and what break are they given in achieving the good life? That is the theme and the thesis. It sounds all right; but who was it said that there was more reality in a louse on a dirty bagman than in all this sorrow for the working class? Granted the poverty, the discomfort, the struggle against odds, no slice of humanity is so dim and sad as *Dead End* observes. They laugh and fight and love one another and, except to the sympathisers from without, their dreams of escape are not more important than the rich grip on life they already signify. It is this that *Dead End* misses. It lacks gusto.

John Grierson. *World Film News.* Jan. 1938, p. 20

For all its magnolias and moonlight, beaux and belles and romantic trappings, *Jezebel* is far from the usual romantic southern tale. It is a penetrating study of character in a setting whose conventional surface handsomeness does not nullify its essential truth and solidity. As in any good movie its excellences came from many sources—good plotting and writing, a director and photographer who know how to make the thing flow along with dramatic pictorial effect, and a cast that makes its story a record of living people. It has enough romantic glamor to interest those who look only upon the surface, enough substance to satisfy those who like the surface to be a truthful expression of depths beneath, and —finally—the ultimate satisfaction of the demands of justice which art can supply though life so seldom does. . . .

It is unusual for a movie to take such a subject as this and handle it so unevasively, with such clean surgical skill. It is not morbid—many people will see it as just an entertaining tale of a spoiled girl who gets what is coming to her, which is a spectacle far from unsatisfying. But it has its pathological aspects for those who can see and appreciate such things, clear and unvarnished, treated realistically and vividly. . . .

William Wyler directed the picture, and its excellence must in the last summing up go back to him. He did a fine creative job.

James Shelley Hamilton. *NBR.* April 1938, pp. 14–15

The movie *Wuthering Heights* came just in time. The film year has been about the leanest in seven—and Sam Goldwyn's version of the novel turns out to be among the best pictures made anywhere. Our sleepyheads in the prints and the industry itself have been apologizing and deprecating and rolling sheep's eyes at the legitimate stage for so long that the habit of playing down movies is ingrained, while even in mildly good theater there seems to be nothing but sky for a limit to critical hurrah. I have enjoyed quite a few of this season's plays, yet most of them don't make more than a good patch on *Wuthering Heights,* for truth, vigor, and thorough expression in the form. Just watch the words go by, however, and count how many times this picture is very respectfully restricted to being, oh quite fine—for a picture.

Pictures made from novels, especially novels everyone is supposed to have read, are usually desperate ventures; but in this case the script-writers were both sober and skillful enough to get a film story out of the book; it was impossible they should not lose some of the solid effect, but on the other hand they have delivered the action from that heavy weight of words. The production was given the best in everything except music, and the best in this case included a free rein to sincere workmanship. From then on it was up to William Wyler's direction, cameras, and cast.

Wyler has many adult jobs to his credit, but more than usual was required of him here, a sustained mood of bleakness and sullen passions. Part of this is achieved in the film by remarks in character, and part by the setting on the Yorkshire moors (some artificiality shows through, reminding you of the superior natural effects of a film like [Victor Saville's] *South Riding*). But the closeness with which the story holds together is ultimately the result of the way director, photographer, and cutters have used what should be called the moving camera, the part of photography that goes beyond a register of things to the position from which they are seen, moved up to, led away from, to the value in tempo and coloring of each strip of film with relation to that of all preceding and following strips—the camera telling a story.

It is a very intricate and wonderful art, and William Wyler's staff have achieved one of its best examples. Without the distraction of trick effects, however stunning, they have taken a story anchored to three main points and with most of its action interior, and given it a pattern of constant forward motion, with overtones maintained throughout the rise of interest and suspense. The art serves its true purpose unobtrusively, and for that reason will not be fully appreciated unless you start asking yourself afterward how else in the world you would have gone about it. [1939]

Otis Ferguson. *The Film Criticism of O.F.* (Temple, 1971), p. 251

[T]he success of *The Best Years of Our Lives* as a major document in Hollywood's picture of America is attributable to the unusual care that has been devoted to the reality of the surface. The camera, above all, catches the exact appearances of the metropolitan background: the orderly and impersonal comfort of an upper middle class apartment, the hard surfaces of a bank, the ugly and cheap profusion of a chain drugstore, the plain facts of a street—all photographed simply as what happens to be really there, without sympathy or revulsion, without "tricks"—almost, in a sense, without art, if one were not conscious all the time of how much arrangement has gone into this matter-of-fact detail. One recognizes everything and in the end this recognition is all the excitement, for what is on the screen becomes finally as accustomed and undramatic as the shabby décor of the theater itself. The actors, too, are so manipulated as to become embodiments of the physical reality of human beings. More clearly than the important events of the plot, one remembers how the actors hold their bodies: Teresa Wright slouched over a stove, so much like a real woman over a real stove that the scene can become almost unpleasant, as it was certainly not intended to be; or Fredric March and Dana Andrews, quarreling across a table, with their muscles set, two stupid men acting as they think proper in what they conceive to be a moment of drama—this, too, was not intended, but the physical appearances have so strong a hold on the director that he is himself exactly on a level with his material: He sees how everything must look, but frequently he cannot see what it really means. [1947]

Robert Warshow. *The Immediate Experience*
(Atheneum, 1970), pp. 156–57

One of the most ambitious, and courageous, films ever to come out of Hollywood, *The Best Years of Our Lives* will probably cause more tears to flow in 1947 than anything else screened during the year. They will be legitimate tears. For this is a drama of our lives and times, produced, written, directed, and acted by men and women who wish us well. It is no olive branch or Christmas wreath they hold out to us. It is a hard-hitting challenge to think through our problems and do justice to our ideals. And not to fail our fallen. . . .

Robert E. Sherwood and William Wyler . . . want to make us recognize ourselves in these questing, struggling people, trying with so much good will and good humor to fight their way through the confusion of forces that govern their lives. Writer and director both equally succeed. Long as is the picture, uncertain as are some of its incidentals, its texture is the very weave of American living today. And toward that way of life it is both strongly critical and warmly affectionate.

Too much cannot be said for William Wyler's direction. In a three hour film, he has achieved a balance and a tempo of episode and incident that hardly ever falter. Shot by shot, its rich complexity is clear, absorbing, and sustained. All of the players are excellent, some of them astoundingly so. Fredric March's performance is the best of all his many fine ones, rich in human values and skilful in characterization. Myrna Loy, Dana Andrews, and Teresa Wright are with the director and writer every minute of their delineations, with Roman Bohnen, Gladys George, and Ray Collins expertly filling in the complicated mosaic. The playing of Harold Russell, one feels, is not playing at all. It is something more eloquent than artistry. It is symbolic of all our loss, and all we have to gain.

One bows to Samuel Goldwyn for his courage in making this film. It is hard to imagine anyone, anywhere, who won't thank him for it. Whoever complains of the happy solutions offered to the problems so strongly posed in it might well ask himself what other solutions we are willing to entertain, for the years of our lives that are ahead.

Richard Griffith. *NBR*. Jan. 1947, pp. 4–5

It takes a film of such quality as *The Heiress* to revive the old issue of play into motion picture. For producer-director William Wyler is that rarest of craftsmen who can take such a drama as this, already completely fulfilled in theatre terms, and convert it to film without ever permitting the play-form to dominate the screen. What he did so successfully with *The Little Foxes* he has repeated with increment in *The Heiress*. . . .

Except for a few new exterior scenes, notably the ball at which Catherine and Morris meet, the script has held firm in spirit and pattern to the Broadway original, confining the major part of its action inside the walls of the doctor's house on Washington Square. Even within these limits there is sufficient potential for movement for the director who knows, as Wyler does, where to look. Shrewdly he pivots his action around the central staircase that leads up two flights to Catherine's room, marking her emotional changes in the way she moves up and down the stairs. The vista of rooms end to end in these narrow houses along the Square provides many variations for the camera, and when their limit is reached there are mirrors to extend the view. In such a setting, with the aid of the long-focus camera the director can deploy his actors for dialogue without appearing to hold the scene in static composition. If the large sliding doors which divide the parlor floor of the mansion are opened and closed a little too often, punctuating the scene in a way to remind us that the theatre is not far away after all, this is only a minor flaw in a visualization which, for all its repose, is almost endlessly beguiling to the eye.

Hermione Rich Isaacs. *Films in Review*.
Feb. 1950, pp. 25–27

William Wyler's *The Heiress*, from the stage success remotely adapted from Henry James' *Washington Square*, is a sadly wasted opportunity. Ruth and Augustus Goetz, using their play as a foundation for the script, make no attempt to replace those overtones of feeling which they had sacrificed for broader theatrical effects. Rather, they simplify still further, to make of James' tragi-comedy only a polished period piece. In the film, the love of the gauche, unattractive Catherine Sloper for the presentable fortune hunter, Morris Townsend, assumes the foreground. Morris, played by Montgomery Clift with far too authentic a charm, becomes for much of the film almost a hero; the cold, bitter Dr. Sloper is reduced to a Washington Square Mr. Barrett; Catherine's relationship to her father is simplified and weakened and, when Morris's defection proves him in the right, her closing in on herself seems rather a theatrical gesture—as, emphatically, does her ultimate rejection of Morris—than a natural development of the character as we have seen it.

. . . Wyler has directed with the same faultless eye for externals. The photography (Leo Tover) makes great play with deep focus, with a camera whose movements become stylised, mechanical and obtrusive through their very meticulous care. Wyler, too, seems to accept the softening of the central situation, the film's fundamental fault: he has allowed *The Heiress* to assume a prettiness, an exhibition of the art director's skill, which can only detract from a story which not only has no need for such devices, but positively rejects them.

Penelope Houston. *Sight & Sound*.
Dec. 1950, pp. 332–33

The film *Carrie* is an attempt to make into romantic melodrama Dreiser's story of two people displaced, and distorted, by social forces. The attempt seems to succeed in the beginning, for the ways people get into trouble are never uninteresting, and a romantic triangle can make a beginning for any sort of story.

But when the second half comes along, it becomes evident that Dreiser was not interested in romantic melodrama, and that script-writers Ruth and Augustus Goetz and Director William Wyler weren't interested in what Dreiser was interested in. They shot the later episodes for the strongest dramatic effect only, despite the fact that the story had stopped following a melodramatic line and had become a sociological study. After the middle of the film each additional episode exploits the audience's hope that things will be brought to a satisfactory conclusion, but they never are. . . .

It seems to this reviewer that the audience is left wondering whether Hurstwood is a victim of neurotic apathy, which is not indicated in the film, or of social forces which are not entirely visible either. The way the film is directed is not really compatible with either interpretation, with its glamorous closeups, heightening—and annoying—crescendos in the musical score, and gratuitous justifications for Carrie's arrivism. . . .

With more realism, with more sociological emphasis, *Sister Carrie* might have made a good, though not a very popular, film. Hurstwood would have had to be weaker from the start, and the camera would have had to go outdoors for a great many long and medium shots to help reveal to us the way people get lost in big cities.

Terence Anderson. *Films in Review*.
March 1952, pp. 134–35

Roman Holiday, shot entirely in Italy—on location in Rome and at the Cinecitta studios—and edited in Hollywood, has a good romantic comedy idea that at one time Capra intended to film. In the transference to a director of impeccable craftsmanship but, apparently, little aptitude for the lightness and rhythm such a subject demands, it has lost a good deal. . . . William Wyler . . . seems to have directed the film as if it were *Carrie* or even *The Heiress*, so slow and un-gay is the tempo, so heavily prolonged the development. The film moves like a great, smooth, polished, crushing machine, and towards the end, with the farewell scenes of Bradley and the Princess bled to the last reaction shot, it becomes positively oppressive.

Roman Holiday is the first film of its genre that Wyler has attempted; and while Capra or, in a different way, Lubitsch could have made something wholly enjoyable from it, it would seem that Wyler's technique is now too ponderously inflexible for such lightweight material. The craftsmanlike detail of the staging, the resourceful care with which Audrey Hepburn's performance has been guided, are in themselves admirable feats, but one cannot help feeling that a butterfly has, unintentionally, been broken on the wheel.

BFI Bulletin. Sept. 1953, p. 132

The Friendly Persuasion (*Allied Artists*) is something quite rare in recent screen history: a family picture (in the sense that it is about a family and also that both in suitability and appeal it is for the family) which is absolutely first-rate in quality.

The family in question is in many ways unique on the screen. They are Quakers living in Southern Indiana during the Civil War. As far as I can remember, this is the first time a movie has dealt with Quakers in full-dress fashion and with dignity. In addition, the setting is unfamiliar.

The particular place and time, however, conspire to provide the film with its most poignant and dramatic moments. Confederate raiders, crossing the Ohio River and burning and pillaging the peaceful countryside, confront the Quaker family with the most agonizing test of their pacifism.

This serious issue, raised toward the end of the film, is not wholly resolved. The older son (Anthony Perkins) takes up a gun and goes off to fight. The father (Gary Cooper) protectively follows him, but finds that his own convictions against killing do not desert him on the battlefield. The mother (Dorothy McGuire), the most articulate advocate of non-resistance, discovers rather humorously that her subconscious mind is far from non-violent.

For the most part the picture, derived from a series of short sketches of the same name by Jessamyn West, is concerned with less solemn matters, with the everyday happenings in the lives of a high-spirited, loving family whose virtues and failings have something to do with their particular religious beliefs but even more to do with the universal fact that they are human beings.

The material is a little tenuous, with incidents ranging from the father's un-Quakerlike urge to race his horse on the way to Sunday meeting to the younger son's (Richard Eyer) feud with the remarkable pet goose. But William Wyler's sure-handed direction consistently illuminates it with a humor, a gentle charm and a feeling for fundamental values that are rare indeed.

Moira Walsh. *America.* Nov. 17, 1956, p. 212

Among the top American directors, William Wyler has perhaps the keenest editing sense of all. Although apparently preferring the adapted stage play as the basis for his pictures, he organizes his scenes with a strong instinct for filmic form. In *The Little Foxes* (1941), for example, the horrifying scene in which Regina permits her husband to die upon the stairs is intensified in Wyler's handling by framing within a single shot a huge, immobile close-up of Regina while, deep in the background, the husband is seen desperately trying to make his way up the stairs. No one knows better when to shift the camera's point of view, when to cut, or how to relate the characters in one shot to those in the next. The relationships may be complex, the action involved, but you never have to wonder where you are in a Wyler picture, or from whose viewpoint you are watching the scene. His sense of film geography, his unfailing precision in the placement of his actors as he cuts from one to the other, give his work a certainty and clarity unmatched by anyone.

Wyler has also developed to perfection a technique that might best be described as cutting within the frame. Realizing that dialogue imposes a slower editing pace than obtained in silent days, he has sought to create the effect of shifting visual patterns by strong regroupings of his characters within the shot, or by sudden changes of background. In the scene of Fredric March's homecoming in *The Best Years of Our Lives* (1945), for example, March enters close to the camera. His wife, Myrna Loy, runs toward him down a long corridor. As she approaches, his daughter, Teresa Wright, moves in from the side and the trio shut out the view of the corridor. Thus, a long-shot has been transformed into a close-up without the need of cutting. Similarly, in *The Heiress* (1949) the constant closing of doors, shutting off room after room as the camera passes through, accomplished very much the same effect. Testing out his dialogue, Wyler felt that repeated cuts would detract both from the importance of the words and the emotional flow of the performances. His solution proved an ideal technique for sound films.

Arthur Knight. *The Liveliest Art* (Macmillan, 1957), pp. 197–98

But there is another . . . type of alteration [in *Wuthering Heights*] which results from what might be called the principle of Hollywood Aristotelianism. According to this always operative, rarely articulated principle, all elements of the film—spectacle, diction, character, and certainly thought—must be subordinated to plot, the prime arbiter. Parker Tyler has pointed out the dangers inherent in "the nonchalant assumption of the usual commercial film that the only necessary formal element is *plot* and that merely conventional 'framing' and clear photography are required for plastic values." While *Wuthering Heights* exhibits certain exceptions to the usual result—what Tyler calls "the vulgar journalistic look and formlessness of standard movie products" —it does omit a number of promising pictorial effects which appear both in the novel and in the original script. These effects, if integrated into the film's total composition, might have supported the drive of sheer incident which the film now has. As it stands, the film is overloaded with medium shots, relieved only occasionally by long shots of the "Castle" or the Heights. In spite of the storms and brooding moors, the physical set-ups of the landscape and the characters are only occasionally allowed to endorse the dramatic event.

George Bluestone. *Novels into Film* (Johns Hopkins, 1957), p. 103

. . . *Ben-Hur* is a "spectacle" and so, one gathers from the critics, must be judged by modest aesthetic standards. (Though, come to think of it, *Intolerance*, *The Birth of a Nation*, and *Potemkin* were also "spectacles.") The big spectacular moments—the seafight, the Roman triumph, the chariot race—failed because Wyler doesn't know how to handle crowds nor how to get a culminating rhythm by cutting. He tries to make up for this lack by huge sets and thousands of extras, but a Griffith can make a hundred into a crowd while a Wyler can reduce a thousand to a confused cocktail party. [1960]

Dwight Macdonald. *D. M. on Movies* (Prentice-Hall, 1969), p. 425

[*Ben Hur*.] [I]n his first epic, Wyler has constructed the most tasteful and visually exciting film spectacle yet produced by an American company. The contribution of the film to whatever history the cinema will ever achieve is the chariot-race sequence, directed by Andrew Marton. Here one perceives the dynamic cinema at work, for the visual splendor, the vigorous, barbaric spirit of ancient Roman civilization is most meaningful to the spectator during these moments. Wyler and Marton have directed this race-of-hatred in what might be called "the Griffith tradition," with an acute sense of editing, natural sound, spectacular imagery, color, and movement. In the chariot race, the excitements of watching symbolic good (the white horses) and evil (the black horses, and spiked wheels) vie with one another, have the timeless melodramatic appeal which reaches audiences everywhere; the simple universal conflict pulls the spectator *into* the action, with the dust of the arena, the roar of chariot wheels and of the crowd. A visual moment of inspired cinema occurs, too, when Ben-Hur drives his victorious chariot past the mangled body of the defeated Messala. He looks back over his shoulder with the same helpless look of wonder that he had earlier directed toward Christ—the horses rear and pull at the reins, Messala rolls bloodily in the dust toward the camera, while beyond the tossing white manes Ben-Hur still stares down; then, suddenly, the horses pull his chariot away. The film achieves something wonderful in these moments, so that most of the scenes of leprosy and religious affirmation which follow appear theatrical and lacking in spirit.

The entry of Ben-Hur into a deserted Judean marketplace is also unusually effective. Accompanied by his afflicted mother and sister, he discovers only a few townspeople running to Pilate's villa to witness Christ's trial. One gets here, briefly, some indication of ingenuity of imagination, and feels that this incident might possibly have occurred in this manner, but the subsequent views of the trial and the "via crucis" are cinema mythology again, complete with thunderstorm-and-miracle.

Albert Johnson. *Film Quarterly*. Spring 1960, pp. 45–46

Come and Get It is the quintessence of what is most American during the period between the wars: the timber-cutting scenes, the virility of Edward Arnold and Joel MacCrea, the charm of the turn of the century saloons, the ambiguous seduction of Francis Farmer, playing a double role, the life of an American society living in comfort and refinement. There is certainly much of Wyler in all this since we find the principle characteristics again in *Jezebel*, which is structured like a tragedy by Racine. What Wyler totally lacked in *Wuthering Heights*, whose staleness announced the academicism of recent years, he totally succeeded with in this film, which was freed—perhaps by John Huston's adaptation—from its theatrical moorings and which remained within its historical framework thanks to the clash of the characters, its cast. . . . It is somewhat of a condensation of all American production from 1930 to 1940.

Come and Get It and *Jezebel* nevertheless are specimens of that theatrical vein that weighed down on most of Wyler's films from 1940 to 1960. When he was able to handle and surmount this theatricality —with the help of Gregg Toland—he provided interesting works. But it would seem that the worm was in the fruit from the beginning, as very quickly, with *The Letter* and *Mrs. Miniver* and *Detective Story*, the heavy and static side of his direction emphasized the coldness that seemed to be the fault of this skillful artisan—too skillful. . . .

Henri Agel. *Romance Américaine* (Editions du Cerf, 1963), p. 54

[*The Collector*] is a very skillful, even artful, tale of a deranged man's weird action, and it does contain also some of the social facts: resentment, defensiveness, inability of the classes to communicate. But it makes important changes. It turns the girl into someone at times much too defensive, and thus, by implication, rather too guilty; it eliminates tellingly dreary details that evoke the Clegg world in all its grubbiness and sterility; it makes Clegg not only pathetic, which he is in the book, but also sympathetic—even his impotence is fudged over, and, most important, it does not connect Clegg's psychic aberrancy with his social background: it shies away from the central accusation, the basic allegory, the coming to power of the petty bourgeoisie as the death of the finer aspects of man.

Consider some typical changes. In the book, much is made of Clegg's garish taste in furniture, clothes, art. Miranda has to smash some awful plaster ducks with which his fine 1623 house is decorated; she can't bear to put on the dresses he buys for her; she cannot begin to make him understand about painting and literature. In the film, the furniture and clothes are just slightly off (clever work by the art director, John

Stoll)—no plaster ducks!—and Clegg's arguments against *The Catcher in the Rye* and a Picasso reproduction emerge rather too convincing. Could it be that the director, William Wyler, was eager not to offend an audience who liked his *Ben Hur* and *The Best Years of Our Lives*, and who, no doubt, also likes plaster ducks? Does Wyler himself have a taste for them? [1965]

John Simon. *Private Screenings* (Macmillan, 1967), pp. 164–65

In America, William Wyler's *Mrs. Miniver* was considered the best dramatic film with a war background. But in Europe, even though it arrived preceded by considerable fame based mostly on the usual shower of Oscars, the movie had only a good commercial success. In truth, the excessive melodrama of the subject and a tiresome rhetoric could not be compensated for on the artistic plane by the convincing interpretations of Greer Garson and Walter Pidgeon.

Lino Lionello Ghirardini. *Il cinema e la guerra* (Maccari, 1965), pp. 218–19

Counsellor-at-Law. John Barrymore seems an unlikely choice for the ghetto-born lawyer of Elmer Rice's play, but this is one of the few screen roles that reveal his measure as an actor; his fabulous "presence" is apparent in every scene; so are his restraint, his humor, and his zest. The material is a success-story-with heartbreak, a typical American well-made play—energetic, naive, melodramatic, and rather touchingly goodhearted. The 1933 production has by now the patina of a period piece, and what a good movie period it was, full of gold-diggers, social climbers, dedicated radicals, etc. William Wyler directed, and despite his later reputation for such "polished" works as *The Little Foxes*, *The Best Years of Our Lives*, *Roman Holiday*, *The Desperate Hours*, etc., I prefer this earlier Wyler, fresh from more than fifty two-reel Westerns, willing to tell his story simply. . . .

Pauline Kael. *Kiss Kiss Bang Bang* (Little, Brown, 1968), pp. 251–52

The film [*Funny Girl*] itself is rotten, but so was the Broadway show. The songs are mediocre, the book worse. (It's based, need I say, on the life of Fanny Brice.) William Wyler, a generally able director, has done his creakiest work here, full of slow sentimental dissolves and strained attempts to make like Minnelli and Donen (for instance, different stanzas of a song sung in different locales). As for the "straight" sequences, it's hard to believe that the man who controlled the hokum so beautifully in the last scene of *Roman Holiday* could have been so paralyzed by hokum here. Harry Stradling, whose camera ladled Technicolor gravy all over *My Fair Lady*, keeps ladling along. Omar Sharif plays Nicky Arnstein. What a performance! Isn't there enough trouble between Jews and Egyptians? [1968]

Stanley Kauffmann. *Figures of Light*
(Harper, 1971), p. 114

Dead End stands as a beautiful document of a nearly vanished consciousness in America. The realism of its tenements was self-conscious, but the concern in the film with social issues was genuine. The film's opening shots—a panoramic sweep of New York City gradually focussing on the river-front slum and its neighboring high rental buildings—was visually striking and to the point. As the camera moved to a close shot of the slum, the realism aimed at by the theatre of Elmer Rice and Clifford Odets came briefly alive on screen: we have common people on an average day. The celebration in the thirties of the common man's tribulations, made dramatic by economic deprivation and stagey by social consciousness, was preserved in part, in *Dead End*.

Andrew Bergman. *We're in the Money*
(NYU, 1971), p. 153

ZINNEMANN, FRED (1907–)

One dries his eyes after *The Search*, but realizes he has seen no ordinary tear-jerker. The film is a profound emotional experience, obviously planned on a high intellectual level, yet somehow not calculated. Despite patent mechanisms of melodrama, *The Search* is so deeply moving as to make criticism and analysis difficult, and perhaps even superfluous. The spectator is too completely caught up by the anguish of the people on the screen to deny them their happy ending. Any other denouement would be crueler to the audience than to the characters themselves.

This is the story of the displaced persons in Europe; the time is now. The early part of the film approaches pure documentary as it describes the routine of UNRAA personnel in dealing with these cases. An off-screen voice—the documentary commentator—explains and expands what the pictures tell us. Then gradually the film's content narrows down to the case of one boy, ten-year-old Karel Malik, and his search for his mother. The documentary sense of reality is maintained; Karel's story may be based on fact. But now the facts are dramatized, personalized and, through the skill of the director, made far more real, more immediate, more meaningful. Eventually the boy does find his mother, which is perhaps the way it should be in fiction. But through that fiction we have the reality of post-war Europe forced home to us; fiction here becomes less a sugar-coating than an emotionalization of that reality.

The technique of *The Search* is very similar to that of Lazar Wechsler's earlier film, *The Last Chance*. Photographing in the American Occupied Zone in Germany, he has again played his story against its authentic background. Metro-Goldwyn-Mayer, which financed *The Search*, added to his company its own director, Fred Zinnemann. An Austrian, he had worked in this country on documentary films; his most notable Hollywood production was *The Seventh Cross*. Happily, Zinnemann seems to have been in complete sympathy with Wechsler's objectives. To him no doubt belongs the credit for the sense of authenticity in the performances.

NBR. April 1948, p. 4

The Men plunges without preliminaries into the heart of its subject and disdains the use of a single flashback. Advancing soldiers are cross-cut into the credit titles while a drum beats on the sound-track. An officer signals them on, a gun rattles: the wounded officer, groaning on the earth, dissolves into the same man lying on a hospital bed in America, hopeless, bitter, crushed—a paraplegic. Zinnemann then cuts to another room in the hospital (which specialises exclusively in the treatment of paraplegics) where the wives and girls of the patients (among them the officer's girl, Teresa Wright) are being informed by the principal doctor (Everett Sloane) that their men, paralysed from the waist down, are as helpless as babies and will have to be trained anew in the primary physical functions. They will also, he informs them, with the rarest of exceptions, be impotent. . . .

Such is the bald story of a remarkable film which explores the relationships of a number of human beings living in circumstances of unusual tension and stress, while affording a dramatically realistic view of the mechanics of their existence. Most of the men are played by actual paraplegics and the film is dedicated to them. The key parts are played by professionals who, with Marlon Brando, gave a good deal of study to the behaviour of paraplegics in the leading U.S. hospital for that affliction. Zinnemann's authority with the non-professional players is expectedly flawless and it is only with his main characters that a literary note is occasionally detected, sometimes in cross-talk between the men, and in an odd scene or so. Zinnemann's refusal to make concessions is exemplified in the scene between Ellen and her well-meaning, un-understanding, common-sense parents, as in the wedding night quarrel: situations that would have fatally trapped most Hollywood directors.

This is not to depreciate the powers of the hospital sequences where the slow process of readjustment is harassed by treacherous hopes, sudden inexplicable physical collapses and occasional tragic ventures into the world of women, moments when the bravado to which the men cling deserts them. . . .

The Men was produced under Stanley Kramer's method of exhaustive preliminary rehearsal before shooting, the reward of which is to be seen in a pre-cutting tautness that pays compliments to Carl Foreman's writing (aside from his virile dialogue) as well as to Zinnemann's direction. We must make the most of *The Men* for, as with any other honest statement about war and its effects, the net outcome is pacifist. And that is a courageous thing to-day. [1950]

Richard Winnington in *Shots in the Dark*, edited by E. C. Ansley and others (Allan Wingate, 1951), pp. 246–47

[W]hile working as a script clerk in Hollywood, Zinnemann was offered the directorial assignment on a picture to be shot entirely in Mexico, *The Wave*. Its producer and cameraman was the great American photographer, Paul Strand.

One of the earliest of the semidocumentary films, *The Wave* described the revolt of Mexican fishermen against intolerable working conditions. Its cast was made up almost entirely of non-professionals; the story was elementary in the extreme. The particular effectiveness of *The Wave* lay in Paul Strand's magnificent photography and Zinnemann's use of non-actors acting out events that might have happened to them in their native environment. *The Wave* represented an approach to film-making that Zinnemann would return to again and again. . . .

Like *The Wave* and *The Search*, *The Men* was also made on the spot, much of it being shot in the Birmingham Veterans' Hospital. In these sequences—the most significant and memorable in the picture—Zinnemann succeeded in moving professional actors in among the patients. His naturalistic style of directing made it impossible to say which were actors, which nonactors. And since Zinnemann prefers to choose unfamiliar film faces for his professionals, Marlon Brando, Jack Webb, Richard Erdman, Arthur Gurado and the others were able to be unobtrusive amid the real casualties of war that surrounded them. No great star's face impairs the authenticity of these hospital scenes.

Films in Review. Jan. 1951, pp. 22–23

The director of *High Noon* is Fred Zinnemann, who might be strong enough for that job. At any rate, he has put this picture together with authority. He works here in what approximates real time (the story runs from a little before eleven to noon; the picture runs for about an hour and forty minutes), which means that he can waste little time on indecision or incidentals.

Zinnemann puts the narrative together from a series of crisp and purposeful scenes that interpret one another like the pins on a strategist's war map. No one bats an eye or rubs an elbow in *High Noon* unless the gesture contributes to the story. The director permits his cameraman a few rather mannered shots of the excellent 1870 frontier-town set, and he is a little too fond of moments so "pregnant with meaning" that all motion is suspended; otherwise his work is impressively unpretentious. The dialogue is sensible; the music, primarily a lugubrious ballad, is appropriate and only occasionally takes the action over from the performers—a vice now most common in Hollywood.

Those, then, are the excellences of *High Noon*, and they are sufficient to make the picture celebrated. But they are all technical. For a movie to be really superior, its content must be taken seriously, and on the level of ideas *High Noon* presents another face.

Robert L. Hatch. *Reporter*. Sept. 16, 1952, p. 38

Carson McCullers' [*The Member of the Wedding*] has reached the screen via a successful Broadway stage adaptation. Whether a satisfactory film could have been made of it seems doubtful—so much here depends on the suggestion of the lonely child's state of mind, of which her outbursts of rage, self-pity and self-condemnation are only the momentary reflection. But if the attempt was to be made, one wishes that the stage version had been by-passed. Apart from Frankie's abortive running away, the action confines itself almost entirely to the single kitchen set, and the all-important atmosphere of the small, stifling Southern town in summer is consequently missing. We are left with a close-up view of Frankie—literally so, since Fred Zinnemann, presumably attempting a sense of intimacy with the characters, uses the close-up to such an extent that, as a dramatic device, it becomes almost meaningless. . . .

This is essentially an actor's film, and Fred Zinnemann, for whom it is something of a departure, has focused attention almost entirely on the players. He adroitly keeps the action moving in the confined set, but he does not bring much of his own personality to the film, and the result is more than a little flat. *The Member of the Wedding* is a failure to be regretted, since it marks another imaginative attempt by the Stanley Kramer Company to venture into unfamiliar, and from the box-office viewpoint possibly dangerous, territory.

BFI Bulletin. April 1953, p. 48

A few years ago, *The Men* and *Teresa* established Fred Zinnemann as the most vital new director in post-war Hollywood. His work was distinguished by adult, sensitive characterisation and by soberly authentic portrayals of the contemporary American scene. Making his films on a small scale and with little-known or non-professional players, Zinnemann managed to dramatise post-war "problem" situations without glibness or sentimentality. He became an acute and accurate reporter, whose films, made in a mood of rueful urgency, seemed to demand sympathy and understanding of their heroes' problems. Without conventional happy endings, these films closed on a hopeful note and implied—without the glibness that a bald statement of their intentions might suggest—that the problems they raised could be met by personal courage and good will.

From Here to Eternity, in which Zinnemann returns to a war theme after an interval of two years, is made in a very different mood. . . .

This is not a theme that one would expect Zinnemann to approach in the hopeful, sympathetic mood of his earlier films; but neither could one expect the negative shrug of indifference with which he seems to have surrendered to its hysteria. He commits himself to no statement of attitude towards his material and supplies only a kind of opportunist's slickness. The tension is piled up in a series of crescendo scenes, each played at full emotional blast, and only isolated moments of rest—the singing of the blues, Clift's impromptu trumpet solo in the bar—really come alive. For the rest, everything is hard, disillusioned, boringly *blasé* in the suggestion that the film's melodramatics present life as it is lived and that one might as well accept it. Only the character of Prewitt—the independent though loyal private who suffers beatings and humiliations without bitterness and retains his devotion to the army—is shown in any depth. One sees vaguely that the director may have seen Prewitt's situation as a reflection of the impasse in which the independent citizen is placed by present-day political America. But the character is too negative to embody any significant attitude, too involved in the plot's arbitrary melodramatic twists to have any wider validity. Montgomery Clift, though miscast, plays him with his customary intelligence and is well supported by Deborah Kerr—unexpectedly at ease as a sexy blonde—Frank Sinatra, Burt Lancaster and Donna Reed. But, good though much of the acting is, and well though isolated sequences are realised, one never really believes in the world the film depicts. Zinnemann seems much happier with less established players and with simpler, less pretentious stories; and he needs a subject he can believe in.

Karel Reisz. *Sight & Sound*. March 1954, pp. 145–46

Not only is this film a major directorial achievement in the career of Fred Zinnemann, but *The Nun's Story* is the best study of religious life ever made in the American cinema. A masterpiece of semidocumentary and character revelation, it covers a period of almost two decades in the life of a young Belgian girl who enters a convent and its atmosphere of interior silence and self-sacrifice. . . .

The entire film exhibits a warmth of cinematic approach and intimate attentiveness to character-detail and background not found to such a complete degree in a Zinnemann film since *The Member of the Wedding*. In all of his works, there has been some touch of documentary, and here, it is particularly discernible in the Brussels madhouse, where violent patients shriek from steaming tubs while a nun sits patiently attending them, and in the film's observations of the native population in the Congo. The sweeping rivers and sounds of Africa, and an amusing sequence showing some native children watching a Christmas service, are impressively contrasted to the autumnal disciplines of the European world.

The leisurely pacing of the film is part of a respectful labor of love, and, surprisingly, only the wartime sequences seem oddly ineffectual. However, this section of the picture is utilized chiefly to further emphasize Sister Luke's growing inability to ignore the impulses of the outside world, and the difficulties of showing the introverted personalities of nuns are managed by astute implication and understatement most of the time, with even the smallest roles brilliantly etched by such performers as Mildred Dunnock, Patricia Collinge, Margaret Phillips and Patricia Bosworth.

Albert Johnson. *Film Quarterly*. Winter 1958, pp. 57–58

Member of the Wedding, which demanded the ultimate in sensitivity, if its stage values were to be preserved, escaped from his [Zinnemann's] grasp. He was handicapped by the necessity to use a patently too mature Julie Harris for the role of Frankie, and perhaps by Stanley Kramer's insistence on artificial studio sets. Artificiality (not helped by the close-ups of Miss Harris) was what was achieved, and yet, analyzed scene by scene, it was difficult to see where he went wrong. The film is more valuable now as a record of the Julie Harris stage performance, and the play itself, and Zinnemann deserves commendation for putting so fragile a work on the screen.

He was forced to use the cumbersom Todd-AO process for *Oklahoma*, and either demonstrated a lack of affinity for the musical form or was hampered by the presences of Rodgers and Hammerstein, as well as an uncongenial cast that included Rod Steiger, Gloria Grahame, and Shirley Jones. The zest needed for the piece was missing, pictorially fetching as the film turned out to be in some of its moments. The sound track blared out the tunes too stridently, and in some of Zinnemann's films one receives the impression that the accompanying musical score is not under his supervision, and is added as underscoring to what is felt might be too delicate for mass consumption.

Hollis Alpert. *The Dream and the Dreamers* (Macmillan, 1962), p. 159

If Wilder is the American screen's reigning social commentator, Fred Zinnemann is, currently, its finest pictorialist. There is a rightness, even an inevitability, about his choice of shots and his editing which mark him as a sensitive worker, without pretense of afflatus. Beginning with *The Search*, in 1948, he has made a series of understated, perfectly toned films, focusing quietly on the needs of the individual in a mass society that is constantly threatening to him. His best works, *The Men*, *From Here to Eternity*, *High Noon*, *A Hatful of Rain*, *The Nun's Story*, and even *The Sundowners* have been unblinking studies in threatened integrity; his greatest virtue has been his ability to place his protagonists in a carefully realized social context without letting it overwhelm them or him.

Richard Schickel. *Movies* (Basic, 1964), p. 185

I turn with relief to *A Man for All Seasons,* which may not be a film for all seasons, but certainly is a godsend in this particularly impoverished one. I have written a good deal elsewhere (*The Hudson Review, Theatre Arts*) about this commendable but somewhat less than considerable play; in adapting his work for the screen, Robert Bolt once again both idealized and oversimplified Thomas More, who was, at times, both more religiously fanatical and broadly facetious than Bolt's protagonist. By giving us such a flawless man, Bolt gives us a flawed play and film. From the film, moreover, some of the play's strongest or wittiest lines have been excised. . . .

But I digress. *A Man for All Seasons* suffers from the usual ills that plague a play adapted to the screen. Neither Bolt, nor his director, Fred Zinnemann, was able to do much about that. The outdoor scenes always have that feel of, "Oh, yes, that was thrown in to make it more of a movie!" about them, and Zinnemann's direction is decent but plodding. When, in the trial scene, the camera shuttles swiftly across the faces of the spectators, it seems rather as if Zinnemann had suddenly remembered that he had forgotten to put the art taint in. One device, though, is effective. A bird in a tree sings against a delicate pale blue sky. Cut to More and the headsman on the scaffold, against the same sky. But one bird does not make a summer, to say nothing of all seasons. [1966]

John Simon. *Private Screenings* (Macmillan, 1967), pp. 262–63

Perhaps I was a reviewer of little faith in producer-director Fred Zinnemann during the first twenty minutes of *A Man for All Seasons.* We are shown scenes of extraordinary beauty in the lovely color photography of Ted Moore, scenes that have the quality of a magnificent pageant as Cardinal Wolsey's letter is taken by messenger on the Thames from Hampton Court to Sir Thomas More's manor in Chelsea. And at the manor we are introduced in a merry family gathering to More, his wife and daughter, his good friend the Duke of Norfolk, the job-seeking young Richard Rich, and several others including Matthew the household steward. The Cardinal's letter is a summons to come at once. And we make the return trip, gliding on the Thames in the attractive scenery to Hampton Court where Wolsey (made enormously fat as Orson Welles fills the screen in his handsome scarlet robe) expresses his displeasure with More for More's unwillingness, flat refusal, in fact, to intercede with the Pope to declare King Henry's marriage to Catherine null. The argument ends in a stalemate; but we know Wolsey will fight for Henry VIII who wants to marry his mistress, Anne Boleyn; and we know Thomas More is a man of high principle who will follow his conscience. And then once again we are rowed on the Thames in all that pretty, colorful scenery—back to the Chelsea manor where the stern Catholic father refuses to allow William Roper to marry Margaret More if Will continues his heretical beliefs.

Along about this time I was convinced that Fred Zinnemann was turning Robert Bolt's thoughtful stage play into an elaborate pageant about sixteenth-century England. I was wrong of course; and I should have realized that the maker of such outstanding films as *The Search, The Men, High Noon, From Here to Eternity, The Nun's Story, The Sundowners,* and others was a man of high purpose and integrity and was more interested in the drama of people than in easy though handsome spectacle. Quite rightly in his direction of *A Man for All Seasons,* Zinnemann is taking his time and setting the stage for the circumstance and inner drama that is to come, a drama that is not so much a conflict between King Henry who divorces Catherine, marries Anne, and makes himself head of the Church in England, and Thomas More who refuses to swear to the Act of Succession, as it is a drama about a man's conscience. Perhaps because Zinnemann develops this drama so slowly and carefully, it becomes all the more forceful when it gets to its final scenes in the Tower, at the trial and on the scaffold.

Philip T. Hartung. *Commonweal.*
Dec. 23, 1966, p. 349

High Noon. It could be, as some film enthusiasts tell us, a poem of force comparable to the *Iliad.* On the other hand, it might be a portentous account of what the reviewers called "a moment of crisis" for a little cow town. Gary Cooper is the marshal who fights alone for law and order when the town is paralyzed by fear. Much has been made of the film's structure: it runs from 10:40 A.M. to high noon (coinciding with the running time of the film); of the stark settings and the long shadows; of the screen writer Carl Foreman's build-up of suspense and his psychological insights. I'm inclined to think his insights are primer sociology passing from dramatic motive, that the town's cowardice is Q.E.D. . . . and that the Western form is being used for a sneak civics lesson. Given this hokum for what it is, it's good, and Fred Zinnemann's direction is excellent. . . .

Pauline Kael. *Kiss Kiss Bang Bang*
(Little, Brown, 1968), pp. 280–81

In all fairness to Zinnemann, his direction is about as effectively expert here as it was ineffectively expert in *Behold a Pale Horse.* Every frame is etched and chiseled in terms of the most precise placement of characters, colors, costumes, and period decor. As an academic exercise, *A Man for All Seasons* will probably be snapped up by the 16-millimeter catalogues unless there are purists who still object to filmed stage plays. The film will probably look better in 16-millimeter. Zinnemann avoids close-ups and sweeping camera movements like the plague, and some of his imagery with stone lions evokes Eisenstein's *October.* On the whole, Zinnemann's visual style is recessive in that everyone is always seen at a safe distance. I don't like this style particularly. It's safe, tactful, and tentative for a director who doesn't want to get too involved with his characters. Yet it is probably wise for this project. Scofield and Bolt don't really take close-ups. They lack feeling and empathy. Scofield is a virtuoso on the stage, where the dry inflections of his voice can ripple across the footlights with layers and layers of expressive irony and biting cynicism. When you look at his face on the screen, however, you get a guilty desire to look somewhere else. . . .

Andrew Sarris. *Confessions of a Cultist*
(S&S, 1970), p. 279

FILMOGRAPHIES

Frank Borzage (1893–1961)

Flying Colors (1918); *Until They Get Me* (1918); *The Gun Woman* (1918); *Shoes That Danced* (1918); *Innocents' Progress* (1918); *Society for Sale* (1918); *An Honest Man* (1918); *Who Is to Blame?* (1918); *The Ghost Flower* (1918); *The Curse of Iku* (1918); *Toton* (1919); *Prudence of Broadway* (1919); *Whom the Gods Destroy* (1919); *Humoresque* (1920); *The Duke of Chimney Butte* (1921); *Get Rich Quick Wallingford* (1922); *Bank Day* (1922); *Silent Shelby* (1922); *Billy Jim* (1922); *The Good Provider* (1922); *Valley of Silent Men* (1922); *The Pride of Palomar* (1922); *Children of Dust* (1923); *Nth Commandment* (1923); *Song of Love* (1923); *The Age of Desire* (1924); *Secrets* (1924); *The Lady* (1925); *Daddy's Gone a' Huntin'* (1925); *Wages for Wives* (1925); *The Circle* (1925); *Lazybones* (1925); *Marriage License* (1926); *The First Year* (1926); *The Dixie Merchant* (1926); *Early to Wed* (1926); *Seventh Heaven* (1927); *Street Angel* (1928); *The River* (1929); *Lucky Star* (1929); *They Had to See Paris* (1929); *Song o' My Heart* (1930); *Liliom* (1930); *Bad Girl* (1931); *Doctors' Wives* (1931); *As Young As You Feel* (1931); *A Farewell to Arms* (1932); *After Tomorrow* (1932); *Young America* (1932); *A Man's Castle* (1933); *Secrets* (1933); *No Greater Glory* (1934); *Little Man What Now* (1934); *Flirtation Walk* (1934); *Living on Velvet* (1935); *Stranded* (1935); *Shipmates Forever* (1935); *Desire* (1936); *Hearts Divided* (1936); *History Is Made at Night* (1937); *Green Light* (1937); *The Big City* (1937); *Mannequin* (1937); *Three Comrades* (1938); *The Shining Hour* (1938); *Disputed Passage* (1939); *The Mortal Storm* (1940); *Strange Cargo* (1940); *Flight Command* (1940); *Smilin' Through* (1941); *The Vanishing Virginian* (1941); *Seven Sweethearts* (1942); *Stage-door Canteen* (1943); *His Butler's Sister* (1943); *Till We Meet Again* (1944); *The Spanish Main* (1945); *I've Always Loved You* (1946); *The Magnificent Doll* (1946); *That's My Man* (1947); *Moonrise* (1948); *China Doll* (1958); *The Big Fisherman* (1959)

Richard Brooks (1912–)

Crisis (1950); *The Light Touch* (1951); *Deadline U.S.A.* (1952); *Battle Circus* (1953); *Take the High Ground* (1953); *The Last Time I Saw Paris* (1954); *Blackboard Jungle* (1955); *The Last Hunt* (1956); *The Catered Affair* (1956); *Something of Value* (1957); *The Brothers Karamazov* (1958); *Cat on a Hot Tin Roof* (1958); *Elmer Gantry* (1960); *Sweet Bird of Youth* (1962); *Lord Jim* (1964); *The Professionals* (1966); *In Cold Blood* (1967)

Clarence Brown (1890–)

The Last of the Mohicans (with Jacques Tourneur—1920); *The Great Redeemer* (1920); *The Foolish Matron* (with Jacques Tourneur—1921); *The Light in the Dark* (1922); *Don't Marry for Money* (1923); *The Acquittal* (1923); *The Signal Tower* (1924); *Butterfly* (1924); *Smouldering Fires* (1925); *The Eagle* (1925); *The Goose Woman* (1925); *Kiki* (1926); *Flesh and the Devil* (1926); *The Trail of '98* (1928); *Woman of Affairs* (1929); *Wonder of Women* (1929); *Navy Blues* (1929); *Anna Christie* (1930); *Romance* (1930); *Inspiration* (1931); *A Free Soul* (1931); *Possessed* (1931); *Emma* (1932); *Letty Lynton: The Son-Daughter* (1932); *Looking Forward* (1933); *Night Flight* (1933); *Sadie McKee* (1934); *Chained* (1934); *Anna Karenina* (1935); *Ah, Wilderness!* (1935); *Wife Versus Secretary* (1936); *The Gorgeous Hussy* (1936); *Conquest* (1937); *Of Human Hearts* (1938); *Idiot's Delight* (1939); *The Rains Came* (1939); *Edison the Man* (1940); *Come Live with Me* (1941); *They Met in Bombay* (1941); *The Human Comedy* (1943); *The White Cliffs of Dover* (1944); *National Velvet* (1945); *The Yearling* (1946); *Song of Love* (1947); *Intruder in the Dust* (1949); *To Please a Lady* (1950); *Angels in the Outfield* (1951); *When in Rome* (1951); *Plymouth Adventure* (1952)

Tod Browning (1882–1962)

Which Woman (1918); *The Deciding Kiss* (1918); *The Eyes of Mystery* (1918); *Revenge* (1918); *The Legion of Death* (1918); *Unpainted Woman* (1919); *The Wicked Darling* (1919); *The Exquisite Thief* (1919); *Set Free* (1919); *Brazen Beauty* (1919); *Petal on the Current* (1919); *The Virgin of Stamboul* (1920); *Bonnie, Bonnie Lassie* (1920); *Outside the Law* (1921); *No Woman Knows* (1921);

The Wise Kid (1922); *Man under Cover* (1922); *Under Two Flags* (1922); *Drifting* (1923); *White Tiger* (1923); *The Day of Faith* (1923); *The Dangerous Flirt* (1924); *The Unholy Three* (1925); *The Mystic* (1925); *Dollar Down* (1925); *Silk Stocking Sal* (1925); *The Road to Mandalay* (1926); *The Black Bird* (1926); *The Show* (1927); *The Unknown* (1927); *London after Midnight* (1927); *Big City* (1928); *West of Zanzibar* (1928); *East Is East* (1929); *The Thirteenth Chair* (1929); *Paid* (1930); *Dracula* (1931); *The Iron Man* (1931); *Freaks* (1932); *Fast Workers* (1933); *Mark of the Vampire* (1935); *The Devil-Doll* (1936); *Miracles for Sale* (1939)

Frank Capra (1897–   )

The Strong Man (1926); *Tramp, Tramp, Tramp* (1926); *Long Pants* (1927); *For the Love of Mike* (1927); *That Certain Feeling* (1928); *So This Is Love* (1928); *The Matinee Idol* (1928); *The Way of the Strong* (1928); *Say It with Sables* (1928); *Submarine* (1928); *Power of the Press* (1928); *The Younger Generation* (1929); *The Donovan Affair* (1929); *Flight* (1929); *Ladies of Leisure* (1930); *Rain or Shine* (1930); *Dirigible* (1931); *The Miracle Woman* (1931); *Platinum Blonde* (1931); *Forbidden* (1932); *American Madness* (1932); *The Bitter Tea of General Yen* (1933); *Lady for a Day* (1933); *It Happened One Night* (1934); *Broadway Bill* (1934); *Mr. Deeds Goes to Town* (1936); *Lost Horizon* (1937); *You Can't Take It with You* (1938); *Mr. Smith Goes to Washington* (1939); *Meet John Doe* (1941); *Why We Fight* (World War II documentaries—1942–1945); *Arsenic and Old Lace* (1944); *It's a Wonderful Life* (1946); *State of the Union* (1948); *Riding High* (1950); *Here Comes the Groom* (1951); *A Hole in the Head* (1959); *A Pocketful of Miracles* (1961)

John Cassavetes (1929–   )

Shadows (1960); *Too Late Blues* (1962); *A Child Is Waiting* (1962); *Faces* (1968); *Husbands* (1969); *Minnie and Moskowitz* (1972)

Charles Chaplin (1889–   )

(Only those films actually directed by Chaplin are listed.)

Caught in a Cabaret (with Mabel Normand—1914); *Caught in the Rain* (1914); *A Busy Day* (1914); *The Fatal Mallet* (said to have been co-directed by Mabel Normand and Mack Sennett—1914); *Her Friend the Bandit* (with Mabel Normand—1914); *Mabel's Busy Day* (with Mabel Normand—1914); *Mabel's Married Life* (with Mabel Normand—1914); *Laughing Gas* (1914); *The Property Man* (1914); *The Face on the Barroom Floor* (1914); *Recreation* (1914); *The Masquerader* (1914); *His New Profession* (1914); *The Rounders* (1914); *The New Janitor* (1914); *Those Love Pangs* (1914); *Dough and Dynamite* (1914); *Gentlemen of Nerve* (1914); *His Musical Career* (1914); *His Trysting Place* (1914); *Getting Acquainted* (1914); *His Prehistoric Past* (1914); *His New Job* (1915); *A Night Out* (1915); *The Champion* (1915); *In the Park* (1915); *A Jitney Elopement* (1915); *The Tramp* (1915); *By the Sea* (1915); *Work* (1915); *A Woman* (1915); *The Bank* (1915); *Shanghaied* (1915); *A Night in the Show* (1915); *Charlie Chaplin's Burlesque on Carmen* (1915); *Police* (1916); *The Floorwalker* (1916); *The Fireman* (1916); *The Vagabond* (1916); *One A.M.* (1916); *The Count* (1916); *The Pawnshop* (1916); *Behind the Screen* (1916); *The Rink* (1916); *Easy Street* (1917); *The Cure* (1917); *The Immigrant* (1917); *The Adventurer* (1917); *A Dog's Life* (1918); *The Bond* (1918); *Triple Trouble* (from an unfinished work called *Life*—1918); *Shoulder Arms* (1918); *Sunnyside* (1919); *A Day's Pleasure* (1919); *The Kid* (1921); *The Idle Class* (1921); *Pay Day* (1922); *The Pilgrim* (1923); *A Woman of Paris* (originally titled *Public Opinion*—1923); *The Gold Rush* (1925); *The Circus* (1928); *City Lights* (1931); *Modern Times* (1936); *The Great Dictator* (1940); *Monsieur Verdoux* (1947); *Limelight* (1942); *A King in New York* (1957); *The Countess from Hong Kong* (1967)

James Cruze (1884–1942)

Too Many Millions (1918); *Valley of the Giants* (1919); *Roaring Road* (1919); *The Dub* (1919); *Alias Mike Morgan* (1919); *You're Fired* (1919); *Love Burglar* (1919); *Hawthorne of the U.S.A.* (1920); *The Lottery Man* (1920); *Mrs. Temple's Telegram* (1920); *An Adventure in Hearts* (1920); *Terror Island* (1920); *What Happened to Jones* (1920); *The Dollar a Year Man* (1921); *Food for Scandal* (1921); *Always Audacious* (1921); *Charm School* (1921); *A Full House* (1921); *Crazy to Marry* (1921); *One Glorious Day* (1922); *Is Matrimony a Failure?* (1922); *The Dictator* (1922); *The Old Homestead* (1922); *Thirty Days* (1922); *The Covered Wagon* (1923); *Hollywood* (1923); *Ruggles of Red Gap* (1923); *To the Ladies* (1923); *The Garden of Weeds* (1924); *The Fighting Coward* (1924); *The City that Never Sleeps* (1924); *The Enemy Sex* (1924); *Merton of the Movies*

(1924); *The Goose Hangs High* (1925); *Beggar on Horseback* (1925); *Welcome Home* (1925); *Marry Me* (1925); *The Pony Express* (1925); *Mannequin* (1926); *The Waiter from the Ritz* (1926); *Old Ironsides* (1926); *Marriage* (1926); *We're All Gamblers* (1927); *On to Reno* (1927); *The City* (1927); *Gone Wild* (1927); *Red Mark* (1928); *Excess Baggage* (1928); *Mating Call* (1928); *Man's Man* (1929); *Once a Gentleman* (1930); *The Great Gabbo* (1930); *She Got What She Wanted* (1930); *Salvation Nell* (1931); *Washington Merry-go-round* (1932); *If I Had a Million* (with King Vidor, Ernst Lubitsch, Norman Z. McLeod, Stephen S. Roberts, William A. Seiter, Norman Taurog, Bruce Humberstone—1932); *Sailor Be Good* (1933); *Race-track* (1933); *I Cover the Waterfront* (1933); *Mr. Skitch* (1933); *David Harum* (1934); *Their Big Moment* (1934); *Helldorado* (1935); *Two-fisted* (1935); *Sutter's Gold* (1936); *The Wrong Road* (1937); *Prison Nurse* (1938); *Gangs of New York* (1938); *Come on Leather-necks* (1938)

George Cukor (1899–)

Grumpy (with Cyril Gardner—1930); *Virtuous Sin* (with Louis Gasnier—1930); (*The Royal Family of Broadway* (with Cyril Gardner —1930); *Tarnished Lady* (1931); *Girls About Town* (1931); *One Hour with You* (with Ernst Lubitsch—1932); *What Price Hollywood?* (1932); *A Bill of Divorcement* (1932); *Rockabye* (1932); *Our Betters* (1933); *Dinner at Eight* (1933); *Little Women* (1933); *David Copperfield* (1935); *Sylvia Scarlet* (1935); *Romeo and Juliet* (1936); *Camille* (1936); *Holiday* (1938); *Zaza* (1939); *Gone with the Wind* (replaced by Sam Wood, then Victor Fleming—1939); *The Women* (1939); *Susan and God* (1940); *The Philadelphia Story* (1940); *A Woman's Face* (1941); *Two-faced Woman* (1941); *Her Cardboard Lover* (1942); *Keeper of the Flame* (1942); *Resistance and Ohm's Law* (documentary—1943); *Gaslight* (1944); *Winged Victory* (1944); *Desire Me* (codirector, uncredited—1946); *A Double Life* (1947); *Edward, My Son* (1948); *Adam's Rib* (1949); *A Life of Her Own* (1950); *Born Yesterday* (1950); *The Model and the Marriage Broker* (1951); *The Marrying Kind* (1951); *Pat and Mike* (1952); *The Actress* (1953); *It Should Happen to You* (1954); *A Star Is Born* (1954); *Bhowani Junction* (1956); *Les Girls* (1957); *Wild Is the Wind* (1957); *Song without End* (replaced the late Charles Vidor—1959); *Heller in Pink Tights* (1960); *Let's Make Love* (1960); *The Chapman Report* (1962); *My Fair Lady* (1964), *Justine* (1969); *Travels with My Aunt* (1972)

Michael Curtiz (1888–1962)

Good Time Charlie (1927); *The Moon of Israel* (1927); *Tenderloin* (1928); *The Glad Rag Doll* (1929); *Madonna of Avenue A* (1929); *The Gamblers* (1929); *Hearts in Exile* (1929); *Noah's Ark* (1929); *Mammy* (1930); *Under a Texas Moon* (1930); *The Matrimonial Bed* (1930); *A Soldier's Plaything* (1930); *Bright Lights* (1930); *River's End* (1930); *God's Gift to Women* (1931); *The Mad Genius* (1931); *The Woman from Monte Carlo* (1932); *The Strange Love of Molly Louvain* (1932); *Alias the Doctor* (1932); *Cabin in the Cotton* (with William Keighley—1932); *Doctor X* (1932); *20,000 Years in Sing Sing* (1933); *The Mystery of the Wax Museum* (1933); *The Keyhole* (1933); *Private Detective 62* (1933); *Goodbye Again* (1933); *The Kennel Murder Case* (1933); *Female* (1933); *Mandalay* (1934); *Jimmy the Gent* (1934); *The Key* (1934); *British Agent* (1934); *Black Fury* (1935); *The Case of the Curious Bride* (1935); *Captain Blood* (1935); *Little Big Shot* (1935); *Front Page Woman* (1935); *The Walking Dead* (1936); *The Charge of the Light Brigade* (1936); *Stolen Holiday* (1937); *Mountain Justice* (1937); *Kid Galahad* (1937); *The Perfect Specimen* (1937); *Gold Is Where You Find It* (1938); *Sons of Liberty* (1938); *The Adventures of Robin Hood* (with William Keighley—1938); *Four's a Crowd* (1938); *Four Daughters* (1938); *Angels with Dirty Faces* (1938); *Dodge City* (1939); *Daughters Courageous* (1939); *The Private Lives of Elizabeth and Essex* (1939); *Four Wives* (1939); *Virginia City* (1940); *The Sea Hawk* (1940); *Santa Fe Trail* (1940); *The Sea Wolf* (1941); *Dive Bomber* (1941); *Captains of the Clouds* (1942); *Yankee Doodle Dandy* (1942); *Casablanca* (1942); *Mission to Moscow* (1943); *This Is the Army* (1943); *Passage to Marseilles* (1944); *Janie* (1944); *Roughly Speaking* (1945); *Mildred Pierce* (1945); *Night and Day* (1946); *Life with Father* (1947); *The Unsuspected* (1947), *Romance on the High Seas* (1948); *My Dream Is Yours* (1949); *Flamingo Road* (1949); *The Lady Takes a Sailor* (1949); *The Breaking Point* (1950); *Bright Leaf* (1950); *Young Man with a Horn* (1950); *Force of Arms* (1951); *Jim Thorpe, All American* (1951); *I'll See You in My Dreams* (1952); *The Story of Will Rogers* (1952); *The Jazz Singer* (1952); *Trouble Along the Way* (1953); *The Boy from Oklahoma* (1954); *The Egyptian* (1954); *White Christmas* (1954); *We're No Angels* (1955); *The Vagabond King* (1956); *The Scarlet Hour* (1956); *The Best Things in Life Are Free* (1956); *The Helen Morgan Story* (1957); *King Creole* (1958); *The Proud Rebel* (1958); *The Hangman* (1959); *The Man in the Net* (1959); *A Breath of Scandal* (1959); *The Adventures of Huckleberry Finn* (1960); *Frances of Assisi* (1961); *The Comancheros* (1961)

Cecil B. De Mille (1881–1959)

The Squaw Man (1914); *The Call of the North* (1914); *The Virginian* (1914); *What's His Name* (1914); *The Man from Home* (1914); *Rose of the Rancho* (1914); *The Girl of the Golden West* (1915); *The Warrens of Virginia* (1915); *The Unafraid* (1915); *The Captive* (1915); *The Wild Goose Chase* (1915); *The Arab* (1915); *Chimmie Fadden* (1915); *Kindling* (1915); *Carmen* (1915); *Chimmie Fadden Out West* (1915); *The Cheat* (1915); *The Golden Chance* (1915); *Temptation* (1916); *The Trail of the Lonesome Pine* (1916); *The Heart of Nora Flynn* (1916); *Maria Rosa* (1916); *The Dream Girl* (1916); *Joan the Woman* (1917); *Romance of the Redwoods* (1917); *The Little American* (1917); *The Woman God Forgot* (1917); *The Devil Stone* (1917); *The Whispering Chorus* (1918); *Old Wives for New* (1918); *We Can't Have Everything* (1918); *Till I Come Back to You* (1918); *The Squaw Man* (1918); *Don't Change Your Husband* (1919); *For Better, for Worse* (1919); *Male and Female* (1919); *Why Change Your Wife?* (1920); *Something to Think About* (1920); *Forbidden Fruit* (1921); *The Affairs of Anatol* (1921); *Fool's Paradise* (1921); *Saturday Night* (1922); *Manslaughter* (1922); *Adam's Rib* (1923); *The Ten Commandments* (1923); *Triumph* (1924); *Feet of Clay* (1924); *The Golden Bed* (1925); *The Road to Yesterday* (1925); *The Volga Boatman* (1926); *The King of Kings* (1927); *The Godless Girl* (1929); *Dynamite* (1929); *Madame Satan* (1930); *The Squaw Man* (1931); *The Sign of the Cross* (1932); *This Day and Age* (1933); *Four Frightened People* (1934); *Cleopatra* (1934); *The Crusades* (1935); *The Plainsman* (1937); *The Buccaneer* (1938); *Union Pacific* (1939); *North West Mounted Police* (1940); *Reap the Wild Wind* (1942); *The Story of Dr. Wassell* (1944); *Unconquered* (1947); *Samson and Delilah* (1949); *The Greatest Show on Earth* (1952); *The Ten Commandments* (1956)

William Dieterle (1893–1973)

(American films only.)

The Last Flight (1931); *Her Majesty, Love* (1931); *Man Wanted* (1932); *Jewel Robbery* (1932); *The Crash* (1932); *Six Hours to Live* (1932); *Scarlet Dawn* (1932); *Lawyer Man* (1932); *Grand Slam* (1933); *Adorable* (1933); *Devils in Love* (1933); *Female* (1933); *From Headquarters* (1933); *Fashions of 1934* (with Busby Berkeley—1934); *Fog over Frisco* (1934); *Madame Du Barry* (1934); *The Firebird* (1934);

The Secret Bride (1935); *Dr. Socrates* (1935); *A Midsummer Night's Dream* (with Max Reinhardt—1935); *The Story of Louis Pasteur* (1935); *Concealment* (1935); *Men on Her Mind* (1935); *The White Angel* (1936); *Satan Met a Lady* (1936); *The Great O'Malley* (1937); *Another Dawn* (1937); *Life of Emile Zola* (1937); *Blockade* (1938); *Juarez* (1939); *Hunchback of Notre Dame* (1939); *The Story of Dr. Ehrlich's Magic Bullet* (1940); *A Dispatch from Reuters* (1940); *All That Money Can Buy* (1941); *Syncopation* (1942); *Tennessee Johnson* (1942); *Kismet* (1944); *I'll Be Seeing You* (1944); *Love Letters* (1945); *This Love of Ours* (1945); *The Searching Wind* (1946); *Duel in the Sun* (with King Vidor—1947); *The Accused* (1948); *Portrait of Jenny* (1948); *Rope of Sand* (1949); *Paid in Full* (1950); *Dark City* (1950); *September Affair* (1950); *Peking Express* (1951); *Red Mountain* (1951); *Boots Malone* (1952); *The Turning Point* (1952); *Salome* (1953); *Volcano* (1953); *Elephant Walk* (1954); *Joseph and His Brethren* (unreleased—1954); *Magic Fire* (1956); *The Loves of Omar Khayyam* (1957); *Friday the Thirteenth* (unreleased—1957); *John Paul Jones* (1959)

Allan Dwan (1885–   )

(The following list is only a partial one for the early years.)

Wildflower (1914); *The Straight Road* (1914); *A Girl of Yesterday* (1915); *Jordan Is a Hard Road* (1915); *The Pretty Sister of Jose* (1915); *The Dancing Girl* (1915); *David Harum* (1915); *Betty of Greystone* (1916); *The Habit of Happiness* (1916); *The Half-breed* (1916); *The Good Bad Man* (1916); *Manhattan Madness* (1916); *An Innocent Magdalene* (1916); *Panthea* (1917); *The Fighting Odds* (1917); *A Modern Musketeer* (1918); *Mr. Fix-it* (1918); *Bound in Morocco* (1918); *He Comes up Smiling* (1918); *Cheating Cheaters* (1919); *Soldiers of Fortune* (1919); *The Dark Star* (1919); *Getting Mary Married* (1919); *Luck of the Irish* (1920); *A Splendid Hazard* (1920); *The Forbidden Thing* (1920); *The Perfect Crime* (1921); *A Broken Doll* (1921); *In the Heart of a Fool* (1921); *The Scoffer* (1921); *The Sin of Martha Queed* (1922); *Superstition* (1922); *Robin Hood* (1922); *Zaza* (1923); *Glimpses of the Moon* (1923); *Lawful Larceny* (1923); *Big Brother* (1923); *Her Love Story* (1924); *Manhandled* (1924); *A Society Scandal* (1924); *The Wages of Virtue* (1924); *Argentine Love* (1924); *Night Life in New York* (1925); *Stage Struck* (1925); *Coast of Folly* (1925); *Sea Horses* (1926); *Padlocked* (1926); *Tin Gods* (1926); *Summer Bachelors* (1926); *The Music Master* (1927); *The Joy Girl* (1927); *East Side, West Side* (1927); *French Dressing* (1928); *Big Noise* (1928); *The Iron Mask*

(1929); *Tide of Empire* (1929); *Frozen Justice* (1929); *The Far Call* (1929); *South Sea Rose* (1929); *What a Widow!* (1930); *Man to Man* (1931); *Chances* (1931); *Wicked* (1931); *While Paris Sleeps* (1932); *Her First Affair* (1933); *Counsel's Opinion* (1933); *The Morning After* (1934); *Black Sheep* (1935); *Beauty's Daughter* (1935); *The Song and Dance Man* (1936); *Human Cargo* (1936); *High Tension* (1936); *Fifteen Maiden Lane* (1936); *Woman Wise* (1937); *That I May Live* (1937); *One Mile from Heaven* (1937); *Heidi* (1937); *Rebecca of Sunnybrook Farm* (1938); *Josette* (1938); *Suez* (1938); *The Three Musketeers* (1939); *The Gorilla* (1939); *Frontier Marshall* (1939); *Sailor's Lady* (1940); *Young People* (1940); *Trail of the Vigilantes* (1940); *Look Who's Laughing* (1941); *Rise and Shine* (1941); *Friendly Enemies* (1942); *Here We Go Again* (1942); *Around the World* (1943); *Abroad with Two Yanks* (1944); *Up in Mabel's Room* (1944); *Brewster's Millions* (1945); *Getting Gertie's Garter* (1945); *Rendezvous with Annie* (1946); *Calendar Girl* (1947); *Northwest Outpost* (1947); *Driftwood* (1947); *The Inside Story* (1948); *Angel in Exile* (with Philip Ford—1948); *Sands of Iwo Jima* (1949); *Surrender* (1950); *Belle Le Grand* (1951); *The Wild Blue Yonder* (1951); *I Dream of Jeannie* (1952); *Montana Belle* (1952); *The Woman They Almost Lynched* (1953); *Sweethearts on Parade* (1953); *Flight Nurse* (1953); *Silver Lode* (1954); *Cattle Queen of Montana* (1954); *Passion* (1954); *Escape to Burma* (1955); *Pearl of the South Pacific* (1955); *Tennessee's Partner* (1955); *Slightly Scarlet* (1956); *Hold Back the Night* (1956); *The River's Edge* (1957); *The Restless Breed* (1957); *Enchanted Island* (1958); *The Most Dangerous Man Alive* (1961)

Robert J. Flaherty (1884–1951)

Nanook of the North (1922); *Moana of the South Seas* (with Frances Hubbard Flaherty—1926); *The Pottery-Maker* (1925); *The Twenty-four Dollar Island* (1926–27); *White Shadows in the South Seas* (with W. S. Van Dyke—1928); *Tabu* (with F. W. Murnau—1929); *Industrial Britain* (with John Grierson—1933); *Man of Aran* (with Frances Hubbard Flaherty—1934); *Elephant Boy* (with Zoltan Korda; location direction only—1937); *The Land* (1941); *Louisiana Story* (1948)

Victor Fleming (1883–1949)

When the Clouds Roll By (1920); *The Mollycoddle* (1920); *Mamma's Affair* (1921); *Woman's Place* (1922); *Red Hot Romance* (1922); *Lane That Had No Turning* (1922); *Anna Ascends* (1922); *Dark*

Secrets (1923); *Law of the Lawless* (1923); *To the Last Man* (1923); *Call of the Canyon* (1923); *Empty Hands* (1924); *The Code of the Sea* (1924); *A Son of His Father* (1925); *Adventure* (1925); *The Devil's Cargo* (1925); *Lord Jim* (1925); *Blind Goddess* (1926); *Mantrap* (1926); *Rough Riders* (1927); *Way of All Flesh* (1927); *Hula* (1927); *Abie's Irish Rose* (1928); *The Awakening* (1928); *Wolf Song* (1929); *The Virginian* (1929); *Common Clay* (1930); *Renegades* (1930); *Around the World in 80 Minutes* (1931); *The Wet Parade* (1932); *Red Dust* (1932); *White Sister* (1933); *Bombshell* (1933); *Treasure Island* (1934); *Reckless* (1935); *The Farmer Takes a Wife* (1935); *Captains Courageous* (1937); *Test Pilot* (1938); *The Wizard of Oz* (1939); *Gone with the Wind* (replaced George Cukor and Sam Wood—1939); *Dr. Jekyll and Mr. Hyde* (1941); *Tortilla Flat* (1942); *A Guy Named Joe* (1943); *Adventure* (1945); *Joan of Arc* (1948)

John Ford (1895–1973)

(Only films actually directed by Ford. Early films released under name of Jack Ford.)

Lucille, the Waitress (1914); *The Tornado* (1917); *The Trail of Hate* (1917); *The Scraper* (1917); *The Soul Herder* (1917); *Cheyenne's Pal* (1917); *Straight Shooting* (1917); *The Secret Man* (1917); *A Marked Man* (1917); *Bucking Broadway* (1917); *The Phantom Riders* (1918); *Wild Women* (1918); *Thieves' Gold* (1918); *The Scarlet Drop* (1918); *Hell Bent* (1918); *Delirium* (1918); *A Woman's Fool* (1918); *Three Mounted Men* (1918); *Roped* (1919); *The Fighting Brothers* (1919); *Bare Fists* (1919); *A Fight for Love* (1919); *By Indian Post* (1919); *The Gun Packer* (1919); *Riders of Vengeance* (1919); *The Last Outlaw* (1919); *The Outcasts of Poker Flat* (1919); *The Ace of the Saddle* (1919); *The Rider of the Law* (1919); *A Gun Fightin' Gentleman* (1919); *Marked Men* (1919); *The Prince of Avenue A* (1920); *The Girl in No. 29* (1920); *Hitchin' Posts* (1920); *Just Pals* (1920); *The Big Punch* (1921); *The Freeze Out* (1921); *The Wallop* (1921); *Desperate Trails* (1921); *Action* (1921); *Sure Fire* (1921); *Jackie* (1921); *Little Miss Smiles* (1922); *Silver Wings* (with Edwin Carewe—1922); *The Village Blacksmith* (1922); *The Face on the Barroom Floor* (1923); *Three Jumps Ahead* (1923); *Cameo Kirby* (first film to use name *John* Ford—1923); *North of Hudson Bay* (1923); *Hoodman Blind* (1923); *The Iron Horse* (1924); *Hearts of Oak* (1924); *Lightnin'* (1925); *Kentucky Pride* (1925); *The Fighting Heart* (1925); *Thank You* (1925); *The Shamrock Handicap* (1926); *3 Bad Men* (1926); *The Blue Eagle* (1926); *Upstream* (1927); *Mother Machree*

(1928); *Four Sons* (1928); *Hangman's House* (1928); *Napoleon's Barber* (1928); *Riley the Cop* (1928); *Strong Boy* (1929); *The Black Watch* (1929); *Salute* (1929); *Men Without Women* (1930); *Born Reckless* (1930); *Up the River* (1930); *The Seas Beneath* (1931); *The Brat* (1931); *Arrowsmith* (1931); *Air Mail* (1932); *Flesh* (1932); *Pilgrimage* (1933); *Dr. Bull* (1933); *The Lost Patrol* (1934); *The World Moves On* (1934); *Judge Priest* (1934); *The Whole Town's Talking* (1935); *The Informer* (1935); *Steamboat 'Round the Bend* (1935); *The Prisoner of Shark Island* (1936); *Mary of Scotland* (1936); *The Plough and the Stars* (1936); *Wee Willie Winkie* (1937); *The Hurricane* (1937); *The Adventures of Marco Polo* (uncredited sequence—1938); *Four Men and a Prayer* (1938); *Submarine Patrol* (1938); *Stagecoach* (1939); *Young Mr. Lincoln* (1939); *Drums Along the Mohawk* (1939); *The Grapes of Wrath* (1940); *The Long Voyage Home* (1940); *Tobacco Road* (1941); *Sex Hygiene* (Army documentary—1941); *How Green Was My Valley* (1941); *The Battle of Midway* (Navy documentary—1942); *Torpedo Squadron* (1942); *December 7th* (Navy documentary—1943); *We Sail at Midnight* (Navy documentary—1943); *They Were Expendable* (with Robert Montgomery—1945); *My Darling Clementine* (1946); *The Fugitive* (with Emilio Fernandez—1947); *Fort Apache* (1948); *Three Godfathers* (1948); *She Wore a Yellow Ribbon* (1949); *When Willie Comes Marching Home* (1950); *Wagonmaster* (1950); *Rio Grande* (1950); *This Is Korea!* (Navy documentary—1951); *What Price Glory* (1952); *The Quiet Man* (1952); *The Sun Shines Bright* (1953); *Mogambo* (1953); *Hondo* (uncredited segment—1953); *The Long Gray Line* (1955); *Mister Roberts* (with Mervyn Le Roy—1955); *The Bamboo Cross* (1955); *Rookie of the Year* (1955); *The Searchers* (1956); *The Wings of Eagles* (1957); *The Rising of the Moon* (1957); *So Alone* (1958); *The Last Hurrah* (1958); *Gideon of Scotland Yard* (made in G. B.—1959); *Korea* (1959); *The Horse Soldiers* (1959); *The Colter Craven Story* (1960); *The Alamo* (with John Wayne—1960); *Sergeant Rutledge* (1960); *Two Rode Together* (1961); *The Man Who Shot Liberty Valance* (1962); *Flashing Spikes* (1962); *How the West Was Won* (Civil War sequence—1963); *Donovan's Reef* (1963); *Cheyenne Autumn* (1964); *Young Cassidy* (finished and signed by Jack Cardiff—1965); *Seven Women* (1966)

John Frankenheimer (1930–   )

The Young Stranger (1956); *The Young Savages* (1961); *Birdman of Alcatraz* (1962); *All Fall Down* (1962); *The Manchurian Candidate*

(1962); *The Train* (1963); *Seven Days in May* (1964); *Seconds* (1966); *Grand Prix* (replaced John Sturges—1967); *The Extraordinary Seaman* (1967); *The Fixer* (1968); *The Gypsy Moths* (1969); *The Horsemen* (1970); *The Iceman Cometh* (1973)

D. W. Griffith (1875–1948)

(The following list is only a partial one for the years from 1908 to 1914.)

The Adventures of Dollie (1908); *For the Love of Gold* (1908); *After Many Years* (1908); *The Taming of the Shrew* (1908); *The Song of the Shirt* (1908); *A Story of the Underworld* (1908); *Father Gets in the Game* (1908); *Edgar Allan Poe* (1909); *The Curtain Pole* (1909); *The Politician's Love Story* (1909); *The Voice of the Violin* (1909); *The Medicine Bottle* (1909); *The Drunkard's Reformation* (1909); *The Suicide Club* (1909); *Resurrection* (1909); *The Cricket on the Hearth* (1909); *What Drink Did* (1909); *The Violin Maker of Cremona* (1909); *The Lonely Villa* (1909); *Her First Biscuits* (1909); *A Convict's Sacrifice* (1909); *The Mended Lute* (1909); *The Sealed Room* (1909); *1776, or The Hessian Renegades* (1909); *In Old Kentucky* (1909); *Leather Stockings* (1909); *Pippa Passes* (1909); *A Change of Heart* (1909); *In the Watches of the Night* (1909); *Through the Breakers* (1909); *Lines of White on a Sullen Sea* (1909); *Nursing a Viper* (1909); *The Restoration* (1909); *The Light that Came* (1909); *The Red Man's View* (1909); *A Corner in Wheat* (1909); *In Old California* (1910); *As It Is In Life* (1910); *The Unchanging Sea* (1910); *Ramona* (1910); *The Thread Destiny* (1910); *In the Season of Buds* (1910); *A Child of the Ghetto* (1910); *The Face at the Window* (1910); *Muggsy's First Sweetheart* (1910); *The House with Closed Shutters* (1910); *The Usurer* (1910); *Rose o' Salem Town* (1910); *The Iconoclast* (1910); *That Chink at Golden Gulch* (1910); *The Message of the Violin* (1910); *Waiter No. 5* (1910); *The Lesson* (1910); *The Two Paths* (1911); *The Italian Barber* (1911); *His Trust* (1911); *His Trust Fulfilled* (1911); *The Manicure Lady* (1911); *What Shall We Do with Our Old* (1911); *Fisher Folk* (1911); *The Lily of the Tenements* (1911); *The Heart of a Savage* (1911); *A Decree of Destiny* (1911); *The Lonedale Operator* (1911); *The Spanish Gypsy* (1911); *Paradise Lost* (1911); *How She Triumphed* (1911); *Enoch Arden* (1911); *The Primal Call* (1911); *Fighting Blood* (1911); *The Last Drop of Water* (1911); *The Squaw's Love* (1911); *The Revenue Man and the Girl* (1911); *Her Awakening* (1911); *The Battle* (1911); *Through Darkened Vales* (1911); *The Miser's Heart* (1911); *The*

Failure (1911); *A Terrible Discovery* (1911); *For His Son* (1912); *A Mender of Nets* (1912); *The Goddess of Sagebrush Gulch* (1912); *A Girl and Her Trust* (1912); *The Female of the Species* (1912); *The Lesser Evil* (1912); *The Old Actor* (1912); *A Temporary Truce* (1912); *Lena and the Geese* (1912); *Man's Lust for Gold* (1912); *Man's Genesis* (1912); *The Sands of Dee* (1912); *A Change of Spirit* (1912); *A Pueblo Legend* (1912); *An Unseen Enemy* (1912); *A Feud in the Kentucky Hills* (1912); *The Musketeers of Pig Alley* (1912); *My Baby* (1912); *Friends* (1912); *The Massacre* (1912); *The New York Hat* (1912); *The God Within* (1912); *Greed* (1912); *The One She Loved* (1912); *A Child of the Ghetto* (1912); *Broken Ways* (1913); *The Sheriff's Baby* (1913); *The Mothering Heart* (1913); *The Battle at Elderbush Gulch* (1913); *Judith of Bethulia* (1913); *The Battle of the Sexes* (1913); *The Escape* (1914); *Home Sweet Home* (1914); *The Avenging Conscience* (1914); *The Birth of a Nation* (1915); *Intolerance* (1916); *Hearts of the World* (1918); *The Great Love* (1918); *The Greatest Thing in Life* (1918); *A Romance of Happy Valley* (1919); *The Girl Who Stayed at Home* (1919); *Broken Blossoms* (1919); *True Heart Susie* (1919); *The Fall of Babylon* (1919); *The Mother and the Law* (1919); *Scarlet Days* (1919); *The Greatest Question* (1919); *The Idol Dancer* (1920); *The Love Flower* (1920); *Way Down East* (1920); *Dream Street* (1921); *Orphans of the Storm* (1922); *One Exciting Night* (1922); *The White Rose* (1923); *America* (1924); *Isn't Life Wonderful?* (1924); *Sally of the Sawdust* (1925); *That Royle Girl* (1925); *Sorrows of Satan* (1926); *Drums of Love* (1928); *The Battle of the Sexes* (1928); *Lady of the Pavements* (1929); *Abraham Lincoln* (1930); *The Struggle* (1931)

Henry Hathaway (1898–)

Wild Horse Mesa (1933); *Heritage of the Desert* (1933); *Under the Tonto Rim* (1933); *Sunset Pass* (1933); *Man of the Forest* (1933); *To the Last Man* (1933); *Come on Marines* (1934); *The Last Round-up* (1934); *Thundering Herd* (1934); *The Witching Hour* (1934); *Now and Forever* (1934); *Lives of A Bengal Lancer* (1935); *Peter Ibbetson* (1935); *Trail of the Lonesome Pine* (1936); *Go West, Young Man* (1936); *Souls at Sea* (1937); *Spawn of the North* (1938); *The Real Glory* (1939); *Johnny Apollo* (1940); *Brigham Young* (1940); *The Shepherd of the Hills* (1941); *Sundown* (1941); *Ten Gentlemen from West Point* (1942); *China Girl* (1942); *Home in Indiana* (1944); *Wing and a Prayer* (1944); *Nob Hill* (1945); *The House on 92nd Street* (1945); *The Dark Corner* (1946); *13 rue Madeleine* (1946); *Kiss of*

Death (1947); *Call Northside 777* (1948); *Down to the Sea in Ships* (1949); *The Black Rose* (1950); *You're in the Navy Now* (1951); *Rawhide* (1951); *14 Hours* (1951); *The Desert Fox* (1951); *Diplomatic Courier* (1952); *Niagara* (1953); *White Witch Doctor* (1953); *Prince Valiant* (1954); *Garden of Evil* (1954); *The Racers* (1955); *The Bottom of the Bottle* (1956); *23 Paces to Baker Street* (1956); *Legend of the Lost* (1957); *From Hell to Texas* (1958); *Woman Obsessed* (1959); *Seven Thieves* (1960); *North to Alaska* (1960); *How the West Was Won* (with John Ford and George Marshall—1963); *Circus World* (1964); *The Sons of Katie Elder* (1965); *Nevada Smith* (1966); *The Last Safari* (1967); *5-Card Stud* (1968); *True Grit* (1969)

Howard Hawks (1896–)

The Road to Glory (1926); *Fig Leaves* (1926); *The Cradle Snatchers* (1927); *Paid to Love* (1927); *A Girl in Every Port* (1928); *Fazil* (1928); *The Air Circus* (1928); *Trent's Last Case* (1929); *The Dawn Patrol* (1930); *The Criminal Code* (1931); *The Crowd Roars* (1932); *Scarface* (also known as *Shame of a Nation*—1932); *Tiger Shark* (1932); *Today We Live* (1933); *Twentieth Century* (1934); *Viva Villa!* (completed and signed by Jack Conway—1934); *Barbary Coast* (1935); *Ceiling Zero* (1936); *The Road to Glory* (1936); *Come and Get It* (with William Wyler—1936); *Bringing Up Baby* (1938); *Only Angels Have Wings* (1939); *His Girl Friday* (1940); *The Outlaw* (uncredited, with Howard Hughes—1940); *Sergeant York* (1941); *Ball of Fire* (1941); *Air Force* (1943); *To Have and Have Not* (1944); *The Big Sleep* (1946); *Red River* (1948); *A Song Is Born* (1948); *I Was a Male War Bride* (also known as *You Can't Sleep Here*—1949); *The Big Sky* (1952); *Monkey Business* (1952); *O'Henry's Full House* ("The Ransom of Red Chief" episode—1952); *Gentlemen Prefer Blondes* (1953); *The Land of the Pharaohs* (1955); *Rio Bravo* (1959); *Hatari!* (1962); *Man's Favorite Sport?* (1964); *Red Line 7000* (1965); *El Dorado* (1967)

Alfred Hitchcock (1899–)

(Only films made after his arrival in U.S.)

Rebecca (1940); *Foreign Correspondent* (1940); *Mr. and Mrs. Smith* (1941); *Suspicion* (1941); *Saboteur* (1942); *Shadow of a Doubt* (1943); *Lifeboat* (1943); *Bon Voyage* (1944); *Adventure Malgache* (1944);

Spellbound (1945); *Notorious* (1946); *The Paradine Case* (1947); *Rope* (1948); *Under Capricorn* (1949); *Stage Fright* (1951); *Strangers on a Train* (1951); *I Confess* (1952); *Dial M for Murder* (1954); *Rear Window* (1954); *To Catch a Thief* (1955); *The Man Who Knew Too Much* (1955); *The Trouble with Harry* (1956); *The Wrong Man* (1957); *Vertigo* (1958); *North by Northwest* (1959); *Psycho* (1960); *The Birds* (1963); *Marnie* (1964); *Torn Curtain* (1966); *Topaz* (1969); *Frenzy* (made in G.B.—1969)

John Huston (1906–)

The Maltese Falcon (1941); *In This Our Life* (1942); *Across the Pacific* (1942); *Report from the Aleutians* (documentary—1942); *The Battle of San Pietro* (documentary—1944); *Let There Be Light* (documentary—1945); *The Treasure of the Sierra Madre* (1948); *Key Largo* (1948); *We Were Strangers* (1949); *The Asphalt Jungle* (1950); *The Red Badge of Courage* (1951); *The African Queen* (1952); *Moulin Rouge* (1953); *Beat the Devil* (1954); *Moby Dick* (1956); *A Farewell to Arms* (replaced by Charles Vidor—1957); *Heaven Knows, Mr. Allison* (1957); *The Barbarian and the Geisha* (1958); *The Roots of Heaven* (1958); *The Unforgiven* (1960); *The Misfits* (1961); *Freud* (1962); *The List of Adrian Messenger* (1963); *The Night of the Iguana* (1964); *The Bible* (1966); *Casino Royale* (David Niven footage only—1967); *Reflections in A Golden Eye* (1967); *Sinful Davey* (1969); *A Walk with Love and Death* (1969); *The Kremlin Letter* (1970); *Fat City* (1972)

Thomas H. Ince (1880–1924)

(Ince was a producer as well as a director, and there is no agreement as to which of the many films produced by his studio can be attributed to him.)

Their First Understanding (1910); *The New Cook* (1911); *Little Neils* (1911); *Tobacco* (1911); *The Silver Dollar* (1911); *The New Look* (1912); *Across the Plains* (1912); *The Deserter* (1912); *Soldier's Honor* (1912); *The Squaw* (1912); *A Woman of the East* (1912); *Shadow of the Past* (1912); *Custer's Last Fight* (1912); *Ambassador's Envoy* (1913); *Tongues of Flame* (1913); *Pride of the South* (1913); *Free and Equal* (1914); *The Bargain* (1914); *The Wrath of the Gods* (1914); *The Battle of Gettysburg* (1914); *Two-gun Hicks* (1914);

The Typhoon (1914); *The Gangsters and the Girl* (1914); *Painted Souls* (1914); *The Iron Strain* (1915); *The Despoiler* (1915); *The Italian* (1915); *The Coward* (1915); *Carmen of the Klondike* (1915); *Between Men* (1915); *The Three Musketeers* (1915); *Civilization* (1916); *The Fugitive* (1916); *The Aryan* (1916); *Primal Lure* (1916); *Honor's Altar* (1916); *Moral Fabric* (1916); *The Patriot* (1916); *The Dividend* (1916); *Payment* (1916); *Lieutenant Danny* (1916); *Flying Colors* (1917); *Until They Get Me* (1917); *The Clodhopper* (1917); *The Hired Man* (1918); *Blue Blazes Rawdon* (1918); *The Old Swimming Hole* (1921); *Human Wreckage* (1923)

Rex Ingram (1892–1969)

The Great Problem (1916); *His Robe of Honor* (1918); *Humdrum Brown* (1918); *Shore Acres* (1920); *Under Crimson Skies* (1920); *The Day She Paid* (1920); *The Four Horsemen of the Apocalypse* (1921); *Hearts Are Trumps* (1921); *The Conquering Power* (1921); *Turn to the Right* (1922); *The Prisoner of Zenda* (1922); *Trifling Women* (1922); *Where the Pavement Ends* (1923); *Scaramouche* (1923); *The Arab* (1924); *Mare Nostrum* (1926); *The Magician* (1926); *A Garden of Allah* (1927); *Three Passions* (1929); *Baroud* (made in North Africa—1932)

Elia Kazan (1909–)

It's Up to You (1941); *A Tree Grows in Brooklyn* (1945); *Boomerang!* (1947); *The Sea of Grass* (1947); *Gentleman's Agreement* (1947); *Pinky* (1949); *Panic in the Streets* (1950); *A Streetcar Named Desire* (1952); *Viva Zapata!* (1952); *Man on a Tightrope* (1952); *On the Waterfront* (1954); *East of Eden* (1955); *Baby Doll* (1956); *A Face in the Crowd* (1957); *Wild River* (1960); *Splendor in the Grass* (1961); *America America* (1964); *The Arrangement* (1969)

Buster Keaton (1895–1966)

(Only those films actually directed by Keaton.)

The High Sign (with Eddie Cline—1920); *One Week* (with Eddie Cline—1920); *Convict 13* (with Eddie Cline—1920); *The Scarecrow* (with Eddie Cline—1920); *Neighbors* (with Eddie Cline—1920); *The*

Haunted House (with Eddie Cline—1921); *Hard Luck* (with Eddie Cline—1921); *The Goat* (with Malcolm St. Clair—1921); *The Electric House* (with Eddie Cline; unfinished—1921); *The Playhouse* (with Eddie Cline—1921); *The Boat* (with Eddie Cline—1921); *The Paleface* (with Eddie Cline—1921); *Cops* (with Eddie Cline—1922); *My Wife's Relations* (with Eddie Cline—1922); *The Blacksmith* (with Malcolm St. Clair—1922); *The Frozen North* (with Eddie Cline—1922); *Daydreams* (with Eddie Cline—1922); *The Electric House* (with Eddie Cline—1922); *Balloonatics* (with Eddie Cline—1923); *The Love Nest* (with Eddie Cline—1923); *The Three Ages* (with Eddie Cline—1923); *Our Hospitality* (with Jack Blystone—1923); *Sherlock Junior* (1924); *The Navigator* (with Donald Crisp—1924); *Seven Chances* (1925); *Go West* (1925); *The Battling Butler* (1926); *The General* (with Clyde Bruckman—1926)

Henry King (1888–)

23½ Hours Leave (1919); *A Fugitive from Matrimony* (1919); *Haunting Shadows* (1919); *The White Dove* (1920); *Uncharted Channels* (1920); *One Hour Before Dawn* (1920); *Help Wanted—Male* (1920); *Dice of Destiny* (1920); *When We Were 21* (1921); *Mistress of Shenstone* (1921); *Salvage* (1921); *The Sting of the Lash* (1921); *Tol'able David* (1921); *The Seventh Day* (1922); *Sonny* (1922); *The Bond Boy* (1922); *Fury* (1922); *The White Sister* (1923); *Romola* (1924); *Sackcloth and Scarlet* (1925); *Any Woman* (1925); *Stella Dallas* (1925); *Partners* (1926); *The Winning of Barbara Worth* (1926); *The Magic Flame* (1927); *The Woman Disputed* (with Sam Taylor—1928); *She Goes to War* (1929); *Hell's Harbor* (1930); *Eyes of the World* (1930); *Lightnin'* (1930); *Merely Mary Ann* (1931); *Over the Hill* (1931); *The Woman in Room 13* (1932); *State Fair* (1933); *I Loved You Wednesday* (1933); *Carolina* (1934); *Marie Galante* (1934); *One More Spring* (1935); *Way Down East* (1935); *The Country Doctor* (1936); *Ramona* (1936); *Lloyds of London* (1937); *Seventh Heaven* (1937); *In Old Chicago* (1938); *Alexander's Ragtime Band* (1938); *Jesse James* (1939); *Stanley and Livingstone* (1939); *Little Old New York* (1940); *Maryland* (1940); *Chad Hanna* (1940); *A Yank in the RAF* (1941); *Remember the Day* (1941); *The Black Swan* (1942); *The Song of Bernadette* (1944); *Wilson* (1944); *A Bell for Adano* (1945); *Margie* (1946); *The Captain from Castille* (1947); *Deep Waters* (1948); *The Prince of Foxes* (1949); *Twelve O'clock High* (1950); *The Gunfighter* (1950); *I'd Climb the Highest Mountain*

(1951); *David and Bathsheba* (1952); *Wait till the Sun Shines Nellie* (1952); *O'Henry's Full House* ("The Gift of the Magi" episode—1952); *The Snows of Kilimanjaro* (1952); *King of the Khyber Rifles* (1954); *Untamed* (1955); *Love Is a Many-splendored Thing* (1955); *Carousel* (1956); *The Sun Also Rises* (1957); *The Bravados* (1958); *This Earth Is Mine* (1959); *Tender Is the Night* (1962)

Stanley Kramer (1913–)

Not As a Stranger (1954); *The Pride and the Passion* (1956); *The Defiant Ones* (1958); *On the Beach* (1959); *Inherit the Wind* (1960); *Judgment at Nuremberg* (1961); *It's a Mad Mad Mad World* (1963); *Ship of Fools* (1965); *Guess Who's Coming to Dinner* (1967); *The Secret of Santa Vittoria* (1969)

Stanley Kubrick (1928–)

Day of the Fight (documentary—1949); *The Flying Padre* (documentary—1951); *Fear and Desire* (1953); *Killer's Kiss* (1955); *The Killing* (1956); *Paths of Glory* (1957); *Spartacus* (1960); *Lolita* (1962); *Dr. Strangelove* (1964); *2001: A Space Odyssey* (1968); *Napoleon* (1971); *A Clockwork Orange* (1972)

Gregory La Cava (1892–1952)

The New Schoolteacher (1924); *Restless Wives* (1924); *Womanhandled* (1925); *Let's Get Married* (1926); *So's Your Old Man* (1926); *Say It Again* (1926); *Paradise for Two* (1927); *Running Wild* (1927); *Tell It to Sweeney* (1927); *The Gay Defender* (1928); *Feel My Pulse* (1928); *Half a Bride* (1928); *Saturday's Children* (1929); *Big News* (1929); *His First Command* (1930); *Laugh and Get Rich* (1931); *Smart Woman* (1931); *Symphony of Six Million* (1932); *Age of Consent* (1932); *The Half-naked Truth* (1932); *Gabriel over the White House* (1933); *The Affairs of Cellini* (1934); *What Every Woman Knows* (1934); *Private Worlds* (1935); *She Married Her Boss* (1935); *My Man Godfrey* (1936); *Stage Door* (1937); *Fifth Avenue Girl* (1939); *The Primrose Path* (1940); *Unfinished Business* (1941); *Lady in a Jam* (1942); *Living in a Big Way* (1947)

Fritz Lang (1890–   )

(American films only.)

Fury (1936); *You Only Live Once* (1937); *You and Me* (1938); *The Return of Frank James* (1940); *Western Union* (1941); *Moontide* (codirector, uncredited—1941); *Man Hunt* (1941); *Confirm or Deny* (codirector, uncredited—1941); *Hangmen Also Die* (1943); *Ministry of Fear* (1944); *The Woman in the Window* (1944); *Scarlet Street* (1945); *Cloak and Dagger* (1946); *Secret Beyond the Door* (1948); *House by the River* (1950); *Winchester 73* (replaced by Anthony Mann —1950); *An American Guerrilla in the Philippines* (also known as *I Shall Return*—1950); *Rancho Notorious* (1952); *Clash by Night* (1952); *The Blue Gardenia* (1953); *The Big Heat* (1953); *Human Desire* (1954); *Moonfleet* (1955); *While the City Sleeps* (1956); *Beyond a Reasonable Doubt* (1956)

Mervyn Le Roy (1900–   )

No Place to Go (1927); *Flying Romeos* (1928); *Harold Teen* (1928); *Naughty Baby* (1929); *Hot Stuff* (1929); *Broadway Daddy* (1929); *Little Johnny Jones* (1930); *Playing Around* (1930); *Show Girl in Hollywood* (1930); *Numbered Men* (1930); *Broken Dishes* (1930); *Top Speed* (1930); *Little Caesar* (1930); *Gentlemen's Fate* (1931); *Broadminded* (1931); *Too Young to Marry* (1931); *Five Star Final* (1931); *Local Boy Makes Good* (1931); *Tonight or Never* (1931); *I Am a Fugitive from a Chain Gang* (1932); *High Pressure* (1932); *Heart of New York* (1932); *Two Seconds* (1932); *Big City Blues* (1932); *Three on a Match* (1932); *Hard to Handle* (1933); *Tugboat Annie* (1933); *Elmer the Great* (1933); *Gold Diggers of 1933* (1933); *The World Changes* (1933); *Heat Lightning* (1934); *Hi Nellie* (1934); *Happiness Ahead* (1934); *Sweet Adeline* (1934); *Oil for the Lamps of China* (1935); *Page Miss Glory* (1935); *I Found Stella Parish* (1935); *Anthony Adverse* (1936); *Three Men on a Horse* (1936); *The King and the Chorus Girl* (1937); *They Won't Forget* (1937); *Fools for Scandal* (1938); *Waterloo Bridge* (1940); *Escape* (1940); *Blossoms in the Dust* (1941); *Unholy Partners* (1941); *Random Harvest* (1942); *Johnny Eager* (1942); *Madame Curie* (1943); *Thirty Seconds over Tokyo* (1944); *Without Reservations* (1946); *Homecoming* (1948); *Little Women* (1949); *Any Number Can Play* (1949); *In the Good Old Summertime* (1949); *East Side, West Side* (1949); *Quo Vadis* (1951);

Lovely to Look At (with Vincente Minnelli—1952); *Million Dollar Mermaid* (with Busby Berkeley—1952); *Latin Lovers* (1953); *Rose-marie* (1954); *Strange Lady in Town* (1955); *Mister Roberts* (with John Ford—1955); *The Bad Seed* (1956); *Toward the Unknown* (1956); *No Time for Sergeants* (1958); *Home before Dark* (1958); *The FBI Story* (1950); *Wake Me When It's Over* (1960); *The Devil at Four O'clock* (1961); *A Majority of One* (1961); *Gypsy* (1962); *Mary, Mary* (1963); *Moment to Moment* (1966); *Downstairs at Ram-sey's* (1969); *The Thirteen Clocks* (1970)

Anatole Litvak (1902–)

(American films only.)

The Woman I Love (1937); *Tovarich* (1937); *The Amazing Dr. Clit-terhouse* (1938); *The Sisters* (1938); *The Roaring Twenties* (replaced by Raoul Walsh—1939); *Confessions of a Nazi Spy* (1939); *Castle on the Hudson* (1940); *All This and Heaven Too* (1940); *City for Con-quest* (1940); *Out of the Fog* (1941); *Blues in the Night* (1941); *This Above All* (1942); *Why We Fight* series (World War II documentaries: *The Nazis Strike*, 1942; *Divide and Conquer*, 1943; *The Battle of Russia*, 1943; *The Battle of China*, 1944; *War Comes to America*, with Frank Capra, 1945); *The Long Night* (1947); *Sorry, Wrong Number* (1948); *The Snake Pit* (1949); *Decision Before Dawn* (1951); *Act of Love* (1954); *The Deep Blue Sea* (1955); *Anastasia* (1956); *The Journey* (1959); *Goodbye Again* (1961); *Five Miles to Midnight* (1963); *The Night of the Generals* (1967)

Frank Lloyd (1889–1960)

(Partial listing.)

A Tale of Two Cities (1917); *Les Misérables* (1918); *Madame X* (1920); *Oliver Twist* (1922); *The Sin Flood* (1922); *The Eternal Flame* (1923); *The Sea Hawk* (1924); *Dark Streets* (1926); *The Divine Lady* (1929); *East Lynne* (1930); *Passport to Hell* (1932); *Cavalcade* (1933); *Berkeley Square* (1933); *Mutiny on the Bounty* (1935); *Under Two Flags* (1936); *Maid of Salem* (1937); *Wells Fargo* (1937); *If I Were King* (1939); *Rulers of the Sea* (1939); *The Tree of Liberty* (1940); *The Lady from Cheyenne* (1941); *This Woman Is Mine* (1941); *The Spoilers* (1942); *Blood on the Sun* (1945); *The Shanghai Story* (1954); *The Last Command* (1955)

Pare Lorentz (1905–)

(Only those films actually directed by Lorentz.)

The Plow That Broke the Plains (1936); *The River* (1937); *The Fight for Life* (1940); *Ecce Homo!* (unfinished)

Ernst Lubitsch (1892–1947)

(American films only.)

Rosita (1923); *The Marriage Circle* (1924); *Three Women* (1924); *Forbidden Paradise* (1924); *Kiss Me Again* (1925); *Lady Windermere's Fan* (1925); *So This Is Paris* (1926); *The Student Prince* (1927); *The Patriot* (1928); *Eternal Love* (1928); *The Love Parade* (1929); *Paramount on Parade* (1930); *Monte Carlo* (1930); *The Smiling Lieutenant* (1931); *The Man I Killed* (also known as *Broken Lullaby*—1932); *One Hour with You* (directed by George Cukor from Lubitsch plan and signed by Lubitsch—1932); *Trouble in Paradise* (1932); *If I Had a Million* (with King Vidor, James Cruze, Norman Z. McLeod, Stephen S. Roberts, William A. Seiter, Norman Taurog, Bruce Humberstone—1932); *Design for Living* (1933); *The Merry Widow* (1934); *Angel* (1937); *Bluebeard's Eighth Wife* (1938); *Ninotchka* (1939); *The Shop Around the Corner* (1940); *That Uncertain Feeling* (1941); *To Be or Not to Be* (1942); *Heaven Can Wait* (1943); *Cluny Brown* (1946); *That Lady in Ermine* (completed by Preminger after Lubitsch's death—1948)

Sidney Lumet (1924–)

Twelve Angry Men (1957); *Stage Struck* (1958); *That Kind of Woman* (1959); *The Fugitive Kind* (1959); *View from the Bridge* (1962); *Long Day's Journey into Night* (1962); *Fail Safe* (1964); *The Pawnbroker* (1965); *The Hill* (1965); *The Group* (1966); *Bye Bye Braverman* (1968); *The Sea Gull* (1968); *The Appointment* (1969); *Klute* (1971); *Child's Play* (1972); *The Offence* (1973); *Serpico* (1973)

Leo McCarey (1898–1969)

The Sophomore (1929); *Red Hot Rhythm* (1929); *Let's Go Native* (1930); *Wild Company* (1930); *Part Time Wife* (1930); *Indiscreet*

(1931); *The Kid from Spain* (1932); *Duck Soup* (1933); *Six of a Kind* (1934); *Belle of the Nineties* (1934); *Ruggles of Red Gap* (1935); *The Milky Way* (1936); *The Awful Truth* (1937); *Make Way for Tomorrow* (1937); *Love Affair* (1939); *Once upon a Honeymoon* (1942); *Going My Way* (1944); *The Bells of St. Mary's* (1945); *Good Sam* (1948); *My Son John* (1952); *An Affair to Remember* (1957); *Rally Round the Flag, Boys* (1958); *Satan Never Sleeps* (1962)

Rouben Mamoulian (1897–)

Applause (1929); *City Streets* (1931); *Dr. Jekyll and Mr. Hyde* (1932); *Love Me Tonight* (1932); *Queen Christina* (1933); *Song of Songs* (1933); *We Live Again* (1934); *Becky Sharp* (replaced Lowell Sherman—1935); *The Gay Desperado* (1936); *High, Wide and Handsome* (1937); *Golden Boy* (1939); *The Mark of Zorro* (1940); *Blood and Sand* (1941); *Rings on Her Fingers* (1942); *Summer Holiday* (1948); *The Wild Heart* (replaced Michael Powell, but uncredited—1951); *Silk Stockings* (1957); *Porgy and Bess* (replaced by Otto Preminger—1959)

Joseph L. Mankiewicz (1909–)

(Only those films actually directed by Mankiewicz.)

Dragonwyck (1946); *Somewhere in the Night* (1947); *The Late George Apley* (1946); *The Ghost and Mrs. Muir* (1947); *Escape* (1948); *A Letter to Three Wives* (1949); *House of Strangers* (1949); *No Way Out* (1950); *All About Eve* (1950); *People Will Talk* (1951); *Five Fingers* (1952); *Julius Caesar* (1953); *The Barefoot Contessa* (1954); *Guys and Dolls* (1955); *The Quiet American* (1957); *Suddenly Last Summer* (1959); *Cleopatra* (replaced various directors—1963); *The Honey Pot* (1967); *Couples* (1969); *The Bawdy Bard* (1969); *There Was a Crooked Man* (1970)

Lewis Milestone (1895–)

Seven Sinners (1925); *The Caveman* (1925); *The New Klondike* (1926); *Two Arabian Knights* (1927); *The Garden of Eden* (1928); *The Racket* (1928); *The Betrayal* (1929); *New York Nights* (1929); *All Quiet on the Western Front* (1930); *Hell's Angels* (with Howard Hughes—1930); *The Front Page* (1931); *Rain* (1932); *Hallelujah, I'm a Bum!* (1933); *The Captain Hates the Sea* (1934); *Paris in the Spring* (1935); *Anything Goes* (1936); *The General Died at Dawn* (1936); *Night of Nights* (1940); *Of Mice and Men* (1940); *Lucky Partners* (1940); *My Life with Caroline* (1941); *Edge of Darkness* (1943); *The North Star* (1943); *The Purple Heart* (1944); *A Walk in the Sun* (1945); *The Strange Love of Martha Ivers* (1946); *Guest in the House* (codirector, uncredited—1946); *Arch of Triumph* (1947); *No Minor Vices* (1948); *The Red Pony* (1949); *Halls of Montezuma* (1950); *Kangaroo* (1952); *Les Misérables* (1952); *Melba* (1953); *They Who Dare* (1955); *King Kelly* (uncompleted—1957); *Pork Chop Hill* (1959); *Ocean's Eleven* (1960); *Mutiny on the Bounty* (replaced Carol Reed—1962)

Vincente Minnelli (1902–)

Cabin in the Sky (1943); *I Dood It* (1943); *Meet Me in St. Louis* (1944); *The Clock* (1945); *Yolanda and the Thief* (1945); *Ziegfeld Follies* (1946); *Undercurrent* (1946); *The Pirate* (1948); *Madame Bovary* (1949); *Father of the Bride* (1950); *An American in Paris* (1951); *Father's Little Dividend* (1951); *The Bad and the Beautiful* (1953); *The Story of Three Loves* (the "Mademoiselle" episode—1953); *The Band Wagon* (1953); *The Long, Long Trailer* (1954); *Brigadoon* (1954); *Cobweb* (1955); *Kismet* (1955); *Lust for Life* (1956); *Tea and Sympathy* (1956); *Designing Woman* (1957); *Gigi* (1958); *The Reluctant Debutante* (1958); *Some Came Running* (1959); *Bells Are Ringing* (1960); *Home from the Hill* (1960); *Four Horsemen of the Apocalypse* (1962); *Two Weeks in Another Town* (1962); *The Courtship of Eddie's Father* (1963); *Goodbye Charlie* (1964); *The Sandpiper* (1965); *On a Clear Day You Can See Forever* (1969)

F. W. Murnau (1889–1931)

(American films only.)

Sunrise (1927); *Four Devils* (1928); *Our Daily Bread* (also known as *City Girl*—1930); *Tabu* (with Robert Flaherty—1931)

Mike Nichols (1931–)

Who's Afraid of Virginia Woolf? (1967); *The Graduate* (1968); *Catch-22* (1969); *Carnal Knowledge* (1971); *The Day of the Dolphin* (1973)

Arthur Penn (1922–)

The Left-Handed Gun (1957); *The Miracle Worker* (1962); *The Train* (some action shots only—1963); *Mickey One* (1964); *The Chase* (1965); *Bonnie and Clyde* (1967); *Alice's Restaurant* (1969); *Little Big Man* (1970)

Edwin S. Porter (1870–1941)

(Partial listing.)

The Life of an American Fireman (1902); *Uncle Tom's Cabin* (1903); *The Great Train Robbery* (1903); *The Bold Bank Robbery* (1903); *The Ex-Convict* (1904); *White Caps* (1904); *The Kleptomaniac* (1905); *The Miller's Daughter* (1904); *How Jones Lost His Roll* (1905); *The Night Before Christmas* (1905); *Dream of a Rarebit Fiend* (1905); *The Seven Ages* (1906); *A Tale of the Sea* (1906); *Rescued from an Eagle's Nest* (1907); *Alice's Adventures in Wonderland* (1910); *The Count of Monte Cristo* (1912); *In the Bishop's Carriage* (with Dawley —1913); *Hearts Adrift* (1914); *A Good Little Devil* (1914); *The Eternal City* (1914); *Tess of the Storm Country* (1914)

Otto Preminger (1906–)

Under Your Spell (1936); *Danger—Love at Work* (1937); *Margin for Error* (1943); *In the Meantime, Darling* (1944), *Laura* (1944); *A Royal Scandal* (also known as *Czarina*—1945); *Fallen Angel* (1945); *Centennial Summer* (1946); *Forever Amber* (1947); *Daisy Kenyon* (1947); *That Lady in Ermine* (begun and signed by Ernst Lubitsch—1948); *The Fan* (1949); *Whirlpool* (1949); *Where the Sidewalk Ends* (1950); *The Thirteenth Letter* (1950); *Angel Face* (1953); *The Moon Is Blue* (1953); *River of No Return* (1954); *Carmen Jones* (1954); *The Court-Martial of Billy Mitchell* (1955); *The Man with the Golden Arm* (1955); *Saint Joan* (1957); *Bonjour Tristesse* (1958); *Porgy and Bess* (replaced Rouben Mamoulian—1959); *Anatomy of a Murder* (1959); *Exodus* (1960); *Advise and Consent* (1962); *The Cardinal* (1963); *In Harm's Way* (1965); *Bunny Lake Is Missing* (1965); *Hurry Sundown* (1966); *Skidoo!* (1968)

Robert Rossen (1908–1966)

(Only those films actually directed by Rossen.)

Johnny O'Clock (1947); *Body and Soul* (1947); *All the King's Men* (1949); *The Brave Bulls* (1951); *Mambo* (1955); *Alexander the Great* (1956); *Island in the Sun* (1956); *They Came to Cordura* (1959); *The Hustler* (1961); *Lilith* (1964)

Victor Seastrom (1879–1960)

(American films only.)

Name the Man (1924); *He Who Gets Slapped* (1924); *Confessions of a Queen* (1925); *The Tower of Lies* (1925); *The Scarlet Letter* (1926); *The Divine Woman* (1928); *The Wind* (1928); *Masks of the Devil* (1928); *A Lady to Love* (1930)

Mack Sennett (1880–1960)

(Because of the number of titles involved, readers are referred to the 180-page filmography in Davide Turconi's *Mack Sennett: il "re delle comiche,"* Edizioni dell'Ateneo, Rome, 1961.)

Josef von Sternberg (1894–1969)

The Salvation Hunters (1925); *The Exquisite Sinner* (1925); *The Sea Gull* (also called *A Woman of the Sea*—1926); *Underworld* (1927); *The Last Command* (1928); *The Dragnet* (1928); *The Docks of New York* (1929); *The Case of Lena Smith* (1929); *Thunderbolt* (1929); *The Blue Angel* (*Der Blaue Engel*—1930); *Morocco* (1930); *Dishonored* (1931); *An American Tragedy* (1931); *Shanghai Express* (1932); *Blonde Venus* (1932); *The Scarlet Empress* (1934); *The Devil Is a Woman* (1935); *Crime and Punishment* (1935); *The King Steps Out* (1936); *Claudius* (unfinished—1937); *Sergeant Madden* (1939); *The Shanghai Gesture* (1941); *The Town* (1943); *Jet Pilot* (1951); *Macao* (1952); *Anatahan* (1953)

George Stevens (1905–)

The Cohens and the Kellys in Trouble (1933); *Bachelor Bait* (1934); *Alice Adams* (1934); *Kentucky Kernels* (1934); *Laddie* (1935); *Swing Time* (1936); *Quality Street* (1937); *A Damsel in Distress* (1937); *Vivacious Lady* (1938); *Gunga Din* (1939); *Vigil in the Night* (1940); *Penny Serenade* (1941); *Woman of the Year* (1942); *The Talk of the Town* (1942); *The More the Merrier* (1943); *I Remember Mama* (1948); *A Place in the Sun* (1951); *Something to Live For* (1952); *Shane* (1953); *Giant* (1956); *The Diary of Anne Frank* (1959); *The Greatest Story Ever Told* (1965); *The Only Game in Town* (1970)

Erich von Stroheim (1885–1957)

Blind Husbands (1918); *The Devil's Passkey* (1919); *Foolish Wives* (1922); *Merry-Go-Round* (replaced by Rupert Julian—1922); *Greed* (1925); *The Merry Widow* (1925); *The Wedding March* (Parts 1 and 2—1928); *Queen Kelly* (1928); *Walking down Broadway* (completed by someone else and released as *Hello Sister*—1933)

John Sturges (1911–)

Thunderbolt (with William Wyler; service film later exhibited publicly—1945); *The Man Who Dared* (1946); *Shadowed* (1946); *Alias Mr. Twilight* (1947); *For the Love of Rusty* (1947); *Keeper of the Bees* (1947); *Best Man Wins* (1948); *Sign of the Ram* (1948); *The Walking Hills* (1949); *Mystery Street* (1950); *The Capture* (1950); *The Magnificent Yankee* (1950); *Right Cross* (1950); *Kind Lady* (1951); *The People Against O'Hara* (1951); *It's a Big Country* ("The Census Takers" sketch—1951); *The Girl in White* (1952); *Jeopardy* (1953); *Escape from Fort Bravo* (1953); *Fast Company* (1953); *Bad Day at Black Rock* (1955); *Underwater* (1955); *The Scarlet Coat* (1955); *Backlash* (1956); *Gunfight at the O.K. Corral* (1957); *The Obsessed* (uncompleted—1957); *The Spirit of St. Louis* (replaced by Billy Wilder—1957); *The Old Man and the Sea* (replaced various directors—1958); *The Law and Jake Wade* (1958); *Last Train from Gun Hill* (1959); *Never So Few* (1959); *The Magnificent Seven* (1960); *By Love Possessed* (1961); *Sergeants Three* (1962); *The Great Escape*

(1963); *A Girl Named Tamiko* (1963); *The Satan Bug* (1965); *The Hallelujah Trail* (1965); *Grand Prix* (replaced by John Frankenheimer —1967); *The Hour of the Gun* (1967); *Ice Station Zebra* (1968); *Marooned* (1969)

Preston Sturges (1898–1959)

The Great McGinty (1940); *Christmas in July* (1940); *The Lady Eve* (1941); *Sullivan's Travels* (1942); *The Palm Beach Story* (1942); *Miracle at Morgan's Creek* (1944); *Hail the Conquering Hero* (1944); *The Great Moment* (1944); *Mad Wednesday* (1947); *Unfaithfully Yours* (1948); *The Beautiful Blonde from Bashful Bend* (1949); *The French They Are a Funny Race* (also known as *The Notebooks of Major Thompson*—1955)

Maurice Tourneur (1876–1961)

(American films only.)

Mother (1914); *The Man of the Hour* (1914); *The Wishing Ring* (1914); *The Pit* (1914); *Alias Jimmy Valentine* (1915); *The Cub* (1915); *Trilby* (1915); *The Ivory Snuff Box* (1915); *A Butterfly on the Wheel* (1915); *The Pawn of Fate* (1916); *The Hand of Peril* (1916); *The Closed Road* (1916); *The Rail Rider* (1916); *The Velvet Paw* (1916); *A Girl's Folly* (1917); *The Whip* (1917); *The Pride of the Clan* (1917); *The Poor Little Rich Girl* (1917); *The Undying Flame* (1917); *The Law of the Land* (1917); *Exile* (1917); *Barbary Sheep* (1917); *The Rise of Jennie Cushing* (1917); *Rose of the World* (1918); *A Doll's House* (1918); *The Blue Bird* (1918); *Prunella* (1918); *Sporting Life* (1918); *Woman* (1918); *The White Heather* (1919); *The Broken Butterfly* (1919); *The Life Line* (1919); *My Lady's Garter* (1920); *Treasure Island* (1920); *The Great Redeemer* (1920); *The White Circle* (1920); *Deep Waters* (1920); *The Last of the Mohicans* (with Clarence Brown—1920); *The Bait* (1921); *The Foolish Matrons* (with Clarence Brown—1921); *Lorna Doone* (1922); *While Paris Sleeps* (1923); *The Christian* (1923); *The Isle of Lost Ships* (1923); *The Brass Bottle* (1923); *Jealous Husbands* (1923); *Torment* (1924); *The White Moth* (1924); *Never the Twain Shall Meet* (1925); *Clothes Make the Pirate* (1925); *Aloma of the South Seas* (1926); *Old Loves and New* (1926); *The Mysterious Island* (1926)

W. S. Van Dyke (1899–1944)

Men of the Desert (1918); *Gift o' Gab* (1918); *Lady of the Dugout* (1919); *According to Hoyle* (1922); *Boss of Camp No. 4* (1922); *Forget Me Not* (1922); *Little Girl Next Door* (1923); *Miracle Workers* (1923); *Loving Lies* (1923); *You Are in Danger* (1923); *Half-a-dollar Bill* (1924); *The Beautiful Sinner* (1925); *Gold Heels* (1925); *Hearts and Spurs* (1925); *The Trail Rider* (1925); *The Ranger of the Big Pines* (1925); *The Timber Wolf* (1925); *The Desert's Price* (1925); *The Gentle Cyclone* (1926); *War Paint* (1926); *Winners of the Wilderness* (1927); *California* (1927); *Heart of the Yukon* (1927); *Eye of the Totem* (1927); *Foreign Devils* (1927); *Spoilers of the West* (1927); *Wyoming* (1928); *Under Black Eagle* (1928); *White Shadows in the South Seas* (with Robert J. Flaherty—1928); *The Pagan* (1929); *Trader Horn* (1931); *Never the Twain Shall Meet* (1931); *Guilty Hands* (1931); *Cuban Love Song* (1931); *Tarzan* (1932); *The Ape Man* (1932); *Night World* (1932); *Penthouse* (1933); *Eskimo* (1933); *The Prizefighter and the Lady* (1933); *Laughing Boy* (1934); *Manhattan Melodrama* (1934); *The Thin Man* (1934); *Hide-out* (1934); *The Painted Veil* (1934); *Forsaking All Others* (1935); *Naughty Marietta* (1935); *I Live My Life* (1935); *Rose Marie* (1936); *San Francisco* (1936); *His Brother's Wife* (1936); *The Devil Is a Sissy* (1936); *Love on the Run* (1936); *After the Thin Man* (1936); *Personal Property* (1937); *They Gave Me a Gun* (1937); *Rosalie* (1937); *Marie Antoinette* (1938); *Sweethearts* (1938); *Stand Up and Fight* (1939); *It's a Wonderful World* (1939); *Andy Hardy Gets Spring Fever* (1939); *Another Thin Man* (1939); *I Take This Woman* (1940); *I Love You Again* (1940); *Bitter Sweet* (1940); *Rage in Heaven* (1941); *The Feminine Touch* (1941); *Shadow of the Thin Man* (1941); *Dr. Kildare's Victory* (1941); *I Married an Angel* (1942); *Cairo* (1942); *Journey for Margaret* (1942)

King Vidor (1894–)

The Turn in the Road (1918); *Better Times* (1919); *The Other Half* (1919); *Poor Relations* (1919); *The Jack-knife Man* (1919); *The Family Honor* (1920); *The Sky Pilot* (1921); *Love Never Dies* (1921); *Conquering the Women* (1921); *Woman, Wake Up* (1921); *The Real Adventure* (1922); *Dusk to Dawn* (1922); *Alice Adams* (1922); *Peg o' My Heart* (1922); *The Woman of Bronze* (1923); *Three Wise Fools*

(1923); *Wild Oranges* (1923); *Happiness* (1923); *Wine of Youth* (1924); *His Hour* (1924); *Wife of a Centaur* (1924); *Proud Flesh* (1925); *The Big Parade* (1925); *La Bohème* (1925); *Bardelys the Magnificent* (1926); *The Crowd* (1927); *Show People* (1928); *The Political Flapper* (also known as *The Patsy*—1928); *Hallelujah!* (1929); *Not So Dumb* (1930); *Billy the Kid* (1930); *Street Scene* (1931); *The Champ* (1931); *If I Had a Million* (with James Cruze, Ernst Lubitsch, Norman Z. McLeod, Stephen S. Roberts, William A. Seiter, Norman Taurog, Bruce Humberstone—1932); *Bird of Paradise* (1932); *Cynara* (1932); *The Stranger's Return* (1933); *Our Daily Bread* (1934); *The Wedding Night* (1934); *So Red the Rose* (1935); *The Texas Rangers* (1936); *Stella Dallas* (1937); *The Citadel* (1938); *Northwest Passage* (1939); *Comrade X* (1940); *H. M. Pulham, Esq.* (1941); *An American Romance* (1944); *Duel in the Sun* (with William Dieterle—1947); *On Our Merry Way* (with Leslie Fenton—1947); *The Fountainhead* (1949); *Beyond the Forest* (1949); *Lightning Strikes Twice* (1951); *Japanese War Bride* (1952); *Ruby Gentry* (1952); *Man without a Star* (1955); *War and Peace* (1956); *Solomon and Sheba* (1959)

Raoul Walsh (1892–)

Life of Villa (1912); *The Regeneration* (1915); *Carmen* (1915); *Honor System* (1916); *Blue Blood and Red* (1916); *The Serpent* (1916); *Betrayed* (1917); *The Conqueror* (1917); *The Pride of New York* (1917); *The Innocent Sinner* (1917); *Silent Lie* (1917); *Woman and the Law* (1918); *This Is the Life* (1918); *The Prussian Cur* (1918); *On the Jump* (1918); *Every Mother's Son* (1918); *I'll Say So* (1918); *Evangeline* (1919); *Should a Husband Forgive?* (1919); *From Now On* (1920); *The Deep Purple* (1920); *The Strongest* (1920); *The Oath* (1921); *Serenade* (1921); *Kindred of the Dust* (1922); *Lost and Found* (1923); *The Thief of Bagdad* (1924); *East of Suez* (1925); *The Spaniard* (1925); *The Wanderer* (1926); *The Lucky Lady* (1926); *The Lady of the Harem* (1926); *What Price Glory?* (1926); *The Monkey Talks* (1927); *The Loves of Carmen* (1927); *Sadie Thomson* (1928); *The Red Dance* (1928); *Me Gangster* (1928); *Hot for Paris* (1929); *In Old Arizona* (with Irving Cummings—1929); *The Cockeyed World* (1929); *The Big Trail* (1930); *The Man Who Came Back* (1931); *Women of All Nations* (1931); *Yellow Ticket* (1931); *Wild Girl* (1932); *Me and My Gal* (1932); *Sailor's Luck* (1933); *The Bowery* (1933); *Going Hollywood* (1933); *Under Pressure* (1935); *Baby Face Harrington* (1935); *Every Night at Eight* (1935); *Klondike Annie* (1936); *Big Brown Eyes* (1936); *Spendthrift* (1939); *You're in the Army Now* (1937); *When Thief Meets Thief* (1937); *Artists and Models* (1937); *Hitting a New High* (1937); *College Swing* (1938); *St. Louis Blues* (1939); *The Roaring Twenties* (replaced Anatole Litvak—1939); *Dark Command* (1940); *They Drive by Night* (1940); *High Sierra* (1941); *The Strawberry Blonde* (1941); *Manpower* (1941); *They Died with Their Boots on* (1941); *Desperate Journey* (1942); *Gentleman Jim* (1942); *Background to Danger* (1943); *Northern Pursuit* (1943); *Uncertain Glory* (1944); *Objective Burma* (1945); *Salty O'Rourke* (1945); *The Horn Blows at Midnight* (1945); *San Antonio* (with David Butler—1945); *The Man I Love* (1946); *Pursued* (1947); *Cheyenne* (1947); *Stallion Road* (with James V. Kern—1947); *Silver River* (1948); *One Sunday Afternoon* (1948); *Fighter Squadron* (1948); *Colorado Territory* (1949); *White Heat* (1949); *Along the Great Divide* (1951); *Captain Horatio Hornblower* (1951); *Distant Drums* (1951); *Glory Alley* (1952); *The World In His Arms* (1952); *Blackbeard the Pirate* (1952); *The Lawless Breed* (1952); *Sea Devils* (1953); *A Lion Is in the Streets* (1953); *Gun Fury* (1953); *Saskatchewan* (1954); *Battle Cry* (1955); *The Tall Men* (1955); *The Revolt of Mamie Stover* (1956); *The King and Four Queens* (1956); *Band of Angels* (1957); *The Naked and the Dead* (1958); *The Sheriff of Fractured Jaw* (1958); *A Private's Affair* (1959); *Esther and the King* (1960); *Marines, Let's Go!* (1961); *A Distant Trumpet* (1963)

Andy Warhol (1930–)

(Only those films actually directed by Warhol.)

Kiss (1963); *Andy Warhol Films Jack Smith Filming "Normal Love"* (1963); *Tarzan and Jane Regained Sort Of* (1964); *Dance Movie* (1964); *Haircut* (1964); *Eat* (1964); *Blow Job* (1964); *Batman Dracula* (filmed 1964—never released); *Empire* (1964); *Henry Geldzahler* (1965); *Salome and Delilah* (filmed 1963—never released); *Soap Opera* (filmed 1964—never released); *Couch* (1966); *Shoulder* (filmed 1964); *Mario Banana* (1965); *Harlot* (1965); *13 Most Beautiful Women* (filmed 1964–1965); *13 Most Beautiful Boys* (filmed 1964–1965); *50 Fantastics and 50 Personalities* (filmed 1964–1966); *Taylor Mead's Ass* (filmed 1964); *Ivy and John* (filmed 1965); *Suicide* (filmed 1965); *Screen Test #1* (filmed 1965); *Screen Test #2* (1965); *The Life of Juanita Castro* (1965); *Drunk* (filmed 1965); *Horse* (1965); *Poor Little Rich Girl* (1965); *Vinyl* (1965); *Bitch* (filmed 1965); *Restaurant* (filmed 1965); *Kitchen* (1966); *Prison* (filmed 1965); *Face* (1966); *Afternoon* (filmed 1965); *Beauty #2* (1965);

Space (filmed 1965); *Outer and Inner Space* (1966); *My Hustler* (1965); *Camp* (1965); *Paul Swan* (filmed 1965); *Hedy* (filmed 1965); *The Closet* (filmed 1965); *More Milk, Evette* (1966); *Lupe* (1966); *Bufferin* (filmed 1966); *Eating Too Fast* (filmed 1966—sound version of *Blow Job*); *The Velvet Underground and Nico* (1966); *Chelsea Girls* (1966); *Four Stars* (1967); *I, a Man* (1967); *Bike Boy* (1967); *Nude Restaurant* (1967); *The Loves of Ondine* (1968—originally part of *Four Stars*); *Lonesome Cowboys* (1969); *Sleep* (1964); *Blue Movie* (1969); *Schraft's Commercial* (1969); *Surfing Movie* (filmed 1968); *L'Amour* (with Paul Morrissey—1973)

Orson Welles (1915–)

Too Much Johnson (film frame for stage production—1938); *Citizen Kane* (1941); *It's All True* (unreleased—1942); *The Magnificent Ambersons* (1942); *Journey into Fear* (signed by Norman Foster—1943); *The Stranger* (1946); *The Lady from Shanghai* (1947); *Macbeth* (1948); *Othello* (1952); *Mr. Arkadin* (also called *Confidential Report*—1955); *Touch of Evil* (1957); *The Trial* (1962); *Chimes at Midnight* (also called *Falstaff*—1966); *The Immortal Story* (for French television—1968)

William Wellman (1896–)

The Man Who Won (1923); *Second Hand Love* (1923); *Big Dan* (1923); *The Vagabond Trail* (1924); *Cupid's Fireman* (1924); *Not a Drum Was Heard* (1924); *The Circus Cowboy* (1924); *When Husbands Flirt* (1926); *The Boob* (1926); *The Cat's Pajamas* (1926); *You Never Know Women* (1926); *Wings* (1927); *Legion of Condemned* (1928); *Ladies of the Mob* (1928); *Beggars of Life* (1928); *Chinatown Nights* (1929); *The Man I Love* (1929); *Woman Trap* (1929); *Dangerous Paradise* (1930); *Young Eagles* (1930); *Maybe It's Love* (1930); *Steel Highway* (also called *Other Men's Women*—1930); *The Public Enemy* (1931); *Star Witness* (1931); *Night Nurse* (1931); *Safe in Hell* (1931); *Love Is a Racket* (1932); *Hatchet Man* (1932); *So Big* (1932); *Purchase Price* (1932); *The Conquerors* (1932); *Frisco Jenny* (1933); *Central Airport* (1933); *Lady of the Night* (also called *Midnight Mary*—1933); *Lily Turner* (1933); *College Coach* (1933); *Heroes for Sale*; *Wild Boys of the Road* (1933); *Looking for Trouble* (1934); *Stingaree* (1934); *The President Vanishes*

(1934); *The Call of the Wild* (1935); *Robin Hood of El Dorado* (1935); *Small Town Girl* (1936); *A Star Is Born* (1937); *Nothing Sacred* (1937); *Men with Wings* (1938); *Beau Geste* (1939); *The Light That Failed* (1939); *Reaching for the Sun* (1940); *Roxie Hart* (1942); *The Great Man's Lady* (1942); *Thunderbirds* (1942); *Ox-bow Incident* (1943); *Lady of Burlesque* (1943); *Buffalo Bill* (1944); *Air Ship Squadron #4* (service film later released to public—1944); *This Man's Navy* (1945); *Story of G.I. Joe* (1945); *Gallant Journey* (1946); *Magic Town* (1947); *The Iron Curtain* (1948); *Happy Years* (1948); *The Next Voice You Hear* (1949); *Battleground* (1949); *Across the Wide Missouri* (1950); *Westward the Women* (1950); *Yellow Sky* (1951); *My Man and I* (1952); *Island in the Sky* (1953); *The High and the Mighty* (1954); *Track of the Cat* (1954); *Blood Alley* (1955); *Goodbye, My Lady* (1956); *Darby's Rangers* (1958); *Lafayette Escadrille* (also called *Hell Bent for Glory*—1958)

Billy Wilder (1906–   )

(American films only.)

The Major and the Minor (1942); *Five Graves to Cairo* (1943); *Double Indemnity* (1944); *The Lost Weekend* (1945); *The Emperor Waltz* (1947); *A Foreign Affair* (1948); *Sunset Boulevard* (1950); *Ace in the Hole* (also titled *The Big Carnival*—1951); *Stalag 17* (1953); *Sabrina* (1954); *The Seven Year Itch* (1955); *The Spirit of St. Louis* (replaced John Sturges—1957); *Love in the Afternoon* (1957); *Witness for the Prosecution* (1957); *Some Like It Hot* (1959); *The Apartment* (1960); *One, Two, Three* (1961); *Irma La Douce* (1963); *Kiss Me, Stupid* (1964); *The Fortune Cookie* (1966); *The Private Life of Sherlock Holmes* (1969); *Avanti* (1972)

William Wyler (1902–   )

Lazy Lightning (1926); *Stolen Ranch* (1926); *Blazing Days* (1927); *Hard Fists* (1927); *Straight Shootin'* (1927); *The Border Cavalier* (1927); *Desert Dust* (1927); *Thunder Riders* (1928); *Anybody Here Seen Kelly?* (1928); *The Shakedown* (1929); *Come Across* (1929); *Love Trap* (1929); *Hell's Heroes* (1930); *The Storm* (1930); *A House Divided* (1932); *The Old Dark House* (1932); *Tom Brown of Culver* (1932); *Her First Mate* (1933); *Counsellor at Law* (1933); *Glamour* (1934); *The Good Fairy* (1935); *The Gay Deception* (1935); *Come and Get It* (with Howard Hawks—1936); *Dodworth* (1936); *These Three* (1936); *Dead End* (1937); *Jezebel* (1938); *Wuthering Heights* (1939); *The Letter* (1940); *The Westerner* (1940); *The Little Foxes* (1941); *Mrs. Miniver* (1942); *The Memphis Belle* (service film later exhibited publicly—1943); *The Fighting Lady* (service film later exhibited publicly—1944); *Glory for Me* (service film later exhibited publicly—1945); *Thunderbolt* (with John Sturges; service film later exhibited publicly—1945); *The Best Years of Our Lives* (1946); *The Heiress* (1949); *Detective Story* (1951); *Carrie* (1952); *Roman Holiday* (1953); *The Desperate Hours* (1955); *Friendly Persuasion* (1956); *Thieves' Market* (uncompleted—1957); *The Big Country* (1958); *Ben Hur* (1960); *The Children's Hour* (1962); *The Collector* (1965); *How to Steal a Million* (1966); *Funny Girl* (1968); *The Liberation of L. B. Jones* (1970)

Fred Zinnemann (1907–)

Short subjects (1938–1942):
A Friend Indeed (1938); *The Story of Dr. Carver* (1938); *That Mothers Might Live* (1938); *Tracking the Sleeping Death* (1938); *They Live Again* (1938); *Weather Wizards* (1939); *While America Sleeps* (1939); *Help Wanted!* (1939); *One Against the World* (1939); *The Ashcan Fleet* (1939); *Forgotten Victory* (1939); *The Old South* (1940); *The Way in the Wilderness* (1940); *The Great Meddler* (1940); *Forbidden Passage* (1941); *Your Last Act* (1941); *The Lady or the Tiger?* (1942)

Features:
The Wave (1937); *Kid Glove Killer* (1942); *Eyes in the Night* (1942); *The Seventh Cross* (1944); *Little Mr. Jim* (1946); *My Brother Talks to Horses* (1947); *The Search* (1948); *Act of Violence* (1949); *The Men* (1950); *Teresa* (1951); *High Noon* (1952); *The Member of the Wedding* (1952); *From Here to Eternity* (1953); *Oklahoma!* (1955); *A Hatful of Rain* (1957); *The Nun's Story* (1959); *The Sundowners* (1960); *Behold a Pale Horse* (1963); *A Man for All Seasons* (1966); *The Day of the Jackal* (1973)

COPYRIGHT ACKNOWLEDGMENTS (*continued from page iv*)

BASIC BOOKS, INC. For excerpts from *Movies: The History of an Art and an Institution* by Richard Schickel, © 1964 by Richard Schickel. Published by Basic Books, Inc., Publishers, New York.

ANDREW BERGMAN. For excerpts from *We're in the Money*.

ROBERT BINGHAM. For excerpt from the review on *Baby Doll* in *The Reporter*.

THE BODLEY HEAD. For excerpts from *Charlie Chaplin* by Louis Delluc.

KNOX BURGER. For excerpts from reviews by Dan Wakefield published in *The Atlantic Monthly*.

JONATHAN CAPE LIMITED. For excerpts from *The Film Till Now* and *Celluloid* by Paul Rotha.

DOROTHY CHAMBERLAIN. For excerpts from *The Film Criticism of Otis Ferguson*.

COMMENTARY. For excerpts from reviews by William Pechter. Reprinted from *Commentary* by permission. Copyright © 1970, 1971 by the American Jewish Committee.

COMMONWEAL PUBLISHERS CO., INC. For excerpts from articles by Philip T. Hartung and by Colin L. Westerbeck published in *Commonweal*.

THE CONDÉ NAST PUBLICATIONS INC. For excerpts from articles by Ann Birstein on *Guess Who's Coming to Dinner*, © 1968; by Arthur Schlesinger, Jr. on *Catch-22*, © 1970, on *The Sea Gull*, © 1969, on *2001*, © 1968, on *The Fixer*, © 1968, on *Carnal Knowledge*, © 1970, on *Faces*, © 1969, published in *Vogue*; from "The Screen" by Pare Lorentz, copyright © 1932, 1933, from "Field Generals of the Film" by Harvey Alan Potamkin, copyright © 1932, published in *Vanity Fair*. All articles copyrighted by The Condé Nast Publications Inc.

ALISTAIR COOKE. For excerpts from articles published in *Sight & Sound*.

COWARD, MCCANN & GEOGHEGAN, INC. For excerpts from *The Art of the Motion Picture* by Jean Benoit-Levy. Copyright © 1946 by Jean Benoit-Levy. Reprinted by permission.

CUE MAGAZINE. For excerpt from review by William Wolf of *2001*.

DAVID DENBY. For excerpts from reviews published in *The Atlantic Monthly*.

DELACORTE PRESS. For excerpts from *Behind the Screen* by Kenneth Macgowan. Copyright © 1965 by the Estate of Kenneth Macgowan. Reprinted by permission of the publisher.

THE DIAL PRESS. For excerpts from *Movies into Film* by John Simon, copyright © 1971 by John Simon. Reprinted by permission of the publisher.

DOUBLEDAY & COMPANY, INC. For excerpts from *The Film Director as Superstar* by Joseph Gelmis, copyright © 1970 by Joseph Gelmis. From *Howard Hawks* by Robin Wood, copyright © 1968 by Robin Wood. Reprinted by permission of the publisher.

E. P. DUTTON & CO., INC. For excerpts from *The American Cinema* by Andrew Sarris, published in a paperback edition by E. P. Dutton. Copyright © 1968 by E. P. Dutton & Co., Inc. From *The Lubitsch Touch* by Herman Weinberg, copyright © 1968 by Herman Weinberg. First published 1968 by E. P. Dutton & Co., Inc. in a paperback edition. From *Josef von Sternberg* by Herman G. Weinberg, copyright © 1967 by Herman Weinberg. Used with permission of the publisher.

ENCOUNTER. For excerpts from articles by Eric Rhode and John Weightman.

FARRAR, STRAUS & GIROUX, INC. For excerpts from *Slouching Towards Bethlehem* by Joan Didion.

MARVIN FELHEIM. For excerpt from review of Chaplin's *A King in New York* published in *The Reporter*.

FILM COMMENT. For excerpt from "Preston Sturges in the Thirties" by Andrew Sarris published in *Film Comment*. Copyright © 1970 Film Comment Publishing Corp., used by permission.

FILM CULTURE. For its generous permission to reprint excerpts from numerous articles.

FILM HERITAGE. For excerpts from articles by Alan Casty and G. Charles Niemeyer.

GROSSET & DUNLAP, INC. For excerpts from *Agee on Film*: Vol. I. by James Agee. Copyright © 1958 by The James Agee Trust.

HARCOURT BRACE JOVANOVICH, INC. For excerpts from *The Innocent Eye* by Arthur Calder-Marshall; from *Film Form* by Sergei Eisenstein.

HARPER & ROW, PUBLISHERS, INC. For excerpts from *Figures of Light* by Stanley Kauffmann, copyright © 1968 by Stanley Kauffmann. From *A World on Film* by Stanley Kauffmann, copyright © 1966 by Stanley Kauffmann. From *Twenty-four Times a Second* by William S. Pechter, copyright © 1971 by William S. Pechter. From *The Seven Lively Arts* by Gilbert Seldes, copyright 1924 by Harper & Row, Publishers, Inc., renewed 1952 by Gilbert Seldes. Reprinted by permission of the publisher.

ROBERT L. HATCH. For excerpts from articles published in *The Reporter*.

HOLT, RINEHART AND WINSTON, INC. For excerpts from *The Talkies* by Arthur Edwin Krows. Copyright 1930 by Holt, Rinehart and Winston, Inc. Copyright © 1958 by Arthur Edwin Krows. From *Screening the Sexes* by Parker Tyler, copyright © 1972 by Parker Tyler.

HOLIDAY. For excerpt from review by Al Hine published in *Holiday Magazine*. Copyright © 1950. The Curtis Publishing Co. Reprinted by permission.

HORIZON PRESS. For excerpts from *The Crazy Mirror* by Raymond Durgnat, copyright © 1970. From *Sex, Psyche, etcetera in the Film* by Parker Tyler, copyright © 1969. Reprinted by permission of the publisher.

INDIANA UNIVERSITY PRESS. For excerpts from *Billy Wilder* by Axel Madsen; from *Literature and Film* by Robert Richardson; from *Buster Keaton* by David Robinson.

LEWIS M. ISAACS, JR. For excerpt from an article by Stark Young published in *New Republic*. Reprinted by permission of executor of the Will of Stark Young, copyright owner.

JOHNS HOPKINS UNIVERSITY PRESS. For excerpt from *Novels into Film* by George Bluestone.

WALTER KERR. For excerpt from his article published in *Theatre Arts*.

LITTLE, BROWN AND COMPANY. For excerpts from *Kiss Kiss Bang Bang* by Pauline Kael, copyright © 1965, 1966, 1967, 1968 by Pauline Kael. From *I Lost It at the Movies* by Pauline Kael, copyright © 1962, 1965 by Pauline Kael. From *Going Steady* by Pauline Kael, copyright © 1968, 1969, 1970 by Pauline Kael. Reprinted by permission of Atlantic-Little, Brown and Co.

LIVERIGHT PUBLISHING CORPORATION. For excerpts from *American Film Criticism* by Stanley Kauffmann. Copyright © 1972 by Stanley Kauffmann. Reprinted by permission of Liveright Publishing Corporation.

MCCALL'S. For excerpts from articles by Frankie McKee Robins.

MCGRAW-HILL BOOK COMPANY. For excerpt from *The Hollywood Musical* by John Russell Taylor and Arthur Jackson, copyright © 1971 by Martin Secker & Warburg, Ltd. Used by permission of McGraw-Hill Book Company.

MACMILLAN PUBLISHING CO., INC. For excerpts from *The Dream and the Dreamers* by Hollis Alpert, copyright © 1962 by Hollis Alpert. From *The Name Above the Title* by Frank Capra, copyright © 1971 by Frank Capra. From *Horror!* by Drake Douglas, copyright © 1966 by Drake Douglas. From *The Livliest Art* by Arthur Knight, copyright © 1957 by Arthur Knight. From *Private*

Screenings by John Simon, copyright © 1962, 1963, 1964, 1965, 1966, 1967 by John Simon. Reprinted by permission of Macmillan Publishing Co., Inc.

STEVEN MARCUS. For excerpt from "Where We Came In" published in *The Reporter*.

THE MUSEUM OF MODERN ART. For excerpts from *Film Notes* edited by Eileen Bowser, copyright © 1969 The Museum of Modern Art. From *Cukor & Co./ The Films of George Cukor and His Collaborators* by Gary Carey, copyright © 1971 by The Museum of Modern Art. From *George Stevens: an American Romantic* by Donald Richie, copyright © 1970 by The Museum of Modern Art. From *The Films of Josef Sternberg* by Andrew Sarris, copyright © 1966 by The Museum of Modern Art. All rights reserved. Excerpts reprinted by permission of The Museum of Modern Art, New York.

THE NATION. For excerpts from reviews by Alexander Bakshy, Harold Clurman, Robert Hatch, Franz Hoellering, William Troy; from *Negative Space* by Manny Farber.

THE NATIONAL BOARD OF REVIEW OF MOTION PICTURES, INC. For its generous permission to reprint excerpts from numerous articles published in *National Board of Review* and *Films in Review*.

NEWSWEEK. For excerpt from review on Henry Hathaway.

THE NEW YORK TIMES. For excerpts from an article on Stanley Kubrick by Renata Adler, copyright © 1968 by The New York Times Company. From numerous articles © 1932, '35, '36, '39, '40, '47, '48, '49, '58, '62, '66, '69, '72. Reprinted by permission.

HAROLD OBER ASSOCIATES. For excerpts from a review of *A Face in the Crowd* by Marya Mannes published in *The Reporter*.

WILLIAM S. PECHTER. For excerpts from "With-It Movies" published in *Commentary*.

PHOTOPLAY. For numerous excerpts from reviews published in *Photoplay*.

PRAEGER PUBLISHERS, INC. For excerpts from *Allan Dwan* by Peter Bogdanovich; from *Fritz Lang in America* by Peter Bogdanovich; from *Film Essays* by Sergei Eisenstein; from *Arthur Penn* by Robin Wood.

PRENTICE-HALL, INC. For excerpts from *Dwight Macdonald on Movies* by Dwight Macdonald. Copyright © 1969 by Dwight Macdonald.

G. P. PUTNAM'S SONS. For excerpts from *That Marvel—The Movie* by Edward S. Van Zile.

QUIGLEY PUBLISHING COMPANY, INC. For excerpts from *Decency in Motion Pictures* by Martin Quigley; from *Motion Picture Almanac*.

THE REPORTER. For excerpts from "The Shakespeare Boom" by Robert Bingham, copyright 1955 by The Reporter Magazine Company. From "A Child Bride, A Wide Globetrotter" by Robert Bingham, copyright 1957 by The Reporter Magazine Company. From "A Monarch in Exile" by Marvin Felheim, copyright 1957 by The Reporter Magazine Company. From "Three Movies from Africa," "Gary Cooper a Tragic Hero," "Chaplin: the Trouble with Being a Myth," by Robert Hatch, copyright 1952 by Fortnightly Publishing Co. From "A Highly Peculiar Film" by Jay Jacobs, copyright 1959 by The Reporter Magazine Company. From "Where We Came In" by Steven Marcus, copyright 1959 by The Reporter Magazine Company. From "The Twilight of an Aging Prodigy" by Gerald Weales, copyright 1958 by The Reporter Magazine Company. From "The Tame and Wooly West" by Gerald Weales, copyright 1961 by The Reporter Magazine Company.

FRANKIE MCKEE ROBINS. For excerpts from reviews of *Portrait of Jenny, Little Women*, published in *McCall's*.

HENRY T. ROCKWELL. For excerpts from reviews by Robert E. Sherwood, published in *Life*.

Paul Rotha. For excerpts from *The Film Till Now* and from *Celluloid.*

Charles Scribner's Sons. For excerpts from "Motion Pictures" by Gilbert Seldes published in *Scribner's Magazine.*

Sight and Sound. For its generous permission to reprint excerpts from numerous articles.

Simon & Schuster, Inc. For excerpts from *Graham Greene on Film* by Graham Greene. From *The Movies* by Richard Griffith and Arthur Mayer, copyright © 1957, 1970 by Arthur Mayer and the estate of Richard Griffith. From *Confessions of a Cultist* by Andrew Sarris, copyright © 1961, 1962, 1963, 1964, 1965, 1966, 1967, 1968, 1969, 1970 by Andrew Sarris. From *Second Sight* by Richard Schickel, copyright © 1965, 1966, 1967, 1968, 1969, 1970, 1971, 1972 by Richard Schickel. From *The Public Arts* by Gilbert Seldes. Reprinted by permission of Simon & Schuster.

Stein and Day. For excerpts from *Movie Man* by David Thomson. Copyright © 1967 by David Thomson. Reprinted by permission of Stein and Day/ Publishers.

Teachers College Press. For excerpts from Lewis Jacobs *The Rise of the American Film: A Critical History* with an Essay, "Experimental Cinema in America, 1921-1947." New York: Teachers College Press, 1968; copyright 1939, 1948, and 1967 by Lewis Jacobs. Reprinted by permission of the publisher.

Temple University Press. For excerpts from *The Film Criticism of Otis Ferguson* by Otis Ferguson. Copyright © 1971 by Temple University. All rights reserved.

Frederick Ungar Publishing Co., Inc. For excerpts from *The Cinematic Imagination* by Edward Murray and from *The Age of the American Novel*: The Film Aesthetics of Fiction between Two Wars by Claude-Edmonde Magny.

Universe Books. For excerpts from *Experimental Cinema* by André Bazin.

University of California Press. For excerpts from *One Reel a Week* by Fred Balhofer and Arthur C. Miller; from *John Ford* by Peter Bogdanovich; from *Stroheim* by Joel W. Finler; from *Grierson on Documentary* edited by Forsyth Hardy; from *The Films of Orson Welles* by Charles Higham. Originally published by the University of California Press; reprinted by permission of the Regents of the University of California. For excerpts from articles published in *Film Quarterly* by Gideon Bachmann, Spring 1961, pp. 56-57; by Ernest Callenbach, Winter 1958, pp. 45-46, Summer 1963, p. 50; by Arlene Croce, Winter 1958 pp. 43, 45; by Stephen Farber, Fall, 1967, pp. 60-61; by Henry Goodman, Summer 1960, pp. 50-51; by Lawrence Grauman, Spring 1961, p. 53; by Albert Johnson, Winter 1958, pp. 54-55 and 57-58; Spring 1959, pp. 32-33; Summer 1959, pp. 42-43; Winter 1961, p. 50; Spring 1960, p. 40 and pp. 45-46; by Colin Young, Spring 1959, pp. 10-11, Fall 1959, pp. 12-13. Copyright by The Regents of the University of California. Reprinted by permission.

University of Oklahoma Press. For excerpts from *Motion Pictures: Development of an Art from Silent Films to the Age of Television* by A. R. Fulton, copyright 1960 by the University of Oklahoma Press. From *World of Laughter: The Motion Picture Comedy Short: 1910-1930* by Kalton C. Lahue, copyright 1966 by the University of Oklahoma Press. From *Pare Lorentz and the Documentary Film* by Robert L. Snyder, copyright 1968 by University of Oklahoma Press. From *The Movies in the Age of Innocence* by Edward Wagenknecht, copyright 1962 by the University of Oklahoma Press. By permission of the publisher.

Variety. For excerpts from reviews on Dwan, Litvak, McCarey, Walsh, Wellman.

THE VELVET LIGHT TRAP. For excerpts from review of "Sex and Character in *Klute*" by Jonathan Stutz; on *Carnal Knowledge* by Mike Wilmington; on *Mildred Pierce* by Jonathan Davis.

THE VILLAGE VOICE. For excerpts from "Griffith: Not Only Great, but Good" by John Belton, copyright 1971 by The Village Voice, Inc. From "Movie Journal" by Jonas Mekas, copyright 1959 by The Village Voice, Inc. From "Films in Focus" by Andrew Sarris, copyright 1965 by The Village Voice, Inc. Reprinted by permission of *The Village Voice*.

DAN WAKEFIELD. For excerpts from reviews on *Skidoo, Lonesome Cowboys, Alice's Restaurant* published in *The Atlantic Monthly*.

PAUL WARSHOW. For excerpts from *The Immediate Experience*.

GERALD WEALES. For excerpts from reviews on *Touch of Evil*, and *The Misfits* published in *The Reporter*.

HERMAN WEINBERG. For excerpts from *Saint Cinema;* from reviews published in *Sight & Sound*.

ALLAN WINGATE, LTD. For excerpts by Gavin Lambert from *Shots in the Dark*, edited by E. C. Ansley et al.

INDEX OF CRITICS AND FILM TITLES

Names of critics and films are cited on the pages given. When a film title is included here for a director not covered in this volume, the full name of the director is provided.